"Project Cens... dia traction should in fact drive the reporting ag...... ......s outlet. These 25 stories are clearly the most consequential ...... what is scary in looking at the list is how obvious it is that s...... ts of these th...... ...........t governments and corporat... ......... Project C...... significant stories." —...... *Beauty Myth*; *The End o......*

"The syst......sored has been an impor......*ople's History of the United States*

"Project Censored . . . has evolved into a deep, wide, and utterly engrossing exercise to unmask censorship, self-censorship, and propaganda in the mass media." —Ralph Nader, consumer advocate, lawyer, author

"[Project Censored] is a clarion call for truth telling."—Daniel Ellsberg, *The Pentagon Papers*

"[Project Censored] shows how the American public has been bamboozled, snookered, and dumbed down by the corporate media. It is chock-full of 'ah-ha' moments where we understand just how we've been fleeced by banksters, stripped of our civil liberties, and blindly led down a path of never-ending war." —Medea Benjamin, author of *Drone Warfare*, and cofounder of Global Exchange and CODEPINK

"Project Censored . . . not only shines a penetrating light on the American Empire and all its deadly, destructive, and deceitful actions, it does so at a time when the Obama administration is mounting a fierce effort to silence truth-tellers and whistleblowers. Project Censored provides the kind of fearless and honest journalism we so desperately need in these dangerous times."—Peter Kuznick, professor of history, American University, and coauthor, with Oliver Stone, of *The Untold History of the United States*

"The world needs more brave whistleblowers and independent journalists in the service of reclaiming democracy and challenging the abuse of power. Project Censored stands out for its commitment to such work." —Deepa Kumar, author of *Islamophobia and the Politics of Empire* and professor of media studies at Rutgers University

"Project Censored brings to light some of the most important stories of the year that you never saw or heard about. This is your chance to find out what got buried." —Diane Ravitch, author of *The Death and Life of the Great American School System*

"Most journalists in the United States believe the press here is free. That grand illusion only helps obscure the fact that, by and large, the US corporate press does not report what's really going on, while tuning out, or laughing off, all those who try to do just that. Americans—now more than ever—need those outlets that do labor to report some truth. Project Censored is not just among the bravest, smartest, and most rigorous of those outlets, but the only one that's wholly focused on those stories that the corporate press ignores, downplays, and/or distorts." —Mark Crispin Miller, author, professor of media ecology, New York University

"At a time when the need for independent journalism and for media outlets unaffiliated with and untainted by the government and corporate sponsors is greater than ever . . . we are fortunate to have an ally like Project Censored."—Dahr Jamail, independent journalist

"Those who read Project Censored are in the know." —Cynthia McKinney, former member of the US House of Representatives

"[Project Censored's] efforts to continue globalizing their reporting network could not be more timely or necessary."—Kristina Borjesson, award-winning freelance journalist

"Project Censored continues to do the work they've been persistently pursuing since 1976: Exposing the secrets that those in power would prefer to keep hidden and the corruption that should be scandalous, but isn't, because the corporate media won't cover it." —David Rovics, musician and activist

"Project Censored is one of the organizations that we should listen to, to be assured that our newspapers and our broadcasting outlets are practicing thorough and ethical journalism."—Walter Cronkite, anchor, *CBS Evening News*, 1962-1981

"One of the most significant media research projects in the country." —I. F. Stone, American muckraker

"A terrific resource, especially for its directory of alternative media and organizations . . . Recommended for media collections." —*Library Journal*

"This book is evidence of Project Censored's profoundly important work in educating readers on current events and the skills needed to be a critical thinker." —*Publishers Weekly*, on *Censored 2014*

"A distant early warning system for society's problems." —*American Journalism Review*

# CENSORED 2017

Fortieth Anniversary Edition

## Mickey Huff and Andy Lee Roth
### with Project Censored

Foreword by
## Mark Crispin Miller

Cartoons by
## Khalil Bendib

**Seven Stories Press**
New York • Oakland

Seven Stories Press
140 Watts Street
New York, NY 10013
www.sevenstories.com

ISBN 978-1-60980-715-3 (paperback)

ISBN 978-1-60980-716-0 (electronic)

ISSN 1074-5998

9 8 7 6 5 4 3 2 1

Book design by Jon Gilbert

Printed in the USA

*Ben H. Bagdikian*
*(1920–2016)*

Journalist of conscience,
pioneering critic of corporate media consolidation, and
champion of the public's right to know

*Media power is political power . . . To give citizens a choice in
ideas and information is to give them a choice in politics: If a
nation has narrowly controlled information, it will soon have
narrowly controlled politics.*

from *The Media Monopoly*, by Ben H. Bagdikian

Bagdikian served as a Project Censored judge
from 1976–2000

# PUBLISHER'S NOTE

That Project Censored has survived and thrived for forty years is a testament to this incredible team of people and also to the enduring power of the idea that monitoring news censorship can keep our democracy going. Real democracy in America is constantly under assault, but the simple fact that Project Censored exists means that the kind of investigative reporting the Project celebrates, and the publications that support investigative reporting, have a forum and even a reward for their efforts and talent and sacrifice.

I remember meeting intrepid reporters like Gary Webb and Sidney Wolfe and so many others through Project Censored, including young journalists who were being celebrated for a story they'd written and it may have been the first time a story they'd written had a life beyond initial publication. And it felt great, like we were on the winning team.

So much of this kind of research and nonfiction writing happens in isolation, even extending to and including publication. I remember that, often, it was at the Project Censored Awards that writer and publisher met in person for the first time.

For four decades Project Censored has also initiated thousands of college students into the world of censorship and investigative reporting, not only at Sonoma State University where the Project was founded in 1976, but also at dozens of colleges and universities around the country.

Under successive directors, founder Carl Jensen, then Peter Phillips, and now Mickey Huff with Andy Lee Roth, the Project has continued its work as one of America's strongest alternative media institutions.

As Project Censored's publisher through all but one of the years that they have produced an annual volume of censored stories, *Censored*, I've been amazed at the resilience and joyfulness this organization has shown, year after year. Forever young, and ever more important, Project Censored makes us all better-informed and more empowered as citizens.

—Dan Simon, Publisher, Seven Stories Press

# Contents

CHAPTER 2: Déjà Vu: Strolling Down Memory Hole Lane
by Susan Rahman and Sheila Beasley, Larkin Bond, Katie Kolb, Stephanie
Lee, Caitlin McCoy, Alexander Olson, Elizabeth Ramirez, Kenny Rodriguez,
Karina Seiler, Claudia Serrano, Kady Stenson, Karl Wada; with Mickey Huff

CHAPTER 3: The Corporate Media's War on Reality: Faux Elections and the
Facade of DeMockracy: Junk Food News and News Abuse for 2015–16
by Nolan Higdon with Mickey Huff, and student researchers Hanna
Begnell, Taylor Bledsoe, Aimee Casey, Alexandra Castillo, Daniel Cerezo,
Daniel Cervantez, Lauren Freeman, Mitchell Graham, Josh Gorski, Kyle
Hunt, Jaspreet Kang, Justin Lascano, Brandy Miceli, George Petrucci, Sarah
Powell, Jared Rodda, Edwin Sevilla, Chandler Saul, Sebastian Trucios, Jacob

CHAPTER 4: Media Democracy in Action
by Mnar Muhawesh (MintPress News), Peter B. Collins (*The Peter Collins
Show*), Eric Draitser (Stop Imperialism), Abby Martin (*The Empire Files*),
Darcey Rakestraw (Food & Water Watch), Susan Rahman and Eliana Dimo-

CHAPTER 5: Contested Visions, Imperfect Information, and the Persistence of
Conspiracy Theories

CHAPTER 6: Played by the Mighty Wurlitzer: The Press, the CIA, and the
Subversion of Truth

CHAPTER 7: Selling Empire, War, and Capitalism: Public Relations Propaganda
Firms in Service to the Transnational Capitalist Class
by Peter Phillips, with Ratonya Coffee, Robert Ramirez, Mary Schafer, and

# "Our Free Press" as a Clear and Present Danger

## Why We Need Project Censored Forty Years Later

Mark Crispin Miller

**I**

Concerning what we call "the media" today, it is the best of times, it is the worst of times. First, the worst. . . .

I've been studying the US press since it elected Ronald Reagan back in 1980. Since then, our "free press" has often failed completely to keep We the People properly informed, instead colluding, avidly, in one state propaganda drive after another (with some of us trying, vainly, to oppose it).

Let me be clear: throughout those years, as even now, there was much excellent work produced by serious reporters. But when the chips were down, the state about to strike, and people needing most to hear some truth, there wasn't any to be heard—at least not enough to make a difference.

Thus our "free press" unanimously justified the 1983 invasion of Grenada, the 1989 invasion of Panama, the first US Gulf War in 1990 (unanimously hailing it as a miraculous success), and the intervention in Yugoslavia in 1999 (unanimously blacking out the horrors of NATO's "humanitarian" bombing there).

Such unity against The Enemy dates back to World War I, when our free press was first systematically deployed for propaganda purposes. To treat us *not* as citizens to be informed, but as *subjects to be mobilized for war,* was the purpose of most "news" about "the Hun" in World War I, the Soviets from 1917, the first Red Scare in 1919, and, eventually, the long Cold War, pitting *us* against the Red Colossus that would crush our freedom, rights and property—and our free press.

There is, of course, some irony in that last threat because "our free press" *itself* was often just as bellicose, authoritarian, repetitive and *hostile to dissent* as its chained counterparts behind the "Iron Curtain." Far from hailing those who tell the awful truth, as in *All the President's Men*, the US press has often banished them. In 1939, George Seldes, veteran foreign correspondent, was savaged by newspapers nationwide for blasting their fantastic claims about the Soviet invasion of Finland, in a four-part series that no major magazine would touch, so it ended up in the *New Masses* (where it was mostly read by Communists). Although his study was confirmed by the Institute for Propaganda Analysis at Columbia University, Seldes realized that he would never find a proper readership unless he went *outside* the daily press, and so he started up *In Fact*, his independent newsletter, which ran from 1940 to 1950.[1]

I. F. Stone had a similar experience in 1952, on the publication of *The Hidden History of the Korean War*—a meticulous dissection of precisely how *and why* the US had allowed that war to start, and then kept it going. Because his book went far beyond the usual story of the war's beginning ("North Korean aggression"), and noted the atrocities by US forces (as in "Operation Killer"), it was turned down by over two dozen publishers; and when it finally did come out on Monthly Review Press, our "free press" largely greeted it with *silence*—until a hit piece by liberal journalist Richard Rovere in the *New York Post*, which pushed Stone out into the wilderness for years, forcing him to follow Seldes's lead with *I. F. Stone's Weekly*, which ran from 1953 to 1971.[2]

Nor was it only wayward journalists who got that treatment. "Some long-cherished illusions of mine about the great free press in our country underwent a painful reappraisal during this period," wrote Jim Garrison, noting how, in 1967, the media went after him *en masse* for seeking to crack open the conspiracy to murder President John F. Kennedy: "As far as I could tell, the reports and editorials in *Newsweek*, *Time*, the *New York Times*, the *New York Post*, the *Saturday Evening Post* and on and on were indistinguishable," all deploying the same abusive memes—"irresponsible," "ambitious," "circus"—to tarnish him, and cloud the issue. (Garrison got much the same reception on NBC's *The Tonight Show*, where he more than held his own against an oddly hostile Johnny Carson.)[3]

Thus, from World War I until the eve of September 11, 2001, "our free press" was more a nice idea than a reality, as *"our" real* press, for the most part, failed repeatedly, and often with calamitous effects, to keep We the People properly informed about the doings of our government, so as to help us keep it under our control. Instead, throughout that century the US press, with rare exceptions, served the interests of the state *against* the people, while keeping the people completely in the dark about it.

It's history that we badly need to know, and not because it's over—on the contrary. That history may help us grasp why "our free press" today is even worse than it was back when the United States was still a semi-functional democracy. Now that the Cold War is formally over, leaving "us" supreme throughout the world, "our free press" is more authoritarian, repressive, and irrational than ever—far less like what the Framers had in mind than what George Orwell satirized as "the Ministry of Truth" in *1984*.

## II

Like that dystopian bureaucracy, the US press today repeatedly asserts that "black is white," and "2 + 2 = 5," while tuning out whatever facts might somehow complicate the story.

### "A forcefulness not seen since the Cold War"

Take Russia—that is, the "resurgent Russia" that "invaded Ukraine" and then "seized Crimea," out of Vladimir Putin's "obsessive quest to make Russia great again," a "dangerous obsession" deeply threatening not only to "Ukraine's fledgling democracy," but also to "European peace and stability," and "world peace" overall ("Russia has bolstered its military and asserted itself on the world stage with a forcefulness not seen since the Cold War, ratcheting up tensions with the West"), and so on.[4]

Thus "our free press" has turned the truth completely upside-down. Contrary to that image of Ukraine as Putin's trembling prey, with *his* designs endangering "world peace," the hard truth is that the US struck first, by managing the coup that *ended* "Ukraine's fledgling democracy"—ousting the elected president in favor of a junta rife with neo-Nazi activists and neoliberal technocrats (cf. Chile, c. 1973).

All this the US press unanimously misreported as a "revolution" by "pro-Europe Ukrainians" clamoring for Western freedom and prosperity—a pretty story that the press maintained by leaving out whatever ugly details didn't fit it. Despite the glaring evidence of rampant neo-Nazi violence throughout that "revolution," and the overt Nazi pedigree of certain parties angling to take power, the *Times, Washington Post, Time,* Daily Beast, and others laughed it off as "Russian propaganda."[5]

That this "revolution" *was* a US-sponsored coup came clear on February 7, 2014, when someone posted a bugged phone chat between Victoria Nuland, an assistant secretary of state, and Geoffrey Pyatt, US ambassador to Ukraine. The two discussed the crisis not as interested observers but as managers, with Nuland loftily deciding which of Ukraine's pols should "go into the government," and which should not (and if Europe won't help seal the deal, well: "Fuck the EU").[6]

More evidence of high manipulation came out a month later, in a hacked conversation between Urmas Paet, Estonia's foreign minister, and Catherine Ashton, European Union chief of foreign policy. Paet was troubled by some news about the slaughter in Maidan Square on February 20, 2014, when snipers had killed scores of protesters— a massacre attributed to the police force of Viktor Yanukovych, Ukraine's pro-Russian president, forcing him to flee the country. But "all the evidence" now told a different story—and the new regime would not look into it: "It's really disturbing that . . . they don't want to investigate what exactly happened," Paet said, noting a "stronger and stronger understanding," among Ukrainians, that, "behind [the] snipers . . . it was not Yanukovych, but it was somebody from the new coalition."[7]

"Our free press" either spiked those stories outright, or downplayed and distorted them.[8] Having thus rewritten the beginning of the crisis, they took to hammering Putin endlessly for his "invasion of Ukraine" and "seizure of Crimea"—two now-notorious crimes that never happened.

While Russia did provide the separatists in East Ukraine with some light arms, and Russian nationals have joined the fighters on their own, so far all "evidence" of an "invasion of Ukraine" has been exposed as fake.[9] Nor did Putin "seize" Crimea, but held a referendum there, so voters could choose whether to join the new regime in Kiev, or stay with Russia— and they voted overwhelmingly (95.7 percent) to stay: a startlingly lopsided outcome that the exit polls confirmed, while the vote was certified as honest by a team of international observers.[10]

Gallup reconfirmed that preference three months later, and a German pollster reconfirmed it yet again some eight months after that; even *Forbes* conceded that "the Crimeans are happy right where they are," while the State Department and the *Times* keep pointing to that "annexation" as another Russian crime against humanity.[11]

Thus, again, "our free press" stands united with a state intent on war—a partnership more dangerous than ever, given Russia's massive nuclear capacity. The propaganda makes it hard for most of us to see "Euromaidan" for what it really was—a first strike by the United States: Ukraine now holds de facto membership in the North Atlantic Treaty Organization (NATO), putting that belligerent alliance right in Putin's face (despite the US promise, back in 1990, not to move it "one inch eastward").

And that is only one of several provocations by the US (and EU) since 2014, all ignored or understated by our corporate press. As I write this, the existential danger of that serial harassment has been making news online—and nowhere else. On May 31, 2016, a group of Russians living in America published "A Russian Warning," which included this passage:

> We now feel that it is our duty, as Russians living in the US, to warn the American people that they are being lied to, and to tell them the truth. And the truth is simply this: If there is going to be a war with Russia, then the United States will most certainly be destroyed, and most of us will end up dead.[12]

Beyond its urgent point, that warning is significant for what it says about the US press today, and its decline from an imperfect medium of information *for* the people into a near-total weapon of the state *against* the people. That "our free press" would just churn out that propaganda, rather than expose its lies, investigate its motives, and explain its dangers, tells us that the US press itself is just as captive to the state as Russia's under Stalin, or China's now, or North Korea's, although the bond here is informal, or covert.

## "Our free press" as a clear and present danger

While ever fewer of us recall them, and very few can even picture them, there have been moments when our journalists were not all hitmen on behalf of US foreign policy. Even those who shared the basic creed of Cold War anticommunism (journalists more tractable than Stone and Seldes) could sometimes probe specific policies, and talk to "enemies" with some respect. Since such professional detachment can be hard in time of war, those moments mostly came in times of peace, or once the war had lost its promise: in the 1930s, the postwar 1940s, the early 1960s (under JFK), and in that vital interval from 1968 (the Tet Offensive) to 1980 ("Morning in America").

The US press today is something else—an outright adjunct of the State Department and the Pentagon (and an implicit adjunct of the Central Intelligence Agency [CIA]). While there are still tough journalists out there, they've mostly been ejected from the cockpits of our journalistic Air Force, somewhat like Stone and Seldes long ago: e.g., Seymour Hersh, once at the *Times*, now writes for the *New Yorker* and *London Review of Books*; Robert Parry, once at AP and *Newsweek*, now runs Consortiumnews, an independent website; and Sharyl Attkisson, once at CBS, now has a syndicated TV show on Sundays.

Such ousters have now left "our free press" wholly unified in its commitment to "report" whatever tripe the state may hand them, from Putin's "seizure of Crimea" and "invasion of Ukraine," to Assad's "barrel bombs" and "moderate opposition," to North Korea's hack of Sony Pictures, to (brace yourself) the "Tiananmen Square Massacre"—a bloodbath that the *Times* et al. have been "remembering" poignantly since 1989, notwithstanding all those witnesses who claim there wasn't one (including Nicholas Kristof, the *Times*' own Beijing bureau chief).[13] As US naval forces fence with

China's in the South China Sea, the "memory" of "Tiananmen" helps make that distant provocation (as if China had its navy in the Caribbean) seem wholly justified, and worth the risk.

And while such propaganda readies us for war, so does the media's inexorable projection of the USA as everything that Russia/China/North Korea/Syria are *not*—i.e., a democratic nation spreading peace and freedom everywhere. The press maintains that myth of national benevolence with stories like the one about the three good-lookin' troops—two white, one black—who took out that Islamist on the train in France (not something you see every day!), and countless scenes of soldierly benevolence among the locals in Afghanistan. Hollywood keeps selling us the same heroic story.

And yet it's not so much by running any such material that the *Times* et al. sustain this myth of national benevolence. Rather, it's primarily through what they *don't* report that "our free press" depicts the USA as wholly good and always in the right, *protecting* people everywhere, like those three dudes did on that train in France (and like Ben Affleck does in *Argo*).

Thus the US press purveys a version of world history as heavily redacted as a Federal Bureau of Investiation file released through proper channels. Search the archives of the *Times* et al., and try to find some mention of the US and/or CIA in what you'll read or watch about the hellhole that is Guatemala, or Honduras, or Angola, or El Salvador, or Haiti, or about the genocidal massacre in Indonesia back in 1965, or about the brutal era of "the generals" in Brazil (1964–85), or about those tortured under Pinochet in Chile (1973–90), or about the memory of the junta's "dirty war" in Argentina (1976–83), or about the bloody modern history of Iran, or Greece, or Congo, or South Africa—just to name a few of all those places where "we" did lasting harm that most of us have never heard of—because our schools won't go there, either.

Nor does the US press provide an honest view of our own modern history. While always quick to yell when Russians "whitewash the system's horrors" under Stalin, the *Times* et al. say little of "the system's horrors" over here. *The Times* has mentioned MKULTRA—the CIA's horrific mind control program—twice since 1999 (once in the Arts section, once in a Religion column), while "Operation Chaos," the

CIA's domestic spying program under presidents Lyndon B. Johnson and Richard Nixon, has not come up since 1985. *The Times* has always been far less inclined to note such "horrors" than to *defend* the Agency, as it infamously did in 1996, when it joined the *Washington Post* and *Los Angeles Times* in attacking Gary Webb's exposé of the CIA's involvement in the cocaine trade out of Nicaragua.

Recently the *Times* has gone much further in abetting CIA propaganda. On July 8, 2016, in a mood piece on the panic throughout Dallas after the mass shooting of policemen there, the Gray Lady offered this astonishing historical aside:

> Fifty-plus years ago, the gunman in Dallas was a troubled ex-Marine with a mail order rifle. This time, the police said it was a troubled former Army reservist with more serious weaponry who was identified as Micah Johnson, 25.[14]

Thus "America's Newspaper of Record" bluntly reaffirmed the thesis of the Warren Report—that a lone, troubled gunman with a military background assassinated JFK—an official fantasy that decades of meticulous research have long since thoroughly debunked. That the *Times* would take that stand *again,* despite its manifest absurdity, suggests that there are certain stories that "our free press" ("left" press included) *will not tell,* no matter how well-documented, even though—or, it would seem, *because*—those stories are the *most* important for us all, concerning the survival of American democracy, as well as our survival on this Earth.

Far from giving them the close attention they deserve, the press keeps trying to kill those stories by dismissing them as "conspiracy theories"—a tactic that the CIA devised in 1967, precisely to discredit new books questioning the Warren Report. As Lance deHaven-Smith explains in *Conspiracy Theory in America,* from that point on the epithet was used increasingly to stifle all discussion—and to chill investigation by the press—of many crimes committed by the agents of a state intent on war abroad and "order" here at home, despite the Constitution, and the laws.[15]

And so, having laughed off the conspiracy to kill John Kennedy (and thereby let 'er rip in Vietnam, and keep the Cold War boiling), "our free press" did the same with Robert Kennedy's assassination, then Martin Luther King's. And after the 1970s—an interim when state conspiracy did not seem so far-fetched, what with Watergate and the Church Committee hearings into CIA and FBI abuses—the press mocked on, "debunking" the October Surprise, and minimizing Iran/Contra, and attacking Gary Webb for his "conspiracy theory" about the CIA's drug-running, and pooh-poohing the idea that TWA Flight 800 had been accidentally shot down by the US Navy. And then "our free press" outdid its awesome whitewash of the Kennedy assassination by accepting the official story of 9/11, and mocking those who question it, just as with the Warren Report since 1964.

The press has done the same with our computerized elections, brightly certifying the official count in contest after contest, however bad the smell, and even when the evidence of electronic fraud is overwhelming. Although they've had their eyes shut since the 1970s,[16] it was not until 2000—the year Bush/Cheney *took* the White House—that the US press began to jeer election fraud as a conspiracist delusion, as they've been doing ever since, right through the flagrant manufacture of Hillary Clinton's "victory" over Bernie Sanders in 2016 (a fraud denied with equal vigor by the *Nation* and the *New York Times*).[17]

Thus the US press consistently blacks out what we most need to know, about the doings of our government, the true intentions of our "enemies," and the condition of our own democracy—and that's not all. While putting us at risk collectively by courting war, "our free press" also puts us each at personal risk, by blacking out all inconvenient truths about our health.

By "inconvenient," I mean "damaging to corporate profits." Thus the US press, with few exceptions, once routinely blacked out any news about the risks of smoking, since the press depended on its lavish advertising revenues from the cigarette industry. As we all know from TV shows like *Mad Men*, such commercial censorship kept people dangerously unaware of what their smokes were doing to them, back when roughly half the population smoked, including most reporters, and many doctors.

Although the press no longer advertises cigarettes, it still routinely blacks out inconvenient truths—a profitable reflex far *more* lethal than it was back in the 1950s, since what we don't know now can kill us even if we never smoke, get lots of exercise, and eat organic.

Thus, while we all know about the health risks of junk food, high-caffeine drinks, and alcohol, we all *don't* know the true extent of Fukushima's toxic effluent, right here in the United States, or about the risks of radiation from our cell phones, as well as our TVs, radios and microwaves—and WiFi (whose use in nursery schools was banned in France in January 2016). Worse yet, we all *don't* know the dangers of the very "healthcare" that's supposed to keep us well, since "our free press" is even more protective of Big Pharma (and the Centers for Disease Control) than it was of "Big Tobacco" fifty years ago; and so it jeers alternative therapies as "quackery" while skirting the risks of profitable drugs.

## III

And so, concerning what we call "the media" today, these are, without a doubt, the worst of times. Yet they're the best of times as well; because, while "our free press" has never lied so much, or buried so much truth, it's never been so easy for so many to see through those lies, and to dig up so much truth themselves.

This is one great advantage of our digital technology: that it enables us to fact-check all that propaganda in a flash, and find the other side, or sides, of every story—even those that seem, at first, to be the *only* story. Whereas, fifty years ago, you would have had to trek outside the state's hermetic fiction of the Kennedy assassination, to visit certain libraries, or witnesses, or other students of the crime, today it's possible to do all that, or much of it, online—moving instantly beyond the *Times*/CNN story of the latest crackpot gunman, "upset victory," enemy aggression or whatever else, to get some different sense of what, if anything, went down.

This is not to minimize the disadvantages of this new virtual mobility. While "the truth is out there," first of all, there's also tons of crap out there—including lots of propaganda tailor-made precisely for that sphere. And while it keeps us all in touch with one another, we're also *dis*connected by this new virtual "community," and all too easily distracted "there" as well (and also under absolute surveillance, with every search recorded).

Nevertheless, our digital capacities have freed us, or *can* free us, from the tyranny of those official narratives, allowing us to *test* them as we never could before; and this has weakened the authority of those who craft those stories, and who try to force them on us by assuring us that any *other* narrative is a "conspiracy theory"—a meme that isn't as intimidating as it used to be, especially for younger people.

In short, our digital technology enables us to slip the bonds of "our free press," and do what Project Censored has been doing so brilliantly, and teaching all the rest of us to do, for forty years—finding out those stories that we *need* to know, for our own good, and for the good of all, and that we *would* know, if our own press, or its masters, didn't censor them.

---

MARK CRISPIN MILLER is Professor of Media, Culture and Communication at New York University, and publisher of News from Underground (markcrispinmiller. com). His books include *Boxed In: The Culture of TV*, *The Bush Dyslexicon: Observations on a National Disorder*, and *Fooled Again: The Real Case for Election Reform*. He is also editor of the Forbidden Bookshelf series for Open Road Integrated Media.

An extended version of this Foreword appears as an article at www.projectcensored.org.

## Notes

1   George Seldes, *Tell the Truth and Run* (New York: Greenberg, 1953).
2   D.D. Guttenplan, *American Radical: The Life and Times of I.F. Stone* (New York: Farrar, Straus and Giroux, 2009), pp. 265-67. See also Bruce Cumings' preface to *I.F. Stone, The Hidden History of the Korean War, 1950-1951* (Boston: Little, Brown, 1988), pp. xi-xiii.
3   Jim Garrison, *On the Trail of the Assassins* (New York: Skyhorse Publishing, 2012), p. 161. Garrison appeared on *The Tonight Show* on January 31, 1968, https://www.youtube.com/watch?v=h1cZCIDwiuA
4   "resurgent Russia": e.g., Nicholas Kulish and Sara Rhodin, "In Ukraine, Fear of Being a Resurgent Russia's Next Target," *New York Times*, August 16, 2008; Steven Erlanger, "NATO steps back into the U.S.S.R.," *New York Times*, May 22, 2014; and Steven Erlanger, "Tested by Russia, NATO Struggles to Stay Credible," *New York Times*, May 31, 2016; "obsessive quest," "dangerous obsession": "Vladimir Putin's Dangerous Obsession" (editorial), *New York Times* , May 19, 2016.
    "Ukraine's fledgling democracy": Joerg Forbrig, "Ukraine's political suicide," Politico, February 5, 2016, (http://www.politico.eu/article/ukraine-political-suicide-government-corruption-conflict/). According to Forbrig, "Russia . . . attacked Ukraine, annexed Crimea, stoked separatism in Donbas, and terrorized the rest of the country."
    "Russia has bolstered": Catrin Einhorn, Hannah Fairfield and Tim Wallace, "Russia Rearms for a New Era," *New York Times*, December 24, 2015.

5 "In support of those Russian-sponsored militias in Eastern Ukraine, now backed by growing ranks of Russian troops and weapons [sic], Moscow has created a *fantasy that plays on Russian victimization*," write the editors of the *Washington Post*. "*By this rendering, the forces backing Ukraine's government in Kiev are fascists and neo-Nazis*, a portrayal that Mr. Putin personally advanced on Friday, when he likened the Ukrainian army's attempts to regain its territory to the Nazi Siege of Leningrad in World War II, an appeal meant to inflame Russians' already overheated nationalist emotions" (emphasis added). "Putin's propaganda keeps Russians in the dark about Ukraine and more" (editorial), August 31, 2014.

6 The audio of the conversation is on YouTube, at https://www.youtube.com/watch?v=KIvRljAaNgg, and the BBC posted a transcript: "Ukraine crisis: Transcript of leaked Nuland-Pyatt call," BBC, February 7, 2014, http://www.bbc.com/news/world-europe-26079957.

7 The audio of the Paet/Ashton conversation is on YouTube, at https://www.youtube.com/watch?v=kkC4Z67QuCo. For a transcript (the audio is hard to follow), see Prof. Martin Hellman's blog, *Defusing the Nuclear Threat*, June 19, 2014, https://nuclearrisk.wordpress.com/2014/06/19/transcript-of-estonian-fm-bombshell-revelation/.

8 As reported (briefly) by the *Times* et al., the Nuland/Pyatt exchange made news, not for what it said about the US hand behind the "Maidan Revolution," but as a case of Russian perfidy, the State Department charging (with no evidence) that Russian hands had done the hacking: "Certainly we think this is a new low in Russian tradecraft," State's spokeswoman told the *Times* (Peter Baker, "U.S. Points to Russia as Diplomats' Private Call Is Posted on Web," *New York Times*, February 6, 2014).

9 For example, see "Evidence of undercover Russian troops in Ukraine debunked," Human rights investigations, April 22, 2014, https://humanrightsinvestigations.org/2014/04/22/evidence-of-undercover-russian-troops-in-ukraine-debunked/; Kurt Nimmo, "NYT caught creating fake war propaganda in Ukraine just like Iraq," Infowars, April 24, 2014, http://www.infowars.com/nyt-issues-back-page-retraction-on-russian-troops-in-ukraine-photos/; Michel Chossudovsky, "Obama is a Liar. Fake NATO Evidence. OSCE Confirms that No Russian Troops, No Tanks, Have Crossed the Russia-Ukraine Border," Global Research, September 4, 2014; http://www.globalresearch.ca/obama-is-a-liar-fake-nato-evidence-osce-confirms-that-no-russian-troops-no-tanks-have-crossed-the-russia-ukraine-border/5399457; Raul Ilargi Meijer, "The Bogus Narrative about Russia's 'Invasion' of Ukraine—Still Not a Shred of Evidence," David Stockman's Contra Corner, February 14, 2015; http://davidstockmanscontracorner.com/the-bogus-narrative-about-russias-invasion-of-ukraine-still-not-a-shred-of-credible-evidence/.

As a stalwart British adjunct of America's "free press," the *Guardian* has struggled manfully to find some evidence of an "invasion," thereby reconfirming that there isn't any. For example, see Ewen MacAskill, "Does US evidence prove Russian special forces are in eastern Ukraine?" *Guardian*, April 22, 2014.

10 "Crimea exit poll: About 93% back Russia union," BBC News, March 16, 2014.

As for the verdict of the international observers, it's hard to find reports unbiased one way or the other, and the story overall was heavily blurred to start with by the refusal of the Organization for Security and Cooperation in Europe (OSCE) to recognize the de facto Crimean government, and, therefore, to send observers there, as that government invited them to do.

For an impartial survey of the findings by those monitors who *did* observe the vote—and a (grudging) acknowledgement that it was evidently honest—see Ken Hanly, "Op-Ed: The Crimea referendum and International observers," *Digital Journal*, March 22, 2104, http://www.digitaljournal.com/news/politics/op-ed-the-crimea-referendum-and-international-observers/article/377812

11 Kenneth Rapoza, "One Year After Russia Annexed Crimea, Locals Prefer Moscow to Kiev," *Forbes*, March 20, 2015. That calm assessment evidently nettled someone higher up at *Forbes* (or higher than that), as it was fiercely countered ten days later: Andrea Chalupa, "One Year Later in Crimea: Polls Don't Tell the Whole Story," *Forbes*, March 30, 2015.

12 "A Russian Warning," Cluborlov, May 31, 2016, http://cluborlov.blogspot.com/2016/05/a-russian-warning.html

13 "Based on my observations in the streets, neither the official account nor many of the foreign versions are quite correct. There is no massacre in Tiananmen Square, for example, although there is plenty of killing elsewhere." Nicholas Kristof, "China Update: How the Hardliners Won," *New York Times*, November 12, 1989. (That admission comes at the tail-end of a very long article.)

Kristof's view was privately confirmed by an unnamed Chilean diplomat (who, working for the government of Gen. Pinochet, would not have been too soft on China). His "eye-witness account" was noted in two cables from the US embassy in Beijing to the State Department: Included in the cache of documents released by WikiLeaks in June, 2011, those two cables were ignored by "our free press," appearing only in the *Telegraph*. See Deirdre English, "Tiananmen Square 'massacre' was a myth," *Workers World*, June 29, 2011, http://www.workers.org/2011/world/tiananmen_0707/.

See also Jay Mathews, "The Myth of Tiananmen and the Price of Passive Press," *Columbia Journalism Review*, September/October, 1998; Gregory Clark, "Sri Lanka and Tiananmen: Time to Accept the Truth," *Japan Times*, June 11, 2009; and "A Student's Account of the Tiananmen Incident," *Multiple Texts*, May 26, 2009, http://multipletext.com/2009/5_Tiananmen_incident_witness.htm.

That there was lethal violence *beyond* the Square there is no doubt—although the evidence suggests a scene more complicated than the simple "massacre" invoked by "our free press" ad infinitum. (There was intense street fighting all throughout Beijing, with many soldiers killed along with protesters.) While it would serve us all—Chinese and Americans alike—to know the truth about what happened in Beijing, it obviously wouldn't serve the propaganda purposes behind those endless "memories" of that "massacre."

14 Richard Fausset and Campbell Robertson, "On Dallas Streets, Fearful Bystanders and Chilling Historical Echoes," July 8, 2016, *New York Times*, http://www.nytimes.com/2016/07/09/us/dallas-shooting-scene-chaos.html?_r=0.

15 Lance DeHaven-Smith, *Conspiracy Theory in America* (Austin: University of Texas Press, 2013).

16 See James Collier and Kenneth Collier, *Votescam: The Stealing of America* (Victoria House Press, 1992), available in print via http://www.votescam.org, and as an e-book from Open Road Integrated Media (http://www.openroadmedia.com/series/forbidden-bookshelf/).

17 Collier and Collier, *Votescam*.

On the theft of the 2004 election, see John Conyers et al., *What Went in Ohio: The Conyers Report on the 2004 Presidential Election* (Chicago: Chicago Review Press, 2005); Mark Crispin Miller, *Fooled Again: The Real Case for Electoral Reform*, paperback edition (New York: Basic Books, 2006); Steve Freeman and Joel Bleifuss, *Was the 2004 Presidential Election Stolen? Exit Polls, Election Fraud, and the Official Count* (New York: Seven Stories Press, 2006); Robert J. Fitrakis, Harvey Wasserman and Steven Rosenfeld, *What Happened in Ohio: A Documentary Record of Theft and Fraud in the 2004 Election* (New York: New Press, 2006); Richard Hayes Phillips, *Witness to a Crime: A Citizen's Audit of an American Election* (Election Defense Alliance, 2006), available for download at http://electiondefensealliance.org/richard_hayes_phillips.

On election fraud in the United States since 2004, see Mark Crispin Miller, ed. *Loser Take All: Election Fraud and the Subversion of American Democracy* (New York: Ig Publishing, 2006); See also the ongoing work of Bob Fitrakis and Harvey Wasserman at Free Press (http://freepress.org/profile/bob-fitrakis-and-harvey-wasserman), Greg Palast (http://www.gregpalast.com), Bev Harris (BlackBoxVoting.org), and Richard Charnin (https://richardcharnin.wordpress.com), and the 2016 documentary *I Voted?* (directed by Jason Grant Smith).

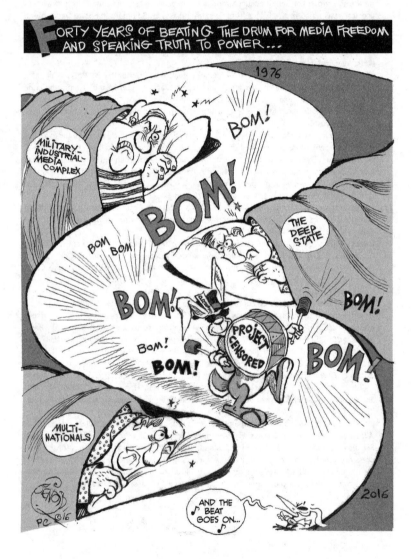

# Introduction

Andy Lee Roth and Mickey Huff

In his introduction to the first edition of *The Media Monopoly*, Ben H. Bagdikian reported that, when a small group of fifty corporate chiefs control "more than half the information and ideas" that reach the American people, "it is time for Americans to examine the institutions from which they receive their daily picture of the world."[1]

For forty years, Project Censored has done its part to contribute to this critical examination. Since 1976, when Carl Jensen established Project Censored, its participants have sought to provide a systematic critique of US corporate news media, drawing attention to how corporate reporting often limits the accepted scope of public debate on crucial public affairs and social issues to a narrow range of perspectives that reflect conventional political narratives and serve corporate interests. More specifically, over five decades, Project Censored has systematically documented approximately one thousand significant news stories, covered by independent journalists and news outlets, that the corporate media have either ignored altogether, or covered in only partial (i.e., incomplete and/or slanted) ways.[2] Documenting a diversity of censored or underreported news topics and stories, the Project—like Bagdikian's work—has consistently sought to educate the public about the crucial role of a free press and independent journalism for robust democracy. As Bagdikian frequently reminded the American public: Media power is political power.

Ben Bagdikian died in Berkeley, California on March 11, 2016. Remembering his distinguished career—which encompassed among its highlights a Peabody Award and a Pulitzer Prize, a pivotal part in the 1971 publication of the Pentagon Papers, and service as editor of the *Washington Post* and, subsequently, as dean of the Graduate School of Journalism at the University of California-

Berkeley—we dedicate the fortieth anniversary edition of *Censored* to Ben Bagdikian.

By 2004, when Bagdikian published the final edition of his pioneering study, *The New Media Monopoly*, the consolidation of media ownership had intensified to the point that he imagined the owners of the five remaining predominant media corporations "could fit in a generous phone booth." This imaginary phone booth would have held the chiefs of Time Warner, Disney, Viacom, News Corp, and Bertelsmann. "Their steady accumulation of power in the world of news, radio, television, magazines, books, and movies," Bagdikian wrote, "gave them a steady accumulation of power in politics."[3]

The Pew Research Center's "State of the News Media 2016" report reads like a continuation of the themes and concerns that Bagdikian addressed. The Center introduced its thirteenth annual report by observing how US newsrooms continue to undergo market-driven "tectonic shifts" that impact news audiences in both direct and not-so-obvious ways. For example, smaller budgets continue to lead to smaller newsrooms; five big technology companies—including Google, Facebook, and Yahoo, but not a single journalism outlet—now account for 65 percent of the money generated by online advertising; and the "tug and pull" between tech and journalism companies leaves it unclear what the future of the media industry will ultimately mean for "the public's ability to stay informed."[4] Original news reporting and writing are two fundamental tasks still performed by news organizations—rather than by tech companies. However, as the 2016 Pew report also noted, "Well reported news stories" are "not worth much" without "strong distribution and curation channels."[5]

Increasing the public's awareness of and appreciation for the best *independent* journalism is another aim that Project Censored has sought to fulfill throughout its forty-year history. Put another way, the Project has always balanced its *critique* of flawed corporate news coverage and censorship with an *affirmation* of the good work done by independent journalists and the news outlets that publish or broadcast their reporting.[6] Although Project Censored's annual listing of the most underreported stories can be interpreted as a damning critique of the corporate news media's blind spots and self-serving interests, it can also be read as evidence of the living legacy among independent reporters and news outlets of what Carl Jensen liked to call "good old-fashioned muckraking."[7]

Through the annual *Censored* yearbook, the Project's website, its weekly radio program, a pair of feature-length documentary films, and a packed calendar of public events, faculty members, college and university students, and media freedom activists affiliated with Project Censored consistently bring to greater public attention the independent news stories, journalists, and outlets that thrive outside the narrow spectrum of news and public affairs content provided by the corporate media. As we have suggested in previous *Censored* volumes, these independent journalists and outlets, along with Project Censored itself, constitute a developing *networked fourth estate*, characterized by both expert reporting that truly serves the public and economically viable, increasingly digital channels of curation and distribution.[8]

## INSIDE *CENSORED 2017*

The Project has covered a lot of ground in the past forty years—highlighting courageous independent journalism, fighting censorship, calling out Junk Food News, celebrating media democracy in action, deconstructing propaganda, and educating generations of students about the importance of critical media literacy—all in an effort to strengthen and make more democratic our Republic. This year, we continue these traditions in a volume that not only speaks truth to power, but also demonstrates that seeking and speaking truth *is* power. It is the power that We the People possess, and we must use our rights of free speech and especially the free press to inform ourselves as we strive to uphold the principles of social justice.

The book's first chapter calls attention to the Top 25 most important underreported and censored stories of the past year. These independent news stories, researched by hundreds of students and their respective faculty at close to two dozen colleges across the US and in Canada, vetted in several stages and ultimately voted on and selected by our esteemed panel of judges, represent the kind of reporting we need to be a functional self-governing society. This year's list reveals not only some of the major challenges we face in the US and around the world—from rampant militarism, corporate influence, and government corruption; to ongoing assaults on civil liberties and human rights; to the impacts of climate change—it also illuminates the efforts undertaken to address these issues, highlighting social justice success stories and those who remain steadfast and hopeful in the face of such adversity.

In Chapter 2, what we call Censored Déjà Vu, Susan Rahman and her students at College of Marin, with the assistance of students from Diablo Valley College and the University of California, Davis, revisited past censored stories to see if the corporate media have discovered them yet. Some stories were eventually picked up, albeit with lag time, while others have remained forgotten, as if tossed in one of George Orwell's memory holes from *1984*. This year, for our fortieth anniversary, we asked our twenty-eight judges to vote on what they thought were the most significant of the Project's number one stories, going all the way back to 1976. The six stories that received the most votes are those we revisited this year, and they represent a cross section of the many underreported news stories that the Project has highlighted since its inception. We trace the development of these stories and topics, including the Myth of Black Progress, Ocean Acidification, Corporate Crime, Wealth Inequality, and No Habeas Corpus for "any person," analyzing their status in terms of media coverage and the public's responses to these critical issues. One of the stories our judges selected relates to the primary concern of Project Censored: the media itself. Ben Bagdikian's "Information Monopoly" story from 1987, warning against the increasing concentration of media ownership, is as timely and relevant as ever.

Chapter 3 is our annual Junk Food News and News Abuse report. Nolan Higdon and student researchers from five colleges investigated the corporate media's "War on Reality," using the presidential election season as a case study. The authors present an empty calorie Junk Food News menu of ubiquitous sensationalism, vapid coverage, and trivial distractions, as well as the skewed framing, glaring biases, and prevalent propaganda masquerading as journalism that we at Project Censored call News Abuse. From Trump trumping everyone in coverage to Clinton's coronation by the press, reporting about the primaries was among the worst we've encountered in recent history. In fact, a Harvard study on media election coverage, published just as our book was completed, revealed many of the same bleak findings and failings of the corporate press.[9] Pointing out the tabloid character and proselytizing aims of what often passes as "news" has become an online phenomenon, having spawned its own set of social media memes; but it all started with the Project's founder, Carl Jensen, in 1983 when he coined the term "Junk Food News," or "Twinkies for the brain."

Chapter 4, "Media Democracy in Action," provides welcome contrast to Junk Food News and News Abuse. Consistent with this year's #1 *Censored* story, on the global presence of US military forces, this year's chapter highlights reporting on US imperialism by Mnar Muhawesh of MintPress News, Eric Draitser of Stop Imperialism, and Abby Martin, host of *The Empire Files*. Their independent reporting consistently addresses this third rail, adding critical perspective and a diversity of voices so absent from corporate news coverage. Dovetailing with *Censored* story #14, on FBI surveillance, Peter B. Collins reminds us how the FBI and local police departments now employ legal powers, originally intended to target terrorists, against nonviolent activists. Collins champions the role of whistleblowers, acting in the public interest, whose truth telling serves as a corrective to a failing system. Regular followers of Project Censored will no doubt already be familiar with the crucial work done by Food & Water Watch. Here, Darcey Rakestraw provides an inside look at how the organization has so successfully countered corporate spin on fracking and water contamination, agriculture, and water privatization. These examples not only provide inspiration but also offer lessons that other media-savvy activists can use to advance their own work. Finally, Susan Rahman and Eliana Dimopoulos introduce another kind of media democracy. Their article describes how the combination of service learning and universal design challenges traditional educational models and promotes greater inclusivity.

In Chapter 5, "Contested Visions, Imperfect Information, and the Persistence of Conspiracy Theories," Susan Maret tackles, like few can, the difficult but significant topic of government secrecy and the formation of conspiracy theories. Maret, an expert on government secrecy, charts out varied definitions of "Conspiracy Theory" (CT) and the many problems surrounding CT research. She quotes historian Kathryn Olmsted, who noted that "[w]hen citizens cannot trust their government to tell the truth, when they are convinced that public officials routinely conspire, lie, and conceal their crimes, they become less likely to trust the government to do anything. The result is a profoundly weakened polity, with fewer citizens voting and more problems left unaddressed for a future generation that is ever more cynical about the possibility of reforms." Maret's work aims to address these challenges and proposes "nine patterns that take the scholarly community to task on its framing and views of conspiracy theories." She suggests "a pressing need for new directions in critical and interpretive research and methods," and offers "a set of recommendations . . . for the research community to consider in its future study of CTs." Ultimately, Maret believes that in a post-9/11 world, "these approaches form the basis for a more holistic understanding of the ways conspiracy theories propagate and memetically crawl through social systems in response to imperfect publicity and transparency."

In Chapter 6, "Played by the Mighty Wurlitzer: The Press, the CIA, and the Subversion of Truth," veteran Project contributor Brian Covert focuses on the history and role of one of America's most secretive institutions and its influence over the news media. In other words, it isn't just corporate owners and advertisers who have an interest in shaping public opinion for profit via the press; the so-called Deep State, or secret government departments and agencies, also aided in the engineering of opinion in support of US Cold War and anti-communism policies. Readers familiar with the history of CIA propaganda efforts may recall "Operation Mockingbird," but Covert's research reveals that this may have only been a minor project. He focuses more specifically on the network of CIA assets in the media that could play the press, and thus the public, like a Mighty Wurlitzer. Covert argues that the CIA cast a long shadow over America's so-called free press, and in newsrooms around the world. Despite the declared cessation of various CIA programs, or their specific names, the history uncovered by Covert provides vital context for developing a deeper understanding of the relationships between major news media outlets and government agencies, as well as a more sophisticated framework with which to critique media control, censorship, and propaganda in the present.

Former Project Censored director Peter Phillips returns to the pages of *Censored* this year with more research on the global elites and their power structures. In Chapter 7, "Selling Empire, War, and Capitalism: Public Relations Propaganda Firms in Service to the Transnational Capitalist Class," Phillips, along with research assistants from Sonoma State University, investigates the executives and clients of the most powerful public relations firms in the world, and argues how the extremely wealthy of the planet pursue their imperial interests at the expense of the rest of us with the help of massive PR propaganda campaigns.

Chapter 8, "Remote Control: Electronic Surveillance and the Demise of Human Dignity" by Elliot D. Cohen, debunks the official government narrative—conventionally reproduced by the corporate news media—that current US government surveillance practices preempt terrorist attacks without threatening civil liberties. Cohen tracks the history of the US surveillance system, which now aims for "total information awareness," considering how newly developing technologies augur a future social order that would threaten the very basis of human dignity. How to avoid this dystopian end? Cohen identifies eleven specific points about the NSA's mass surveillance program that journalists should consistently emphasize in order to educate the American public. The media thus play a crucial role in protecting human freedom, he argues, but ultimately the American people must act to hold their government accountable.

Continuing on the theme of surveillance and civil rights, in Chapter 9, attorney Shahid Buttar reminds readers of President Dwight D. Eisenhower's prescient 1961 Farewell Address. In "Ike's Dystopian Dream, and How It Came True," Buttar writes of the omnipresence of the military, security, and surveillance industrial complex and its impact on democratic culture and civil liberties. "The connection between police surveillance . . . and the militarization it enables and advances . . . may escape the attention of an observer unaware of Eisenhower's warning. But it emerges in stark relief when informed by Ike's warning that 'in every city . . . the very structure of our society' would be influenced by corporate profit motives fueling military operations essentially seeking new targets to justify themselves." Buttar makes the important connection of the impacts militarization and surveillance have on a purportedly free society, stating, "When vulnerable community members are intimidated into silence by the knowledge that their voices and concerns will be publicized or retained, it is not merely they who suffer. The theory of democracy animating the First Amendment presupposes the importance and primacy of public debate, not only as an exercise of a speaker's rights but also to satisfy the rights of listeners to hear from all voices, grow informed by their perspectives, and make better reasoned judgments as participants in the political process."

In the book's closing chapter, we return to one of the Project's main missions over the past forty years, that of media education. This past year, we partnered with the Action Coalition for Media Education (ACME) and the graduate program in Media Literacy and Digital Culture (MLDC) at Sacred Heart University in Connecticut as part of our ongoing commitment to education. In this chapter, Bill Yousman, director of the MLDC program, asks "Who's Afraid of Critical Media Literacy?" Yousman explains what is so crucial about the term "critical" in the context of media literacy education. It means not merely knowing about media systems, but also critiquing and deconstructing them, which he differentiates from simply "bashing media." Yousman discusses critical media literacy in the context of critical theories of society, communication, and culture. He argues that "critical media literacy goes beyond more conservative approaches to media education by starting with the recognition that media perform not just as information and entertainment but even more crucially as the voice of the powerful in society. Critical media literacy also adopts the position that this voice can and should be challenged by alternative voices. Advocating for justice and social transformation is thus central to a critical media literacy approach." At Project Censored, we couldn't agree more.

## DAILY EXPERIENCE AND DEMOCRATIC EXPECTATIONS

The top story in Project Censored's 1987 list of underreported news, "The Information Monopoly," drew heavily on reporting by Ben Bagdikian, published in *Extra!* (the newsletter of Fairness and Accuracy In Reporting) and the *Multinational Monitor* (founded by Ralph

Nader). Project Censored's synopsis quoted Bagdikian's warning: "A shrinking number of large media corporations now regard monopoly, oligopoly, and historic levels of profit as not only normal, but as their earned right. In the process, the usual democratic expectations for the media—diversity of ownership and ideas—have disappeared as the goal of official policy and, worse, as a daily experience of a generation of American readers and viewers."[10] Thirty years on, Bagdikian's analysis remains salient.[11]

Throughout the pages of *Censored 2017*—not to mention across its forty-year history—Project Censored has sought to shape and elevate the public's democratic expectations. Now more than perhaps at any previous period in US history, independent journalists and news outlets make it possible for our society's members to experience, on a daily basis, a broad spectrum of high quality news reporting not shaped by corporate filters.

But news is unlikely to improve our lives, much less our society, if its readers and viewers understand themselves only as readers and viewers. The daily experience of democracy that Bagdikian understood to hinge on diverse media ownership and a broad spectrum of ideas becomes more real and meaningful when each of us realizes our potentially *active* role in our digitally connected, media-saturated nation and world.

At its best, news not only helps us *understand* human events and the forces that shape them, but also motivates us to engage our skills and passions in order to *improve* the human condition and the world that supports us. The authors whose work is featured here exemplify that dual mission. We offer *Censored 2017* with the hopes that it will inform and inspire not only those who have already been doing this work for some time, but also a new generation that may live to see an age beyond the corporate media's information monopoly. Together we can sustain and build the independent news institutions that will ultimately allow us to transform our daily picture of the world.

## Notes

1   Ben H. Bagdikian, *The Media Monopoly* (Boston: Beacon Press, 1983), xix.
2   The first chapter of this volume features twenty-five of these news stories. The Project Censored website archives all forty years of the Project's annual top 25 underreported story lists. See http://projectcensored.org/top-25-censored-stories-of-all-time/.

3    Ben H. Bagdikian, *The New Media Monopoly* (Boston: Beacon Press, 2004), 27, 28.

4    Amy Mitchell and Jesse Holcomb, "State of the News Media 2016," Pew Research Center, June 15, 2016, http://www.journalism.org/2016/06/15/state-of-the-news-media-2016/.

5    Mitchell and Holcomb, "State of the News Media 2016."

6    For a non-trivial assessment of what constitutes "good work" in a profession, and the factors that promote or impede it, see Howard Gardner, Mihaly Csikszentmihalyi, and William Damon, *Good Work: When Excellence and Ethics Meet* (New York: Basic Books, 2001). The authors define "good work" as "work of expert quality that benefits the broader society." (p. ix).

7    See, for example, Carl Jensen, "What Happened to Good Old-Fashioned Muckracking?" in *Into the Buzzsaw: Leading Journalists Expose the Myth of a Free Press*, ed. Kristina Borjesson (Amherst, MA: Prometheus Books, 2002), 333–50.

8    Yochai Benkler coined the term "networked fourth estate" to describe a diverse movement of organizationally decentralized journalism that is challenging the previous dominance of an elite-controlled, centralized, top-down mass media. See Yochai Benkler, "WikiLeaks and the Networked Fourth Estate," in *Beyond WikiLeaks: Implications for the Future of Communications, Journalism and Society*, eds. Benedetta Brevini, Arne Hintz, and Patrick McCurdy (New York: Palgrave Macmillan, 2013), 11–34; and Andy Lee Roth and Project Censored, "Breaking the Corporate News Frame through Validated Independent News Online," in *Media Education for a Digital Generation*, eds. Julie Frechette and Rob Williams (New York and London: Routledge, 2016), 173–186.

9    Thomas E. Patterson, "Pre-Primary News Coverage of the 2016 Presidential Race: Trump's Rise, Sanders' Emergence, Clinton's Struggle," Shorenstein Center on Media, Politics and Public Policy (John F. Kennedy School of Government, Harvard University), June 13, 2016, http://shorensteincenter.org/pre-primary-news-coverage-2016-trump-clinton-sanders/.

10   Ben Bagdikian, "The 50, 26, 20 . . . Corporations That Own Our Media," *Extra!* (Fairness and Accuracy In Reporting), June 1, 1987, http://fair.org/extra/the-50-26-20-corporations-that-own-our-media/.

11   For an update on Project Censored's 1987 "Information Monopoly" coverage, see Chapter 2 of this volume.

# CHAPTER 1

# The Top *Censored* Stories and Media Analysis of 2015–16

Compiled and edited by Andy Lee Roth

## INTRODUCTION

The image of "unfiltered" news is powerful.[1] For forty years, Project Censored has worked to expose and oppose news censorship, and to champion independent journalists and news outlets as alternatives to the filtered version of news identified by Edward S. Herman and Noam Chomsky's "propaganda model."[2]

So in March 2016 when a tech incubator known as Jigsaw announced the launch of Unfiltered.news, an online tool for tracking "important global stories and perspectives that may not be covered in your location," we at the Project noted the development with interest.[3] Unfiltered.news uses data from Google News to provide a visualization of news topics that are popular globally but underreported in the user's location or a location selected by the user. Google News tracks over seventy-five thousand news outlets in more than thirty-eight languages. (Jigsaw is a subsidiary of Alphabet, which also owns Google.)

To determine what news is "less reported" in a region, Unfiltered.news uses an algorithm that compares "the number of times a topic is mentioned worldwide against the number of times it is mentioned in that location." The result, according to the website, is "a cross-lingual signal for who is saying what in the world's media." The site features a timeline that allows users to track how coverage of a topic has changed over time. Using Google Translate, the site allows users to read headlines in any of forty different languages.

Noting that search engines, social media, and news aggregators are "great at surfacing information close to our interests" but limited by the topics people choose to follow, not to mention the languages they can read, Jigsaw's Izzie Zahorian and C. J. Adams framed Unfiltered.news as an effort to counter the "news bubble" that otherwise "shapes our perspective and awareness of the world."[4]

This all sounded great. But there are limitations to the data. Thus, as the Unfiltered.news site acknowledged, topics (e.g., Zika virus) do not map to larger concepts (such as health), and the number of times a topic is mentioned does not necessarily correspond to its importance.[5] A deeper issue with how Unfiltered.news works was not acknowledged on its website: like the search engines and social media that Jigsaw's Zahorian and Adams found limiting, Unfiltered.news also relies on an algorithm to determine the news stories it shows us. Interesting and useful though it may prove to be, Unfiltered.news is another example of what Mark Frary of the *Index on Censorship* meant when he wrote, "Technology companies are deciding which news items you see online."[6] (For more on Frary's article and the role of algorithms in shaping what news we see, see *Censored* story #4, "Search Engine Algorithms and Electronic Voting Machines Could Swing 2016 Election," below).

Of course, there is at least one other way to track news stories that go underreported, as readers who have followed Project Censored over the years know and appreciate. Since 1976, beginning with Professor Carl Jensen and the students in his courses at Sonoma State University, faculty members and students affiliated with the Project have produced an annual list of important news stories reported by independent journalists and news outlets that have been either ignored or only partially covered in the corporate press. Beginning in 2009–10, professors Peter Phillips and Mickey Huff launched Project Censored's campus affiliates program, which expanded the annual research of underreported stories to approximately two dozen college and university campuses around the US and the world.[7]

Though technology plays an increasingly important role in the identification and evaluation of stories Project Censored reviews as Validated Independent News stories, our experience over decades suggests that no algorithm can take the place of the critical thinking and media literacy skills that students (and their faculty mentors) employ and develop in determining whether a news story should be considered "underreported" or not. (For specifics on the yearlong, five-stage review process by which Project Censored determines each year's top *Censored* stories, see "A Note on Research and Evaluation of *Censored* News Stories," below.) Powerful though Jigsaw's Unfiltered.news algorithm may be, it still renders the user relatively passive in making judgments about whether or not a given news topic or story is actually underreported.

The 2015–16 list of the most underreported news stories in this chapter represents the collective efforts of 221 students and 33 faculty members from 18 college and university campuses across the US and Canada, who identified and vetted the 235 Validated Independent News stories from which this volume's top *Censored* stories were drawn. A panel of 28 esteemed judges voted to determine the rank order of the Top 25 list.

From the global presence of US military forces (*Censored* story #1) to the "Crisis in Evidence-Based Medicine" (story #2) and the FBI's Preventing Violent Extremism in Schools program (story #14), from the links between climate change and gender inequality (story #15) to the "Walmarting" of public education (story #20), the stories reported by independent journalists and identified, vetted, and summarized by Project Censored–affiliated students and faculty highlight significant public issues about which most residents of the US are likely to be uninformed. Although each individual story is important in its own right, we present an annual list of these stories to raise public awareness about the limits of corporate news coverage and to increase public appreciation for the importance of a truly independent press.

As in previous years, for each of the following *Censored* story synopses, we identify not only the names and publication sources of the original news stories, but also the names and campus affiliations of the students and faculty members who vetted the stories. We identify the student researchers and faculty evaluators by name as evidence of the collective, human effort required to systematically track underreported news topics—a task that simply cannot be achieved indirectly by outsourcing the analysis and judgment to an algorithm, no matter how sophisticated it may be. The crediting of students and faculty is also intended to inspire additional students and teachers who want to do this kind of work themselves to join us. Those interested can learn more about how to do so in this volume (see "How to Support Project Censored" in the back matter) or online (under "Censorship Guide for Teachers," on our website's homepage, http://projectcensored.org/).

The brief synopses that follow are not meant to replace the original news reports on which they are based. Instead, they summarize the stories' key points, hopefully in ways that lead interested readers back to the journalists' original reports. These independent journalists and news organizations deserve your support, and the otherwise under-reported stories that they cover demand your engagement.

ACKNOWLEDGMENTS: Special thanks to Tom Haseloff, Brandy Miceli, Kamila Janik, and Kylene Biaggi for assistance in the final review of this year's Censored stories.

## A NOTE ON RESEARCH AND EVALUATION OF
## *CENSORED* NEWS STORIES

How do we at Project Censored identify and evaluate independent news stories, and how do we know that the Top 25 stories that we bring forward each year are not only relevant and significant, but also trustworthy? The answer is that each news story candidate undergoes rigorous review, which takes place in multiple stages during each annual cycle. Although adapted to take advantage of both the Project's expanding affiliates program and current technologies, the vetting process is quite similar to the one Project Censored founder Carl Jensen established forty years ago.

Story candidates are initially identified by Project Censored professors and students, or are nominated by members of the general public, who bring them to the Project's attention through our website.[8] Together, faculty and students vet each story candidate in terms of its importance, timeliness, quality of sources, and corporate news coverage. If it fails on any one of these criteria, the story is not included.

Once Project Censored receives the story candidate, we undertake a second round of judgment, using the same criteria and updating the review to include any subsequent competing corporate coverage. Stories that pass this round of review get posted on our website as Validated Independent News stories (VINs).[9]

In early spring, we present all VINs in the current cycle to the faculty and students at all of our affiliate campuses, and to our national and international panel of judges, who cast votes to winnow the story candidates from several hundred to twenty-five.

Once the Top 25 list has been determined, Project Censored student interns begin another intensive review of each story using LexisNexis and ProQuest databases. Additional faculty and students contribute to this final stage of review.

The Top 25 finalists are then sent to our panel of judges, who vote to rank them in numerical order. At the same time, these experts—including media studies professors, professional journalists, and a former commissioner of the Federal Communications Commission, among others—offer their insights on the stories' strengths and weaknesses.[10]

Thus, by the time a story appears in the pages of *Censored*, it has undergone at least five distinct rounds of review and evaluation.

Although the stories that Project Censored brings forward may be socially and politically controversial—and sometimes even psychologically challenging—we are confident that each is the result of serious journalistic effort, and therefore deserves greater public attention.

# THE TOP CENSORED STORIES AND
# MEDIA ANALYSIS OF 2015–16

## 1.

## US Military Forces Deployed in 70 Percent of World's Nations

Nick Turse, "A Secret War in 135 Countries," *Tomdispatch*, September 24, 2015, http://www.tomdispatch. com/blog/176048/.

Nick Turse, "The Stealth Expansion of a Secret US Drone Base in Africa," *Intercept*, October 21, 2015, https://theintercept.com/2015/10/21/stealth-expansion-of-secret-us-drone-base-in-africa/.

Nick Turse, "American Special Operations Forces Have a Very Funny Definition of Success," *Nation*, October 26, 2015, http://www.thenation.com/article/american-special-operations-forces-have-a-very-funny-definition-of-success/.

**Student Researchers:** Scott Arrow (Sonoma State University) and Bri Silva (College of Marin)

**Faculty Evaluators:** Robert McNamara (Sonoma State University) and Susan Rahman (College of Marin)

If you throw a dart at a world map and do not hit water, Nick Turse reported for *Tomdispatch*, the odds are that US Special Operations Forces "have been there sometime in 2015." According to a spokesperson for Special Operations Command (SOCOM), in 2015 Special Operations Forces (SOF) were deployed in 147 of the world's 195 recognized nations, an increase of eighty percent since 2010. "The global growth of SOF missions has been breathtaking," Turse wrote.

As SOCOM commander General Joseph Votel told the audience of the Aspen Security Forum in July 2015, more SOF troops are deployed to more locations and are conducting more operations than at the height of the Afghan and Iraq wars. In Turse's words, "Every day, in around 80 or more countries that Special Operations Command will not name, they undertake missions the command refuses to talk about."

Calculated in 2014 constant dollars, the SOCOM budget has more than tripled since 2001, when funding totaled $3 billion. By 2015, SOCOM funding had risen to nearly $10 billion. That figure, Turse noted, did not include additional funding from specific military branches, which SOCOM estimated to amount to another $8 billion annually, or other undisclosed sums that were not available to the Government Accountability Office.

Every day, Turse wrote, "America's most elite troops are carrying out missions in 80 to 90 nations." The majority of these are training missions, "designed to tutor proxies and forge stronger ties with allies." Training missions focus on everything from basic rifle marksmanship and land navigation to small unit tactics and counter-terrorism operations. For example, between 2012 and 2014, Special Operations Forces carried out five hundred Joint Combined Exchange Training (JCET) missions in as many as sixty-seven countries per year. Officially, JCETs are devoted to training US forces, but according to a SOCOM official interviewed by Turse, these missions also "foster key military partnerships with foreign militaries" and "build interoperability between U.S. SOF and partner-nation forces." JCETs, Turse wrote, "are just a fraction of the story" when it comes to multinational overseas training operations. In 2014, Special Operations Forces organized seventy-five training operations in thirty countries, a figure projected to increase to ninety-eight exercises by the end of 2015, according to the Office of the Under Secretary of Defense.

In addition to training, Special Operations Forces also engage in "direct action." Counterterrorism missions, including what Turse described as "low-profile drone assassinations and kill/capture raids by muscled-up, high-octane operators," are the specific domains of Joint Special Operations Command (JSOC) forces, such as the Navy's SEAL Team 6 and the Army's Delta Force.

Africa has seen the greatest increase in SOCOM deployments since 2006. In that year, just 1 percent of special operators deployed overseas went to Africa. As of 2014, that figure had risen to 10 percent. In the *Intercept*, Turse reported on the development by US forces of the Chabelley Airfield in the East African nation of Djibouti. "Unbeknownst to most Americans and without any apparent public announcement," Turse wrote in October 2015, "the U.S. has recently taken steps to transform this tiny, out-of-the-way outpost into an 'enduring' base, a key hub for its secret war, run by the U.S. military's Joint Special Operations Command (JSOC), in Africa and the Middle East." Chabelley, he reported, has become "essential" to secret US drone operations over Yemen, southwest Saudi Arabia, Somalia, and parts of Ethiopia and southern Egypt. Aerial images of Chabelley taken between April 2013 and March 2015 testify to the significant expansion of the base and the presence of drones, though officials refused to respond to questions about the number and types of drones based there. As Turse summarized, "The startling transformation of this little-known garrison in this little-known country is in line with U.S. military activity in Africa, where, largely under the radar, the number of missions, special operations deployments, and outposts has grown rapidly and with little outside scrutiny."[11]

If, as Turse reported, SOCOM has "grown in every conceivable way from funding and personnel to global reach and deployments" since 9/11, has its expansion resulted in significant success? In an October 2015 report for the *Nation*, Turse reported skepticism from a number of experts in response to this question. According to Sean Naylor, the author of *Relentless Strike*, a history of Joint Special Operations Command, JSOC operations are "a tool in the policymaker's toolkit," not a "substitute for strategy." JSOC may have had an impact on the history of Iraq—where its forces captured Saddam Hussein, killed Uday and Qusay Hussein, and "eviscerated" al-Qaeda in Iraq—but, as Turse wrote, impacts are not the same as successes. Similarly, Andrew Bacevich, a Vietnam veteran and author of *Breach of Trust: How Americans Failed Their Soldiers and Their Country*, told Turse, "As far back as Vietnam . . . the United States military has tended to confuse inputs with outcomes. Effort, as measured by operations conducted, bomb tonnage dropped, or bodies counted, is taken as evidence of progress made. Today, tallying up the number of countries in which Special Operations forces are present repeats this error."

Corporate media have not covered the massive expansion of Special Operations Forces around the globe, much less raised critical questions about whether these missions result in meaningful accomplishments. The increase that has taken place over the past five to ten years is not "breaking" news, and so it has gone all but completely unreported by the corporate press. Instead, the global presence of US military personnel is typically treated as the unspoken background for more dramatic reports of specific military operations or policy decisions. Thus, for example, in October 2015, *Time* magazine ran a graphic documenting "places with some of the most significant numbers" of US military personnel stationed "in over 150 countries across the world."[12] However, the *Time* map of the world featured just nine points—none of which were located in Africa—and the entire graphic ran as a sidebar to the primary story, about President

Obama's announcement to maintain the current number of troops in Afghanistan through most of 2016, which reversed his earlier plan to withdraw most military personnel by the end of his presidency.

## 2.

### Crisis in Evidence-Based Medicine

Richard Horton, "What is Medicine's 5 Sigma?," *Lancet* 385, no. 9976, April 11, 2015, http://www.thelancet.com/pdfs/journals/lancet/PIIS0140-6736%2815%2960696-1.pdf.

Charlie Cooper, "Anti-Depressant was Given to Millions of Young People 'After Trials Showed It was Dangerous,'" *Independent*, September 16, 2015, http://www.independent.co.uk/life-style/health-and-families/health-news/anti-depressant-was-given-to-millions-of-young-people-after-trials-showed-it-was-dangerous-10504555.html.

Sarah Boseley, "Seroxat Study Under-Reported Harmful Effects on Young People, Say Scientists," *Guardian*, September 16, 2015, https://www.theguardian.com/science/2015/sep/16/seroxat-study-harmful-effects-young-people.

**Student Researchers:** Joshua Gill-Sutton and Adaeze Iroka (San Francisco State University)

**Faculty Evaluator:** Kenn Burrows (San Francisco State University)

In April 2015, the *Lancet's* editor, Richard Horton, wrote, "Something has gone fundamentally wrong with one of our greatest human creations." Describing the upshot of a UK symposium held that month on the reproducibility and reliability of biomedical research, Horton summarized the "case against science":

> [M]uch of the scientific literature, perhaps half, may simply be untrue. Afflicted by studies with small sample sizes, tiny effects, invalid exploratory analyses, and flagrant conflicts of interest, together with an obsession for pursuing fashionable trends of dubious importance, science has taken a turn towards darkness... The apparent endemicity of bad research behaviour is alarming.

Horton is not the first editor of a prominent medical journal to raise these concerns. In 2009, Marcia Angell, a former editor of the *New England Journal of Medicine*, made comparable claims in an article for the *New York Review of Books*:

> It is simply no longer possible to believe much of the clinical research that is published, or to rely on the judgment of trusted physicians or authoritative medical guidelines. I take

no pleasure in this conclusion, which I reached slowly and reluctantly over my two decades as editor of *The New England Journal of Medicine*.[13]

Countering the pharmaceutical industry's undue influence on the medical profession, Angell concluded, would require "a sharp break from an extremely lucrative pattern of behavior." Horton's *Lancet* editorial echoed Angell's assessment: "Can bad scientific practices be fixed? Part of the problem is that no-one is incentivised to be right. Instead, scientists are incentivised to be productive and innovative."

No biomedical study better epitomizes the corruption and conflicts of interest noted by insider critics like Angell and Horton than Study 329, a now notorious clinical trial published in the *Journal of the American Academy of Child and Adolescent Psychiatry* in 2001. Study 329 reported that paroxetine—marketed by SmithKline Beecham (now GlaxoSmithKline, or GSK) as Paxil in the US and as Seroxat in the UK—was safe and effective for treating depressed children and adolescents. A GSK marketing campaign built on the published study, touting the drug's "remarkable efficacy and safety," led to doctors prescribing Paxil to more than two million US children and adolescents by the end of 2002.

However, within a year of the original report, the US Food and Drug Administration declared Study 329 a "failed trial" because further evidence indicated that adolescents prescribed the drug to treat depression fared no better than those on a placebo. In 2003, UK drug regulators instructed doctors not to prescribe Seroxat to adolescents. In 2012, in what the US Department of Justice described as the "largest health care fraud settlement in U.S. history," GSK paid a $3 billion fine to resolve its liability over fraud allegations and failure to report safety data.[14]

In 2015 the *BMJ* published a major reanalysis of GSK's Study 329.[15] Charlie Cooper of the *Independent* reported that the reanalysis—conducted by an international team of researchers from Australia, Canada, the US, and the UK, and based on thousands of pages of newly available GSK data—"starkly" contradicted the original report's claims. Furthermore, Cooper noted, the reassessment of Study 329 marked "a milestone in the medical community's campaign to open up clinical trial data held by pharmaceutical companies to independent scientific scrutiny."

As Sarah Boseley reported for the *Guardian*, the reanalysis of Study 329 found that paroxetine's beneficial effects were far less, and its harmful effects far greater, than the original study reported. In particular, by examining the full set of clinical trials data, the researchers who conducted the reassessment found that 11 of the 275 children and adolescents on the drug developed suicidal or self-harming behavior. The original study had acknowledged only 5 of these cases. David Healy, a psychiatry professor and one of the reassessment's coauthors, observed, "This is a very high rate of kids going on to become suicidal. It doesn't take expertise to find this. It takes extraordinary expertise to avoid finding it." Boseley's report also documented renewed calls for the *Journal of the American Academy of Child and Adolescent Psychiatry* to retract the original GSK study, whose lead author was Martin Keller of Brown University. Peter Doshi, the *BMJ*'s associate editor, observed, "It is often said that science self-corrects. But for those who have been calling for a retraction of the Keller paper for many years, the system has failed." Neither the journal's editors nor any of the paper's listed authors have intervened to correct the record, and none of the authors have been disciplined, Doshi noted.

Nevertheless, as documented by Charlie Cooper of the *Independent* and Sarah Boseley of the *Guardian*, the reanalysis of the complete set of original clinical trials data for Study 329 is the first major success of a new open data initiative known as Restoring Invisible and Abandoned Trials (RIAT), which has been promoted by the *BMJ*. As Cooper reported, "The *BMJ*'s final judgment on the infamous 'Study 329' represents a symbolic victory for the burgeoning 'open data' movement in health." RIAT is part of a broader movement to force pharmaceutical companies to make all their data available for independent scientific scrutiny. The AllTrials campaign, which calls for open publication of all clinical trials results, now has the backing of over six hundred medical and research organizations, Cooper reported. Boseley's *Guardian* article quoted *BMJ* editor in chief Fiona Godlee, who said that the reanalysis of Study 329 showed "the extent to which drug regulation is failing us." Godlee called for independent rather than industry-funded and -managed clinical trials, as well as legislation "to ensure that the results of all clinical trials are made fully available" to third-party scrutiny. Both news stories noted the cooperation of GlaxoSmithKline in making the original data available for reanalysis. GSK posted seventy-seven thousand pages of de-identified case reports from the trial on a website—though, it should be noted, the company was obliged to do so under the terms of their settlement.

Richard Horton's *Lancet* editorial received no coverage in the US corporate press. The *Washington Post* featured one story on the reanalysis of the original paroxetine study. The article provided a great deal of information about the misrepresentation of the original study—including, for instance, that the discrepancy between the original report and the *BMJ* reanalysis was partly due to "the miscoding of a serious suicide attempt as 'emotional lability,' a temporary condition that involves uncontrollable episodes of crying."[16] However, the *Washington Post* report made only passing mention of the open data movement and did not identify any of the specific initiatives (such as RIAT or AllTrials) by name.[17] Otherwise, the corporate press ignored the reassessment of the paroxetine study.

In May 2014, President Obama signed the Digital Accountability and Transparency Act.[18] Although it requires federal agencies to make data—including funding sources for clinical trials—publicly available, the DATA Act's requirements do not apply to privately funded biomedical research.

## 3.

### Rising Carbon Dioxide Levels Threaten to Permanently Disrupt Vital Ocean Bacteria

Robert Perkins, "Climate Change Will Irreversibly Force Key Ocean Bacteria into Overdrive," *USC News* (University of Southern California), September 1, 2015, https://news.usc.edu/85742/ climate-change-will-irreversibly-force-key-ocean-bacteria-into-overdrive/.

Emma Howard, "Climate Change Will Alter Ocean Bacteria Crucial to Food Chain—Study," *Guardian*, September 2, 2015, http://www.theguardian.com/environment/2015/sep/02/ climate-change-will-alter-ocean-micro-organisms-crucial-to-food-chain-say-scientists.

**Student Researcher:** Ally Spero (Sonoma State University)

**Faculty Evaluator:** Carmen Works (Sonoma State University)

Imagine a car heading toward a cliff's edge with its gas pedal stuck to the floor. That, Robert Perkins wrote, is a metaphor for "what climate change will do to the key group of ocean bacteria known as *Trichodesmium*," according to a study published in the September 2015 issue of *Nature Communications* by researchers at the University of Southern California and Woods Hole Oceanographic Institution.[19]

*Trichodesmium* is found in nutrient-poor parts of the ocean, where it converts nitrogen gas into material that can be used by other forms of life. From algae to whales, all life needs nitrogen to grow. Reporting for the *Guardian*, Emma Howard quoted Eric Webb, one of the study's researchers, who explained how the process of "nitrogen fixation" makes *Trichodesmium* "the fertilising agent of the open ocean."

The study tested the effects of elevated levels of carbon dioxide by subjecting hundreds of generations of *Trichodesmium* bred over a five-year period to $CO_2$ levels predicted for the year 2100 by the Intergovernmental Panel on Climate Change. Responding to increased ocean acidification, the bacteria went into "reproductive overdrive," Howard reported, evolving to grow faster and to produce 50 percent more nitrogen. One consequence of this is that *Trichodesmium* could consume significant quantities of nutrients that are in limited supply in the ocean, such as iron and phosphorus, leaving other organisms that depend on the same nutrients without enough to survive. Alternatively, *Trichodesmium* might consume nutrients at a rate that would lead to its own extinction, leaving other organisms without the nitrogen that the bacteria makes available. Either way, the effects of elevated $CO_2$ levels on the bacteria could trigger catastrophic effects up the marine food chain.

Most significantly, the researchers found that even when the bacteria was returned to lower, present-day levels of carbon dioxide, *Trichodesmium* remained "stuck in the fast lane," a finding that Webb described as "unprecedented in evolutionary biology." The study's lead author, David Hutchins, observed, "Losing the ability to regulate your growth rate is not a healthy thing . . . The last thing you want is to be stuck with these high growth rates when there aren't enough nutrients to go around. It's a losing strategy in the struggle to survive."

The next stages of the team's research involve studying the DNA of *Trichodesmium* to better understand "how and why the irreversible evolution occurs," Perkins reported.

In addition to the coverage noted here, the *Nature Communications* study was reported by Grist, Reuters, and, in the corporate press, by the *Washington Post*.[20]

## 4.

### Search Engine Algorithms and Electronic Voting Machines Could Swing 2016 Election

Robert Epstein, "How Google Could Rig the 2016 Election," *Politico*, August 19, 2015, http://www.politico.com/magazine/story/2015/08/how-google-could-rig-the-2016-election-121548.

Mark Frary, "Whose World are You Watching? The Secret Algorithms Controlling the News We See," *Index on Censorship* 44, no. 4 (December 2015), 69–73. [Extract available via: http://ioc.sagepub.com/content/44/4/69.extract]

Lawrence Norden and Christopher Famighetti, "America's Voting Machines at Risk," Brennan Center for Justice (New York University School of Law), September 15, 2015, https://www.brennancenter.org/publication/americas-voting-machines-risk.

Harvey Wasserman, interview by Amy Goodman, "Could the 2016 Election be Stolen with Help from Electronic Voting Machines?," *Democracy Now!*, broadcast February 23, 2016, transcript, http://www.democracynow.org/2016/2/23/could_the_2016_election_be_stolen.

Bob Fitrakis and Harvey Wasserman, "Is the 2016 Election Already Being Stripped & Flipped?," *Free Press*, March 31, 2016, http://freepress.org/article/2016-election-already-being-stripped-flipped.

**Student Researchers:** Brandy Miceli (San Francisco State University) and Amanda Woodward (University of Vermont)

**Faculty Evaluators:** Kenn Burrows (San Francisco State University) and Rob Williams (University of Vermont)

From search engine algorithms to electronic voting machines, technology provides opportunities for manipulation of voters and their votes in ways that could profoundly affect the results of the 2016 election. In the US, the 2012 presidential election was won by a margin of just 3.9 percent; and, historically, half of US presidential elections have been won by margins under 7.6 percent. These narrow but consequential victory margins underscore the importance of understanding how secret, proprietary technologies—whether they are newly developing or increasingly outdated—potentially swing election results.

Mark Frary, in *Index on Censorship*, describes the latest research by Robert Epstein and Ronald E. Robertson of the American Institute for Behavioral Research and Technology on what they call the Search Engine Manipulation Effect (SEME). Their research focuses on the powerful role played by the secret algorithms (including Google's PageRank and Facebook's EdgeRank) that determine the contents of our Internet search results and social media news feeds.

Epstein and Robertson studied over 4,500 undecided voters in the US and India, using randomized, controlled, double-blind methods, with research subjects who matched as closely as possible each country's electorate. "The results," Frary reported, "were shocking." Epstein and Robertson showed that biased search rankings "could shift the voting preferences of undecided voters by 20% or more." The effect could be greater than 20 percent in some demographic groups, and—perhaps most significantly—this search-ranking bias "could be masked so that people show no awareness of the manipulation."

In an earlier article for *Politico*, Epstein wrote that the Search Engine Manipulation Effect "turns out to be one of the largest behavioral effects ever discovered . . . [W]e believe SEME is a serious threat to the democratic system of government."

Epstein described how the study's measures—including research subjects' trust, liking, and voting preferences—"all shifted predictably" based on information provided by a Google-like search engine that he and Robertson created, which they called Kadoodle. In one of the experiments, Epstein and Robertson documented SEME with real voters during an actual election campaign: in a study involving two thousand eligible undecided voters in India's 2014 Lok Sabha election, they found that "search engine rankings could boost the proportion of people favoring any candidate by more than 20 percent—more than 60 percent in some demographic groups."

Predictably, Google challenged these findings. As Frary reported, a senior vice president at Google, Amit Singhal, responded in *Politico*, "There is absolutely no truth to Epstein's hypothesis that Google could work secretly to influence election outcomes. Google has never ever re-ranked search results on any topic (including elections) to manipulate user sentiment."[21] However, as Frary duly noted,

> Singhal specifically says "re-ranked" rather than "ranked." What he means by this is that the algorithm decides on the ranking of search results and that no one goes in and manipulates them afterwards. Google's stated mission to "organize the world's information and make it universally accessible and useful" should perhaps have a caveat—"as long as our algorithm decides you should see it."

Hidden algorithms shape online content in significantly different ways from more widely recognized concerns about editorial censorship on television and in print. On TV and in print, Frary observed, "there is a person at the heart of the decision process . . . We can imagine how commissioning editors think, but the algorithms behind Facebook and Google are opaque." This concern has led Emily Bell, a journalism professor at Columbia University, to observe, "If there is a free press, journalists are no longer in charge of it. Engineers who rarely think about journalism or cultural impact or democratic responsibility are making decisions every day that shape how news is created and disseminated."[22]

When filtering is financially motivated, secret, and beyond our control, Robert Epstein told *Index on Censorship*, "we should be extremely concerned." Online filtering on massive platforms such as Google and Facebook, he warned, is "rapidly becoming the most powerful form of mind control that has ever existed."

More than 75 percent of online searches in the US are conducted on Google—in other countries Google's share of Internet searches is as high as 90 percent; some 1.5 billion individuals, political parties, businesses, and other organizations now use Facebook. Epstein and Robertson are now researching how to counter SEME. "We found the monster; now we're trying to figure out how to kill it," Epstein wrote in his *Politico* article. These efforts hinge in part on eroding public trust in Google, including our willingness to accept whatever our search results present to us as fact.

As Frary reported, Facebook, Google, and others are "highly secretive about how their algorithms work." Electronic voting machines present similar challenges, as Harvey Wasserman and Bob Fitrakis document.[23] "Electronic voting machines are owned by private corporations . . . And the courts have ruled that the source code on these electronic voting machines is proprietary," Wasserman told Amy Goodman of *Democracy Now!* in February 2016.

In 2016, about 80 percent of the US electorate will vote using outdated electronic voting machines that rely on proprietary software from private corporations, according to a September 2015 study by the Brennan Center for Justice at the New York University School of Law. Forty-three states are using machines that will be at least ten years old in 2016; in fourteen states, machines will be fifteen or more years old. The Brennan Center study identified "increased failures and crashes, which can lead to long lines and lost votes" as the "biggest risk" of outdated voting equipment, while noting that older machines also have "serious security and reliability flaws that are unacceptable today."

"From a security perspective," Jeremy Epstein of the National Science Foundation noted, "old software is riskier, because new methods of attack are constantly being developed, and older software is likely to be vulnerable."[24] Virginia recently decertified an electronic voting system used in twenty-four of its precincts after finding that an external party could access the machine's wireless features to "record voting data or inject malicious data."[25] The investigation also raised concerns over the AccuVote-TSx machine, which is used in over twenty states. In 2014, voters in Virginia Beach observed that when they selected one candidate, the machine would register their selection for a different candidate, due to an "alignment problem."[26]

Amy Goodman of *Democracy Now!* asked Wasserman how voters using electronic voting machines could be sure that their votes are counted. He told her, "They can't be. You cannot verify an electronic voting machine . . . The proprietary software prevents the public from getting access to the actual vote count." In a March 2016 article on the *Free Press* website, Fitrakis and Wasserman wrote that the "veracity of outcomes" in electoral races for the offices of president, US Congress, governorships, state legislatures, county commissioners, and others "will vary from state to state based on the whims and interest of those in charge of the electronic tallies."

On *Democracy Now!* and elsewhere, Wasserman and Fitrakis have advocated universal, hand-counted paper ballots and automatic voter registration as part of their "Ohio Plan" to prevent stripping and flipping in US elections.[27]

Corporate media outlets including CNNMoney, *Fortune*, and the *Washington Post* provided some coverage of Epstein and Robertson's research.[28] In May 2016, the *Huffington Post* published an article by actor and activist Tim Robbins, titled "We Need to Fix Our Broken Election System." "Every broken machine, every disenfranchised voter, every discrepancy between the exit polls and the final results," Robbins wrote, suggests "malfeasance" and "leads to more and more disillusionment that results in less and less voters."[29]

## 5.

### Corporate Exploitation of Global Refugee Crisis Masked as Humanitarianism

Sarah Lazare, "World Bank Woos Western Corporations to Profit from Labor of Stranded Syrian Refugees," AlterNet, February 24, 2016, http://www.alternet.org/labor/world-bank-woos-western-corporations-profit-labor-stranded-syrian-refugees.

Glen Ford, "Turkey and Europe: Human Trafficking on a Scale Not Seen Since the Atlantic Slave Trade," *Black Agenda Radio*, Black Agenda Report, broadcast March 8, 2016, transcript, http://www.blackagendareport.com/turkey_europe_human_trafficking.

**Student Researchers:** Mark Nelson (Sonoma State University), Sean Donnelly (Citrus College), and Elizabeth Ramirez (College of Marin)

**Faculty Evaluators:** Anne Donegan (Santa Rosa Junior College), Andy Lee Roth (Citrus College), and Susan Rahman (College of Marin)

According to a June 2015 United Nations report, sixty million people worldwide are now refugees due to conflict in their home nations.[30] The UN report indicated that during 2014, 1 out of every 122 people was a refugee, internally displaced, or an asylum seeker; and over half of these refugees were children.[31] While Syrian refugees account for the largest number (an estimated 11.5 million people), other places such as Colombia, parts of sub-Saharan Africa, and Asia have large refugee populations that remain largely unreported. According to António Guterres, the UN High Commissioner for Refugees at the time of the report, "We are witnessing a paradigm change, an unchecked slide into an era in which the scale of global forced displacement as well as the response required is now clearly dwarfing anything seen before."[32]

Although the extent of the global refugee crisis has been covered in the corporate media,[33] the exploitation of refugees has been less well covered. In February 2016, Sarah Lazare published an article on AlterNet that warned of the World Bank's private enterprise solution to the Syrian displacement crisis. "Under the guise of humanitarian aid," Lazare wrote, "the World Bank is enticing Western companies to launch 'new investments' in Jordan in order to profit from the labor of stranded Syrian refugees. In a country where migrant workers have faced forced servitude, torture and wage theft, there is reason to be concerned that this capital-intensive 'solution' to the mounting crisis of displacement will establish sweatshops that specifically target war refugees for hyper-exploitation."

According to a World Bank press release by its president, Jim Yong Kim, "We are exploring the creation of special economic zones (SEZs), and encouraging investments in municipal projects and labor-intensive work." According to World Bank materials, the goal is to help alleviate hardships faced by refugees in Jordan by developing five SEZs along the Syrian border. "We are using a holistic approach to addressing the refugee influx through private sector development," Lazare quoted one World Bank spokesperson as saying. However, as Lazare also noted, despite her multiple attempts to obtain more information from the World Bank on the proposed SEZs, specific details remained scant; furthermore, she reported, the history of Jordan's existing special economic zones (operated under a variety of names) is marred by human trafficking, torture, and wage theft, "often in the service of U.S. companies."

"At a time of mass human displacement from ongoing wars," Lazare wrote, "we should be asking hard questions about the political implications of encouraging Western companies to target and profit from the labor of people violently uprooted from their homes." The World Bank program "raises deeper questions about the global responsibility to address the large-scale human harm the West played a role in unleashing" in Syria. Myriam Francois, a journalist and research associate at SOAS, University of London, told Lazare that the development of SEZs in Jordan "will change refugee camps from emergency and temporary responses to a crisis, to much more permanent settlements." The SEZ proposals, Francois said, are "less about Syrian needs and more about keeping Syrian refugees out of Europe by creating (barely) sustainable conditions within the camps which would then make claims to asylum much harder to recognize."

Describing an agreement between Turkey and the European Union to keep millions of refugees from entering Europe as "a deal between devils," Glen Ford of Black Agenda Report said that Turkey has "cashed in on the people it has helped make homeless." As Al Jazeera reported, Turkey accepted $3.3 billion from the European Union (EU) "in return for checking the flow of refugees across the Aegean Sea."[34] Turkey reportedly asked for double that amount to cover the costs of dealing with the refugees. Earlier in March 2016, European Council president Donald Tusk had warned refugees from Asia and Africa, "Do not come to Europe . . . It is all for nothing."[35]

Noting that "the great bulk of Turkey's refugees are victims of Turkey's role in the war against Syria, in alliance with Europe and the United States and the royal oil aristocrats of the Persian Gulf," Ford described human trafficking in Turkey as "on a scale not seen since the Atlantic slave trade."

In addition to the EU money, Turkey has also sought admission to the European Union—and, with this, the right for seventy-five million Turks to enter Europe without visa restrictions—as a condition for controlling its refugee population. Thus, according to Ford, Turkey has engaged in a "vast protections racket trap," effectively agreeing to protect Europe from further incursions by "the formerly colonized peoples whose labor and lands have fattened Europe and its white settler states for half a millennium." However, Ford concluded, "Europeans will never accept Turkey into the fold, because it is Muslim and not-quite-white."

Corporate exploitation of the global refugee crisis is underreported in the popular and corporate press, and often subject to distorted pro-business coverage, as in a September 2015 *Wall Street Journal* article on the number of small businesses and large corporations that are finding ways to profit from the flood of migrants.[36] Unlike Lazare's AlterNet report, the *Journal*'s coverage dealt only with Syrians who had managed to migrate to European countries. According to the *Journal*, private equity groups across Europe were pursuing a new investment opportunity with "promising organic and acquisitive growth potential," the management of camps and services for refugees. "The margins are very low," the article quoted Willy Koch, the retired founder of the Swiss company ORS Service AG, as saying. "One of the keys is, certainly, volume."

## 6.
### Over 1.5 Million American Families Live on Two Dollars Per Person Per Day

Marcus Harrison Green, "1.5 Million American Families Live on $2 a Day—These Authors Spent Years Finding Out Why," *YES! Magazine*, September 24, 2015, http://www.yesmagazine. org/commonomics/13-million-american-families-live-on-2-a-day-these-authors-spent-years-finding-out-why-20150924.

Jared Bernstein, "America's Poorest are Getting Virtually No Assistance," *Atlantic*, September 6, 2015, http://www.theatlantic.com/business/archive/2015/09/welfare-reform-americas-poorest/403960/.

**Student Researcher:** Rupert Watson (Sonoma State University)

**Faculty Evaluator:** Tiffany Scott (Napa Valley College)

According to Kathryn J. Edin and H. Luke Shaefer, sociologists and authors of the book *$2.00/a Day: Living on Almost Nothing in America*, in 2011 more than 1.5 million US families—including three million children—lived on as little as two dollars per person per day in any given month.[37] Edin and Shaefer determined this figure on the basis of data from the US Census Bureau's Survey of Income and Program Participation (SIPP), income data from the federal Supplemental Nutrition Assistance Program (SNAP), additional data on family homelessness, and their own fieldwork in four study sites, including Chicago, Cleveland, and rural communities in Appalachia and the Mississippi Delta.

As Marcus Harrison Green wrote in *YES! Magazine*, their depiction of what poverty truly looks like in the US reads "like a Dickens

novel." As Green noted, US media often neglect the experiences of the poor, making the study's findings "startling for many."[38] From families who depend on their mother making plasma donations twice a week for their income, to others with nothing but a carton of spoiled milk in their refrigerator, Edin and Shaefer documented family households living "from crisis to crisis." One of their informants told Shaefer that she had been beaten and raped and was always "looking out for the next threat."

As Jared Bernstein noted in his September 2015 report for the *Atlantic*, in addition to providing a vivid account of what it's like to live in extreme poverty, Edin and Shaefer's research also offers a policy critique that highlights the long-term consequences of President Bill Clinton's 1996 welfare reform initiative. Since then, Bernstein wrote, "anti-poverty policy in this country has evolved to be 'pro-work,'" with the fateful consequence that "if you're disconnected from the job market, public policy won't help you much at all." As Edin and Shaefer found, the number of families living on less than two dollars per person per day has more than doubled since 1996. The working-age people in their study wanted decent, steady jobs—not only because work was an economic necessity, but also because they understood jobs as a source of dignity for themselves and their families. A "huge flaw" in welfare reform, Bernstein reported, is the "insistence on work without regard to job availability."

The jobs held by members of poor families typically pay low wages with unstable hours and unsafe working conditions, contradicting the consistent assumption of conservative policy agendas that there is "an ample supply of perfectly good jobs" that poor people could have if they really wanted to work. Instead, the extreme poverty documented by Edin and Shaefer is driven by the "state of the low-wage labor market," Shaefer told *YES! Magazine*. "People make the assumption that low-income families don't work or don't want to work." In the Mississippi Delta, Shaefer said, "[w]ork isn't just hard to come by, it's often nonexistent." Otherwise, however, the norm among the families with children that they studied is "a parent who works or has worked recently."

Edin and Shaefer proposed three policy changes to address extreme poverty in the United States. First, policy must start by "expanding work opportunities for those at the very bottom of society." This means improving the quality of the jobs available by raising the minimum wage, stabilizing work schedules, and increasing accountability for labor standards that often go unenforced. It also means countering the ideological assumption that poor people are unwilling to work. Second, policy must address housing instability, which Shaefer described as both a cause and a consequence of extreme poverty. "Parents should be able to raise their children in a place of their own." Third, families must be insured against extreme poverty even when parents are not able to work. Edin and Shaefer proposed to revive and scale up employment programs that were part of the 2009 Recovery Act. As Bernstein reported, "[I]f America's anti-poverty policy framework is founded on work in the paid labor market, and if that labor market doesn't provide the necessary quantity or quality of jobs, public policy must make up the difference."

Corporate coverage of Edin and Shaefer's sociological study of extreme poverty has been limited. In early 2012, *USA Today* published a straightforward report on a previous version of their findings, which indicated 1.46 million families lived on less than two dollars per person per day. *USA Today* quoted a senior research fellow at the conservative Heritage Foundation who disputed Edin and Shaefer's findings: "When you look at that type of family, you don't see the type of deprivation this study suggests."[39] More recently, the *Los Angeles Times* ran an opinion piece by Edin and Shaefer, and the *New York Times* published William Julius Wilson's favorable review of their book in its Sunday Book Review.[40] Wilson, a leading sociologist in the study of poverty, described their book as "an essential call to action," and observed, "the rise of such absolute poverty since the passage of welfare reform belies all the categorical talk about opportunity and the American dream."

## 7.

### No End in Sight for Fukushima Disaster

Dahr Jamail, "Radioactive Water from Fukushima is Leaking into the Pacific," *Truthout*, January 27, 2016, http://www.truth-out.org/news/item/34565-radioactive-water-from-fukushima-is-leaking-into-the-pacific.

Linda Pentz Gunter, "No Bliss in This Ignorance: The Great Fukushima Nuclear Cover-Up," *Ecologist*, February 20, 2016, http://www.theecologist.org/News/news_analysis/2987222/no_bliss_in_this_ignorance_the_great_fukushima_nuclear_coverup.html.

Celine-Marie Pascale, "Vernacular Epistemologies of Risk: The Crisis in Fukushima," *Current Sociology*, March 3, 2016, http://csi.sagepub.com/content/early/2016/03/03/0011392115627284.abstract.

**Student Researcher:** Harrison Hartman (Sonoma State University)

**Faculty Evaluator:** Peter Phillips (Sonoma State University)

Five years after the 9.0 earthquake and tsunami that destroyed the nuclear power plant at Fukushima, Dahr Jamail reported that Tokyo Electric Power Company (TEPCO) officials in charge of the plant continue to release large quantities of radioactive waste water into the Pacific Ocean.[41] Arnold Gundersen, a former nuclear industry senior vice president, called Fukushima "the biggest industrial catastrophe in the history of humankind." As Jamail reported, experts such as Gundersen continue warning officials and the public that this problem is not going away. As Gundersen told Jamail, "With Three Mile Island and Chernobyl, and now with Fukushima, you can pinpoint the exact day and time they started . . . but they never end." Another expert quoted in Jamail's *Truthout* article, M. V. Ramana, a

physicist and lecturer at Princeton University's Program on Science and Global Security and the Nuclear Futures Laboratory, explained, "March 2011 was just the beginning of the disaster, which is still unfolding."

Although the Fukushima plant has been offline since the disaster, uncontrolled fission continues to generate heat and require cooling. The cooling process has produced "hundreds of thousands, if not millions, of tons" of highly radioactive water, Jamail reported. TEPCO has no backup safety systems or proactive plan for dealing with the accumulation of contaminated water, so much of it is released into the Pacific Ocean. Drawing on reports from the *Asahi Shimbun* and Agence France-Presse, Common Dreams reported that, on September 14, 2015, "Despite the objections of environmentalists and after overcoming local opposition from fishermen, the Tokyo Electric Power Co. (TEPCO) pumped more than 850 tons of groundwater from below the Fukushima nuclear power plant into the Pacific Ocean."[42] Each day, according to these reports, TEPCO was pumping approximately 300 tons of groundwater to the surface for treatment before placing it in storage. Officially no water is released into the ocean until it is tested for radioactive content, but many experts are skeptical of this claim. As Jamail reported, "The company has repeatedly come under fire for periodically dumping large amounts of radioactive water."

According to Helen Caldicott, the antinuclear advocate and author, once it is released, "There is no way to prevent radioactive water [from] reaching the western shores of the North American continent and then circulating around the rest of the Pacific Ocean . . . At the moment, it seems like this is going to occur for the rest of time." Radioactive water affects ocean life through a process described by Caldicott as "biological magnification." The effect of radiation expands each step up the food chain—from algae, to crustaceans and small fish, up to the ocean's largest creatures.

While biological magnification may ultimately impact human health, a December 2015 Woods Hole Oceanographic Institution study showed a 50 percent increase in seawater radiation levels 1,600 miles west of San Francisco.[43] That report indicated that these levels are far below what the US government considers dangerous, but Caldicott and other experts question the standards that the US government and other official agencies use to determine safe levels of radiation exposure.

Meanwhile, Linda Pentz Gunter, writing for the *Ecologist*, reported that the Japanese government has kept its citizens "in the dark" from the start of the disaster about high radiation levels and dangers to health. "In order to proclaim the Fukushima area 'safe,'" Gunter wrote, "the Government increased exposure limits to twenty times the international norm," a determination preliminary to Prime Minister Shinzō Abe's stated goal of lifting evacuation orders and forcing displaced Fukushima refugees to return home by March 2017. Government policy is now to "'normaliz[e]' radiation standards," Gunter wrote, and to tell the Japanese people that everything is all right, despite medical or scientific evidence to the contrary.

At a conference in February 2016, prefectural governors urged young people to return to Fukushima. Doing so would facilitate the region's reconstruction and "help you lead a meaningful life," said Fukushima's governor, Masao Uchibori. However, as Gunter reported, young people appear not to be cooperating. Instead, most of the returning evacuees are senior citizens, with stronger traditional ties to the land and their ancestral burial grounds. This creates a further dilemma for local authorities, according to Gunter: Local tax revenues are levied on both individuals and corporations, with nearly a quarter of the taxes collected by local prefectures and municipalities coming from individuals. "The onus is on governors and mayors," she wrote, "to lure as many working people as possible back to their towns and regions in order to effectively finance local public services." Retired senior citizens do not contribute to income tax.

Gunter reported the public remarks of Tetsunari Iida, the founder and executive director of the Institute for Sustainable Energy Policies (ISEP) in Japan: Prime Minister Shinzō Abe "says 'everything is under control' . . . Yes—under the control of the media!" While Iida directed his critique to Japan's press, it could easily apply to US corporate media coverage of Fukushima and its aftermath, as documented by sociologist Celine-Marie Pascale of American University. Pascale conducted a content analysis of more than 2,100 articles, editorials, and letters to the editor on Fukushima published by the *Washington Post*, the *New York Times*, *Politico*, and the *Huffington Post* between March 11, 2011 and March 11, 2013. Her analysis focused on two basic questions: "Risk for whom?" and "Risk from what?" Pascale found that just 6 percent of the articles reported on risk to the general public. "This in itself," she reported, "is a significant finding about the focus of news media during one of the largest nuclear disasters in history."

More specifically, Pascale found that the great majority of news coverage that focused on risks to the public significantly discounted those risks. Sixty-five of the 129 articles that focused on risk to the general population characterized it as being "quite low on the basis of comparisons to other risks or claims of no evidence."[44] An additional forty-four articles characterized risk as low on the basis of uncertain evidence. In other words, assessments of uncertain risk were interpreted by news media as low risk. Over two years, the four major US news outlets that Pascale studied reported just seventeen articles that characterized the disaster as having even "*potentially* high risk to the general population."[45] Pascale concluded:

The largest and longest lasting nuclear disaster of our time was routinely and consistently reported as being of little consequence to people, food supplies, or environments. Impressively this was done systematically across *The New York Times*, *The Washington Post*, *Politico*, and *The Huffington Post*. In short, the media coverage was premised on misinformation, the minimization of public health risks, and the exacerbation of uncertainties.

A flurry of corporate media coverage around the fifth anniversary of the disaster for the most part reproduced the pattern identified by Pascale. For example, as CNBC's anniversary report acknowledged, "Elevated [radiation] levels off the coast of Japan show that the situation is not yet under control, and that the facility is still leaking radiation." But, the report continued, "the levels observed near the United States are below—very far below—those set by health and safety standards, and are also far outstripped by naturally occurring radiation."[46]

In February 2016, the Associated Press and other news outlets reported that three TEPCO executives, including Tsunehisa Katsumata, TEPCO's chairman at the time of the earthquake and tsunami, were formally charged with negligence in the Fukushima nuclear disaster.[47]

## 8.

### Syria's War Spurred by Contest for Gas Delivery to Europe, Not Muslim Sectarianism

Mnar Muhawesh, "Refugee Crisis & Syria War Fueled by Competing Gas Pipelines," MintPress News, September 9, 2015, http://www.mintpressnews.com/migrant-crisis-syria-war-fueled-by-competing-gas-pipelines/209294/.

Student Researcher: Salah Mouazen (Citrus College)

Faculty Evaluators: Andy Lee Roth and Lanette Granger (Citrus College)

At least four years into the crisis in Syria, "most people have no idea how this war even got started," Mnar Muhawesh reported for MintPress News in September 2015.

In 2011–12, after Syrian president Bashar al-Assad refused to cooperate with Turkey's proposal to create a natural gas pipeline between Qatar and Turkey through Syria, Turkey and its allies became "the major architects of Syria's 'civil war.'" The proposed pipeline would have bypassed Russia to reach European markets currently dominated by Russian gas giant Gazprom. As a result, Muhawesh wrote, "The Middle East is being torn to shreds by manipulative plans to gain oil and gas access by pitting people against one another based on religion. The ensuing chaos provides ample cover to install a new regime that's more amenable to opening up oil pipelines and ensuring favorable routes for the highest bidders."

In 2012, the US, UK, France, Qatar, and Saudi Arabia, along with Turkey, began to organize, arm, and finance rebels to form the Free Syrian Army, consistent with long-standing US plans to destabilize Syria. These nations formed a pact, the Group of Friends of the Syrian People, that implemented a sectarian divide-and-conquer strategy to overthrow President Assad. "It's important to note the timing," Muhawesh wrote. "This coalition and meddling in Syria came about immediately on the heels of discussions of an Iran-Iraq-Syria gas pipeline that was to be built between 2014 and 2016 from Iran's giant South Pars field through Iraq and Syria. With a possible extension to Lebanon, it would eventually reach Europe, the target export market."

As MintPress News reported, access to oil and gas—not sectarian differences—is the underlying cause of the violent conflict and humanitarian disaster in Syria. "[T]he war is being sold to the public as a Sunni-Shiite conflict" by the Friends of Syria because, if the public understood the economic interests at stake, "most people would not support any covert funding and arming of rebels or direct intervention."

Based on secret US cables revealed by WikiLeaks, Muhawesh reported that "foreign meddling in Syria began several years before the Syrian revolt erupted." US State Department cables from 2006 documented plans to instigate civil strife that would lead to the overthrow of Assad's government.[48] The leaks revealed the United States has partnered with nations including Saudi Arabia, Turkey, Qatar, and Egypt to fuel Sunni-Shiite sectarianism to divide Syria.[49]

Although there is plenty of coverage in US corporate media about the violence in Syria and the refugee crisis that is sweeping Europe and reaching North America, this coverage has failed to address the economic interests, including control of potentially lucrative gas pipelines, that motivate the US and its allies.[50] Instead, corporate news coverage has characterized the conflict as a battle for democracy that has been hijacked by Sunni-Shiite interests. For example, Oren Dorell of *USA Today* identified "a mind-boggling and dangerous stew of shifting and competing alliances" involved in the Syrian conflict— including groups categorized as progovernment, antigovernment, anti-Islamic State, and "other fighters"—but he did not address the gas interests that, according to Muhawesh's reporting, ultimately underpin the conflict.[51] Instead, much of what passes for news coverage in the corporate press adheres to a pattern that Muhawesh identified and critiqued as simplistic and "Orientalist," framing conflict in the Middle East and especially Syria as sectarian in order "to paint the region and its people as barbaric."

## 9.
### Big Pharma Political Lobbying Not Limited to Presidential Campaigns

Mike Ludwig, "How Much of Big Pharma's Massive Profits are Used to Influence Politicians?" *Truthout*, September 30, 2015, http://www.truth-out.org/news/item/33010-how-much-of-big-pharma-s-massive-profits-are-used-to-influence-politicians.

**Student Researcher:** Harrison Hartman (Sonoma State University)

**Faculty Evaluator:** Debora Paterniti (Sonoma State University)

Pharmaceutical companies have been among the biggest political spenders for years, according to data from the Center for Responsive Politics. As Mike Ludwig of *Truthout* reported, based on CRP data, large pharmaceutical companies made over $51 million in campaign donations during the 2012 presidential election, nearly $32 million in the 2014 elections, and, as of September 2015, they had already put $10 million into the 2016 election. During the 2014 elections, Pfizer led drug companies with $1.5 million in federal campaign donations, followed by Amgen ($1.3 million) and McKesson ($1.1 million).

Although these are large sums of money, campaign donations by large pharmaceutical companies pale in comparison to how much they spend on lobbying politicians and influencing policies outside of elections. As Ludwig reported, according to data gathered on the 2014 election, the industry spent seven dollars on lobbying for every dollar spent on the election. The $229 million spent by drug companies and

their lobbying groups that year was down from a peak of $273 million in 2009, the year that Congress debated the Affordable Care Act.

According to records from MapLight's lobbying database, the Pharmaceutical Research and Manufacturers of America (PhRMA) has been the drug companies' lead lobbying group.[52] Since 2008, PhRMA has spent over $163 million on lobbying, making it the fifth-largest lobbying spender in the nation, outspending powerful defense contractors (such as Boeing and Northrop Grumman), the oil and gas industry (e.g., ExxonMobil), and Koch Industries, among others.[53] Pfizer is among the nation's top 25 lobbying spenders, having spent over $101 million since 2008 and $9.4 million in 2015 alone.[54]

What do big pharmaceutical companies hope to achieve through lobbying? As Ludwig wrote, "lobbying allows Big Pharma to take advantage of Washington's revolving door and directly influence legislation." Specifically, records filed by drug companies and their lobbying groups indicated the industry's top concerns, including policy on patents and trademarks, management of Medicare and Medicaid, and international trade. For example, Ludwig's article described how the pharmaceutical industry sought to persuade the Obama administration to pressure India to tighten its laws on generic drugs. India's less strict patent laws have allowed some manufacturers to make generic versions of drugs used in developing countries to treat HIV/AIDS and hepatitis C, undermining the monopolies created by US patent laws that permit drug companies up to twenty years before generic versions of their drug, which would drive down prices, can enter the market.[55] Pharmaceutical lobbyists also consistently lobby to prevent Medicare from negotiating drug prices. Both Hillary Clinton and Bernie Sanders advocated on behalf of Medicare price negotiations during their 2016 presidential campaigns. A PhRMA press release dramatically said that Clinton's proposed plan would "turn back the clock on medical innovation and halt progress against diseases that patients fear most."

Since Ludwig's September 2015 report, updated records published by the Center for Responsive Politics indicate that the 2016 campaign has followed the pattern of past election seasons. As of May 16, 2016, Pfizer had made $1.27 million in campaign contributions (with 64 percent going to Republican candidates) in 2015–16, followed by Amgen (over $939,000, with 60 percent to Republicans) and Celgene (over $848,000, with nearly 90 percent to Republican or "Conservative" candidates). Pharmaceutical Research and Manufacturers of America made over $242,000 in campaign donations, nearly 75 percent of which has gone to Republican candidates.[56]

As in previous years, the pharmaceutical industry's investment in lobbying has dramatically outpaced its campaign contributions. Based on data from the Senate Office of Public Records, as of April 25, 2016, PhRMA had spent over $5.98 million on lobbying in 2016, followed by Pfizer ($3.28 million), Merck ($3.26 million), and Novartis (over $3.13 million). Collectively, pharmaceutical and health product lobbying for the first months of 2016 (through April 25) totaled over $63.1 million.[57]

As Ludwig wrote, the pharmaceutical industry includes some of the most profitable companies in the world, and the industry has "a clear interest in maintaining the political status quo." While representatives of the industry assure the public that profits go to the research and development of new drugs, a closer examination of Big Pharma's spending on political contributions and, especially, lobbying reveals that it spends hundreds of millions of dollars to influence US politics, health care policy, and international trade.

Although the cost of prescription drugs has been a major issue in the 2016 presidential election campaign, corporate news coverage has failed to report the extent to which the pharmaceutical industry engages in political lobbying. Apart from articles published by CNN and *U.S. News & World Report*, which both drew on data from the Center for Responsive Politics, drug companies' campaign donations have received limited news coverage.[58] Also citing the Center for Responsive Politics, a February 2016 article in the *New York Times* briefly mentioned the amount spent by the pharmaceutical industry on lobbying. Otherwise, this topic appears to have gone significantly underreported, despite the corporate news media's nonstop coverage of the 2016 electoral campaign.[59]

## 10.

### CISA: The Internet Surveillance Act No One is Discussing

Andy Greenberg, "Congress Slips CISA into a Budget Bill That's Sure to Pass," *Wired*, December 16, 2015, http://www.wired.com/2015/12/congress-slips-cisa-into-omnibus-bill-thats-sure-to-pass/.

Sam Thielman, "Congress Adds Contested Cybersecurity Measures to 'Must-Pass' Spending Bill," *Guardian*, December 16, 2015, http://www.theguardian.com/us-news/2015/dec/16/congress-cybersecurity-information-sharing-cisa-spending-bill.

Jason R. Edgecombe, "Interim Guidelines to the Cybersecurity Information Sharing Act," TechCrunch, April 13, 2016, http://techcrunch.com/2016/04/13/interim-guidelines-to-the-cybersecurity-information-sharing-act/.

Violet Blue, "Where the Candidates Stand on Cyber Issues," Engadget, May 13, 2016, http://www.engadget.com/2016/05/13/where-the-candidates-stand-on-cyber-issues/.

**Student Researcher:** Victoria Bespalov (University of Vermont)

**Faculty Evaluator:** Rob Williams (University of Vermont)

On December 18, 2015, President Obama signed the Cybersecurity Information Sharing Act (CISA) into law as part of a two-thousand-page omnibus spending bill. As drafted, CISA was intended to "improve cybersecurity in the United States through enhanced sharing of information about cybersecurity threats, and for other purposes." The act authorized the creation of a system for corporate informants to provide customers' data to the Department of Homeland Security (DHS), which, in turn, would share this information with other federal agencies, including the

Departments of Commerce, Defense (which includes the NSA), Energy, Justice (which includes the FBI), the Treasury (which oversees the IRS), and the Office of the Director of National Intelligence.

As Sam Thielman of the *Guardian* reported, civil liberties experts had been "dismayed" when Congress used the omnibus spending bill to advance some of the legislation's "most invasive" components. Anthony Romero of the American Civil Liberties Union criticized Congress for using the spending bill "to pursue their extremist agendas." "Sneaking damaging and discriminatory riders into a must-pass bill usurps the democratic process," he told the *Guardian*. Lauren Weinstein, who cofounded People For Internet Responsibility, also spoke critically of the legislation: "There is not a culture of security and privacy established in the government yet. You have to have that before you even consider sharing the amounts of data [CISA] would cover." Evan Greer of Fight for the Future called CISA "a disingenuous attempt to quietly expand the US government's surveillance programs."

In July 2015, Senate Majority Leader Mitch McConnell had attempted to attach the bill as an amendment to the annual National Defense Authorization Act, but the Senate blocked this by a vote of 56 to 40.

As Andy Greenberg reported for *Wired*, the final Senate version of the bill removed personal information protections that privacy advocates had fought successfully to have included in a previous version.[60] Greenberg reported that CISA had "alarmed the privacy community" by providing a loophole in privacy laws that would enable intelligence and law enforcement officials to engage in surveillance without warrants. The version of CISA approved in the Senate by a vote of 74 to 21 in October 2015, Greenberg reported, "creates the ability for the president to set up 'portals' for agencies like the FBI and the Office of the Director of National Intelligence, so that companies hand information directly to law enforcement and intelligence agencies instead of to the Department of Homeland Security." Commenting on this aspect of the legislation, Jadzia Butler and Greg Nojeim of the Center for Democracy and Technology wrote, "Information shared for cybersecurity reasons should be used for cybersecurity purposes, but this legislation does not impose this simple requirement."

Greenberg's *Wired* article noted that tech firms—including Apple, Twitter, and Reddit—as well as fifty-five civil liberties groups had opposed the bill, and that, in July 2015, DHS itself warned that the bill would "sweep away privacy protections" while inundating the agency with data of "dubious" value.

In April 2016, Jason R. Edgecombe reported for TechCrunch on the release by DHS and the Department of Justice of additional "Privacy and Civil Liberties Interim Guidelines" to supplement CISA. The interim guidelines aimed to address continued concerns over inadequate privacy safeguards. In particular, the language of CISA required that private entities sharing information with the government only had to protect "information that the entity knows *at the time of sharing* to be personal information or information that identifies a specific person." As Edgecombe observed, "This is a low bar: If the entity doing the sharing isn't aware 'at the time of sharing' that a CTI [cyber threat indicator] identifies a specific person, it is not required to de-identify that information."

The interim guidelines required DHS and other government agencies receiving private information under CISA to review cyber threat indicators for personally identifiable information and to remove it before sharing the data further. As Edgecombe reported, however, the interim guidelines only protect personal information "not directly linked to a cybersecurity threat." And they do not require destruction of personal information unless it is "known not to be directly related to uses authorized under CISA." As he reported, this wording created a "potentially vast loophole," because CISA authorized "a number of law enforcement activities unrelated to cybersecurity." "The best way to prevent personal information from falling into the hands of the feds," Edgecombe concluded, "is for non-governmental entities to decline to share it in the first place." As *Censored 2017* went to press, the DHS/DOJ final guidelines had not yet been made public.

Assessing where presidential candidates Hillary Clinton, Bernie Sanders, and Donald Trump stand on cybersecurity issues, Violet Blue of Engadget reported that, while most people felt that CISA did not go far enough in protecting citizens' privacy, "Clinton felt the law didn't go far enough in facilitating the sharing of data between companies and the government." Sanders voted against CISA. ("Our civil liberties and right to privacy shouldn't be the price we pay for security. #CISA," he tweeted on October 22, 2015.) Though Trump had not taken a specific position on CISA, Blue noted, "Trump is an outspoken supporter of government surveillance." The NSA, he has said, "should be given as much leeway as possible."

In November 2015, NBC News asked, "Why aren't Presidential Candidates Talking about Cybersecurity?" The story noted that Sanders was the only candidate (other than Republican Rand Paul) to oppose CISA, and it included a "quick primer" on CISA that consisted of two sentences.[61] On December 22, 2015, CNBC's Everett Rosenfeld reported on President Obama having signed the "controversial 'surveillance' act," but this report was derivative of Andy Greenberg's previous report for *Wired*.[62]

## 11.
### CIA Warned Bush Administration of Terrorist Attack Prior to 9/11

Chris Whipple, "The Attacks Will be Spectacular," *Politico*, November 12, 2015, http://www.politico.com/magazine/story/2015/11/cia-directors-documentary-911-bush-213353.

Student Researcher: Austin Hamilton (Indian River State College)

Faculty Evaluators: Elliot D. Cohen (Indian River State College) and Mickey Huff (Diablo Valley College)

Based on new interviews with Cofer Black, the former director of the CIA's Counterterrorism Center, and George Tenet, the former director of the CIA, Chris Whipple reported in *Politico* that the George W. Bush administration ignored CIA warnings in the months before 9/11. Noting that neither Black nor Tenet has spoken about the warnings "in such detail until now—or has been so emphatic about how specific and pressing their warnings were," Whipple wrote that, starting in spring 2001, the CIA "repeatedly and urgently" warned the White House that an attack was imminent.[63]

In spring 2001, Tenet and Black proposed to Bush administration officials a plan aimed at ending the threat of al-Qaeda. Known as the "Blue Sky paper," the plan called for covert CIA and military operations against al-Qaeda, "getting into the Afghan sanctuary, launching a paramilitary operation, creating a bridge with Uzbekistan." Tenet told Whipple that the White House responded, "We're not quite ready to consider this. We don't want to start the clock ticking." Whipple interpreted Tenet's account to imply that, in Whipple's words, the White House "did not want a paper trail, to show that they'd been warned." According to Black, Bush's staff was "mentally stuck" in an outdated conception of terrorism. "They were used to terrorists being Euro-lefties," Black told Whipple, making it "very difficult" to communicate the urgency of the CIA's warnings regarding al-Qaeda.

Black recounted for Whipple how, on the morning of July 10, 2001, Richard Blee, who led the CIA's al-Qaeda unit, told Black, "Chief, this is it. Roof's fallen in." According to Black the information was "absolutely compelling," "multiple-sourced," and "the last straw." Black and Blee briefed Tenet, who then called Bush's National Security Advisor, Condoleezza Rice. According to Tenet he told Rice, "I have to come see you."

Whipple reported that Tenet "vividly recalls" the meeting with Rice and her team. (At the time President Bush was on a trip in Boston.) Tenet told Whipple that Blee began by reporting, "There will be significant terrorist attacks against the United States in the coming weeks or months. The attacks will be spectacular. They may be multiple." According to Tenet, Rice asked what should be done, and Black, slamming his fist on the table, told her, "We need to go on wartime footing now!"

In her memoir, Rice wrote that her recollection of the meeting was "not very crisp because we were discussing the threat every day . . . I thought we were doing what needed to be done."[64] Whipple wrote that, in response to an inquiry about her response to the claims by Black and Tenet, Rice's chief of staff told Whipple that she stands by the account in her memoir. Tenet told Whipple he testified about the July 10 meeting with Rice and her team before the 9/11 Commission, but this was not included in the commission's final report. Black told Whipple that the White House's inaction "remains incomprehensible."

At the end of July, Tenet told Whipple, he and his deputies gathered in his conference room at CIA headquarters. According to Tenet, Blee told them, "They're coming here." Tenet described the ensuing silence as "deafening." "You could feel the oxygen come out of the room."

Whipple conducted interviews with George Tenet and Cofer Black for a documentary, *The Spymasters*, about Tenet and the eleven other living former CIA directors. Showtime broadcast the program in November 2015.

## 12.

## Why Our Lives Depend on Keeping 80 Percent of Fossil Fuels in the Ground

Bill McKibben, "Why We Need to Keep 80 Percent of Fossil Fuels in the Ground," *YES! Magazine*, February 15, 2016, http://www.yesmagazine.org/issues/life-after-oil/why-we-need-to-keep-80-percent-of-fossil-fuels-in-the-ground-20160215.

Richard Heinberg, "100% Renewable Energy: What We Can Do in 10 Years," *YES! Magazine*, February 22, 2016, http://www.yesmagazine.org/issues/life-after-oil/100-renewable-energy-what-we-can-do-in-10-years-20160222.

**Student Researcher:** Janzen Adisewojo (San Francisco State University)

**Faculty Evaluator:** Kenn Burrows (San Francisco State University)

The spring 2016 issue of *YES! Magazine* featured articles on the theme "After Oil." Bill McKibben, the founder of 350.org, wrote that, when it comes to climate change, the essential problem is not "industry versus environmentalists, or Republicans against Democrats. It's people against physics." For that reason, the compromises and trade-offs typical of most public policy debates will not work, because "[l]obbying physics is useless." What does physics tell us? McKibben reported that we "have to keep 80 percent of the fossil fuel reserves we know about underground," the aim of a Keep It in the Ground movement that began five years ago.

At that time, McKibben reported, environmentalists engaged in climate policy focused on reducing demand. Such an approach has been making "slow but steady progress." Reducing demand was working, but not quickly enough, so the Keep It in the Ground movement focused on the supply side of climate policy. "We have to leave fossil fuel in the ground," McKibben reported. The world's remaining concentrations of fossil fuels can be understood as "money pits"— untapped coal, gas, and oil could be worth $20 trillion—or as "carbon bombs," which will wreck the planet if they are used. For this reason, the Keep It in the Ground movement has opposed the Keystone pipeline and what would have been the world's largest coal mine in Queensland, Australia, while advocating for colleges and universities, doctors' associations, and churches from around the world to divest from fossil fuels. Blocking pipelines, McKibben wrote, cuts the fuse on the carbon bomb, while divestment campaigns have "driven the necessity of keeping carbon underground from the fringes into the heart of the world's establishment."

With alternatives to fossil fuel becoming increasingly less expensive, "we don't need to win this fight forever," McKibben wrote. Instead, if we can hold off fossil fuel development for "just a few more years . . . we'll have made the transition to clean energy irreversible."

That transition was the focus of Richard Heinberg's article, which reported on what the US could do in the next ten years to transition to 100 percent renewable energy. Heinberg, a Senior Fellow at the Post Carbon Institute, wrote that the transition to renewable energy would be unlike previous energy transitions, which were "additive" and "driven by opportunity, not policy." We still use firewood, even after adding coal and other energy sources, for example. By contrast, the shift to renewable energy would involve trading our currently dominant energy sources for alternative ones "that have different characteristics," entailing "hefty" challenges.

Heinberg and his colleague David Fridley, a scientist in the Energy Analysis Program at Lawrence Berkeley National Laboratory, have analyzed and assessed a variety of already-formulated plans for transitioning to 100 percent renewable energy. In Heinberg's *YES! Magazine* article, he provided a summary of three "levels" of change, tailored to the United States. The first level focused on what can be done "relatively quickly and cheaply," scaling up to the third level, which would take "long, expensive, sustained effort" to implement.

First, the transition would be kick-started by shifting electricity production from coal sources to solar and wind power. Since solar and wind power generate electricity, "it makes sense to electrify as much of our energy usage as we can," Heinberg wrote. Along with retrofitting buildings for energy efficiency and increasing the market share of local organic foods, level one changes "could achieve at least a 40 percent reduction in carbon emissions in 10 to 20 years."

Level two addresses "harder stuff," including some of the consequences of how solar and wind power differ from fossil fuels. Because solar and wind provide intermittent energy, when they become our primary energy sources, we would have to "accommodate that intermittency," for example by significantly increasing "grid-level" energy storage and by timing energy use to coordinate with available sunlight and wind energy. Although most manufacturing already runs on electricity, many raw materials either are fossil fuels or require fossil fuels

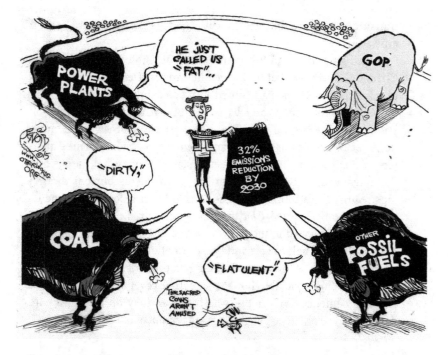

for mining or transportation. "Considerable effort" would be required to replace industrial materials based on fossil fuels. Adding level two changes would achieve "roughly 80 percent reduction in emissions" compared to our current levels, Heinberg reported.

Level three addresses the "really hard stuff." Concrete is currently fundamental for all kinds of construction. Making cement—concrete's crucial ingredient—requires high heat. Theoretically, this could be provided by sunlight, electricity, or hydrogen, but this shift would entail "a nearly complete redesign of the process," Heinberg reported. Similarly, eliminating all fossil fuel inputs from our food system would require not only local organic food (as noted in level one) but also the redesign of the food system "to minimize processing, packaging, and transport." In the transport sector, paving and repairing roads without oil-based asphalt is "possible," but would require "complete redesign" of processes and equipment. Aviation fuels have no good substitute, and air travel might have to be relegated to a "specialty transportation mode," he wrote. Together, however, addressing these most difficult aspects of the transition to renewable energy could get us "beyond zero carbon emissions."

Leading up to and in the aftermath of the United Nations Climate Change Conference that took place in Paris in December 2015, popular and corporate media featured limited coverage of the Keep It in the Ground movement and its issues. An article in the *Huffington Post* quoted the executive secretary of the UN's Framework Convention on Climate Change, Christiana Figueres, as saying, "Three quarters of the fossil fuel reserves need to stay in the ground," a position that illustrated, according to the article, "how the discourse is moving 'upstream,'" from controlling emissions to limiting fossil fuel production.[65] In January 2016, *Time* magazine ran a brief article on a scientific report published in the journal *Nature* that found that 80 percent of coal reserves, half of gas, and one-third of oil reserves could not be used if the world is to avoid global temperatures rising more than two degrees Celsius.[66] Notably, however, the *Time* coverage of this report— just five sentences in length—was based entirely on a much more detailed article on the findings, originally published by the *Guardian*.[67]

## 13.

### US "Vaccine Court" Has Paid Over $3 Billion to Vaccine-Injured Families

Anders Kelto, "Vaccine Court Aims to Protect Patients and Vaccines," *All Things Considered* (NPR), broadcast June 2, 2015, edited transcript, http://www.npr.org/sections/health-shots/2015/06/02/411243242/vaccine-court-aims-to-protect-patients-and-vaccines.

Tracy Seipel, "Vaccine Battles Call New Attention to Obscure Compensation Court," *Marin Independent Journal*, August 2, 2015, http://www.marinij.com/article/NO/20150802/NEWS/150809969.

Jessica Boehm, "Vaccine Injury Fund Tops $3.5 Billion, as Patients Fight for Payment," *Cronkite News* (Arizona PBS), May 8, 2015, http://cronkitenewsonline.com/2015/05/vaccine-injury-fund-tops-3-5-billion-as-patients-fight-for-payment/.

**Student Researchers:** Brittany Oldham, Dorsa Abyaneh, and Emiko Osaka (San Francisco State University)

**Faculty Evaluator:** Kenn Burrows (San Francisco State University)

Since 1988, the US government has paid $3.2 billion to 4,150 individuals and families for injuries and deaths attributed to shots for flu, diphtheria, whooping cough, and other conditions. Though vaccines "remain one of the greatest success stories in public health," Tracy Seipel reported, "for some Americans, rare side effects of inoculations have led to hardship, serious injury, and even death."

As Anders Kelto reported on NPR's *All Things Considered*, high-profile lawsuits against drug companies in the 1980s successfully charged that children immunized with the diphtheria-tetanus-pertussis (DTP) vaccine experienced adverse reactions, including seizures and brain damage, leading to at least two court settlements worth millions of dollars. In response, drug companies threatened to stop producing vaccines for the US market because litigation risks were too great unless the government provided them with "no-fault" protection. NPR quoted Anna Kirkland, a professor of women's studies and political science at the University of Michigan: "There was a real fear that some of our childhood vaccines would no longer be available."

In 1986, that fear led Congress to establish the little-known Office of Special Masters of the US Court of Federal Claims (known informally as the vaccine court) and the National Vaccine Injury Compensation Program. NPR reported that the court administers a "no-fault compensation program that serves as an alternative to the traditional U.S. tort system." As Kirkland explained, the vaccine court served to "shield the vaccine makers from liability." It also created a fund to compensate injured vaccine recipients, through a 75-cent surcharge on every vaccine dose.

As the NPR report explained, "Petitioners don't have to prove that the immunization caused their condition—the court operates under a presumption of causation if the injury develops within a certain period of time." To win a claim, petitioners must provide proof of developing a condition listed on a vaccine injury table. Settlements for conditions not included in the table require a higher burden of proof. But, as Seipel reported, the other restriction that petitioners face is filing within strict time limits. A petition must be filed within three years of the first symptoms, within two years of death, or within four years of the first symptom of a vaccine-related injury that resulted in death.

The problem of the time limit is twofold. First, and most fundamentally, most people simply do not know about the government's vaccine-injury compensation program, and they may not learn about it in time to petition. Second, in cases where parents allege that a vaccine has injured a child of theirs, the full extent of the injury may not be known until the child is older. As Anna Kirkland, the Michigan professor who has studied the vaccine court, told NPR, publicizing the vaccine court and injury compensation program creates a dilemma: Once critics see compensation settlements, they conclude that "vaccines are dangerous and you shouldn't vaccinate." If the court were to achieve greater visibility, especially regarding payouts to injured patients, the public might conclude that vaccines are more generally dangerous than significant research and evidence indicates.

Jessica Boehm of *Cronkite News* reported that vaccine information statements, which include information about both possible side effects and the vaccine compensation program, are provided to patients before each shot. However, few people read the fine print. According to Drew Downing, a lawyer who specializes in vaccine injury cases, "[T]hat's really the only place that the vaccine program is really ever talked about." As Seipel reported, other critics have noted that, when patients seek medical attention for an adverse reaction, they should be informed about the court system and compensation program.

Boehm's *Cronkite News* report indicated that annual revenues of the Vaccine Injury Compensation Trust Fund significantly exceed the amount spent on injury claims through the compensation program. According to Government Accountability Office figures, since 2005 the vaccine court has compensated an average of 190 of the 466 claims it receives each year. During that time, the program's annual budget has averaged $148.7 million. Some critics of the program, Boehm reported, question the program's record of stringent compensation, given that it now maintains a $3.5 billion fund. Others contended that the large trust fund is a "safety net," maintained by the program in the event that the vaccine court might rule to compensate thousands of families, as could have occurred in 2007 when the court began its Omnibus Autism Proceeding to determine whether two types of vaccines triggered autism in children. In 2009 the court ruled against the families, but if it had not the settlement would have required at least that much in compensation. Vaccine-injured victims are entitled to lost wages, medical and rehabilitation expenses, and up to $250,000 in compensation for pain and suffering. For vaccine-related deaths, compensation is limited to $250,000.

Since 2002, the *Washington Post* has published a handful of editorials, opinion pieces, and letters to the editor that have addressed the National Vaccine Injury Compensation Program. In 2009 it ran a front-page article on the vaccine court's finding of no link between vaccines and autism in children.[68] Coverage of the vaccine court and its injury program in the *New York Times* appears to have been limited to a single story from 1994, sourced from the Associated Press, on a new vaccine for whooping cough, which mentioned the program and compensation fund in passing.[69]

## 14.

### FBI's New Plan to Spy on High School Students Across the Country

Sarah Lazare, "The FBI Has a New Plan to Spy on High School Students Across the Country" AlterNet, March 2, 2016, http://www.alternet.org/grayzone-project/fbi-has-new-plan-spy-high-school-students-across-country.

Danielle Jefferis, "The FBI Wants Schools to Spy on Their Students' Thoughts," Just Security, March 11, 2016, https://www.justsecurity.org/29901/fbi-schools-spy-students-thoughts/.

**Student Researcher:** Brandy Miceli (San Francisco State University)

**Faculty Evaluator:** Kenn Burrows (San Francisco State University)

Under new guidelines issued in January 2016, the FBI is instructing high schools across the country to report students who criticize government policies and "Western corruption" as potential future terrorists, Sarah Lazare reported for AlterNet. The new guidelines also warn that young people who are poor, are immigrants, or talk about travel to "suspicious" countries are more likely to commit violence. As Lazare wrote, the FBI's "Preventing Violent Extremism in Schools" guidelines combine "McCarthy-era theories of radicalization"—in which authorities monitor thoughts and behaviors suspected of leading to acts of violent subversion—with elements of a "widely unpopular" and "deeply controversial" British surveillance program, known as Prevent, that monitors Muslim communities and individuals.

The new guidelines depict US high schools as "hotbeds of extremism," Lazare summarized. Claiming that youth "possess inherent risk factors," the FBI guidelines describe high school students as "ideal targets" for recruitment by violent extremists. Educational materials prepared by the FBI for schools indicate that activities ranging from using "unusual language" or "private messaging apps"

The Canary in the Mineshaft of American Democracy

and encryption ("going dark," in FBI speak) to playing online games outside of school could indicate that "someone plans to commit violence."

The guidelines draw on a conveyor belt theory of extremism, which contends that extreme ideas lead to violence, a model tracing back to "the first red scare in America, as well as J. Edgar Hoover's crackdown on civil rights and anti-war activists," Lazare wrote. As Hugh Handeyside, a staff attorney for the American Civil Liberties Union's National Security Project, told Lazare, by broadening the definition of violent extremism, "the FBI is policing students' thoughts and trying to predict the future based on those thoughts."

The guidelines "are almost certainly designed" to target Muslim-American students. "In its caution to avoid the appearance of discrimination," Lazare wrote, "the agency identifies risk factors that are so broad and vague that virtually any young person could be deemed dangerous and worthy of surveillance." Nonetheless, the guidelines' repeated focus on "immigrant" and "diaspora" populations, as well as cultural and religious differences, reveal an underlying agenda. The FBI "consistently invokes an Islamic threat without naming it," Lazare reported. Arun Kundnani, author of *The Muslims Are Coming!: Islamophobia, Extremism, and the Domestic War on Terror*, about Islamophobia, told AlterNet, "In practice, schools seeking to implement this document will end up monitoring Muslim students disproportionately."

Writing for Just Security, an online forum based at the Center for Human Rights and Global Justice at New York University School of Law, Danielle Jefferis of the ACLU's National Security Project reported that "the FBI's request that school officials spy and report on students' ideas and beliefs risks stifling curiosity and free expression, which corrupts the trust that should exist between teachers and students." Though the FBI asserts that it does not want to limit students' freedom of speech, the guidelines encourage school officials to identify students who "engage in communications indicating support for extreme ideologies" or who are "curious about" subject matter that could be deemed extreme.

In calling for schools to create threat assessment teams and to "enhance domain awareness," the FBI engages in what Jefferis characterized as "fear mongering," which "will almost assuredly ratchet up the pressure on school officials to go to law enforcement before seeking out alternatives." This confronts school principals with the false dilemma of choosing between keeping their schools safe or upholding students' rights to freedom of expression and equal protection. Instead, Jefferis concluded, "Our kids are safer, and our communities are stronger, when we work to protect—not erode—our fundamental values and freedoms."

Lazare's AlterNet report was republished by *Salon*. PressTV, the Free Thought Project, MintPress News, and the *Intercept* subsequently ran stories on the FBI's "Preventing Violent Extremism in Schools" guidelines, but US corporate news media appear not to have covered this story in any detail.

## 15.

## Understanding Climate Change and Gender Inequality

Georgie Johnson, "Why Climate Change is a Gender Equality Issue," Greenpeace Energydesk, March 8, 2016, https://energydesk.greenpeace.org/2016/03/08/why-climate-change-gender-equality/.

Student Researcher: Noemi Garcia (Citrus College)

Faculty Evaluator: Andy Lee Roth (Citrus College)

We need to understand climate change through the lens of gender equality, Georgie Johnson reported for Greenpeace's Energydesk in March 2016. As Johnson's report showed, climate change has different impacts on men and women, based on preexisting social and economic inequalities. Because most international efforts to address climate change do not include women, the resulting policies do not take into account the particular challenges that climate change poses for women and girls. This is ironic because, according to a 2014 European Union study, women are more likely than men to be concerned about climate change.

Johnson identified two key factors to understanding climate change and gender. First, women (and other marginalized groups) are affected by climate change disproportionately due to social and economic inequality. For example, women accounted for 61 percent of fatalities caused by Cyclone Nargis in Myanmar in 2008, 70–80 percent in the 2004 Indian Ocean tsunami, and 91 percent in the 1991 cyclone in Bangladesh. As Johnson noted, gender inequality shaped the disproportionate rate at which women and girls died in these disasters. The reasons could be as simple as women not being taught to swim. In more unequal societies, where women do not tend to move in public spaces, adhering to social expectations to stay at home unless chaperoned by a male could lead women to ignore early warning signs to seek safer shelter.

For women who do survive, the aftermath of crises is also dangerous: Women are at greater risk of sexual assault and domestic abuse after natural disasters and in areas of conflict. For example, in the year after Hurricane Katrina hit New Orleans, 80 percent of those left behind in the Ninth Ward were women,[70] and incidents of gender-based violence (including sexual assault and domestic violence) in the state were almost four times higher than before the storm.[71]

Second, and more affirmatively, women can nonetheless offer

"incredibly powerful solutions to climate change," because they comprise nearly three-quarters of the global poor. This makes them "uniquely placed" to share knowledge about climate impacts and to implement solutions. Around the world women are "working to mitigate and adapt to climate change, either through direct on-the-ground solutions or as researchers, organisers and campaigners." For instance, Johnson described women farmers in El Salvador who have harnessed geothermal energy to replace wood and fossil fuels in their communities, reducing 1.8 tons of carbon dioxide emissions per year.[72]

"If we had gender parity in politics," Johnson wrote, "climate change policy might have more teeth."

## 16.

### Over Three-Quarters of Freedom of Information Act Requests Not Fully Answered

Ted Bridis and Jack Gillum, "US Gov't Sets Record for Failures to Find Files When Asked," Big Story (Associated Press), March 18, 2016, http://bigstory.ap.org/article/697e3523003049cdb0847ecf8 28afd62/us-govt-sets-record-failures-find-files-when-asked.

**Student Researcher:** Alexis Marie Tunstad (Citrus College)

**Faculty Evaluator:** Andy Lee Roth (Citrus College)

On his election, President Obama promised greater governmental transparency to the American people. In practice, the Obama administration has set a record for failures to find and produce government documents in response to Freedom of Information Act (FOIA) requests. As Ted Bridis and Jack Gillum reported for the Associated Press's Big Story, in response to FOIA requests, 129,825 times during the 2015 fiscal year—or more than one in every six cases—government searchers said they came up empty-handed. Overall, Bridis and Gillum wrote, "People who asked for records under the law received censored files or nothing in 77 percent of requests, also a record." The 77 percent figure represents a 12 percent increase, compared with the first full year after President Obama's election.

Signed into law by President Lyndon Johnson in 1966, the Freedom of Information Act encourages and enforces government disclosures to citizens and foreigners who request federal records, with exemptions for disclosures that would threaten national security, violate personal privacy, or expose confidential decision-making in certain areas.

Censorship and refusal to disclose are only two parts of a three-piece puzzle, the last being human error. As Bridis and Gillum reported, federal workers and the procedures they use to retrieve requested files also contribute to the problem. Though federal workers are required by law to make a reasonable search for requested files, the means of doing so are left to their discretion. "Skepticism," Bridis and Gillum wrote, has led many experts making FOIA requests to specify "exactly how they want federal employees to search files." Official efforts are reportedly underway to address this issue, by implementing specific guidelines, methods, and even lists of search terms to use.

However, an already overworked government staff will be challenged to implement the recommended improvements. As Bridis and Gillum reported, in 2015 the total number of FOIA requests increased 19 percent, compared to the previous year. During that time the number of new, full-time workers handling FOIA requests rose only 7 percent.

Though the corporate press, including the *New York Times* and the *Los Angeles Times*, have run stories on the Obama administration's efforts to improve government transparency, most of these articles predate the dramatic increase in the number of FOIA requests that the Obama administration has failed to respond to adequately.[73] And, whereas corporate media have focused on the president and his administration, Bridis and Gillum focus on the role of the government agencies actually tasked with responding to FOIA requests. A March 2015 story in the *Washington Post* drew largely from a previous report by Ted Bridis.[74] *U.S. News & World Report* reran Bridis and Gillum's report, as did the *Wall Street Journal*.[75] Notably, however, the *Journal* ran it as an opinion piece.

## 17.

### Deadly Medical Neglect for Immigrants in Privatized US Jails

Seth Freed Wessler, "This Man Will Almost Certainly Die," *Nation*, January 28, 2016, http://www.thenation.com/article/privatized-immigrant-prison-deaths/.

Seth Freed Wessler, "A Guide to Our Investigation of Deaths Inside the Federal Bureau of Prison's Immigrant-Only Facilities," *Nation*, January 28, 2016, http://www.thenation.com/article/a-guide-to-our-investigation-of-deaths-inside-the-federal-bureau-of-prisons-immigrant-only-facilities/.

Seth Freed Wessler, interview by Juan González and Amy Goodman, "'This Man Will Almost Certainly Die': The Secret Deaths of Dozens at Privatized Immigrant-Only Jails," broadcast February 9, 2016, *Democracy Now!*, transcript, http://www.democracynow.org/2016/2/9/this_man_will_almost_certainly_die.

Student Researchers: Aliana Ruiz (Citrus College), Alexandra Castillo (California Maritime Academy), Justin Lascano (Diablo Valley College), and Harrison Hartman (Sonoma State University)

Faculty Evaluators: Nolan Higdon (California Maritime Academy), Andy Lee Roth (Citrus College), and Peter Phillips (Sonoma State University)

Over one hundred inmates in privatized, immigrant-only prisons have died, many in disturbing circumstances involving negligent medical and mental health care, Seth Freed Wessler reported for the *Nation* in January 2016.

Wessler's article documented the deadly consequences of medical neglect in eleven immigrant-only prisons, known as Criminal Alien Requirement facilities. From 1998 to 2014, at least 137 inmates died in these special immigrant-only facilities run by the Corrections Corporation of America, the GEO Group, and the Management and Training Corporation under contract with the Federal Bureau of Prisons (BOP).

Wessler's report was based on more than 9,000 pages of medical records for 103 of the inmates who died in custody since the BOP first opened contract facilities. He fought over two years to obtain these files, using FOIA requests and ultimately a federal lawsuit to compel the BOP to release the records.

The *Nation* convened a panel of twenty-three independent reviewers, including seventeen medical doctors and six psychiatrists, to review the files. In twenty-five cases, multiple reviewers found evidence of inadequate care that likely contributed to an inmate's premature death. By contrast, in just thirty-nine cases did the reviewers find that care had likely been in accordance with recognized medical standards.

Unlike prisons that are run directly by the federal government—including immigration detention centers, where federal authorities typically hold immigrants pending deportation—these private, for-profit institutions are not held to the same standards. "Though the prisons are part of the federal infrastructure, the private contractors that run them operate under a different—and less stringent—set of rules in order to allow cost-cutting innovations," Wessler wrote.[76]

As a result, men with cancer, AIDS, mental illness, and liver and heart disease endured critical delays in care, prison medical units failed to make correct diagnoses of patients with obvious and painful symptoms, and inmates died of treatable diseases that they likely would have survived with access to adequate care.

The medical files documented at least seven suicides in the BOP's immigrant-only contract prisons. One BOP official, speaking on condition of anonymity, told Wessler, "In regular BOP prisons, mental-health treatment is part of the mission, because rehabilitation is part of the mission . . . For criminal-alien prisons, it's just, 'Hold them.'" Seven of the thirteen privatized facilities were not compliant with the standards for adequate mental health care.

Furthermore, licensed vocational nurses (or LVNs, who are meant to function as support staff for registered nurses or medical doctors) were often inmates' sole medical providers. "In 19 of the 103 deaths we reviewed," Wessler wrote, "at least one doctor flagged the overextension of LVNs as an inadequacy in care."

Forty percent of the men held in these prisons were incarcerated for "immigration-related" crimes for which only noncitizens can be convicted, including, for example, trying to re-enter the US after being deported. Until the 1990s, this crime was rarely ever prosecuted. The privatization of US prisons began in the late 1990s, as an effort by President Bill Clinton's administration to reduce the size of the federal workforce and to cut costs in the federal prison system.

An extensive search of corporate media coverage yielded just three somewhat comparable reports, each dating back to 2009, on the subject of inmate deaths in private prisons. Two of those articles were from the *New York Times*, with another from the *Washington Post*.[77] More recently, corporate news has focused on exposing the costs of incarcerating immigrants or comparing the frequency with which illegal immigrants and US citizens are convicted of rape or murder.[78] The deadly medical neglect of inmates in privatized, immigrant-only prisons—as documented by Seth Freed Wessler for the *Nation*—has gone unreported in the US corporate press.

**18.**

## Women's Movements Offer Global Paradigm Shift Toward Social Justice

Rucha Chitnis, "How Women-Led Movements are Redefining Power, from California to Nepal,"
*YES! Magazine*, March 8, 2016, http://www.yesmagazine.org/people-power/how-women-led-
movements-are-redefining-power-from-california-to-nepal-20160308.

**Student Researcher:** Mariah McHugh (San Francisco State University)

**Faculty Evaluator:** Mickey Huff (Diablo Valley College)

From LGBTQ movements and indigenous farming struggles to Black Lives Matter and efforts to create sustainable development, women around the world are leading the way toward greater social justice. In *YES! Magazine*, Rucha Chitnis wrote that, as responses to "corporate power, land grabs, economic injustice, and climate change," women's movements offer "a paradigm shift." Women-led movements have "redefined leadership and development models, connected the dots between issues and oppression, prioritized collective power and movement-building, and critically examined how issues of gender, race, caste, class, sexuality, and ability disproportionately exclude and marginalize." Chitnis's *YES! Magazine* report gave numerous examples of such developments.

One is the National Domestic Workers Alliance (NDWA), which stood in solidarity with the women of Ferguson, Missouri, in opposition to police brutality there. The letter of support from NDWA read in part, "As domestic workers, as women, we know that dignity is everyone's issue and justice is everyone's hope . . . We organize to create a world where every single one of us, domestic workers, black teens, immigrant children, aging grandparents—all of us—are treated with respect and dignity."

Women have long understood that social movements benefit from recognizing the intersections among different forms of oppression. Women around the world are working with a clear and common theme, which Chitnis framed in terms of a 1983 essay by the black lesbian feminist poet, Audre Lorde, "There is No Hierarchy of Oppressions." In that piece Lorde concluded, "I have learned that oppression and the intolerance of difference come in all shapes and sizes and colors and sexualities; and that among those of us who share the goals of liberation and a workable future for our children, there can be no hierarchies of oppression."[79]

On LGBTQ issues, Kimberlé Crenshaw, executive director of

the African American Policy Forum, stated, "People of color within LGBTQ movements; girls of color in the fight against the school-to-prison pipeline; women within immigration movements; trans women within feminist movements; and people with disabilities fighting police abuse—all face vulnerabilities that reflect the intersections of racism, sexism, class oppression, transphobia, ableism, and more."

Another example Chitnis cited comes from India, where Daya-mani Barla, a tribal journalist from Jharkhand, has "led a powerful movement to stop the world's largest steel company, ArcelorMittal, from displacing thousands of indigenous farming communities." Taking into account hydroelectric dams, mining, and extractive industries that have displaced, dispossessed, and impoverished millions of tribal people across India, Barla told *YES! Magazine* that globalization "has given rise to a kind of fascism." But Barla is not "anti-development." Instead, she said, "We want development of our identity and our history. We want that every person should get equal education and healthy life. We want polluted rivers to be pollution free. We want wastelands to be turned green. We want that everyone should get pure air, water, and food. This is our model of development."

After Nepal's devastating April 2015 earthquake, Rita Thapa, a Nepali public health physician, women's rights advocate, and peace activist, saw how women and girls were more vulnerable than their male counterparts.[80] Nevertheless, Thapa told *YES! Magazine* about the crucial role of women in the country's recovery and rebuilding efforts: With "little display of money or power," women held their communities together, feeding the young and old, caring for the sick, and (literally) picking up the rubble. "Everyone can learn from this," Thapa told *YES! Magazine*.

Chitnis summarized, "Whether it is indigenous women in the Amazon fighting corporate polluters and climate change or undocumented Latina domestic workers advocating for worker rights and dignity in California, women's groups and networks are making links between unbridled capitalism, violence, and the erosion of human rights and destruction of the Earth."

## 19.

### Global Epidemic of Electronic Waste

Katie Campbell and Ken Christensen, "On the Trail of America's Dangerous, Dead Electronics," KCTS9/EarthFix, May 9, 2016, http://www.opb.org/news/series/circuit/tracking-dangerous-dead-electronics/.

Katie Campbell and Ken Christensen, "Watchdog Group Tracks What Really Happens to Your 'Recycled' E-Waste," *PBS NewsHour*, PBS, broadcast May 9, 2016, transcript, http://www.pbs.org/newshour/bb/watchdog-group-tracks-what-really-happens-to-your-recycled-e-waste/.

Elizabeth Grossman, "GPS Tracking Devices Catch Major U.S. Recyclers Exporting Toxic E-Waste," *Intercept*, May 10, 2016, https://theintercept.com/2016/05/10/gps-tracking-devices-catch-major-u-s-recyclers-in-improper-e-waste-exports/.

**Student Researcher:** Karl Wada (College of Marin)

**Faculty Evaluator:** Susan Rahman (College of Marin)

Consumers in the US generate an estimated 3.14 million tons of electronic waste annually, according to the US Environmental Protection Agency, and about 40 percent of this—fifty thousand dump trucks a year—goes to be recycled. A 2016 study by the Basel Action Network (BAN), a nonprofit that aims to end the global trade in toxic electronic waste, found that nearly one-third of these devices is exported to developing countries, where the low-tech dismantling of the recycled equipment contaminates the environment and endangers workers, many of whom are children.[81] "People have a right to know where their stuff goes," BAN's executive director Jim Puckett told Katie Campbell and Ken Christensen of KCTS9/EarthFix in May 2016.

From July 2014 to December 2015, BAN installed GPS tracking devices in two hundred used, nonfunctional pieces of computer equipment, delivered the equipment to publicly accessible electronic waste recycling drop-off sites around the US, and then followed what happened to the equipment.

As of May 2016, BAN found that sixty-five of the devices (approximately 32 percent) were exported, rather than recycled domestically. Based on laws in the places where the electronics went, BAN estimated that sixty-two of the devices (31 percent) were likely to be illegal shipments. Puckett told the *Intercept* that the GPS tracking devices are "like little lie detectors . . . They tell their story and they tell it dispassionately."

BAN partnered with Carlo Ratti of the Massachusetts Institute of Technology's Senseable City Lab to determine exactly where the equipment went.[82] Ratti told the *PBS NewsHour* that he and his fellow researchers were surprised by how far waste traveled. Global e-waste flows "actually almost cover the whole planet." Each recycled device in the BAN study traveled an average of 2,500 miles.

Most equipment went to Hong Kong, but BAN tracked devices to ten different countries including China, Taiwan, Pakistan, Mexico, Thailand, Cambodia, and Kenya. Elizabeth Grossman, writing for the *Intercept*, quoted Puckett as describing Hong Kong's New Territories, near the Chinese border, as the "new ground zero" for e-waste processing. As the Chinese government has cracked down on electronic waste imports, Chinese workers have crossed the border to Hong Kong without official documentation to do similar work there.

If improperly disposed, e-waste can release a variety of toxins, including lead, mercury, and cadmium. However, the US only restricts e-waste exports of one type of component, cathode ray tubes. Though many US states prohibit dumping used electronics in landfills and have e-waste recycling programs, no federal law regulates e-waste recycling.

In Hong Kong, Puckett, a Chinese journalist and translator, and a local driver followed a GPS signal to a fence with a sign identifying the land on the other side as farmland. Peering over the fence, Puckett found workers covered in black toner ink—a probable carcinogen associated with respiratory problems—breaking up printers that were piled fifteen feet high across a lot as big as a football field. "There is no protection of this labor force . . . There are no occupational laws that are going to protect them," Puckett said. Earlier, at another site where workers dismantled LCD TVs, they found workers without protective face masks who were unaware of the mercury vapors released when the fluorescent tubes that light the LCD screens break.[83] Even in trace amounts, mercury can be a neurotoxin.

Since 1989, 182 national governments and the European Union have signed the Basel Convention, an international treaty to stop developed countries from dumping hazardous waste in less developed nations. As EarthFix reported, the US is the world's only industrialized country that has not ratified the treaty.

In April 2016, *U.S. News & World Report* published an article anticipating the release of BAN's report, *Disconnect: Goodwill and Dell Exporting the Public's E-waste to Developing Countries*. Otherwise, it has been poorly covered in the US corporate press.[84]

## 20.

## The Walmarting of American Education

Jeff Bryant, "How the Cutthroat Walmart Business Model is Reshaping American Public Education," AlterNet, March 13, 2016, http://www.alternet.org/education/how-cutthroat-walmart-business-model-reshaping-american-public-education?akid=14059.1078898.bMYE-X&rd=1&s rc=newsletter1052509&t=2.

**Student Researcher:** Marc Wilhelm (Diablo Valley College)

**Faculty Evaluator:** Mickey Huff (Diablo Valley College)

In January 2016, Walmart publicized a plan to close 269 of its retail stores. As Jeff Bryant reported for AlterNet, the announcement was significant news in small towns and suburban communities directly affected by the closures, but otherwise it did not garner prominent media attention. "Stories about local communities being devastated by business decisions made in distant headquarters have become a staple of this era," he wrote. At the same time, Bryant reported, the Walton Family Foundation (WFF) announced a five-year strategic plan to spend a billion dollars to support and expand charter schools in thirteen US cities and states. As *Education Week* reported, WFF was "doubling down on its investments in school choice."[85]

Over the past twenty years, WFF has given more than $1.3 billion to K–12 education, according to its own calculations. The WFF boasts that one in four charter schools across the nation has received WFF startup funds.[86] In his AlterNet article, Bryant described how WFF's commitment to charter schools is a product of the Walton family having been "fully inculcated" in the educational philosophy of libertarian economist Milton Friedman and by the "myth of school failure" spread by the Reagan administration.

In 1980, Ronald Reagan campaigned to abolish the Department of Education. One of the landmarks of his presidency was the 1983 report "A Nation at Risk: The Imperative for Educational Reform," which warned against a "rising tide of mediocrity." Though critics have since rebutted many of the report's claims and questioned the validity of its statistical analysis, "A Nation at Risk" was and remains influential. Indeed, John Walton read the report the year it was published and shared it with family members, leading his father, Sam Walton, to announce, "I'd like to see an all-out revolution in education."

In 1995, Friedman argued that "[o]ur elementary and secondary educational system needs to be radically restructured," and that

only by "privatizing a major segment of it" could the restructuring succeed. As Bryant described, "Central to Friedman's ideology was that schools should be thought of as businesses," and their students understood as customers. Friedman's philosophy meshed with the Waltons' business sensibilities, as did a shared animosity toward unions. In this view, businesses—and, by extension, schools—thrive by providing customers with what they want at lower prices than their competitors can offer; and employees—or teachers—remain loyal because of profit-sharing and other options that give them a stake in the business, rather than due to higher wages.

In a related report for *Salon*, excerpted from his book *Schools on Trial*, Nikhil Goyal documented how the New Markets Tax Credit Program, established in 2000 by the Clinton administration, encouraged private investors to "put money into community projects, like the development of new charter schools, in low-income communities."[87] Under the program, such ventures can earn investors a 39 percent federal tax break over seven years. Goyal quoted journalist Juan

González as saying, "The program . . . is so lucrative that a lender who uses it can almost double his money in seven years."

Walmart founder Sam Walton established the Walton Family Foundation (WFF) in 1987 as a philanthropic endeavor. Walmart's vast earnings generate the foundation's money. The Walton family is among the world's richest, with a combined net worth of approximately $150 billion in January 2016.

Although corporate news attended to WFF's $1 billion commitment to charter schools, this coverage often favored charter school expansion, as in an April 2016 CNBC report that spotlighted how charter schools would decrease educational inequality.[88] *Salon* and Valerie Strauss of the *Washington Post* each republished Bryant's AlterNet piece in March 2016.

NOTE: For related coverage of charter schools, see *Censored* story #22, "Department of Education Cooperates with ALEC to Privatize Education," below.

## 21.
### Little Guantánamos: Secretive "Communication Management Units" in the US

Will Potter, "The Secret US Prisons You've Never Heard of Before, " TED video, filmed January 2015, https://www.ted.com/talks/will_potter_the_secret_us_prisons_you_ve_never_heard_of_before.

Will Potter, interview by Sharmini Peries, "'Little Guantanamos' in the US," Real News Network, broadcast October 20, 2015, transcript, http://therealnews.com/t2/index.php?option=com_content&task=view&id=31&Itemid=74&jumival=14945.

Carrie Johnson, "Inmates Try to Revive Lawsuit over Secretive Prison Units," NPR, March 15, 2016, http://www.npr.org/2016/03/15/470430094/inmates-try-to-revive-lawsuit-over-secretive-prison-units.

Chip Gibbons, "Circuit Court Weighs Appeals in 'Communication Management Units' Prison Case," Bill of Rights Defense Committee, March 17, 2016, http://bordc.org/news/circuit-court-weighs-appeals-in-communication-management-units-prison-case/.

**Student Researcher:** Allison Bamford (University of Regina)

**Faculty Evaluator:** Patricia W. Elliott (University of Regina)

In March 2016, inmates from two highly secretive US prisons, known as Communication Management Units (CMUs), appealed a previous summary judgment for the government in their case against the Federal Bureau of Prisons. In March 2015, the US District Court for the District of Columbia had ruled against the prisoners, asserting that

CMUs did not violate inmates' rights because restrictions were "limited in nature" compared to ordinary prison units, and far better than solitary confinement. In their appeal, attorneys for the Center for Constitutional Rights argued that CMUs represent a "fundamental disruption" to prisoners' rights and freedoms.

CMUs have strict regulations against outside communication. Prisoners are isolated from the rest of the prison population, and are limited to four hours of visits per month, none of which permit direct contact, and three phone calls per month (for a total of forty-five minutes), which must be carried out in English. Lawyers representing the CMU inmates argued that the typical time served in a CMU is three to five years, or fifty-five times longer than the average time in administrative detention.

Beginning in 2006, the Federal Bureau of Prisons created CMUs without any written conditions or procedures. Prisoners receive very little information as to why they are transferred to the unit in the first place. They are able to appeal their transfer, but not a single prisoner has ever been released through the appeal process. Without written rules in place, it is suggested that these transfers take place based on discrimination.

In January 2015, the Federal Bureau of Prisons finalized rules regarding who can be sent to CMUs and how the facilities should operate, but as Christie Thompson of the Marshall Project reported, prisoner advocates claimed the new rules imposed "even stricter limits on contact without providing a legitimate way for inmates to appeal being placed under such restrictions."[89]

About 178 inmates are held in CMUs. Nearly 60 percent of them are Muslims, according to Center for Constitutional Rights attorneys representing the prisoners.[90] Journalist Will Potter, who has visited a CMU, told the Real News Network that CMUs are effectively "political prisons for political prisoners." "People are sent to the CMU because of their race, and their religion and their political beliefs," rather than the crimes they have committed, Potter said.

In a January 2015 TED Talk on CMUs, Potter noted that CMU guards call non-Muslim prisoners "balancers," meaning they "help balance the racial numbers, in hopes of deflecting lawsuits." Many of these "balancers" are animal rights and environmental activists.

Journalists are not permitted in CMUs, but Potter was able to visit an imprisoned environmental activist, Daniel McGowan, "as a friend."

There are two known CMUs in the United States, one in Marion, Illinois, and the other in Terre Haute, Indiana. Both operate within larger federal prisons.

In March 2011, NPR ran a two-part investigative report and the *Nation* published a detailed article on CMUs.[91] In 2011 and 2013, the *Huffington Post* published reports by Daniel McGowan, the first of which was written while he was imprisoned in the Marion, Illinois, CMU.[92] The *Huffington Post* has consistently published articles by attorneys with the Center for Constitutional Rights on CCR's efforts to defend prisoners' right to due process and to bring CMU policies in line with constitutional requirements.[93] Otherwise, coverage of CMUs in the popular press is limited to articles such as the *New York Times* report from April 2016, "The Terrorists in U.S. Prisons," which briefly mentioned CMUs and their predominantly Muslim inmates, but did not discuss challenges to the CMUs' constitutionality.[94]

## 22.

### Department of Education Cooperates with ALEC to Privatize Education

Dustin Beilke, "Feds Cheerlead for Charter Schools, Aiding Private Philanthropy's Takeover of America's Public Schools," *PR Watch*, Center for Media and Democracy, January 20, 2016, http://www.prwatch.org/news/2016/01/13019/feds-cheerlead-charter-schools-aiding-private-philanthropy's-takeover-america's.

**Student Researcher:** Karina Seiler (College of Marin)

**Faculty Evaluator:** Susan Rahman (College of Marin)

The Department of Education and school districts throughout the US are working with billionaire families such as the Waltons and Netflix CEO Reed Hastings to undermine public education, Dustin Beilke reported for *PR Watch* in January 2016. Instead of defending public education in pursuit of equity for all students, the Department of Education (DoE) is working with organizations like the American Legislative Exchange Council (ALEC)—an alliance of corporate lobbyists and state legislators—as well as local chambers of commerce to encourage the conversion of public institutions into private charter schools.

A December 2015 DoE presentation showed that the federal government had spent over $3 billion of taxpayer money to boost charter

schools, supporting an uncritical assessment of how effective charter schools actually are. Beilke described the twenty-five-slide overview of the DoE's charter schools program as "an uncritical PR document embracing a magical idea of charter schools."[95]

According to the Center for Media and Democracy (CMD), although many charter schools have failed and closed in the last twenty years, the DoE continues to provide significant funding to promote them. An October 2015 CMD investigation, "Charter School Black Hole," uncovered how much the federal government has invested in charter schools, as well as the DoE's ties to ALEC.[96] As Beilke reported, a slide from the December 2015 DoE overview of its charter school program acknowledged that it had spent $3.3 billion to "fund the start-up, replication and expansion of public charter schools." However, Beilke reported, "CMD was unable to extract this number from DOE despite inquiries and Freedom of Information Act (FOIA) requests since 2014." The actual figure may be higher, because the list of charter schools receiving DoE funding appears to have been incomplete. Overall, the DoE overview suggested that it functions as a "propagandist" for charter schools, Beilke wrote.

According to the CMD report, "laws governing charters have been built by proponents, favoring 'flexibility' over rules," permitting an "epidemic of fraud, waste, and mismanagement that would not be tolerated in public schools." As Beilke concluded, "the Department of Education's charter school agenda matches that of the anti-education, pro-privatization movement that funds and promotes so much of the misinformation about public education."

Corporate media have provided significant coverage of ALEC's involvement in promoting charter schools, including its lobbying efforts, but the role of the DoE has not been well covered in the corporate press. A 2012 *New York Times* article, "Public Money Finds Back Door to Private Schools," mentioned both ALEC and the DoE, but did not establish any connection between them.[97]

NOTE: For related coverage of charter schools, see *Censored* story #20, "The Walmarting of American Education," above.

## 23.
### Modern-Day Child Slavery: Sex Trafficking of Underage Girls in the US

D. Parvaz, "Selling American Girls," Al Jazeera America, December 15, 2015, http://projects. aljazeera.com/2015/12/sex-trafficking/.

**Student Researcher:** Vanessa Anderson (University of Vermont)

**Faculty Evaluator:** Rob Williams (University of Vermont)

In December 2015, D. Parvaz published "Selling American Girls," a seven-part investigative report for Al Jazeera America that documented sex trafficking in the US. Each part of her report examined a different role in the sex trafficking trade and its enforcement, from the prostitutes and their buyers, pimps, and advocates, to law enforcement officers and judges.

Sex trafficking in the US is pervasive. According to the US Department of Justice, human trafficking is the second-fastest-growing criminal enterprise after drug trafficking, with minors constituting roughly half the victims in the US. In 2015, over 4,100 of the 5,544 trafficking cases reported to the National Human Trafficking

Resource Center's hotline involved sex trafficking.[98]

Sex trafficking is also a major component of the underground economy in many American cities. A 2014 study conducted by the Urban Institute found that the underground commercial sex economy in the US produced multimillion-dollar profits. Researchers at the Urban Institute studied eight major US cities—Atlanta, Dallas, Denver, Kansas City, Miami, Seattle, San Diego, and Washington, DC—to estimate that, in each city, the underground sex economy was worth between $39.9 million and $290 million in 2007.[99] "From high-end escort services to high school 'sneaker pimps,'" the report's authors wrote, "the sex trade leaves no demographic unrepresented and circuits almost every major US city."

As Parvaz reported, "The variety of men engaged in purchasing sex across the U.S. is staggering." According to Michael Osborn, chief of the FBI's Violent Crimes Against Children Unit, the FBI focuses on "recovering" the victims of sex trafficking and capturing their pimps, who "represent a national threat" because they move among cities and across states to avoid capture. Buyers (or "johns"), by contrast, tend to remain in local jurisdictions, which the FBI leaves to local law enforcement. Because precincts, counties, and states keep track of john arrests in different ways, if at all, there are no comprehensive statistics for how many are arrested each year. Enforcement tends to be stronger in cases where buyers are charged with soliciting minors. In one study of 134 cases involving prostitutes who were minors, 113 johns were convicted. On average they were sentenced to three years in prison, but served just 1.5 years. Twenty-six percent of those convicted served no time at all.[100]

Many pimps look for children who come from unstable family backgrounds or destitute neighborhoods. According to FAIR Girls, an antitrafficking organization, 70–75 percent of the girls they assisted had histories with foster care systems. Special Agent Renea Green of the Georgia Bureau of Investigation told Al Jazeera America, "We had a trafficker tell us he looked for victims, for girls, walking from the local DFAC [Department of Family and Children Services] office."

While safe harbor laws, which criminalize adults who purchase sex with a minor, have been passed in thirty-four states, according to the Polaris Project these laws tend to vary widely from state to state, leaving many girls treated as criminals rather than as victims.

Sex trafficking in the US has been a focus of corporate news coverage, but reports tend to focus primarily on the prostitutes and their pimps,[101] while neglecting other important issues raised in the Al Jazeera America report, such as the prosecution of buyers and the criminal penalties that girls and young women often face. Most news coverage is from local news outlets, which tend to report specific instances of sex trafficking, rather than discussing the topic in a broader social context.

## 24.
### India's Solar Plans Blocked by US Interests, WTO

Ben Beachy and Ilana Solomon, "The WTO Just Ruled against India's Booming Solar Program," Sierra Club, February 24, 2016, http://www.sierraclub.org/compass/2016/02/wto-just-ruled-against-india-s-booming-solar-program.

Dipti Bhatnagar and Sam Cossar-Gilbert, "World Trade Organisation Smashes India's Solar Panels Industry," Ecologist, February 28, 2016, http://www.theecologist.org/News/news_analysis/2987286/world_trade_organisation_smashes_indias_solar_panels_industry.html.

Charles Pierson, "How the US and the WTO Crushed India's Subsidies for Solar Energy," Counter-Punch, August 28, 2015, http://www.counterpunch.org/2015/08/28/how-the-us-and-the-wto-crushed-indias-subsidies-for-solar-energy/.

**Student Researcher:** Jillian Solomon (San Francisco State University)

**Faculty Evaluator:** Kenn Burrows (San Francisco State University)

The United Nations Conference on Climate Change, held in December 2015 in Paris, featured lofty rhetoric about international cooperation to tackle climate change, including overtures by the US and other nations to include India. Anticipating the Paris summit, World Trade Organization (WTO) director-general Roberto Azevêdo wrote, "The challenge is not to stop trading but to ensure that trade is an ally in the fight against climate change."[102] However, in February 2016, the WTO ruled against India's Jawaharlal Nehru National Solar Mission. In a case initiated by the US in 2013, the WTO found that India's solar initiative, which required that 10 percent of solar cells be produced locally, violated international trade laws. As Dipti Bhatnagar and Sam Cossar-Gilbert of Friends of the Earth International reported in the Ecologist, "The WTO ruling sets a dangerous precedent for countries wanting to support homegrown renewable energy initiatives."

Prime Minister Manmohan Singh launched India's National Solar Mission in 2010. Ben Beachy and Ilana Solomon described how the

National Solar Mission aimed to develop long-term policy, research and development, and domestic production to reduce the cost of solar power generation in India and, ultimately, to increase India's solar capacity to 100,000 megawatts by 2022—a target that would surpass the combined current solar capacity of the world's top five solar-producing countries. By the time of the WTO ruling, the National Solar Mission had already increased India's solar capacity from "nearly nothing" to 5,000 megawatts, Beachy and Solomon reported.

However, US Trade Representative Michael Froman claimed that India's subsidized solar program discriminated against American suppliers, arguing that India's solar plan created unfair barriers to imports of US-made solar panels. Even though India had argued that the program helped it to meet its commitments under the United Nations Framework Convention on Climate Change, the WTO ruling stated that domestic policies in conflict with its rules could not be justified on the basis that they fulfill international climate commitments. As Beachy and Solomon summarized, "antiquated trade rules trump climate imperatives."

On the WTO ruling against India, Froman described the decision as "important" for the message it sent "to other countries considering discriminatory 'localization' policies." But, Beachy and Solomon noted, the US position was "perverse" because "[n]early half of U.S. states have renewable energy programs that, like India's solar program, include 'buy-local' rules that create local, green jobs and bring new solar entrepreneurs into the economy."

This was not the first time the US appealed to the WTO to challenge another nation's domestic climate initiatives. A similar program in Canada, Ontario's Green Energy Act, sought to boost renewable technologies and create clean-energy jobs. Spurred by the US, in 2012 the WTO ruled against the program, which had to be modified to comply with WTO rules.

In February 2016, *Forbes* ran an opinion piece clearly in favor of the WTO ruling (and free trade in general), while a September 2015 article in the *Wall Street Journal* provided coverage of India's position and noting opportunities for foreign companies if the WTO ruled against India's requirement that some solar panels should be produced domestically.[103] A Reuters report on the WTO ruling emphasized the US perspective and provided little detail about India's solar program—accounted for by the claim that "Indian officials were not immediately available to comment," despite basic information about its solar program having been previously available in a variety of public forums.[104]

## 25.
### NYPD Editing Wikipedia on Police Brutality

Kelly Weill, "Edits to Wikipedia Pages on Bell, Garner, Diallo Traced to 1 Police Plaza," *Capital New York* (since renamed *Politico New York*), March 13, 2015, http://www.capitalnewyork.com/article/city-hall/2015/03/8563947/edits-wikipedia-pages-bell-garner-diallo-traced-1-police-plaza; since redirected to http://www.politico.com/states/new-york/city-hall/story/2015/03/edits-to-wikipedia-pages-on-bell-garner-diallo-traced-to-1-police-plaza-087652.

Inae Oh, "The NYPD is Editing the Wikipedia Pages of Eric Garner, Sean Bell," *Mother Jones*, March 13, 2015, http://www.motherjones.com/mojo/2015/03/nypd-editing-wikipedia-pages-eric-garner-sean-bell.

**Student Researcher:** Amber Gerard (Indian River State College)

**Faculty Evaluator:** Elliot D. Cohen (Indian River State College)

In March 2015, Kelly Weill reported in *Capital New York* that computers operating at One Police Plaza, the headquarters of the New York Police Department (NYPD), had been used "to alter Wikipedia pages containing details of alleged police brutality," including the entries for Eric Garner, Sean Bell, and Amadou Diallo. As *Mother Jones* subsequently reported, "The pages have been edited to cast the NYPD in a more favorable light and lessen allegations of police misconduct." According to Weill's report, an NYPD spokesperson indicated that the matter was under internal review.

*Capital New York* identified eighty-five Internet Protocol (IP) addresses associated with the NYPD that had been used to edit or to attempt to delete Wikipedia entries. "Notable" Wikipedia activity was linked to approximately one dozen of those IP addresses, Weill reported.

On the evening of December 3, 2014, after a Staten Island grand jury ruled not to indict NYPD officer Daniel Pantaleo in Eric Garner's death, a computer user on the NYPD headquarters network made multiple edits to the "Death of Eric Garner" Wikipedia entry. For example, edits included changing text that read "push Garner's face into the sidewalk" to "push Garner's head down into the sidewalk." Another edit revised text that read, "Use of the chokehold has been prohibited" to read, "Use of the chokehold is legal, but has been prohibited." As *Mother Jones* noted, additional edits suggested that "Garner's death was his own fault."

On November 25, 2006, undercover NYPD officers fired fifty times at three unarmed men, killing Sean Bell, whose death led to widespread protests against police brutality. On April 12, 2007, a user on the NYPD headquarters network attempted to delete the Wikipedia entry for "Sean Bell shooting incident." On the website's internal "Articles for deletion" page, the user wrote: "[N]o one except Al Sharpton cares anymore."

On three occasions between October 2012 and March 2013, a user on the One Police Plaza network made edits to Wikipedia's "Stop-and-frisk in New York City" entry.

As Weill noted, revisions and counter-revisions are "typical of Wikipedia's self-policing user community." However, those made with NYPD IP addresses seemed to violate Wikipedia's conflict of interest policy involving contributions that promote one's own self-interests.

All of the NYPD edits documented by *Capital New York* were made anonymously (rather than with a Wikipedia account). *Capital New*

*York* developed a computer program to search Wikipedia for all of the anonymous edits made from the range of IP addresses registered to One Police Plaza. Weill concluded by providing a link to a list of all the anonymous Wikipedia edits made by NYPD IP addresses.[105]

The *Washington Post* and *Time* magazine each ran stories based on Weill's original *Capital New York* report.[106]

## Notes

1 This introduction draws on Andy Lee Roth's talk, "Breaking the Corporate News Frame: Toward a New Digital Commons," presented at the annual meetings of the Pacific Sociological Association, in Oakland, California, on April 1, 2016.

2 Edward S. Herman and Noam Chomsky, *Manufacturing Consent: The Political Economy of the Mass Media* (New York: Pantheon Books, 1988), 1–35.

3 Quotation from Unfiltered.news, https://unfiltered.news/about.html. On the launch of Unfiltered.news, see Joseph Lichterman, "A New Data Viz Tool Shows What Stories are being Undercovered in Countries around the World," Nieman Lab, March 18, 2016, http://www.niemanlab.org/2016/03/a-new-data-viz-tool-shows-what-stories-are-being-undercovered-in-countries-around-the-world/.

4 Lichterman, "New Data Viz Tool."

5 For sobering evidence of the lack of correlation between the number of times a topic is mentioned in the news and its importance, see the analysis in Chapter 3 of this volume, on Junk Food News and News Abuse.

6 Mark Frary, "Whose World are You Watching? The Secret Algorithms Controlling the News We See," *Index on Censorship* 44, no. 4 (December 2015), 69–73, quote at 69.

7 On the development of Project Censored's campus affiliates program, see Peter Phillips and Mickey Huff, "Colleges and Universities Validate Independent News and Challenge Censorship," *Censored 2011: The Top 25 Censored Stories of 2009–10*, eds. Mickey Huff, Peter Phillips, and Project Censored (New York: Seven Stories Press, 2010), 355–69; and Andy Lee Roth and Project Censored, "Breaking the Corporate News Frame through Validated Independent News Online," *Media Education for a Digital Generation*, eds. Julie Frechette and Rob Williams (New York and Abingdon: Routledge, 2016), 173–86.

8 For information on how to nominate a story, see "How to Support Project Censored," at the back of this volume.

9 Validated Independent News stories are archived on the Project Censored website at http://www.projectcensored.org/category/validated-independent-news.

10 For a complete list of the national and international judges and their brief biographies, see the acknowledgments section of this book.

11 For previous Project Censored coverage of US military operations in Africa, see Brian Martin Murphy, "The 'New' American Imperialism in Africa: Secret Sahara Wars and AFRICOM," in *Censored 2014: Fearless Speech in Fateful Times*, eds. Mickey Huff, Andy Lee Roth, and Project Censored (New York: Seven Stories Press, 2013), 353–364.

12 Julia Zorthian and Heather Jones, "This Graphic Shows Where U.S. Troops are Stationed around the World," *Time*, October 16, 2015, http://time.com/4075458/afghanistan-drawdown-obama-troops/.

13 Marcia Angell, "Drug Companies & Doctors: A Story of Corruption," *New York Review of Books*, January 15, 2009, http://www.nybooks.com/articles/2009/01/15/drug-companies-doctors-story-of-corruption/. After the *Review* received a letter from a legal representative of one of the researchers described in Angell's article, objecting to the use of the word "corruption" in the headline and text of her review, the *Review*'s editors wrote that "the growing financial dependence of the medical profession on the pharmaceutical industry is profoundly detrimental to sound public, medical, and scientific policy." See The Editors, "A Note to Readers," *New York*

*Review of Books*, February 12, 2009, http://www.nybooks.com/articles/2009/02/12/a-note-to-readers/.

14    "GlaxoSmithKline to Plead Guilty and Pay $3 Billion to Resolve Fraud Allegations and Failure to Report Safety Data," US Department of Justice, Office of Public Affairs, July 2, 2012, https://www.justice.gov/opa/pr/glaxosmithkline-plead-guilty-and-pay-3-billion-resolve-fraud-allegations-and-failure-report.

15    Joanna Le Noury et al., "Restoring Study 329: Efficacy and Harms of Paroxetine and Imipramine in Treatment of Major Depression in Adolescence," *BMJ*, September 16, 2015, http://www.bmj.com/content/351/bmj.h4320.

16    Lenny Bernstein and Ariana Eunjung Cha, "Reanalysis Cites Serious Flaws in 2001 Paxil Study," *Washington Post*, September 17, 2015, A2.

17    Ibid. "The reanalysis was the first in a program by The BMJ to encourage a second look at abandoned or misreported studies to ensure that doctors have accurate information."

18    US Library of Congress, Congressional Research Service, "Summary: S.994—113th Congress (2013–2014)," May 9, 2014, https://www.congress.gov/bill/113th-congress/senate-bill/994.

19    David A. Hutchins et al., "Irreversibly Increased Nitrogen Fixation in Trichodesmium Experimentally Adapted to Elevated Carbon Dioxide," *Nature Communications*, September 1, 2015, http://www.nature.com/ncomms/2015/150901/ncomms9155/full/ncomms9155.html.

20    Suzanne Jacobs, "Climate Change Will Do Strange Things to This Hungry Little Microbe," Grist, September 1, 2015, http://grist.org/science/climate-change-will-do-strange-things-to-this-hungry-little-microbe/; Alex Dobuzinskis, "Climate Change Could Alter Key Ocean Bacteria: A Study," Reuters, September 1, 2015, http://www.reuters.com/article/us-usa-microbes-study-idUSKCN0R149K20150901; Chelsea Harvey, "Climate Change Could Push These Tiny Marine Organisms to Evolve—Irreversibly," *Washington Post*, September 1, 2015, https://www.washingtonpost.com/news/energy-environment/wp/2015/09/01/climate-change-could-push-these-tiny-marine-organisms-to-evolve-rapidly-and-thats-not-necessarily-a-good-thing/.

21    Amit Singhal, "A Flawed Elections Conspiracy Theory," *Politico Magazine*, Politico, August 26, 2015, http://www.politico.com/magazine/story/2015/08/google-2016-election-121766; quoted in Frary, "Whose World," 71. For additional coverage critical of Epstein and Robertson's findings, see Andrew Gelman and Kaiser Fung, "Could Google Rig the 2016 Election? Don't Believe the Hype," Daily Beast, September 21, 2015, http://www.thedailybeast.com/articles/2015/09/21/could-google-rig-the-2016-election-don-t-believe-the-hype.html.

22    Emily Bell, "Silicon Valley and Journalism: Make Up or Break Up?," Reuters Memorial Lecture video, filmed November 11, 2014, posted December 10, 2014, https://podcasts.ox.ac.uk/silicon-valley-and-journalism-make-or-break-reuters-memorial-lecture-2014; quoted in Frary, "Whose World," 73.

23    Robert J. Fitrakis and Harvey Wasserman, *The Strip & Flip Selection of 2016: Five Jim Crows & Electronic Election Theft* (Columbus, OH: CICJ Books, 2016).

24    Quoted in Lawrence Norden and Christopher Famighetti, "America's Voting Machines at Risk," Brennan Center for Justice (New York University School of Law), September 15, 2015, https://www.brennancenter.org/sites/default/files/publications/Americas_Voting_Machines_At_Risk.pdf.

25    Ibid., 5.

26    Ibid., 13.

27    Bob Fitrakis and Harvey Wasserman, "Why We Must Now Adopt the 'Ohio Plan' to Prevent the 'Strip and Flip' of American Elections," *Free Press*, January 23, 2016, http://freepress.org/article/why-we-must-now-adopt-ohio-plan-prevent-strip-and-flip-american-elections.

28    David Goldman, "Google Could 'Rig the 2016 Election,' Researcher Says," CNNMoney, August 20, 2015, http://money.cnn.com/2015/08/20/technology/google-2016-election; Michael Addady, "Researchers Claim that Google Could 'Rig the 2016 Election'," *Fortune*, August 23, 2015, http://fortune.com/2015/08/23/research-google-rig-election/; Craig Timberg, "A Google Effect on Elections?," *Washington Post*, May 13, 2014, A10.

29 Tim Robbins, "We Need to Fix Our Broken Election System," *Huffington Post*, May 5, 2016, http://www.huffingtonpost.com/tim-robbins/fix-our-election-system_b_9847102.html.

30 "World at War: Global Trends, Forced Displacement in 2014," United Nations High Commissioner for Refugees (UNHCR), June 18, 2015, http://unhcr.org/556725e69.html.

31 For previous Project Censored coverage of the global refugee crisis, see "Global Forced Displacement Tops Fifty Million," *Censored* story #14 in *Censored 2016: Media Freedom on the Line*, eds. Mickey Huff, Andy Lee Roth, and Project Censored (New York: Seven Stories Press, 2015), 69–70.

32 "World at War: Global Trends, Forced Displacement in 2014," 3.

33 See, for example, Somini Sengupta, "60 Million People Fleeing Chaotic Lands, U.N. Says," *New York Times*, June 18, 2015, http://www.nytimes.com/2015/06/18/world/60-million-people-fleeing-chaotic-lands-un-says.html; and Griff Witte, "New U.N. Report Says World's Refugee Crisis is Worse Than Anyone Expected," *Washington Post*, June 18, 2015, https://www.washingtonpost.com/world/europe/new-un-report-says-worlds-refugee-crisis-is-worse-than-anyone-expected/2015/06/17/a49c3fc0-14ff-11e5-8457-4b431bf7ed4c_story.html.

34 "Refugee Crisis: EU and Turkey Reach 'Breakthrough' Deal," Al Jazeera, March 8, 2016, http://www.aljazeera.com/news/2016/03/refugee-crisis-eu-turkey-agree-proposal-160308021149403.html.

35 Jennifer Rankin, "'Do Not Come to Europe,' Donald Tusk Warns Economic Migrants," *Guardian*, March 3, 2016, http://www.theguardian.com/world/2016/mar/03/donald-tusk-economic-migrants-do-not-come-to-europe.

36 Anton Troianovski, Manuela Mesco, and Simon Clark, "The Growth of Refugee Inc.," *Wall Street Journal*, September 14, 2015, http://www.wsj.com/articles/in-european-refugee-crisis-an-industry-evolves-1442252165.

37 Kathryn J. Edin and H. Luke Shaefer, *$2.00 a Day: Living on Almost Nothing in America* (New York: Houghton Mifflin Harcourt Publishing Company, 2015).

38 For previous Project Censored coverage of how corporate media neglect to cover poor people, see "Millions in Poverty Get Less Media Coverage Than Billionaires Do," *Censored* story #9 in *Censored 2016*, 61–2.

39 Marisol Bello, "More Than 1.4 Million Families Live on $2 a Day Per Person," *USA Today*, February 24, 2012, http://usatoday30.usatoday.com/news/nation/story/2012-02-23/extreme-poverty-increase/53227386/1.

40 Kathryn Edin and H. Luke Shaefer, "Living on $2 a Day in America," *Los Angeles Times*, September 3, 2015, http://www.latimes.com/opinion/op-ed/la-oe-0903-shaefer-edin-2-dollar-a-day-poverty-20150903-story.html; William Julius Wilson, "'$2.00 a Day,' by Kathryn J. Edin and H. Luke Shaefer," *New York Times Sunday Book Review*, September 2, 2015, http://www.nytimes.com/2015/09/06/books/review/2-00-a-day-by-kathryn-j-edin-and-h-luke-shaefer.html?_r=0.

41 Project Censored has consistently featured independent news coverage of the ongoing Fukushima disaster in our annual listings of the most underreported news stories. For past *Censored* coverage, see "Fukushima Nuclear Disaster Deepens," *Censored* story #5 in *Censored 2016*, 52–4; "Lawsuit Challenges Nuclear Power Industry Immunity from Liability in Nuclear Accidents," *Censored* story #13 in *Censored 2015: Inspiring We the People*, eds. Andy Lee Roth, Mickey Huff, and Project Censored (New York: Seven Stories Press, 2014), 61–62; Brian Covert, "Fukushima Disaster Worse Than Anticipated," *Censored 2015*, 121–5; Elaine Wellin, "Environment and Health," *Censored 2013: Dispatches from the Media Revolution*, eds. Mickey Huff, Andy Lee Roth, and Project Censored (New York: Seven Stories Press, 2012), 91–3; Brian Covert, "On the Road to Fukushima: The Unreported Story behind Japan's Nuclear-Media-Industrial Complex," *Censored 2013*, 387–406; and "The Fairy Tale of Clean and Safe Nuclear Power," *Censored* story #8 in *Censored 2012: Sourcebook for the Media Revolution*, eds. Mickey Huff and Project Censored (New York: Seven Stories Press, 2011), 102–5.

42 Common Dreams staff, "In First, TEPCO Dumps Fukushima Groundwater into Pacific Ocean," Common Dreams, September 15, 2015, http://www.commondreams.org/news/2015/09/15/first-tepco-dumps-fukushima-groundwater-pacific-ocean.

43 "Higher Levels of Fukushima Cesium Detected Offshore," Woods Hole Oceanographic Institution, December 3, 2015, https://www.whoi.edu/news-release/fukushima-higher-levels-offshore.

44 For example, Pascale wrote, "Media practices encouraged publics to understand the largest nuclear disaster in history as no more significant than the radiation produced by the sun."

45 Pascale also found three articles that "challenged dominant media discourses" about radiation and health risks.

46 Robert Ferris, "U.S. Watches as Fukushima Continues to Leak Radiation," CNBC, March 10, 2016, http://www.cnbc.com/2016/03/10/us-watches-as-fukushima-continues-to-leak-radiation.html.

47 Mari Yamaguchi, "3 Former Execs of Utility Charged in Fukushima Disaster," Big Story (Associated Press), February 29, 2016, http://www.bigstory.ap.org/article/eef3ae2b8147470c93a1d2c0dffcf3d8/3-ex-execs-utility-charged-fukushima-disaster.

48 William Roebuck, "Influencing the SARG in the End of 2006," WikiLeaks cable: 06DAMASCUS5399_a, Public Library of US Diplomacy, WikiLeaks, created December 13, 2006, https://wikileaks.org/plusd/cables/06DAMASCUS5399_a.html. "SARG" refers to the Syrian Arab Republic Government.

49 See Robert Naiman, "WikiLeaks Reveals How the US Aggressively Pursued Regime Change in Syria, Igniting a Bloodbath," Truthout, October 9, 2015, http://www.truth-out.org/progressivepicks/item/33180-wikileaks-reveals-how-the-us-aggressively-pursued-regime-change-in-syria-igniting-a-bloodbath.

50 US corporate news coverage of the Ukraine crisis was comparable in that it too downplayed geopolitical oil interests as a source of tension among Russia, the US, and their respective allies, as Nafeez Ahmed has reported. See "US Media Hypocrisy in Covering Ukraine Crisis," Censored story #9 in Censored 2015, 53–5.

51 Oren Dorell, "A Mind-Boggling Stew of Nations is Fighting in Syria's Civil War," USA Today, February 16, 2016, http://www.usatoday.com/story/news/world/2016/02/15/mind-boggling-stew-nations-fighting-syrias-civil-war/80406862/.

52 "Pharmaceutical Research & Manufacturers of America—Lobbying," MapLight, http://maplight.org/us-congress/lobbying/pharmaceutical-research-manufacturers-of-america; for previous Censored coverage of MapLight's work, see Jay Costa and Darby Beck, "MapLight: Revealing Money's Influence on Politics," Censored 2013, 187–9.

53 "Pharmaceutical Research & Manufacturers of America—Lobbying," MapLight.

54 Ibid.

55 See also Mike Ludwig, "Big Pharma Lobbies Hard to End India's Distribution of Affordable Generic Drugs," Truthout, October 10, 2014, http://www.truth-out.org/news/item/26721-big-pharma-lobbies-hard-to-end-india-s-distribution-of-affordable-generic-drugs.

56 "Pharmaceutical Manufacturing, Top Contributors, 2015–2016," Center for Responsive Politics, http://www.opensecrets.org/industries/indus.php?ind=H4300.

57 "Pharmaceuticals/Health Productions, Industry Profile: Summary, 2016," Center for Responsive Politics, http://www.opensecrets.org/lobby/indusclient.php?id=H04&year=2016.

58 Nadia Kounang, "Big Pharma's Big Donations to 2016 Presidential Candidates," CNN, February 11, 2016, http://www.cnn.com/2016/02/11/health/big-pharma-presidential-politics/; Kimberly Leonard, "Hillary Takes Millions in Campaign Cash From 'Enemies,'" U.S. News & World Report, October 14, 2015, http://www.usnews.com/news/articles/2015/10/14/hillary-takes-millions-in-campaign-cash-from-enemies.

59 Robert Pear, "Top Lobbyist for Drug Makers Threads a Thicket of Outrage," New York Times, February 26, 2016, http://www.nytimes.com/2016/02/27/business/top-pharmaceutical-lobbyist-threads-a-thicket-of-outrage.html?_r=0.

60 A House version of the legislation, the "National Cybersecurity Protection Advancement Act of 2015" (H.R. 1731), had generally offered better privacy protections.

61 "CISA supporters say that it could prevent security breaches in the future by encouraging private companies to voluntarily share information on cyberattacks with the government. Opponents don't like the potential for abuse, especially after the details of the National Security Agency's surveillance program were made public." Keith Wagstaff, "Why Aren't Presidential Candidates

Talking About Cybersecurity?," *NBC News*, November 3, 2015, http://www.nbcnews.com/tech/tech-news/why-arent-presidential-candidates-talking-about-cybersecurity-n451826.

62 Everett Rosenfeld, "The Controversial 'Surveillance' Act Obama Just Signed," CNBC, December 22, 2015, http://www.cnbc.com/2015/12/22/the-controversial-surveillance-act-obama-just-signed.html.

63 Whipple distinguished Tenet's detailed interview remarks from the "general terms" in which Tenet had described these events in his 2007 memoir, *At the Center of the Storm: My Years at the CIA* (New York: HarperCollins Publishers, 2007).

64 Condoleezza Rice, *No Higher Honor: A Memoir of My Years in Washington* (New York: Random House, 2011), 67.

65 Mike Sandler, "The Paris Agenda: Leave Fossil Fuels in the Ground, Auction Permits, Protect People," *Huffington Post*, October 28, 2015, http://www.huffingtonpost.com/mike-sandler/the-paris-agenda-leave-fo_b_8404694.html.

66 Elizabeth Barber, "Study: Most Fossil Fuels Must be Left Untouched to Meet Climate Change Target," *Time*, January 7, 2015, http://time.com/3658980/climate-change-fossil-fuels/.

67 Damian Carrington, "Leave Fossil Fuels Buried to Prevent Climate Change, Study Urges," *Guardian*, January 7, 2015, http://www.theguardian.com/environment/2015/jan/07/much-worlds-fossil-fuel-reserve-must-stay-buried-prevent-climate-change-study-says.

68 Shankar Vedantam, "U.S. Court Finds No Link Between Vaccines, Autism," *Washington Post*, February 13, 2009, A1, http://www.washingtonpost.com/wp-dyn/content/article/2009/02/12/AR2009021201391.html.

69 "New Whooping Cough Vaccine is Said to Eliminate Side Effects," *New York Times*, November 25, 1994, A20.

70 Laura Butterbaugh, "Why Did Hurricane Katrina Hit Women So Hard?," *Off Our Backs* 35, no. 9/10 (September–October 2005), 17–19.

71 Jane M. Henrici, Allison Suppan Helmuth, and Jackie Braun, "Women, Disasters, and Hurricane Katrina," Institute for Women's Policy Research (IWPR #D492), August 2010, 2, available online at http://www.iwpr.org/initiatives/katrina-the-gulf-coast.

72 For more on how women's movements are addressing global social problems, see *Censored* story #18, "Women's Movements Offer Global Paradigm Shift toward Social Justice," above.

73 See, for example, Eric Lichtblau, "Report Faults U.S.'s Efforts at Transparency," *New York Times*, March 14, 2010, http://www.nytimes.com/2010/03/15/us/politics/15open.html; and Andrew Malcolm, "A Little Secret about Obama's Transparency," *Los Angeles Times*, March 21, 2010, http://articles.latimes.com/2010/mar/21/nation/la-na-ticket21-2010mar21.

74 Erik Wemple, "AP: Obama Administration 'Sets New Record' for Denying Records," *Washington Post*, March 18, 2015, https://www.washingtonpost.com/blogs/erik-wemple/wp/2015/03/18/ap-obama-administration-sets-new-record-for-denying-records/.

75 Ted Bridis and Jack Gillum, "When It Comes to Providing Government Records the Public Asks to See, the Obama Administration Has a Hard Time Finding Them," *U.S. News & World Report*, March 18, 2016, http://www.usnews.com/news/business/articles/2016-03-18/us-govt-sets-record-for-failures-to-find-files-when-asked; "Transparency and Obama: The Administration Breaks a Freedom of Information Act Record—Not in a Good Way," *Wall Street Journal*, March 20, 2016, http://www.wsj.com/articles/notable-quotable-transparency-and-obama-1458504352.

76 As background on the economics and politics of privatized prisons, see "Private Prison Companies Fund Anti-Immigrant Legislation," *Censored* story #5 in *Censored 2012*, 84, 87–88.

77 Nina Bernstein, "Another Jail Death, and Mounting Questions," *New York Times*, January 27, 2009, http://www.nytimes.com/2009/01/28/us/28detain.html?hp&_r=1; Nina Bernstein and A. E. Velez, "Man's Death in Private Immigration Jail Bares Difficulty of Detention Overhaul," *New York Times*, August 21, 2009, http://query.nytimes.com/gst/fullpage.html?res=9B00E1D91 63AF932A1575BC0A96F9C8B63&pagewanted=all; Nick Miroff, "ICE Facility Detainee's Death Stirs Questions," *Washington Post*, February 1, 2009, http://www.washingtonpost.com/wp-dyn/content/story/2009/01/31/ST2009013101877.html.

78 Catherine E. Shoichet, "Immigrants and Crime: Crunching the Numbers," CNN, July 8, 2015, http://www.cnn.com/2015/07/08/politics/immigrants-crime/; Malia Zimmerman, "Elusive Crime Wave Data Shows Frightening Toll of Illegal Immigrant Criminals," Fox News, September 16, 2015, http://www.foxnews.com/us/2015/09/16/crime-wave-elusive-data-shows-frightening-toll-illegal-immigrant-criminals.html.

79 Audre Lorde, "There Is No Hierarchy of Oppressions," *Interracial Books for Children Bulletin*, 14, no. 3/4 (1983), 9; available online at http://www.pages.drexel.edu/~jc3962/COR/Hierarchy.pdf.

80 See also *Censored* story #15, "Understanding Climate Change and Gender Inequality," above.

81 Jim Puckett, Eric Hopson, Monica Huang, "Disconnect: Goodwill and Dell, Exporting the Public's E-Waste to Developing Countries," E-Trash Transparency Project, Basel Action Network, May 9, 2016, available online at http://www.ban.org/trash-transparency/.

82 The MIT Senseable City Lab created a visualization of the resulting findings; see "Monitour," E-Trash Transparency Project, MIT Senseable City Lab and Basel Action Network, no date, http://senseable.mit.edu/monitour-app/.

83 For the broadcast version of Campbell and Christensen's report, which includes video footage of these scenes, see Katie Campbell and Ken Christensen, "Tracking Down America's Electronic Waste," KCTS9, no date, http://kcts9.org/programs/circuit/tracking-down-america's-electronic-waste.

84 Tom Risen, "America's Toxic Electronic Waste Trade," *U.S. News & World Report*, April 22, 2016, http://www.usnews.com/news/articles/2016-04-22/the-rising-cost-of-recycling-not-exporting-electronic-waste.

85 Arianna Prothero, "Charter Sector to Get $1 Billion from Walton Family Foundation," *Education Week*, January 8, 2016, http://www.edweek.org/ew/articles/2016/01/13/charter-sector-to-get-1-billion-from.html; notably Prothero's article disclosed that WFF "provides grant support for Education Week's coverage of school choice and parent-empowerment issues."

86 For previous *Censored* coverage, see "Education 'Reform' a Trojan Horse for Privatization," *Censored* story #13 in *Censored 2013*, 70–2, and Adam Bessie, "GERM Warfare: How to Reclaim the Education Debate from Corporate Corruption," *Censored 2013*, 271–96.

87 Nikhil Goyal, "Corporate Reformers Wreck Public Schools: Billionaire Foundations and Wall Street Financiers are Not Out to Help Your Kids Learn," *Salon*, February 21, 2016, http://www.salon.com/2016/02/21/corporate_reformers_wreck_public_schools_billionaire_foundations_and_wall_street_financiers_are_not_out_to_help_your_kids_learn/.

88 Javier E. David, "Education Reform 'Good Politics, Good Policy,' School Choice Advocate Says," CNBC, April 30, 2016, http://www.cnbc.com/2016/04/30/education-reform-good-politics-good-policy.html.

89 Christie Thompson, "Another Kind of Isolation," Marshall Project, January 28, 2015, https://www.themarshallproject.org/2015/01/28/another-kind-of-isolation – .be2hzfK4R.

90 "Allow Prisoners to Challenge Placement in Secretive Prison Units, Attorneys Argue," Center for Constitutional Rights, March 15, 2016, http://ccrjustice.org/home/press-center/press-releases/allow-prisoners-challenge-placement-secretive-prison-units.

91 For audio of the first part of the two-part NPR series, along with an accompanying article, see Carrie Johnson and Margot Williams, "'Guantanamo North': Inside Secretive U.S. Prisons," *NPR News Investigations*, NPR, March 3, 2011, http://www.npr.org/2011/03/03/134168714/guantanamo-north-inside-u-s-secretive-prisons; for audio of the second part of the two-part NPR series, along with an accompanying article, see Carrie Johnson and Margot Williams, "Leaving 'Guantanamo North,'" *Morning Edition, NPR News Investigations*, NPR, March 4, 2011, http://www.npr.org/2011/03/04/134176614/leaving-guantanamo-north; Alia Malek, "Gitmo in the Heartland," *Nation*, March 10, 2011, http://www.thenation.com/article/gitmo-heartland/.

92 Daniel McGowan, "Tales from Inside the U.S. Gitmo," *Huffington Post*, May 25, 2011, http://www.huffingtonpost.com/daniel-mcgowan/tales-from-inside-the-us_b_212632.html; Daniel McGowan, "Court Documents Prove I Was Sent to Communication Management Units (CMU) for My Political Speech," *Huffington Post*, June 1, 2013, http://www.huffingtonpost.com/daniel-mcgowan/communication-management-units_b_2944580.html.

93 E.g., Alexis Agathocleous, "'New' Rules for the BOP's Experiment in Social Isolation," *Huffington Post*, March 31, 2015, http://new.www.huffingtonpost.com/the-center-for-constitutional-rights/new-rules-for-the-bops-ex_b_6574136.html; Rachel Meeropol, "Challenging Secretive U.S. Prisons," *Huffington Post*, October 28, 2015, http://new.www.huffingtonpost.com/the-center-for-constitutional-rights/challenging-secretive-us_b_8412230.html.

94 Hannah Fairfield and Timothy Wallace, "The Terrorists in U.S. Prisons," *New York Times*, April 7, 2016, A16, http://www.nytimes.com/interactive/2016/04/07/us/terrorists-in-us-prisons.html?_r=0.

95 The complete slide presentation, titled "The U.S. Department of Education's Charter Schools Program Overview," is accessible online at http://www.prwatch.org/files/oii_csp_datasetppt20151223.pdf.

96 "Charter School Black Hole: CMD Special Investigation Reveals Huge Info Gap on Charter Spending," Center for Media and Democracy, October 2015, http://www.prwatch.org/files/new_charter_school_black_hole_report_oct_21_2015.pdf.

97 Stephanie Saul, "Public Money Finds Back Door to Private Schools," *New York Times*, May 22, 2012, A1, http://www.nytimes.com/2012/05/22/education/scholarship-funds-meant-for-needy-benefit-private-schools.html.

98 "Hotline Statistics," National Human Trafficking Resource Center, https://traffickingresourcecenter.org/states.

99 Meredith Dank et al., "Estimating the Size and Structure of the Underground Commercial Sex Economy in Eight Major US Cities," Urban Institute, March 12, 2014, http://www.urban.org/research/publication/estimating-size-and-structure-underground-commercial-sex-economy-eight-major-us-cities.

100 "Fact Sheet," Demanding Justice Project, 2014, http://sharedhope.org/wp-content/uploads/2014/08/Demanding-Justice-Fact-Sheet1.pdf.

101 See, e.g., Sara Sidner, "Old Mark of Slavery is Being Used on Sex Trafficking Victims," CNN, September 1, 2015, http://www.cnn.com/2015/08/31/us/sex-trafficking-branding/index.html; and Colbert I. King, "Washington D.C.'s Serious Sex-Trafficking Problem," *Washington Post*, January 15, 2016, https://www.washingtonpost.com/opinions/sex-slavery-isnt-just-a-problem-overseas/2016/01/15/bc3acb04-badd-11e5-829c-26ffb874a18d_story.html.

102 Roberto Azevêdo, "World Trade Has an Important Role in Combating Climate Change," *Guardian*, November 23, 2015, https://www.theguardian.com/business/economics-blog/2015/nov/23/world-trade-important-role-low-carbon-economy-wto.

103 Tim Worstall, "U.S. Beats India in WTO Solar Case: Indian Consumers Win," *Forbes*, February 25, 2016, http://www.forbes.com/sites/timworstall/2016/02/25/us-beats-india-in-wto-solar-case-indian-consumers-win/ - 303abdce761f; Rajesh Roy, "WTO Panel Rules Against India's Solar Program," *Wall Street Journal*, September 1, 2015, http://www.wsj.com/articles/wto-panel-rules-against-indias-solar-program-1441112645.

104 Tom Miles, David Lawder, Douglas Busvine, and Manoj Kumar, "U.S. Wins WTO Dispute against India's Solar Rules," Reuters, February 24, 2016, http://www.reuters.com/article/us-india-usa-solar-idUSKCN0VX1Y5.

105 "NYPD IP Addresses with Anonymous Wikipedia Edits," Google Docs, Google, document, https://docs.google.com/document/d/1mcnQZaZCYSYYG0-_uU4i1Fczvj7gn_GkiPjxcdnneRU/edit.

106 Abby Ohlheiser, "Eric Garner's Wikipedia Page Was Edited From an NYPD Computer, NYPD Admits," *Washington Post*, March 16, 2015, https://www.washingtonpost.com/news/post-nation/wp/2015/03/16/eric-garners-wikipedia-page-was-edited-from-an-nypd-computer-the-nypd-admits/; Sam Frizell, "Eric Garner Wikipedia Article Edited from Inside NYPD HQ," *Time*, March 13, 2015, http://time.com/3744657/eric-garner-wikipedia-article-edited-nypd-hq/.

CHAPTER 2

# Censored Déjà Vu
## Strolling Down Memory Hole Lane

Susan Rahman and College of Marin students Sheila Beasley,
Larkin Bond, Katie Kolb, Stephanie Lee, Caitlin McCoy, Alexander
Olson, Elizabeth Ramirez, Kenny Rodriguez, Karina Seiler,
Claudia Serrano, Kady Stenson, Karl Wada; with Mickey Huff and
Teaching/Research Assistant Sierra Shidner of Diablo Valley
College and the University of California, Davis

*"And if all others accepted the lie . . . if all records told the same tale—then the lie passed into history and became truth. Who controls the past . . . controls the future; who controls the present controls the past."*

—George Orwell, *1984*

Each year, Project Censored reviews previously underreported and censored stories from our research and publications in an effort to learn if the corporate media have improved their coverage. Sometimes there are pleasant surprise discoveries of previous stories highlighted by Project Censored being picked up by mass media outlets, which is certainly something we laud. However, the majority of stories highlighted by Project Censored have continued to be ignored by the corporate media. It's as if some of these stories have been tossed into what George Orwell, in his dystopian novel *1984*, described as "the memory hole"—where information past or present that went against the party line could be disappeared into incinerators, literally filling the dustbins of history. This chapter is dedicated to following up on the Project's past Top *Censored* Stories, charting their significance, past to present, and analyzing whether or not they have received the attention they ultimately deserve. In short, we're emptying those dustbins and sifting through what's been overlooked or disappeared as we stroll down memory hole lane.

We decided to take a broader historical view with the Déjà Vu installment this year. In honor of the 40th anniversary of the Project, we thought it would be fitting to go back over the past forty years and choose a handful of our most interesting and timely #1 *Censored* stories and update them. We consulted our panel of esteemed judges, who voted on what they thought were among the most significant top stories in the Project's history. We selected the top six #1 stories that received the most votes. These include:

1. Myth of Black Progress (1977)[1]
2. Corporate Crime of the Century (1979, 2000)[2]
3. Wealth Inequality in 21st Century Threatens Economy and Democracy (2005, 2016)[3]
4. The Information Monopoly (1987, 1996)[4]
5. No Habeas Corpus for "Any Person" (2008)[5]
6. Ocean Acidification Increasing at Unprecedented Rate (2015)[6]

We reflect upon these stories to see if the corporate media has bothered to report about them, and analyze what has or hasn't changed in terms of coverage as well as the vital issues under review. For each story, we provide an original summary, followed by a current update.

We begin in 1977, just after the founding of Project Censored, with "Myth of Black Progress." This article countered the narrative of black social and economic progress in the US two decades after the judicial and legislative outlawing of Jim Crow segregation. This reporting is further underscored by the recent discovery of President Richard Nixon staffer John Ehrlichman's remarks that the war on drugs was intentionally created, in part, to discredit the black power movement and demonize the African American community, while disrupting the actions of those involved, criminalizing selective cultural behaviors, and resulting in the mass incarceration of vast numbers of African Americans.[7] These historical patterns of institutional racism remain four decades later. Despite the election in 2008 of an African American president in the US, the rise of massive social movements like Black Lives Matter, created in response to police brutality and racism in the criminal justice system, indicate that the "Myth of Black Progress" is as relevant in the 21st century as it was in the 1970s.

Another prescient article, from 1979, detailed what was deemed the "Corporate Crime of the Century." This article lays out the long span of corporate brutality used in the pursuit of maximizing profits. This connects to another story from 2000, about how "Multinational Corporations Profit from International Brutality." That trend has persisted to the present day, as many corporations, including corporate media, place more importance on profits than on the people whose interests they claim to serve.

A recurring theme among *Censored* stories is the growing wealth inequality both in the US and worldwide. In 2005, Project Censored's top story was "Wealth Inequality in 21st Century Threatens Economy and Democracy," and in 2016 a related article topped the list, "Half of Global Wealth Owned by the One Percent," based on an Oxfam report that showed the gap between rich and poor ever-increasing. Only sixty-two people, fifty-three of them men, control as much wealth as half of the global population—some 3.6 billion people. Not only is the issue of growing inequality still with us, and worsening, it is still a story that manages to escape the attention of the corporate press and major mass media outlets.

The 1980s marked a time of major shifts in media consolidation. The late media scholar Ben Bagdikian, in his book *The Media Monopoly*, correctly predicted that there would come a day when the bulk of corporate media would be controlled by six entities. It was the Project's top story in 1987, "The Information Monopoly," and again in 1996 a story on media consolidation topped the list, "Telecommunications Deregulation: Closing Up America's 'Marketplace of Ideas.'" Lo and behold, keeping that marketplace of ideas open to all is an ongoing challenge in the present. Bagdikian rightly warned that shrinking ownership and more corporate power falls in line with overall total control by the few of the many, and in this case, that means control of what news We the People can hear, read, and see. That this particular topic is consistently underreported or ignored by the corporate press should surprise no one—among the many things they don't cover with much rigor, their own corporate ascendancy would certainly come first.

In 2008, Project Censored reported on the lessening of habeas corpus rights, and the current update on "No Habeas Corpus for 'Any Person'" notes that, although there have been some court challenges, Barack Obama's administration has done little to restore the rights that were stripped away under President George W. Bush. In fact, through Obama's drone strikes, kill lists, and continued assaults on journalists, whistleblowers, and other civic activists, one might argue that not only has Obama not restored or protected due process rights, he has in fact continued to erode them.

The last of the top *Censored* stories we look at in this chapter is from *Censored 2015*, "Ocean Acidification Increasing at Unprecedented Rate." While this story highlights the consequences of human disregard for other living things, it also offers ways in which, if we cared to, we could address this problem and other problems related to climate change. This would involve redistribution of resources and acknowledgment that many of us need to scale back on our consumption both as individuals and as institutions. Given the significance of climate change, and the evidence supporting it, one wonders if the corporate media will ever get around to providing the kind of news reporting that could very well contribute to motivating humanity to save our shared home—planet Earth.

This brings us full circle, in some ways, back to the few controlling the many and the lack of information readily published and made easily available about the real injustices plaguing our world. But a well-informed society can make a difference. As the founder of Project Censored, Carl Jensen, wrote nearly thirty years ago,

> Indeed the media can make a difference if they want to. They have the power to stimulate the people to clean up the environment; to prevent nuclear proliferation; to force crooked politicians out of office; to reduce poverty; to create a truly equitable society; and, as we have seen, to literally save the lives of millions of human beings. And this is why we must look to, prod, and support a free, open, and aggressive press. This is the real, bottom line issue. For it is the press which determines which issues go on the national agenda for discussion and thought and which don't.[8]

Here, Jensen reminds us that vibrant independent media is not only a seed for change, but a prime vehicle for civic action. Project Censored continues to advocate and agitate for a truly free press in that vein forty years later.

# 1.

## Censored 1977: Myth of Black Progress

SUMMARY: It took a power blackout and the looting of New York City for America to rediscover its ghettos. Just like the time before, it took a massive dose of urban violence to draw attention to the underclass. Though the times have changed, the grievances remain the same. The poverty, disenfranchisement, unemployment, and drug abuse that were a national scandal in the 1960s have only worsened since then.

Half the black population is less than twenty-four years old, and for them the future promises little. Judging by current economic indices, one out of ten young black and brown people in the ghettos will never have a job that provides them with a livelihood or enables them to support a family. This is the human dimension of a black teenage unemployment rate of 40 percent.

Even black people with steady employment are losing ground to their white counterparts. The Department of Labor reports a growing gap between white and black income, with the wages of white workers increasing twice as fast as those of black workers. Ninety-seven percent of all professional jobs are still held by whites, and this has not changed since 1969.

Young black people, particularly in urban areas, are disproportionately affected by policing and incarceration. In New York City today, the number of black youths under 16 who have been arrested is almost ten times what it was in 1950.

"Redlining," the refusal to rent or sell accommodations to particular racial or ethnic groups within specific geographic areas, in combination with financial institutions' discriminatory lending practices, have sealed the fate of most black communities. In contrast to the relative mobility of the white working class, resulting in so-called "white flight," the inner city has become the exclusive preserve of those who cannot afford to leave.

In the 1960s the mass media, following urban uprisings across the country, began to hire black journalists to cover the rise of the Black Power movement. The contributions of black journalists were crucial in articulating the struggles and perspectives of black communities coping with continuing oppression following the Civil Rights Movement and the assassinations of prominent leaders. Today, the role of black journalists in the corporate media has diminished. Fewer opportunities are granted to cover the normal aspects of black life or of the continuing struggle for equality in the day-to-day routine, with black journalists instead frequently expected to fill a tokenistic role within a largely white narrative structure.

Media have failed to see black struggles as an ongoing story and have instead chosen to focus on black communities exclusively for reports of crime or large scale urban violence. This has meant that the social and economic inequality affecting black Americans remains among the most critical Project Censored stories.

UPDATE: Thirty-seven years later, a July 2014 phone poll of 1,009 adults conducted by CBS found that almost eight out of ten polled believed there had been real progress in getting rid of racial discrimination in the United States since the Civil Rights Movement of the 1960s. Only 19 percent of those polled said there hadn't been much progress. However, when that nearly 80 percent majority was broken down along racial lines, a clear divide was evident. Only 59 percent of black Americans believed real progress had been made, compared to 82 percent of whites. Forty-one percent of black Americans polled believed that there was still a lot of discrimination against black Americans, versus 14 percent of whites who believed the same. Sixty-three percent of whites polled believed that black and white Americans had an equal chance of "getting ahead." Only 46 percent of black Americans agreed, while another 46 percent said that whites had an advantage.

The ACLU's page on racial profiling explains that "more than 240 years of slavery and ninety years of legalized racial segregation have led to systemic profiling of blacks in traffic and pedestrian stops."

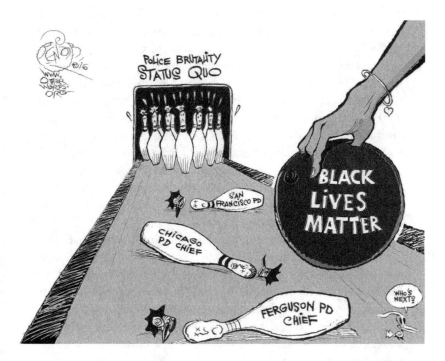

According to Ed Stetzer of *Christianity Today*, in 2013, "Black Americans are incarcerated at nearly six times the rate of whites. If current trends continue, one in three black males born today can expect to spend time in prison during his lifetime." Stetzer goes on to cite the NAACP's Criminal Justice Fact Sheet, which includes the statistic that black Americans constitute nearly 1 million of the 2.3 million people incarcerated in the United States, while black Americans make up less than 15 percent of the overall population.

That black Americans are incarcerated at a far higher rate than their white counterparts is indicative not only of a two-tiered justice system, but of a new form of slavery. In both state and federal prisons a majority of the inmates were convicted of nonviolent crimes, many for petty drug offenses. The so-called "War on Drugs," which might be more aptly referred to as the "War on Minorities," has drastically increased the prison population in the past half-century, and has disproportionally targeted black people.

A prime example of such discriminatory enforcement and sentencing is the federal law that ". . . stipulates five years' imprisonment without possibility of parole for possession of 5 grams of crack . . . and 10 years for possession of less than 2 ounces of rock-cocaine . . ." whereas "[a] sentence of 5 years for cocaine powder requires possession of 500 grams—100 times more than the quantity of rock cocaine for the same sentence." While crack and cocaine are both derived from the same plant, cocaine, being a much more expensive substance, has tended to be bought and consumed by middle- to upper-class white people, while crack has remained more prevalent among lower-class, African American communities. Despite comparable levels of drug use among whites, black communities have been disproportionately targeted by antidrug enforcement.

The rise of the black prison population is directly correlated to the rise of the prison industrial complex, as prison corporations have routinely lobbied for policies that incarcerate more people and keep them locked up for longer. As of 2014, the Centre for Research on Globalization reported that "at least 37 states have legalized the contracting of prison labor to private corporations that mount their operations inside state prisons." This system of contracting out prison labor was created after the Civil War in order to maintain a steady supply of what was essentially slave labor and continues today on a scale comparable to the plantation system of the old South with the drastic expansion of the prison industrial complex.

A study conducted in 2015 by the Ella Baker Center for Human Rights, Forward Together, and Research Action Design, and reported on by the *Guardian*, found that "on average families with an imprisoned relative paid $13,607 in court-related costs. In addition, one in five families who participated in the study reported that they had to take out a loan to cover these costs. One in five families were unable to afford housing expenses due to the loss of income from their loved one's incarceration. Two out of three families had difficulty meeting basic needs as a result of their loved one's conviction and incarceration. 83 percent of family members primarily responsible for these costs were women."

Five decades have passed since the era of legal segregation, yet the divide between black and white Americans has grown even wider. In

"America's Racial Divide, Charted," written during the wake of the Ferguson protests and the death of Michael Brown in 2014, Irwin, Miller and Sanger-Katz examine the startling statistics. Unemployment has remained higher amongst black Americans—regardless of education—than amongst whites for decades, and the gap between the two has remained constant. The racial divide in higher education increased from 10 percent in 1970 to 17 percent in 2012. "In 1983, the median weekly pay of white workers was 18.4 percent higher than that of black workers. Three decades later, the premium had risen to 21.6 percent." While the poverty rate amongst black Americans has fallen, it was about the only example of positive change in the article. As a matter of fact, the wealth gap between white and black Americans has outstripped the wage gap, as white Americans have on average 6.1 times greater wealth than their African American counterparts. In 2015 the numbers remain demonstrative of the myth of black progress. As reported in *Breitbart* by Caroline May in June of 2015, "The unemployment rate for African Americans was nearly twice the national average and more than double the unemployment rate for whites last month, according to new jobs data released . . . by the Bureau of Labor Statistics."

Still more grim are the racial disparities revealed by the statistics of deaths at the hands of police officers or while in police custody. MintPress News did two stories on this subject in 2015, "776 People Killed by Police So Far in 2015, 161 of Them Unarmed" and the follow-up report "Over 1,000 People Killed by Police Since the Beginning of 2015." Both use data compiled by the *Guardian* in a database called The Counted, which tracks police killings throughout the United States. "The Counted database is the most comprehensive information available on police killings, since no US government agency maintains a similar listing." As of May 2, 2016, police have killed 347 people in the United States this year, and of those killed, 75 were African Americans. From January 2015 to May 2016, white Americans have died at the hands of police officers more often than African Americans in terms of simple numbers. "However, activists like the members of the Black Lives Matter movement argue that police kill blacks at a rate disproportionate to their total percentage of the population—an assertion supported by The *Guardian*'s statistics. Police killed almost five black people per every million black residents of the US, compared with about 2 per million for both white and hispanic victims."

We have the numbers. Corporate media choose to focus on isolated stories instead of the systematic oppression of black Americans through both the criminal justice and educational systems in this country. This is no accident, either. A host of American corporations, including but not limited to the Boeing Company and AT&T, profit greatly from the prison industrial complex, in turn benefitting from the discriminatory policies that keep black prison populations high. According to LaMarche, writing for the *Nation*, "For a democracy movement to be worthy of the name, it must recognize the fact that the criminal-justice system is a barrier to the full exercise of citizenship for many marginalized Americans." These systems need an overhaul, and the American people need to look long and hard at the racist narratives that surround them before they can expect Black Progress to be more than just a myth.

## SOURCES:

"Racial Profiling," The American Civil Liberties Union, http://www.aclu.org/issues/racial-justice/race-and-criminal-justice/racial-profiling.

Sarah Dutton, Jennifer De Pinto, Anthony Salvanto, and Fred Backus, "50 Years After Civil Rights Act, Americans See Progress on Race," CBS News, July 1, 2014, http://www.cbsnews.com/news/50-years-after-civil-rights-act-americans-see-progress-on-race/.

Syreeta McFadden, "Government Policies Based on Racist Myths Help Dissolve Black Families," *Guardian*, September 20, 2015, http://www.theguardian.com/commentisfree/2015/sep/20/government-policies-racist-myths-dissolve-black-families/.

Neil Irwin, Claire Cain Miller, and Margot Sanger-Katz, "America's Racial Divide, Charted," *New York Times*, August 19, 2014, http://www.nytimes.com/2014/08/20/upshot/americas-racial-divide-charted.html?_r=0.

Gara LaMarche, "Racial Justice is the Key to Democracy Reform," *Nation*, February 4, 2016, http://www.thenation.com/article/racial-justice-is-the-key-to-democracy-reform/.

Caroline May, "Black Unemployment Nearly Double National Rate, Twice as High as White Unemployment," Breitbart, June 5, 2015, http://www.breitbart.com/big-government/2015/06/05/black-unemployment-nearly-double-national-rate-twice-as-high-as-white-unemployment/.

"Over 1,000 People Killed by Police Since the Beginning of 2015," MintPress News, November 24, 2015, http://www.mintpressnews.com/over-1000-people-killed-by-police-since-the-beginning-of-2015/211529/.

"Criminal Justice Fact Sheet," National Association for the Advancement of Colored People, http://www.naacp.org/pages/criminal-justice-fact-sheet.

Vicky Pelaez, "The Prison Industry in the United States: Big Business or a New Form of Slavery?" Centre for Research on Globalization, March 31, 2014, http://www.globalresearch.ca/the-prison-industry-in-the-united-states-big-business-or-a-new-form-of-slavery/8289.

## 2.

### Censored 1979: The Corporate Crime of the Century

SUMMARY: In November 1979, *Mother Jones*, one of America's leading investigative journals, devoted nearly an entire issue to what it called "The Corporate Crime of the Century." Several aspects of this story have been dealt with in previous Project Censored efforts. But the November *Mother Jones* issue revealed, for the first time, the full scope of American corporate exploitation of Third World countries.

The mass media have yet to explore and expose the international tragedy of what is sometimes called "dumping." While "dumping" may not be technically illegal, it is a widespread practice that endangers the health, lives, and environment of millions of people outside the United States. It is done by American businesses in the name of profit.

Manufacturers of products that are restricted or banned from use in the US can legally export and sell them to countries with fewer health protections. The government allows the export of dangerous chemicals, toxic pesticides, and defective medical drugs and devices, to name just a few such hazardous US products. The US Food and Drug Administration allows drug manufacturers to export banned drugs, stale-dated drugs, and even unapproved new drugs.

Profiting from products difficult or illegal to sell in the US is not limited to pesticides and drugs. As the US nuclear industry encountered difficulties in selling reactors to wary American communities, it turned to sales in countries where dissent can be silenced and political payoffs can bring quick results.

There is an ironic footnote to the story of corporate exploitation of Third World nations. Exporting poisonous pesticides to developing nations, for example, has what author-researcher Leslie Ware called, in *Audubon* magazine, "a boomerang effect." In reference to dumping pesticides in such countries as Guatemala, Nicaragua, Brazil, and Ecuador, Ware points out that "[t]heir use is banned here, but hazardous poisons manufactured by American companies come back to haunt us on the food we import from developing nations." Ten percent of all imported foods (such as coffee, bananas, and tomatoes) are contaminated with illegal levels of pesticide residues. Much of this pesticide contamination comes from America's own exports.

A curious addendum to the report on corporate "dumping" suggests that profit isn't necessarily always the overriding issue for the mass media outlets; rather, it may also matter from where that profit comes. *Mother Jones* submitted an advertisement to *Time* magazine that displayed the "Corporate Crime of the Century" cover. *Time* refused to run the ad because, according to *Mother Jones*, some of the advertising copy "offended" them. Or perhaps it offended some of their higher paying advertising clients.

The failure of the mass media to investigate and expose "The Corporate Crime of the Century" and its future repercussions (potentially more serious than repulsive bananas) on the American people qualified this as the top *Censored* story of 1979.

## Censored 2000: Multinational Corporations Profit from International Brutality

SUMMARY: The Project Censored top story from 2000, "Multinational Corporations Profit from International Brutality," covered the extent of huge transnational corporations' investments and collaborations with countries that violate human rights. Through these business ventures, governments gain the financial means and resources to suppress political dissent and violate individual rights. Though corporations claim that through "constructive engagement" their presence will improve human rights, those rights have been drastically curtailed as corporate investments have funded repressive governments in India, Burma, and Turkmenistan, among many others.

The Internet has been a major instrument in revealing the unethical profit-driven agenda of corporations in continuing dealings with abusive governments. Corporations are aware of the power of perception, and push an environmental, fair trade, and human rights-supporting stance. In July 2000, multibillion-dollar corporations such as Royal Dutch Shell and BP Amoco joined with governments and United Nations agencies to form the UN Global Compact, the world's largest corporate sustainability initiative. The compact has been criticized for setting down principles for human rights, labor, and the environment without taking any steps toward their enforcement. It allows companies to "blue-wash" their image while still violating human rights.

UPDATE: Mass media outlets have shed some light on the practices of green-washing and blue-washing and have begun to highlight efforts by advocates for corporate accountability. During the 2015 United Nations Climate Change Conference held in Paris, the *New York Times* reported on a small contingency of demonstrators who used negative advertising to publicly shame Volkswagen for a green-marketing campaign that contradicted their actual practices. While it is commendable for corporations to make commitments that affect meaningful change, mass media outlets have a powerful opportunity to hold them to task. We do see a trend of corporate media balancing the claims of a company with how they go about initiating and taking responsibility. The problem with this strategy is that it only shames the company and does not hold governments responsible for their share.

In the case of state-owned companies, accountability is especially important as they often operate with disregard for human rights. Reporting for *Foreign Policy*, Michael Hobbes writes, "In Angola, the state-owned oil company, Sonangol, is also the government regulator, responsible for policing conditions in its own sector." In Madagascar, the government tried to lease half the country's arable land to the South Korean company Daewoo Logistics without even asking for payment. Sarah Labowitz, cofounder and codirector of New York University's Stern Center for Business and Human Rights, calls this the "denominator problem." Labowitz points out that many of the garment factories in Bangladesh are owned by politicians, the same people in charge of inspecting them.

These obvious conflicts of interest remain a huge problem facing the movement to bring multinational corporations to task for their abuses. The difficulty, as pointed out by Hobbes, is that these state-owned companies defer questions about human rights to the realm of diplomacy while happily filling the voids left by companies that have been pressured to change their practices or leave. "Every leverage mechanism we have, this entire architecture we've built, is

A RISING TIDE LIFTS ALL BOATS ...

DINA CORP HALLIBURTON BECHTEL BIG OIL ARMAMENT

WAR PROFITEERING

SHIP OF STATE: JOBS, BUDGET DEFICITS, SOCIAL SERVICES

...THE PRIVATE YATCHS, ESPECIALLY!

based on chasing companies back to jurisdictions where regulators, customers, and civil society have the power to punish them." The problem is that the corporations committing human rights violations operate in a void of accountability. Hobbes continues, "these companies aren't subject to any transnational regulatory mechanisms. They don't have to report their activities abroad, and they can't be taken to court in their home jurisdictions."

The world's largest oil and gas companies seem to be using language alone to convince us of their good intentions, and we rely heavily on the media to validate such claims. When taken to task by mass media, corporate green-washing becomes a less effective tool, and state-run companies may at least be called out for their conflicts of interest. There are, however, many examples of human rights abuses that deserve to be examined and have yet to see prosecution.

Corporate media have failed to cover the continuing role of multinational corporations in supporting human rights abuses. In addition, the US courts have failed to hold them accountable for complicity in these violations under the Alien Tort Statute (ATS), part of the Judiciary Act of 1789, which since 1980 has been interpreted to allow non-US citizens to file lawsuits in US federal courts for violations of international law committed outside the US. Mass media failed to research or cover allegations made against Royal Dutch Shell for its complicity with the Nigerian government in extrajudicial killings, torture, and unlawful detainment of Nigerians. Independent news sources have covered the incredible consequences of not holding corporations liable for such egregious abuses.

Corporate media outlets have also failed to cover the human rights abuse case against ExxonMobil and its Indonesian affiliate company. The now fifteen-year case was first brought against ExxonMobil by Indonesians who sought to hold ExxonMobil accountable for human rights abuses committed by military security forces in their direct employment. Corporate media did not report that US courts ruled the case could go forth in 2014 and that, for the first time, corporations could be prosecuted for human rights violations on international soil. Mineral resources have increased the presence of mining companies in Mexico, the Philippines, Guatemala, and Peru, which has fueled government-sanctioned violence as they attempt to either protect resources or move locals off land for corporate mining. Dozens of companies, including Unocal, Ford, and IBM, have been at the receiving end of lawsuits under the ATS for aiding and abetting human rights abuses in Myanmar, apartheid South Africa, and elsewhere, yet none of these cases were thoroughly examined in the corporate media (even though some of the companies settled out of court). Their abuse of human rights went largely unreported. That is, until June 20 of this year when the Supreme Court found in favor of IBM and Ford. Several corporate and establishment media then suddenly discovered the matter, including Reuters, *Fortune*, and the Associated Press.

Another increasing problem with the recent rise of digital technologies is the cooperation of governments and technology companies in designing infrastructure to censor, surveil, and control citizens. Technology companies profit from selling their programs to oppressive governments. The Electronic Frontier Foundation brought attention to the role of Cisco Systems, a powerful US networking company, in facilitating human rights abuses in China by designing the Internet surveillance system "Golden Shield" with a module designed to identify, locate, and prosecute practitioners of Falun Gong. Cisco denies civil liability because selling "internet infrastructure" is regulated and protected under US export laws. Major tech company Hewlett Packard owns EDS Israel, now known as HP Enterprise Services, which provides the Israeli government with the Basel System, the automated biometric access control system that is installed in checkpoints in Gaza and the occupied West Bank. Increasingly, companies are providing oppressive regimes with the technology needed to cut off Internet access and communications, as well as to target dissenters.

A University of Toronto program called Citizen Lab identified that Blue Coat Systems, a security software company, had dual-use devices in dozens of countries, including Syria, Iran, and Sudan. Though these applications are mainly for securing and maintaining networks, they can be abused by restricting access to information and recording private communications. Cutting off Internet communications has been increasing in countries embroiled in civil conflict, following a trend of censorship to silence or stop demonstrators. In 2013, Sudan experienced a total Internet blackout three days after violent protests over rising oil prices, which escalated to a push to oust the current president. The previous year, Egypt, Syria, and Libya experienced Internet blackouts likewise coinciding with political conflicts. Due to the huge scale of these blackouts, it is likely corporations controlling telecommunications actively participated in this censorship. The surveillance industry brings in from $3–5 billion per year, and corporations greatly profit from selling to repressive regimes, directly enabling them to enact further violence upon the citizenry.

SOURCES:

Claire Barthelemy, "Activists Try to Shame Corporations for 'Greenwashing' During the Paris Climate Talks," *New York Times*, December 2, 2015, http://www.nytimes.com/interactive/projects/cp/climate/2015-paris-climate-talks/artists-try-to-shame-corporations-climate-change.
Nate Cardozo and Sophia Cope, "Cisco's Latest Attempt to Dodge Responsibility for Facilitating Human Rights Abuses: Export Rules," Electronic Frontier Foundation, April 18, 2016, https://

www.eff.org/deeplinks/2016/04/ciscos-latest-attempt-dodge-responsibility-facilitating-human-rights-abuses-export.

Hewlett Packard (HP), "Who Profits: The Israeli Occupation Industry", April 2, 2015, http://www.whoprofits.org/company/hewlett-packard-hp.

Michael Hobbes, "The Untouchables: Why It's Getting Harder to Stop Multinational Corporations," *Foreign Policy*, April 11, 2016, http://foreignpolicy.com/2016/04/11/the-untouchables-zimbabwe-green-fuel-multinational-corporations/.

"Kiobel v. Royal Dutch Petroleum," *Oyez*, Chicago-Kent College of Law at Illinois Tech, n.d., https://www.oyez.org/cases/2011/10-1491.

Derek Mead,"Mass Surveillance is Big Business: Corporations are as Good at Spying as Governments," *Motherboard*, November 18, 2013, http://motherboard.vice.com/blog/mass-surveillance-is-big-business-corporations-are-as-good-at-spying-as-governments.

Meghan Neal,"Are Governments Getting Trigger-Happy with the Internet Kill Switch?" *Motherboard*, September 25, 2013, http://motherboard.vice.com/blog/are-governments-getting-trigger-happy-with-the-internet-kill-switch.

Meghan Neal, "Despite Embargoes, 'Terrorist States' Are Still Using American Surveillance Software," *Motherboard*, July 11, 2013, http://motherboard.vice.com/blog/despite-embargoes-terrorist-states-are-still-using-american-surveillance-software.

Scott Price, "Canadian Mining Companies Leave Behind Decades of Violence in Guatemala," *Truthout*, January 15, 2016, http://www.truth-out.org/news/item/34433-canadian-mining-companies-leave-behind-decades-of-violence-in-guatemala.

Thomas Roulet, "Unpicking the Link Between Laissez-faire Economics and Corporate Greenwashing," *Guardian*, May 9, 2014, http://www.theguardian.com/sustainable-business/unpicking-link-laissez-faire-economics-corporate-individualism.

Sara Schonhardt, "Exxon Mobil Sued in US Court for Alleged Indonesian Human Rights Abuses," *Alaska Dispatch News*, April 26, 2013, http://www.adn.com/article/20130426/exxon-mobil-sued-us-court-alleged-indonesian-human-rights-abuses.

Jonathan Stempel, "Indonesia Torture Case vs Exxon Mobil Revived," Reuters, July 08, 2011, http://www.reuters.com/article/us-exxonmobil-indonesia-idUSTRE7676I120110708.

Jen Wilton, "Violence in Mexico: Where Corporations and Human Rights Collide," *Contributoria*, May 2015, http://www.contributoria.com/issue/2015-05/54f4d6eed077e7c21b00001c/.

# 3.

## Censored 2005: Wealth Inequality in 21st Century Threatens Economy and Democracy

SUMMARY: In the late 1970s, wealth inequality, while stabilizing or increasing slightly in other industrialized nations, increased sharply and dramatically in the United States. While it is no secret that such a trend has been taking place, it is rare to see a TV news program announce that the top 1 percent of the US population now owns about a third of the wealth in the country. Discussion of this trend takes place, for the most part, behind closed doors.

During the short boom of the late 1990s, conservative analysts asserted that, yes, the gap between rich and poor was growing, but that incomes for the poor were still increasing over previous levels. Today most economists, regardless of their political persuasion, agree that the data over the last twenty-five to thirty years is unequivocal:

The top 5 percent is capturing an increasingly greater portion of the pie while the bottom 95 percent is clearly losing ground, and the highly touted American middle class is fast disappearing.

According to economic journalist David Cay Johnston, author of *Perfectly Legal*, this trend is not the result of some naturally-occurring, social Darwinist "survival of the fittest." It is the product of legislative policies carefully crafted and lobbied for by corporations and the super-rich over the past twenty-five years.

New tax shelters in the 1980s shifted the tax burden off of capital and onto labor. As tax shelters rose, the amount of federal revenue coming from corporations fell (from 35 percent during the Eisenhower years to 10 percent in 2002). During the deregulation wave of the 1980s and '90s, members of Congress passed legislation (often without reading it) that deregulated much of the financial industry. These laws took away, for example, the powerful incentives for accountants to behave with integrity or for companies to put away a reasonable amount in pension plans for their employees—resulting in the well-publicized (too late) scandals involving Enron, Global Crossing, and others.

A series of reports released in 2003 by the UN and other global economy analysis groups warn that further increases in the imbalance in wealth throughout the world will have catastrophic effects if left unchecked. The balance of poverty is shifting quickly from rural to urban areas as the world's population moves from the countryside to the city. Currently, almost one-sixth of the world's population lives in slum-like conditions. The UN warns that unplanned, unsanitary settlements threaten both political and fiscal stability within developing countries, where urban slums are growing faster than expected. UN-Habitat reports that unless governments work to control the current unprecedented spread in urban growth, a third of the world's population will be slum dwellers within thirty years.

In developing countries, the concentration of key industries profitable to foreign investors requires that people move to cities, while forced privatization of public services strip them of the ability to become stable or move up financially once they arrive. Meanwhile, the strict repayment schedules mandated by the global institutions make it virtually impossible for poor countries to move out from under their burden of debt. "In a form of colonialisation that is probably more stringent than the original, many developing countries have become suppliers of raw commodities to the world, and fall further and further behind," says one UN analyst. World economists conclude that if enough of the world's nations reach a point of economic failure, such a situation could collapse the entire global economy.

## Censored 2015: Half of Global Wealth Owned by the 1 Percent

SUMMARY: In January 2015, Oxfam International, a nonprofit organization that aims to eliminate poverty, published a report stating that 1 percent of the global population will own more wealth than the rest of the 99 percent combined by 2016. The Oxfam report provided evidence that extreme inequality is not inevitable, but is, in fact, the result of political choices and economic policies established and maintained by the power elite, wealthy individuals whose strong influence keeps the status quo rigged in their own favor. In addition to reporting the latest figures on global economic inequality and its consequences, the Oxfam study outlined a nine-point plan that governments could adopt in creating new policies to address poverty and economic inequality.

According to the Oxfam report, the proportion of global wealth owned by the 1 percent has increased from 44 percent in 2009 to 48 percent in 2014, and it is projected to reach 50 percent in 2016. In October 2014, a prior Oxfam report, "Even It Up: Time to End Extreme Inequality," revealed that the number of billionaires worldwide had more than doubled since the 2009 financial crisis, showing that, although those at the top have recovered quickly, the vast majority of the world's population are far from reaping the benefits of any recent economic recovery. Even more staggering, the world's richest eighty-five people now hold the same amount of wealth as half the world's poorest population. "Failure to tackle inequality will leave hundreds of millions trapped in poverty unnecessarily," the report's authors warned.

Oxfam calculated that taxing billionaires just 1.5 percent of their wealth "could raise $74 billion a year, enough to fill the annual gaps in funding needed to get every child into school and to deliver health services in the world's poorest countries."

Corporate coverage of the two Oxfam reports has been minimal in quantity and problematic in quality. A few corporate television networks, including CNN, CBS, MSNBC, ABC, FOX, and C-SPAN covered Oxfam's January report, according to the TV News Archive. CNN had the most coverage, with approximately seven broadcast segments; however, these stories were never aired during primetime. At CBS and MSNBC the coverage was similar. Fox also covered the story, once questioning Oxfam's motives for releasing the report just before the 2015 annual meeting of the World Economic Forum in Davos, Switzerland. *Forbes* was consistently critical in its coverage of the two Oxfam reports.

In sum, much of the corporate news coverage was brief, broadcast at odd hours (either late at night or early in the morning when not many people were watching), questioned the report, and/or focused on Obama's tax reforms rather than the Oxfam reports' contents. In contrast with independent news coverage, none of the televised stories addressed details of the Oxfam reports, such as the organization's nine-point plan for changes. The Oxfam studies received better coverage in the international press at places like the BBC.

UPDATE: The corporate media have finally started to report on the ever-widening gap between the richest 1 percent of the world's population and everyone else. However, such coverage often only scratches the surface of the full scope of economic inequality. Although polls have shown that a majority of Americans believe that the level of income inequality is too high, a study done by economist Ray Fisman found that most politicians, Democrat and Republican alike, are unwilling to shape policies that would reduce inequality. Fisman and his colleagues concluded that "elites were much less willing to sacrifice efficiency for equality than the average American was." Most policymakers think of programs that benefit the middle and lower classes as a waste of resources.

Since 1981, the number of people living in poverty has increased tremendously. Most mainstream economists attribute income inequality to an increased demand for highly skilled workers in high tech industries. Matt Vidal, a Senior Lecturer in Work and Organisations at King's College London and editor in chief of *Work in Progress*, studied the economies of Canada, the UK, and the US and found that income inequality had risen almost continuously in the US since the 1970s. In Canada it had been stable for two decades until the 1990s, while inequality in the UK grew faster than in the US until 1990, at which point it has since remained relatively stable. This information complicates the mainstream, skill-biased explanation, and points instead to the culpability of those who shape political and economic policies. According to Vidal, the main causes of income inequality are de-unionization, outsourcing, and the market-determination of wages. These factors have increased the use of part-time and temporary employment, while wages for low-skilled workers have been lowered as much as possible as per market-determination.

Wages for middle- and lower-class workers have not risen to reflect increased productivity or to offset inflation, while those at the top of the economic food chain have seen their annual income increase at unprecedented rates. In the article "Inequality Against Democracy: 10 Facts about the 0.01 Percent," Richard Eskow states that between the years 1979 and 2012, "after accounting for inflation, the productivity of the average American worker increased about 85 percent" but "the inflation-adjusted wage of the median worker rose only about 6 percent, and the value of the minimum wage fell 21 percent." By contrast, in the past forty-some-odd years, the income for the top 1 percent has grown by 275 percent, and CEOs now earn as much as 373 times more than the average American worker. All the while, the costs of housing, higher education, health care, and retirement have risen exponentially. Further compounding the issues of income inequality is the reality that the richest individuals, and corporations, do not pay anywhere near their fair share of taxes.

Many suggest that by simply taxing the wealthiest households, revenues would significantly increase, and investing in the expansion of "wealth-building across the economy" would be a feasible option. According to Lynn Stuart Parramore, without meaningful political change our democracy will continue to be undermined, "social cohesion blown apart, economies destabilized, social mobility stalled, and many other important aspects of our personal and public lives degraded, including our health."

Journalist Bob Lord has proposed three changes to our system of taxation that would have profound effects in restructuring the economy so that it would work for the many, and not just for the few. First, he suggests an increase to taxation on investment income, which essentially only affects the richest Americans. Second, the income tax rates for the super-rich must be increased considerably. Third, the loopholes in the estate tax system should be eradicated and an increase on the estate tax rate enacted. It has become abundantly clear that, despite what proponents of Reaganomics would like us to believe, granting a low tax burden to corporations and the super-rich does not benefit the middle and lower classes. Furthermore, when the most affluent individuals stash their money in overseas tax-havens, it is obviously impossible for their wealth to "trickle-down" to improve the economy.

On April 3, 2016, the world witnessed one of the biggest data leaks in history, the Panama Papers, released by the International Consortium of Investigative Journalists. The US Department of the Treasury received anonymous information that exposed tax evasions by a slew of governments, politicians, celebrities, and private individuals worldwide. The Panama Papers are only one example of how many wealthy people use offshore tax havens in order to reduce, or completely avoid, income taxes. The law firm exposed by the data leak, Mossack Fonseca, is one of the largest providers of offshore services. Law firms that specialize in tax-havens for the super-rich have hindered the economic progress in poor countries like Syria and Uganda. Uganda spent years trying to force Heritage Oil and Gas, a Channel Islands-based business, to pay taxes after selling its assets in Uganda to Tullow Oil, but they refused to do so. Aided by Mossack Fonseca, the company managed to avoid paying $404 million in taxes, until finally legally forced to do so more than four years later. During the period of this large-scale tax evasion, hospitals around the oil field lacked the funds needed to provide even the most basic care. Patients were treated on the hospital floor and were required to bring their own gloves and cotton balls; otherwise they were sent home without receiving care. The $404 million that Heritage Oil and Gas avoided paying represents more than the Ugandan government's annual health budget. The Panama Papers have provided undeniable proof that some companies and individuals are "extracting more money from an economy without actually adding to the growth," and the results are often disastrous.

While the Panama Papers do not identify as many US offenders, there have been other exposés that detail citizens of the United States who have clearly evaded paying taxes. Gabriel Zucman's book, *The Hidden Wealth of Nations: The Scourge of Tax Havens*, reports that "US citizens have at least $1.2 trillion stashed offshore, costing $200 billion a year worldwide in lost tax revenue from wealthy individuals." This information is significant because it provides the 99 percent with indisputable evidence of the 1 percent's illegal activities, and from this basis we can demand that our governments take action and hold these companies and individuals accountable.

With the US presidential election upon us, it is troubling to confront the fact that Donald Trump is now the Republican nominee.

His business practices are on par with many of those exposed by the Panama Papers, so it almost goes without saying that his presidency would continue this detrimental practice. His advances in the political arena with the stated intention of "making direct change on behalf of the 'public interests'" because our "democratic system needs better representation" have been, quite frankly, absurd. Democratic candidate Bernie Sanders pointed out that the top tenth of the 1 percent owns approximately 50 percent of the world's income, and that this trend towards such a high concentration of wealth has happened over the last six presidential cycles. It has been predicted that if we continue along this path by 2040 wealth inequality will rise to 9,000 times its current levels, so the average household in the top hundredth of 1 percent will be worth over $250 million. And that much wealth in the pockets of the few means that much less for everyone else.

## SOURCES:

"62 People Have as Much Wealth as World's 3.6B Poorest, Oxfam Finds Ahead of Davos," Reuters, January 17, 2016, http://www.cnbc.com/2016/01/17/62-people-have-as-much-wealth-as-worlds-36b-poorest-oxfam-finds-ahead-of-davos.html.

Richard Eskow, "Inequality Against Democracy: 10 Facts about the 0.01 Percent," *Huffington Post*, February 1, 2016, http://www.huffingtonpost.com/rj-eskow/inequality-against-democr_b_9133250.html.

Melissa Kearney and Phillip Levine, "Income Inequality, Social Mobility, and the Decision to Drop Out of High School," *Brookings Papers on Economic Activity*, March 10, 2016, http://www.brookings.edu/about/projects/bpea/papers/2016/kearney-levine-inequality-mobility.

Joe McCarthy, "What the Panama Papers Have to Say about Inequality and Poverty," *Global Citizen*, April 4, 2016, https://www.globalcitizen.org/en/content/what-the-panama-papers-have-to-say-about-inequalit/.

Chuck Collins, "The Panama Papers Expose the Hidden Wealth of the World's Super-Rich," *Nation*, April 5, 2016, http://www.thenation.com/article/panama-papers-expose-the-hidden-wealth-of-the-worlds-super-rich/.

Sara Rimer, "Power Brokers Care More about Efficiency Than Equality," *BU Today*, February 4, 2016, http://www.bu.edu/today/2016/income-inequality-ray-fisman/.

"The Panama Papers," *The International Consortium of Investigative Journalists*, April 3, 2016, website, https://panamapapers.icij.org/.

Miles Weiss, "Steve Cohen Has a New Firm That's Allowed to Take Outside Money," *Bloomberg*, April 14, 2016, http://www.bloomberg.com/news/articles/2016-04-14/steve-cohen-has-a-new-firm-that-s-allowed-to-take-outside-money.

Rick Baum, "During Obama's Presidency Wealth Inequality Has Increased and Poverty Levels are Higher," *Counterpunch*, February 26, 2016, http://www.counterpunch.org/2016/02/26/during-obamas-presidency-wealth-inequality-has-increased-and-poverty-levels-are-higher/.

Bob Lord, "Inequality Will Increase until There's a Revolution," *Counterpunch*, April 28, 2016, http://www.counterpunch.org/2016/04/28/inequality-will-increase-until-theres-a-revolution/.

Matt Vidal, "What's Behind the Rise in Income Inequality? Technology or Class Struggle," *Counterpunch*, March 17, 2016, http://www.counterpunch.org/2016/03/17/whats-behind-the-rise-in-income-inequality-technology-or-class-struggle/.

Gabriel Zucman, *The Hidden Wealth of Nations: The Scourge of Tax Havens* (Chicago: University of Chicago Press, 2015).

Mortimer B. Zuckerman, "Making a Mockery of the American Dream," *US News & World Report*, March 27, 2015, http://www.usnews.com/opinion/articles/2015/03/27/income-inequality-makes-a-mockery-of-the-american-dream.

Lynn Stuart Parramore, "Is the 1% Really the Problem?," AlterNet, April 11, 2016, http://www.alternet.org/economy/1-really-problem.

## 4.

## Censored 1987: The Information Monopoly

SUMMARY: In 1982, media expert Ben Bagdikian completed research for his book, *The Media Monopoly*, which talked about how fifty corporations controlled at least half of the media business. But when completing a revision of this book for a second edition by December 1986, the number of corporations controlling much of the media business had shrunk down to twenty-nine, followed by twenty-six just half a year later when Bagdikian wrote an article on the subject for *Extra!*, the publication of media watchdog Fairness and Accuracy In Reporting. Based upon the predictions of Wall Street analysts, Bagdikian warned that by the 1990s the number of corporations controlling most of our media would shrink down to just six firms.

This rapidly increasing centralization of media ownership has raised questions about the public's access to a diversity of opinion. By the end of the 1980s, Bagdikian found that fewer than fifteen corporations controlled most of the circulation of daily papers around the country, with fewer than a dozen companies controlling the book business, a handful of firms controlling most of the magazine business (with *Time* magazine accounting for about 40 percent of that industry's revenues), and only three networks (Capital Cities/ABC, CBS, and NBC) having majority access to television audiences.

What makes this situation even worse is the conflict of interest among interlocking boards of directors for major corporations. A study conducted by Peter Dreier and Steven Weinberg found interlocking directorates in major newspaper chains, such as Gannet (sharing directors with Merrill Lynch, Standard Oil of Ohio, 20th Century Fox, Kerr-McGee, and Kellogg Company, among others), The New York Times (interlocked with Bristol Myers, Charter Oil, American Express, IBM, and Sun Oil, among others), and Time Inc. (interlocked with Mobil Oil, AT&T, American Express, and most major international banks.)

Despite the information uncovered by Bagdikian and others, the impact of the monopolization of information on a free society continues to be ignored by the mass media. Even worse, publishers' traditional tendency of avoiding controversy tends to promote censorship among writers, journalists, editors, and news directors.

Warned Bagdikian: ". . . a shrinking number of large media corporations now regard monopoly, oligopoly, and historic levels of profit as not only normal, but as their earned right. In the process, the usual democratic expectations for the media—diversity of ownership and ideas—have disappeared as the goal of official policy and, worse, as a daily experience of a generation of American readers and viewers."

UPDATE: Media expert Ben Bagdikian was vindicated when he stated that only six conglomerates would control 90 percent of what we read, watch, and listen to. As of today, among some of their holdings, News Corp owns Fox, the *Wall Street Journal*, and the *New York Post*; Disney owns ABC, ESPN, Pixar, Miramax, and Marvel Studios; Viacom owns MTV, Nickelodeon, BET, CMT, and Paramount Pictures; CBS owns Showtime, the Smithsonian Channel, NFL.com, Simon & Schuster; Time Warner owns CNN, HBO, TBS, and Warner Brothers; and finally, Comcast owns NBCUniversal, AT&T Broadband, Universal Studios, and Universal Parks. These companies provide the majority of Americans with their sole source of entertainment and information, though the latter may often be better described as either misinformation or disinformation.

As the number of major conglomerates that control broadcasting and telecommunications services has shrunk from fifty different corporations to just six within the span of only twenty years, the big question is: How have only a handful of corporations consolidated all of the major television networks and nearly every major news outlet?

During his presidency, Bill Clinton, influenced by the lobbying efforts of the communications and media industries, signed into law with great fanfare the Telecommunications Act of 1996. The top story of that year for Project Censored was "Telecommunications Deregulation: Closing Up America's 'Marketplace of Ideas.'" This act eased restrictions on media cross-ownership, allowing for just one corporation or person to own multiple media businesses, such as broadcast

and cable stations, newspapers, and websites. While the stated intention of the law was to increase competition by reducing regulation, it instead strengthened corporations more than even insiders anticipated. The use of mergers as well as the buyouts of smaller, yet still powerful, corporations has created a media oligopoly. While some have supported this as free market competition, many others believe that the government should regulate this industry in order to prevent monopolies and promote media diversity. Opponents of the Telecommunications Act of 1996 have focused on the history of the Federal Communications Commission (FCC), a federal office established by the Communications Act of 1934 to regulate all interstate and international communications media in the US.

Since its conception in 1934, the FCC claimed that all broadcast media is the official property of the federal government. In the 1960s and '70s, with the help of Congress, the FCC created new regulations that prevented companies from owning alternative media outlets within the same market and determining that no company could own more than seven broadcast networks. During the 1980s, however, the

FCC and Congress moved towards media deregulation. New provisions gave broadcast companies the opportunity to own up to twelve networks and eliminated restrictions on content, such as the amount of advertising. Whereas broadcast networks were once required to provide "fair" coverage by giving equal time to opposing viewpoints, in 1987 the FCC removed those regulations. This reduced the FCC's responsibilities and obligations to the public and gave more power and liberty to the major broadcast networks.

Following a number of Senate hearings that studied the effects of media consolidation, several media organizations petitioned Congress in 2003 to allow for complete deregulation. Later that year, the FCC changed their rules again, this time allowing media organizations to potentially own up to 45 percent of the media in a single market and formally removing restrictions that called for media organizations to serve in the public's interest. This time, however, Congress repealed these deregulatory decisions, concerned that more deregulation would further encourage the formation of monopolies. As a result, the federal appeals court ruled that the FCC would have to rewrite its restrictions. This only heightened debates between congressional committees and members of the FCC backed by major media representatives. Finally, the FCC was permitted to remove restrictions that prevented major media agencies from purchasing one another.

As a result of the Telecommunications Act of 1996, as well as numerous deregulations by the FCC, mass media consolidation, otherwise known as media oligopoly, became legal within the radio, newspaper, and television industries. Prior to 1996, iHeartMedia, previously known as Clear Channel, owned just forty stations. Once this deregulation act was signed into effect, iHeartMedia came to own 1,240 stations, becoming thirty times more powerful than was previously legal. Gannett, a company that holds many local newspapers at its mercy, owns more than 1,000 newspapers and 600 magazines nationwide, including *USA Today*, one of the highest-circulating periodicals in the United States. News Corp, a company that managed to avoid paying $875 million in taxes as recently as 2010, owns the top newspapers on three continents, including the *Wall Street Journal* in North America, the *Sun* in Europe, and the *Australian* in Australia. In 2009 the NBC-Comcast merger guaranteed control of one-fifth of the total hours of all daily broadcasts and a monopoly in eleven major US markets. These mergers, and others like them, are what have led to the consolidation of 70 percent of the cable industry.

Net neutrality is also in jeopardy as a result of this mass media oligopoly. Net neutrality entails a lack of restrictions on Internet content and ensures that all data is treated equally, no matter who created it. Net neutrality allows start-up companies to supplant their competitors in a free market. Ending net neutrality would allow two major conglomerates, Comcast and Time Warner, as well as other big companies such as Cox, AT&T, and Verizon, to essentially construct a two-tiered Internet through the creation of monopolies. These corporations would be able to charge certain technology companies for the ability to more quickly send their data to consumers. Smaller, less established, companies that do not have the funds to pay a premium to them would then be relegated to the "slow lane" of the Internet. One of the most dangerous implications of this system is that it would allow big businesses to restrict usage for alternative news media outlets on the Internet, and thus silence dissenting political views.

By controlling most of the news and entertainment around the world, these major conglomerates are able to successfully deliver propaganda, social programming, and perpetual crisis narratives to the public, without much of the public being consciously aware of this situation. As fewer and fewer corporations gain even more power to dictate what the public watches, hears, and reads, the access to accurate and unbiased information, to diverse and substantial journalism, is being greatly diminished.

Media conglomerates have spent tens of millions of dollars lobbying the government to do away with the few remaining regulations that prevent their total control of the dissemination of information. If the public can discourage our government from allowing even further deregulation of media industries, it could help potentially create space for actual journalism. However, considering that President Obama appointed Tom Wheeler, former lobbyist for the cable industry, as the chairman of the FCC, the future of net neutrality and of investigative journalism may be tenuous at best.

But as this book goes to publication, there is some hope and good news for those who believe in a truly free press and the right to access information. A Federal Appeals Court ruled in favor of the FCC upholding net neutrality rules, protecting, for now, an open Internet. We must fight to maintain this openness, as it directly impacts our ability to know and understand the world around us and to be meaningfully self-governing.

## SOURCES:

Ashley Lutz, "These 6 Corporations Control 90% of the Media in America," *Business Insider*, June 14, 2012, http://www.businessinsider.com/these-6-corporations-control-90-of-the-media-in-america-2012-6

"Bernie Sanders on Media Ownership & Telecommunications," *FeelTheBern.org*, n.d.,http://feelthebern.org/bernie-sanders-on-media-ownership-and-telecommunications/

"Last Week Tonight with John Oliver: Net Neutrality (HBO)," YouTube video, 13:18, from season 1 episode 5 of *Last Week Tonight with John Oliver*, broadcast June 1, 2014, posted by "LastWeekTonight," uploaded June 1, 2014, https://www.youtube.com/watch? v=fpbOE0RrHyU.

Michael Corcoran, "Democracy in Peril: Twenty Years of Media Consolidation under the Telecommunications Act," *Truthout*, February 11, 2016, http://www.truth-out.org/news/item/34789-democracy-in-peril-twenty-years-of-media-consolidation-under-the-telecommunications-act.

Micah L. Issitt, "Media Consolidation: An Overview," in *Points Of View: Media Consolidation*, March 1, 2016, 1. Points of View Reference Center (EBSCO), web, accessed May 1, 2016, http://connection.ebscohost.com/c/articles/23413102/media-consolidation-overview.

Alina Selyukh, "US Appeals Court Upholds Net Neutrality Rules in Full," NPR, June 14, 2016, http://www.npr.org/sections/thetwo-way/2016/06/14/471286113/u-s-appeals-court-holds-up-net-neutrality-rules-in-full.

## 5.

## Censored 2008: No Habeas Corpus for "Any Person"

SUMMARY: With the approval of Congress and no outcry from the corporate media, the Military Commissions Act (MCA) signed by President George W. Bush on October 17, 2006, ushered in trial by military commission law for US citizens and noncitizens alike. While corporate media, including a lead editorial in the *New York Times* on October 19, 2006, gave false comfort that we, as American citizens, would not be the victims of the draconian measures legalized by this Act—such as military roundups and lifelong detention with no rights or constitutional protections—journalist Robert Parry pointed to text in the MCA that allowed for the institution of a military alternative to the constitutional justice system for "any person" regardless of American citizenship. The MCA effectively did away with habeas corpus rights for "any person" arbitrarily deemed to be an "enemy of the state." The judgment over who is deemed an "enemy combatant" has been left to the sole discretion of the president.

The oldest human right defined in the history of English-speaking civilization is the right to challenge governmental power of arrest and detention through the use of habeas corpus laws, considered to be the most critical part of the Magna Carta, signed by King John of England in 1215. That an 800-year legal mainstay could be wiped out in the swipe of a pen with little fanfare in the 21st century is troubling, to say the least.

Besides allowing "any person" to be swallowed up by the MCA, the law prohibits detainees once inside from appealing to the traditional American courts until after prosecution and sentencing, which could translate into an indefinite imprisonment. Other constitutional protections in the Bill of Rights, such as a speedy trial, the right to reasonable bail, and the ban on "cruel and unusual punishment," would likewise seem to be beyond a detainee's reach.

In one of the most chilling public statements ever made by a US Attorney General, Alberto Gonzales opined at a Senate Judiciary Committee hearing on January 18, 2007, "The Constitution doesn't say every individual in the United States or citizen is hereby granted or assured the right of habeas corpus. It doesn't say that. It simply says the right shall not be suspended."

More important than its sophomoric nature, Parry warned, was that Gonzales's statement suggested he was still searching for arguments to make habeas corpus optional, subordinate to the president's executive powers that Bush's neoconservative legal advisers claimed to be virtually unlimited during "time of war."

UPDATE: In 2008, the US Supreme Court found Section 7 of the Military Commissions Act unconstitutional, allowing detainees to challenge their detentions. The restoration of some of the right to habeas corpus was covered in *Salon* on June 12, 2008, and the next day the *New York Times* reported on the 5-4 ruling. The *Times* also addressed numerous petitions, and called for better handling of evidence and due process for detainees. The article they published was a more honest and valid representation of the issue than the coverage from 2006.

The *Huffington Post* has covered current issues with the MCA and the injustices that detainees are facing during their trials. The Act

takes away the right to fire one's own lawyer without "good cause," which has been problematic for detainees who don't trust their lawyers. In addition to torture, solitary confinement, and lack of access to proper medical care and contact with their families, these flaws in the Act directly stand in the way of proper justice.

As of April 2016, the *Miami Herald* has covered the recent proposal for the Military Commissions Act Amendments of 2016. These amendments aim to improve the efficiency and accountability of the legal process. They are "fully in alignment with the interests of justice and consistent with our American values of fairness in judicial processes."

The *Huffington Post* covered the story of Abu Zubaydah in April 2016. Zubaydah was accused of being Osama bin Laden's senior lieutenant and second-in-command for al-Qaeda. He was one of the first people detained and tortured under the Military Commissions Act. He was waterboarded, lost his right eye, and was a "ghost prisoner" hidden from the world and even the International Committee of the Red Cross, in violation of the Geneva Conventions. Following the introduction of evidence of his innocence, many charges were dropped, and after the Supreme Court ruling, his lawyers were able to file a habeas corpus petition. Unfortunately, seven years later it has yet to be ruled on, and he is still being detained.

In May 2016, Michael Ratner, the former president of the Center for Constitutional Rights, who played an instrumental part in challenging the MCA and prompting the Supreme Court to rule that the denial of habeas corpus was unconstitutional, passed away. The *New York Times* and other major news outlets covered his death, and in the process shedding some further light on the Military Commissions Act.

SOURCES:

Daphne Eviatar, "A Cloud Hanging Over the Military Commissions," *Huffington Post*, February 17, 2016, http://www.huffingtonpost.com/daphne-eviatar/a-cloud-hanging-over-the_b_9255672.html.

Rebecca Gordon, "The Al-Qaeda Leader Who Wasn't," *Huffington Post*, April 25, 2016, Accessed May 14, 2016, http://www.huffingtonpost.com/rebecca-gordon/abu-zubaydah_b_9771034.html.

Linda Greenhouse, "Justices, 5-4, Back Detainee Appeals for Guantánamo," *New York Times*, June 13, 2008, http://www.nytimes.com/2008/06/13/washington/13scotus.html?_r=0.

Glenn Greenwald, "Supreme Court Restores Habeas Corpus, Strikes Down Key Part of Military Commissions Act," *Salon*, June 12, 2008, http://www.salon.com/2008/06/12/boumediene/.

Sam Roberts, "Michael Ratner, Lawyer Who Won Rights for Guantánamo Prisoners, Dies at 72," *New York Times*, May 11, 2016, http://www.nytimes.com/2016/05/12/us/michael-ratner-lawyer-who-won-rights-for-guantanamo-prisoners-dies-at-72.html?_r=0.

Carol Rosenberg, "Sept. 11 Trial by Skype? Pentagon Seeks to Hold Some Guantánamo Hearings by Video from U.S.," *Miami Herald*, April 20, 2016, http://www.miamiherald.com/news/nation-world/world/americas/guantanamo/article72965207.html#storylink=cpy.

## 6.

Censored 2015: Ocean Acidification Increasing at Unprecedented Rate

SUMMARY: It's well known that burning fossil fuels in the form of coal, oil, and natural gas releases carbon dioxide ($CO_2$) into the air. Less understood is that a quarter of this carbon dioxide—about twenty trillion pounds each year—is absorbed by the oceans. Writing for the *Seattle Times*, Craig Welch invited readers to "imagine every person on earth tossing a hunk of $CO_2$ as heavy as a bowling ball into the sea. That's what we do to the oceans every day." As Welch and others reported, this carbon dioxide is changing the ocean's chemistry faster than at any time in human history, in ways that have potentially devastating consequences for both ocean life and for humans who depend on the world's fisheries for their health and livelihood.

When $CO_2$ mixes with seawater, it lowers the pH levels of the water, making it more acidic and sour. In turn, this erodes some animals' shells and skeletons and robs the water of ingredients that those animals require for healthy development. Known as ocean acidification, this phenomenon, Welch wrote, "is helping push the seas toward a great unraveling that threatens to scramble marine life on a scale almost too big to fathom, and far faster than first expected."

The impacts of ocean acidification have been most pronounced in the Arctic and Antarctic, because cold, deep seas absorb the most carbon dioxide. Julia Whitty reported for *Mother Jones* that humans have enjoyed a free ride so far: "The ocean has swallowed our atmospheric carbon dioxide emissions and slowed global warming during the past few critical decades while we dithered in disbelief." Now, however, the average acidity of surface ocean waters worldwide is more than 30 percent greater than it was at the start of the Industrial Revolution. As ocean acidification impacts the abundance, productivity, and distribution of Arctic marine species, these changes are likely to affect the culture, diet, and livelihoods of indigenous Arctic peoples and other populations in or around the Arctic.

Craig Welch, in his "Sea Change" article for the *Seattle Times*, wrote, "The most-studied animals remain those we catch. Little is known about the things they eat." This points to another problematic dimension of ocean acidification. Despite the potential magnitude of the problem—as ocean acidification is changing the chemistry of the world's oceans faster than ever before, and faster than the world's leading scientists had predicted—there is little funding for research on ocean acidification and its effects. As Welch reported, "Combined nationwide spending on acidification research for eight federal agencies, including grants to university scientists by the National Science Foundation, totals about $30 million a year—less than the annual budget for the coastal Washington city of Hoquiam, population 10,000."

UPDATE: Little has been written on this story since it was published, but a recent article by Deborah Sullivan Brennan in the *Los Angeles Times* expresses the severity of ocean acidification as it reaches dangerously high levels. One of the biggest concerns about the dramatic change in acidity levels is how much they are affecting the world's coral reefs. Coral bleaching, caused by climate change, is a direct result of temperature increases in the ocean, which absorbs around 93 percent of the increasing heat from the Earth. Studies show that the current water temperature in the ocean has increased by about 1.8–3.6° F. El Niño's distribution of warm waters across the oceans has compounded the issue of coral bleaching, and has led to some of the worst coral bleaching on record in the Pacific Ocean. Coral reefs lose their color because, when they are under stress from conditions such as higher temperatures, they expel a colored algae called zooxanthellae, which produces the oxygen, glucose, glycerol and amino acids required for the coral's survival. About 95 percent of the reefs from Cairns, Australia to New Guinea suffer from coral bleaching, and only four out of the 520 reefs show no evidence of being affected by the high acidity levels.

Fortunately, coral bleaching can be reversed, but it would require living conditions in the oceans to return to normal, with added recovery time. Coral reefs are instrumental to the health of the world's oceans, as they are home to about a quarter of all marine species while covering less than 0.2 percent of the ocean. Coral is made out of calcium carbonate and undergoes a process called calcification in order to grow or produce more coral. The rising acidity of the ocean makes it difficult for calcification to occur and corrodes the calcium carbonate shells of many other creatures. If ocean acidification continues unabated, coral and many other species of marine wildlife could be extinct within a century.

Other marine critters in danger as a result of increased acidity levels include clams, oysters, mussels, and, crucially, various species of plankton. A 2015 study conducted by MIT found that by 2100 ocean acidification will cause many species of plankton to completely die off. Scientists have only recently discovered the role of plankton in the global ecosystem, and have determined that they provide half of the world's supply of oxygen. If the ocean water doesn't become more alkaline in the near future, many species could become extinct. As human activity has emitted increasing levels of carbon dioxide into the atmosphere, the acidity of the ocean's surface waters has increased by about 30 percent since the late-18th century. At this rate, it is projected that, by the end of this century, surface ocean waters could be almost 150 percent more acidic.

Due to the way the Pacific Ocean circulates, the waters of the West Coast are going through an acidification process that is twice as fast as the rest of the world, and the rest of the world's ocean acidification has been far from slow. However, there are a few methods that may slow down the process of ocean acidification. One possible solution to address this issue is to plant more seagrass. This particular plant absorbs carbon dioxide and uses that energy to reproduce. Seagrass has the ability to change the chemistry of the water and a large amount could help reduce the impact of acidification.

Another method which might reverse the effects of ocean acidification is to reduce the amount of pollution that travels through the storm drains and rivers which can exacerbate the intensity of acidification. Common chemicals such as nitrogen and phosphorus have been introduced to the ocean waters, and these chemicals contribute to the high acidity levels by attracting and supporting the lives of algae. Algae decrease oxygen levels in the water, making it more difficult to control the acidity in the ocean, so cutting down on algae by cutting down on chemical pollutants may indirectly solve the problem of acidification.

Another possible solution is to release bubbles of compressed air along the seafloor to help strip carbon dioxide from the water. This process requires a higher concentration of carbon dioxide being dissolved in the water than the air that is being bubbled through, to mimic the composition of the atmosphere. This idea could help vulnerable coastal ecosystems cope with the sudden changes, but it remains too costly at the moment to apply to the rest of the world's oceans.

Undoubtedly, the cost of doing nothing about ocean acidification and climate change will likely be far greater in the long run than any methods enacted today, not only to the ocean life but to all of life on Earth.

# SOURCES:

"Australia's Great Barrier Reef Hit by 'Worst' Bleaching," *BBC News*, March 29, 2016, http://www.bbc.com/news/world-australia-35914009.

"Ocean Acidification Putting Marine Life at Risk, Study Says," *Santa Cruz Sentinel*, March 18, 2016, http://www.santacruzsentinel.com/environment-and-nature/20160318/ocean-acidification-putting-marine-life-at-risk-study-says.

Jennifer Chu, "Ocean Acidification May Cause Dramatic Changes to Phytoplankton," *MIT News*, July 20, 2015, http://news.mit.edu/2015/ocean-acidification-phytoplankton-0720.

Jade Boyd, "Study: Ocean Acidification Already Slowing Coral Reef Growth," Rice University, February 25, 2016, http://news.rice.edu/2016/02/25/study-ocean-acidification-already-slowing-coral-reef-growth-2/.

Deborah Sullivan Brennan, "West Coast Fisheries are at Risk as Climate Change Disturbs the Ocean's Chemistry," *Los Angeles Times*, April 19, 2016, http://www.latimes.com/science/la-me-oceans-acid-20160419-story.html.

Deirdre Lockwood, "Bubbles Could be a Targeted Remedy for Ocean Acidification," *Chemical & Engineering News*, April 1, 2016, http://cen.acs.org/articles/94/web/2016/03/Bubbles-targeted-remedy-ocean-acidification.html.

Brandon Miller, "Dramatic Images Reveal Coral Bleaching in Great Barrier Reef," CNN, March 23, 2016, http://www.cnn.com/2016/03/22/weather/great-barrier-reef-coral-bleaching/.

Avaneesh Pandey, "Ocean Acidification Killed Off More than 90 Percent of Marine Life 252 Million Years Ago: Study," *International Business Times*, republished and available via *Raw Story*, April 10, 2015, http://www.rawstory.com/2015/04/ocean-acidification-killed-off-more-than-90-percent-of-marine-life-252-million-years-ago-study/.

"West Coast Scientists Urge Immediate Action to Combat Ocean Acidification," *Daily Breeze*, April 8, 2016, http://www.dailybreeze.com/environment-and-nature/20160408/west-coast-scientists-urge-immediate-action-to-combat-ocean-acidification.

Luiz A. Rocha, "Ocean Acidification is Already Damaging Coral Reefs," *Huffington Post*, February 25, 2016, http://www.huffingtonpost.com/luiz-a-rocha/ocean-acidification-is-al_b_9309502.html.

SUSAN RAHMAN is a mother and professor of behavioral science at College of Marin. She lives with her daughter, Jordan; partner, Carlos; and two dogs, Rosie and Phoebi, in Northern California.

# Notes

1   The Project Censored number one story for 1977, "Myth of Black Progress," viewed online at http://projectcensored.org/1-myth-of-black-progress/.

2   The Project Censored number one story for 1979, "The Corporate Crime of the Century," viewed online at http://projectcensored.org/1-the-corporate-crime-of-the-century/; and the Project Censored number one story for 2000, "Multinational Corporations Profit from International Brutality," viewed online at http://projectcensored.org/1-multinational-corporations-profit-from-international-brutality/?doing_wp_cron=1466282448.3221879005432128906250.

3   The Project Censored number one story for 2005, "Wealth Inequality in 21st Century Threatens Economy and Democracy," viewed online http://projectcensored.org/1-wealth-inequality-in-21st-century-threatens-economy-and-democracy/; and the Project Censored number one story for 2016, "Half of Global Wealth Owned by the 1 Percent," viewed online at http://projectcensored.org/1-half-of-global-wealth-owned-by-the-1-percent/.

4   The Project Censored number one story for 1987, "The Information Monopoly," viewed online at http://projectcensored.org/1-the-information-monopoly/; and the Project Censored number one story for 1996, "Telecommunications Deregulation: Closing Up America's 'Marketplace of Ideas,'" viewed online at http://projectcensored.org/1-telecommunications-deregulation-closing-up-americas-marketplace-of-ideas/.

5   The Project Censored number one story for 2008, "No Habeas Corpus for 'Any Person,'" viewed online at http://projectcensored.org/1-no-habeas-corpus-for-any-person/.

6   The Project Censored number one story for 2015, "Ocean Acidification Increasing at Unprecedented Rate," viewed online at http://projectcensored.org/1-ocean-acidification-increasing-unprecedented-rate/.

7   Dan Baum, "Legalize It All: How to Win the War on Drugs," *Harper's Magazine*, April 2016, online at https://harpers.org/archive/2016/04/legalize-it-all/.

8   Carl Jensen, "Project Censored: Giving Unreported News the Attention It Deserves," in *Context: The Ecology of Media from Storytelling to Telecommunications* 23, Fall 1989, online at http://www.context.org/iclib/ic23/jensen/.

# CHAPTER 3

# The Corporate Media's War on Reality

## Faux Elections and the Facade of DeMockracy: Junk Food News and News Abuse for 2015–16

Nolan Higdon with Mickey Huff, and student researchers Hanna Begnell, Taylor Bledsoe, Aimee Casey, Alexandra Castillo, Daniel Cerezo, Daniel Cervantez, Lauren Freeman, Mitchell Graham, Josh Gorski, Kyle Hunt, Jaspreet Kang, Justin Lascano, Brandy Miceli, George Petrucci, Sarah Powell, Jared Rodda, Edwin Sevilla, Chandler Saul, Sebastian Trucios, Jacob Trutanich, Mark Yolangco; these students are from California State University East Bay, California State University Maritime Academy, Diablo Valley College, Las Positas College, and San Francisco State University.

*"If... the public does not receive all the information it needs to make informed decisions, then some form of news blackout is taking place... some issues are over-looked (what we call 'censored') and other issues are over-covered (what we call 'junk food news')."*

—Carl Jensen, founder, Project Censored[1]

## JUNK FOOD NEWS AND NEWS ABUSE: A BRIEF HISTORY

*How in the world could Richard Nixon be re-elected to the presidency after taking part in Watergate?* When Sonoma State University (SSU) professor Carl Jensen asked this question in 1976, few could have predicted that he would turn it into an education project that transformed the lives of thousands of students and millions of readers. Jensen's research concluded that Nixon was held to no noteworthy media scrutiny during his 1972 re-election bid because the corporate media ignored Watergate. However, the independent press had continued to note Nixon's involvement in the crime, and eventually Nixon resigned.

Most academics would have completed a study like Jensen's, published it, and begun the next project. Not Jensen. Jensen sought to ameliorate the societal problem of citizens receiving information from a propagandistic and inaccurate corporate media system. He began having his students compare corporate and independent news coverage every semester to document what was and was not being covered by corporate media. The top twenty-five independent news stories that were ignored by the corporate press were published in an annual list distributed for public consumption. Their project was dubbed *Project Censored: The News that Didn't Make the News*, and it is now a forty-year bastion of media and democracy in action.

Some journalists and editors in the corporate media took issue with Jensen, arguing that the stories were not "censored" as he claimed, but due to time and space constraints could not be published, a decision they defended as part of "news judgment." Jensen researched their claim and concluded that the corporate media often covered trivial and non-newsworthy stories at the expense of newsworthy stories. He called such coverage Junk Food News. Once again Jensen could have just let his research speak for itself, but instead he added a list of the corporate media's Junk Food News to Project Censored's annual publications.

When Jensen retired, Dr. Peter Phillips, a sociology professor at SSU, became the director of Project Censored. Phillips was convinced that the corporate media peddled propaganda that misinformed and misguided the public to adopt positions against their interests. Like Jensen, Phillips had his students investigate how mass media disseminate inaccurate and propagandistic stories. They began to document such instances and called them News Abuse, which refers to the corporate media stories that were newsworthy, but presented in a slanted, partial, or trivial manner.

As of 2016, the Junk Food News and News Abuse chapter focuses on the relationship between corporate media and social justice, equity, and diversity. This chapter, as part of celebrating the forty years of Project Censored, returns to the topic that was the genesis of Jensen's idea: the relationship between media and presidential elections.

This year, we analyze the 2016 presidential primaries to illuminate the prevalence and use of Junk Food News and News Abuse in the corporate press. This year's chapter examines Republican presidential candidate and billionaire Donald Trump's twenty-four-hour cycle of Junk Food News. All of his outlandish behavior has been covered *ad nauseam* at the expense of far more newsworthy stories—not to mention other candidates, including third parties. The chapter concludes with a News Abuse study of how the corporate press peddles, misrepresents, and/or ignores stories of state crimes against democracy and human rights, as well as racism, sexism, and Islamophobia in the context of the presidential election, all while convincing the public to coronate Hillary Clinton as the Democratic Party presidential candidate.

## STATE OF THE SNOOZE

The past year's news cycle saw both positive and negative signs about the influence of corporate media. For example, only 6 percent of the public has a positive view of the press in the US. That is roughly the same approval rating for Congress.[2] However, most people still trust television news and social media to inform them about key issues of the day, including the 2016 presidential election.[3] This is problematic, considering that those corporate outlets tend to slant their content toward the interests of those in power.[4] Analysts argue this is why voters vote with the wealthy rather than for their own economic interests.[5] Censorship remained a problem during the 2015–2016 news cycle.

In fact, a Pew Research Center study found that millennials (those born between 1982–2004) are more supportive of censoring speech and expression than the older generations.[6] About 40 percent of millennials supported some form of censorship on free speech. For example, when South Carolina police officer Ben Fields slammed a young woman on the ground in a classroom because she would not leave her desk, the only person arrested was fellow student Niya Kenny, who acted as a whistleblower by videotaping the violent act.[7] Furthermore, when Fields was fired for the incident—thanks in part to Kenny's video—students protested his firing by wearing shirts that read "Free Fields" and "Bring Back Fields."[8] The students' behavior may not be shocking, considering that they were raised on corporate media messages that normalized the views of those in power, from curtailing civil liberties via the USA PATRIOT Act to National Security Agency (NSA) spying, while privileging state secrets by attacking whistleblowers like Edward Snowden and Chelsea Manning.[9] This culture of censorship is so pervasive that the Central Intelligence Agency's (CIA) Inspector General felt comfortable publicly claiming that the agency "accidently" deleted its only copy of the US Senate's damning report about the CIA's illegal use of torture.[10]

The inculcation of a generation in accepting censorship has allowed for the further decaying of the fourth estate. For example, when police slammed a CBS reporter for doing his job of covering a Trump rally, attendees screamed, "Go back to Iraq," rather than note that police were arresting a journalist for using his First Amendment right of freedom of the press.[11]

In fact, last year, new evidence reminded the public of how censorship and media propaganda is not only prevalent, but morally questionable and at times even deadly. Newly declassified documents prove that conservative icon William F. Buckley, Jr. and his magazine, the *National Review*, constructed a false image of Chilean dictator Augusto Pinochet for Americans in the 1970s. This included covering up the thousands of individuals murdered in Chile under his rule and two people who were murdered in Washington, DC by a car bomb Pinochet had ordered. Buckley wanted to promote the false narrative that Pinochet's rightwing assault on leftists was promoting freedom. As a result, he helped hide a multitude of human rights abuses and thousands of deaths from the US public.[12]

This type of framing is a form of propaganda and censorship that continues to the present. One startling recent example is that of the Fox News terrorist analyst who was arrested for impersonating a CIA agent on the network for over a decade.[13] In the course of that decade, Fox News did irreparable damage to the public by having this person falsely inform viewers about foreign policy, civil liberties, and the CIA. However, no one at Fox was or ever has been arrested for impersonating a journalist. Meanwhile, Brian Williams, who completely fabricated multiple tales, including being in a helicopter crash in Iraq, to improve his public image, returned to the helm of the election desk for MSNBC during the election news cycle.[14] Perhaps Williams brushed up on basic journalism school principles while on suspension.

The corporate press did discuss the important issue of censorship, but much of that discussion focused on it being a problem in other nations, and not the US. For example, the corporate media hammered Turkey for banning any coverage of "terror" bombings, and Russian President Vladimir Putin for censoring various news broadcasts.[15] At the same time, in the US, CNN openly practiced censorship when it suspended global affairs correspondent Elise Labott for offering a critical perspective on the US policy toward Syria.[16] Like Russia, the US also practices state censorship. In another example, from 2016, reporters were banned from the Virginia State Senate floor. They were literally told it was illegal for them to be present and report on those in power while they are making key decisions.[17]

Since Jensen developed Project Censored, new forms of censorship have arisen in the digital age. For example, just this past year, Outskirts Press (in conjunction with Amazon.com) censored a serial killer's autobiography, Robert DeNiro was pressured to remove a controversial film on vaccines from his own film festival, and University of California, Davis paid hundreds of thousands of dollars for a public relations firm to censor images and scrub the Web of one of their officers using unnecessary force against peaceful protesters in 2011.[18] In a particularly egregious example of digital censorship, social media platform Facebook blocked a leak of 7,000 Hillary Clinton emails from whistleblower organization WikiLeaks.[19] Facebook was also caught earlier this year specifically censoring some conservative sources on news feeds and trending stories. This kind of social media censorship is worrisome, considering that a majority of US citizens now claim to receive their news from Facebook and other social media platforms.[20]

This past year has provided such a dismal display of journalistic failures by the corporate press that it even drew the ire of some of those who have participated in and benefitted from its dysfunction. For example, Fox News host Greta Van Susteren was so enraged by the pathetic election coverage that she wrote a surprisingly astute article on how those who work in corporate media are largely unaware of the real anger that gave rise to the Donald Trump and Bernie Sanders campaigns because they spend too much time with those in power.[21] Let that statement sink in for a moment. Other reporters who retired from the press, such as Andrew Sullivan and Keith Olbermann, were so dismayed by the corporate media coverage of the primaries that they publicly announced that they felt a "civic duty" to come out of retirement and cover the elections.[22] Finally, President Barack Obama, who has benefitted from the corporate media's celebrity culture, lambasted the corporate media for covering the election like a celebrity reality show. He said, "What I'm concerned about is the degree to which reporting and information starts emphasizing the spectacle and the circus. Because that's not something we can afford . . . The American people, they've got good judgment, they've got good instincts—as long as they get good information."[23] Judging by the contents of this chapter, the American people are still waiting for that kind of information.

## JUNK FOOD NEWS

Earlier this year, in the wake of the Panama Papers, people in countries around the world sought to remove leaders from power for their knowledge of and/or participation in hiding offshore monies to avoid taxation. Meanwhile, in the US, Americans were immersed in a vapid celebrity-worshipping culture, one that has invaded nearly every facet of life—even infecting the democratic process and elections.[24] Even as the two leading corporate party candidates for presidential nomination were both under legal clouds of potential investigations, looming indictments, and other controversies, corporate media focused more on bread and circus acts, serving up a full menu of Junk Food News and News Abuse in lieu of real, hard-hitting election year journalism. A brief sampler platter of distractions include the Fox News panel that debated if mathematics should be required in schools; the NBC reporter who touted the network's ethics before storming into the home of murder suspects in San Bernardino; and the Fox debate over Ronald Reagan that concluded with pot George Will and kettle Bill O'Reilly calling each other a "hack."[25] In other words, corporate media served up an anemic news diet.

Trivial stories and celebrity demagoguery were mainstays of the 2016 presidential primary season. While Americans stayed glued to the corporate media's embarrassing exercise in entertainment deceitfully presented as democracy, the independent press published numerous newsworthy stories. For one key example, consider how the corporate media focused on election gossip and some of the aforementioned non-issues while diminishing their coverage of police violence. The independent press, however, continued to cover police killings of unarmed people of color that terrorize communities around the country.[26] Comparably, while the corporate media argued that democracy depends on choosing between Hillary Clinton and Donald Trump, the independent press covered real displays of civic action, like the Democracy Spring, a protest movement against the influence of money in politics. In April of 2016, seven hundred people were arrested in Washington, DC as part of these protests, which received little-to-no corporate media coverage.[27] So, while some of the Junk Food News of the 2016 presidential primary season may make one laugh, it is only funny until one realizes that the joke is on us—We the People.

### The Trump Card

Trump first appeared in the Junk Food News section of Project Censored in the 1990 story "The Marital Woes of Donald and Ivana Trump." Now in 2015–16, Trump has moved from a junk husband to a junk candidate. In the summer of 2015, the corporate media began to notice the profitable potential of the reality television star's presidential campaign.[28] Consumers were captivated by Trump's outrageous behavior. In fact, Les Moonves, chairman of the board, president, and CEO of CBS, admitted that Trump coverage led to increased profits when he noted, "I've never seen anything like this, and this [is] going to be a very good year for us . . . Sorry. It's a terrible thing to say. But,

bring it on, Donald. Keep going . . . [I]t may not be good for America, but it's damn good for CBS."[29] In fact, former CBS anchorman Dan Rather warned that Trump and the media act as business partners.[30] The corporate media's obsession with The Donald helped change the US democratic process to an unholy hybrid of *Keeping Up with the Kardashians* and *American Idol*.[31] In fact, 75 percent of Americans agreed that the corporate media covered Trump too often.[32]

Viewers had reason to be upset with the corporate media coverage. On the road to presumptive party nomination at the convention, Trump, more than any candidate from either major corporate party, dominated the election coverage. In fact, by spring, Trump had received nearly triple the coverage of Hillary Clinton.[33] That equates to $2 billion in free coverage for Trump.[34] For example, in a single twenty-four-hour news cycle, a story about or ad for Trump ran sixty times on Fox, MSNBC, and CNN at no cost to Trump.[35] In fact, MSNBC was so overjoyed to interview Trump on his private jet that they played the interview seventy-nine times over a three day period.

This is problematic, considering that studies have shown that the more a candidate is covered, the higher they rise in the polls.[36]

In comparison to Trump, the Sanders campaign received only one-third of the amount of media coverage.[37] In actual airtime, Trump's campaign received eighty-one times more airtime than Sanders.[38] Perhaps one of the most glaring examples of this media snub would be from March 2016, when Fox, CNN, and MSNBC decided to cover every candidate's primary election speech except for Sanders'.[39] Instead of covering Sanders's speech, they had a camera on an empty podium waiting for Trump to arrive and give his speech.[40] We'll let the reader make the inference there.

However, curiously, earlier in the month, there was no shortage of corporate media coverage of Sanders—so long as that coverage was negative. In one egregious example, the *Washington Post* ran sixteen hit pieces on Sanders's campaign in as many hours between March 6 and 7, which just so happened to be on the cusp of an important Democratic candidate debate in Flint, Michigan. This wasn't the first time the *Post* targeted Sanders, either. One wonders what relationship the owner of the *Washington Post*, Amazon CEO Jeff Bezos, might have with Clinton, as in her final year as Secretary of State, Bezos's company received a $16.5 million contract from the US State Department. Further, Amazon received a ten-year $600 million contract from several intelligence agencies, including the CIA, an organization which Sanders stated he wanted to abolish in 1974 and which he still has serious issues with at present.[41] Sanders's analysis and information was literally trumped by the US corporate deep state media.[42] As Les Moonves of CBS said, "Bring it on, Donald. Keep going . . ."

## Trump's Bad Blood with Megyn Kelly

The junk coverage of Trump was heavily focused on his public fights and insults. He called Senator Ted Cruz "Lyin' Ted" and Senator Marco Rubio a "lightweight choker."[43] The corporate media's favorite battle, though, was Trump's war with the host of Fox News's the *Kelly File*, Megyn Kelly. In August 2015, the bad blood began when Kelly moderated a Republican primary debate and confronted Trump about his sexist comments about women, which included phrases such as "'fat pigs,' 'dogs,' 'slobs,' and 'disgusting animals.'"[44] Trump attacked Kelly and the question rather than explain his actions. He then publicly stated that "[t]here was blood coming out of her eyes, blood coming out of her wherever."[45] Rather than ignore his comments, the corporate media dedicated a massive amount of coverage to the story, "Megyn Kelly Going on Vacation Following Heated GOP Debate and Donald Trump 'Blood' Comments." Days after the episode with Trump, Kelly announced her ten-day vacation plans. The corporate media reported on Kelly with stories such as "R&R for Megyn Kelly."[46] The coverage of Kelly and Trump's war came at the expense of a *Common Dreams* story titled "As of Today, Humanity Has Exhausted its 2015 Supply of Natural Resources," arguing that the world is operating on an "ecological deficit—accumulating carbon dioxide in the atmosphere and depleting the planet for future generations."[47] This story is far more newsworthy than the Trump and Kelly war for its imperative implications regarding the future sustainability of life as we know it on Earth.

The corporate media continued to manufacture the Trump and Kelly war through early 2016. Fox, the *New York Times*, the *Washington Post*, and others covered how Trump had asked via Twitter that "everybody" boycott her show because it's "always a hit on Trump!"[48] He projected onto Kelly that she was "sick, & the most overrated person on TV."[49] Trump's tweets distracted from such stories as "Choking to Death in Detroit: Flint Isn't Michigan's Only Disaster" by Zoë Schlanger writing for *Newsweek*. Her article reported that a large amount of civilians with asthma living in Detroit, Michigan, are literally choking to death.[50] Again, this environmental reality, which could ultimately impact millions in more heavily polluted US cities, was ignored to focus on a war of words between a reality TV star turned presidential candidate and a Fox "news" personality.

### Bring a Wife to a Dud Fight?

In addition to Kelly versus Trump, the corporate media dedicated precious time and space to "The Wife Feud." By late March of 2016, the Republican presidential primary ignored policy in favor of debating who had a more attractive wife. The high school banter began when an anti-Trump super PAC released a campaign advertisement that included a provocative picture of Trump's wife, Melania. Trump responded by posting a picture of his wife with captions that compared her to Cruz's wife, Heidi.[51] Trump took to Twitter, writing, "Be careful, Lyin' Ted, or I will spill the beans on your wife!" The reference to Cruz's wife received a reserved reaction from Cruz on Twitter, "Donald, real men don't attack women. Your wife is lovely, and Heidi is the love of my life." The episode could have died there, but hours later Cruz tweeted that Trump was "a sniveling coward," and tweeted to "leave Heidi the hell alone." The 140-character war was covered by MSNBC, Fox, CNN, the *New York Times*, and others.[52] "The Wife Feud" distracted from Tariq Ali's story, written for *CounterPunch*, titled "Joker Rules: The Crackdown on Press Freedom in Turkey." Ali wrote about how Turkey was attempting to punish him for calling the president of Turkey a joker.[53] Stories about threatened press freedoms are exactly what people need to be aware of, as they are, dare say, still more newsworthy than even "The Wife Feud."

## Size Matters

When the corporate media was not covering Trump's distracting feuds, they were covering his junk, literally, in an exquisite example of a Junk Food News story. In March of 2016, the corporate media became obsessed with the story, "Trump and the Small Hands Equals Small Manhood Myth, or Reality?" It began when Republican presidential candidate Marco Rubio implied that Trump's penis must be small because he has small hands. At the following debate, Trump addressed the remark while on stage with Rubio, stating, "I guarantee you there's no problem."[54] ABC, CNN, CBS, NBC, *Time*, *Variety*, and others dedicated a massive amount of coverage to the debate over Trump's junk, with titles such as "Donald Trump Defends Size of His Penis," "Trump Defends Making His Manhood a Big Issue," and "The History Behind the Donald Trump 'Small Hands' Insult."[55] While the corporate press was fixated on the alleged size of Trump's junk, Medea Benjamin and Rebecca Green, writing for *Foreign Policy in Focus*, reported that newly released documents exposed how then-Secretary of State Hillary Clinton provided arms to Saudi Arabia.[56]

The story gave rise to questions about Clinton's war-hawk mentality, financial corruption, and her hypocritical claims that she represents women's interests, while weaponizing a country that heavily limits women's rights.[57] Their report circulated across the independent press, but the corporate media evidently felt that presidential penile speculation was more important.

## Trivial and Factless

Even when Trump did not supply fodder for the corporate media, they simply invented Junk Food News discussions about Trump. For example, on April 19, 2016, Trump won the New York State Republican primary. The victory was unsurprising, considering it was his home state and no polls predicted a tight race, let alone a loss for Trump. Rather than shift their coverage to a newsworthy story, such as election fraud and voter suppression claims in New York during the primary, the corporate media focused on how Trump's victory speech in New York was "presidential."[58] The night of the primary, the corporate media began a week-long discussion about how Trump was shedding his insulting buffoonery and gruff behavior in order to be taken seriously as a candidate. They even broke down his speech, noting that he used verbs instead of adjectives and placed both hands on the podium when he spoke.[59] Perhaps if they had spent less time studying his stance and vocabulary, they could have fact-checked him. Five reporters at the *Huffington Post* looked at a 12,000-word transcript of a one-hour Trump speech and found that he made seventy-one claims that were "inaccurate, misleading or deeply questionable."[60] However, even when outlets such as NPR criticized Trump for his false remarks, they were quick to distance themselves from being seen as a legitimate news organization by emphasizing that it was a contributor, and not a journalist, who made the critique.[61] One problem with NPR's statement stands out—the contributor in question was actually Cokie Roberts, and whether one likes or agrees with her or not, she is a longtime journalist and analyst (and one who worked at NPR until 1992). While Roberts opined on Trump's candidacy and what it meant for the Republican Party, she did so with the evidence that he makes wildly inaccurate claims. Regardless of her views on the elec-

tion, her discussion of Trump's falsehoods constituted demonstrably factual statements. While NPR focused on Roberts' possible partisanship, they seemed to miss the thesis of her discussion—that Trump peddles relentless falsehoods and it's the media's job to note that. It was as if NPR was apologizing for reporting accurately about reality. It is enough to make one's head swirl.

### Cruzin' for a Porno

Junk Food News has evolved since Jensen first developed the concept. While it has not become any more informative, it now exists in a variety of media, and certainly propagates on the Internet more than ever before. The Internet is where junk is created, discussed, shared, and sometimes circulated and picked up by the traditional corporate press. For example, in February 2016, online media buzzed with a rumor that Republican presidential candidate Ted Cruz was the Zodiac Killer. Memes appeared on social media featuring Cruz side by side with a sketch of the murder suspect. It took off like wildfire, with numerous articles and conspiracies associated with Cruz and the Zodiac popping up on the Web. Then a Florida poll revealed that just over one-third of Florida voters claimed they were unsure whether or not Cruz was the Zodiac Killer.[62] Cruz's wife, Heidi, responded, noting that "[t]here's a lot of garbage out there . . . Well, I've been married to him for 15 years and I know pretty well who he is."[63] MSNBC mused over whether or not Cruz made a veiled reference to the Zodiac conspiracy during his appearance on *Jimmy Kimmel Live!*[64] Cruz became the center of similar Internet fodder after an image of twenty-one-year-old Searcy Hayes passed around social media because she resembled Cruz, while she was a guest on the tabloid talk show *Maury*. This vapid social media post was soon picked up by corporate media.[65] The press coverage helped launch Hayes to instant fame, which included a $10,000 deal to record a six-minute scene in a pornographic film.[66]

## Feeling the Bird

Similar to the Cruz Internet distractions, in March 2016, the corporate media was fixated on how a bird landed on Bernie Sanders's podium at his Portland, Oregon rally.[67] Reportedly, there was "thunderous applause of the crowd," with "a Disney princess meme tak[ing] flight," as a result.[68] After the bird landed, Sanders said, "I think there may be some symbolism here. I know it doesn't look like it, but that bird is really a dove asking us for world peace. No more wars."[69] The freak occurrence of a bird landing, which happens only irregularly, was covered by CNN, *US News & World Report*, *Fortune*, the *New York Post*, the *Huffington Post*, the *Washington Post*, *Vanity Fair*, and *USA Today*, among others.[70] That it happened in Portland, home of the popular cable comedy program *Portlandia*, contributed to the generation of countless memes based on one of the show's skits and songs, "Put a Bird on It." For the corporate media, "Birdie Sanders" was born, which seemed to garner more attention than his speeches or policy positions.

While the corporate media was engulfed in Birdie coverage, the independent outlet the *Intercept* released their report, "Israeli Rights Group Releases Video of Army Medic Executing Wounded Palestinian

Suspect."[71] The story, which reported the execution of an unarmed and injured Palestinian by an Israeli soldier, reiterates ongoing tensions between Israelis and Palestinians, as well as demonstrates human rights abuses by the US-backed Israeli forces. Near 2015's end, Human Rights Watch published documentation of violence and tension between Israelis and Palestinians throughout the year, stating that "Palestinians killed at least 17 Israeli civilians and 3 Israeli soldiers, and injured 87 Israeli civilians and 80 security officers in the West Bank and Israel as of November 27. Israeli security forces killed at least 120 and injured at least 11,953 Palestinian civilians in West Bank, Gaza, and Israel as of the same date, including bystanders, protesters, and suspected assailants."[72] If only a birdie would land on a podium in the West Bank, perhaps the media might begin to pay some attention.

## NEWS ABUSE

*"And I think the American people are going to have to say to NBC and ABC and CBS and CNN, 'You know what, forget the political gossip. Politics is not a soap opera. Talk about the real damn issues facing this country.'"*

—Bernie Sanders to Rachel Maddow on MSNBC[73]

During the 2016 election cycle, the corporate media was not just peddling junk disguised as journalism, but propaganda disguised as news. The corporate media inserted themselves into stories just like the camerawoman who tripped escaping refugees from Syria.[74] They inundated viewers with a barrage of outdated and inaccurate adages, such as "the parties will have to listen to the people" and "this is an historic election" to distract from the corporate hijacking of the democratic process. In fact, the corporate media censored the pervasive corporate influence on the democratic process, from the role of so-called dark money to the news media itself. For example, MSNBC and CNN edited out several lines from a video where Sanders attacked the corporate media for failing to fulfill its role in reporting all-important issues in the election, including the issue of corporate media biases.[75]

The corporate media's refusal to delineate between fact and opinion, slant and bias, perspective and falsehood, allowed the election coverage to co-opt serious issues of equity and social justice including racial and gender prejudice, immigration, climate change, human rights, sexuality, and civil liberties. Furthermore, it allowed for political falsehoods to permeate the corporate media echo chamber, such as Rubio's claim that welders have a higher income than those who major in philosophy, or Trump's claims that he predicted 9/11, that Mexico was sending rapists to the US, that Obama was taking 200,000 Syrian refugees, that a table full of steaks, water, and wine prove he is a successful business man, and that he helped move a Ford Motor plant from Mexico to Ohio.[76]

Youth and social media played a major role in the presidential primary, as they have since 2008. A GOP pollster argued that the youth are terrifyingly liberal.[77] In fact, by mid-March 2016, Sanders had received 1.5 million youth votes; that is more than Clinton and Trump combined.[78] Still, the corporate media worked to spread cynicism among the youth. For instance, MSNBC's Joe Scarborough said that the youth should not waste their time supporting Sanders when the race is already "rigged" for Clinton.[79] This cynicism ignores several prominent youth-led victories, such as when Maine became the first state to abolish superdelegates.[80] Rather than take the youth acrimony seriously, the Clinton campaign went on the defensive. Bill Clinton ignored how his policies contributed to the present climate of discontent among the youth, and instead blamed them for their current state of affairs. He argued that, had they voted to prevent a Republican Congress in 2010, there would not be so many problems facing the nation.[81] Similarly, in the digital age, it is not just television that spreads apathy and support for a corporate candidate, but corporate-run social media. For example, a Clinton super PAC and lobbyist group wrote a pro-Clinton op-ed for Atlanta, Georgia, Mayor Kasim Reed, paying handsomely to spread the op-ed across the Internet. The article offered few facts in denouncing Bernie Sanders.[82] In a similar case, a Clinton super PAC, Correct The Record, is "pledging to spend $1 million to 'push back against' users on Twitter, Facebook, Reddit, and Instagram" who criticize Clinton.[83]

The 2015–16 election coverage news cycle was a stunning example of News Abuse in action. Since Phillips coined the term, the forms and tools that shape America's News Abuse have changed, but the propaganda and deceit remain constant. In the 2015–16 news cycle, the corporate media slanted coverage to coronate Clinton as the Democratic presidential nominee. This year's News Abuse study examines the corporate media's coverage of the Democratic primary.

## The Clinton Coronation

Before the primary season even began, the corporate media were touting the narrative that Clinton was the frontrunner for the Democratic Party presidential nomination. They made this claim despite the fact that, since late 2015, Bernie Sanders led in numerous national polls over every Republican by more points than Clinton.[84] The corporate media narrative that Clinton was the frontrunner became self-fulfilling after their coverage included misleading delegate counts, slanted analysis, a redefining of progressivism, censorship of a corrupted party committing state crimes against democracy, and a premature declaration of her victory before the primary was over and the convention even held. This is the result of a codependency Clinton and the corporate media seem to have fostered with one another.

## Clinton and the Media

Since she led the 1990s health care debate, Hillary Clinton and the corporate press have cultivated a mutually dependent relationship. Clinton needs positive media coverage to reverse her poor public image. Polling has found that 50 percent of the US population have a negative view of Clinton, and only 22 percent of the population hold a favorable image of the former Secretary of State.[85] Clinton spent over $1 million on online trolls with the purpose of "correcting" the negative statements about her.[86] She tried to manage public perception by maintaining a close relationship with the press. According to CNN's Brian Stelter, in April 2015, before her announcement was official or a single primary speech had been delivered, Clinton met with members of the corporate media to discuss her talking points. The guests included "ABC's George Stephanopoulos, MSNBC's Joe Scarbor-

ough, and a half-dozen reporters from CNN . . ." among dozens of
others from corporate news outlets.[87] Additionally, one of Clinton's
top financial supporters, Haim Saban, bought out the satirical news
website, the *Onion*, and Clinton's daughter, Chelsea, is on the board
of directors for InterActivCorp (IAC), a company that partially owns
*Newsweek*, the *Daily Beast*, and numerous other news outlets.[88]

One clear reason the corporate press maintains a friendly relationship with the Clintons is that the Democratic Party and Comcast have
vested economic interests. For instance, Comcast owns NBC and provides airtime to Democrats that support policies favorable to Comcast, such as trade deals, on MSNBC and shows like the *Tonight Show
Starring Jimmy Fallon* and *Saturday Night Live*. Clinton and Obama
have both been beneficiaries of this slanted coverage.[89] In another
example, Precision Strategies, a firm largely responsible for Clinton's
campaign, sent its cofounder, Stephanie Cutter, on to NBC News'
*Meet the Press* to express her support for Clinton and her opposition
to Sanders, without clearly stating during the broadcast that she is on

Clinton's payroll. Cutter is one of numerous examples of pro-Clinton talking heads consuming corporate media time and space without revealing their economic interests.[90]

Clinton's rapport with the press has resulted in favorable coverage that hides or excuses her indiscretions. For example, *New York Times* columnist Nicholas Kristof wrote, "As we head toward the general election showdown, by all means denounce Hillary Clinton's judgment and policy positions, but let's focus on the real issues. She's not a saint but a politician, and to me, this notion that she's fundamentally dishonest is a bogus narrative."[91] Kristof's contradictory piece took precious time to tell voters that politicians lie, and Clinton lies, but that the voters should trust her. Moreover, Fairness and Accuracy In Reporting (FAIR) found that on the night of the first Democratic presidential primary debate, the corporate press pundits unanimously declared Clinton the winner, but the online polls showed that voters by margins as high as 65 percent believed that Sanders had won the debate.[92] Also, the pro-Clinton slant in the corporate press was on full display when her rival Sanders appeared on MSNBC's *Hardball with Chris Matthews*. The interview quickly became a debate over Sanders's proposals.[93] Clinton has experienced nothing similar. Perhaps Matthews's favoritism stems from his wife, Kathleen Matthews, being a financial supporter for Hillary Clinton.[94] Lastly, CBS used a Harvard poll to show how Clinton had a six-point lead over Sanders, but the actual poll stated something entirely different. Sanders had 41 percent of the vote among millennial voters, and a six-point lead over Clinton.[95] According to the corporate media, accuracy seems to matter about as much as honesty, and they have fostered strained relations with both.

During the election cycle, corporate media inundated Americans with opinion, popularity, and delegate polls, and then used the results to legitimize Clinton's inevitable victory narrative. Polling dominated a majority of election coverage, yet often polls have proven to be incredibly inaccurate and to contain no newsworthy information.[96] Common pitfalls in polling include the types of questions posed, the methods of collection, and the lack of random samples.[97] In addition, a poll's data can quickly be rendered obsolete. For example, the polls in the month leading up to the Michigan primary incorrectly predicted defeat for Sanders.[98] In a rare appearance on CNN, Pacifica's *Democracy Now!* host Amy Goodman criticized the use of polls in corporate media election coverage and recommended diverting those resources into substantial candidate research and investigation.[99] Rather than fulfill Goodman's request, the corporate media continued to use the polls as a form of News Abuse, and to ignore that Clinton's inevitable victory narrative was dependent upon their slanted coverage.[100] According to a study in 2015, Clinton amassed 80 percent of Democratic Party airtime.[101] The correlation between amount of air time and poll numbers suggests that the disparity in coverage favoring Clinton made her party coronation, inevitably, a self-fulfilling corporate media prophecy.[102]

The manipulations, omissions, and outright lies were compounded by the corporate media's convoluted coverage of the already confusing Democratic primary nomination system. To become the Democratic presidential nominee, a candidate must win 2,383 delegates. Delegates are pledged supporters of candidates, while superdelegates are free to vote for any candidate in their party. Superdelegates hold a lot of power, since they can swing the results to nominate the candidate who did not receive the majority of votes during the primary. As if this undemocratic dilemma isn't complex enough, states that hold caucuses rather than primaries revert to a coin-toss when the candidates receive an equal amount of delegates.[103] Corporate media were not entirely clear on how this process worked, and certainly didn't deign to suggest for whom it was beneficial.

As this book goes to the publisher in June 2016, we note that the superdelegate votes are not cast until the Democratic National Convention in late July. However, the corporate media reached out to superdelegates to find out how they would vote before the primary began. The corporate media assessed that there were nearly five hundred superdelegates voting for Clinton before the primary began, which is almost 25 percent of the delegates she needed to declare victory.[104] Even though the superdelegates can change their minds any time before July's convention, the corporate media continued to count the superdelegates in their primary tally between Sanders and Clinton.[105] As a result, the corporate media sent a message that Clinton was so far ahead in delegates that Sanders's campaign was futile.[106] In a classic

display of News Abuse, the corporate press included superdelegates to demonstrate Clinton's lead, but did not include undeclared superdelegates in the amount of delegates remaining. This coverage meant that viewers saw a lead for Clinton that was larger than what actually existed and an amount of remaining delegates for Sanders that was fewer than what actually existed. The corporate media delegate count is an example of the most dishonest and inherently undemocratic News Abuse, as they prematurely, even falsely, declared Clinton the victor in the primary.

Despite lacking enough pledged delegates to clinch the nomination, the corporate press declared Clinton the victor in the Democratic Party primary on June 6, 2016, the night before six states, including delegate-rich California and New Jersey, had their primaries.[107] The announcement came after a two-week period where Sanders was leading in many polls, including in California, and it had been announced that Clinton was under an FBI investigation. The announcement of her perceived nomination, which ran on CNN,

MSNBC, CBS, *New York Times, Huffington Post, Associated Press*, and more, included a graphic that had been created and approved between the corporate media and the Clinton campaign the weekend before the announcement.[108] The announcement was especially odd considering that they based the result on the primary in Puerto Rico that had voted two days earlier, not to mention the corporate press took months to calculate and add in the Washington State delegates which went to Sanders, who had won nearly 70 percent of the vote. Nonetheless, as voters went to the polls on June 7, 2016, the corporate press told them it was useless to vote, Clinton had won, and that citizens should recognize the historic event of the first woman to be a presidential nominee for a major (corporate-backed) party. In fact, the corporate media announced Clinton as the winner of the California primary by nearly 400,000 votes despite the fact that another 2.6 million ballots had still not been counted by mid-June. As of this writing, several California counties have already flipped for Sanders, that is, once all the ballots were counted.[109] What a novel approach it would be, to actually count all the ballots in an election *before* declaring a winner.

## Re-defining Progressivism

In another form of News Abuse, during the campaign cycle, the corporate media slanted their coverage to declare Clinton as a progressive. In the corporate media narrative, the Democrats represent the far left and Republicans the far right. The presidential race on the Democratic side demonstrated that the Clinton Democrats are indistinguishable from the moderate Republicans in the problematic left/right binary metric. However, as part of the coronation of Clinton, the corporate media continued to spin their tales of "the progressive" Clinton while bashing Sanders as "unrealistic."

The term "progressive" generally refers to an individual who seeks to use government to protect equality and individual liberty in the face of small-government traditionalists. Clinton's history and public statements leave no doubt that she is not a progressive. She has repeatedly held anti-progressive views until public sentiment overwhelmingly opposes those views. For example, she opposed same-sex marriage until 2013 and actively promoted fracking until 2016.[110] She also did not fight for progressive causes when she was in a position to make a difference. For example, she refused to speak up against Walmart's opposition to unions while she was on the board of Walmart for six years, and as Secretary of State she was decidedly hawkish on foreign affairs.[111]

Clinton is so emblematic of a non-progressive philosophy that she has garnered support from several prominent neo-conservatives and individuals that utterly oppose the progressive agenda. For example, billionaire Charles Koch, a notorious scourge of leftists as he infuses the political system with cash to further his corporate agenda at the expense of progressive change, has said that Clinton is the best candidate for conservatives.[112] Similarly, the conservative *Wall Street Journal* has referred to Clinton as "The Conservative Hope."[113] In fact, fifty-six business leaders, many of whom are Republicans, have endorsed Clinton for the Presidency.[114]

Clinton went to great lengths to conceal her anti-progressive perspectives. She refused to publicly release her paid speeches to Wall Street bankers and has literally blasted electronic noise so loud at some of her private events that the press cannot hear her speeches to wealthy donors.[115] Furthermore, she is a favorite of Wall Street, which donated $4.2 million for her primary campaign alone.[116] Similarly, Clinton has received millions in donations from Donald Trump, who is possibly "The Least Charitable Billionaire," as well as Jeb Bush's education company.[117] Her anti-progressive agenda is so well known that supporters have taken to claiming that Clinton is a "closet progressive." This means that everything she does and says publicly is not progressive, but voters should believe without evidence that once in office her progressive ideals will come out.[118] One wonders if she also has a great deal to offer the public on some swampland for sale in Florida.

The corporate media falsified Clinton's progressive credentials by ignoring the influence of corporate cash on the Clinton campaign. Missing from the corporate media coverage is any discussion of why the plutocracy donates to the Clinton campaign. Clinton has argued that the money she receives, such as $675,000 from Goldman Sachs, does not influence her policies.[119] She holds up her support of the

2010 Dodd-Frank Wall Street Reform and Consumer Protection Act (usually referred to simply as the "Dodd-Frank Act") as evidence of her anti-Wall Street corruption credentials. However, the act was so influenced by banking and corporate lobbying that it provides regulators with no real power or tools to hold banks accountable. As a result, the "prosecutions of financial and other professionalized crimes in the United States are at their lowest level in 20 years."[120] Clinton also cited her support for the Affordable Care Act as evidence of her progressive qualifications, but did not mention that many of her advisers and contributors worked vigorously to oppose it.[121] She also opposed an actual progressive proposal for healthcare reform, one supported by a majority of doctors and nurses, for single-payer health coverage.

During the 2016 election cycle, the corporate press tirelessly framed Clinton as a progressive and Sanders as unrealistic. In the face of mounting criticism about her lack of progressive credentials, Clinton declared, "I'm a progressive who gets things done."[122] The line was meant to insinuate that even though she is not as progressive as Sanders, or not at all, she wants to accomplish goals. Rather than point out the ridiculous nature of her non sequitur, the corporate press followed her line by attacking Sanders and arguing that Clinton is a progressive. For example, New York Times columnist Paul Krugman commonly used the phrase "very serious people" to pejoratively attack Republicans, but in the 2016 campaign he used it against Sanders.[123] In addition, the Washington Post, in the midst of publishing sixteen negative articles about Sanders in a span of sixteen hours, falsely asserted that Sanders's education plan would cost $3.27 trillion.[124] The Washington Post is owned by the CEO of Amazon, Jeff Bezos, who has (as we noted earlier) recently secured contracts with the CIA worth $600 million; though perhaps it is a coincidence that Bezos's media company would viciously attack a candidate who has publicly criticized the CIA.[125] Other outlets falsified the impact of Sanders's proposed plans. For example, the New York Times claimed that leftist economists have concluded that Sanders's proposals are economically impossible. However, the same economists actually admitted that they have no evidence to determine the impact of some of Sanders's proposals.[126] Rather than point out that Sanders is a real progressive and reveal the false nature of the long-held corporate media narrative that says Democrats are the party of the far left, the corporate press assailed Sanders as unrealistic and Clinton as a progressive, further obfuscating the rightward shift of the Democratic Party establishment.

## Party Corruption

As part of the Clinton coronation, the corporate media did not widely report on or demand accountability for the colluding efforts of the Clinton campaign, Democratic Party, White House, and plutocracy in general to undermine Sanders's bid for the Democratic nomination. Despite the corporate media narrative that Democrats are the liberal or left wing (read: the anti-corporate party), the Democratic National Committee (DNC) is directed by mass corporate funding and influence.[127] For example, one of the biggest companies and highest-ranking corporations among consumer discontent, Comcast, has a special seat at the Democratic Convention.[128] Similarly, many of the superdelegates supporting Clinton are corporate lobbyists who are paid by private prison corporations, private health care insurers opposed to the Affordable Care Act, and even Rupert Murdoch's News Corp.[129] Furthermore, the former Congressman Barney Frank will be overseeing the DNC platform creation while managing a major bank.[130] The Sanders campaign has demonstrated that there is a large contingent of real progressives in the US who recognize and oppose the corporate agenda of the DNC. However, their voices have mostly gone unheard. In fact, the DNC packed convention committees with delegates who created a platform that largely supports the corporate agenda of the DNC. Just a few of the delegates are progressive Sanders supporters despite the fact that Sanders garnered over 40 percent of the primary vote.[131]

While the corporate interests of the Democratic Party and the corporate media aligned, top party officials worked to coronate Clinton. For example, Clinton has held numerous off-the-record meetings with President Obama while running for the presidency.[132] Since they are off the record, the press does not know what inside scoops about policy and intelligence Obama has provided to Clinton but not Sanders. Similarly, Clinton conducted a secret meeting with Senator Elizabeth Warren of Massachusetts, which likely contributed to Warren endorsing her, despite the fact that she has criticized most of what Clinton stands for and has to date been most ideologically aligned with Sanders.[133] Other Democratic Party officials were publicly outspoken in their attacks on Sanders. Former Congressman Barney Frank attempted to discredit Sanders by implying that he is only helping the GOP retake the White House.[134] House Minority leader Nancy Pelosi (D-California) attacked Sanders's "Medicare for All" proposals.[135] Other Democratic Party officials claimed that any voter who opposes Clinton only does so because they are sexist. For example, Madeleine Albright insured her supporters that, "[t]here's a special place in hell for women who don't help each other."[136] One wonders if there is also a special place in hell for Albright, who, as Secretary of State under President Bill Clinton, stated in an interview on CBS's 60 *Minutes* regarding US-backed sanctions that led to the deaths of half a million Iraqi children, ". . . we think the price is worth it."[137] When suggesting women ought support a strong female candidate, perhaps Albright could have been referring to an actually progressive female candidate, one the corporate media has largely ignored, Dr. Jill Stein, the Green Party candidate for president.

Lastly, at Clinton's aid, the corporate press excused the party and state crimes against democracy perpetrated in the Democratic primary. The Democratic Party has used a slew of rules to curtail success by the Sanders campaign, attempting to exclude him from primary ballots in Washington, DC, ignoring party insiders' and Sanders supporters' demands for a recount at the Nevada convention, and suspending Sanders's access to the party database.[138] In New York, some citizens were forbidden to vote in the primary because they did not change their party affiliation to the Democratic Party before the October deadline, a full six months before the primary. However, even for those who had been registered Democrats well in advance, a New York judge found that voters had been purged for unknown reasons.[139] The scale of voter suppression in just Brooklyn, New York is estimated at 126,000 voters.[140] There are also reports that some voting sites had incomplete voter lists and that others purged entire buildings of voters.[141] Nonetheless, Clinton was declared victorious in New York. She also won in Massachusetts by 1 percent of the vote, even though her husband illegally campaigned in a polling area.[142] There were also issues of delegate switching in Iowa and voter suppression in Arizona as voters' party affiliations were mysteriously changed.[143] Lastly, in California, numerous voters registered as Independent reported being told by poll workers that they were not allowed to vote in the Democratic primary.[144] All of these "mysterious" anomalies just happened to favor Clinton.

Despite the overwhelming evidence of party corruption, the corporate press portrayed Sanders supporters as delusional. In fact, Charles P. Pierce, writing for *Esquire*, proclaimed, "If anybody thinks that, somehow, [Sanders] is having the nomination 'stolen' from him, they are idiots. And, no, I don't want to talk about it."[145] Establishment liberals like Krugman of the *New York Times* called Sanders's supporters delusional for continuing the race.[146] The *New York Times* and *US News & World Report* ran headlines that stated "Bernie Sanders Should Drop Out Now" and "Bernie's Dropout is Hillary's Move."[147] However, Krugman and other corporate media shills seem unaware that Sanders supporters believe the system is rigged and want to change it, not respect it and operate within it.

In Nevada, the corporate press lambasted Sanders supporters for the problems with the election, rather than criticizing the Democratic Party. In May 2016, Sanders supporters protested that the Nevada State Democratic Party had ignored attendees and had changed the state convention rules to undermine the vote count, which had favored Sanders.[148] The ruckus caused the convention to close early. Corporate media and the Democratic Party made unsubstantiated and disproven claims that there was violence at the convention, including a chair being thrown.[149] However, no chairs were actually thrown. In fact, the journalist who originally reported the story, Jon Ralston of PBS, was fired for falsifying the story.[150] Ralston is a major contributor to corporate news outlets such as MSNBC and Fox News. Thus, the corporate media and Democratic Party leaders treated the falsified story as fact and then denounced Sanders and his supporters. They cited dubious, anonymous aggressive texts and phone calls that Nevada party leaders received. Sanders appropriately released a statement that condemned those infractions. However, the corporate press and then-DNC chairwoman Debbie Wasserman Schultz chided the apology as insufficient.[151] Comparably, the *Washington Post* spread fear among Democrats about Sanders's supporters by claiming that his letter denouncing violence read like "an open threat to the Democratic establishment."[152] Yet the corporate media coverage ignored that the real culprit behind the Nevada convention's disintegration was the DNC, who hijacked democracy by falsifying election results. Furthermore, the only candidate who had a supporter arrested for violence was actually Clinton. Actor Wendell Pierce, a Clinton supporter, reportedly assaulted a female Sanders supporter.[153]

### Concluding the Coronation

Since 2015, the corporate media has acted to coronate Hillary Clinton as the Democratic presidential nominee. This is a sheer abuse of the power of the media, but not shocking given the overlapping interests of the Clintons, the Democratic Party establishment, and corporate America, which includes many in the corporate press. It is difficult to find an equally egregious example of where the corporate media not only ignored but justified a massive political party suppression of one candidate. As of June 2016, the corporate press pointed to the votes favoring Clinton to argue that the Democratic Party system is not rigged against Sanders. However, this in itself is a piece of propaganda.[154] It ignores that a citizen's vote is as valuable as the information behind it. With so many voters being misinformed by a corporate media system which denounced Sanders while it coronated Clinton, it is not a surprise that Clinton managed to accumulate more votes. The only surprise is that these propagandists can call themselves journalists.

## CONCLUSION

The 2016 election cycle demonstrated that the corporate media peddling of Junk Food News and News Abuse has continued into the digital age. In fact, as this chapter goes to publication, a Harvard study by Thomas Patterson, Harvard's Bradlee Professor of Government and the Press, in conjunction with the Shorenstein Center on Media, Politics and Public Policy, drew many of the same conclusions as

Project Censored regarding unequal and biased coverage during the 2016 primary season.[155] However, the palpable voter anger illustrated an acute awareness about the negative impact of corporate media on society. While the millennial generation appears to have some grasp on the problematic nature of the US democratic system, it will take years and multiple election cycles to determine whether or not the millennials will begin the steps to repair that system.

Carl Jensen and his successors created a service-learning program in Project Censored that has left an indelible mark on generations of educators, students, activists, and citizens. It has taught them that these abuses not only exist, but also that they have the power, tools, and resources to stop and/or undermine them. This seems to ring true in contemporary youth-dominated movements such as Democracy Spring, Black Lives Matter, LGBTQI Rights, Fight for $15, Occupy, Youth Climate Movement, DREAMers, and more. Project Censored, with its many supporters and partners, has continued Jensen's legacy of building awareness and cultivating civil action for equity in society by aligning itself with the youth and contemporary social justice and public education movements. Among the best ways the Project believes it is possible to promote democracy in action is through critical media literacy education, perhaps the strongest means for fighting against censorship and propaganda in their numerous guises while supporting a truly independent and free press.

---

NOLAN HIGDON is a professor of English and Latin American and US history in the San Francisco Bay Area. His academic work focuses on nationalism, propaganda, and critical media literacy education. He sits on the board of the Media Freedom Foundation and is the originating coordinator for the Global Critical Media Literacy Project. He has contributed chapters to numerous Project Censored volumes as well as Stephen Lendman's *Ukraine: How the US Drive for Hegemony Risks World War III* (2014). He has published articles on media and propaganda including "Disinfo Wars: Alex Jones' War on Your Mind" (2013), "Millennial Media Revolution" (2014), and "Justice For Sale" (2015). He has been a guest on national radio and television programs and is a frequent guest cohost for The Project Censored Radio Show.

MICKEY HUFF is director of Project Censored and professor of Social Science and History at Diablo Valley College, where he cochairs the History Department. His more complete bio is at the end of this volume.

# Notes

1   "The Invisible Hand of the Media," American Patriot Friends Network, no date, http://www.apfn.org/THEWINDS/arc_features/media/disinfo9-97.html.

2   Nick Visser, "Hardly Anyone Trusts the Media Anymore," *Huffington Post*, April 18, 2016, accessed May 16, 2016, www.huffingtonpost.com/entry/trust-in-media_us_57148543e4b06f35cb6fec58.

3   Damon Beres, "You Won't Believe America's Most Trusted Source for Election News," *Huffington Post*, February 4, 2016, accessed May 16, 2016, www.huffingtonpost.com/entry/pew-election-2016-study_us_56b36741e4b08069c7a6322b?utm_hp_ref=tw.

4   Sean McElwee, "The NYT's 1 Percent Problem: Media Bias Goes Much Deeper than Fox News vs MSNBC," *Salon*, June 6, 2015, accessed May 16, 2016, www.salon.com/2015/06/06/yes_the_media_is_biased_but_its_not_just_about_democrats_and_republicans/.

5   Ibid.

6   Robby Soave, "Millennials More Likely to Support Censorship of Offensive Speech Than Older Americans," *Hit and Run Blog*, November 20, 2015, accessed May 16, 2016, https://reason.com/blog/2015/11/20/millennials-more-likely-to-support-censo.

7   Bethania Palma Markus, "SC Student Arrested for Recording School Cop's Violent Assault on Classmate Sitting in Her Desk," *Raw Story*, October 27, 2015, accessed May 16, 2016, www.rawstory.com/2015/10/sc-student-arrested-for-recording-school-cops-violent-assault-on-classmate-sitting-in-her-desk/.

8   Ollie Gillman, "Students Protest IN SUPPORT of Cop Who Dragged Schoolgirl, 16, from Her Desk and Threw Her Across Classroom," *Daily Mail*, October 31, 2015, accessed May 16, 2016, www.dailymail.co.uk/news/article-3298748/Students-protest-fired-cop-dragged-schoolgirl-16-desk-threw-classroom-job-back.html.

9   Project Censored has covered these topics in the last 15 books it has published; see also Kevin Gosztola, "'60 Minutes' Pushes National Security Propaganda to Cast Snowden, Manning as Traitors," Shadow Proof, November 9, 2015, accessed May 16, 2016, https://shadowproof.com/2015/11/09/60-minutes-pushes-national-security-propaganda-to-cast-snowden-manning-as-traitors/.

10  Julian Hattem, "CIA Watchdog 'Accidentally Destroyed' Copy of 'Torture Report,'" Hill, May 16, 2016, accessed June 9, 2016, thehill.com/policy/national-security/280002-cia-watchdog-accidentally-destroyed-only-copy-of-torture-report.

11  M. David and Jackson Marciana, "CBS Reporter Arrested at Trump Rally Told 'Go Back to Iraq' Before Cops Slammed Him to the Ground," *Counter Current News*, March 13, 2016, accessed May 16, 2016, http://countercurrentnews.com/2016/03/cops-arrested-reporter-at-a-trump-rally/.

12  Jeet Heer, "When Will National Review Apologize for Cooperating with Murderous Dictator Augusto Pinochet?" *New Republic*, October 9, 2015, accessed May 16, 2016, https://newrepublic.com/article/123073/national-review-should-apologize-cooperating-augusto-pinochet.

13  Ian Simpson, "Fox News Guest Analyst Arrested on Charges of Lying about Working for CIA," *Business Insider*, October 15, 2015, accessed May 16, 2016, www.businessinsider.com/fox-news-guest-analyst-arrested-for-lying-about-working-for-cia-2015-10.

14  Gabriel Arana, "Brian Williams Returns to TV—But He's Not Talking about Himself," *Huffington Post*, September 22, 2015, accessed May 16, 2016, www.huffingtonpost.com/entry/brian-williams-returns_us_5601bdcce4b0fde8b0d03a9.

15  Charlotte Alfred, "Why Turkey Bans News about Terror Bombings," *Huffington Post*, January, 13, 2016, accessed May 16, 2016, www.huffingtonpost.com/entry/turkey-media-blackout-istanbul-bombing_us_56957080e4b086bc1cd5a364.

Eline Gordts, "Putin's Press: How Russia's President Controls the News," *WorldPost*, October 24, 2015, accessed May 16, 2016, www.huffingtonpost.com/entry/vladimir-putin-russia-news-media_us_56215944e4b0bce34700b1df.

16    Glenn Greenwald, "CNN Punished Its Own Journalist for Fulfilling a Core Duty of Journalism," *Common Dreams*, November 20, 2015, accessed May 16, 2016, www.commondreams.org/views/2015/11/20/cnn-punished-its-own-journalist-fulfilling-core-duty-journalism.

17    Dominique Mosbergen, "Virginia Lawmakers Ban Reporters from State Senate Floor, Prompting Transparency Concerns," *Huffington Post*, January 14, 2016, www.huffingtonpost.com/entry/reporters-virginia-state-senate_us_56974d1ae4b0b4eb759d3e6a?utm_hp_ref=tw.

18    Michael McLaughlin, "Amazon Yanks Serial Killer's Book after Outrage," *Huffington Post*, February 24, 2016, accessed May 16, 2016, www.huffingtonpost.com/entry/robert-pickton-amazon_us_56ce316be4b0871f60ea067d?utm_hp_ref=tw.

      Tom Boggioni, "Filmmakers Cry 'Censorship' after Robert DeNiro Boots Anti-Vaxx Movie from Film Festival," *Raw Story*, March 27, 2016, accessed May 16, 2016, https://www.rawstory.com/2016/03/filmmakers-cry-censorship-after-robert-deniro-boots-anti-vaxx-movie-from-film-festival/.

      Sam Stanton and Diana Lambert, "UC Davis Spent Thousands to Scrub Pepper-Spray References from Internet," *Sacramento Bee*, April 13, 2016, accessed May 16, 2016, http://www.sacbee.com/news/local/article71659992.html.

19    Michaela Whitton, "Wikileaks Drops Hillary Email Bomb That Could End Her Campaign but FB Censored It," *Anti-Media*, March 21, 2016, accessed May 16, 2016, http://theantimedia.org/wikileaks-drops-hillary-email-bomb-that-could-end-her-campaign-but-fb-censored-it/.

20    Julia Greenberg, "Facebook and Twitter Really are Where People Get Their News," *Wired*, July 14, 2015, accessed May 16, 2016, www.wired.com/2015/07/facebook-twitter-really-people-get-news/.

21    Greta Van Susteren, "Why the Media Got It Wrong about Trump and Sanders Phenomena," *Huffington Post*, May 6, 2016, accessed May 16, 2016, www.huffingtonpost.com/greta-van-susteren/why-the-media-got-it-wrong-about-trump-and-sanders-phenomena_b_9856390.html.

22    Michael Calderone, "Andrew Sullivan Returning to Cover Trump-Fueled 2016 Race out of 'Civic Duty,'" *Huffington Post*, April 1, 2016, accessed May 16, 2016, http://www.huffingtonpost.com/2016/04/01/andrew-sullivan-returns-donald-trump_n_9595408.html.

23    Doina Chiacu with reporting by Jeff Mason and Susan Heavey, "Obama Urges Scrutiny of Donald Trump's Record: 'This is Not Entertainment,'" *Huffington Post*, May 6, 2016, accessed May 16, 2016, http://www.huffingtonpost.com/entry/obama-donald-trump_us_572cc8e6e4b096e9f0912765.

24    Andy Greenberg, "How Reporters Pulled Off the Panama Papers, the Biggest Leak in Whistleblower History," *Wired*, April 4, 2016, accessed May 16, 2016, https://www.wired.com/2016/04/reporters-pulled-off-panama-papers-biggest-leak-whistleblower-history/.

25    David Edwards, "'Who Needs Algebra?': Fox News Panel Debates Whether Math Should be Required in School," *Raw Story*, March 30, 2016, accessed May 16, 2016, www.rawstory.com/2016/03/who-needs-algebra-fox-news-panel-debates-whether-math-should-be-required-in-school/.

      Michael Calderone, "NBC Reporter Touts Network's Ethics before Broadcasting Live from inside San Bernardino Suspects' Apartment," *Huffington Post*, December 4, 2015, accessed May 16, 2016, www.huffingtonpost.com/entry/nbc-live-tv-images-san-bernardino-shooting-suspects_566d3bce4b072e9d1c5f047.

      "'You're a Hack': Fox's Bill O'Reilly and George Will Spar over Killing Reagan," *Media Matters for America*, November 6, 2015, accessed May 16, 2016, video and transcript, http://mediamatters.org/video/2015/11/06/youre-a-hack-foxs-bill-oreilly-and-george-will/206695.

26    Nick Wing and Julie Craven, "Cops are Still Killing People, but the Nation Has Stopped Paying Attention," *Huffington Post*, April 18, 2016, accessed May 16, 2016, http://www.huffingtonpost.com/2016/04/17/police-shootings-2016_n_9721758.html.

27    "Media Blackout Continues as 700+ Arrests Reported in Front of the U.S. Capitol," *MRK Report*, April 14, 2016, accessed May 16, 2016, https://mrkreport.com/2016/04/14/media-blackout-continues-as-700-arrests-reported-in-front-of-the-u-s-capitol/.

28  Gabriel Arana, "Trump is a 'Ratings Machine.' Does That Justify the Media's Binge?" *Huffington Post*, August 21, 2015, accessed May 16, 2016, http://www.huffingtonpost.com/entry/trump-phenomenon_55d6fea2e4b00d8137edde58?kvcommref=mostpopular.

      Gabriel Arana, "Blame the Media for Donald Trump's Rise in the Polls," *Huffington Post*, July 22, 2015, accessed May 16, 2016, www.huffingtonpost.com/entry/blame-the-media-for-donald-trumps-rise-in-the-polls_us_55afd21ee4b08f57d5d34cfo.

29  Nick Visser, "CBS Chief Les Moonves Says Trump's 'Damn Good' for Business," *Huffington Post*, March 1, 2016, accessed May 16, 2016, www.huffingtonpost.com/entry/les-moonves-donald-trump_us_56d52ce8e4b03260bf780275.

30  Marina Fang, "Dan Rather Worries That The Media Has Become 'A Business Partner Of Donald Trump'" *Huffington Post*, June 26, 2016, accessed July 9, 2016, www.huffingtonpost.com/entry/dan-rather-donald-trump_us_576ff802e4b017b379f63ec8?section=

31  Gabriel Arana, "NBC Nabs Trump Interview, and MSNBC Plays It on Seemingly Infinite Loop," *Huffington Post*, August 17, 2015, accessed May 16, 2016, http://www.huffingtonpost.com/entry/nbc-nabs-trump-interview-plays-it-on-seemingly-infinite-loop_us_55d23bd0e4b0ab468d9e09b0.

32  Dylan Bryers, "Donald Trump Has Had Too Much Media Coverage, 75% of Americans Say," CNNMoney, March 31, 2016, accessed April 19, 2016, http://money.cnn.com/2016/03/31/media/trump-media-pew-survey.

33  Zach Cartwright, "Amy Goodman Blasts CNN for Airing Trump's Empty Stage Instead of Sanders' Speech," U.S. Uncut, March 20, 2016, http://usuncut.com/politics/amy-goodman-calls-media-blacking-bernies-speech/.

34  Michael Calderone, "Donald Trump Has Received Nearly $2 Billion in Free Media Attention," *Huffington Post*, March 15, 2016, http://www.huffingtonpost.com/entry/donald-trump-2-billion-free-media_us_56e83410e4b065e2e3d75935.

35  Michael Calderone, "Donald Trump Shouldn't Have Bothered Buying Airtime. Cable News Ran His Ad 60 Times for Free," *Huffington Post*, January 5, 2016, http://www.huffingtonpost.com/entry/donald-trump-cable-news-airtime_us_568c0d96e4b014efe0dbe5a4.

36  James Warren, "Media to Blame for the Rise of Trump? Two Political Scientists Think So," *Poynter*, July 21, 2015, accessed May 16, 2016, www.poynter.org/2015/media-to-blame-for-the-rise-of-trump-two-political-scientists-think-so/359303/.

37  Will Bunch, "More Americans Support Bernie Than The Donald—but He Gets 1/23 the TV Coverage," *Philadelphia Daily News*, December 10, 2015, http://www.philly.com/philly/blogs/attytood/More-Americans-support-Bernie-than-The-Donald----but-he-gets-123-the-TV-coverage.html.

38  Eric Boehlert, "ABC World News Tonight Has Devoted Less Than One Minute to Bernie Sanders' Campaign This Year," Media Matters for America, December 11, 2015, http://mediamatters.org/blog/2015/12/11/abc-world-news-tonight-has-devoted-less-than-on/207428#disqus_thread.

39  Jon Queally, "Blackout Tuesday: The Bernie Sanders Speech Corporate Media Chose Not to Air," Common Dreams, March 16, 2016, http://www.commondreams.org/news/2016/03/16/blackout-tuesday-bernie-sanders-speech-corporate-media-chose-not-air.

    Zach Cartwright, "Amy Goodman Blasts CNN."

40  Jon Queally, "Blackout Tuesday."

41  Matthew Phelan, "Amazon is the Scariest Part of the CIA's New Amazon Cloud Storage," *Gawker*, July 21, 2014, http://blackbag.gawker.com/amazon-is-the-scariest-part-of-the-cias-new-amazon-clo-1605847721.

42  Adam Johnson, "Washington Post Ran 16 Negative Stories on Bernie Sanders in 16 Hours," Fairness and Accuracy In Reporting, March 8, 2016, http://fair.org/home/washington-post-ran-16-negative-stories-on-bernie-sanders-in-16-hours/

    Dylan Sevett, "Here's Washington Post's Coverage of Bernie Sanders Since the Debate. Do You Spot an Agenda?" U.S. Uncut, March 8, 2016, https://usuncut.com/politics/washington-post-bias-against-bernie-sanders/.

43   Jenna Johnson, "Donald Trump Creates a New Nickname for Marco Rubio: 'Lightweight Choker,'" *Washington Post*, November 10, 2015, accessed May 16, 2016, https://www.washingtonpost.com/news/post-politics/wp/2015/11/10/donald-trump-creates-a-new-nickname-for-marco-rubio-lightweight-choker/.

44   Nick Corasaniti, "Fox News Slams Donald Trump for 'Sick Obsession' with Megyn Kelly," *New York Times*, March 18, 2016, accessed May 16, 2016, http://www.nytimes.com/politics/first-draft/2016/03/18/fox-news-slams-donald-trump-for-sick-obsession-with-megyn-kelly/.

45   Evelyn Rupert, "Trump Offers Belated Defense of Megyn Kelly 'Blood' Comment," Hill, May 6, 2016, accessed May 16, 2016, thehill.com/blogs/blog-briefing-room/news/279097-trump-offers-belated-defense-of-megyn-kelly-blood-comment.

46   Megyn Kelly, "R & R for Megyn Kelly," *The Kelly File*, Fox, video and transcript, filmed August 12, 2015, published August 13, 2015, accessed May 16, 2016, http://nation.foxnews.com/2015/08/13/r-r-megyn-kelly.

47   Sarah Lazare, "As of Today, Humanity Has Exhausted Its 2015 Supply of Natural Resources," Common Dreams, August 13, 2015, accessed May 16, 2016, http://www.commondreams.org/news/2015/08/13/today-humanity-has-exhausted-its-2015-supply-natural-resources.

48   Nick Corasaniti, "Fox News Slams Donald Trump."
     Erik Wemple, "Proof Positive of Donald Trump's Deranged Obsession with Megyn Kelly," *Washington Post*, March 21, 2016, accessed May 16, 2016, https://www.washingtonpost.com/blogs/erik-wemple/wp/2016/03/21/proof-positive-of-donald-trumps-deranged-obsession-with-megyn-kelly/.

49   Nick Corasaniti, "Fox News Slams Donald Trump."

50   Zoë Schlanger, "Choking to Death in Detroit: Flint Isn't Michigan's Only Disaster," *Newsweek*, March 30, 2016, http://www.newsweek.com/2016/04/08/michigan-air-pollution-poison-southwest-detroit-441914.html.

51   Paul Waldman, "Ted Cruz and Donald Trump are Fighting over Their Wives. This was Inevitable.," *Washington Post*, March 25, 2016, accessed April 17, 2016, https://www.washingtonpost.com/blogs/plum-line/wp/2016/03/25/ted-cruz-and-donald-trump-are-fighting-over-their-wives-this-was-inevitable/.

52   Mika Brzezinski, "Mika to Cruz, Trump: Move On from Wife Feud," video clip from *Morning Joe*, MSNBC, March 24, 2016, accessed May 16, 2016, www.msnbc.com/morning-joe/watch/mika-to-cruz-trump-move-on-from-wife-feud-651367491745.
     "Cruz Calls Trump a 'Sniveling Coward' over Wife Tweet," *Fox News*, March 24, 2016, www.foxnews.com/politics/2016/03/24/cruz-calls-trump-sniveling-coward-over-wife-tweet.html.
     Patrick Healy, "Donald Trump and Ted Cruz Continue Clash over Spouses," *New York Times*, March 27, 2016, accessed May 16, 2016, www.nytimes.com/politics/first-draft/2016/03/27/donald-trump-and-ted-cruz-continue-clash-over-spouses/.
     Theodore Schleifer and Julia Manchester, "Donald Trump Makes Wild Threat to 'Spill the Beans' on Ted Cruz's Wife," CNN, March 24, 2016, www.cnn.com/2016/03/22/politics/ted-cruz-melania-trump-twitter-donald-trump-heidi.

53   Tariq Ali, "Joker Rules: The Crackdown on Press Freedom in Turkey," *CounterPunch*, March 25, 2016, accessed May 16, 2016, http://www.counterpunch.org/2016/03/25/joker-rules-the-crackdown-on-press-freedom-in-turkey/.

54   Gregory Krieg, "Donald Trump Defends Size of His Penis," CNN, March 4, 2016, accessed May 16, 2016, http://www.cnn.com/2016/03/03/politics/donald-trump-small-hands-marco-rubio/.

55   Emily Shapiro, "The History behind the Donald Trump 'Small Hands' Insult," *ABC News*, March 4, 2016, accessed May 16, 2016, http://abcnews.go.com/Politics/history-donald-trump-small-hands-insult/story?id=37395515.
     Jen Christensen, "Trump and the Small Hands Equals Small Manhood Myth, or Reality?" CNN, March 8, 2016, accessed May 16, 2016, http://www.cnn.com/2016/03/08/health/trump-small-hands-penis/.

F. Brinley Bruton, "Donald Trump Makes His Penis a Campaign Issue During Debate," *NBC News*, March 4, 2016, accessed May 16, 2016, http://www.nbcnews.com/politics/2016-election/donald-trump-makes-his-penis-campaign-issue-during-debate-n531666.

"Social Media Explodes after Donald Trump Talks about His Penis Size During GOP Debate," CBS, March 3, 2016, accessed May 16, 2016, http://newyork.cbslocal.com/2016/03/03/donald-trump-penis-size/.

Gregory Krieg, "Donald Trump Defends Size of His Penis," CNN, March 4, 2016, accessed May 16, 2016, http://www.cnn.com/2016/03/03/politics/donald-trump-small-hands-marco-rubio/.

Philip Rucker and Robert Costa, "Donald Trump: 'My Hands are Normal Hands,'" *Washington Post*, March 21, 2016, accessed May 16, 2016, https://www.washingtonpost.com/news/post-politics/wp/2016/03/21/donald-trump-my-hands-are-normal-hands/.

"Donald Trump Discusses Penis Size at GOP Debate (Watch)," *Variety*, March 3, 2016, accessed May 16, 2016, http://variety.com/2016/biz/news/donald-trump-penis-gop-debate-rubio-video-1201722389.

Daniel White, "Watch Trump Talk about His Private Parts at the Debate," *Time*, March 3, 2016, accessed May 16, 2016, http://time.com/4247366/republican-debate-donald-trump-small-hands-penis/.

56   Medea Benjamin and Rebecca Green, "Hillary Clinton's State Department Armed Saudi Arabia to the Teeth," *Foreign Policy in Focus*, March 8, 2016, http://fpif.org/hillary-clintons-state-department-armed-saudi-arabia-teeth/.

57   George Greenwood, "Five Things That Saudi Arabian Women Still Cannot Do," *Independent*, December 15, 2015, accessed May 16, 2016, http://www.independent.co.uk/news/world/middle-east/five-things-that-saudi-arabian-women-still-cannot-do-a6765666.html.

58   Deirdre Fulton, "Voting Problems Plague High-Stakes Primary Day in New York," Common Dreams, April 19, 2016, accessed May 16, 2016, www.commondreams.org/news/2016/04/19/voting-problems-plague-high-stakes-primary-day-new-york.

59   Jason Linkins, "Media Goes Gaga after Trump Takes a Night Off from Jackassery," *Huffington Post*, April 20, 2016, www.huffingtonpost.com/entry/donald-trump-presidential_us_5717b784e4b0c9244a7a8c94.

60   Dana Liebelson, Jennifer Bendery, and Sam Stein, "Donald Trump Made Up Stuff 71 Times in an Hour," *Huffington Post*, March 30, 2016, accessed May 16, 2016, www.huffingtonpost.com/entry/donald-trump-fact-check_us_56fc375fe4b0daf53aee9175.

61   David Folkenflik, "NPR Clarifies Cokie Roberts' Role after Anti-Trump Column," *NPR Morning Edition*, March 14, 2016, www.npr.org/sections/thetwo-way/2016/03/14/470340825/npr-clarifies-cokie-roberts-role-after-anti-trump-column.

62   Tessa Stuart, "Is Ted Cruz the Zodiac Killer? Maybe, Say 38 Percent of Florida Voters," *Rolling Stone*, February 26, 2016, accessed May 16, 2016, http://www.rollingstone.com/politics/news/is-ted-cruz-the-zodiac-killer-maybe-say-38-percent-of-florida-voters-20160226#ixzz4802OdlnR.

63   Paige Lavender, "Heidi Cruz Responds to Accusation Her Husband is the Zodiac Killer," *Huffington Post*, May 2, 2016, accessed May 16, 2016, www.huffingtonpost.com/entry/heidi-cruz-zodiac-killer_us_57279a39e4b0b49df6abe85b.

64   Anna Merod, "Ted Cruz Jokes about Hitting Trump with a Car on 'Jimmy Kimmel,'" MSNBC, March 31, 2016, accessed May 16, 2016, www.msnbc.com/msnbc/ted-cruz-jokes-about-hitting-trump-car-jimmy-kimmel.

65   Sophia Rosenbaum, "'Female Ted Cruz' is Making a Porno," *New York Post*, April 24, 2016, nypost.com/2016/04/24/female-ted-cruz-is-making-a-porno/.

66   David Moye, "Female Ted Cruz Lookalike Agrees to Do Porn for $10,000," *Huffington Post*, April 23, 2016, accessed May 16, 2016, www.huffingtonpost.com/entry/ted-cruz-lookalike-porn_us_571aa703e4b0d4d3f7237467.

67 Lauren Dake, "Call Him Birdie Sanders: Bird Interrupts Oregon Rally to Thunderous Applause," *The Guardian*, March 25, 2016, http://www.theguardian.com/us-news/2016/mar/25/bernie-sanders-rally-bird-portland-oregon-portlandia.

68 Elyse Wanshel, "A Bird Lands on Bernie Sanders' Podium, and a Disney Princess Meme Takes Flight," *Huffington Post*, March 28, 2016, http://www.huffingtonpost.com/entry/bernie-sanders-bird-meme-disney-princess-birdiesanders_us_56f944dbe4b0143a9b48a229.
  Lauren Dake, "Call Him Birdie Sanders."

69 Daniella Diaz, "Watch a Bird Make an Uninvited Appearance at Sanders Rally," CNN, March 26, 2016, http://www.cnn.com/2016/03/25/politics/bernie-sanders-bird-portland-oregon-symbolism/.

70 Aaron Blake, "Stephen Colbert Knows Why That Bird REALLY Landed on Bernie Sanders's Lectern," *Washington Post*, March 29, 2016, https://www.washingtonpost.com/news/the-fix/wp/2016/03/29/stephen-colbert-gets-to-the-bottom-of-why-that-bird-really-landed-on-bernie-sanderss-podium/.
  Mary Bowerman, "Crowd Goes Wild after Small Bird Lands on Bernie Sanders' Podium," *USA Today*, March 26, 2016, http://www.usatoday.com/story/news/nation-now/2016/03/26/watch-small-bird-lands-bernie-sanders-podium/82289730/.
  Charles Bramesco, "Small Bird Lands on Bernie Sanders' Lectern Mid-Speech, Brings Crowd to Their Feet," *Vanity Fair*, March 26, 2016, accessed April 21, 2016, http://www.vanityfair.com/news/2016/03/birdie-sanders.
  Daniella Diaz, "Watch a Bird Make an Uninvited Appearance."
  Rachel Dicker, "Why is the Internet Still Obsessed with #BirdieSanders?" *US News & World Report*, March 28, 2016, accessed April 21, 2016, http://www.usnews.com/news/articles/2016-03-28/birdiesanders-hashtag-trends-after-bird-lands-on-bernie-sanders-podium-at-a-rally.
  Dan Mennella, "Bernie Sanders' Perfect Response When a Bird Crashed His Speech," *New York Post*, March 25, 2016, accessed April 21, 2016, http://nypost.com/2016/03/25/bernie-sanders-perfect-response-when-a-bird-crashed-his-speech/.
  David Z. Morris, "Sanders, and a Bird, Become Twitter Gold," *Fortune*, March 27, 2016, accessed April 21, 2016, http://fortune.com/2016/03/27/bernie-bird-twitter-gold/.
  Elyse Wanshel, "A Bird Lands on Bernie Sanders' Podium."

71 Robert Mackey, "Israeli Rights Group Releases Video of Army Medic Executing Wounded Palestinian Suspect," *Intercept*, March 24, 2016, accessed April 21, 2016, https://theintercept.com/2016/03/24/israeli-rights-group-releases-video-soldier-executing-wounded-palestinian-suspect/.

72 "Israel/Palestine: Events of 2015," *Human Rights Watch*, no date, accessed April 21, 2016, https://www.hrw.org/world-report/2016/country-chapters/israel/palestine.

73 Daniel Marans, "Sanders Calls Out MSNBC's Corporate Ownership—In Interview on MSNBC," *Huffington Post*, May 7, 2016, http://www.huffingtonpost.com/2016/05/07/bernie-sanders-asks-who-owns-msnbc_n_9862836.html.

74 Justin Salhani, "Camerawoman Sues the Syrian Refugee She Tripped, and Facebook," Think Progress, October 23, 2015, http://thinkprogress.org/world/2015/10/23/3715394/camerawoman-who-tripped-syrian-refugee-now-plans-to-sue-him/.

75 Lee Fang, "Cable News Edits Out Rousing Sanders Attack on Vapid Media Coverage," *Intercept*, October 14 2015, https://theintercept.com/2015/10/14/cable-news-edits-out-rousing-sanders-attack-on-vapid-media-coverage/.

76 Clayton Youngman, "Marco Rubio Said Wrongly That Welders Make More Money Than Philosophers," Politifact, November 11, 2015, www.politifact.com/truth-o-meter/statements/2015/nov/11/marco-rubio/marco-rubio-welders-more-money-philosophers/.
  Jan Schwartz, "Trump: Mexico Not Sending Us Their Best; Criminals, Drug Dealers and Rapists are Crossing Border," RealClearPolitics, June 16, 2015, www.realclearpolitics.com/video/2015/06/16/trump_mexico_not_sending_us_their_best_criminals_drug_dealers_and_rapists_are_crossing_border.html.

"Donald Trump Dominates List of 2015's Biggest Lies," *FactCheck.org*, republished by *Huffington Post*, December 21, 2015, www.huffingtonpost.com/entry/2015-biggest-lies_us_56787039e4b014efe0d66a79.

Jill Colvin, "Trump Displays Steak, Water, Wine to Defend Business Record," *Salon*, March 9, 2016, www.salon.com/2016/03/09/trump_displays_steak_water_wine_to_defend_business_record/.

77  Jon Schwarz, "Top GOP Pollster: Young Americans are Terrifyingly Liberal," *Intercept*, February 24, 2016, https://theintercept.com/2016/02/24/top-gop-pollster-young-americans-are-terrifyingly-liberal/.

78  Aaron Blake, "74-Year-Old Bernie Sanders's Remarkable Dominance among Young Voters, in 1 Chart," *Washington Post*, March 17, 2016, https://www.washingtonpost.com/news/the-fix/wp/2016/03/17/74-year-old-bernie-sanderss-amazing-dominance-among-young-voters-in-1-chart/.

79  Scott Eric Kaufman, "Joe Scarborough: Why Even Vote for Bernie Sanders When the Race is Already 'Rigged' for Hillary Clinton?" *Salon*, April 11, 2016, www.salon.com/2016/04/11/joe_scarborough_why_even_vote_for_bernie_sanders_when_the_race_is_already_rigged_for_hillary_clinton/.

80  Tom Cahill, "It's Official—the First Democratic Convention Just Abolished Superdelegates," U.S. Uncut, May 7, 2016, usuncut.com/politics/maine-democratic-party-just-got-rid-superdelegate-system/.

81  Michael McAuliff, "Bill Clinton Blames Millennials for Anger, Economy, Congress," *Huffington Post*, April 21, 2016, www.huffingtonpost.com/entry/bill-clinton-blames-millennials_us_57191d13e4b0d0042da88c9f.

82  Deirdre Fulton, "Pro-Clinton Super PAC Caught Astroturfing on Social Media, Op-Ed Pages," Common Dreams, May 6, 2016, http://www.commondreams.org/news/2016/05/06/pro-clinton-super-pac-caught-astroturfing-social-media-op-ed-pages.

83  Ben Collins, "Hillary PAC Spends $1 Million to 'Correct' Commenters on Reddit and Facebook," *Daily Beast*, April 21, 2016, www.thedailybeast.com/articles/2016/04/21/hillary-pac-spends-1-million-to-correct-commenters-on-reddit-and-facebook.html.

84  "Bump for Trump as Carson Fades in Republican Race, Quinnipiac University National Poll Finds; Clinton, Sanders Surge in Matchups with GOP Leaders," Quinnipiac University National Poll, December 2, 2015, accessed May 16, 2016, https://www.qu.edu/news-and-events/quinnipiac-university-poll/national/release-detail?ReleaseID=2307.

Ryan Rifai, "Polls: Sanders Has More Potential to Beat Trump," Al Jazeera, May 14, 2016, accessed May 16, 2016, www.aljazeera.com/indepth/features/2016/05/polls-sanders-potential-beat-trump-160514170035436.html.

85  Andrea Germanos, "Wow. Americans Really, Really Don't Like Trump or Clinton; New Gallup poll shows the two as among the worst rated presidential candidates," Common Dreams, July 01, 2016, accessed July 9, 2016, www.commondreams.org/news/2016/07/01/wow-americans-really-really-dont-trump-or-clinton

Lisa Lerer and Emily Swanson, "Hillary Clinton Has a Likability Problem," *US News & World Report*, April 8, 2016, accessed May 16, 2016, http://www.usnews.com/news/politics/articles/2016-04-08/ap-gfk-poll-many-dislike-clinton-but-more-disdain-trump.

86  Tom Cahill, "BUSTED: Pro-Clinton Super PAC Caught Spending $1 Million on Social Media Trolls," U.S. Uncut, April 21, 2016, accessed May 11, 2016, http://usuncut.com/politics/clinton-super-pac-busted/.

87  Warner Todd Huston, "Hillary Has Secret Meeting with Media Stars to Hand Deliver Approved Talking Points," *Right Wing News*, April 13, 2015, accessed May 11, 2016, rightwingnews.com/democrats/hillary-has-secret-meeting-with-media-stars-to-hand-deliver-approved-talking-points/.

Staff, "Hillary Clinton Campaign Wines & Dines Media at Off-Record Dinners," *Breitbart*, April 12, 2015, accessed May 11, 2016, www.breitbart.com/big-journalism/2015/04/12/hillary-clinton-campaign-wines-dines-media-at-off-record-dinners/.

88   Claire Bernish, "Hillary's Top Donor Just Bought the Onion—Started Publishing Propaganda Immediately," Free Thought Project, February 18, 2016, accessed May 11, 2016, http://thefreethoughtproject.com/hillarys-top-donor-buys-onion-starts-publishing-propaganda-immediately/#hJoGJLEF4VUyR3Ft.01.
      Julianne Pepitone, "Chelsea Clinton joins IAC board," CNN, September 26, 2011, accessed July 9, 2016, money.cnn.com/2011/09/26/technology/chelsea_clinton_IAC/.

89   Adam Johnson, "Comcast-Funded Website Plugs Comcast-Owned TV Show Promoting Comcast-Backed Trade Pact," Fairness and Accuracy In Reporting, June 11, 2016, accessed June 16, 2016, http://fair.org/home/comcast-funded-website-plugs-comcast-owned-tv-show-promoting-comcast-backed-trade-pact/.

90   Lee Fang, interview by Amy Goodman, "Lee Fang: TV Pundits Praise Hillary Clinton on Air, Fail to Disclose Financial Ties to Her Campaign," *Democracy Now!*, transcript, February 26, 2016, accessed April 20, 2016, http://m.democracynow.org/stories/15991.

91   Robert Parry, "Is Hillary Clinton 'Honest'? (A Response to Kristof)," Common Dreams, April 24, 2016, accessed May 11, 2016, www.commondreams.org/views/2016/04/24/hillary-clinton-honest-response-kristof.

92   Gunar Olsen, "Pundits Thought Clinton Beat Sanders—but Did Viewers?" Fairness and Accuracy In Reporting, October 14, 2015, accessed May 11, 2016, http://fair.org/home/pundits-thought-clinton-beat-sanders-but-did-viewers/.

93   Bernie Sanders, interview by Chris Matthews, "Sanders: 'I'm Not an Inside-the-Beltway Guy,'" video clip from *Hardball with Chris Matthews*, MSNBC, February 25, 2016, accessed April 21, 2016, http://www.msnbc.com/hardball/watch/sanders-i-m-not-an-inside-the-beltway-guy-631560771760.

94   Joanna Mueller, "Hardball Host May Have to Answer for His Clinton Bias," Liberal America, February 25, 2016, accessed April 21, 2016, http://www.liberalamerica.org/2016/02/25/hardball-host-may-have-to-answer-for-his-clinton-bias/.

95   TsoDog, "WTF? CBS Reverses Sanders:Clinton Numbers from Harvard Poll," Daily Kos blog, December 15, 2015, accessed April 23, 2016, http://www.dailykos.com/story/2015/12/15/1460422/-WTF-CBS-reverses-Sanders-Clinton-numbers-from-Harvard-poll.

96   Joseph P. Williams, "The Problem with Polls," *US News & World Report*, September 28, 2015, accessed May 16, 2016, www.usnews.com/news/the-report/articles/2015/09/28/why-public-opinion-polls-are-increasingly-inaccurate/.
      Herbert J. Gans, "Public Opinion Polls Do Not Always Report Public Opinion," Neiman Journalism Lab, April 29, 2013, accessed May 16, 2016, http://www.niemanlab.org/2013/04/public-opinion-polls-do-not-always-report-public-opinion/.

97   Brian Stryker, "Can We Trust Polls without Cellphones Anymore?" *Huffington Post*, March 6, 2014, accessed May 16, 2016, http://www.huffingtonpost.com/brian-stryker/can-we-trust-polls-withou_b_4880127.html/.
      Herbert J. Gans, "Public Opinion Polls."
      Reid Wilson, "The Problem with Modern Polling, in One Chart," *Washington Post*, March 12, 2014, accessed May 16, 2016, https://www.washingtonpost.com/blogs/govbeat/wp/2014/03/12/the-problem-with-modern-polling-in-one-chart/
      Cliff Zukin, "What's the Matter With Polling?" *New York Times*, June 20, 2015, www.nytimes.com/2015/06/21/opinion/sunday/whats-the-matter-with-polling.html?_r=0.

98   Harry Enten, "What the Stunning Bernie Sanders Win in Michigan Means," FiveThirtyEight, March 9, 2016, accessed May 16, 2016, www.fivethirtyeight.com/features/what-the-stunning-bernie-sanders-win-in-michigan-means/.

99   David Edwards, "Amy Goodman Scorches CNN for an 'Obsession with Polls': 'Are We Telling People What to Think?'" Raw Story, February 21, 2016, www.rawstory.com/2016/02/amy-goodman-scorches-cnn-for-an-obsession-with-polls-are-we-telling-people-what-to-think/.

100  H. A. Goodman, "Bernie Sanders Will Become President, Despite Rigged Debate Schedules, Skewed Polls, and Clinton's 'Inevitability,'" *Huffington Post*, December 11, 2015, www.huffingtonpost.com/h-a-goodman/bernie-sanders-will-become-president_b_8780730.html?utm_hp_ref=tw.

101  Rich Noyes, "Study: Hillary Gets the Most Press; Bernie and Biden Get the Best Press," Media Research Center, October 6, 2015, accessed May 16, 2016, http://www.mrc.org/media-reality-check/study-hillary-gets-most-press-bernie-and-biden-get-best-press.

102  James Warren, "Media to Blame for the Rise of Trump?"

Gabriel Arana, "Blame the Media for Donald Trump's Rise in the Polls," *Huffington Post*, July 22, 2015, accessed May 16, 2016, www.huffingtonpost.com/entry/blame-the-media-for-donald-trumps-rise-in-the-polls_us_55afd21ee4b08f57d5d34cf0.

David Rothschild, "Understanding How Polls Affect Voters," *Huffington Post*, October 26, 2012, www.huffingtonpost.com/david-rothschild/understanding-how-polls-affect-voters_b_2009034.html.

103  Domenico Montanaro, "Coin-Toss Fact-Check: No, Coin Flips Did Not Win Iowa for Hillary Clinton," NPR, February 2, 2016, accessed May 11, 2016, www.npr.org/2016/02/02/465268206/coin-toss-fact-check-no-coin-flips-did-not-win-iowa-for-hillary-clinton.

104  Andi O'Rourke, "Hillary Clinton is Already Winning the Democratic Race Even before the Iowa Caucus Begins," *Bustle*, January 31, 2016, accessed June 9, 2016, www.bustle.com/articles/138820-hillary-clinton-is-already-winning-the-democratic-race-even-before-the-iowa-caucus-begins.

105  Seth Abramson, "Clinton Delegate Lead Down to 194, Even as Dramatic Miscounting of Delegates by Media Continues," *Huffington Post*, April 17, 2016, accessed May 9, 2016, http://www.huffingtonpost.com/seth-abramson/clintons-delegate-lead-do_b_9711160.html.

smmaher, "No Bernie is Not 'Less Competitive Than He Appears,'" Daily Kos blog, April 11, 2016, accessed May 16, 2016, http://www.dailykos.com/story/2016/4/11/1513599/-No-Bernie-is-not-less-competitive-than-he-appears.

106  Zach Cartwright, "Bernie Sanders Has a Lot More Delegates Than the Media is Telling You," U.S. Uncut, April 18, 2016, accessed May 9, 2016, http://usuncut.com/politics/bernie-delegates-accurate-count/.

107  Kevin Gosztola, "Establishment Media Commit Massive Act of Malpractice and Claim Clinton 'Clinched,'" Shadow Proof, June 7, 2016, accessed June 9, 2016, https://shadowproof.com/2016/06/07/establishment-news-media-commit-massive-act-of-malpractice-claim-clinton-clinched/.

108  "Sanders Supporters Cry Foul over Clinton's Suspicious 'Secret Win' Email," Common Dreams, June 7, 2016, accessed June 9, 2016, www.commondreams.org/news/2016/06/07/sanders-supporters-cry-foul-over-clintons-suspicious-secret-win-email.

109  John Myers, "There are More Than 2.5 Million Uncounted Ballots Left from Tuesday's Statewide Primary," *Los Angeles Times*, June 10, 2016, accessed June 11, 2016, www.latimes.com/politics/la-pol-ca-california-primary-there-are-more-than-2-5-million-1465520381-htmlstory.html.

110  Jeff Cohen, "Hillary Clinton Turns Stand-Up Comic: 'I'm a Progressive Who Gets Things Done,'" Common Dreams, February 4, 2016, http://www.commondreams.org/views/2016/02/04/hillary-clinton-turns-stand-comic-im-progressive-who-gets-things-done.

111  Brian Ross, Maddy Sauer, and Rhonda Schwartz, "Clinton Remained Silent as Wal-Mart Fought Unions," *ABC News*, January 31, 2008, http://abcnews.go.com/Blotter/clinton-remained-silent-wal-mart-fought-unions/story?id=4218509.

112  "Charles Koch: Clinton Might Make Better President Than Republican Candidates," *Huffington Post*, April 23, 2016, http://www.huffingtonpost.com/entry/koch-clinton-president-republicans_us_571c35c5e4b0d912d5fee371.

113  Bret Stephens, "Hillary: The Conservative Hope," *Wall Street Journal*, May 9, 2016, http://www.wsj.com/article_email/hillary-the-conservative-hope-1462833870-lMyQjAxMTI2NjE0MDYxNzA5Wj.

114  Emily Peck, "56 Successful Business Leaders, Including Republicans, Now Back Hillary Clinton Apparently, "The Apprentice" didn't sell them on Donald Trump's management skills." *Huffington Post*, June 23, 2016, accessed July 9, 2016, www.huffingtonpost.com/entry/business-leaders-endorse-clinton_us_576c0b84e4b0b489bb0c9e91?section=

115 Seth Abramson, "Release of Clinton's Wall Street Speech Could End Her Candidacy for President," *Huffington Post*, April 15, 2016, http://www.huffingtonpost.com/seth-abramson/release-of-clintons-wall-street-speeches_b_9698632.html

Hillary Hanson, "Hillary Clinton Accused of Using Static Noise to Conceal Fundraising Speech," *Huffington Post*, April 9, 2016, http://www.huffingtonpost.com/entry/hillaryclinton-static-noise-speech_us_570930dae4b0836057a16748.

116 Brody Mullins and Rebecca Ballhaus, "Financial Sector Gives Hillary Clinton a Boost," *Wall Street Journal*, May 8, 2016, http://www.wsj.com/articles/financial-sector-gives-hillary-clinton-a-boost-1462750725.

117 Erin Dooley, "Donald Trump Says His Money Drew Hillary Clinton to His Wedding," *ABC News*, August 7, 2015, http://abcnews.go.com/Politics/trump-money-drew-hillary-clinton-wedding/story?id=32936868.

"Trump: The Least Charitable Billionaire," Smoking Gun, April 12, 2011, http://www.thesmokinggun.com/documents/celebrity/trump-least-charitable-billionaire-109247.

Marcia Dunn, "There's Something Fishy about Donald Trump's Charitable Donations," *Business Insider*, August 2, 2015, http://www.businessinsider.com/theres-something-fishy-about-donald-trumps-charitable-donations-2015-8.

Lee Fang, "Hillary Clinton Paid by Jeb Bush's Education Company," *Intercept*, May 18, 2015, https://theintercept.com/2015/05/18/hillary-clinton-paid-jeb-bushs-education-company/.

118 Jonathan Cohn, "Hillary Clinton is a Progressive Democrat, Despite What You May Have Heard," *Huffington Post*, May 8, 2016, http://www.huffingtonpost.com/entry/hillary-clinton-progressive_us_572cca08e4b0bc9cb0469098.

119 Lee Fang, "Hillary Clinton Laughs When Asked if She Will Release Transcripts of Her Goldman Sachs Speeches," *Intercept*, January 23, 2016, https://theintercept.com/2016/01/23/clinton-goldman-sachs-laugh/.

120 Aaron Rupar, "Hillary Clinton Says Obama Took on Wall Street. The Facts Don't Back Her Up.," ThinkProgress, February 11, 2016, http://thinkprogress.org/politics/2016/02/11/3749007/hillary-wall-street-debate/.

121 Lee Fang, "Top Hillary Clinton Advisers and Fundraisers Lobbied against Obamacare and Dodd-Frank," *Intercept*, February 8, 2016, https://theintercept.com/2016/02/08/hrc-inner-circle-lobbyists/.

122 Ibid.

123 Thomas Palley, "How the Democratic Party Establishment Suffocates Progressive Change," Campaign for America's Future, March 21, 2016, https://ourfuture.org/20160321/how-the-democratic-party-establishment-suffocates-progressive-change.

124 Adam Johnson, "Washington Post Ran 16 Negative Stories on Bernie Sanders."

Dean Baker, "Washington Post Won't Let Journalistic Integrity Stand in the Way of Scaring You Away from Sanders," Fairness and Accuracy In Reporting, October 1, 2015, http://fair.org/home/washington-post-wont-let-journalistic-integrity-stand-in-the-way-of-scaring-you-away-from-sanders/.

125 Lukas I. Alpert and Jack Marshall, "Bezos Takes Hands-On Role at Washington Post," *Wall Street Journal*, December 20, 2015, accessed May 16, 2016, www.wsj.com/articles/bezos-takes-hands-on-role-at-washington-post-1450658089.

Adam Johnson, "Washington Post Ran 16 Negative Stories on Bernie Sanders."

126 Doug Henwood, "NYT Rounds Up 'Left-Leaning Economists' for a Unicorn Hunt," Fairness and Accuracy In Reporting, February 17, 2016, accessed May 16, 2016, http://fair.org/home/nyt-rounds-up-left-leaning-economists-for-a-unicorn-hunt/.

Zach Cartwright, "Economists Who Bashed Bernie Sanders' Tax Plan Admit They're Clueless: 'We're Not Really Experts,'" U.S. Uncut, March 5, 2016, accessed May 16, 2016, http://usuncut.com/politics/sanders-shoots-down-tpc-analysis-of-tax-plan/.

Dean Baker, "NYT Invents Left-Leaning Economists to Attack Bernie Sanders," Beat the Press (blog) at the Center for Economic and Policy Research, February 16, 2016, http://cepr.net/blogs/beat-the-press/nyt-invents-left-leaning-economists-to-attack-bernie-sanders.

127 Jacqueline Pine, "The DNC Just Declared War on Bernie Sanders' Political Revolution," U.S. Uncut, February 12, 2016, accessed May 16, 2016, http://usuncut.com/news/the-dnc-opens-the-gates-to-unlimited-wall-street-funding/.

128 Zach Cartwright, "The DNC Joins Arms with America's Most Hated Company to Host National Convention," U.S. Uncut, May 10, 2016, accessed May 16, 2016, http://usuncut.com/politics/democratic-national-convention-comcast/.

129 Zach Cartwright, "This Superdelegate Just Confirmed Sanders Supporters' Worst Fears," U.S. Uncut, February 16, 2016, accessed May 16, 2016, http://usuncut.com/politics/vermont-superdelegate/.

130 Clark Mindock and David Sirota, "Wall Street Money: Barney Frank to Oversee Democratic Platform while Running Big Bank," *International Business Times*, May 9, 2016, accessed May 16, 2016, http://www.ibtimes.com/political-capital/wall-street-money-barney-frank-oversee-democratic-platform-while-running-big-bank.

131 "DNC Packed Democratic Convention Committees with Clinton Supporters—Sanders," RT (Russia Today), May, 6, 2016, accessed May 16, 2016, https://www.rt.com/usa/342130-sanders-dnc-clinton-convention/.

132 Charlie Spiering, "Obama Hosts Secret White House Meeting with Hillary Clinton," *Breitbart*, December 7, 2015, accessed May 16, 2016, www.breitbart.com/big-government/2015/12/07/obama-hosts-secret-white-house-meeting-hillary-clinton/.
    Kevin Liptak, "Clinton and Obama Have Another Secret Lunch," CNN, December 7, 2015, accessed May 16, 2016, www.cnn.com/2015/12/07/politics/obama-hillary-clinton-lunch/.

133 David McCabe, "Clinton and Warren's Secret Meeting," Hill, February 17, 2015, http://thehill.com/blogs/ballot-box/232942-hillary-clinton-and-elizabeth-warren-met-one-on-one-in-december.

134 Sophia Tesfaye, "Barney Frank Unloads on Pro-Sanders Progressives: Says They're Only Helping GOP Win," *Salon*, July 23, 2015, accessed April 15, 2016, http://www.salon.com/2015/07/23/barney_frank_unloads_on_pro_sanders_progressives_says_theyre_only_helping_gop_win/.

135 Brent Budowsky, "Sanders Surge Panics Washington Establishment," Common Dreams, January 29, 2016, accessed April 20, 2016, http://www.commondreams.org/views/2016/01/29/sanders-surge-panics-washington-establishment.

136 Ryan Buxton, "Bernie Sanders' Wife, Jane, Calls Madeleine Albright's Comments 'Unfortunate and Disturbing,'" *Huffington Post*, February 10, 2016, http://www.huffingtonpost.com/entry/jane-sanders-madeleine-albright-gloria-steinem_us_56bbb603e4b0b40245c540ce?utm_hp_ref=tw.

137 Rahul Mahajan, "We Think the Price is Worth It," Fairness and Accuracy In Reporting, November 1, 2001, http://fair.org/extra/we-think-the-price-is-worth-it/.

138 Harper Neidig, "DC Votes to Put Sanders on Primary Ballot," Hill, April 5, 2016, accessed May 16, 2016, http://thehill.com/blogs/ballot-box/dem-primaries/275224-dc-council-votes-to-put-sanders-on-primary-ballot.
    Tim Hains, "Chaos at Nevada Democratic Convention; State Party Chair Flees Building as Sanders Supporters Demand Recount," RealClearPolitics, May 15, 2016, accessed May 16, 2016, www.realclearpolitics.com/video/2016/05/15/chaos_at_nevada_democratic_convention_dnc_leaders_flee_building_as_sanders_supporters_demand_recount.html.
    Hugh Wharton, "The Democratic Party Just Sabotaged Bernie Sanders' Campaign . . . Again," U.S. Uncut, March 30, 2016, accessed May 16, 2016, http://usuncut.com/news/bernie-sanders-washington-dc/.
    Aaron C. Davis, "No, Bernie Sanders was Not Kicked Off the D.C. Ballot," *Washington Post*, March 30, 2016, accessed May 16, 2016, https://www.washingtonpost.com/local/dc-politics/no-bernie-sanders-was-not-kicked-off-the-dc-ballot/2016/03/30/53be925c-f6c6-11e5-8b23-538270a1ca31_story.html.
    Samantha Lachman and Cristian Farias, "Bernie Sanders' Campaign Reaches Voter Data Deal with Democratic National Committee," *Huffington Post*, December 18, 2015, http://www.

huffingtonpost.com/entry/sanders-sues-dnc_us_56748b06e4b06fa6887d883e?utm_hp_ref=tw

Gabriel Debenedetti and Annie Karni, "Chaos in the Democratic Presidential Primary," *Politico*, December 18, 2015, accessed April 20, 2016, http://www.politico.com/story/2015/12/sanders-campaign-threatens-to-sue-dnc-216942.

Pete Voelker, "Is the Democratic Party Rigging the Election for Hillary Clinton?" *VICE*, December 19, 2015, accessed April 23, 2016, http://www.vice.com/read/the-democratic-party-hillary-clinton-bias-goes-way-beyond-data?utm_source=vicefbus.

139 Nathan Francis, "New York Primary Lawsuit Update: In Potential Win for Bernie Sanders Supporters, Judge Declares Voters Wrongly Purged from Democratic Party Rolls May Still be Able to Vote," Inquisitr News, April 19, 2016, accessed May 9, 2016, http://www.inquisitr.com/3012582/new-york-primary-lawsuit-update-voters-wrongly-purged-from-democratic-party-rolls-may-still-be-able-to-vote-judge-declares/.

Chris White, "Voter Registration Purge Alleged in New York Primary, Judge to Hold Hearing," LawNewz, April 19, 2016, accessed May 10, 2016, http://lawnewz.com/high-profile/breaking-judge-to-hold-hearing-on-emergency-lawsuit-filed-over-alleged-ny-voter-registration-fraud/.

140 Gregory Krieg, "Sanders Campaign, New York Officials Cry Foul after New York Voters Report Issues," CNN, April 20, 2016, accessed May 9, 2016, http://www.cnn.com/2016/04/19/politics/new-york-primary-voter-problem-polls-sanders-de-blasio/.

Tom Cahill, "New York's Mayor Responds as Brooklyn Voter Purge Doubles to 126,000," U.S. Uncut, April 19, 2016, accessed May 10, 2016, http://usuncut.com/politics/nyc-mayor-responds-to-brooklyn-voter-purge/.

141 Gregory Krieg, "Sanders Campaign, New York Officials Cry Foul."

AJ Vicens, "The Story of the Great Brooklyn Voter Purge Keeps Getting Weirder," *Mother Jones*, April 22, 2016, accessed May 11, 2016, http://m.motherjones.com/politics/2016/04/new-york-primary-voter-purge.

142 Bob Fredericks, "Why Nearly 100,000 People are Calling for Bill Clinton's Arrest," *New York Post*, March 3, 2016, http://nypost.com/2016/03/03/why-85000-people-are-calling-for-bill-clintons-arrest/.

143 Chuck Ross, "Report: Iowa Democratic Party Unilaterally Shifted Delegates from Bernie to Hillary," *Daily Caller*, February 5, 2016, http://dailycaller.com/2016/02/05/report-iowa-democratic-party-unilaterally-shifted-delegates-from-bernie-to-hillary/.

Nathan Wellman, "All Hell is Breaking Loose at Arizona Election Fraud Hearing," U.S. Uncut, March 28, 2016, http://usuncut.com/politics/arizona-election-fraud-hearing-chaos/.

Lauren McCauley, "Clinton Claims Victory but Arizona's Voting Fiasco Dubbed 'National Disgrace,'" Common Dreams, March 23, 2016, http://www.commondreams.org/news/2016/03/23/clinton-claims-victory-arizonas-voting-fiasco-dubbed-national-disgrace.

delphine, "Myths about Election Irregularities and Suppression in Arizona (Update II)," Daily Kos blog, March 23, 2016, http://m.dailykos.com/stories/2016/3/23/1505343/-Myths-About-Election-Irregularities-and-Suppression-in-Arizona.

Amanda Girard, "Arizona Secretary of State Confirms Election Fraud Happened in State Primary (VIDEO)," U.S. Uncut, March 30, 2016, http://usuncut.com/politics/arizona-election-fraud-primary/.

144 bwh0345, "Voter Suppression in California," Daily Kos blog, June 7, 2016, accessed June 11, 2016, www.dailykos.com/story/2016/6/7/1535829/-Voter-Suppression-in-California.

145 Charles P. Pierce, "It's Time for Bernie's People to Calm Down," *Esquire*, May 16, 2016, accessed May 16, 2016, www.esquire.com/news-politics/politics/news/a44904/nevada-democratic-convention/.

146 Scott Eric Kaufman, "Paul Krugman: Delusional Sanders Supporters Don't Understand Reality Any Better Than Their Candidate," *Salon*, May 18, 2016, accessed May 18, 2016, www.salon.com/2016/05/18/paul_krugman_delusional_sanders_supporters_dont_understand_reality_any_better_than_their_candidate/.

147 Lara M. Brown, "Bernie Sanders Should Drop Out Now," *New York Times*, April 20, 2016, accessed May 16, 2016, www.nytimes.com/roomfordebate/2016/04/20/should-bernie-sanders-call-it-quits/bernie-sanders-should-drop-out-now.

Jonathan C. Rothermel, "Bernie's Dropout is Hillary's Move." *US News & World Report*, April 27, 2016, accessed May 16, 2016, www.usnews.com/opinion/articles/2016-04-27/hillary-clinton-should-offer-bernie-sanders-a-return-for-dropping-out.

148 Stephanie Dube Dwilson, "Nevada Democratic Convention: Stories of Voter Suppression," Heavy, May 15, 2016, accessed May 18, 2016, heavy.com/news/2016/05/nevada-democratic-convention-what-happened-roberta-lange-delegates-election-fraud-videos-recount-denied/.

149 Tim Hains, "Cenk Uygur: 'CNN Never Showed You' What Really Happened at Nevada Dem Convention," RealClearPolitics, May 17, 2016, accessed May 18, 2016, www.realclearpolitics.com/video/2016/05/17/cenk_ugyur_cnn_never_showed_you_what_really_happened_at_nevada_dem_convention.html.

150 Zach Cartwright, "Nevada Reporter Who Falsely Claimed Sanders Supporters Threw Chairs Just Got What He Deserves," US Uncut, June 21, 2016, accessed July 9, 2016, usuncut.com/politics/nevada-reporter-chair-throwing/.

151 Jonathan Easley "DNC Chairwoman Chides Sanders," Hill, May 17, 2016, accessed May 18, 2016, thehill.com/blogs/ballot-box/presidential-races/280300-dnc-chairwoman-chides-sanders.

152 Chris Cillizza, "This Bernie Sanders Statement on the Nevada Convention Reads Like an Open Threat to the Democratic Establishment," *Washington Post*, May 17, 2016, accessed May 18, 2016, https://www.washingtonpost.com/news/the-fix/wp/2016/05/17/bernie-sanders-is-mad-as-hell-and-hes-not-going-to-take-it-anymore-at-least-in-nevada/.

153 G.A. Casebeer, "Are CNN, MSNBC and NYT Covering Up Wendell Pierce's Assault of Sanders Supporters?" Bern Report, May 16, 2016, accessed May 16, 2016, thebernreport.com/are-cnn-and-msnbc-covering-up-wendell-pierces-assault-of-sanders-supporters/.

154 "The Situation Room with Wolf Blitzer," CNN, June 8, 2016.

155 Thomas E. Patterson, "Pre-Primary News Coverage of the 2016 Presidential Race: Trump's Rise, Sanders' Emergence, Clinton's Struggle," Shorenstein Center on Media, Politics, and Public Policy (Kennedy School of Government, Harvard University), June 13, 2016, http://shorensteincenter.org/pre-primary-news-coverage-2016-trump-clinton-sanders/.

# CHAPTER 4

# Media Democracy in Action

Contributions by Mnar Muhawesh (MintPress News), Peter B.
Collins (*The Peter Collins Show*), Eric Draitser (Stop Imperialism),
Abby Martin (*The Empire Files*), Darcey Rakestraw (Food & Water
Watch), Susan Rahman and Eliana Dimopoulos (College of Marin);
introduction by Andy Lee Roth

*Not everything that is faced can be changed; but nothing
can be changed until it is faced.*

—James Baldwin[1]

In 1962 James Baldwin wrote, "We live in a country in which words
are mostly used to cover the sleeper, not to wake him up." Baldwin
addressed the role for writers, and especially novelists, in helping a
nation's members to understand themselves and their country. The
great novelist, Baldwin proposed, was distinguished by the effort "to
tell as much of the truth as one can bear, and then a little more."[2]

These insights apply equally to our era's most outstanding journalists and their work. At its best, investigative reporting challenges us
to wake up and face what Baldwin described with remarkable under-
statement as "particulars" that "are not very attractive."

In 2002 Peter Phillips, Project Censored's second director, introduced the phrase "Media Democracy in Action" as a tagline for the
organization's work. In the preface to *Censored 2003*, after identifying
a crisis of freedom of information in the US, Phillips described media
democracy in action in terms of emerging opportunities for truth and
discovery: "We can share and tell our stories. We can find our own news
and report our victories."[3] This was a vision of journalism as a progressive social movement, not limited to professional reporters or bound by
establishment conventions of depersonalization and balance.[4]

The following yearbook marked the debut of a chapter titled "Media Democracy in Action," which covered "the everyday activism of grassroots media groups all across the nation."[5] These groups demonstrated how media *analysis* and media *activism* fortify each other. Each yearbook since *Censored 2004* has featured a chapter that underscores this point by highlighting the contributions and successes of individuals and organizations that exemplify media democracy in action.

In this year's chapter, Mnar Muhawesh of MintPress News, Eric Draitser of Stop Imperialism, and Abby Martin, host of *The Empire Files*, each challenge us to confront the reality of US imperialism, and its consequences. Their engaged news judgment introduces us to a broad spectrum of people who oppose the American empire, voices consistently marginalized or excluded by the narrow, corporate version of who counts as newsworthy. Similarly, Peter B. Collins reminds us how the FBI and local police departments now employ legal powers, originally intended to target terrorists, against nonviolent activists. "What we do know about the creeping American police state," he writes, "would still be secret if it weren't for courageous whistleblowers." A public that understands the importance of whistle-blowing, as a corrective mechanism for a failing system, will be more likely to support protections for whistle-blowers, and to hold government and corporate officials to account for the hard truths that whistle-blowers expose.

Darcey Rakestraw describes how Food & Water Watch has successfully countered corporate spin on fracking and water contamination, agriculture, and water privatization. She writes, "Sustained and smart use of research, organizing, and communications tools can help advocates make a meaningful contribution to media narratives—even in the face of massive amounts of industry advertising and PR dollars." Her examples of Food & Water Watch's successes provide not only inspiration but also lessons that can be adapted to effective media activism on other pressing social problems.

Though previous "Media Democracy in Action" chapters have highlighted the good work of independent reporters and news organizations, Susan Rahman and Eliana Dimopoulos introduce another kind of media democracy. They describe how a combination of two revolutionary programs in higher education, service learning and universal design, challenges traditional educational models and promotes greater inclusivity. Rahman and Dimopoulos describe how these programs "help students grow into citizens and community members who believe in the value of helping others, who may differ from them, with compassion."

The contributors to this year's chapter urge us to face our society's most pressing social problems. Furthermore, their examples show us that in many cases—indeed, far more frequently than corporate media would lead us to believe—positive change is possible.

## MINTPRESS NEWS AND "BEHIND THE HEADLINE": UNFLINCHING, UNCENSORED INVESTIGATIVE JOURNALISM

Mnar Muhawesh

My journey in social justice activism and journalism began when I was just a few years old. I marched with my family in Minneapolis, Minnesota, against Israel's illegal occupation and apartheid policies. With an ethnic Palestinian background and having been educated from a young age about the importance of human rights, I soon experienced oppression firsthand when my family moved to Palestine for almost four years.[6]

There, I witnessed disturbing war crimes and atrocities and saw the systemic discrimination suffered by my Palestinian classmates and family. I suffered directly under military occupation and martial law, witnessing Palestinian children being shot at with rubber bullets, militarized checkpoints, and planes firing missiles at homes in Ramallah. I returned to the United States as a young teen in 2001, suffering from PTSD and anxiety. Despite these conditions, my experience in Palestine made me passionate about opposing warfare, imperialism, and oppression.

In the immediate aftermath of 9/11, I protested the US invasions of Afghanistan and Iraq, despite facing intense Islamophobia and bigotry at school. While most American teenagers were unable to locate Iraq or Palestine on a map, I turned to the media to keep informed about wars overseas, only to find pervasive dehumanization of our wars' victims. While suffering from PTSD and anxiety from living under Israeli occupation, and from school bullying for being Muslim following the 9/11 attacks, I found courage and catharsis to pursue journalism as a way to speak up for those who don't have a voice, especially those living in war.

Even then, I knew that journalism was the means I wanted to pursue to help reeducate the public about US wars and to build bridges to help my fellow Americans understand people around the world, especially those who are victims of corporate exploitation and war.

After launching a blog featuring local news and exclusive interviews, in 2009 I broke barriers by becoming the first American TV journalist to report and anchor the news while wearing a hijab. But, after briefly interning at KARE 11, NBC's Minneapolis/St. Paul affiliate, I became disillusioned by the limitations that the corporate media put on me. It was obvious that corporate journalists have to answer to advertisers and, in many cases, to political agendas before they serve the needs of the people.

In 2012 I left TV news to expand my blog into MintPress News, a global journalism start-up site offering issue-based reporting with a focus on special-interest groups, big business lobbying efforts, and how Wall Street influences our domestic and foreign policies and drives US warfare and imperialism. Through the lenses of social justice and human rights, MintPress examines the effects these forces have on democracy and freedoms as defined by the Constitution. Every day, MintPress brings important stories and unique analysis from a team of freelance journalists and writers located around the country and world. With outlets such as BuzzFeed and the *Huffington Post* leading online news media with fast-food headlines, sponsored by special interests and lacking in journalistic ethics, part of MintPress's mission has been to set an example as a profitable news agency that never sacrifices journalistic integrity.

In August 2013 MintPress revealed that Syrian rebels were suspected of using Saudi-supplied chemical weapons in Ghouta, casting doubt on official claims of chemical weapons use by the Assad government.[7] Despite an organized campaign to discredit MintPress and our reporting at the time, this breaking story had a significant impact on US foreign policy, including preventing an all-out war with Syria. The report cemented MintPress's reputation as a source of unflinching, uncensored investigative journalism. We continue to hold our elected officials accountable through uncompromising reporting and analysis.

Four years after founding MintPress, I am returning to TV, bringing the same dedication to truth and journalistic integrity that's distinguished MintPress News: *Behind the Headline*, a weekly thirty-minute program that began airing in April 2016 on Free Speech TV, a network that reaches more than forty million American households through DISH Network, DirecTV, and Roku set-top boxes. *Behind the Headline* is currently being structured as a citizen-supported non-profit project.

Each program highlights important issues and stories that the corporate media ignore, and amplifies the voices of fascinating independent thinkers and newsmakers who are usually silenced by the media, including activists for peace and inclusion, government whistle-blowers, and third-party presidential candidates who prioritize the needs and interests of people and the environment.

---

MNAR A. MUHAWESH is the founder and editor in chief of MintPress News, and the host of *Behind the Headline*, a new citizen-supported TV program launched in April 2016 on Free Speech TV.

## NO SYSTEM CORRECTION IN SIGHT

Peter B. Collins

My work in recent years has been informed in many ways by courageous whistle-blowers who have striven to expose lawbreaking, fraud, mismanagement, and other wrongdoings in America's law enforcement, intelligence, and military sectors. These brave individuals never thought they would wear the badge of "whistleblower," and the list includes an array of agencies: FBI, CIA, NSA, DEA, DHS, TSA, the State Department, and many branches of the Pentagon.

While most administration insiders can strategically leak classified information to advance their political or propaganda goals, the crackdown on whistle-blowers has been severe and broad-based. It's no secret that the Obama Justice Department has relentlessly pursued the principled leakers tagged as whistle-blowers, and often, traitors.

Chelsea Manning will be in Leavenworth for decades, and Ed Snowden doesn't dare leave asylum in Russia. Many lesser-known whistleblowers have lost their livelihoods and pensions, and seen their savings dwindle as they pay hefty legal fees that can double or triple as the government drags out resolution.

In almost every case, these veterans of government service were honoring the terms of their employment and their security clearance agreements, and believed that reporting through "the proper channels" would earn them plaudits, and maybe a promotion. Instead, virtually all of them have been subjected to retaliation that is disproportionate and heavy-handed—and often appears to be illegal. The legitimate secrecy of security operations is used, illegitimately, to punish dedicated public employees whose reports of wrongdoing are embarrassing or challenge internal or external politics.

In many of these cases, we see a massive diversion of resources, including personnel, to silence whistle-blowers and intimidate them into submission. In one outrageous case, when Julia Davis, who worked for Homeland Security at the border near San Diego, alerted her superiors to suspicious traffic at the border, they ignored her. Following protocols, she next reported her concerns to the FBI. That enraged her superiors, who initiated a campaign of heavy surveillance of Davis, which culminated in a warrantless helicopter raid on her home with twenty-seven armed men in SWAT mode. For doing her job, Davis was treated like an enemy.

Many whistle-blowers know that their own cases will not likely be resolved in their favor. But they hope that the risks they take, and the costs they incur, will eventually lead to a system correction; that a latter-day Senator Frank Church will hold hearings that expose the systemic problems and pierce the veil of secrecy that provides immunity to those who violate the law under color of authority.[8] They believe in our system, and that its subversion is a temporary condition that will be rectified when the pendulum swings from oppression to liberty. It's happened before, but seems unlikely to recur in the foreseeable future.

During the final years of the Nixon administration, I hosted a late-night talk show on WLS-FM in Chicago, owned by the ABC network. Covering the Watergate scandal that led to Nixon's resignation, the revelations of the Church Committee about CIA assassinations, and the FBI's sweeping domestic counterintelligence program, COIN-TELPRO, I learned about the dark underbelly of our intelligence and law enforcement agencies. Congress passed some reforms that amounted to a system correction. The reforms were not comprehensive or airtight, but for a time it seemed that we were reclaiming our constitutional rights at home while cutting back on the export of orchestrated mayhem.

It wasn't long though, before we returned to form. President Jimmy Carter, who signed the reform laws written by the Senate's Church Committee and the House's Pike Committee, secretly authorized the covert war in Afghanistan that bogged down the Soviet Union and saw the US using mujahideen mercenaries in covert operations. Ronald Reagan went deep with the Iran-Contra schemes, despite the clear congressional ban on support for the Contras.

Since 9/11, we've experienced the vertical integration of domestic law enforcement, with expansive powers—some authorized, some arrogated—conferred on the FBI and local police agencies. The powers and tools that were purported to only target terrorists are routinely used against nonviolent First Amendment activists, run-of-the-mill criminals, and some whistle-blowers. Despite muscular efforts to maintain secrecy, what we do know about the creeping American police state would still be secret if it weren't for courageous whistle-blowers.

It's been over three years since former NSA analyst Russell Tice told Sibel Edmonds and me that he had seen wiretap installation orders for phones associated with members of the Senate Intelligence Committee, Supreme Court members and nominees, and other top government officials. Using all available channels, public and private, I have shared this information with more than a dozen members of Congress, thinking that they would at least fight to preserve their own rights under the separation of powers doctrine. In a 2014 interview, Senator Jeff Merkley, an Oregon Democrat who has authored amendments to limit domestic surveillance, became uncomfortable when

Tice's statements were shared with him, and signaled his aide to end the interview.

We are overdue for a system correction, but our present political leaders display no interest in restoring constitutional rule, perhaps because the NSA and FBI have collected some dirt on those leaders. For now, we must rely on principled whistle-blowers to expose wrong-doing and fight for our constitutional rights.

PETER B. COLLINS is a veteran radio host from San Francisco. You can listen to his podcasts, including interviews with many whistle-blowers, at peterbcollins.com. He is working with Sibel Edmonds and others to launch Newsbud.com an independent, publicly funded media site

## THE NECESSITY OF AN ALTERNATIVE TO THE "ALTERNATIVE" MEDIA

Eric Draitser

Although it was already fall, the air was still warm and sticky, the leaves yet to turn their customary burnt reds and browns, and I was at Zuccotti Park in Lower Manhattan in the first days of Occupy Wall Street, or what would come to be known as the "Occupy Movement." How could I not be? This was the revolution! This was the moment we'd all been waiting for.

I was there, in the eye of the political storm, with airy thoughts of Rosa Luxemburg fluttering through my mind, her imagined voice forcefully whispering:

> The mass strike is the first natural, impulsive form of every great revolutionary struggle of the proletariat and the more highly developed the antagonism is between capital and labor, the more effective and decisive must mass strikes become . . . The mass strike is . . . a universal form of the proletarian class struggle resulting from the present stage of capitalist development and class relations.[9]

It was clear—this was our mass strike upsurge.

The day had finally arrived when a people's movement had organized to take on the burning issues of the day—economic exploitation and oppression, the police state, and the military-industrial-financial complex and its endless imperialist wars—and I wanted to be there. After all, it was at that very moment that the US war machine was raining death and destruction on the people of Libya in the name of freedom and democracy, just as it had in Iraq, Afghanistan, and countless other lands before them.

I knew the importance of seizing the moment to drive home the point that those bombs were being dropped on Libya by one arm of the same diseased corpus that saddled us with debt, drove down our wages, foreclosed on our homes, and imposed austerity on us at every turn. Surely I would find allies at Occupy; surely there'd be media (especially alternative media) ready to finally counter the dominant narrative about that war and connect it to the burgeoning movement; surely this was the opening salvo of our resistance.

It didn't take long, however, to realize that the assemblage of student activists, and even many of the veterans of past protest movements, were either blissfully unaware of the reality of the US-NATO war on Libya happening at the very instant that they were gathered together to talk about solidarity, social justice, and resistance to corporations and capitalism, or they were totally misinformed by both the corporate media and alternative media. I couldn't believe it. Here I was at "ground zero" of a radical, revolutionary movement, and no one even wanted to discuss actions in solidarity with victims of the very same imperial establishment that we were allegedly opposing.

I was told that Gaddafi was a dictator; we weren't there to talk about war; we should be in solidarity with the (US-NATO backed) "revolutionaries"; and that I was being an agitator for demanding that we take a stand publicly and immediately. I was dumbfounded. How could this be?

It became clear to me almost immediately that amid all the triumphalism, and all the celebrations of the latest and greatest in protest movements, something was clearly and unmistakably wrong. The Left, progressive, antiestablishment media had utterly failed in its sole duty: to challenge power in the service of social justice. Instead, what I now call the pseudo-alternative media had become a willing cheerleader for the Empire. Sure they were willing to focus on Occupy as it ticked off every Left activist box: young people with guitars, a drum circle, lack of demands and leadership, etc. But they were unwilling to touch the blood-soaked elephant in the room: imperialism. The same people who had protested endlessly from well-funded soapboxes against George W. Bush and his criminal war in Iraq had seemingly become the sentinels at the gates of the pro-war Left sanctuary.[10]

It was at that moment that I knew an alternative to the alternative media was needed, one that could be trusted to take anti-imperialism seriously; one that could be both uncompromising and indefatigable on issues of war and peace. I also knew that such an outlet needed to be financially independent. It could not be bankrolled by the traditional foundation liberals who righteously oppose Republican wars but go conspicuously missing when liberal Democrats wage similar wars. When I looked around at all the biggest names in the alternative media, I found that every single one of them was funded by either Wall Street financiers (Open Society Foundations of George Soros, the Ford Foundation, the MacArthur Foundation, etc.) or by foreign governments (Al Jazeera, Russia Today, Press TV, etc.).[11] And while any of those outlets might be useful and do good work in specific cases, none could be regarded as truly independent. It had to be me.

So I started StopImperialism.org with one goal in mind: provide thoughtful analysis from a leftist, anti-imperialist perspective, and try to provide content that could be used to fight the all too necessary information war against the corporate and alternative media establishment online.

But it wasn't just about putting out the analysis for others to learn from and disseminate; it was about countering the pervasive influence of controlled media narratives in the online space. I had seen how social media had been manipulated during the Libyan war and the start of the war on Syria, when suddenly thousands of Twitter accounts magically materialized to demand military intervention on the part of the Empire to effectuate the fall of Muammar Gaddafi and Bashar al-Assad, as if by some wave of a wand these countries had become hotbeds of social media activism.

And I remembered a story from February of that year (2011) that explained how the US government contracted for the development of software that could create multiple fake social media accounts for the purposes of swaying public opinion and promoting propaganda in the highly influential social media space.[12] I knew that some of the most influential bloggers driving the alternative-media narrative on Libya and Syria had been proved to be hoaxes, such as the so-called "Gay Girl in Damascus," who in June of 2011 had been exposed by Electronic Intifada[13] and the *Washington Post*.[14] These were just a few of many examples of precisely the sort of misinformation and disinformation that I wanted StopImperialism.org, my podcasts and writings, and all my other work to counter.

Of course I knew that this was only one aspect of a much more complex and multifaceted problem that pointed to the interconnected series of challenges faced by those trying to undermine the dominant narrative by chipping away at the edifice of information control. With the so-called "mainstream" media owned and controlled almost entirely by six corporations—what the late Ben Bagdikian, Pulitzer prize–winning journalist and former dean of the Graduate School of Journalism at UC Berkeley, described as a "cartel"[15]—one had to see the corporate media as an arm of the establishment, the public relations wing of the Empire.

Simultaneously, I had come to realize that the foundation-funded, pseudo-alternative media could not be trusted either, as it had eagerly disseminated pro-war propaganda against Libya and Syria under the guise of "humanitarian intervention," or what US Ambassador to the United Nations Samantha Power insidiously termed "Responsibility to Protect" (R2P)—a deceptive term to justify war using the laughably tragic pretext of protecting civilians.[16] It had become clear to me that the Wall Street–linked foundations funding these pseudo-alternative media outlets were simply another tentacle of the same establishment that controls the corporate media. In effect, the alleged alternative was no alternative at all, merely a different flavor of the same poison pill.

And so it was here, outside the corporate frame and its so-called alternative, where I decided to plant a flag, to draw the proverbial line in the sand. And I continue to do so. There is nothing particularly extraordinary in what StopImperialism.org is, or what I do with my other projects such as CounterPunch Radio, the podcast I produce in partnership with another bastion of truly independent alternative media. But it does seem to be needed. I produce my work totally independently, without any financial or technical assistance from anyone. I have no staff, no interns, no advertisers, and certainly no profits. I merely produce the best-quality analysis and commentary I can. No more, no less.

---

ERIC DRAITSER is an independent political analyst, editor of StopImperialism.org, and host of CounterPunch Radio. His work focuses primarily on politics, geopolitics, and the role of imperialism in the modern world. Draitser's articles have appeared in many publications both in the US and internationally, and have been translated into more than a dozen languages. He is a regular contributor to TeleSUR, CounterPunch, RT, Truthout, WBAI, and a variety of other media outlets. His work on the origins and evolution of the conflict in Ukraine was recently featured in *The Palgrave Encyclopedia of Imperialism and Anti-Imperialism*. He is based in New York City.

## REVOLUTIONARY TRUTH-TELLING IN TODAY'S MEDIA CLIMATE: *THE EMPIRE FILES*

### Abby Martin

From fracking dangers to Internet freedom, the stories that most affect people's lives are routinely repressed, backpaged, and distorted. Americans' lack of information is not due to some vast, hidden conspiracy—it's the consequence of an open conspiracy under capitalism, where the CEOs and business owners of media conglomerates work to maintain only one interest: profit.

The corporate takeover of the fourth estate has gutted any semblance of democracy. What started as a free public service became a fire sale in the age of neoliberalism. Telecom companies began tightening their grip on the market by eating each other, resulting in only six corporations now controlling 90 percent of all information in the US.

The government has a lot at stake in how this information is managed, and the corporate media can't control the masses effectively without its close cooperation. Beyond its own borders, the US war machine deploys subversive media outlets and the propaganda of regime change on behalf of US business interests, polluting the airwaves from Europe to Cuba.

Corporate media and the political establishment work side by side to propagandize the public and manufacture consent for corporate Empire. For decades, DC journalists have been far more concerned with preserving their access and career paths than with doing their jobs. Despite the mantra about America's great free press, so-called mainstream journalists who go against the line are quickly demoted or fired—just ask Phil Donahue or Cenk Uygur.

The hypocrisy that drives this problem is amplified in the world's so-called greatest democracy, but it certainly isn't unique to America. Across the Western world, state governments work in concert with their corporate media in order to maintain the status quo of neoliberalism, capitalism, and endless war. Thankfully, some nations have advanced to buck this crushing system.

While the US media has promoted the interests of US corporate rulers, one of the biggest challenges to this information war in the past decade has been the creation of media projects from nations charting a different path. Many countries around the world not under the boot of the United States have launched their own media offensives, threatening the grip of the hierarchy.

Russia Today (RT), for instance, is a state-funded media outlet specifically designed to deliver the Russian perspective and to target the US government's endless hypocrisies. The US government recognizes the threat, even holding State Department briefings on how to combat the damage RT is doing to its image.

Revolutions, elections, and changing political dynamics have allowed other countries to develop alternative, leftist media platforms. One such example is TeleSUR, and its English language branch, TeleSUR English, a collaborative project among several Latin American countries that formed to promote the fight against Western domination. Created in 2005 as the "Latin socialist answer to CNN," TeleSUR is an entity cooperatively run between the states of Venezuela, Cuba, Nicaragua, Argentina, Bolivia, and Uruguay.

TeleSUR's answer to US propaganda and the Western-backed corporate interests in their own countries is a media that highlights the voices of the oppressed and the people's movement against imperialism. Just like other networks that challenge the Empire's conventional wisdom, TeleSUR is dismissed as "propaganda" by the establishment and those unwilling to comprehend the need for revolutionary truth-telling platforms in today's suffocating media climate.

Aside from the relentless smear campaign against TeleSUR for its affiliations, its entire existence is now threatened by Latin America's changing political climate.

After the November 2015 election of right-wing president Mauricio Macri in Argentina—one of TeleSUR's biggest funders—Macri's administration not only pulled all state funds from TeleSUR, but also censored its coverage, and ultimately removed TeleSUR from Argentina's airwaves.

The December 2015 right-wing victory in the National Assembly of Venezuela, the heart of and largest source of funds for TeleSUR, has put the network's total elimination high on the government's list of priorities. Newly elected politicians have even threatened TeleSUR journalists publicly at press conferences.

Aiding the offensive are US economic sanctions to help undermine government projects like TeleSUR, threatening the very lifeblood of one of the world's only remaining international leftist media outlets.

This is the context of global media censorship: a world run and shaped by the economic and military Empire of the United States, with its junior partners, collaborators, and puppets lined up behind them. These media offensives are weapons in the very real war to expand and tighten US domination.

It's with this understanding that I chose to join TeleSUR and create *The Empire Files*, a weekly documentary series that records the brutal reality of living under the shadow of American hegemony.

It's difficult to inform the masses in America about the disastrous consequences of Empire when most are conditioned by corporate media to believe that they live in the "greatest country in the world," and that the US is a righteous moral arbiter of human rights. But with over 800 US military bases littering the world, it's an undeniable fact that America is the world's most powerful, far-reaching Empire in human history.

Cementing itself as militarily supreme after terrorizing the planet with its use of two nuclear weapons, the US Empire has subverted the democratic processes of dozens of countries, undermined the people the world over, and installed countless dictators loyal to its will.

In Latin America alone, the US military has intervened 56 times to determine the destiny of other nations, in each case thwarting political self-determination in the targeted country. To ensure access to super-profits for US business across the region, the US even created the School of the Americas (now known as the Western Hemisphere Institute for Security Cooperation). Since 1946, this institution has trained tens of thousands of indigenous soldiers—many of whom have gone on to become some of history's most brutal dictators—and death squads that have committed egregious war crimes against leftists, peasants, and students.[17] Americans understand less about this bloody history thanks to corporate media bias, but in fact these atrocities are comparable to today's ISIS massacres.

Many of the migrants fleeing to the US today are victims of these dirty wars. Today's public debates on immigration often fail to acknowledge the role of US military intervention throughout Latin America in manufacturing the current crisis along the US-Mexico border, which results in thousands of casualties every year, turning our southern desert into a graveyard.

A constant introspective investigation of the US Empire is a mandatory task for journalists. *The Empire Files* takes as its starting point the fact that every issue facing people and the planet, here and abroad, is rooted in this global situation: the supremacy of the US Empire, enforcing its economic order for the benefit of the 0.1% through the pervasive reach of its brutal military might.

As the US Empire marches forward to strangle every drop of profit from the world, it employs an array of weapons spanning from television to drones. We must craft our own weapons of information in order to expose this global reality to the people who have the power to change it.

---

ABBY MARTIN is the creator of *The Empire Files* on TeleSUR and former host of *Breaking the Set* on RT America. She founded the citizen journalism project Media Roots and sits on the board of the Media Freedom Foundation/Project Censored.

# FOOD & WATER WATCH: COMMUNICATING IN THE PUBLIC INTEREST

Darcey Rakestraw

Food & Water Watch is an independent organization that illuminates how corporate power influences our access to safe food and clean, affordable water. Additionally—and perhaps more importantly—we organize people to take action to pressure decision makers to provide the proper oversight to serve the public interest. Using a blend of policy research, organizing, and media outreach, we've been able to effectively publicize how the oil and gas industry, the food and agriculture industry, and the private water industry in particular are influencing public policy in ways that serve profits, not people. Raising awareness about these issues is key to the political organizing that must happen to protect communities and the environment.

Much of this work is about debunking corporate spin through media outreach and the web. Working to inject our issues into the media is key to unspooling narratives on issues like energy and biotechnology that are carefully woven by millions in industry marketing dollars. Below are a few of the issues that Food & Water Watch have helped shift the conversation by prioritizing communication to the media.

## Hydraulic Fracturing and Drinking Water Contamination

For many years, the oil and gas industry has convinced many opinion leaders—including the Obama administration and big environmental organizations—that the way to clean energy is more fossil fuels. Ads on Sunday morning talk shows touted natural gas as a "bridge fuel," a cleaner alternative to coal until we can ramp up renewables. That was the public line to build support for more hydraulic fracturing, or fracking, a form of extreme energy extraction that has harmed communities, public health, and the environment. Furthermore, it's not a bridge—it's a form of energy that will keep us hooked on fossil fuels and that will run the clock out on switching to truly clean energy to avert climate catastrophe.

One of the many much-debated issues with fracking in the media has been pollution of wells in rural communities where fracking is occurring. In June 2015 the Environmental Protection Agency released a report on contamination in drinking water. While the report itself confirmed instances of contamination, the top-level finding communicated to the media in the report's press materials was that there had been no "widespread, systemic" contamination of drinking water from fracking, as if widespread contamination should be the bar.

It is no surprise that spin was the major takeaway in most news stories published about the report when it was initially published. The finding is also unsurprising given the problems with the study design itself. Geoffrey Thyne, a geochemist and a former member of the EPA Science Advisory Board (a group of independent scientists charged with reviewing agency science) said, "This was supposed to be the gold standard. But they went through a long bureaucratic process of trying to develop a study that is not going to produce a meaningful result."[18] Neela Banerjee at InsideClimate News reported in March 2015 that the EPA had been unable to collect the data it needed from the industry: "The EPA's failure to answer the study's central question partly reflects the agency's weakness relative to the politically potent fossil fuel industry."[19]

Food & Water Watch submitted lengthy comments highlighting the disconnect between the agency's misleading top line and the actual findings of the study. In late October, we brought together allies, including affected individuals, to testify at the EPA's Science Advisory Board meetings for reviewing the study. The testimonies applied pressure on the EPA to revisit its conclusions that no "widespread, systemic" contamination had occurred. Affected individuals including Ray Kemble and Craig Stevens, from Dimock, Pennsylvania; Ron Gulla, from Hickory, Pennsylvania; John Fenton, from Pavillion, Wyoming; and Steve Lipsky, from Parker County, Texas, all spoke before the panel, and according to Food & Water Watch researcher Hugh MacMillan, their testimonies struck a chord with the independent scientists on the advisory board:

One after another, the scientists, engineers and even some

of the industry representatives took issue with the Obama EPA's finding. The panelists saw that "widespread, systemic" was a meaningless phrase. They emphasized the "local" and "severe" impacts that were outlined in the study and that were recounted in the public testimonies by Kemble, Stevens, Gulla, Fenton, and Lipsky. And one after another, the panelists noted how the study was plagued at every turn by "uncertainties and data limitations."

In a cathartic moment, toward the end of the second day, one of the panelists offered up a rewrite of the study's major findings that captured all of these sentiments, and the panelists erupted in applause. It is safe to say the Obama Administration was not expecting rapturous applause from the panel in support of turning the top line finding on its head.[20]

Since that meeting, which Food & Water Watch publicized on its website and through media outreach to reporters who had written about the initial release of the study in June, we've been able to shift the media narrative by helping shed light on the controversy. The panel reviewing the EPA study has echoed Food & Water Watch's comments from August, and responded to the testimonies from affected residents by asking the agency to clarify the scientific basis of its "widespread, systemic" line and asking it to include extensive summaries of the high-profile cases of contamination in Pavillion, Wyoming; Dimock, Pennsylvania; and Parker County, Texas, that the agency inexplicably left out of its one thousand page study.

In November, the *Pittsburgh Post-Dispatch* reported:

> According to the peer-reviewed document by the 30-member Science Advisory Board, the EPA's primary conclusion to its June draft study—that fracking has not caused "widespread, systemic impacts on drinking water resources in the United States"—isn't supported by the cited data, which has gaps and deficiencies.[21]

Food & Water Watch has worked closely with several other journalists to drive the story forward. This episode shows how tireless oversight of the process—in this case, leading extensive public comments critical of the study, organizing affected individuals to come and testify during the peer-review of the study, and targeted media outreach—has successfully countered what looked like a huge public relations victory for the oil and gas industry when the study was first released.

## Agriculture

Food and agriculture is big business, and the industry drives media narratives around everything from livestock drugs that enable factory farming to genetically modified organisms (GMOs). Industry science drives regulatory approval, and in many cases, little independent research exists. That's where Food & Water Watch research comes in.

Food & Water Watch scrutinized the development and regulatory oversight of controversial livestock drugs and shed light on a disturbing fact: many of the scientific journals where research is published and disseminated to media have strong ties to the industry. Industry groups play a large role in the production of scientific literature, authoring journal articles, funding academic research, and also serving as editors, sponsors, or directors of scientific journals where much of this research is published. Many academic journals have failed to establish or enforce rules requiring conflict of interest disclosure. According to the Food & Water Watch report, *Corporate Control in Animal Science Research*, the influence this industry wields over every aspect of scientific discourse has allowed potentially unsafe animal drugs—including growth promoters for beef cattle as well as arsenic-based drugs (the latter of which have since been removed from the market)[22]—to reach the market with virtually no independent scrutiny.

A similar influence is wielded at the university level in agriculture research across the country—including at publicly funded land-grant universities—which more and more steers research priorities to serve corporate interests. Food & Water Watch issued a report in 2012, *Public Research, Private Gain*, that outlined some of the conflicts of interests inherent in corporate funding of agricultural research:

Private-sector funding not only corrupts the public research mission of land-grant universities, but also distorts the science that is supposed to help farmers improve their practices and livelihoods. Industry-funded academic research routinely produces favorable results for industry sponsors. Because policymakers and regulators frequently voice their need for good science in decision-making, industry-funded academic research influences the rules that govern their business operations.

The report notes how land-grant universities today depend on industry to underwrite research, endow faculty chairs, sponsor departments, and finance new construction. For example, one Cornell professor was a paid Monsanto consultant while also publishing journal articles promoting the benefits of recombinant Bovine Growth Hormone (rBGH) for dairy farms. His research was used in Monsanto's regulatory submissions to the US Food and Drug Administration. Candy manufacturer Mars donated more than $15 million for nutrition research at the University of California to study the nutritional benefits of cocoa, which the company then used to promote the benefits of eating chocolate.[23]

The report was the topic of an Associated Press article in June 2012, which led to more interest in the issue by other news organizations, including Harvest Public Media, providing fresh media scrutiny to this conflict of interest that continues today.[24]

The financial relationships between researchers and their industry sponsors are not always disclosed in published scientific papers—or at all. In March 2016 a WBEZ news investigation revealed that a University of Illinois professor had taken nearly $60,000 over the course of two years from Monsanto to travel, write, and speak about GMOs—including lobbying federal officials on industry-related regulations. The professor avoided disclosure through a series of university loopholes, including passing the money through the University of Illinois Foundation, effectively exempting it from disclosure.[25]

## Attacks by Water Companies

Food & Water Watch helps communities ward off the advances of private water companies, which seek to operate local systems while also providing a profitable return to their investors. But handing over control of water systems has lead to a raw deal for consumers, who often suffer worse service at a higher cost, and privatization takes away local control over this precious resource. The workforce may also be cut, resulting in fewer workers to make needed ongoing repairs. Food & Water Watch has provided copious research to educate communities and local government officials about the issue, and has helped over three dozen communities resist water privatization.

And the industry is fighting back. In 2015 it launched a website, Truthfromthetap.com, which asks, "Why are activists meddling with your drinking water?" and offers several attacks on various advocacy groups including Food & Water Watch. A seemingly innocuous educational site to the undiscerning visitor, it's actually sponsored by the National Association of Water Companies (NAWC). Composed of large US water companies and the US subsidiaries of multinational corporations like Suez, the NAWC has been a member of the American Legislative Exchange Council (ALEC), which promotes model legislation that helps the bottom lines of its corporate supporters—including industry-friendly measures like deregulation and privatization.

Aware that people—particularly journalists—searching for information about water privatization online might come across this attack site, we posted a response entitled, "Truth from the Tap: A Water Industry PR Blitz."[26] We search-optimized the title and the content to help ensure that people searching for information about this website would find information about the private water industry and failed water privatizations. It was also republished on AlterNet.[27]

Similar industry attacks on our organization in other forms of media have offered us a platform, ironically, to talk about the failures of water privatization and the motive of the lobby group. For example, in Atlantic City (where state legislation that could force water privatization was being considered), the head of the NAWC, Michael Deane, devoted an entire op-ed in the local paper to attacking Food & Water Watch. We used our opportunity to respond to the attacks by pointing out how private water was no solution for Atlantic City, and highlighted the failure of privatization in other communities. We also shed light on NAWC's involvement in ALEC. Our response concludes, "In light of Deane's hollow attacks on Food & Water Watch, and his inability to set forth a vision for private water in Atlantic City—not to mention all of the risks of privatization and the industry's profit motive—readers should ask themselves whether they believe private water companies are the best ones to solve Atlantic City's water woes."[28]

## Conclusion

These are just three examples of how we work to shift the debate in the media, and just a few of the tactics we can use to shed light on corporate influence over policies affecting our food, water, and environment. Sustained and smart use of research, organizing, and communications tools can help advocates make a meaningful contribution to media narratives—even in the face of massive amounts of industry advertising and PR dollars.

---

DARCEY RAKESTRAW is the communications director at Food & Water Watch, a national advocacy organization

## SOCIALLY JUST PATHWAYS TO INCLUSIVITY VIA SERVICE LEARNING AND UNIVERSAL DESIGN

Susan Rahman and Eliana Dimopoulos

Project Censored has long been a champion of equity through student engagement and empowerment. Students involved in the Project's Validated Independent News program, for example, challenge status quo assumptions about whose stories are newsworthy, and they call out the limitations of the corporate elite's top-down model of journalism. Project Censored celebrates news told from multiple perspectives—including, especially, those that the corporate media have marginalized or excluded—and it provides opportunities for students' direct participation in media analysis and activism. Diverse voices are welcome.

Like Project Censored, service learning and universal design challenge established norms, by calling into question traditional models of education and promoting greater inclusivity.

## Service Learning as a Tool for Social Change

Service learning is an approach to education that merges community service and academic curriculum via classroom learning.[29] This process allows students to gain hands-on practical experience in their field of study, coordinated with classroom study of the field's theoretical foundations. As research demonstrates, service learning provides many benefits to students. Service learning helps students:

- To shift understandings of civic engagement, by providing them with structured opportunities to become meaning-makers and change-agents in their communities
- To apply theory to practice, while developing valuable work experience
- To create pathways for cooperative models of engagement
- To promote social and environmental responsibility via innovative learning environments

For example, one study found that service learning fostered a student's heightened sense of competency in the areas of work ethic, patience, diversity, and fairness.[30] Another study found that students participating in service learning courses maintained higher grade point averages (GPAs) than students enrolled in traditional curricula.[31] Research conducted at UCLA found that service learning enhanced not only students' academic performance (measured by GPA, writing skills, and critical-thinking skills) but also their values (measured in terms of commitment to activism and sensitivity to diversity and difference), leadership and interpersonal skills, and their likelihood of choosing a service-oriented career.[32] Finally, traditionally underserved student populations frequently benefit from service learning opportunities.[33] Beyond the direct benefits to students, service learning partnerships create useful connections between educational institutions and their neighboring communities.

Teachers can incorporate service learning into their curricula in a variety of ways. Ideally, the institution would have a coordinator who helps facilitate placing students in community organizations. On many college campuses, a coordinator works as a liaison among students, community partners, and faculty. Alternatively, in the absence of an officially designated coordinator, teachers can do this independently.

This has been the case at our institution. Neighboring agencies have been identified over time, and a list of these agencies is provided to students who enroll in the service learning course. Students then choose an agency from this list. Once placed, students spend sixty hours in the agency, in addition to twenty classroom hours.

Various models of service learning are available. Faculty who incorporate service learning into their curricula have great flexibility. There is no one right way to incorporate it into a curriculum.[34] With that in mind, here are some suggestions based on our experience:

▸ Make sure to have the students in placement for a minimum of twenty hours. This is a minimum for them to become significantly involved in an agency's work, and to have a meaningful experience.

▸ Establish a coordinator who works as the liaison between students and their community organizations. This creates a more cohesive experience for all participants.

▸ Make sure to connect what students are doing in the field with the course material. This connection is essential; without it, the experience may still be meaningful for students, but it falls short of service learning's full potential to transform students' understandings of civic engagement.

▸ Prepare activities and assignments that assess outcomes. For students, these could include an ongoing journal, a term paper, and/or a class presentation. Community organizations should also be provided with opportunities to assess outcomes of the service learning relationship.

Student feedback is a critical tool for assessment. Many students report high levels of satisfaction with their service learning efforts, in terms of mastering a course's stated learning outcomes and changes in their quality of life. Here are representative testimonies from students of ours:

> We discussed so many social and interpersonal issues in her classes. We talked about drug and alcohol addiction, the necessity for vulnerability in becoming a better human being, and the many ways the current system can fail to service everyone. We also discussed what we, as individuals, as students, as volunteers for these non-profits could do to bridge that gap between government-provided services and people's needs.

> Volunteering has given me a lot of satisfaction. Helping others has also helped me grow.

> Through the Fieldwork class, I found myself engaging in extracurricular activities that I would never have dreamed possible. This was a challenging course, intended to inspire students to think outside the box.

As a teaching tool, service learning is highly effective. On a grander scale, it also serves as a means to facilitate social change. At our institution, the service learning program is intentionally focused on community, equity, and social justice. Mutual benefit—for both students and the organizations they come to serve—is crucial, but the ultimate objective is loftier still. Through our institution's service learning program, we aim to help students grow into citizens and community members who believe in the value of helping others, who may differ from them, with compassion.

Our model is not unique. Many institutions build service learning into their academic curricula with an eye toward social justice. For example, De Anza College, in California's South Bay has built the Vasconcellos Institute for Democracy in Action (VIDA) into its curriculum. The program is named after former California State Senator John Vasconcellos, known for his commitments to civic engagement and public education. VIDA's mission is "to empower students to become agents of change in their communities and beyond; to foster education that meets the needs of the communities we serve; and to help develop pathways to meaningful participation in local, state, and federal government decision making processes."[35]

## Universal Design as a Framework for Service Learning and Social Justice

Universal Design for Learning (UDL) offers a framework to address many social justice challenges. By rethinking the traditional one-to-many classroom hierarchy, UDL principles can highlight and support service learning goals. UDL espouses three principles for addressing inequitable, "one size fits all" curricula: engagement, representation, and action and expression.[36] These principles align with service learning both in methodology and practice. Both examine and question established educational norms and experiences, as well as seeking to create and promote equitable supports for underserved populations. Arising from the intersection of assistive technology and pedagogy, universal design has its roots in breaking down barriers found in educational institutions' hidden curricula.[37]

Universal design's value is in its scope and scalability: It can be either a tool in the service learning toolbox or the toolbox itself. Simply speaking, universal design's methodology is rooted in equity and social justice; moreover, these overarching principles can be applied practically to service learning placements. As an example, a service learning placement in a media services outlet that produces captions and descriptive transcripts for multimedia offers an opportunity to gain insight into communities other than the student's own. Students in this particular placement often report increased awareness and understandings that parallel current accessibility research and findings. For example, such students may come to appreciate the differences between an impairment and a disability: whereas not being able to hear can be the result of an anatomical impairment, the absence of universally designed media to provide equitable access is a socially created disability.[38]

As mission and methodology, universal design and service learning can be used in tandem, revisiting the VIDA's charge above, "to empower students to become agents of change in their communities and beyond."

SUSAN RAHMAN is a mother and professor of behavioral sciences at College of Marin. Her interest in service learning stems from years of witnessing student engagement and civic responsibility grow as a result of the experience. She lives with her daughter, Jordan; partner, Carlos; and two dogs, Rosie and Phoebi, in Northern California.

ELIANA DIMOPOULOS is the assistive technologist and co-coordinator of the LGBTIQQ Safe Space at College of Marin as well as an independent scholar. She has also worked as a literacy educator, donated her time to various community nonprofit organizations, and climbed both Mt. Fuji-san and the Gorges du Verdon. Her current work is focused on the intersection of educational technology, disability law, and policy.

## Notes

1   James Baldwin, "As Much Truth as One Can Bear," *New York Times,* January 14, 1962, 38.

2   Ibid, 1.

3   Peter Phillips, "Preface," *Censored 2003: Media Democracy in Action* (New York: Seven Stories Press, 2002), 11.

4   On the pitfalls of depersonalization and balance as means to achieve journalistic objectivity, see Robert M. Entman, "Objectivity, Slant, and Bias in the News," in *Democracy without Citizens* (New York: Oxford University Press, 1989), 30–38.

5   Peter Phillips, DaveyD, Marc Sapir, and Project Censored, "Media Democracy in Action," in *Censored 2004,* ed. Peter Phillips and Project Censored (New York: Seven Stories Press, 2003), 181-217, quote at 181.

6   Mnar Muhawesh, "What the Media's Getting Wrong about Israel and Palestine—and Why It Matters," MintPress News, July 10, 2014, http://www.mintpressnews.com/mnar-muhawesh-what-the-medias-getting-wrong-about-israel-and-palestine-and-why-it-matters/193607/.

7   Dale Gavlak and Yahya Ababneh, "Syrians in Ghouta Claim Saudi-Supplied Rebels Behind Chemical Attack," MintPress News, August 29, 2013, http://www.mintpressnews.com/witnesses-of-gas-attack-say-saudis-supplied-rebels-with-chemical-weapons/168135/.

8   In 1975, US Senator Frank Church headed the Senate's Select Committee to Study Governmental Operations with Respect to Intelligence Activities. The committee, often referred to as the Church Committee, published a series of reports on alleged abuses of law and power by the CIA, NSA, and FBI, and recommended reform of these agencies' intelligence gathering practices.

9   Rosa Luxemburg, *The Mass Strike, the Political Party, and the Trade Unions,* trans. Patrick Lavin (Detroit: Marxist Educational Society of Detroit, 1925), Ch. 7. Online see: https://www.marxists.org/archive/luxemburg/1906/mass-strike/ch07.htm.

10  Bruce Dixon, "Are Democracy Now!'s Libyan Correspondents Feeding Us the State Department and Pentagon Line on Libya?," Black Agenda Report, October 5, 2011, http://www.blackagendareport.com/content/are-democracy-nows-libyan-correspondents-feeding-us-state-department-and-pentagon-line-libya.

11  For analysis of how "philanthropic practices allow the dominant classes to generate knowledge about society and regulatory prescriptions," see Nicolas Guilhot, "Reforming the World: George Soros, Global Capitalism and the Philanthropic Management of the Social Sci-

ences," *Critical Sociology*, 33, no. 3 (2007): 447–77. Since the late twentieth century, Guilhot writes, a new transnational strata of financial elites has used philanthropy as "a privileged strategy for generating new forms of 'policy knowledge'" that converge with their interests.

12  Darlene Storm, "Army of Fake Social Media Friends to Promote Propaganda," *PC World*, February 23, 2011, http://www.computerworld.com/article/2470594/endpoint-security/army-of-fake-social-media-friends-to-promote-propaganda.html.

13  Ali Abunimah, "New Evidence about Amina, the 'Gay Girl in Damascus' Hoax," Electronic Intifada, June 12, 2011, https://electronicintifada.net/blogs/ali-abunimah/new-evidence-about-amina-gay-girl-damascus-hoax.

14  Elizabeth Flock and Melissa Bell, "Tom MacMaster, the Man behind 'A Gay Girl in Damascus:' 'I Didn't Expect the Story to Get So Big,'" *Washington Post*, June 13, 2011.

15  PBS Independent Lens, "Democracy on Deadline," http://www.pbs.org/independentlens/democracyondeadline/mediaownership.html.

16  Robert Parry, "Samantha Power: Liberal War Hawk," Consortium News, June 15, 2015, https://consortiumnews.com/2015/06/15/samantha-power-liberal-war-hawk/.

17  Abby Martin, "The U.S. School That Trains Dictators & Death Squads," *Empire Files* (TeleSUR English), December 5, 2015, https://www.youtube.com/watch?v=GUtumGkoE6Q.

18  Neela Banerjee, "Can Fracking Pollute Drinking Water? Don't Ask the EPA," InsideClimate News, March 2, 2015, http://insideclimatenews.org/news/02032015/can-fracking-pollute-drinking-water-dont-ask-epa-hydraulic-fracturing-obama-chesapeake-energy.

19  Ibid.

20  Hugh MacMillan, "How the Wheels Fell Off the EPA's Fracking Study," Food & Water Watch, November 2, 2015, http://www.foodandwaterwatch.org/insight/how-wheels-fell-epa%E2%80%99s-fracking-study.

21  Don Hopey, "Board Questions EPA Report on Fracking," *Pittsburgh Post-Gazette*, November 28, 2015. http://powersource.post-gazette.com/powersource/2015/11/28/Advisory-board-raises-issues-on-EPA-fracking-report/stories/201511300044.

22  *Corporate Control in Animal Science Research*, Food & Water Watch, April 2015, http://www.foodandwaterwatch.org/insight/corporate-control-animal-science-research.

23  *Public Research, Private Gain*, Food & Water Watch, April 2012, http://www.foodandwaterwatch.org/insight/public-research-private-gain.

24  Alan Scher Zagier, "Corporations Boost Agricultural Research Funding," Associated Press, June 7, 2012, http://www.northjersey.com/news/health-news/corporations-boost-agricultural-research-funding-1.446574?page=all; "Corporations Boost Agricultural Research Funding," Harvest Public Media, June 7, 2012, http://harvestpublicmedia.org/article/1246/corporations-boost-agricultural-research-funding/5.

25  Monica Eng, "Why Didn't an Illinois Professor Have to Disclose GMO Funding?" WBEZ, March 15, 2016, https://www.wbez.org/shows/wbez-news/u-of-i-professor-did-not-disclose-gmo-funding/eb99bdd2-683d-4108-9528-de1375c3e9fb.

26  Darcey Rakestraw, "Truth from the Tap: A Water Industry PR Blitz," Food & Water Watch, April 28, 2015, http://www.foodandwaterwatch.org/news/truth-tap-water-industry-pr-blitz.

27  Darcey Rakestraw, "Water Industry Launches Attack on Water Democracy, Promotes Privatization," AlterNet, April 29, 2015, http://www.alternet.org/environment/water-industry-launches-attack-water-democracy-promotes-privatization.

28  Michael Deane, "Quit the Private Water Scare Tactics in Atlantic City," *Press of Atlantic City*, March 23, 2016, http://www.pressofatlanticcity.com/opinion/commentary/michael-deane-quit-the-private-water-scare-tactics-in-atlantic/article_6eadd87f-85ff-54d0-8254-80a9efd68812.html; Lena Smith, "Private Water Industry Offers Attacks, Not Solutions for Atlantic City," *Press of Atlantic City*, March 30, 2015, http://www.pressofatlanticcity.com/opinion/commentary/lena-smith-private-water-industry-offers-attacks-not-solutions-for/article_c44ae048-31a8-5eb9-8336-86db4037973f.html.

29  Wendy A. Lascell, "Academic Service-Learning Faculty Handbook," State University of New York, Oneonta, 2014, http://www.oneonta.edu/academics/csrc/PDFs/SL_Handbook_Lascell_2014.pdf.

30  Alexander W. Astin, Lori J. Vogelgesang, Elaine K. Ikeda, and Jennifer A. Yee, "How Service Learning Affects Students," Higher Education Research Institute, UCLA, January 2000, http://heri.ucla.edu/pdfs/hslas/hslas.pdf.

31  Comfort O. Okpala, Leon Sturdivant and Linda Hopson, "Assessment of the Impact of Service Learning on Academic Growth of College Students," *Journal of College Teaching & Learning*, 6, no. 4 (July/August 2009), 65-8, http://www.cluteinstitute.com/ojs/index.php/TLC/article/view/1156.

32  Astin, et al., " How Service Learning Affects Students."

33  Wanda Kanwischer, Amanda Lilgreen, and Monica Saralampi, "Service Learning as a College Involvement and Success Strategy for Underserved Student Populations," *Journal for Civic Commitment*, 23 (March 2015), http://ccncce.org/articles/service-learning-as-a-college-involve-ment-and-success-strategy-for-underserved-student-populations/.

34  For another, complementary perspective on integrating service learning and Project Censored, see Michael I. Niman, "Service Learning: The SUNY-Buffalo State and Project Censored Partnership," in *Censored 2015: Inspiring We the People*, eds. Andy Lee Roth and Mickey Huff (New York: Seven Stories Press, 2014), 193-8.

35  Vasconcellos Institute for Democracy in Action, De Anza College, no date, https://www.deanza.edu/vida/.

36  *Universal Design in Higher Education: From Principles to Practice*, 2e, ed. Sheryl E. Burgstahler (Cambridge, MA: Harvard Education Press, 2015), 37.

37  "Hidden curriculum" refers to values or behaviors that students learn indirectly through the structure of a schooling system and the methods of teaching used in it. These hidden curricula often perpetuate systemic educational inequalities. See, for example, the contributions to *The Hidden Curriculum in Higher Education*, ed. Eric Margolis (New York and London: Routledge, 2001).

38  Jane K. Seale, *E-Learning and Disability in Higher Education: Accessibility Research and Practice*, 2e, (New York and London: Routledge, 2014), 11-13.

# CHAPTER 5

# Contested Visions, Imperfect Information, and the Persistence of Conspiracy Theories

Susan Maret

As I write this chapter for Project Censored's fortieth anniversary, philosopher David Ray Griffin's talk "9/11: The Myth and the Reality" plays in the background. In this YouTube video, Griffin addresses "nine of the major myths contained in the official story about 9/11."[1] Myth 3, for example, argues that the attacks of September 11 were "such a big operation, involving so many people, [they] could not have been kept a secret, because someone involved in it would have talked by now." As support for Myth 3, Griffin compares the official narrative about 9/11 with the secrecy of the "Manhattan Project to create the atomic bomb, and the war in Indonesia in 1957, which the United States government provoked, participated in, and was able to keep secret from its own people until a book about it appeared in 1995."[2]

On the surface, these connections with secrecy appear convincing. US government secrecy *did* become institutionalized through the regulation of information related to bombmaking, so much so that ideas and inventions were not merely marked classified, they came into existence "born classified". This concept "grew quite naturally out of the American experience in World War II. The atomic bomb project was one of the best kept secrets of the war."[3] As for the dark history of the Indonesian war as cited by Griffin, and documented by scholars Audrey R. Kahin and George McTurnan Kahin in their *Subversion as Foreign Policy: The Secret Eisenhower and Dulles Debacle in Indonesia*, this too has plausible roots in government secrecy. In part, Kahin and Kahin's research was made possible by the *Foreign Relations of the United States* (*FRUS*), published by the Office of the Historian, US State Department. In the graduate course I teach on secrecy and intellectual freedom, we study the dynamics of *FRUS*, generally described as the "official documentary historical record of major US foreign policy decisions and significant diplomatic activity."[4] *FRUS* is constructed from public and formerly classified records of the National Security Council, the intelligence community, the Departments of Defense and State, and the private papers of policymakers involved in formulating US foreign policy. A special nine-member committee, comprised of scholars and archivists with security clearances, review records for inclusion in *FRUS*.[5] *FRUS* has been criticized for its historical inaccuracy as well as for its significant time lag in publishing subject volumes.[6] History by delay aptly describes *FRUS*' time lag, described in 1983 as growing at "an alarming rate: fifteen years in the 1920s and 1930s, by the late 1950s the gap had grown to twenty years, and today is closer to thirty."[7] In its 2015 report, the Advisory Committee on Historical Diplomatic Documentation noted that the "series has never averaged a 30-year lag time, and the current average exceeds 35 years."[8]

I use these cases alongside Griffin's Myth 3 to illustrate that government policies and events often *do* reveal themselves as records seep from federal bodies, Freedom of Information Act requests, and leaks, which all have power to transmute fragmented official accounts into public histories. Once wedded to secrecy, the post-WWII Operations Sunset, Paperclip, and Gladio, the role of the US in the overthrow and assassinations of foreign leaders, multiple CIA Cold War projects (e.g., Artichoke, MKNAOMI, MKULTRA), the exploits of CIA director Allen Dulles, decades-long rumors of NSA surveillance, the Bush administration's plan to bomb Al Jazeera, and CIA-run black sites in Europe—turned out to be authentic.[9]

At this point, it is possible to identify several key features of conspiracy theory ideation and formation: *one, the past imprints on the present*. While it is no longer the same world, *it is*. The past, like one technology of yesteryear, the acetate transparency, overlays the present and shapes perceptions and tests relationships; and *two, it is often difficult to dismiss conspiracy theories (CTs) merely on the basis of what is known now in terms of publicly available knowledge.* In the parallel government, where regulatory secrecy runs course with partial publicity and transparency, histories are written over decades and constructed on redacted, fragmented, perhaps even faulty information. None of my comments regarding Myth 3 should imply I support Griffin's claim; what I am interested in pointing out is the nature of imperfect information, which carries with it the potential to create suspicion, which as Jeremy Bentham observed, "always attaches to mystery. It thinks it sees a crime where it beholds an affectation of secrecy; and it is rarely deceived."[11] Historian Kathryn S. Olmsted offers a more contemporary view of suspicion and conspiracies, one that is compatible with my discussion in this chapter:

> More often, however, the culture of suspicion created by the revelations of government conspiracies undermines democracy. When citizens cannot trust their government to tell the truth, when they are convinced that public officials routinely conspire, lie, and conceal their crimes, they become less likely to trust the government to do anything. The result is a profoundly weakened polity, with fewer citizens voting and more problems left unaddressed for a future generation that is ever more cynical about the possibility of reforms.[12]

In this chapter, I discuss these ideas, as well as offer a sketch of information conditions that affect the development and evolution of CTs. I then offer a brief review of the research literature regarding conspiracies, conspiracy theorists, and conspiracy theory-making. I propose nine patterns that take the scholarly community to task for its framing and views of CTs. These patterns explore the underlying dynamics that potentially lead to the building of conspiracy theories and suggest a pressing need for new directions in critical and interpretive research and methods. The patterns are also a set of recommendations, or what might be seen as a manifesto for the research community to consider in its future study of CTs.

# TRUST NO ONE

Research by the American National Election Studies, Pew Research Center, and scholars such as Russell J. Dalton indicate that trust in government, including but not limited to the US government, has declined since the 1950s.[13] Sociologist Anthony Giddens likens trust to "a form of faith in which confidence vested in probable outcomes expresses a commitment to something."[14] Building conceptually on Giddens, we can delineate trust as dependence upon some individual or body because *we are not in a position to know everything*.[15] If secrecy has the ability to modify relationships, including relations between citizens and their government, then the ability to trust or distrust does as well.[16] While it may reduce social complexity, trust "simplifies life by the taking of a risk. [17] However, the identification of risks, responding to risk, and risk taking are highly dependent on information; information as knowledge communicated becomes the central means that enables connection—it then becomes a "key question *who* gets what information, by *what* means, and in *what* order, about *whom* and *what*, and for *what* purpose."[18] A two-way street, trust is a mutuality, for in entrusting government, citizens take risks in choosing leadership in exchange for political stability and protection from "critical situations," or those "circumstances of radical disjuncture of an unpredictable kind" which may affect individuals and institutions.[19] Therefore, trust is directly connected to the state of knowledge and security, no matter what side of the fence one is on.[20]

A review of US information policies finds persistent use of conditions of information such as secrecy,[21] blowback,[22] censorship,[23] lying,[24] plausible deniability, "colors" of propaganda,[25] redaction, misinformation,[26] disinformation,[27] eyewash,[28] and hearsay.[29] Reclassification of previously declassified records[30] and removal of personal papers from special collections to review "security material"[31] add to this problem. Over the course of US history, these information conditions have become *de facto* national security information policies used to cloak details of assassinations, clandestine programs, covert surveillance,[32] human experimentation,[33] torture,[34] careless environmental practices,[35] weapons research and development, election fraud, interference with the media, and "cultural pathologies" of certain federal agencies.[36] Yet other conditions, such as the "twisting" of language, also contribute to the concealment of information in order to meet some objective and sway public opinion. Not quite propaganda, but a "tampering of communications" nevertheless, an example of twisting is the differently worded classified and unclassified versions of the National Intelligence Estimate to select members of Congress that led to the invasion of Iraq in 2003.[37]

Additional scenarios, such as poor preservation and organization of information, risk communication during crises and disasters (e.g., 9/11, the Flint water crisis, the Fukushima nuclear disaster, Hurricane Katrina, the Sandy Hook shooting, and the nuclear crisis at Three Mile Island) and institutional failures (e.g., the FBI's destruction of the Koresh compound in Waco, or the financial crisis of 2007–08) are often interpreted as secrecy, active censorship, and much worse. Moreover, what Ulrich Beck described in 1992 as the "enabling power of catastrophes" with their endless state of emergencies (e.g., homeland and national security) have now become a normal state.[38] Threat level conditions bring "totally new kinds of challenges to democracy," one of which is the post-9/11 range of surveillance, which includes vigorous collection of biometric data and monitoring of communications.[39] This new normal reflects a "tendency to legitimate totalitarianism of hazard prevention."[40] These "critical situations" may contribute to lack of trust in official accounts, which have the potential to lead to speculation, fictions, rumors, and the formation of CTs as a passive form of protest and rejection of "legitimate knowledge."

Christopher L. Hinson lumps many of the categories listed above as *negative information actions*, or "the willful and deliberate act designed to keep government information from those in government and the public entitled to it."[41] While these information conditions are surely negative in the sense of tempering and arresting the flow of information, it must be acknowledged there are legitimate reasons for the use of some, or all of these conditions, one among them, state security. One scholar suggests that in cases of government information restriction, officials share select details accompanied with a timeline projecting when information can be publicly released in full.[42] However, even with the best of intentions, moderating the flow of information impedes understanding of policies, modifies public trust, and with it, the ability to exercise oversight.

CTs are perhaps intensified by the "mixed media culture," with its "varying standards of journalism, and a fascination with inexpensive, polarizing argument."[43] The late Gary Webb saw journalistic integrity and the production of news influenced by "nervous editors" who avoid reporting controversial stories unless a reporter obtained "an admission of wrongdoing (preferably written) or an official government report confirm[ed] the story's charge."[44] This "new rule," as Webb terms it, overwrote traditional methods of journalism where a reporter "diligently investigated the issue, used named sources, found supporting documentation, and [if] you honestly believed it was true, you went with it."[45] I'll let Mr. Webb speak for himself in recounting firsthand how the shift from traditional journalistic methods influence the public right to know, morphing into a kind of censorship that is subtle and insidious:

> . . . stories about serious, unacknowledged abuses [no longer] get printed, and eventually reporters learn not to waste their time turning over rocks if no one will officially confirm when something hideous slithers out. And once that happens, they cease being journalists and become akin to the scribes of antiquity, whose sole task was to faithfully record the pharaoh's words in clay. It is this latter standard that was championed by Abrams in the Tailwind case and to some extent by *San Jose Mercury News* editor Jerry Ceppos in the case of my "Dark Alliance" series in 1996. Under these new rules, it isn't enough anymore for a reporter to have on-the-record sources and supporting documentation. Now they must have something called "proof." Investigative stories must be "proven" in order to reach the public; having "insufficient evidence" is now cause for retraction and dismissal.[46]

It is under these complex information conditions that I propose that CTs occur within social systems that are not only imperfect in terms of publicity and transparency, but suffer from a "security obsession." Many of the information conditions as listed above, I conjecture, enable CTs, thereby influencing public trust. Zygmunt Bauman outlines the problem in a far more cohesive way:

> To sum up, perhaps the most pernicious, seminal and long-term effect of the security obsession (the "collateral damage" it perpetrates) is the sapping of mutual trust and the sowing and breeding of mutual suspicion. With lack of trust, border-lines are drawn and with suspicion, they are fortified with mutual prejudices and recycled into frontlines. The deficit of trust inevitably leads to a wilting of communication; in avoiding communication, and the absence of interest in its renewal, the "strangeness" of strangers is bound to deepen and acquire ever darker and more sinister tones which in turn disqualifies them even more radically as potential part-ners in dialogue and the negotiation of a mutually safe and agreeable mode of cohabitation.[47]

In short, put together and over decades, these conditions, cou-pled with technology platforms that place demands on information seeking skills and literacies, create an environment ripe for specula-tive thinking, conflicting perspectives, alternative research avenues, *and* conspiracy theory building.[48]

## OF CONSPIRACIES AND CONSPIRACY THEORISTS

The popular and interdisciplinary research literature on conspiracy theories, as many theories themselves, is richly imaginative and descriptive.[49] The one "truth" is that no definitive theory or model offers a completely satisfactory explanation of what constitutes a conspiracy, or how CTs are constructed, propagated, and become entrenched within social systems.

*Conspiracies* in US law "include the fact that regardless of its statu-tory setting, every conspiracy has at least two elements: (1) an agree-ment (2) between two or more persons. Members of the conspiracy are also liable for the foreseeable crimes of their fellows committed in furtherance of the common plot. Moreover, statements by one con-spirator are admissible evidence against all."[50] Conspiracies then, as noted by Julian Assange, "take information about the world in which they operate (the conspiratorial environment), pass through the conspirators and then act on the result."[51] Assange categorizes conspiracies as a type of "cognitive device" that contain "inputs (information about the environment), a computational network (the conspirators and their links to each other) and outputs (actions intend[ed] to change or maintain the environment)."[52] An example that supports Assange's views of conspiracy are the graceful, revealing drawings by conceptual artist Mark Lombardi, whose own death in 2000 propelled numerous CTs.[53] Lombardi's "maps" envision social networks, or the "narrative structures" as Lombardi explained his work, underlying among other subjects, political leaders, spy agencies, and their role in covert financing and shadow banking, the global drug trade, and terrorism.[54]

A *conspiracy theorist* is characterized as an individual who "actively investigates whether conspiracies have taken place or are taking place, and when and if he discovers them tries to publicly identify the conspirators."[55] Theorists are depicted as "victims of cognitive failure," not necessarily suffering from irrationality or mental illness, but from a "crippled epistemology" due to a "sharply limited number of (relevant) informational sources."[56] Theorists are also often categorized as conservative and holding fundamentalist beliefs.[57] Husting and Orr argue the label *conspiracy theorist* functions symbolically, "protecting certain decisions and people from question in arenas of political, cultural, and scholarly knowledge construction."[58] The authors conclude the phrase conspiracy theorist acts a "transpersonal strategy of exclusion."[59]

The seeds of popular and scholarly framing of CTs can be traced to Karl Popper's "conspiracy theory of society" and Richard Hofstadter's "paranoid style," often used as boilerplates in the framing of conspiracy theory building by certain individuals and groups.[60] It is the paranoid style, representative of a "conspiratorial mind," which Hofstadter describes as "manifest on the extreme right wing, among those I have called pseudoconservatives, who believe that we have lived for a generation in the grip of a vast conspiracy."[61] The paranoid style is intended by Hofstadter as "pejorative ... the paranoid style has a greater affinity for bad causes than good."[62] Hofstadter claimed the paranoid style appears in "waves of different intensity" as "an old and recurrent mode of expression in our public life which has frequently been linked with movements of suspicious discontent and whose content remains much the same even when it is adopted by men of distinctly different purposes."[63] Although Hofstadter did not expressly make the link between anti-intellectualism and the advance of conspiracy theories, in the 1950s other researchers made this connection.[64]

Richard O. Curry notes that "fear of conspiracy is most intense during periods of national crisis," especially "when traditional social and moral values are undergoing change."[65] CTs are linked to political extremism and viewed as instrumental in planting the seeds of terrorism, although this connection is inconclusive.[66] The 2006 *National Security Strategy of the United States of America*, for example, links terrorism with CTs, stating that "terrorists recruit more effectively from populations whose information about the world is contaminated by falsehoods and corrupted by conspiracy theories."[67] Conspiracy theorists are further organized into left- and right-wing ideologies as reported in the Department of Homeland Security's (DHS) withdrawn, controversial *Domestic Extremism Lexicon*.[68] DHS marks left-wing extremists as "a movement of groups or individuals that embraces anticapitalist, Communist, or Socialist doctrines and seeks to bring about change through violent revolution rather than through established political processes," while right-wing extremists are defined as a movement or individuals "who can be broadly divided into those who are primarily hate-oriented, and those who are mainly antigovernment and reject federal authority in favor of state or local authority."[69] DHS's attempt at defining extremism is thorny at best, as there exists no one accepted definition of extremism across law, international agreement, and the scholarly literature.

Perhaps there is another way to consider conspiracy theorists and their theories. Former director of the Information Security Oversight Office (ISOO) William J. Leonard offers a compelling view, one that raises questions regarding democratic values and the rise of extremism:

> Our continuing failure to isolate the extremists is due, in part, to the worldwide perception that we continue to vio-

late our own values and ideals, especially as they relate to human dignity and the rule of law. This perception was fostered by some of our own government officials when they refused during the Bush years to plainly state that physically restraining an individual and forcing his lungs to slowly fill up with water constitutes torture. They did this, in part, by hiding behind the classification system—by stating that to acknowledge limits to interrogation techniques used by our intelligence services (but not our military) would somehow disclose classified information—and thus harm our national security.[70]

This brief review suggests that certain CTs refer to the past, some are focused on subjects in the present, and some CTs merge the past with the present; still other CTs are characterized in the research literature as having the capacity to "triumph in the future if they are not disturbed in their plans by those with information about their sinister doings."[71] Thus historical context plays "a decisive role in the genesis and elaboration" of CTs,[72] although some researchers have gone so far as to speculate that CTs may constitute a "necessary part of capitalism and democracy."[73] Finally, while it is productive to think of CTs like "doorways into major social and political issues defining U.S. (and global) political culture since the end of the cold war," CTs are doorways, *period*.[74]

## WHAT IS A CONSPIRACY THEORY?

There is no single agreed-on definition of conspiracy theory. Definitions and descriptions of CTs are abundant, ranging from "the unnecessary assumption of conspiracy where other explanations are more probable," to the "belief that an organization made up of individuals or groups was or is acting covertly to achieve some malevolent end," and a "hypothesis that some events were caused by the intractable secret machinations of undemocratic individuals."[75] Under the former George W. Bush administration, the US State Department's Bureau of International Information characterized CTs as "vast, powerful, evil forces," that are "secretly manipulating events . . . this fits the profile of a conspiracy theory, which is rarely true, even though such theories have great appeal and are often widely believed. In reality, events usually have much less exciting explanations."[76] CTs are portrayed as "poisoned discourse," which "encourages a vortex of illusion and superstition," and framed as explanations of "important events that hypothesize . . . the intentional deception and manipulation of those involved in, affected by, or witnessing these events."[77] CTs have also been defined as a:

> Proposed explanation of an historical event, in which conspiracy (i.e., agents acting secretly in concert) has a significant role. Furthermore, the conspiracy postulated by the proposed explanation must be a conspiracy to bring about the historical event which it purports to explain . . . the proposed explanation must conflict with an "official" explanation of the same historical event.[78]

CTs concern "specific people or groups of people, acting with purposes that are undisclosed or outside accountability or even examination by others," and/or an "effort to explain some event or practice by reference to the machinations of powerful people, who attempt to conceal their role (at least until their aims are accomplished)."[79] This latter definition, crafted by Cass Sunstein and Adrian Vermeule, is contested by David Ray Griffin. Griffin suggests that a "generic" definition pulled from a common dictionary might better serve as a basis for understanding CTs. Griffin proposes that "to hold a conspiracy theory about some event is, therefore, simply to believe that this event resulted from, or involved, such an agreement. This, we can say, is the generic meaning of the term."[80] Another flexible definition is suggested by Olmsted, who notes the statutory/legal roots of conspiracy: conspiracies "occur when two people collude to abuse power or break the law. A conspiracy theory is a proposal about a conspiracy that may or may not be true; it has not yet been proven."[81]

Conspiracy theories are also framed as "*counter*theories: that is, they are always posed in opposition to official accounts of suspicious events."[82] CTs are depicted as "knowledge-producing discourse characterized by a collection of statements and texts shaped within and by different (para) institutional contexts which promote a particular knowledge about the world."[83] The "prototypical" CT, according to Rob Brotherton, is an "unanswered question," for a CT "assumes nothing [is] as it seems . . . it portrays the conspirators as preternaturally competent and as unusually evil; it is founded on anomaly hunting, and is ultimately irrefutable."[84] CTs function both as a part of suppressed knowledge and as a basis for stigmatization, involving stigmatized knowledge, or "claims to truth that the claimants regard as verified despite the marginalization of those claims by the institutions that conventionally distinguish between knowledge and error—universities, communities of scientific researchers and the like."[85] The use of "conspiracy theory" is often used as a "reframing device that neutralizes questions about power and motive while turning the force of challenges back onto their speakers, rendering them unfit public interlocutors."[86] These and other definitions aside, Steve Clarke identifies several benefits of CTs, for the conspiracy theorist "challenges us to improve our social explanations," while also helping to "maintain openness in society."[87]

This brief tour of the CT research literature identifies certain themes such as suspicion, paranoia, distrust, insecurity, uncertainty, secrecy, and power over information. These definitions also suggest *asymmetries in information* between "conspirators" and outsiders that occur under regimes of imperfect information flows. One further characterization of CTs by philosopher Charles Pigden offers an additional consideration of how we might respond to conspiracy theories as narratives that "couldn't possibly happen in free societies that have an open media and freedom of information laws." That is, are "transparent" and democratically elected governments capable of hatching loathsome, rights-infringing secret schemes? We know from historians, journalists, whistleblowers, and human rights workers the answer is yes. Pigden demands that we consider the possibility that conspiracy theories reflect a failure of the democratic process, specifically a collapse of the checks and balances that are derived from public participation:[88]

> The concept of a conspiracy theory as it is commonly employed is a chauvinist construct. It is not to be understood

in terms of governments generally, but in terms of Western governments, and recent Western governments at that. When people say or imply that conspiracy theories ought not to be believed, what they actually mean (in so far as they have a coherent idea) is that we should not believe theories that postulate evil schemes on the part of recent or contemporary Western governments (or government agencies) and that run counter to the current orthodoxy in the relevant Western countries.[89]

## THE PATTERNS THAT CONNECT[90]

Discussed below are patterns that appear in the research literature and in CTs as socially-produced artifacts. These nine patterns identify recurring themes and underlying processes in the scholarly literature and within conspiracy communities as knowledge communities that gather, interpret, produce, and disseminate knowledge:[91]

PATTERN 1: We require better definitions of what constitutes a conspiracy theory. The very notion of conspiracy theory brings to mind sociologist Ulrich Beck's "zombie categories," wherein an idea lives on even after it is long dead.[92] It is time to throw off the dead weight of Popper and Hofstadter. As we've witnessed from our brief exploration of CTs, "conspiracy theory" is a cup too full with countless definitions and theories. There is a desperate need to differentiate CTs that involve institutional failures and malfeasance from those that arise in other environments, such as accounts that are racist, sexist, homophobic, or promote violence. Critical differentiations will lead to better tracing of information flows and targeted use of research methods.

PATTERN 2: Building on Pattern 1, scholarly analyses that lump together CTs as if they are "like" narratives perpetuate ignorance and misunderstanding. For example, many works cited in this chapter discuss the moon landing, Elvis sightings, Heaven's Gate suicides, alien abductions, the death of Princess Diana, climate denial, state crimes, and various politically-motivated assassinations as if all of these conspiracy theories are similar. To treat all CTs as identical in origin and scope is to contaminate the sample. CTs involving "alien technology," for example, might belong in critiques of government secrecy if they concern secret weapons research and development, or unexplained phenomena found in declassified records.[93] Alien abduction narratives are usually not CTs, nor are paranormal or Fortean phenomena (unexplained naturally occurring phenomena). All of these subjects, however, suggest that "the question of how one knows what one knows cannot be ignored."[94]

Select CTs that intersect with conditions of information and cases of "administrative evil,"[95] political and state crimes (e.g., State Crimes Against Democracy or SCADs[96]), and institutional failures variously outlined in the social science literature as atrophy of vigilance, bureaucratic slippage, and recreancy, should be considered in a different way.[97] These CTs, which range from political assassinations, experiments on unwitting subjects, and destabilization of governments, to 9/11 as a "controversial possible SCAD," point to power relations at work in society, and how decisions are made in closed, powerful, secretive groups that may be guilty of corruption.[98] Some of these groups may indeed constitute secret societies (e.g., CFR, Trilateral Commission, Bilderberg Group, Seldes's 1000 Americans, Mills's power elite, Domhoff's "who rules," the military industrial complex, or the surveillance industrial complex).[99]

PATTERN 3: Lack of research and follow-through to fully characterize and frame specific CTs undermines confidence in findings among researchers and the public. One glaring example involves the JFK assassination, often portrayed in the scholarly literature as the gold standard of CTs. Below I use the House Select Committee on Assassinations (HSCA) conspiracy conclusion to chart the failure of the scholarly community to fully trace the trajectory of CTs and to examine its own approaches.

Measurement studies cited as "proof" that JFK conspiracy theorists suffer from "biased assimilation" leading to "attitude polarization" are only slightly more puzzling than the widespread ignorance of the HSCA's findings.[100] The HSCA was organized out of the Senate

Select Committee to Study Governmental Operations with Respect to Intelligence Activities (Church Committee) investigation of CIA covert assassination programs. The HSCA's extensive investigation began in 1976 and concluded in 1979, resulting in twelve volumes of testimony, research, and exhibits. A review of the scholarly sources cited in this chapter found that *no* researchers concerned with CTs, either their ideation or disputing them, cited the HSCA's highly significant findings that President John F. Kennedy was "probably assassinated as a result of a conspiracy." According to its report, the HSCA was "unable to identify the other gunman or the extent of the conspiracy."[101]

HSCA determined, among other matters, that the Secret Service "was deficient in the performance of its duties;" it also concluded that the Department of Justice "failed to exercise initiative in supervising and directing the investigation by the Federal Bureau of Investigation of the assassination."[102] Although the HSCA's conclusions regarding the acoustical evidence from the Dallas police Dictabelt recordings remain a matter of contention, the Commission raised significant questions that go unanswered today. Eyewitness testimony, the Harper fragment, bystander James Tague's cheek injury, discrepancies in matching rifles, the Warren Commission's Exhibit 399, analysis of photographs taken by witnesses, and the three films taken by bystanders, including Abraham Zapruder, are only some of the unresolved issues among scholars, journalists, and citizen researchers. This pattern suggests that outright debunking is never scholarship; it is a step beyond the necessary skepticism that any critical inquiry must include.

PATTERN 4: The creation of conspiracy theory is tied to sense-making. Sense-making, a concept developed by Brenda Dervin in 1972, starts from an assumption that "reality is neither complete nor constant but rather filled with fundamental and pervasive discontinuities or gaps."[103] Sense making involves the inference that, while individuals interact with time and space, their "information seeking and using behaviors (both internal and external) can remain static, can change responsively, and can even change chaotically."[104] Dervin's sense-making is critical to further understanding of CTs in terms of how individuals use factizing to "make their worlds" through what Dervin terms "proceduring, a designing called making facts."[105] Sense-making challenges the notion that there is "one right way to produce knowledge."[106] As it relates to the formation of CTs, sense-making suggests the "forces of power in society and in organizations . . . prescribe acceptable answers and make disagreeing with them, even in the face of the evidence of one's own experience, a scary and risky thing to do. Even more difficult is when the forces of power flow through an organization or system hidden and undisclosed."[107]

PATTERN 5: Building on Pattern 4 and my discussion so far, government secrecy propels individuals to utilize mosaic building in order to construct theories about events and actions. Mosaic building advances sense-making in the piecing together of "disparate items of information, though individually of limited or no utility" that, nonetheless, "take on added significance when combined with other items of information."[108] My use of mosaic building to understand CTs draws on Paul Solomon's concept of information mosaics, but adapts his idea of "indicated patterns of actions" on the basis of *CIA v. Sims*.[109] In this case, the Supreme Court held that the CIA had authority to withhold information requested through Freedom of Information Act (FOIA) concerning researchers and institutions contracted by the Agency in its MKULTRA projects. The Court argued that "an observer who is knowledgeable about a particular intelligence research project, such as MKULTRA, could, upon learning that the research was performed at a certain institution, deduce the identities of the protected individual researchers."[110] After consulting with institutions and researchers contracted to work on MKULTRA, the CIA disclosed the names of fifty-nine institutions that agreed to disclosure, but the Agency did not reveal any individual researchers' names. The CIA then refused to disclose the remaining information, claiming that researchers and affiliated institutions were "intelligence sources" as intended by the National Security Act of 1947, and therefore that the Agency could withhold the information pursuant to FOIA Exemption 3.[111]

Conspiracy theorists flip the switch in taking disparate pieces of information from a wide variety of sources, including public (open source) information and declassified, redacted documents. Using the mosaic concept allows for speculation that, in some cases, takes hold as a counter-narrative. Out of disparate pieces of information, working histories reconstruct past events and actions to create new history. This follows Brian Keeley's observation that individuals engaged in producing CTs typically seek to tie together seemingly unrelated events.[112] The potential knowledge-producing ability of the mosaic identified in *CIA v. Sims* is an essential part of conspiracy theory building, a process that also includes the risk of adopting faulty beliefs as well as far-reaching assumptions and conclusions.

PATTERN 6: Building on Giddens's observation that "all human beings are knowledgeable agents," conspiracy theorists are fundamentally researchers and archivists.[113] Byford writes that "conspiracy theorists do not see themselves as raconteurs of alluring stories, but as investigators and researchers. That is why the conspiracy thesis will usually be embedded within a detailed exposition of plausible and verifiable historical facts."[114] Depending on the CT, those individuals or knowledge communities that investigate CTs are citizen-scientists, citizen-journalists, and "barefoot" researchers.[115] For example, JFK assassination researchers created vast libraries through the Assassination Archives and Research Center, Black Op Radio, and the Mary Ferrell Foundation.[116] Citizens for Truth about the Kennedy Assassination (CTKA) published one of the only accounts of the three-and-a-half-week Rev. Martin Luther King, Jr. civil suit, *Coretta Scott King, et al v. Loyd Jowers, et al*, conducted in 1999 in Memphis. Jim Douglass reported on the trial for *Probe Magazine*, which is published by CTKA. Neither the civil case nor the jury's decision as quoted below were widely reported in the (corporate) mainstream media:

> In answer to the question did Loyd Jowers participate in a conspiracy to do harm to Dr. Martin Luther King, your answer is yes. Do you also find that others, including governmental agencies, were parties to this conspiracy as alleged by the defendant? Your answer to that one is also yes. And the total amount of damages you find for the plaintiffs entitled to [*sic*] is one hundred dollars. Is that your verdict?

THE JURY: Yes (In unison)[117]

Still other citizens have created Freedom of Information Act (FOIA) archives to monitor US government information policies.[118] The *Corbett Report*, hosted by alternative media researcher James Corbett, and former FBI translator Sibel Edmonds's *Boiling Frogs Post* both investigate off-grid news stories and produce a weekly podcast. The controversial Alex Jones and his Infowars team produce films, books, and a podcast. Jones, who we might describe as sometimes suffering from Hofstadter's "curious leap in imagination," nevertheless conducts research and produces knowledge.[119] Various UFO groups, including the former ParaNet[120] and the Center for UFO Studies (CUFOS), founded by astronomer J. Allen Hynek, employ the Hynek Classification System, which rates the visibility or proximity of unidentified aerial objects. Mutual UFO Network (MUFON) utilizes the Vallee Classification System developed by astronomer Dr. Jacques Vallee.[121]

PATTERN 7: Conspiracy theories involve a certain level of syncretism, or the combination or fusion of beliefs, culture, and language to form new meanings. For example, Michael A. Hoffman II and Loren Coleman employ the concept of *twilight language* to identify hidden meanings, symbolic connections, and "cues" behind certain events such as mass shootings.[122] Twilight language, borrowed from Tantric Buddhism, is "written in a highly oblique and obscure literary form . . . designed to conceal its contents from non-practitioners."[123] Other examples of syncretism are the use of the Trivium Method of Critical Thinking.[124] The notion of *New World Order*, a term borrowed from H.G. Wells, was popularized in George H.W. Bush's 1991 State of the Union address, and then morphed into CT usage.[125] The use of *false flag*, a term from military strategy, has consistently been part of CT discourse since the 9/11 attacks. The mash-up of Hegel's *thesis, antithesis, and synthesis* evolved into CT usage as "problem-reaction-solution." Conspiracy theorists understand this characterization as a way that regimes manufacture a problem, encourage a targeted reaction, and propose a specific explanation, action, or (orchestrated) solution, often without democratic participation.

PATTERN 8: Following Pattern 7, a hallmark of CTs is the development of specialized language or discourse in describing complex social phenomena. Language is often borrowed from other contexts (Pattern 7), but can also arise spontaneously in response to events and actions. Terms such as the *mental health national spy complex, spyporn*, and *suicided* (a possible state-sanctioned murder of a person who is officially reported as committing suicide) represent specific worldviews on the nature of authority and distrust in official accounts.

PATTERN 9: Like a Russian nesting doll, or *matryoshka*, CTs often consist of theories within theories. For instance, theories about the 9/11 attacks often comprise multiple, originally independent CTs, including controlled demolition, Building 7 and real estate mogul Larry Silverstein, an "inside job" by the Bush administration, the role of the "dancing Israelis," North American Aerospace Defense Command (NORAD)'s delayed scrambling of F-15 fighters, an alleged Dick Cheney stand-down order, an alleged order to shoot down Flight 93 made by Cheney, letters containing anthrax sent to Senate Judiciary Committee Chairman Patrick Leahy and Senate Majority Leader Tom Daschle, and Operation Northwoods's false flag. The 9/11 case is but one example of how one theory morphs into multiple, connected theories—thus suggesting Lombardi's narrative structures—each with its own distinct dynamics and information flow. CTs, then, are a *web of relations*. This pattern, like many of the patterns outlined here, illustrate that to fully grasp the nature of CTs we must follow the trail from beginning to end. We must painstakingly chart the forensics of conspiracy theories from their origins through to their manifestation on whatever medium or platform they occur.

## FINAL THOUGHTS

This chapter discussed conditions of information and their role in conspiracy theory making. I reviewed the research literature on conspiracies, conspiracy theorists, and conspiracy theories, and introduced nine patterns that lay a conceptual groundwork for thinking about conspiracy theories. As I have argued here, the research community desperately needs not only new definitions and models of CTs, but also a framework within which to critically examine state apparatuses that may be responsible for fostering conspiracy theories. We need to trace the sources and the roles of potentially corrupted and missing information, whether from governments, corporations, media, groups, or individuals, that lead to the production of CTs. We can take from Ulrich Beck the need for an "integrative" cognitive sociology as it relates to the study of CTs, for this kind of sociology consists of "all the admixtures, amalgams and agents of knowledge in their combination and opposition, their foundations, their claims, their mistakes, their irrationalities, their truth and, in the impossibility of their knowing, the knowledge they lay claim to."[126] My discussion also suggests the need for the scholarly community to reassess CTs as they "arise in exclusion and proceed as information-seeking on the part of the outs about the ins."[127]

We can accomplish these directions in a few ways: first, by applying theories across disciplinary boundaries,[128] and second, by utilizing methods that place researchers in dialogue with conspiracy theorists and the direct knowledge they produce. The point is that we researchers "can find out, not with perfect accuracy, but better than zero, what people think they are doing, what meanings they give to the objects and events and people in their lives and experience. We do that by talking to them, in formal or informal interviews, in quick exchanges while we participate in and observe their ordinary activities, and by watching and listening."[129] In the post-9/11 universe, these approaches form the basis for a more holistic understanding of the ways conspiracy theories propagate and memetically crawl through social systems in response to imperfect publicity and transparency.

---

SUSAN MARET, PHD, is a Lecturer at the School of Information, San Jose State University. Maret's interest in CTs stems from a research agenda focused on investigating secrecy as the concealment of information and forms of secrecy. Since 2006, Maret has taught a graduate-level course on secrecy and intellectual freedom, which examines the historical, legal, regulatory, and policy structures underlying government secrecy. With Jan Goldman, Maret is coeditor of *Government Secrecy: Classic and Contemporary Readings* (Libraries Unlimited, 2009) and editor of *Government Secrecy; Research in Social Problems and Public Policy* 19 (Emerald, 2011). She is also coeditor with Jan Goldman of *Intelligence and Information Policy for National Security: Key Terms and Concepts* (Rowman & Littlefield, 2016).

*The author wishes to thank Ivan Greenberg, Mickey Huff, EB, BEB, RC, and MK for their thoughtful comments and suggestions on this chapter. Project Censored thanks Tom Haseloff, sociology major at UC Berkeley, for additional proofreading and formatting assistance.*

## Notes

1   David Ray Griffin, "9/11: The Myth and the Reality," lecture given to the Progressive Democrats of the East Bay, Oakland, CA, March 30, 2006, transcript, http://www.911truth.org/911-the-myth-and-the-reality/. YouTube video at https://www.youtube.com/watch?v=z9UwsSXwTYg.
2   Ibid.
3   Richard G. Hewlett, "The 'Born-Classified' Concept in the US Atomic Energy Commission," US House of Representatives, Committee on Government Operations, *The Government's Classification of Private Ideas: Thirty-fourth Report* (Washington, DC: Government Printing Office, 1980), 173–87.
4   "Historical Documents: *Foreign Relations of the United States* (FRUS)," US Department of State, Office of the Historian, no date, accessed May 5, 2016, http://history.state.gov/historicaldocuments.
5   "Authority and Responsibilities" and "Meeting Notes," US Department of State, Advisory Committee on Historical Diplomatic Documentation, no date, accessed May 5, 2016, https://history.state.gov/about/hac/intro and https://history.state.gov/about/hac/meeting-notes, respectively.
6   See David N. Gibbs, "Misrepresenting the Congo Crisis," *African Affairs* 95, no. 380 (July 1996), 453–59; and William B. McAllister, Joshua Botts, Peter Cozzens, and Aaron W. Marrs, *Toward "Thorough, Accurate, and Reliable": A History of the Foreign Relations of the United States Series* (US Department of State, Office of the Historian, Bureau of Public Affairs, 2015), http://static.history.state.gov/frus-history/ebooks/frus-history.pdf.
7   Lorraine M. Lees and Sandra Gioia Treadway, "Review: A Future for Our Diplomatic Past? A Critical Appraisal of the Foreign Relations Series," *Journal of American History* 70, no. 3 (December 1983), 621–29.
8   "Report of the Advisory Committee on Historical Diplomatic Documentation, January 1–December 31, 2014," US Department of State, Advisory Committee on Historical Diplomatic Documentation, April 19, 2015, accessed May 7, 2016, https://www.fas.org/sgp/advisory/state/hac2014.html.
9   David Talbot, *The Devil's Chessboard: Allen Dulles, the CIA, and the Rise of America's Secret Government* (New York: HarperCollins, 2015); James Bamford, *The Puzzle Palace: A Report on America's Most Secret Agency* (Boston: Houghton Mifflin, 1982); David Leigh and Richard Norton-Taylor, "MPs Leaked Bush Plan to Hit al-Jazeera," *Guardian*, January 9, 2006, accessed May 4, 2016, http://www.theguardian.com/media/2006/jan/09/Iraqandthemedia.politicsandiraq.
10  Publicity is described by Jeremy Bentham as "exposure—the completest exposure of the whole system of procedure—whatever is done by anybody, being done before the eyes of the universal public." See Jeremy Bentham, *The Works of Jeremy Bentham, vol. 2, Published Under the Superintendence of His Executor John Bowring.* (London, Simpkin, Marshall, 1843), 19; Transparency on the other hand, is a "process operating differently in different contexts" (416) but also "a process of requiring persons in relations of community with others to account for their actions, understandings and commitments as regards matters directly relevant to those relations" (414). See Roger Cotterrell, "Transparency, Mass Media, Ideology and Community," *Cultural Research* 3, no. 4 (1999): 414-426.

11   Jeremy Bentham, "Of Publicity," in *Political Tactics*, edited by Michael James and Cyprian Blamires (Oxford: Clarendon Press), 29-44.

12   Kathryn S. Olmsted, "Government Secrecy and Conspiracy Theories," in *Government Secrecy; Research in Social Problems and Public Policy* 19, ed. Susan Maret (Bingley, UK: Emerald Group Publishing, 2011), 91–100.

13   See data compiled from American National Election Studies (http://www.electionstudies.org/); "Beyond Distrust: How Americans View Their Government," Pew Research Center, November 23, 2015, http://www.people-press.org/2015/11/23/beyond-distrust-how-americans-view-their-government/; Russell J. Dalton, "The Social Transformation of Trust in Government," *International Review of Sociology* 15, no. 1 (2005), 133–54, doi: 10.1080/03906700500038819.

14   Anthony Giddens, *The Consequences of Modernity* (Stanford, CA: Stanford University Press, 1990), 27.

15   A simplified Kantian argument.

16   Georg Simmel, "The Sociology of Secrecy and of Secret Societies," *American Journal of Sociology* 11, no. 4 (January 1906), 441–98.

17   Niklas Luhmann, *Trust and Power* (New York: John Wiley and Sons, 1979), 71.

18   Ulrich Beck, *Risk Society: Towards a New Modernity*, tr. Mark Ritter (Thousand Oaks, CA: Sage, 1992), 218. See also Leon Festinger, *A Theory of Cognitive Dissonance* (Stanford, CA: Stanford University Press, 1962), 10.

19   Anthony Giddens, *The Constitution of Society: Outline of a Theory of Structuration* (Berkeley, CA: University of California Press, 1984), 61.

20   See Beatrice De Graaf and Cornel Zwierlein, "Historicizing Security—Entering the Conspiracy Dispositive," *Historical Social Research/Historische Sozialforschung* 38, no. 1 (2013), 46–64.

21   As the intention of concealment of information. See Georg Simmel, "The Sociology of Secrecy."

22   That is, deception involving information planted outside the US by a government source or intelligence agency. The information then "blows back" to that agency or within government, having the potential to mislead officials and the public. See US House of Representatives, Permanent Select Committee on Intelligence, *The CIA and the Media: Hearings before the Subcommittee on Oversight of the Permanent Select Committee on Intelligence, House of Representatives, Ninety-Fifth Congress, First and Second Sessions, December 27, 28, 29, 1977, January 4, 5, and April 20, 1978* (Washington, DC: US Government Printing Office, 1978) and Loch K. Johnson, "The CIA and the Media," *Intelligence and National Security* 1, no. 2 (1986), 143–69.

23   Many definitions exist; the definition that seems most relevant to my discussion is from Cull, Culbert, and Welch, where censorship takes two forms: 1. Selection of information to support a particular viewpoint, or 2. Deliberate manipulation or doctoring of information to create an impression different from the original one intended. Nicholas J. Cull, David Culbert, and David Welch, *Propaganda and Mass Persuasion: A Historical Encyclopedia, 1500 to the Present* (Santa Barbara, CA: ABC-CLIO, 2003).

24   Lying (lies) are outlined as a form of deception, but not all forms of deception are lies. See Sissela Bok, *Lying: Moral Choice in Public and Private Life* (New York: Vintage Books, 1999).

25   "Black" or covert propaganda concerns false sources accompanied by lies, fabrications, and deceptions. Direct propaganda must be preceded by propaganda that is sociological in character, slow, general, seeking to create a climate, an atmosphere of favorable preliminary attitudes. "Gray" propaganda relates to a source that may or may not be correctly identified, and the accuracy of the information is uncertain, and often used to embarrass an enemy or competitor. "White" or overt propaganda is defined as a source that is correctly identified and communicates accurate information, and there is an attempt to build credibility. See Nicholas J. Cull, David Culbert, and David Welch, *Propaganda and Mass Persuasion*.

26   Defined as information "presented as truthful initially but that turns out to be false later." See Stephan Lewandowsky et al., "Misinformation, Disinformation, and Violent Conflict: From Iraq and the 'War on Terror' to Future Threats to Peace," *American Psychologist* 68, no. 7 (October 2013), 487, doi: 10.1037/a0034515.

27   Marchetti and Marks describe "black propaganda and disinformation as virtually indistinguishable. Both refer to the spreading of false information in order to influence people's opinions or actions. Disinformation is a special type of black propaganda ('outright lies') which hinges on absolute secrecy and which is usually supported by false documents." See Victor Marchetti and John D. Marks, *The CIA and the Cult of Intelligence* (New York: Knopf, 1974), 164–67.

28   A CIA practice of disseminating internal memos that contain false information. There is no marking of "eyewashed" documents "distinguishing them from legitimate records being examined by the CIA's Inspector General, turned over to Congress or declassified for historians." See Greg Miller and Adam Goldman, "'Eyewash': How the CIA Deceives Its Own Workforce about Operations," *Washington Post*, January 31, 2016, accessed May 15, 2016, https://www.washingtonpost.com/world/national-security/eyewash-how-the-cia-deceives-its-own-workforce-about-operations/2016/01/31/c00f5a78-c53d-11e5-9693-933a4d31bcc8_story.html.

29   For example, in *Al-Adahi v. Obama*, the District Court rejected evidence submitted by US government lawyers, deeming it hearsay based on third party accounts. See *Alla Ali Bin Ali Ahmed, et al., Petitioners v. Barack H. Obama, et al., Respondents*, Civil Action No. 05-1678 (GK), Memorandum Opinion, US District Court for the District of Columbia, May 11, 2009, accessed May 2, 2016, https://ecf.dcd.uscourts.gov/cgi-bin/show_public_doc?2005cv1678-220, 8.

30   That is, the restoration of security classification to information previously declassified. See *Declassification in Reverse: The US Intelligence Community's Secret Historical Document Reclassification Program*, ed. Matthew Aid, National Security Archive, February 21, 2006, accessed May 1, 2016, http://www.gwu.edu/~nsarchiv/NSAEBB/NSAEBB179/.

31   Jefferson Morley, "How the CIA Writes History," *Intercept*, April 25, 2016, accessed May 11, 2016, https://theintercept.com/2016/04/25/how-the-cia-writes-history/.

32   See Ivan Greenberg, *Surveillance in America: Critical Analysis of the FBI, 1920 to the Present* (Lanham, MD: Lexington Books, 2012) and Laura Poitras, director, *Citizenfour* (documentary film), New York: Radius-TWC, 2014.

33   See for example, Jonathan D. Moreno, *Undue Risk: Secret State Experiments on Humans* (New York: Routledge, 2013); John D. Marks, *The Search for the 'Manchurian Candidate': The CIA and Mind Control, The Secret History of the Behavioral Sciences* (New York: W.W. Norton & Company, 1991), and the final report of the committee, convened by the Clinton administration, to report on the use of human beings as subjects of federally-funded research using ionizing radiation, Advisory Committee on Human Radiation Experiments, "ACHRE Report," US Department of Energy Openness Program, October 1995, accessed May 5, 2016, https://ehss.energy.gov/ohre/roadmap/achre/summary.html.

34   For example, US Senate Select Committee on Intelligence, "Committee Study on Central Intelligence Agency's Detention and Interrogation Program," released by Dianne Feinstein, US Senate Select Committee on Intelligence Chairman, December 9, 2014, accessed May 5, 2016, http://www.feinstein.senate.gov/public/index.cfm/senate-intelligence-committee-study-on-cia-detention-and-interrogation-program.

35   See the infamous Area 51 case, *Kazsa v. Browner*, Nos. 96-15535, 96-15537, 96-16047, 96-16892, 96-16895, 96-16930 and 96-16933, United States Court of Appeals, Ninth Circuit, January 8, 1998, accessed May 15, 2016, http://caselaw.findlaw.com/us-9th-circuit/1129437.html. Through Presidential Determination No. 95-45 (October 10, 1995), the Clinton administration exempted the Groom Lake facility from RCRA provisions that would require disclosure of environmental practices.

36   Amy Zegart, "9/11 and the FBI: The Organizational Roots of Failure," *Intelligence and National Security* 22, no. 2 (2007), 165–84, doi: 10.1080/02684520701415123.

37   Carl J. Friedrich, *The Pathology of Politics: Violence, Betrayal, Corruption, Secrecy, and Propaganda* (New York: Harper and Row, 1972); J. William Leonard, "The Corrupting Influence of Secrecy on National Policy Decisions," *Government Secrecy: Research in Social Problems and Public Policy* 19, ed. Susan Maret (Bingley, UK: Emerald Group Publishing, 2011), 421–34.

38   Ulrich Beck, *Risk Society*, 79.

39 Ibid., 80; Also see Gabe Rottman, "Massive FBI Biometric Database Must be Subject to Appropriate Public Scrutiny," Center for Democracy and Technology, May 31, 2016, accessed June 1, 2016, https://cdt.org/blog/massive-fbi-biometric-database-must-be-subject-to-appropriate-public-scrutiny/.

40 Ulrich Beck, Risk Society, 80.

41 Christopher L. Hinson, "Negative Information Action: Danger for Democracy," American Behavioral Scientist 53, no. 6 (February 2010), 826–47, doi: 10.1177/0002764209353276.

42 Dennis F. Thompson, "Democratic Secrecy," Political Science Quarterly 114, no. 2 (1999), 181–93, doi: 10.2307/2657736. Also see Sissela Bok, Secrets: On the Ethics of Concealment and Revelation (New York: Vintage Books, 1989).

43 Bill Kovach and Tom Rosenstiel, Warp Speed: America in the Age of Mixed Media (New York: Century Foundation, 1999), 5–8. Also see trust-in-government data compiled from American National Election Studies (http://www.electionstudies.org/), Pew Research Center, "Beyond Distrust," and Russell J. Dalton, "The Social Transformation of Trust in Government."

44 Gary Webb, "New Rules for the New Millennium," You are Being Lied To: The Disinformation Guide to Media Distortion, Historical Whitewashes and Cultural Myths, ed. Russ Kick (New York: Disinformation Company, 2001), 38–39.

45 Ibid., 39.

46 Ibid.

47 Zygmunt Bauman, Collateral Damage: Social Inequalities in a Global Age (Cambridge, UK/ Malden, MA: Polity, 2011), 70.

48 So many literacies: Critical media literacy, historical, information, media-information, research, scientific, and visual literacy. Of note is the Framework for Information Literacy which defines information literacy as the ability to "recognize when information is needed and have the ability to locate, evaluate and use effectively the needed information." One of the principles of the Framework is that "authority is constructed and contextual." See the Association of College and Research Libraries, Framework for Information Literacy for Higher Education, February 2, 2015, accessed April 11, 2016, http://www.ala.org/acrl/sites/ala.org.acrl/files/content/issues/infolit/Framework_ILHE.pdf.

UNESCO defines media-information literacy as the ability to "interpret and make informed judgments as users of information and media, as well as to become skillful creators and producers of information and media messages in their own right. Media and information literate citizens must have a good understanding of the functions of the media in a democratic society including a basic knowledge of concepts such as freedom of speech, the free press and the right to information." See Martin Scott, Guidelines for Broadcasters on Promoting User-Generated Content and Media and Information Literacy (London: Commonwealth Broadcasting Association, 2009), 10, accessed April 11, 2016, http://www.unesco.org/new/en/communication-and-information/resources/publications-and-communication-materials/publications/full-list/guidelines-for-broadcasters-on-promoting-user-generated-content-and-media-and-information-literacy/.

49 For example, see Jovan Byford, Conspiracy Theories: A Critical Introduction (Basingstoke, England/New York: Palgrave Macmillan, 2011); Mark Fenster, Conspiracy Theories: Secrecy and Power in American Culture, revised ed. (Minneapolis, MN: University of Minnesota Press, 2008); various essays in Conspiracy Nation: The Politics of Paranoia in Postwar America, ed. Peter Knight (New York: New York University Press, 2002), Timothy Melley, Empire of Conspiracy: The Culture of Paranoia in Postwar America (Ithaca, NY; London: Cornell University Press, 2000), and Ted Goertzel, "Belief in Conspiracy Theories," International Society of Political Psychology 15, no. 4 (December 1994), 731–42, doi: 10.2307/3791630.

50 Charles Doyle, "Federal Conspiracy Law: A Brief Overview (Report R41223)," Congressional Research Service, January 20, 2016, accessed May 15, 2016, https://www.fas.org/sgp/crs/misc/R41223.pdf.

51 Julian Assange, State and Terrorist Conspiracies, iq.org, November 10, 2006, accessed April 15, 2016, https://cryptome.org/0002/ja-conspiracies.pdf.

52 Ibid., 3.

53   Patricia Goldstone, "The Artist Who Obsessed the FBI," *Daily Beast*, December 13, 2015, accessed May 2, 2016, http://www.thedailybeast.com/articles/2015/12/13/the-artist-who-obsessed-the-fbi.html.

54   Mark Lombardi, *Global Networks*, ed. Judith Richard, text by Robert Hobbs (New York: Independent Curators International, 2003) and Patricia Goldstone, *Interlock: Art, Conspiracy, and the Shadow Worlds of Mark Lombardi* (Berkeley, CA: Counterpoint Press, 2015).

55   David Coady, "Are Conspiracy Theorists Irrational?" *Episteme* 4, no. 2 (2007): 193–204, doi: 10.3366/epi.2007.4.2.193.

56   Steve Clarke, "Conspiracy Theories and Conspiracy Theorizing," *Philosophy of the Social Sciences* 32, no. 2 (June 2002): 131–50, doi: 10.1177/004931032002001; Cass R. Sunstein and Adrian Vermeule, "Conspiracy Theories," *Harvard Public Law Working Paper No. 08-03; U of Chicago, Public Law Working Paper No. 199; U of Chicago Law & Economics, Olin Working Paper No. 387*, January 15, 2008, accessed May 5, 2016, http://papers.ssrn.com/sol3/papers.cfm?abstract_id=1084585.

57   Research by Skocpol and Williamson identified members of the Tea Party as "overwhelmingly conservative Republicans" that manufacture "conspiratorial concerns [that] can seem harmless, but they have real policy consequences." Vanessa Williamson, "The Tea Party and the Remaking of Republican Conservatism," *Eurozine*, October 29, 2012, accessed May 15, 2016, http://www.eurozine.com/articles/2012-10-29-williamson-en.html.

58   Gina Husting and Martin Orr, "Dangerous Machinery: 'Conspiracy Theorist' as a Transpersonal Strategy of Exclusion," *Symbolic Interaction* 30, no. 2 (2007), 127–50.

59   Ibid.

60   Two works that started it all: Karl R. Popper, *The Open Society and its Enemies, Volume Two: Hegel and Marx* (New York: Routledge, 1945) with its discussion of the "conspiracy theory of society," and Richard Hofstadter, *The Paranoid Style in American Politics and Other Essays* (New York: Knopf, 1965).

61   Richard Hofstadter, *The Paranoid Style*, xi. In other parts of his essay, Hofstadter notes the paranoid style "is not always right-wing," 3.

62   Ibid., 5.

63   Ibid., 6.

64   Scholars at a 1955 conference sponsored by Goddard College on the topic of anti-intellectualism identified anxiety, rumor, an overemphasis on security, and "distrust of intellectuals in government" as an affront to rationality; this seems more in line with Popper's conspiracy theory of society than Hofstadter's work, but it is Hofstadter's influence that later takes hold in the research literature attached to CTs. See various articles in the *Journal of Social Issues* 11, no. 3 (1955) and Richard Hofstadter, *Anti-Intellectualism in American Life* (New York: Knopf, 1963).

65   Richard O. Curry, "Introduction," in *Conspiracy: The Fear of Subversion in American History*, eds. Richard O. Curry and Thomas M. Brown (New York: Holt, Rinehart and Winston, 1972), viii–ix. Also see David Brion Davis, *The Fear of Conspiracy; Images of Un-American Subversion from the Revolution to the Present* (New York: Cornell University Press, 1971); Geoffrey Cubitt, *The Jesuit Myth: Conspiracy Theory and Politics in Nineteenth-Century France* (Oxford: Clarendon Press, 1993); and *Conspiracy Theories in American History: An Encyclopedia*, ed. Peter Knight (Santa Barbara, CA: ABC-CLIO, 2003).

66   Jan-Willem van Prooijen, André P.M. Krouwel, and Thomas V. Pollet, "Political Extremism Predicts Belief in Conspiracy Theories," *Social Psychological and Personality Science* 6, no. 5 (July 2015), 570–78, doi: 10.1177/1948550614567356; and see Jamie Bartlett and Carl Miller, *The Power of Unreason: Conspiracy Theories, Extremism and Counter-terrorism* (London: Demos, 2010), accessed May 5, 2016, http://www.demos.co.uk/files/Conspiracy_theories_paper.pdf?1282913891. Also see Matt Apuzzo, "Who Will Become a Terrorist? Research Yields Few Clues," *New York Times*, March 27, 2016, accessed May 27, 2016, http://www.nytimes.com/2016/03/28/world/europe/mystery-about-who-will-become-a-terrorist-defies-clear-answers.html

67   White House, *The National Security Strategy of the United States of America*, March 2006, http://nssarchive.us/NSSR/2006.pdf.

68  US Department of Homeland Security, *Domestic Extremism Lexicon*, March 26, 2009, accessed May 5, 2016, https://fas.org/irp/eprint/lexicon.pdf. Due to public outcry, the *Lexicon* changed titles in 2011, with a reduced number of categories and definitions. See US Department of Homeland Security, *Domestic Terrorism and Homegrown Violent Extremism Lexicon*, November 10, 2011, accessed May 5, 2016, https://publicintelligence.net/domestic-terrorism-and-homegrown-violent-extremism-lexicon/.

69  Ibid.

70  J. William Leonard, "The Corrupting Influence of Secrecy," 429.

71  Dieter Groh, "The Temptation of Conspiracy Theory, or: Why Do Bad Things Happen to Good People? Part II: Case Studies," in *Changing Conceptions of Conspiracy*, eds. Carl F. Graumann and Serge Moscovici (Springer New York, 1987), 15–37.

72  Michael Barkun, *A Culture of Conspiracy: Apocalyptic Visions in Contemporary America* (Berkeley: University of California Press, 2013), 3.

73  Mark Fenster, *Conspiracy Theories*, 11.

74  Jack Z. Bratich, *Conspiracy Panics: Political Rationality and Popular Culture* (Albany, NY: SUNY Press, 2008), 6.

75  David Aaronovitch, *Voodoo Histories: The Role of the Conspiracy Theory in Shaping Modern History* (New York: Riverhead Books, 2010), 6; Michael Barkun, *A Culture of Conspiracy*, 3; Michael Albert, "Conspiracy Theory," *Z Magazine*, August 1, 1995, accessed April 28, 2016, https://zcomm.org/zmagazine/conspiracy-theory-by-michael-albert/.

76  US Department of State, "How to Identify Misinformation," USINFO, archived page from the Wayback Machine, accessed May 5, 2016, http://wayback.archive.org/web/20050427002601/http://usinfo.state.gov/media/Archive_Index/Identifying_Misinformation.html.

77  Daniel Pipes, *Conspiracy: How the Paranoid Style Flourishes and Where It Comes From* (New York: Simon and Schuster, 1999); Lee Basham, "Living with the Conspiracy," *Philosophical Forum* 32, no. 3 (2001), 265–80, doi: 10.1111/0031-806X.00065.

78  David Coady, "Conspiracy Theories and Official Stories," *International Journal of Applied Philosophy* 17, no. 2 (2003), 197–209, doi: 10.5840/ijap200317210.

79  Jon W. Anderson, "Conspiracy Theories, Premature Entextualization, and Popular Political Analysis," *Arab Studies Journal* 4, no. 1 (1996), 96–102, http://www.jstor.org/stable/27933679; Cass R. Sunstein and Adrian Vermeule, "Conspiracy Theories: Causes and Cures," *Journal of Political Philosophy* 17, no. 2 (June 2009), 202–27, doi: 10.1111/j.1467-9760.2008.00325.x.

80  David Ray Griffin, *Cognitive Infiltration: An Obama Appointee's Plan to Undermine the 9/11 Conspiracy Theory* (Northampton, MA: Olive Branch Press, 2011), 2.

81  Kathryn S. Olmsted, *Real Enemies: Conspiracy Theories and American Democracy, World War I to 9/11* (New York/Oxford: Oxford University Press, 2009), 3.

82  Lance deHaven-Smith, "Beyond Conspiracy Theory: Patterns of High Crime in American Government," *American Behavioral Scientist* 53, no. 6 (February 2010), 795–825, doi: 10.1177/0002764209353274.

83  Clare Birchall, *Knowledge Goes Pop: From Conspiracy Theory to Gossip* (New York/Oxford: Berg Publishers, 2006), 34.

84  Rob Brotherton, *Suspicious Minds: Why We Believe Conspiracy Theories* (New York: Bloomsbury Publishing, 2015), 80.

85  Michael Barkun, *A Culture of Conspiracy*, 27, 26.

86  Gina Husting and Martin Orr, "Dangerous Machinery," 146.

87  Steve Clarke, "Conspiracy Theories and Conspiracy Theorizing," 148.

88  See Robert A. Dahl, *Democracy and Its Critics* (New Haven, CT: Yale University Press, 1989).

89  Charles R. Pigden, "Conspiracy Theories and the Conventional Wisdom," *Episteme* 4, no. 2 (2007), 219–32, doi: 10.3366/epi.2007.4.2.219.

90  The idea of pattern is liberally taken from Gregory Bateson, *Mind and Nature: A Necessary Unity* (New York: Dutton, 1979). In this work, Bateson discusses patterns as communication in providing context and meaning; pattern making—and order—both occur through information.

91  Taken from Peter M. Haas, "Introduction: Epistemic Communities and International Policy Coordination," *International Organization* 46, no. 1 (1992), 1–35.

92  Ulrich Beck and Elisabeth Beck-Gernsheim, *Individualization: Institutionalized Individualism and Its Social and Political Consequences* (Thousand Oaks, CA: SAGE, 2002), 202–12.

93  See for example, puzzlement by government authorities as to the nature of "UFOs" as reported in documents in the *Declassified Documents Reference System* (DDRS). One document I received under FOIA (I wanted to verify the provenance of the memo) from the CIA in 2015 is a memo written in 1952 by Gen. Walter B. (Bedell) Smith to members of the Psychological Strategy Board on the subject of unidentified flying objects. The sixteen-page memo, which can be found on the Web, discusses among other matters, the National Security Council's recognition "as a national security problem our present limited capabilities in making prompt positive visual or mechanical identification of flying objects." The memo discusses the objects as "having possible implications for psychological warfare" and raises questions as to the Soviet Union's "present level of knowledge regarding these phenomena." See Walter B. Smith to Director, Psychological Strategy Board, 1952, Director of Central Intelligence, Memorandum Subject: "Flying Saucers," CIA -RDP81R00560R000100020017-2, approved for release April 4, 2001, https://www.cia.gov/library/readingroom/docs/DOC_0000015338.pdf.

94  Ron Westrum, "Social Intelligence about Anomalies: The Case of UFOs," *Social Studies of Science* 7, no. 3 (August 1977), 271–302, doi: 10.1177/030631277700700302.

95  Adams and Balfour write that "the masking of administrative evil suggests that evil also occurs along another continuum: from acts committed in relative ignorance to those committed knowingly and deliberately, or what we would characterize as masked and unmasked evil." See Guy B. Adams and Danny L. Balfour, *Unmasking Administrative Evil* (Armonk, New York: M.E. Sharpe, 2015), 12.

96  See for example Morton H. Halperin, Robert L. Borosage, Jerry J. Berman, and Christine M. Marwick, *The Lawless State: The Crimes of the US Intelligence Agencies* (Penguin Books, 1976) and Lance deHaven-Smith, "When Political Crimes are Inside Jobs: Detecting State Crimes Against Democracy," *Administrative Theory & Praxis* 28, no. 3 (September 2006), 330–55, http://www.jstor.org/stable/25610803, who offer cases of such crimes. DeHaven-Smith outlines SCADs as "concerted actions or inactions by public officials that are intended to weaken or subvert popular control of their government ... SCADs include not only election tampering, vote fraud, government graft, political assassinations, and similar crimes when they are initiated by public officials, but also subtle violations of democratic processes and prerequisites" (333). SCADs also entail "political assassination, false-flag terrorism, election theft, military provocation, and contrived crises in industry, finance, energy, and public health" (Lance deHaven-Smith, Alexander Kouzmin, Kym Thorne, and Matthew T. Witt, "The Limits of Permissible Change in U.S. Politics and Policy: Learning from the Obama Presidency," *Administrative Theory & Praxis* 32, no. 1 (2010), 134–40, doi: 10.2753/ATP1084-1806320110). Lance deHaven-Smith, *Conspiracy Theory in America* (Austin, TX: University of Texas Press, 2013) also discusses SCADs and their relationship with CTs.

97  *Atrophy of vigilance* is the decline over time in regulatory surveillance; in *bureaucratic slippage*, there is a "tendency for broad policies to be altered through successive reinterpretation, such that the ultimate implementation may bear little resemblance to legislated or other broad statements of policy intent"; and *recreancy*, where "persons entrusted with the operation of systems may have failed to carry out their responsibilities with the necessary vigor." Atrophy of vigilance and recreancy are concepts devised by sociologist William R. Freudenburg; bureaucratic slippage was conceptualized by Bill Freudenburg and Robert Gramling. For an overview, see Susan Maret, "Freudenburg Beyond Borders: Recreancy, Atrophy of Vigilance, Bureaucratic Slippage, and the Tragedy of 9/11," *William R. Freudenburg, A Life in Social Research; Research in Social Problems and Public Policy* 21, ed. Susan Maret (Bingley, United Kingdom: Emerald Group Publishing Limited, 2011), 201–23.

98  Lance deHaven-Smith, *Conspiracy Theory in America*, 149.

99  Based on Georg Simmel, "The Sociology of Secrecy."

100 John W. McHoskey, "Case Closed? On the John F. Kennedy Assassination: Biased Assimilation of Evidence and Attitude Polarization," *Basic and Applied Social Psychology* 17, no. 3 (1995), 395–409, doi: 10.1207/s15324834basp1703_7.

101 The HSCA's conspiracy finding was perhaps in part riding a wave that began with Mark Lane's influential 1966 book *Rush to Judgment* (New York: Holt, Rinehart and Winston, 1966), which suggested the assassination was the result of a conspiracy. Lane's book is cited in the HSCA's volume 6: US House of Representatives, Select Committee on Assassinations, *Investigation of the Assassination of President John F. Kennedy, Appendix to Hearings before the Select Committee on Assassinations of the U.S. House of Representatives, Ninety-fifth Congress, Second Session: Volume VI, Photographic Evidence* (Washington, DC: US Government Printing Office, 1979).

102 US House of Representatives, Select Committee on Assassinations, *Final Report of the Select Committee on Assassinations, U.S. House of Representatives, Ninety-fifth Congress, Second Session: Summary of Findings and Recommendations* (Washington, DC: US Government Printing Office, 1979), 194.

103 Brenda Dervin, "An Overview of Sense-Making Research: Concepts, Methods and Results to Date," presentation at the International Communication Association Annual Meeting, Dallas, TX, May 1983.

104 Brenda Dervin, "Sense-Making's Journey from Metatheory to Methodology to Method: An Example Using Information Seeking and Use as Research Focus." In *Sense-Making Methodology Reader: Selected Writings of Brenda Dervin*, ed. Brenda Dervin, Lois Foreman-Wemet, and Eric Lauterbach (Cresskill, NJ: Hampton, 2003): 153.

105 Brenda Dervin, "Chaos, Order and Sense-Making: A Proposed Theory for Information Design," in *Information Design*, ed. Robert Jacobsen (Cambridge, MA: MIT Press, 1999), 41.

106 Brenda Dervin, "On Studying Information Seeking Methodologically: The Implications of Connecting Metatheory to Method," *Information Processing & Management* 35, no. 6 (1999), 727–750, doi: 10.1016/S0306-4573(99)00023-0.

107 Brenda Dervin, "Sense-making Theory and Practice: An Overview of User Interests in Knowledge Seeking and Use," *Journal of Knowledge Management* 2, no. 2 (November 1998), 36–46, doi: 10.1108/13673279810249369.

108 David E. Pozen, "The Mosaic Theory, National Security, and the Freedom of Information Act," *Yale Law Journal* 115 (2005), 628–79, http://www.yalelawjournal.org/pdf/358_ft038tb4.pdf.

109 Paul Solomon, "Information Mosaics: Patterns of Action that Structure," in *Exploring the Contexts of Information Behaviour; Proceedings of the 2nd International Conference on Research in Information Needs, Seeking, and Use in Different Contexts*, eds. Thomas D. Wilson and David K. Allen (London: Taylor Graham, 1999).

110 *CIA v. SIMS*, No. 83-1075, United States Supreme Court, April 16, 1985, at note 3, http://caselaw.findlaw.com/us-supreme-court/471/159.html.

111 *Sims v. CIA*, Nos. 82-1945, 82-1961, United States Court of Appeals, District of Columbia Circuit, June 10, 1983, http://www.leagle.com/decision/1983804709F2d95_1775/SIMS%20v.%20C.I.A. .

112 Brian L. Keeley, "Of Conspiracy Theories," *Journal of Philosophy* 96, no. 3 (1999), 109–26.

113 Anthony Giddens, *The Constitution of Society*, 281.

114 Jovan Byford, *Conspiracy Theories: A Critical Introduction*, 88.

115 As I intend it here, barefoot research is a form of action research. Barefoot is derived from the barefoot medicine tradition in China, where rural communities included a lay person with basic medical knowledge. These practitioners were not trained physicians, but had knowledge of alternative forms of healing and disease prevention.

116 At http://aarclibrary.org/about-the-aarc/, http://blackopradio.com, and https://www.maryferrell.org/pages/Documents.html, respectively.

117 See *Probe Magazine*, http://www.ctka.net/probeframes.html; *Coretta Scott King, et al v. Loyd Jowers, et al.*, Case No. 97242, Circuit Court of Shelby County, Tennessee for the 13th Judicial District at Memphis, December 9, 1999. A transcript of the proceedings is available at the King Center's site, http://www.thekingcenter.org/civil-case-king-family-versus-jowers.

118  Such as Black Vault (http://www.theblackvault.com/), Government Attic (http://www.governmentattic. org), Memory Hole (http://thememoryhole2.org/), and MuckRock (https://www.muckrock.com/).

119  Hofstadter, *The Paranoid Style*, 24.

120  "Accomplishments," ParaNet Information Services, Inc., August 21, 2002, via the Wayback Machine, accessed May 15, 2016, http://wayback.archive.org/web/20030212055308/http://www.paranetinfo.com/accomplishments.html.

121  Vallee has attempted to merge the two classification systems. See Jacques F. Vallee, *A System of Classification and Reliability Indicators for the Analysis of the Behavior of Unidentified Aerial Phenomena*, jacquesvallee.net, April, 2007, accessed May 15, 2016, http://www.jacquesvallee.net/bookdocs/classif.pdf.

122  See Michael Hoffman, "Twilight Language Glossary in the Case of the Umpqua Shooter," On the Contrary (blog), October 1, 2015, http://revisionistreview.blogspot.com/2015/10/twilight-language-in-case-of-umpqua.html. Coleman's site is at http://copycateffect.blogspot.com/.

123  John Peacock, "Tantric Writings," in *Buddhism: The Illustrated Guide*, ed. Kevin Trainor (New York: Oxford University Press, 2004), 208–11.

124  See "Trivium: Resources for the Trivium Method of Critical Thinking and Problem Solving, Useful to the Peace Revolution Curriculum," Tragedy and Hope, no date, accessed May 17, 2016, https://tragedyandhope.com/trivium/.

125  George H.W. Bush, "Address Before a Joint Session of the Congress on the State of the Union," American Presidency Project, January 29, 1991, accessed May 5, 2016, http://www.presidency.ucsb.edu/ws/?pid=19253.

126  Ulrich Beck, *Risk Society*, 55.

127  Jon W. Anderson, "Conspiracy Theories, Premature Entextualization."

128  Such as securitization, "which predominantly examines how security problems emerge, evolve and dissolve." Thierry Balzacq, "Constructivism and Securitization Studies," in *The Routledge Handbook of Security Studies*, eds. Myriam Dunn Cavelty and Victor Mauer (Abingdon, UK/New York: Routledge, 2010), 56–72.

129  Based on Herbert Blumer. See Howard S. Becker, "The Epistemology of Qualitative Research," in *Essays on Ethnography and Human Development: Context and Meaning in Social Inquiry*, eds. Richard Jessor, Anne Colby, and Richard Schweder (Chicago: University of Chicago Press, 1996), 53–71.

# CHAPTER 6

# Played by the Mighty Wurlitzer

## The Press, the CIA, and the Subversion of Truth

Brian Covert

A journalist in the US specializing in national security issues, Ken Dilanian, found himself under the harsh glare of the media spotlight in September 2014, when it was revealed that he had been collaborating with press officers of the United States government's Central Intelligence Agency (CIA) in the shaping and publishing of his news stories for the *Los Angeles Times*, one of the most influential daily newspapers in the nation.

An exposé by the *Intercept* online magazine showed how, in private e-mail messages to CIA public affairs staff, Dilanian had not only shared entire drafts of his stories with the agency prior to publication, but had also offered to write up for the CIA on at least one occasion a story on controversial US drone strikes overseas that would be "reassuring to the public" and "a good opportunity" for the CIA to put its spin on the issue.[1]

And Dilanian was not alone. Other e-mail messages, though heavily redacted by the CIA, showed that reporters from other major US news organizations likewise had cooperative relationships with the agency.

Meanwhile, across the Atlantic Ocean that same month, a veteran journalist in Germany was blowing the whistle on his own profession. Udo Ulfkotte, a former news editor with the *Frankfurter Allgemeine Zeitung*, one of the largest newspapers in Germany, revealed how he had cooperated over the years with the German Federal Intelligence Service and the CIA itself in the planting of false news stories as a "non-official cover" and a media "propagandist."[2]

That cooperation, which he claimed was approved by his bosses at the newspaper, included putting his own byline on news stories that had originated with intelligence agencies (such as an article about former Libyan President Muammar Gaddafi allegedly building poison gas factories), and accepting free travel and other gifts.[3] It was understood by reporters for major news companies in other European countries as well, Ulfkotte said, that cooperating with agencies like the CIA could boost a reporter's career: "You don't bite the hand that feeds you. That's where corruption starts."[4]

But that corruption is nothing new. The close ties between the institution of the press and the premier spy agency of the USA date back nearly seventy years to the time of the CIA's establishment. Officially, those ties were known from the late 1940s onward as the agency's "Propaganda Assets Inventory"—an institutional Rolodex of sorts, with companies and individuals that could be counted on to cooperate with the CIA. Within the agency, those propaganda assets were known more casually as a part of a "Mighty Wurlitzer" network.[5] This top-secret intelligence version of the famous movie theater organ used academics, artists, labor union members, students, and many others to be played at will as part of the soundtrack for what the CIA saw as a cultural war with America's enemies abroad during the Cold War period.

Members of the US and foreign press, with their direct access to mass audiences, were considered to be especially valuable tools and allies in that cultural war. The CIA's Mighty Wurlitzer, at its peak years later, reportedly had hundreds of institutions and individuals of the press being played at its fingertips, and could boast, in the words of one CIA official, of having "at least one newspaper in every foreign capital at any given time."[6]

Relations between the news media and the CIA over the past seven decades, in fact, have extended far deeper than have ever been reported by the US news media, researched by academia, or admitted to by the American government. This retrospective report attempts to fill in some of the gaps of that obscured history, drawing on news archives, public and private documents, and the author's original investigation—along with the work of the relatively few journalists and scholars who have tried to bring the truth of the issue before the public over the years.

While not totally exhaustive in scope, this report does bring together for the first time a number of the stories and events that have escaped close scrutiny in the wide shadow of the CIA, and that have long been shelved or shunned by the US news media.

## "THE UBIQUITOUS HARRY KERN"

Among the CIA's many Cold War–era assets in the US news media, few have moved through the ranks of high governmental and corporate power, both within the US and abroad, and still operated well below the radar of the watchdog American press for decades, than a top editor of *Newsweek* magazine by the name of Harry Frederick Kern.

In the immediate postwar years following Japan's defeat in World War II, Kern, in his capacity as the foreign affairs editor for *Newsweek*, played a leading role in reversing the official "reform" policies for Japan that were being carried out by the occupation forces under US General Douglas MacArthur—policies that included breaking up Japan's financial-industrial combines, the *zaibatsu*, that were closely allied with the Japanese military during the Pacific war against the US and its allies, and putting leading Japanese figures in prison as suspected war criminals and accomplices in the war effort.

Kern did this through a barrage of negative coverage of the US occupation of Japan in the pages of *Newsweek*, while serving at the same time as chief organizer for the American Council on Japan (ACJ), a New York–based lobby group made up of ultraconservative elements within the US government and military and on Wall Street that vowed to "safeguard and promote the best interests of the United States" in Japan.[7] The goal of Kern and the ACJ was nothing less than to slam the brakes on Washington's reform policies for Japan, which they viewed as a socialistic revival of New Deal–type policies that could potentially keep Wall Street from recouping its massive prewar investment losses from Japan.

Working closely with the ACJ early on in getting its message out was Wall Street attorney Frank Wisner, who would soon become the chief architect of the CIA's Mighty Wurlitzer network of media assets and front companies.[8]

Through persistent lobbying on both sides of the Pacific Ocean, Kern and the ACJ managed in a short time to help change the direction of the US occupation of Japan, and by the end of 1948 a "reverse course" had overtaken the earlier reform plans as a cornerstone of the Truman Doctrine under US president Harry Truman, putting Japan squarely in the US politico-economic sphere of influence.[9]

Allen Dulles was named CIA director in 1953, and it was not long before Kern and the new CIA chief were addressing each other directly on a first-name basis on matters far beyond Japan. In one exchange in 1955, Kern, writing on Newsweek letterhead, broached with Dulles the idea of newly creating "a real crusading anti-Communist paper in Arabic" as a way to counter Soviet propaganda in the Middle East region.[10] Kern closed the letter with a request to meet Dulles personally in Washington to pass along to him "a most interesting and provocative proposal" from the Saudi Arabian ambassador in the US involving "questions of [foreign] policy." The letter indicates that Dulles and Kern were to meet a couple weeks later in the presence of a "Mr. Roosevelt"—most likely Kermit Roosevelt, Jr., a CIA official who had played a key role two years before in a CIA-sponsored coup that restored the former shah of Iran, Mohammad Reza Pahlavi, to power.[11]

In 1956, after a long and eventful career as a senior editor at Newsweek, Kern shed his journalistic cover and went into business on his own as a political fixer and economic broker, putting his old contacts on Wall Street and in Washington to good use. He started a New York–based consulting firm, Foreign Reports Inc., that focused on governmental and corporate clients in Japan and the Middle East, especially the oil-producing nations of Iran and Saudi Arabia.[12]

But Kern's movements abroad were not going unnoticed. In 1966, ten years after he had left Newsweek, the British embassy in Cairo, Egypt, cabled its Foreign Office back in London that Kern "runs an intelligence machinery for the oil companies in the [Middle East] region and cooperates in this with the CIA," noting Kern's efforts in helping to boost the image of King Faisal, the anticommunist monarch of Saudi Arabia.[13]

The US government was also keeping track of the former journalist. "The ubiquitous Harry Kern has appeared coming from Saudi

Arabia where he has apparently sought to persuade King [Faisal] to underwrite a major Arab public relations campaign in the US," read a confidential memo from the US embassy in Cairo to the Department of State in Washington, DC, a few years later. Kern also discreetly passed on to US officials at that time the concerns of the Japanese government over severe oil restrictions on Japan due to Egypt's closure of the Suez Canal.[14]

Kern's connections extended as far as the White House in Washington, DC. In November 1976, shortly after Jimmy Carter's election as US president, Kern relayed to the president-elect a direct message from the crown prince (and future king) of Saudi Arabia concerning ongoing peace talks between Israel and Palestine.[15]

Kern eventually branched out from the international oil consulting business to include the burgeoning US military aircraft industry overseas. It was not uncommon at the time for Kern to be seen visiting the posh Copacabana nightclub in Tokyo, where some of the most famous American singers of the day performed.[16] The VIP-only club was reputed to be a hotbed of espionage in those days, attracting as it did political leaders and corporate executives from around the globe, including representatives of leading military aircraft manufacturers from the United States seeking to secure ever more lucrative deals with the government of Japan.[17]

One of those military aircraft makers, the New York–based Grumman Corporation, became the focus of a major scandal in Japan in 1979, and Harry Kern soon became a familiar figure to the Japanese public as a parliamentary investigation unfolded and his role in the scandal was revealed. News media in Japan reported that an unusually high 40 percent commission was supposedly meant for Kern by Grumman's Tokyo agent, the Nissho Iwai trading firm, for each Grumman Hawkeye E-2C plane sold to Japan's military. That commission, it was reported, was ostensibly to be passed on by Kern to one or more Japanese government officials to help secure the Grumman aircraft deals.

In March 1979, as the Grumman scandal continued breaking wide open in Japan, Kern made a discreet overture to the White House to have the official Japanese investigation shut down. Declassified documents show that Kern contacted Zbigniew Brzezinski, then National Security Council (NSC) advisor to US President Carter, and requested a personal meeting with Brzezinski concerning the Grumman scandal.[18] In a meeting in Washington, DC, with NSC aide Nicholas Platt soon afterward, Kern warned that he would talk if he were forced to clear his name in the Grumman scandal. This included, Kern said, possibly releasing evidence that could implicate prominent Japanese political figures as well as US embassy officials based in Tokyo regarding the sale of Grumman aircraft to the government of Japan.[19]

According to Platt, Kern suggested that the US government might be able to avert a full-blown political crisis with the Grumman investigation in Japan by "influencing the Japanese judiciary to close the case." Platt responded that Kern's role in the Grumman affair was "not an appropriate White House matter" and that it was best left up to the proper legal channels to handle in the US and Japan. Kern disagreed, saying "this was more than just a judiciary matter."[20]

In the end, no public official in Japan was ever implicated in the Grumman scandal and no American linked to the US military aircraft maker, including Kern, was found guilty of any wrongdoing.

Records show that Kern was merely slowed down, not stopped, by the Grumman scandal and the extensive Japanese media coverage of his secretive activities. Within a few years Kern was actively back in the military aircraft game with the help of Samyr Souki, a former *Newsweek* colleague and ex–press spokesman for the Egyptian embassy in Washington, DC. Documents obtained by the author indicate that by 1984, Kern and Souki were secretly pitching to Japanese officials the benefits of buying F-20 Tigershark fighter jets made by the Northrop Corporation, a leading US military aircraft manufacturer. At one point, Kern, then based in Washington, DC, and Souki, based in Paris, France, acted as intermediaries for a Northrop vice president in the US to directly make his company's sales pitch in Japan for the American-made jets.[21]

No evidence has surfaced to date that the "ubiquitous" Harry Kern had any kind of contractual relationship with the CIA; he appears to have served the spy agency over the years more in an advisory role as a high-level informant. In any case, Kern's special place among CIA media assets would go unreported by his former peers in the US corporate press for decades, before finally catching up with him amidst a flurry of exposés of the CIA that broke out in the 1970s.

## BRAINWASHED

As the postwar years of the 1940s gave way to the 1950s, the Mighty Wurlitzer media propaganda network created by Frank Wisner, the ex–Wall Street lawyer now serving as a CIA deputy director, was being operated out of a harmless-sounding section of the CIA called the Office of Policy Coordination. By 1952, Wisner's office had more than 2,800 operatives working in forty-seven CIA stations around the globe, with a budget of $82 million and rising. Wisner, by all accounts, had a particular obsession to "orchestrate" news reports through his Mighty Wurlitzer network.[22]

Prominent at that time among the many US and foreign journalists who secretly lent their professional services to Wisner's Wurlitzer was Edward Hunter, a New York–based veteran news correspondent with legitimate war-reporting credentials behind him. It was Hunter who first introduced a new and frightening word—"brainwashing"— into the American lexicon in a newspaper article in the *Miami Daily News* of Florida in September 1950, just a few months after the US entered the Korean War.[23] In explaining the Chinese reeducation camps of the time, Hunter came up with this new word by taking the two Chinese characters for "wash" and "brain," and injecting them with a political bias that did not exist in the original Chinese meaning of the word *xi nao*.

In news and opinion articles, books, and even testimony in the US Congress, Hunter played a leading role in the brainwashing scare that seemed to pervade American society in the 1950s. He raised public fears about what he called a new, insidious weapon of thought control and manipulation on a mass scale never seen before: refined techniques practiced by the governments of China and other enemies of the USA of literally washing people's minds clean and reformatting their brains with the ideology of communism. The ultimate target of such brainwashing, warned Hunter, was the American people.[24]

Unbeknownst to the public at large at the time, however, Hunter had worked for the psychological warfare division of the Office of

Strategic Services (OSS), the forerunner of the CIA, for two years during World War II.[25] After the war, he was employed by the CIA in its Office of Policy Coordination (home of the Mighty Wurlitzer operations) for at least one year.[26] This apparently included a stint as a reporter at the Hong Kong bureau of *Newsweek* magazine at a time when Hunter was doing research for his first book, *Brain-washing in Red China*, published in 1951. Hunter's status as a CIA agent was reportedly known at the time by the *Newsweek* foreign affairs editor in New York, the esteemed Harry Kern.[27]

Hunter's writings on brainwashing, while generally gaining little traction in the US scientific community, nevertheless fed right into the CIA's push to fight a new "brain warfare" front against America's enemies in the early 1950s, as declared by then CIA director Allen Dulles, and motivated the agency in ensuing years to delve even more deeply into secret mind-control experiments of its own.[28] But it was the US corporate news media that played the most critical role of all by widely reporting on and giving much-needed credibility to Hunter's unscientific, sensational accounts of brainwashing to an unknowing American public.

In the 1960s Hunter publicly aligned himself with the extremist "radical right" political movement in the USA that spoke openly of violent overthrow of the government under President John F. Kennedy.[29] It was not until Hunter's death in 1978 that his past CIA employment was finally reported by the Associated Press wire service (in contrast to the *Washington Post*, which neglected to mention any such employment in its own obituary on Hunter).[30] Today the CIA's website refers to the late Hunter as a "journalist and onetime CIA officer," and a collection of his old brainwashing-related Chinese propaganda materials is still preserved by an American consortium of university libraries.[31]

So, was the big brainwashing scare of the 1950s part of some CIA propaganda campaign? It is entirely possible, though the available evidence so far remains inconclusive. What is certain is that the term Edward Hunter conceived and publicized through the American media, "brainwashing," remains deeply embedded in popular culture around the world many years later.

## WORKING THE MIGHTY WURLITZER

*The New York Times* was an especially rich source of media assets and friendly informants for the Mighty Wurlitzer in the 1950s, from the very top of the company all the way down through the ranks of news reporters. Among the most valuable of them was Julius Ochs Adler, general manager of the *Times* and nephew of a past owner of the paper. As such, Adler oversaw the business side of the newspaper's operations and had direct access to the editorial side at the highest levels as well.

Adler also happened to be a close personal friend of CIA director Allen Dulles, going all the way back to their undergraduate years together at Princeton University decades earlier. Dulles and Adler dispensed with formalities in business letters, addressing each other on a casual first-name basis as "Julie" and "Allie."[32] When the *New York Times* published an editorial in early 1953 praising US President Dwight Eisenhower's "excellent choice" in appointing Dulles as director of the CIA, Adler bubbled with delight, and Dulles asked him to personally thank editor-in-chief Charles Merz and "my other friends at the *Times*"; Adler promised he would.[33]

Adler served the role of CIA informant on at least one occasion, when he passed along to Dulles information about members of the National Council Against Conscription, a US antiwar group formed in the 1940s. Dulles and Adler then made plans to meet soon afterward in Washington, DC, to further discuss the matter privately.[34]

Meanwhile, in the *New York Times* newsroom, regular beat reporters were being actively sought out for recruitment by CIA officers. *Times* reporter Wayne Phillips, for one, was approached in 1952 by CIA agent Richard Suter with an offer to help get the reporter transferred to a new overseas posting in Moscow, Russia, through a "working arrangement" that the agent claimed the CIA had in place with Arthur Hays Sulzberger, then publisher of the *New York Times*. Phillips turned the offer down.[35]

The CIA had much better luck that same summer with Donald Allan, a *Times* city reporter in his late twenties, who took up the CIA's offer and soon announced his departure to his editors, never telling them that he was recruited by the CIA. Allan was secretly dispatched by the agency to Rome, Italy, where he took day jobs with other major American news companies (which had their own histories of cooperating with the spy agency) to protect his deep-cover work as a CIA agent by night.[36]

Higher up the editorial ladder, James Reston, a prominent *New York Times* correspondent and former US government propaganda officer during World War II, founded his own news magazine, the *Reporter*, together with Max Ascoli, an immigrant scholar from Italy. The New York–based biweekly magazine, with an editorial stance that was both liberal and anticommunist, featured the writings of liberal and conservative authors, scholars, and political figures of the day.

Unknown to most readers and subscribers, however, was the fact that the *Reporter* was a reliable asset for the CIA. Before and after Allen Dulles joined the spy agency, the magazine's staff were sending prepublished proofs of stories to Dulles for his checking in advance. "It is generous of you to give it a once-over for us," *Reporter* managing editor Philip Horton wrote to Dulles of one particular article about the Nuremberg trials of World War II, "and we appreciate it enormously."[37] Before joining the *Reporter*, Horton had earlier served as the first CIA station chief in Paris, France.[38]

Ascoli, cofounder of the *Reporter*, sent to Dulles the prepublished proofs of a particularly controversial story about China that the magazine was planning to run. Dulles, in his official capacity as CIA director, later made a pitch to the head of the New York–based Council on Foreign Relations (CFR), the most influential think tank in the US, to allow Ascoli to join the organization as a regular member.[39]

## "Mysterious Doings": The Harkness Series

By 1954 the CIA was coming under fire for the agency's role in the coups against the governments of Iran and Guatemala, as well as from red-baiters of the political Far Right in the US who suspected the CIA was hiring communist spies as agents. A natural choice for the CIA, then, was to turn to the US corporate press for help.

News media companies and individual journalists up to then had been mostly used by the CIA for propaganda purposes against a common enemy abroad: the scourge of communism. In a marked change of direction, the press was now to be used by the CIA to also protect and promote the spy agency's image at home in the USA. Doing the first honors were Richard Harkness and Gladys Harkness, a famous husband-wife media team.

Richard Harkness was well known to many American TV viewers at the time as Washington, DC, news correspondent for the NBC television network, to his journalistic peers as president of the Radio and Television Correspondents Association, and privately to CIA director Allen Dulles as a personal friend. Gladys Harkness had credentials as a past writer for the United Press wire service and as an NBC correspondent. The series that the Harknesses set out to write together for the *Saturday Evening Post* weekly magazine offers a rare inside look into the workings of the CIA's Mighty Wurlitzer media network of that time.

Documents show a close coordination between the Harknesses, the *Post* editorial team, and the CIA, from the interview access to Dulles through to the taking of photographs and editing of the story's rough draft.[40] In August 1954, as the series was being prepared for publication, *Saturday Evening Post* managing editor Robert Fuoss assured Dulles's top aide that CIA officials would have a chance to preview the story before it went to press: "[Y]ou lads can be sure of seeing the piece by one route or another."[41]

Dulles was "somewhat surprised" to hear that the original story had been stretched out to three parts, and contacted author Richard Harkness at a mountain ranch in rural Wyoming (where the Harknesses were then on vacation), asking to see the expanded story drafts if any sensitive changes had been made. Richard Harkness telegrammed Dulles back, reassuring the CIA director that the *Saturday Evening Post* planned to publish the stories "virtually as you read [them]," and asked Dulles to contact the chief editor of the *Post* to give the CIA's official security clearance on the story. "And now, for those mountain trout!" Harkness gleefully closed in a letter to Dulles.[42] The serious work of a watchdog American press would have to wait for another day.

When the series finally did get published in the *Saturday Evening Post* a few months later, it was heavily promoted by the *Post* and advertised widely in print media across the US as the "first exclusive report on the CIA."[43]

Running in three consecutive issues of the *Post* from October 30 to November 13, 1954, under the title of "America's Secret Agents: The Mysterious Doings of CIA," the series of lengthy stories set something of a high-water mark for CIA-press collaboration up to that time. Reading less like a journalistic scoop and more as dictated stenography, the Harkness series in the *Post* cited at great length the agency's successes in its coup operations abroad and in foiling communist infiltration of its own ranks at home. For the grand finale, part three of the series was devoted exclusively to Allen Dulles, covering everything from his childhood to his heroic World War II service in the OSS to his most efficient running of the CIA as the agency's "master spy."[44]

## EXPOSED

The first in-depth journalistic account of a world most US citizens knew little about—the intelligence and espionage apparatus of the nation, with the CIA at its center—was published in 1964 in a book titled *The Invisible Government* by newspaper reporters David Wise and Thomas B. Ross, shining a media spotlight on some very uncomfortable places for the CIA and sparking renewed public criticism of the agency.[45]

Within the CIA, according to a confidential memo from around that time, the "rising clamor" in the air prompted CIA officials to review the way they had been utilizing the press in the past.[46] That confidential 1965 memo listed the names of twenty prominent American reporters, editors, and media company owners with whom high-ranking CIA official Ray Cline had been meeting and briefing for some years. (Cline, then a deputy director of the agency, had been the CIA's chief analyst during the Cuban missile crisis three years earlier in 1962.)

Among those listed on the memo as having had regular contact with Cline and the CIA were Katharine Graham, then publisher of the *Washington Post* newspaper and *Newsweek* magazine; Chalmers Roberts, the *Post*'s chief diplomatic correspondent, and other *Post* editorial staff; columnist C. L. Sulzberger of the *New York Times* (nephew of former *Times* owner Arthur Hays Sulzberger), and other *Times* editorial staff; and Walter Lippmann, originator of the term "Cold War," who was then a columnist for the *Los Angeles Times*. Two media assets who were especially active in CIA covert operations—columnist Stewart Alsop, then with the *Saturday Evening Post*, and his older brother Joseph Alsop, a columnist with the Publishers' Newspaper Syndicate—were also on the list, along with journalists representing the NBC television network, the *Wall Street Journal*, *Time* magazine, *Fortune* magazine, *US News & World Report* magazine, and the United Features Syndicate service.

The only person on the list of twenty media elites who was meeting with CIA official Cline as a "regular official contact" for on-the-record briefings was Joseph Alsop. All the others were contacted unofficially and discreetly: a "quiet cultivation" of sources, as Cline put it in one case.[47]

## Ramparts Revelations

It was the more radicalized US independent/alternative press of the 1960s, namely the San Francisco–based monthly magazine *Ramparts*, that stepped into the corporate media void in March 1967 to take the first in-depth look into one aspect of the Mighty Wurlitzer propaganda network. *Ramparts* revealed the CIA's fifteen-year bankrolling of the United States National Student Association (NSA), a federation of American college and university student governments formed in the late 1940s, and the domestic funding of the NSA by CIA-affiliated foundations.[48]

A year after that groundbreaking *Ramparts* investigation, the magazine came very close to busting another CIA operation wide open—this time a media front company across the ocean in Europe that was a vital part of the agency's Mighty Wurlitzer media network.

A young American writer in his mid-twenties by the name of Daniel Schechter, who had been studying at the London School of Economics and was allied with the antiapartheid South African exile community in Britain, was investigating a story in 1968 for *Ramparts* about Forum World Features (FWF), a London-based news syndication service that supplied several articles a week to about 150 newspapers in fifty countries, including to major press companies in the

USA. Schechter was convinced at the time that FWF was part of the CIA's larger and more well-known front organization, the Paris-based Congress for Cultural Freedom.[49]

The British director of FWF met with Schechter, showed him all the company's glossy promotional materials, and even escorted him to the company's genuine-looking business office in downtown London to see for himself. Schechter's suspicions were apparently assuaged, and he did not pursue that story for *Ramparts*.

But if he had continued digging, Danny Schechter the Media Dissector (as he was popularly known in later years[50]) would likely have struck gold, since Forum World Features was perhaps the CIA's most prized media front company at the time. FWF had already passed out of the hands of the CIA-sponsored Congress for Cultural Freedom by then, and was being secretly funded at that point by John Hay Whitney—an American multimillionaire who had served in the past as US ambassador to Britain and as publisher of the *New York Herald Tribune* newspaper—through a CIA "proprietary" firm that was legally registered in the US state of Delaware.

The former vice president and treasurer of the London-based Forum World Features at one time had, in fact, been a career CIA officer from the US named Robert Gene Gately. He had earlier worked undercover in Tokyo for both the US magazine *Newsweek* and *Asia Magazine*, a Hong Kong–based publication. Later transferred to the CIA station in Bangkok, Thailand, Gately went on to become an expert of sorts on terrorism and something of a "legendary" CIA covert-operations figure in conservative American political circles.[51]

## Opening Closets of the Past

A sign of what was in store for the CIA in the 1970s came early on in the decade when Seymour Freidin, a respected news veteran then working as London bureau chief for the Hearst Newspapers media chain in the US, became the first American journalist to be outed by colleagues in the news industry as a CIA operative.

As the Watergate scandal was unfolding in the nation's capital, Jack Anderson, investigative columnist for the *Washington Post*, exposed journalist Freidin as a highly paid undercover operative for the election campaigns of Republican Party presidential candidate Richard Nixon in 1968 and 1972—and before that, as a "valued informant" paid by the CIA at a time when Freidin was working in Europe as a news correspondent in the 1950s and 1960s. Freidin had reportedly gone as far as helping out with sensitive negotiations in Switzerland between then-US President Eisenhower and Russian leaders at the Geneva Summit of 1955.[52]

Shortly after the Anderson stories broke in the *Washington Post*, then CIA director William Colby, in an effort to put the agency's own preventive spin on any further damaging disclosures, leaked to the *Post*'s rival newspaper, the conservative *Washington Star-News*, the outlines of an even bigger story: that at least forty full-time news reporters, freelance journalists, and correspondents for trade publications were still on the CIA's payroll or were secretly cooperating with the spy agency in some way.[53]

Though it listed none of those journalists by name, the *Star-News* story noted that most of those paid reporter-agents were American citizens working in various cities around the world as freelance "stringers"—contributors to major new outlets as a cover for their spy work—and that the CIA intended to keep using them as assets in the future. CIA director Colby, however, issued a new directive that immediately cut off the paid services of a handful of regular staff employees of major US news organizations whose identities, if publicly exposed, could "seriously compromise the integrity of the American press and possibly cripple its ability to function overseas."[54]

When Stuart H. Loory, a university journalism professor and former White House correspondent for the *Los Angeles Times*, decided to write up a more comprehensive report on CIA-press relations, he was warned to stay away from such a story by both CIA sources and his colleagues in the press. Loory persisted, and ended up getting the first real exposé of the CIA's Mighty Wurlitzer media network, which he identified as such, published in 1974 as the cover story of the *Columbia Journalism Review*, the respected bimonthly journal serving as the voice of the American media establishment.[55]

It took a few more years, but by summer 1977 the American news media started opening their own closet doors in earnest, and when they did a host of skeletons came tumbling out.

Independent journalists Joe Trento and Dave Roman broke open a new angle of the media-CIA story when they reported on extensive cooperation with the CIA dating back to the 1950s by the San Diego–based Copley Press Inc. company, which then owned nine newspapers in the US, including its flagship *San Diego Union* and *San Diego Evening Tribune* papers, and a subsidiary newswire company, Copley News Service (CNS).[56]

CNS had no less than twenty-three of its news staff on the payroll of the CIA over a two-decade period, it was reported, with the company also providing news-gathering credentials to CIA and other agents as part of their cover. The company's owner, the late right-wing publishing scion James Copley, had founded the news service back in the mid-1950s for the express purpose of helping the CIA with intelligence-gathering activities—as "the eyes and ears" against "the Communist threat in Latin and Central America" for "our intelligence services"—as a personal favor to then US President Eisenhower.[57]

## Bernstein's Big Story

The final breach of the dam holding back the decades-long secrets of the press's ties with the CIA came a couple months later in October 1977 when Carl Bernstein, still riding high on his acclaimed reporting on the Watergate scandal for his former employer, the *Washington Post,* and his two books on the subject with *Post* colleague Bob Woodward, filed the most in-depth report to date on the CIA's Mighty Wurlitzer media network. Bernstein's 25,000-word story was published in the New York–based magazine *Rolling Stone* as a thirteen-page spread, headlined "The CIA and the Media."[58]

Bernstein cited about 400 journalists as having worked in some way or another with the CIA over the years—about ten times the number that the agency had officially admitted to up to then.

Among the notable exposures in Bernstein's report was that of Harry Kern, the "ubiquitous" ex–*Newsweek* magazine foreign affairs editor who had played a leading role in helping to secure Japan's postwar alliance with the US. CIA sources told Bernstein that Kern's dealings with the spy agency had been extensive, and Malcolm Muir, the former editor-in-chief and president of *Newsweek,* confirmed that

Kern (along with Ernest Lindley, the magazine's Washington, DC bureau chief) "regularly checked in with various fellows in the CIA."[59]

Kern's past ties to CIA director Allen Dulles and his brother, US Secretary of State John Foster Dulles, were also confirmed, but Kern denied any formal working relationship. "To the best of my knowledge, nobody at *Newsweek* worked for the CIA," Kern told Bernstein. "The informal relationship was there. Why have anybody sign anything? What we knew we told them [the CIA] and the State Department. . . . When I went to Washington, I would talk to [John Foster Dulles] or Allen Dulles about what was going on. . . . We thought it was admirable at the time. We were all on the same side."[60]

The CBS television network was confirmed by Bernstein as having been the CIA's most valuable broadcast media asset. William Paley, as CBS president, and CIA director Allen Dulles worked out a system of collaboration that was then passed down through the ranks of other CBS executives and editors, and dutifully carried out: a system of CBS providing cover for CIA employees, including at least one well-known overseas correspondent, Austin Goodrich, and several stringers; giving CIA officers full access to the CBS film library and to raw video outtakes; and even setting up a private phone line between CBS and the CIA.[61]

Although Bernstein did not go into much detail about his own former employer, the *Washington Post*, he did report in *Rolling Stone* that *Post* publisher Philip Graham was told by the CIA, upon the newspaper's purchase of *Newsweek* magazine back in 1961, that the magazine was sometimes used by the spy agency for cover purposes. Which probably would not have bothered Philip Graham much anyway, since he and his wife, Katharine Graham (future publisher of the *Post*), had been the best of friends with CIA official Frank Wisner, the architect of the agency's worldwide Mighty Wurlitzer propaganda network, and his wife Polly.[62]

But out of all the CIA's press company assets, as reported in *Rolling Stone*, the most valuable one was undoubtedly the *New York Times*. Under secret arrangements between *Times* publisher Arthur Hays Sulzberger and CIA director Dulles, around ten CIA employees were provided cover as editorial staff members of the newspaper from 1950 to 1966.[63] Sulzberger had signed a secrecy agreement with the

CIA in the 1950s, telling only a select few of the *Times* editorial staff about the company's cooperation with the agency.

Once-private documents show that Dulles—before, during, and after his time at the CIA from the early 1950s to the early 1960s—had indeed enjoyed a close personal and professional relationship with the reigning Sulzberger family of the *New York Times*, corresponding on a first-name basis and meeting regularly over the years with *Times* publisher Arthur Hays Sulzberger, and with his son (and future *Times* president/publisher) Arthur Ochs Sulzberger, and his nephew C.L. Sulzberger, the *Times* columnist.[64]

### The *Times* Follows Up

Stung by the exposures in Bernstein's *Rolling Stone* article, the *New York Times* responded a couple months later by publishing its own in-depth investigation of CIA-media ties at home and abroad in a series of lengthy stories that was carried over three consecutive days on the paper's front page. While obviously intended as a face-saving measure for America's newspaper of record, the detailed research and investigation by reporter John M. Crewdson and other *Times* staffers nevertheless delivered a devastating blow to the wall of secrecy long surrounding the CIA's assets in the press.

Titled "CIA: Secret Shaper of Public Opinion," the series reported how for three decades the CIA had been actively engaged in an "unremitting, though largely unrecognized" effort to manipulate foreign opinion in favor of US policy in other nations. The news media played an important role in that effort, the *Times* noted, with the CIA having owned or financially subsidized more than fifty newspapers, news services, radio stations, and other periodicals, both in the USA and abroad, for propaganda purposes or to provide a believable cover for CIA agents.[65] Since World War II, an estimated thirty to one hundred US journalists for various news organizations had worked concurrently as paid undercover intelligence agents for the CIA, at least a dozen unpaid journalists for major companies were used as "valued sources of information or assistance" for the CIA, and a dozen others were full-time CIA officers secretly working abroad as credentialed employees of US press companies.[66]

Especially in European and Asian countries, the *Times* reported, the CIA had set up a number of its own proprietary newspaper companies and invested lots of money in other legitimate newspapers. "We 'had' at least one newspaper in every foreign capital at any given time," according to an anonymous CIA official, adding that in cases where newspapers were not owned outright or subsidized heavily by the CIA, they were infiltrated with agents who could influence which news stories got published and which ones were not printed.[67]

As one CIA official explained in the *Times* series, the agency had initiated many of its past working relationships with journalists with a promise of "eternal confidentiality"—that their identities would be protected forever. The agency intended to keep that promise, and would continue to refuse to talk about its past media connections "in perpetuity."[68]

All in all, the *Times* series concluded, more than 800 news and public information organizations and individuals, not to mention a dozen or so US publishing houses that printed many of the estimated 1,000 books subsidized or produced by the CIA, could be counted as part of the CIA's international "communications empire" at its peak in the 1960s.[69]

At the end of the series, the *Times* published an editorial criticizing the CIA's past use of the press: "Practically as well as philosophically, this was wrong," the newspaper acknowledged. The editorial welcomed the recently announced policy by CIA director Stansfield Turner that henceforth, barring the occasional exception, the CIA would no longer use journalists formally employed by US news companies as paid CIA agents and that CIA officers could no longer join news media companies as cover to hide their spying activities.[70] At the same time, the CIA intended to continue using "unpaid relationships" with journalists or others working in the press on a voluntary basis.

## INQUIRIES AND INVESTIGATIONS

The longstanding CIA-media links were an open secret for decades in official circles in Washington, DC, but it was not until the independent/alternative and corporate press in the US began exposing those links to the light of day in the 1970s that the US Congress felt compelled to look into the situation. Several major congressional investigations and other internal reports in the 1970s and 1990s dealt specifically with the issue of the press and the CIA.

## The Pike and Church Committees

The first official look into the Mighty Wurlitzer media network as a part of the worldwide covert operations of the CIA began in a big way in 1975 with two congressional investigative bodies: a US House of Representatives intelligence committee chaired by Otis Pike (D-New York) and a US Senate intelligence committee led by Frank Church (D-Idaho).

But from the start, both committees gave the press-CIA relationship comparatively short shrift in their hearings, despite that relationship being a key component of the CIA's international clandestine operations.

The Pike Committee devoted only a dozen paragraphs throughout its extensive report to CIA manipulation of the press, with the contents mostly rehashing what had already been reported elsewhere or admitted to by the CIA.[71] The committee's final recommendation was that US foreign intelligence agencies should be barred from paying journalists to be spies and from using media companies for purposes of cover—except in cases of "the occasional or casual furnisher of news stories or articles to the news media."[72]

Pike, the committee chairman, refused to go along with the CIA's attempts to censor or otherwise influence the overall direction of the committee's investigation, and in the end paid the price for it. The committee's final report was printed up in early 1976 but suppressed by the US House of Representatives before it could reach the public. Though most of the report was leaked at the time to the New York–based *Village Voice* newspaper by *CBS News* reporter Daniel Schorr, the Pike Committee report in its entirety still remains officially unreleased today.

Unlike the Pike Committee, the Senate intelligence committee chaired by Frank Church acquiesced to the CIA's censoring of information and various other conditions and managed to get its final report published.[73] The Church Committee did confirm that at least fifty American journalists or other employees of companies had had a secret working relationship with the CIA. Those US journalists were part of a much larger "network of several hundred foreign individuals around the world who provide intelligence for the CIA and at times attempt to influence foreign opinion through the use of covert propaganda."[74] Under the new rules on CIA use of the press by then CIA director Stansfield Turner, the Church Committee noted, fewer than half of those fifty American journalists would be terminated as CIA assets.

What the Church Committee never told the public, however, was just how much it had compromised in its dealings with the CIA. Frank Church and his committee decided not to question any reporters, editors, publishers, or broadcasting executives whose names surfaced during its investigation, and likewise, the committee made no mention in its final report of about 400 journalists (identities protected by the CIA) who had worked closely with the agency in the past. The Church Committee report also downplayed the influence of the CIA-press relationship on actual news content in the US, and the influential role of news media owners and executives who made that relationship possible.[75]

In February 1976, just before the Church Committee issued its final report, the *Washington Post* ran a front-page exclusive by its national security affairs reporter, Walter Pincus (himself a CIA operative back in the late 1950s and early 1960s), in which the CIA, under then director George H. W. Bush, announced it would no longer use any reporters who were formally accredited with an American news organization as paid assets for the agency, but left a loophole for reporters in other countries as well as freelancers and other contributors to be used by the CIA.[76]

The Church Committee, to its credit, did recommend in its final report that the CIA be prohibited by law from using journalists with US news organizations as paid assets, yet mentioned nothing about the CIA using foreign news companies or reporters as assets.[77] Despite its many shortcomings regarding the media-CIA relationship in particular, the Church Committee investigation did have one long-term effect: it marked the beginning of the end of the thirty-year-long tryst between the US corporate press industry and the CIA under the umbrella of the Mighty Wurlitzer propaganda network.

## The Aspin and Huddleston Hearings

The ink was barely dry on the Church Committee's report in early 1976 when a renewed public outcry over the *Rolling Stone* exposé by Carl Bernstein the following year led to a whole new investigation in Congress. But this time, for the first time ever, the specific target of the inquiry was to be the press and the CIA. Taking its cue from the title of Bernstein's article, a House of Representatives intelligence subcommittee chaired by Les Aspin (D-Wisconsin) convened a fresh round of hearings in Washington, DC, under the official title of "The CIA and the Media."[78]

During a series of six public hearings from December 1977 to April 1978, the Aspin Subcommittee took public testimony from current and past CIA directors and officers, from US ambassadors stationed abroad, and from working journalists in the field. Aspin set the tone of his hearings at the outset: the proceedings would be about determining "the proper relationship between the media and the CIA"— not about revealing the identities of journalists still working for the CIA or uncovering more of the agency's past abuses of the press.[79]

Ray Cline, now retired as a CIA deputy director, claimed in his testimony before the subcommittee to have "exchanged views and information with literally hundreds and hundreds of American journalists as well as many foreign ones" over three decades. Cline testified that "it is entirely natural that there should be close relations" between the CIA and the press.[80] For their part, the journalists who testified at the Aspin Subcommittee hearings, representing several major American news companies, were unanimous in rejecting the idea of a press-CIA working relationship.

The hearings closed with testimony by then CIA director Stansfield Turner, who reconfirmed his recent directive of November 1977: barring the occasional exception (to be decided by him), both accredited journalists and freelance stringers for US news companies would no longer be used as paid CIA agents, and CIA officers could not use US news companies as cover for their covert operations. But, Turner added, "I don't think there is a . . . great danger here to the US public if we have a relationship with foreign media people."[81] And any "unpaid relationships" between the press and the CIA would continue as before.

At the end of it all, the historic Aspin Subcommittee hearings, as the first US congressional inquiry devoted solely to the issue of the press and the CIA, were concluded with no investigation even attempted into the CIA's long history of media manipulation and no official recommendations made about preventing such manipulation from happening again in the future.

In the Senate, meanwhile, the CIA-press connection was being taken up as only one part of a series of public hearings, headed by Walter Huddleston (D-Kentucky) of the US Senate Select Committee on Intelligence, concerning the power wielded by the CIA under the proposed "National Intelligence Reorganization and Reform Act of 1978."[82] Among the heavyweights testifying at the bill's series of Senate hearings were three former directors of the CIA and a host of well-known journalists associated with major media companies such as the Associated Press and United Press International wire services, *CBS News*, the *Los Angeles Times*, and the *Washington Post*.

There was a general consensus among those media people against any kind of formal working relationship with the CIA in their profession. One journalist who chafed under the notion of Congress further tightening any rules concerning CIA-press relations was Philip L. Geyelin, then editorial page editor for the *Washington Post*. Geyelin, during his testimony to the committee on behalf of the American Society of News Editors, admitted that back in 1950, as a *Wall Street Journal* reporter, he had taken a one-year leave of absence from his company to work for the CIA.[83]

In the end, no final recommendations were ever made in the Senate bill specifically concerning relations between the press and the CIA. The bill eventually proved to be too controversial all the way around concerning the expanding powers of the CIA, and never went any further than the committee hearings.

## CIA Openness Task Force

Thirteen years later, in 1991, newly appointed CIA director Robert Gates, in a bid to quell criticisms of his past record with the CIA and to help clean up the agency's public image, set up a "Task Force on Greater CIA Openness" to promote a kinder, gentler spy agency.

The task force soon sent to Gates a fifteen-page internal memorandum listing various areas of focus for the agency's Public Affairs Office (PAO), the CIA's face to the outside world, showing that the CIA of the 1990s had lost none of its old charm when it came to actively working over the American press:

> PAO now has relationships with reporters from *every* major wire service, newspaper, news weekly, and television network in the nation. This has helped us turn some "intelligence failure" stories into "intelligence success" stories, and it has contributed to the accuracy of countless others. In many instances, we have persuaded reporters to postpone, change, hold, or even scrap stories that could have adversely affected national security interests or jeopardized sources and methods.[84]

The task force suggested that the CIA give more background briefings to "a greater number of print and electronic media journalists. . . . Keep PAO as the conduit for these efforts and ensure that media across the US, not only those in the Washington, DC area, are aware of our program." The agency's public affairs staff was also advised to invite journalists to CIA headquarters in Virginia—both to give occasional guest lectures to CIA employees as well as to receive an "unclassified background briefing" from the CIA in times of major international events, such as the Persian Gulf War.

CIA director Gates, in his response to the agency's moves toward more openness, agreed with all the news media–related recommendations except for one: "CIA should not give groups of reporters unclassified background briefings when there is a major international event."[85]

## Council on Foreign Relations Report

A few years on, in early 1996, the influential Council on Foreign Relations set up its own task force to reappraise the various restrictions on the CIA that were supposedly keeping the agency from doing its job more effectively. The twenty-eight-member CFR task force included several ex-CIA officials, as well as past and current representatives of the elite American media establishment.

The CFR's task force report, *Making Intelligence Smarter*, was released soon afterward.[86] It called for more "risk-taking" in CIA operations abroad to give the agency the needed tools to better do its clandestine work, including, the report vaguely said, reviewing the "limits on the use of non-official covers for hiding and protecting those involved in clandestine activities." According to the head of the task force, CFR president Richard N. Haass (a former senior member of the National Security Council under past US President George H.W. Bush), those "non-official covers" referred to the use of journalists and their news organizations, as well as members of the clergy and their religious organizations, as cover for CIA covert operations.

*Washington Post* national security affairs reporter Walter Pincus, the admitted past CIA operative, soon came out with an exclusive story, leaked by the CIA: the agency, using an "exceptions" clause in CIA policy dating back two decades, had been using journalists all along since the 1970s as part of its spy operations.[87]

The ever-vigilant American news media and prominent US press-support organizations were caught totally off guard by the news. Exceptions for reporter-spies? What exceptions? But for those in the US corporate press who had bothered to look, the two-page CIA in-house directive—approved in November 1977 by then CIA director Stansfield Turner around the time of the congressional Aspin hearings on the CIA and the media—had been on the record ever since then. The final paragraph of the so-called Turner Directive, stating that the final judgment on using the press for spy purposes rested with the director of the CIA, read simply, "No exceptions to the policies and prohibitions stated above may be made except with the specific approval of the [Director of Central Intelligence]."[88] It was a loophole big enough to drive a truck through and the CIA had done just that, right under the noses of the US watchdog press.

Howls of surprise and indignation arose in the US corporate news media and from press-support organizations. Both houses of the US Congress, feeling the heat from the press and the public, were forced once again to address the issue.

Representative Bill Richardson (D-New Mexico), a member of the House Intelligence Committee, chose to push a bill through Congress that strictly prohibited the CIA by law from using members of the American press as paid assets in any clandestine operation. But just before the bill was passed into law, Richardson inserted an additional "waiver" into the bill to allow a US president the power to override that restriction when necessary.[89]

The Richardson bill was a partial victory at best for freedom of the press. Now the CIA director and the US president were the only ones who could legally decide when to allow CIA agents and American professional journalists to work together in CIA covert activities. But even bigger, decades-old loopholes were left untouched by the bill: the CIA's longstanding use of accredited journalists in foreign countries and freelance journalists as spies.[90]

Senator Arlen Specter (R-Pennsylvania), chairman of the Senate Select Committee on Intelligence, chose to convene a one-day hearing on the issue a couple months later in July 1996. Then CIA director John Deutch testified before the committee that he was opposed to any kind of outright ban on the CIA and the press working together, and he maintained the right to use "exceptional waivers" in some cases when the CIA would need the secret services of an American journalist.[91]

At the end of the day, the Senate hearing in 1996, like most of the other congressional inquiries since the 1970s, concluded with no formal recommendations of any kind—and marked the last time that the US Congress would bother looking into the critical issue of the CIA's relationship with the news media.


## COMING CLEAN

The last rites were being pronounced in the late 1970s and early 1980s over the CIA's Mighty Wurlitzer media network and its once-powerful sway over the workings of the press, both internationally and domestically in the USA. "Much of the Wurlitzer is now dismantled," the *New York Times* reported, while within the CIA, the Mighty Wurlitzer was considered "now silent."[92]

But the reverberations continued long after the propaganda machine had given up its ghost. The 1980s found the CIA still using some journalists as part of its covert operations.[93] A sitting director of the CIA, William Casey, was serving as a major shareholder in a media company that bought out the much larger ABC television network.[94] And Katharine Graham, board chairwoman and chief executive officer of the *Washington Post*, stood on the stage of the CIA auditorium at agency headquarters in Langley, Virginia, and assured her audience that she understood their pain.

"It's an inescapable irony of democratic government that official secrecy is necessary to preserve liberty," Graham said. "We live in a dirty and dangerous world. There are some things the general public does not need to know and shouldn't. The government must have a classification system and should discipline employees who violate security regulations."[95] Graham defended the role of a free press in society, but also acknowledged that the *Post* had occasionally censored its own news stories on national security grounds at the US government's behest.

Fast-forward to 2014, and a *Los Angeles Times* reporter is exposed as cooperating with the CIA in the shaping of news stories, while a veteran journalist in Germany boldly blows the whistle on the lingering ghosts of the CIA's Cold War–era propaganda network. That old network may be for the most part downsized or dismantled, but all the available evidence today points to an ongoing relationship between the CIA and the press that is as well-connected as ever in the digital age.

The year 2017 marks seven decades since the establishment of the Central Intelligence Agency. It also marks more than twenty years since the last serious look into the press and the CIA was taken by the US Congress, and forty years since the last significant exposures of that relationship by the American independent/alternative media and corporate press.

The kinds of activities that were at the core of the CIA's media propaganda network of the past—paying US journalists as a part of spy operations or having CIA agents secretly work for US news companies—are today barred under the CIA's own internal regulations and by law. But two people have the power to brush those restrictions aside and allow the official use of US journalists as spies: the director of the CIA and the president of the United States. The CIA's use of professional journalists in countries outside the US and the use of freelance journalists (American or otherwise) as media assets is considered allowable, as is the use of any journalist on an unpaid, voluntary basis.

The whole story of the CIA and the US news media remains untold today, wrapped in a collusion of silence by a Fourth Estate that does not want to air its own dirty laundry and risk losing even more credibility among the public, by a Congress that is reluctant to confront and curtail the clandestine operations of the nation's most powerful spy agency, and by a CIA that has vowed to keep its media assets off-limits to public scrutiny "in perpetuity." While it is clear that the CIA has brazenly played the press under its former Mighty Wurlitzer media network, it is equally clear in the light of recent history that the institution of the free press in the USA has been more than willing at times to be played.

Major media institutions like the *New York Times* are quick to point an accusatory finger at other parties when it comes to improprieties, but are slow to confess and admit to their own. But the onus today is now on such elite media organizations to come clean once and for all about the "inseparable relationship" (as the *Washington Post* termed it) between the CIA and the press, and the disreputable role played by the American news media in the past in corrupting the free flow of factual information and subverting the truth in both the United States and countries around the world.[96]

The traditionally close relationship between the media and the CIA is about much more than an ethical lapse here or a conflict of interest there: it goes straight to the heart of what an independent-minded, responsible, and open press should and should not be in any nation. Nearly seventy years after the original creation of the Mighty Wurlitzer propaganda network—after all the exposed secrets, congressional hearings, task force reports, and hidden histories—the time is ripe now for a full accounting of that network, with nothing less than the existence of the press as a pillar of democratic societies at stake in the twenty first century.

BRIAN COVERT is an independent journalist and author based in western Japan. He has worked for United Press International (UPI) news service in Japan, as a staff reporter and editor for English-language daily newspapers in Japan, and as a contributor to Japanese and overseas newspapers and magazines. He is currently a lecturer in the Department of Media, Journalism, and Communications at Doshisha University in Kyoto.

# Notes

1   Ken Silverstein, "The CIA's Mop-Up Man: L.A. Times Reporter Cleared Stories with Agency before Publication," *Intercept*, September 4, 2014, https://theintercept.com/2014/09/04/former-l-times-reporter-cleared-stories-cia-publication/. See also Michael Muskal, "Ex-Tribune Reporter Said to Have 'Collaborative' Relationship with CIA," *Los Angeles Times*, September 4, 2014, http://www.latimes.com/nation/nationnow/la-na-nn-tribune-dilanian-20140904-story.html.

2   Peter Oliver, "'Bought Journalism': German Bestseller Reveals CIA Pay Western Media for Spin & Bias," YouTube video, posted by Russia Today (RT), September 28, 2014, https://www.youtube.com/watch?v=015BZCcURa4. For the full interview with Udo Ulfkotte, see "German Journo: European Media Writing Pro-US Stories under CIA Pressure," *Russia Today*, October 18, 2014, https://www.rt.com/news/196984-german-journlaist-cia-pressure/.

3   Ralph Lopez, "Editor of Major Newspaper Says He Planted Stories for CIA," *Digital Journal*, January 26, 2015, http://www.digitaljournal.com/news/world/editor-of-major-german-newspaper-says-he-planted-stories-for-cia/article/424470.

4   Eric van de Beek, "Our Exclusive Interview with German Editor Turned CIA Whistleblower," *Russia Insider*, October 17, 2014, http://russia-insider.com/en/germany/our-exclusive-interview-german-editor-turned-cia-whistleblower/ri531. See also Udo Ulfkotte, interview by Adam Lesak, "'German Politicians are US Puppets,'" *Oriental Review*, November 7, 2014, http://orientalreview.org/2014/11/07/german-politicians-are-us-puppets/.

5   Frederick L. Wettering, "(C)overt Action: The Disappearing 'C,'" *International Journal of Intelligence and CounterIntelligence* 16, no. 4 (2003), 561.

6   Quoted in John M. Crewdson, "Worldwide Propaganda Network Built by the C.I.A.," *New York Times*, December 26, 1977, A37, http://jfk.hood.edu/Collection/Weisberg%20Subject%20Index%20Files/C%20Disk/CIA%20Reporters%20New%20York%20Times%20Series%2012-25-77/Item%2007.pdf.

7   "Council on Japan Formed to Foster Interests of U.S.," *Berkshire Eagle* (Pittsfield, MA), April 21, 1948, 19.

8   John G. Roberts, "America and the Making of Japan Inc.," *Nation*, February 13, 1982, 173. For more on Wisner and CIA ties to other ACJ members, see also Glenn Davis and John G. Roberts, *An Occupation Without Troops: Wall Street's Half-Century Domination of Japanese Politics* (Tokyo: Yenbooks, 1996), 67, 93–94, 112–14.

9   A highly recommended source on this subject is Howard B. Schonberger, *Aftermath of War: Americans and the Remaking of Japan, 1945–1952* (Kent, OH: Kent State University Press, 1989), esp. 134–60.

10  Letter from Harry F. Kern to Allen Dulles, July 21, 1955, Box 36, Folder 5, Allen W. Dulles Papers, Department of Rare Books and Special Collections, Princeton University Library, http://findingaids.princeton.edu/collections/MC019/c00590.

11  Ibid. Kermit Roosevelt, Jr. was a grandson of former US president Theodore Roosevelt.

12  Foreign Reports Inc. official website, http://www.foreignreports.com. The company, based in Washington, DC, is currently headed by Nathaniel Kern, son of Harry Kern.

13  Quoted in Timothy Mitchell, *Carbon Democracy: Political Power in the Age of Oil* (London/New York: Verso Books, 2011), 212.

14  "Subject: Possible Japanese Assistance to Egypt," memorandum from US embassy in Cairo to US Secretary of State, December 8, 1973, National Archives and Records Administration (NARA), Washington, DC, https://aad.archives.gov/aad/createpdf?rid=37667&dt=2472&dl=1345.

15  "Saudi Arabian Position Regarding a Middle Eastern Settlement," memorandum from Zbigniew Brzezinski to US president-elect Jimmy Carter, November 23, 1976, Foreign Policy Folder, Container 2, Jimmy Carter Presidential Library & Museum, http://www.jimmycarterlibrary.gov/digital_library/sso/148878/2/SSO_148878_002_02.pdf.

16 Robert Whiting, *Tokyo Underworld: The Fast Times and Hard Life of an American Gangster in Japan* (New York: Vintage Books, 1999), 182.

17 Ibid., 180–82.

18 Letter from Harry F. Kern to National Security Advisor Zbigniew Brzezinski, March 1, 1979, Digital National Security Archive, accessed January 14, 2016, http://www.proquest.com/products-services/databases/dnsa.html.

19 "Subject: Harry Kern and the Grumman Scandal," National Security Council memorandum from Nicholas Platt to NSC Deputy National Security Advisor David Aaron, March 8, 1979, Digital National Security Archive, accessed January 14, 2016, http://www.proquest.com/products-services/databases/dnsa.html.

20 Ibid.

21 Letter from Harry F. Kern to Osamu Kaihara (former Japanese government official) concerning the visit of Northrop senior vice president Robert Gates to Tokyo, dated June 17, 1986. Northrop never could sell a single F-20 jet to any country in the world, not even to the Pentagon in the USA, and in 1986 ended up scrapping production of the aircraft.

22 Evan Thomas, *The Very Best Men: The Daring Early Years of the CIA* (New York: Simon & Schuster, 2006), 63.

23 Edward Hunter, "'Brain-Washing' Tactics Force Chinese into Ranks of Communist Party," *Miami Daily News*, September 24, 1950. This article is generally acknowledged as being the origin of the word and concept of "brainwashing" in American popular culture. (CIA ties to other news staff of the *Miami Daily News* would surface in later years.)

24 See Edward Hunter, *Brainwashing: The Story of Men Who Defied It* (New York: Farrar, Straus and Cudahy, 1956), https://archive.org/details/brainwashingstoroohuntrich, as well as Hunter's testimony before the Committee on Un-American Activities, House of Representatives, Eighty-Fifth Congress, Second Session, *Communist Psychological Warfare (Brainwashing)— Consultation with Edward Hunter, Author and Foreign Correspondent* (Washington, DC: Government Printing Office, 1958), https://archive.org/details/communistpsychol1958unit.

25 This was later confirmed by Hunter in an interview with a Cleveland radio station around the mid-1960s. See Bob Purse, "Edward Hunter on Brainwashing," WFMU's Beware of the Blog, September 5, 2010, http://blog.wfmu.org/freeform/2010/09/edward-hunter-on-brainwashing.html.

26 Federal Bureau of Investigation (FBI) file no. HQ 118-4047 notes that Hunter was employed by the CIA in 1949 and 1950, according to information provided to the author by US independent researcher Ernest Lazar. (Lazar's extensive work in getting FBI files released under the Freedom of Information Act can be viewed at https://archive.org/details/lazarfoia.) For a reference to Hunter's status as a CIA officer, see James Reston, "John Paton Davies' Motives Mystery in 'Tawny Pipit' Case," *New York Times*, December 9, 1953, A5.

27 John M. Crewdson, "C.I.A. Established Many Links to Journalists in U.S. and Abroad," *New York Times*, December 27, 1977, A40, http://www.nytimes.com/1977/12/27/archives/cia-established-many-links-to-journalists-in-us-and-abroad-cias.html. For background, see also Edward Hunter, *Brain-washing in Red China* (New York: Vanguard Press, 1951), https://archive.org/details/Brain-Washing_in_Red_China_Edward_Hunter.

28 Matthew W. Dunne, *A Cold War State of Mind: Brainwashing and Postwar American Society* (Amherst, MA: University of Massachusetts Press, 2013), 13–14. See also a 1981 interview with ex-CIA director Richard Helms by journalist David Frost, National Archives and Records Administration (NARA), Washington, DC, https://catalog.archives.gov/id/7283099.

29 A highly recommended source on Hunter's ties to the radical right is Jeffrey H. Caufield, *General Walker and the Murder of President Kennedy: The Extensive New Evidence of a Radical-Right Conspiracy* (Moreland Hills, OH: Moreland Press, 2015), http://jeffreycaufield.com.

30 Associated Press, "Edward Hunter, Author, Dies," *Democrat and Chronicle* (Rochester, NY), June 25, 1978, 6C. See also "Edward Hunter, Writer and Editor," *Washington Post*, June 26, 1978, C4.

31 Hayden B. Peake, "The Intelligence Officer's Bookshelf," Central Intelligence Agency, May 21, 2007, https://www.cia.gov/library/center-for-the-study-of-intelligence/csi-publications/csi-

studies/studies/vol51no1/the-intelligence-officers-bookshelf.html. For Hunter's propaganda collection, see "Chinese Pamphlets: Political Communication and Mass Education in China," Association of Research Libraries, October 5, 2007, http://www.celebratingresearch.org/libraries/crl/politcomm.shtml.

32   According to correspondence between Julius Ochs Adler and Allen Dulles, 1946–1955, Box 1, Folder 7, Allen W. Dulles Papers, Department of Rare Books and Special Collections, Princeton University Library, http://findingaids.princeton.edu/collections/MC019/c00008.

33   "Right Man for the Job" (editorial), *New York Times*, January 27, 1953, A24. See also correspondence between Julius Ochs Adler and Allen Dulles, January 26–February 2, 1953, Allen W. Dulles Papers, Princeton University Library.

34   According to correspondence between Julius Ochs Adler and Allen Dulles, October 16–21, 1953, Allen W. Dulles Papers, Princeton University Library.

35   John M. Crewdson, "C.I.A. Tried in 50's to Recruit Times Man," *New York Times*, January 31, 1976, A28, http://www.nytimes.com/1976/01/31/archives/cia-tried-in-50s-to-recruit-times-man.html.

36   "A Young Reporter's Decision to Join C.I.A. Led to Strain, Anger and Regret," *New York Times*, December 27, 1977, A41, http://www.nytimes.com/1977/12/27/archives/a-young-reporters-decision-to-join-cia-led-to-strain-anger-and.html.

37   Letter from Philip Horton to Allen Dulles, February 23, 1950, Box 48, Folder 18, Allen W. Dulles Papers, Department of Rare Books and Special Collections, Princeton University Library, http://findingaids.princeton.edu/collections/MC019/c00858.

38   Hugh Wilford, *The Mighty Wurlitzer: How the CIA Played America* (Cambridge, MA: Harvard University Press, 2008), 231.

39   Correspondence between Max Ascoli and Allen Dulles, April 8–12, 1952, and letter from Allen Dulles to Walter H. Mallory of the Council on Foreign Relations, February 12, 1955, Box 1, Folder 3, Allen W. Dulles Papers, Department of Rare Books and Special Collections, Princeton University Library, http://findingaids.princeton.edu/collections/MC019/c00004.

40   Correspondence between Richard L. Harkness and Allen Dulles, August 6–13, 1954, Box 31, Folder 2, Allen W. Dulles Papers, Department of Rare Books and Special Collections, Princeton University Library, http://findingaids.princeton.edu/collections/MC019/c00469.

41   Letter from Robert Fuoss to Colonel Stanley Grogan, August 9, 1954, Box 31, Folder 2, Allen W. Dulles Papers, Department of Rare Books and Special Collections, Princeton University Library, http://findingaids.princeton.edu/collections/MC019/c00469.

42   Correspondence between Richard L. Harkness and Allen Dulles, August 9–13, 1954, Allen W. Dulles Papers, Princeton University Library.

43   Advertisement in *Detroit Free Press* (Detroit, MI), October 26, 1954, 14.

44   Richard and Gladys Harkness, "America's Secret Agents: The Mysterious Doings of CIA" [part three], *Saturday Evening Post*, November 13, 1954, 30, 132–34. The Harknesses later went on to put their husband-wife media spin skills to good use as US government employees in the 1970s, serving as press officers for the "war on drugs" campaign declared by the administration of US President Richard Nixon.

45   David Wise and Thomas B. Ross, *The Invisible Government* (New York: Random House, 1964). Wise was Washington, DC bureau chief for the *New York Herald Tribune* and Ross worked at the Washington bureau of the *Chicago Sun-Times*.

46   "Subject: Ray Cline's Efforts with Certain of the Press to Improve Public Confidence in Agency," Memorandum for the Deputy Director, Central Intelligence Agency, September 17, 1965, https://www.cia.gov/library/readingroom/document/cia-rdp80b01676r001700030003-0.

47   Ibid.

48   Sol Stern, "A Short Account of International Student Politics & the Cold War with Particular Reference to the NSA, CIA, etc.," *Ramparts*, March 1967, 29–39, http://www.unz.org/Pub/Ramparts-1967mar-00029?View=PDF.

49   The episode with Schechter is recalled in Brian Crozier, *Free Agent: The Unseen War 1941–1991* (London: Harper Collins, 1993), 75. For extensive background on the CIA's links with the Con-

gress for Cultural Freedom, see Frances Stonor Saunders, *Who Paid the Piper?: The CIA and the Cultural Cold War* (London: Granta Books, 1999).

50 Bill Lichtenstein, "Remembering the News Dissector," *Boston Globe*, April 24, 2015, https://www.bostonglobe.com/opinion/2015/04/24/remembering-news-dissector/cfMbWUiBPiMNSX6MHydCBO/story.html.

51 For more on Gately's role in Forum World Features, see Crozier, *Free Agent*, 63–64, 68–71. For a related story (apparently planted in Gately's hometown newspaper as part of his CIA cover), see "Sandie Grad Heads Feature Syndicate," *Amarillo Globe-Times* (Amarillo, TX), December 29, 1966, 22. For a reference to Gately's stint with the CIA in Thailand, see "Consultations for Political Counselor Petree," cable from US embassy in Bangkok to US embassy in Tokyo, Public Library of US Diplomacy, WikiLeaks, dated January 16, 1974, https://wikileaks.org/plusd/cables/1974BANGKO00862_b.html. For an online chat with Gately, see "Global Focus: Talk about Terrorism," Washingtonpost.com, August 5, 1999, http://www.washingtonpost.com/wp-srv/inatl/zforum/99/inatl080599.htm. For mention of Gately's "legendary" CIA status, see "The Buzz," Foundation for the Defense of Democracies, circa 2006, http://www.defenddemocracy.org/media-hit/the-buzz1/.

52 For the exposures by Jack Anderson in his "Washington Merry-Go-Round" syndicated column, see Jack Anderson and Les Whitten, "Watergate Mystery Man Identified," *Washington Post*, August 28, 1973, B13, http://jfk.hood.edu/Collection/White%20Materials/Watergate/Watergate%20Items%2005979%20to%2006627/Watergate%2006151.pdf, and Jack Anderson, "Nixon Spy Also Worked for '68 Campaign," *Washington Post*, September 4, 1973, B13, http://jfk.hood.edu/Collection/White%20Materials/Watergate/Watergate%20Items%2006228%20to%2006519/Watergate%2006281.pdf.

53 For the full *Washington Star-News* story, see Oswald Johnston, "CIA Uses American Journalists as Undercover Agents," *Raleigh Register* (Beckley, WV), November 30, 1973, 1–2. See also Associated Press, "Colby Leaked CIA-Journalist Story; House Disclosure Rapped," *Daily Reporter* (Dover, OH), January 27, 1976, A1, A3.

54 Johnston, "CIA Uses American Journalists as Undercover Agents."

55 Stuart H. Loory, "The CIA's Use of the Press: A 'Mighty Wurlitzer,'" *Columbia Journalism Review* 3, no. 3 (September–October 1974), 9–18. Loory died in 2015.

56 Joe Trento and Dave Roman, "The Spies Who Came in from the Newsroom," *Penthouse* 12, no. 8 (August 1977), 45–46, 50. See also Matt Potter, "Copley's Deadly Cuba Ties," *San Diego Reader*, December 18, 2014, http://www.sandiegoreader.com/news/2014/dec/18/ticker-copley-cuba/#.

57 Trento and Roman, "The Spies Who Came in from the Newsroom," 45.

58 Carl Bernstein, "The CIA and the Media," *Rolling Stone*, October 20, 1977, 55–67, http://carlbernstein.com/magazine_cia_and_media.php.

59 Ibid., 63.

60 Ibid. Harry Kern died in 1996 in Bethesda, Maryland.

61 Ibid., 61–63. See also Matt Schudel, "Austin Goodrich, Cold War CIA Officer and CBS Correspondent, Dies at 87," *Washington Post*, July 6, 2013, https://www.washingtonpost.com/local/obituaries/austin-goodrich-cold-war-cia-officer-and-cbs-correspondent-dies-at-87/2013/07/06/65c40166-e59f-11e2-80eb-3145e2994a55_story.html.

62 Ibid. See also Katharine Graham, *Personal History* (London: Phoenix Press, 2001), 177–78.

63 Bernstein, "The CIA and the Media," 60–61.

64 Correspondence between Arthur Hays Sulzberger, et al, and Allen Dulles, 1948–1964, Box 54, Folder 2, Allen W. Dulles Papers, Department of Rare Books and Special Collections, Princeton University Library, http://findingaids.princeton.edu/collections/MC019/c01041.

65 John M. Crewdson, "The C.I.A.'s 3-Decade Effort to Mold the World's Views," *New York Times*, December 25, 1977, A1, http://jfk.hood.edu/Collection/Weisberg%20Subject%20Index%20Files/C%20Disk/CIA%20Reporters%20New%20York%20Times%20Series%2012-25-77/Item%2003.pdf.

66 Ibid., A1, A12.

67 Crewdson, "Worldwide Propaganda Network Built by the C.I.A.," A37.

68  Crewdson, "The C.I.A.'s 3-Decade Effort to Mold the World's Views," A1.

69  Crewdson, "Worldwide Propaganda Network Built by the C.I.A.," A1, A37, and Crewdson, "C.I.A. Established Many Links to Journalists in U.S. and Abroad," A1, A40.

70  "The Reporter and the Spy" (editorial), *New York Times*, December 27, 1977, A34. See also George Lardner Jr., "CIA Announces New Rules for Dealing with Journalists," *Washington Post*, December 3, 1977, A4.

71  Aaron Latham (introduction), "The CIA Report the President Doesn't Want You to Read," *Village Voice*, February 16, 1976, 84, 88, http://jfk.hood.edu/Collection/Weisberg%20 Subject%20Index%20Files/P%20Disk/Pike%20Committee%20Report%20Village%20 Voice/Item%2005.pdf.

72  *CIA: The Pike Report* (Nottingham, UK: Spokesman Books, 1977), 275. This is reportedly the only complete version of the unreleased Pike Committee report to be published in book form.

73  United States Senate, Select Committee to Study Governmental Operations with Respect to Intelligence Activities, *Foreign and Military Intelligence, Book I: Final Report* [Church Committee report] (Washington, DC: US Government Printing Office, 1976), https://archive.org/details/finalreportofselo1unit.

74  Ibid., 192.

75  Bernstein, "The CIA and the Media," 65–67.

76  Walter Pincus, "CIA Ends Use of Reporters," *Washington Post*, February 12, 1976, A1. For more on the CIA-Pincus relationship, see Walter Pincus, "'I was Subsidized by the CIA,'" *Boston Globe*, February 17, 1967, 11.

77  US Senate, Select Committee to Study Government Operations, *Final Report*, 456.

78  United States House of Representatives, Permanent Select Committee on Intelligence, Subcommittee on Oversight, *The CIA and the Media: Hearings Before the Subcommittee on Oversight of the Permanent Select Committee on Intelligence, House of Representatives, Ninety-fifth Congress, First and Second Sessions, December 27, 28, 29, 1977, January 4, 5, and April 20, 1978* (Washington, DC: US Government Printing Office, 1978), https://babel.hathitrust.org/cgi/pt?id=md p.39015039053452;view=1up;seq=3.

79  Ibid., 3.

80  Ibid., 61.

81  Ibid., 309, 333–34.

82  United States House of Representatives, Permanent Select Committee on Intelligence, *National Intelligence Reorganization and Reform Act of 1978: Hearings Before the Select Committee on Intelligence of the United States Senate, Ninety-fifth Congress, Second Session on S. 2525, National Intelligence Reorganization and Reform Act of 1978, April 4, 5, 19, 25; May 3, 4, 16; June 15, 21; July 11, 18, 20 and August 3, 1978* (Washington, DC: US Government Printing Office, 1978), http://www.intelligence.senate.gov/sites/default/files/hearings/952525.pdf.

83  Ibid., 166. For more on Geyelin's past ties with the CIA, see also Philip L. Geyelin, "It's Up to the Press, Not Congress, to Police CIA Ties," *Washington Post*, May 21, 1978, B1, https:// www.washingtonpost.com/archive/opinions/1978/05/21/its-up-to-the-press-not-congress-to-police-cia-ties/16418f52-a70b-4b7d-92d1-773f0ef9c8cb/.

84  "Subject: Task Force Report on Greater CIA Openness," Memorandum from the Task Force on Greater CIA Openness to the Director of Central Intelligence, Central Intelligence Agency, December 20, 1991, 6–8, http://nsarchive.gwu.edu/NSAEBB/ciacase/EXB.pdf. Emphasis in the original.

85  "Subject: Task Force Report on Greater CIA Openness," Memorandum from the Director of Central Intelligence to the Deputy Director for Administration, et al, Central Intelligence Agency, January 6, 1992, 3, http://nsarchive.gwu.edu/NSAEBB/ciacase/EXC.pdf.

86  Council on Foreign Relations, Report of an Independent Task Force, *Making Intelligence Smarter: The Future of U.S. Intelligence* (New York: Council on Foreign Relations, January 1996), http://www.cfr.org/intelligence/making-intelligence-smarter/p127. See also http://fas.org/irp/cfr.html.

87  Walter Pincus, "'Loophole' Revealed in Prohibition on CIA Use of Journalistic Cover," *Washington Post*, February 16, 1996, A24, https://www.washingtonpost.com/archive/

politics/1996/02/16/loophole-revealed-in-prohibition-on-cia-use-of-journalistic-cover/
e5416f68-6af1-4a87-9ca6-c50632c1a6a6/. See also Walter Pincus, "CIA to Retain Right to Use Journalistic Cover," *Washington Post*, February 17, 1996, A6, https://www.washingtonpost.com/archive/politics/1996/02/17/cia-to-retain-right-to-use-journalistic-cover/c5b2f40b-0d65-4ea7-9523-621fb0adc109/. Pincus earned a reputation a few months later as "the CIA's house reporter"; see John McCaslin, "Inside the Beltway: Drink to Your Health," *Washington Times*, July 31, 1996, A10.

88  "New Regulations Approved on CIA Relations with U.S. News Media," directive by CIA director Stansfield Turner, Central Intelligence Agency, as reprinted in US House of Representatives, Permanent Select Committee on Intelligence, Subcommittee on Oversight, *The CIA and the Media* hearings, 333–34, https://babel.hathitrust.org/cgi/pt?id=mdp.39015039053452;view=1up;seq=337.

89  John Diamond/Associated Press, "Bill Prohibits CIA from Using Reporters as Spies," *Anniston Star* (Anniston, AL), May 23, 1996, 15A. See also Kate Houghton, "Subverting Journalism: Reporters and the CIA," Committee to Protect Journalists, February 1997, https://www.cpj.org/attacks96/sreports/cia.html.

90  David Wise, "Loopholes that Allow Journalists to Spy," *Los Angeles Times*, May 11, 1997, M2, http://articles.latimes.com/1997-05-11/opinion/op-57675_1_american-journalists. See also "House Intelligence Bill Limits CIA's Ability to Use Journalists," Reporters Committee for Freedom of the Press, June 17, 1996, http://www.rcfp.org/browse-media-law-resources/news/house-intelligence-bill-limits-cias-ability-use-journalists.

91  United States Senate, Select Committee on Intelligence, *CIA's Use of Journalists and Clergy in Intelligence Operations: Hearing Before the Select Committee on Intelligence of the United States Senate, One Hundred Fourth Congress, Second Session on CIA's Use of Journalists and Clergy in Intelligence Operations, Wednesday, July 17, 1996* (Washington, DC: US Government Printing Office, 1996), https://archive.org/details/ciasuseofjournaloounit.

92  See Crewdson, "Worldwide Propaganda Network Built by the C.I.A.," 1A, and "CIA 'Mighty Wurlitzer' is Now Silent," Central Intelligence Agency, November 2, 1980, https://www.cia.gov/library/readingroom/document/cia-mighty-wurlitzer-now-silent.

93  "C.I.A. Head Approved Use of Journalists 3 Times," *Washington Post*, February 29, 1980, A7, and Judith Miller, "C.I.A. on Using Journalists," *New York Times*, June 9, 1982, B14, http://www.nytimes.com/1982/06/09/us/cia-on-using-journalists.html.

94  "Casey Stake in Capital Cities," *New York Times*, March 27, 1985, D6, http://www.nytimes.com/1985/03/27/business/casey-stake-in-capital-cities.html. See also Doug Henwood, "Capital Cities/ABC," Fairness and Accuracy in Reporting (FAIR), March 1, 1990, http://fair.org/extra/capital-citiesabc/.

95  Katharine Graham, "Secrecy and the Press," transcript of speech delivered at CIA headquarters, Langley, VA, November 16, 1988, https://catalog.archives.gov/id/7283275.

96  Bill Richards, "CIA and the Press: Inseparable Relationship," *Washington Post*, December 30, 1977, A4, http://jfk.hood.edu/Collection/Weisberg%20Subject%20Index%20Files/C%20Disk/CIA%20Reporters/Item%2009.pdf.

# CHAPTER 7

# Selling Empire, War, and Capitalism

## Public Relations Propaganda Firms in Service to the Transnational Capitalist Class

Peter Phillips, with research support by Sonoma State University students Ratonya Coffee, Robert Ramirez, Mary Schafer, and Nicole Tranchina

*If those in charge of our society—politicians, corporate executives, and owners of press and television—can dominate our ideas, they will be secure in their power. They will not need soldiers patrolling the streets. We will control ourselves.*

—Howard Zinn[1]

In his 1952 book *Public Relations*, Edward Bernays, one of the primary founders of public relations (PR) in the US, defined PR as information provided to the public to modify attitudes and actions towards various institutions.[2] Bernays stated that PR creates favorable opinions towards ideas, products, and persons, which could include good will between people, and increased sales of products. More commonly the practice of public relations is referred to as "helping an organization and its public adapt mutually to each other."[3] Bernays explained the nature of the business of public relations in his chapter entitled the "The Engineering of Consent":

it is impossible to overestimate the importance of engineering consent, it affects almost every aspect of our daily lives. When used for social purposes, it is among our most valuable contributions to the efficient functioning of society. But the techniques can be subverted: demagogues can utilize them for antidemocratic purposes as successfully as those who employ them for socially desirable ends.[4]

In the shadow of World War II, Bernays clearly discerned the possibilities of the dark side of PR.[5]

Propaganda, a tool closely aligned with public relations, is defined as the dissemination of ideas and information for the purpose of inducing or intensifying specific attitudes and actions.[6] Propaganda is generally categorized into various subgroups, including religious, political, commercial, literary, wartime, and Cold War varieties, and has been widely used by the Central Intelligence Agency (CIA) and other government agencies to advance political, social, and economic interests.[7]

The war propaganda film *The Green Berets*, released in 1968 at the height of the Vietnam War, demonstrates Hollywood's relentless production of propaganda in support of US military policies. The US Department of Defense (DoD) was concerned that *The Green Berets* would look so much like propaganda that they asked the producers to remove credits at the end thanking the Department of Defense and the US Army for their generous assistance.[8] The influence of the government, and especially the Pentagon, on Hollywood is long-standing and continues to this day. Recent films such as *Argo*, *Zero Dark Thirty*, and *The Interview* are just a few examples of ongoing and deliberate US government propaganda efforts accomplished via Hollywood's willing participation.[9]

Propaganda is particularly prevalent in the lead-up to war, when governments attempt to persuade the public of the necessity and desirability of wide-scale destruction at massive public costs, and the involvement of public relations firms in spreading pro-war propaganda has been well-documented.[10] The Rendon Group has been cited as one of the primary PR firms supporting US propaganda efforts in Iraq. In the 1980s, the Rendon Group created public relations propaganda for the ousting of President Manuel Noriega in Panama. They shaped international support for the first Gulf War, and in the

1990s helped to create the Iraqi National Congress political party. The Rendon Group also provided the images that shaped support for a permanent war on terror, including the toppling of the statue of Saddam, the fabricated heroic rescue of Private Jessica Lynch, and various dramatic tales of weapons of mass destruction. Pentagon documents show thirty-five contracts with the Rendon Group between 2000 and 2004 worth a total of fifty to one hundred million dollars.[11]

David Altheide and Jennifer Grimes trace the history of how the Project for the New American Century, a neoconservative think tank, helped plan the propaganda campaign for the Iraq War.[12] A recent journal article by David Guth reports on the history of the debate over propaganda and public diplomacy, focusing on the diversion stories and outright lies employed by the George W. Bush Administration to build support for the Iraq War. This issue has been the focus of numerous books over the past decade, including some by scholars at the Center for Public Integrity and PR Watch.[13]

By definition, propaganda and public relations both attempt to change the public's views, beliefs, and feelings about various issues, ideas, and products. Both propaganda and PR seek to change behaviors and ideas among the masses in support of the agendas of the institutions initiating the actions.

A number of researchers have asserted that the focus of propaganda and public relations is really the same.[14] Corporate Watch writes:

> powerful and pervasive public relations firms ensure that pro-corporate stories and perspectives dominate journalistic output. PR firms and other corporate lobbying agencies ensure that corporate-friendly messages are given preferential treatment within the corridors of power. The upshot is a climate in which market dominance over ever increasing aspects of our lives is often accepted as common-sense, rather than challenged as a cause of suffering and inequality.[15]

In addition, Ryszard Lawniczak believes that this pro-corporate perspective extends internationally, giving the public relations industry a global role in the political economy of marketing.[16] Public relations firms and governments have increasingly overlapped, especially since 9/11. In this regard, it makes perfect sense to study the transnational impacts of propaganda and public relations, not in isolation (as they no longer tend to be mutually exclusive), but by combining studies of the two fields into the term "Public Relations Propaganda."

The public relations propaganda (PRP) industry has experienced phenomenal growth since 2001 after several years of steady consolidation. There are three publicly traded mega-PRP corporations. In order of largesse, the firms are Omnicom Group, WPP, and Interpublic Group of Companies (IPG). Together, these firms employ 214,000 people in over 170 countries, annually collecting some thirty-five billion dollars in revenue. Not only do these firms control a massive amount of wealth, they possess a network of connections in powerful international institutions with direct links to the corporate media, governments, multinational corporations, and global policy-making bodies.

## PROPAGANDA MODEL OF CORPORATE MEDIA AND PRP FIRMS

In *Manufacturing Consent* (1988), Edward S. Herman and Noam Chomsky claim that, because media is firmly imbedded in the market system, it reflects the class values and concerns of its owners and advertisers.[17] According to Herman and Chomsky, the media maintain a corporate class bias through five systemic filters: concentrated private ownership; a strict bottom-line profit orientation; overreliance on governmental and corporate sources for news; a primary tendency to avoid offending the powerful; and an almost religious worship of the market economy, strongly opposing alternative beliefs and ideologies. These filters limit what will become news in society and set parameters on acceptable coverage of daily events.

Media consolidation and the expansion of PRP firms inside news corporations in the world today have resulted in a far more deliberate form of news management. The corporate media is deeply interlocked with the military-industrial complex and policy elites in the US/European/Asian transnational corporate class, and the media is increasingly dependent upon various governmental and PRP sources to generate news. Maintenance of a continuous news cycle requires a constant feed and an ever-entertaining supply of stimulating events and breaking news clips and sound bites. The twenty-four-hour news shows on MSNBC, Fox, and CNN maintain constant contact with the White House, Pentagon, and PRP companies representing both government and private corporations.

Corporate media consolidation has provided the opportunity for PRP firms to emerge as orchestrators of global information and news. Journalists are taking an increasingly dependent secondary position to PRP firms and government press releases in corporate news media. The world today faces a PRP-military-industrial media empire so powerful and complex that, in the majority of news venues, basic truths about world events are concealed, skewed, or simply not reported at all. The result is news managed by government and PRP firms—often interlocked—including the release of specific stories intended to build public support as well as the deliberate noncoverage of news stories that may undermine capitalist goals. It was estimated thirteen years ago that up to 80 percent of all news stories in corporate media were sourced from or directly influenced by PRP firms.[18] PRP penetration into corporate media has only increased to the present day.

PRP firms provide a variety of services to major corporations and institutions in the world. Brand enhancement and sales is undoubtedly one of the key services. However, companies also offer much more, including research and crisis management for corporations and governments, public information campaigns, web design and promotions, and corporate media placement. Hill & Knowlton Strategies of WPP proudly brags on their website that they service 50 percent of the *Fortune* Global 500 companies from their offices in forty countries.[19] Hill & Knowlton, along with Omnicom Group's Fleishman and Hillard, have been the key PRP firms working with Monsanto to protect its brand Roundup, which contains the herbicide glyphosate, recently declared a probable human carcinogen by the World Health Organization. Roundup is the most widely used herbicide in the world, being sold in over 130 countries. As countries begin to restrict its use, PRP firms gear up to protect Monsanto's profits.[20]

WPP's Hill & Knowlton is also well known for its early involvement with the Council for Tobacco Research (CTR), originally set up in 1954 to counter the *Reader's Digest* 1952 report linking tobacco smoking to cancer. The CTR was described by the *Wall Street Journal* in 1993 as producing the "longest running misinformation campaigns in US business history."[21]

It was WPP's Burson-Marsteller that created the front group Global Climate Coalition (GCC), which operated from 1989 to 2001.[22] The GCC was set up to help the oil and auto industries downplay the dangers of global warming. Initial members of the coalition included Amoco, American Petroleum Institute, Chevron, Chrysler, Exxon, Ford, General Motors, Shell, and Texaco. In addition, Burson-Marsteller created the front group Californians for Realistic Vehicle Standards in 1998 to oppose restrictions on car emissions.[23] PRP firms continue to this day to offer services and front groups designed to block public safety laws or progressive legislation that might interfere with corporate profits.

Global Counsel, a WPP advisory firm, provides political consultation to investors regarding risk, regulations, and policymaking in various regions of the world. In a recent report, Global Counsel described the results of the World Trade Organization's 10th Ministerial Conference held in Nairobi, Kenya, in December 2015. World Trade Organization (WTO) agreements in 2015 were described as the "most significant package of reforms in trade of agricultural goods ever agreed." Declines in tariffs and expansion of free trade were key elements of the agreements, reproducing precisely the exploitative conditions that have kept Africa impoverished and beholden to Western powers for decades.[24] In another report on their website, Global Counsel offers insider information on private equity investment in Africa.

The PRP industry continuously promotes products that are a danger to humanity. PRP firms offer brand enhancement worldwide for numerous tobacco, alcohol, junk food, and pharmaceutical products. As we examine the lists of clients for the big three PRP firms below, it is clear that unhealthy foods constitute the largest category of products PRP firms advertise worldwide.

# GOVERNMENT PRP CONTRACTING

The PRP industry holds significant power. The ease with which the American population accepted the invasion of Iraq was the outcome of a concerted effort involving the government, DoD contractors, PRP firms, and the corporate media. Public relations and propaganda were crucial in selling the 2003 Iraq War.[25] These institutions are the instigators and main beneficiaries of a permanent war on terror. The importance of these companies' connections lies in the fact that prominent segments of the power elite and the US national security state have the money and resources to articulate their propaganda repeatedly to the American people and the world, until those messages become self-evident truths and conventional wisdom.

From 2007 to 2015 the US federal government spent over $4 billion on PRP services.[26] The US employs 3,092 public relations officers in 139 agencies. An additional $2.2 billion goes to outside firms for PRP, polling, research, and market consulting.[27] The top PRP firms in the world reaped hundreds of millions of US dollars in 2014: Laughlin, Marinaccio & Owens made $87.98 million,[28] WPP's Young & Rubicam Group made $57.5 million, WPP's Ogilvy Public Relations Worldwide made $47.93 million, Omnicom Group's Fleishman-Hillard made $42.4 million, Gallup made $42 million—and those are only the most well-known firms. It was WPP's Burson-Marsteller who won a $4.6 million contract with the US Department of Homeland Security in 2005 to develop public awareness and education for a major emergency, disaster, or terrorist attack in Washington, DC.[29]

Before the first Gulf War, a propaganda spectacle took place courtesy of WPP's Hill & Knowlton. The firm was hired by Citizens for a Free Kuwait and eventually received nearly $10.8 million to conduct one of the largest and most effective public relations campaigns in history. Hill & Knowlton helped create a national outrage against Iraq by the public recounting of horrifying events supposedly caused by Iraqi soldiers after they had invaded Kuwait. A young woman named Nayirah claimed in congressional testimony, and before a national audience, that she saw "Iraqi soldiers come into the [Kuwait] hospital with guns, and go into the room where 15 babies were in incubators. They took the babies out of the incubators, and left the babies on the cold floor to die."[30] What the public was not told is that Nayirah was the daughter of Kuwait's ambassador to the US. The public also wasn't told that her performance was coordinated by the White House and choreographed by the US public relations firm Hill & Knowlton on behalf of the Kuwait government.[31]

Johan Carlisle, the author of the *Covert Action Quarterly* article quoted in the previous paragraph, went on to write that "... [f]ormer CIA official Robert T. Crowley, the Agency's long-time liaison with corporations," acknowledged that "Hill & Knowlton's overseas offices ... were perfect 'cover' for the ever-expanding CIA. Unlike other cover jobs, being a public relations specialist did not require technical training for CIA officers." Furthermore, the CIA, Crowley admitted, used its Hill & Knowlton connections to "put out press releases and make media contacts to further its positions ... Hill & Knowlton employees at the small Washington office and elsewhere distributed this material through CIA assets working in the United States news media."[32] Carlisle emphasized that,

> [s]ince the CIA is prohibited from disseminating propaganda inside the US, this type of 'blowback'—which former CIA officer John Stockwell and other researchers have often traced to the Agency—is illegal. While the use of US media by the CIA has a long and well-documented history, the covert involvement of PR firms may be news to many.[33]

The CIA invests in a PRP firm that monitors social media as part of the CIA's effort to access more "open source intelligence." The firm is known as Visible Technologies and has offices in New York, Seattle, and Boston. The firm was created in 2005, and in 2006 developed a partnership with WPP. Visible Technologies helps the CIA monitor information that gets overlooked in the massive number of online activities. The company is keeping track of influential Internet posters and how foreign posters view news events. Although the CIA gathers information through this firm that is legally open for anyone to view, media outlets have raised concerns over the possibility that the CIA may use the information for illegal political purposes. These political purposes could include unauthorized domestic investigations into public figures. Visible Technologies can monitor over half a million sites every day. These sites include any open social websites, such as Twitter or Flickr. Visible Technologies already works with companies such as Microsoft and Verizon, keeping track of positive and negative feedback on their products.[34]

Omnicom's PRP firm Ketchum was recently hired by the Honduran government to whitewash its dismal human rights record after the US-backed military coup in 2009. Ketchum is now providing crisis management PRP services to Honduras after the assassination of renowned human rights movement leader Berta Cáceres. Ketchum also runs two front groups promoting the safety of GMOs, paid for by Monsanto, DuPont, and other biotech firms.[35]

University of California, Davis hired PRP firm Nevins & Associates in 2013 for the "eradication of references to the pepper spray incident in search results on Google for the University and the Chancellor." UC Davis spent $175,000 to diminish Internet coverage of the widely reported brutal pepper spraying of student protestors on November 18, 2011.[36]

## THE PRP INDUSTRY AND TRANSNATIONAL CAPITALISM

The American ruling class has long been determined to be a mostly self-perpetuating elite that maintains its influence through policy-making institutions such as the National Association of Manufacturers, the US Chamber of Commerce, the Business Council, Business Roundtable, the Conference Board, American Enterprise Institute for Public Policy Research, the Council on Foreign Relations, and other business-centered groups and think tanks.[37] These associations have long dominated policy decisions within the US government.[38]

Capitalist power elites exist around the world. The globalization of trade and capital brings the world's elites into increasingly interconnected relationships—to the point that sociologists now theorize the development of a transnational capitalist class (TCC). In one of the pathbreaking works in this field, *The Transnational Capitalist Class* (2000), Leslie Sklair argued that globalization elevated transnational corporations to more influential international roles, with the result that nation-states became less significant than international agreements developed through the World Trade Organization and other international institutions.[39] Emerging from these multinational corporations was a transnational capitalist class, whose loyalties and interests, while still rooted in their corporations, were increasingly international in scope.

William Robinson further investigated these conditions in his books, *A Theory of Global Capitalism: Production, Class, and State in a Transnational World* (2004) and *Global Capitalism and the Crisis of Humanity* (2014).[40] Robinson claimed that 500 years of capitalism had led to a global epochal shift in which all human activity is transformed into capital. In this view, the world has become a single market, in which social relationships are privatized. He saw the TCC as increasingly sharing similar lifestyles, patterns of higher education, and consumption. The global circulation of capital is at the core of this international bourgeoisie, who operate in oligopolistic clusters around the world. These clusters of elites form strategic transnational alliances through mergers and acquisitions with the goal of increased concentration of wealth and capital. The process creates a polyarchy of hegemonic elites. The concentration of wealth and power at this level tends to over-accumulate, leading to speculative investments and manufactured wars. The TCC makes efforts to correct and protect its interests through global organizations like the World Bank, International Monetary Fund, the Group of Seven (G7) and the Group of Twenty (G20), World Social Forum, Trilateral Commission, Bilderberg Group, Bank for International Settlements, and other transnational associations. Robinson claims that within this system nation-states become little more than population containment zones, and the real power lies with the decision makers who control global capital.[41]

At the head of the transnational capitalist class is what David Rothkopf calls the "superclass." In his book, *Superclass: The Global Power Elite and the World They are Making* (2008), Rothkopf argued that the superclass constitutes 6,000 to 7,000 people, or 0.0001 percent of the world's population.[42] They are the Davos-attending, private jet-flying, megacorporation-interlocking, policy-building elites of the world—people at the absolute peak of the global power pyramid.

Another recent work on the TCC is William K. Carroll's *The Making of a Transnational Capitalist Class* (2010).[43] Carroll's work focused on the consolidation of the transnational corporate-policy networks between 1996 and 2006. He used a database of the boards of directors of the world's 500 largest corporations, showing the concentrated interconnectedness of key corporations and increasingly small number of people involved. According to this analysis, the average size of corporate boards has dropped from 20.2 to 14.0 during the ten years of his study. Furthermore, financial organizations have increasingly become the center of these networks. Carroll argued that the TCC at the centers of these networks benefit from extensive ties to each other, thus providing both the structural capacity and class consciousness necessary for effective political solidarity. It is for this segment of the TCC that PRP firms are providing services, propagandizing the globe with messages reflecting the ideologies, class interests, and core values of the TCC global empire of power and wealth.

In 2014, my students and I decided to identify the people on the boards of directors of the top ten asset management firms and the top ten most centralized corporations. Because of overlaps, this amounts to a total of thirteen firms, which collectively have 161 directors on their boards. We think that this group of 161 individuals represents the financial core of the world's transnational capitalist class. They collectively manage $23.91 trillion (2014) in funds and operate in nearly every country in the world. They are the center of the financial capital that powers the global economic system. Western governments and international policy bodies work in the interests of this financial core to protect the free flow of capital investment anywhere in the world. This group of 161 people, with a few thousand of their elite friends and colleagues, control $100 trillion, or half the world's wealth.[44]

The TCC represents the interests of several hundred thousand millionaires and billionaires who comprise the richest people in the top 1 percent of the world's wealth hierarchy. Ironically, this extreme accumulation of concentrated capital at the top creates a continuing problem for the TCC, who must scour the world for new investment opportunities that will yield adequate returns (7–10 percent). War is one use for over-accumulated capital. A permanent war on terror offers a unique opportunity for the TCC to loan capital at a profit to governments for military actions, and to participate in rebuilding efforts made necessary by war. The collection of taxes on working peoples' incomes to pay for permanent war results in increasing pressure toward neoliberal governmental austerity measures, which further impoverishes the 99 percent and transfer yet more wealth to the world's 1 percent.

The consolidation of global capitalism and the emerging formation of a transnational capitalist class creates ever-greater opportunities for PRP firms. As capital consolidates, there are increasing needs for new investment opportunities, concentrated surplus capital, and continued growth and expansion. PRP firms provide market stimulation for growing sales and the creation of psychological demands for various goods among the world's masses. Even the 3.5 billion people living on less than three dollars a day are encouraged to spend wages on feel-good products like Coke and cigarettes.

A global war on terrorism requires a continuing ideological justification aimed at the mass of people who instinctively favor peace. PRP firms provide an ongoing rationalization for war by servicing government propaganda activities, military contractors, pro-war Hollywood films, and the marketing of war toys, cartoons, and related products. The techniques for marketing brands are essentially the same as for marketing war. Creative, emotional, and visually stimulating ads are continually cranked out, featuring families with loving young children in danger from foreign threats, and protected by official authorities, homeland security, police, or military. *America's Navy—the Shield* is a perfect example of such a blatantly propagandistic, fear-mongering ad, first aired, uncoincidentally, during the 2014 Army-Navy football game.[45]

## OMNICOM GROUP, WPP, INTERPUBLIC GROUP—GLOBAL BEHAVIOR MODIFICATION AND MIND CONTROL

The big three global PRP firms are key contributors to the total hegemony of capitalism in the world today. PRP firms and their corporate media partners aid corporations, governments, and non-governmental organizations (NGOs) in an unrelenting ideological assault on and pacification of the minds of the masses throughout the world. The overall message encourages the continued acquisition of material products and consumption, expanded desire for a life of luxury, fear of others (including terrorists, criminals, and any other usefully threatening peoples), the support of police states, acceptance of a permanent war on terror, and a view of private corporations as essential elements of democracy. This is what Noam Chomsky called engineering opinion and parading enemies.[46]

Additionally, PRP firms offer continuing brand enhancement worldwide for numerous tobacco, alcohol, junk food, and pharmaceutical products. They work to skew the facts of urgent crises in health and the environment to not only maintain but also increase the sales and production of indisputably harmful commodities.

WPP's TNS Company reveals its propagandist reach when it states that

> the needs of citizens are changing rapidly. Government policies and social programs need to respond to these changing needs. And in an age of economic uncertainty there is increased pressure for accountability of expenditure—on governments, political parties and NGOs. TNS has the leading political and social research unit in the world. With over 500 dedicated social researchers in more than 40 countries, TNS Political & Social is uniquely placed to conduct research on any social issue, in any environment. We assist decision makers in a wide range of policy areas: health, education, social services, environment, labor market, family policy, public transport, road safety, justice, community integration—to name a few. We provide political parties with strategic advice during elections and conduct social polling in many countries around the world.[47]

Likewise, WPP's Glover Park Group (GPG) in Washington, DC, does not shy away from flaunting their abilities as corporate power brokers, reporting on their website under "Understanding and Influencing Washington:"

No other firm is as effective at achieving winning policy outcomes for its clients. We know the issues inside and out. We have decades of experience in government, from the halls of Congress to the upper echelons of Democratic and Republican administrations. We fundamentally understand today's decision-makers and what drives them. . . . GPG's Government Affairs group helps clients develop and execute legislative and regulatory strategies to advance their goals in Washington at every level and in every branch and agency of government.[48]

Without telling us the brands they promote, WPP's Sudler and Hennessey claim on their website that they have been "proudly pushing drugs for 75 years."[49]

The following data on the big three PRP firms was acquired through extensive research from the hundreds of websites they control. It is a consolidated view of the core brands, agencies, and services offered by Omnicom Group, WPP, and Interpublic Group, the three largest PRP firms shaping consumer habits and socioeconomic policies throughout the world today.

## OMNICOM GROUP

Omnicom Group, based in New York, had an annual revenue of $15.1 billion in 2015, with 74,000 employees in over 200 agencies representing a group of subsidiaries, affiliates, and quasi-independent agencies such as BBDO Worldwide, DDB Worldwide, TBWA Worldwide, GSD&M, Merkley & Partners, and Zimmerman & Partners Advertising, as well as Fleishman-Hillard, Integer Group, and Rapp through Omnicom's Diversified Agency Services division. Omnicom is represented at the Council of Foreign Relations in the US.[50]

The inception of Omnicom Group has roots back to 1891 when George Batten opened the George Batten Company in New York. The following year, Batten hired William Johns as his assistant. Johns became the first president of the American Association of Advertising Agencies, and, upon Batten's death in 1918, took the position as president of the Batten Company. The George Batten Company merged with BDO in 1928, and the group was renamed Batten, Barton, Durstine & Osborn (BBDO). BBDO went on to expand around the world, merging with other PRP agencies and forming Omnicom in the 1980s. In 1991, Omnicom's revenue increased to $1.2 billion, and it has progressively increased since then, year after year. Presently, Omnicom serves over 5,000 brands among every sector of service and has over 1500 agencies in over 100 countries.

## OMNICOM GROUP—MAJOR CLIENTS

### Governments and Government-Funded Organizations

Alberta, Barcelona, Brazil, British Columbia, Brooklyn, Royal Brunei Airlines, California Housing Finance Agency, California Lottery, Chicago, China, Colombia, Congo, Dubai Tourism, Ecuador, Egypt, Georgia (country), Houston Airport, Illinois Lottery, Korea Tourism Organization, Library of Congress, Los Angeles, Mauritius, Mexico, Miami-Dade County, Montreal, Munich Airport, New Orleans, New York Police Department, New York State Energy Research and Development Authority, Tourism New Zealand, Nicaragua, Nigeria, Peru, Portugal, Qatar, Spain, Toronto Transit, UNICEF, US Mint, Veterans Affairs, Vienna, Washington State Department of Health, Zurich

### NGOs, Nonprofits, and Universities

Ad Council, Alcola Foundation, American Academy of Actuaries, American International University, American Lung Association, American Petroleum Institute, American Public Transportation Association, American Red Cross, Argosy University, Big Sisters, Boy Scouts of America, California Almond Board, California Endowment, California Raisin Marketing Board, California Table Grape Commission, Campaign for Tobacco-Free Kids, Canadian Cancer Society, Canadian Nuclear Association, Canadian Tourism Commission, Cancer Research Center, Cancer Research UK, Catholic Health Council, Chiropractic Association, Cincinnati Children's Hospital, College of the Holy Cross, Cornell University, Council on Foreign

Relations, Dairy Association, Democratic Governors Association, Doctors Without Borders, Ford Foundation, Howard Jarvis Taxpayers Association, Howard University, Impact Iran, International Pharmaceutical Federation, James Irvine Foundation, John F. Kennedy Center, Kaiser Permanente, Lupus Foundation of America, Montanans for Free and Fair Elections, Mt. Sinai Medical Center, National Association of Broadcasters, National Audubon Society, National Breast Cancer Foundation, National Hockey League, Packard Foundation, Pew Center, Robert Wood Johnson Foundation, Rockefeller Foundation, Rotary International, Ryukoku University, Salvation Army, San Francisco Bowl, Sydney Opera House, Special Olympics, Sundance Film Festival, Telecom Italia, Tony Awards, United Nations Foundation, University of California, Berkeley, University of Phoenix, University of Washington, US Centers for Disease Control and Prevention, Vancouver Convention Center, World Bank, World Heath Organization, YMCA

## Major Corporations and Brands

3M, 7-Eleven, 7 Up, A&E Entertainment, AAA, Adidas, Adobe, Aetna, AirAsia, Air France, Alaska Airlines, Albertsons, Alka-Seltzer, American Airlines, American Express, Amstel, Anheuser-Busch, Anthem, Apple, Arby's, Argos, Arm & Hammer, Arthur Andersen, Aspen Holdings, AT&T, Bacardi, Bank of America, Barnes & Noble, Bayer, Ben and Jerry's, Berkshire Hathaway, Best Buy, Best Western, BlackBerry, BlackRock, Blue Diamond Almonds, BMW, Bose, Bridgestone, British Airlines, Burger King, Cadillac, Campbell's, Canadian Pacific, Canon, Capital One, Captain Morgan, Carta Blanca, Chase Bank, Cheetos, Chevrolet, Chrysler, Cisco, Citibank, Clorox, Coca-Cola, Colgate, Comcast, ConocoPhillips, Converse, Coppertone, Corning, Costco, Covergirl, Crown Royal, CVS, Dicks Sporting Goods, DirecTV, Disney, Dole, Downy, Dreyer's, Dr Pepper, Dunlop, Duracell, Dutch National Bank, eBay, The Economist, Embassy Suites, Equinox, ESPN, ExxonMobil, Facebook, FedEx, Ford, Fry's Electronics, G4S, Gatorade, General Electric, General Mills, Genentech, Gillette, Glad, Godiva, Goodyear, Google, Gucci, H&R Block, Häagen-Dazs, Hallmark, Hampton Inn, Harley-Davidson, HBO, Head & Shoulders, Heineken, Heinz, Hennessy, Hertz, Hewlett-Packard, Hilton, Holiday Inn, Horizon Organic, Hormel, Hovis, Humana, Hyatt Hotels, Hyundai, IBM, IKEA, Ingersoll Rand, Instagram, Intel, Jack Daniels, JCPenny, Jeep, Johnnie Walker, Johnson & Johnson, Kellogg's, Kia, Kimberly-Clark, Kleenex, Kmart, Kotex, Land Rover, Lay's, Levi's, Lexus, Lowe's, Macy's, Madison Square Garden, Major League Baseball, Marathon, Marriott, Mars, Marshalls, MasterCard, Maxwell House, Mazda, McDonald's, McGraw-Hill, Mercedes-Benz, Merck, Microsoft, MillerCoors, Mitsubishi, Monsanto, Morgan Stanley, Motorola, Nasdaq, National Car Rental, NBC, Nestea, Nestlé, Netflix, Newcastle Brown Ale, Newman's Own, Nice 'N Easy, Nickelodeon, Nike, Nintendo, Nissan, Nokia, Novartis, Pacific Gas and Electric, Panasonic, Panda Express, PayPal, Peet's Coffee & Tea, Pepsi, PetSmart, Pfizer, Philips, Pizza Hut, PlayStation, PNC Bank, Popeyes, Porsche, Prada, Procter & Gamble, Quaker Oats, RadioShack, Ritz, Rolex, Safeway, Saks Fifth Avenue, Sam's Club, Samsung, Sears, Sharp, Siemens, Sirius Satellite Radio, Smirnoff, Sol, Sony, Southwest Airlines, Sprint, Staples, Starbucks, State Farm, Subaru, Subway, Sun Life, Tanqueray, Target, Telenet, Telstra, Teva, Thai Airlines, Thomson Reuters, Thrifty Car Rental, Tide, Time Warner Cable, T-Mobile, TNT (network), Toshiba, Toyota, Toys "R" Us, Twitter, Uncle Ben's, Unilever, United Airlines, UPS, U.S. Bank, Verizon, Virgin, Visa, Volkswagen, Walgreens, Wall Street Journal, Walmart, Wells Fargo, Wendy's, Western Union, Whirlpool, Whole Foods, Williams-Sonoma, Wrigley, Xerox, Yahoo, YouTube, Zenith, Ziploc

## WPP

WPP is a conglomerate of over 125 of the world's leading PRP and marketing firms, in fields that include advertising, media investment management, consumer insight, branding and identity, health care communications, direct digital promotion, and relationship marketing. WPP, a London-based conglomerate with an annual revenue of $12.2 billion for 2015, employs around 190,000 people in 3,000 offices across 112 countries. WPP is a strategic partner with the World Economic Forum.

WPP was formed in 1985 when Martin Sorrell took control of a shell company, Wire & Plastic Products PLC. It made its first acquisitions in

1986, buying ten marketing services companies by year-end. In 1987, WPP bought the J. Walter Thompson agency and, in 1989, the Ogilvy Group.[51] During 2000–2002, WPP acquired Young & Rubicam Inc. and The Tempus Group, and continued to buy up stakes in a number of Chinese and other Asian businesses. The Group continues to expand its reach through acquisitions, joint ventures, and partnerships, with investments in China, Brazil, Singapore, the UK, and the US. Primary subsidiaries of WPP include Blanc & Otus, Burson-Marsteller, Cohn & Wolfe, Dewey Square Group, Finsbury, Grey Group, Hill & Knowlton, National Public Relations, and Ogilvy Public Relations.

While over half of the 125 websites for WWP subsidiaries only mention a few of their clients, if any, many make proud boasts when it comes to their largest clients. WPP represents several thousand brands worldwide, and our list below is but a sampling of those brands to give readers an idea of how far their influence reaches in the global capitalist market.

## WPP Client List

GOVERNMENTS AND GOVERNMENT-FUNDED ORGANIZATIONS

Australian Defense Force, BBC, BC Hydro, British Council, British Library, British Olympic Association, Citizens Information Board (Dublin), Disability Federation of Ireland, Dubai Food Festival, Dubai Shopping Festival, Failte Ireland, India Ministry of Tourism, Insolvency Services of Ireland, International Monetary Fund, Kansas City Union Station, Jordan, Lobbying (Regulator of Lobbying in Ireland), Minnesota State Lottery, NATO, Natural History Museum (London), New Jersey State Lottery, Referendum Commission (Ireland), Rio 2016 Olympics, Royal Mail, Tennessee Department of Tourism, UNICEF, UPS, US Marine Corps, US State Department, Washington Lottery

NGOS, NONPROFITS, AND UNIVERSITIES

AARP, Amsterdam Gay Pride, Australian Museum, Bangor University, Bath Rugby, Beirut Digital District, British Lung Association, Campaign for Tobacco-Free Kids, Canadian Breast Cancer Foundation, Clinton Foundation, Danish Football Association, DeVry University, English Athletics, Global Entrepreneurship Summit, GB

Rowing Team, Hamburg AIDS Foundation, International Olympic Committee, Irish Blood Transfusion Service, Irish Cancer Society, James Beard Foundation, Jewish Colorado, LTA British Tennis, Minnesota State Lottery, Mobile World Congress, Museum of London, National September 11 Memorial and Museum, National Standards Authority of Ireland, NFL, Obama for America, Open Connectivity Foundation, Population Services International, The Prince's Trust, Psykiatrifonden, Rotary Club, Royal Institution of Chartered Surveyors, Sons of Norway, Strayer University, Trinity College Dublin, University of Wales, World Economic Forum, World Rugby, Wounded Warrior Project, Youth Sports Trust (UK)

## MAJOR CORPORATIONS AND BRANDS

3M, 7-Eleven, A&W Restaurants, Abbot Downing, Absolut, Adidas, Adobe, Advertising Age, Aetna, Allegheny Health Network, Allegiance Health, Allstate, Amazon, American Express, American Swiss, Amtrak, ANGA (America's Natural Gas Alliance), AOL, Argos, Ascot, Ask.com, AstraZeneca, Audi, Avis, Avon, AXA Life Invest, Bank of America, Bank of England, Bankers Life, Barclays, Baxter International, Bayer, Belvedere Vodka, Bentley, Berghaus, Best Buy, BG Group, Blinkbox, Blue Cross Blue Shield Association, BMW, Boeing, Bose, Boxfresh, British American Tobacco, British Gas, Brown-Forman, British Land, Britvic, Budweiser, Bulleit Bourbon, Bupa, Cadillac, Campbell's, Canon, Capital One, Cargill, Castle Lite, Carlsberg, Carphone Warehouse, CBS, Chase Bank, Chivas Regal, Choice Hotels, Cirque du Soleil, Cisco, Citibank, Citroën, Club Orange, CNN, Coca-Cola, Colgate, Comcast, Commonwealth Bank, Converse, Crayola, Credit Suisse, Dailymotion, Danone, Darden Restaurants, Dasani, Datalex, Del Monte, Dell, Direct Energy, DirecTV, Discover, Disney, Downy, Ducati, Dunkin' Donuts, Dunlop, DuPont, ECCO, Evans Cycles, EVA Air, European Tour (golf), Eurostar, Facebook, Fanagans Funeral Directors, Fanta, Ferrari, Ferrero, Fiat, Finansbank, Fine Gael, Finlandia, Forbes, Ford, Gap, General Electric, General Mills, Gillette, Ginsters, Geocon (engineering), GlaxoSmithKline, Glenlivet, Golden Globes, Goodyear, Google, Grammy Awards, Grey Goose, GroupM, Halls, Hasbro, Hawaiian Airlines, Hawaiian Gardens Casino, Healthline Networks, Hearst, Heineken,

Hennessy, Hershey's, Hertz, HIHO, Hobart Corporation, Holiday Inn, Hollywood Fashion Secrets, Home Depot, Honda, Honeywell, Hootsuite, Hotel Tonight, HSBC, Hyundai, IKEA, Imperial Tobacco, Infiniti, Intel, Intelligent Energy, Ipsen, Isuzu, Interpublic Group, iProspect (digital media), *Irish Examiner*, J&B Scotch, Jack Daniel's, Jägermeister, Jaguar, Japan Tobacco International, Johnnie Walker, Johnson & Johnson, Kellogg's, Kentucky Fried Chicken, Kenwood, Khashoggi Holding, Kimberly-Clark, Kmart, Kraft, Kubota, Lady Speed Stick, Lamborghini, Levi's, LexisNexis, Lexus, Lincoln, L.L. Bean, L'Oréal, Lotus Cars, Lowe's, Lumber Liquidators, Luxgen, Macy's, MasterCard, Match.com, Mattel, Maxim, Mazda, McDonald's, Med 4 Home, Merck, Microsoft, MillerCoors, Mitsubishi, Mobile Marketer, Moccona, Mondelēz International, Monsanto, Motorola, MTM, Mundipharma International, NBC, Nedbank, Nestea, Nestlé, Netmarble, Network Rail (UK), New York Life Insurance Company, Nextel, Nike, Nissan, Nobia, Nokia, Novant Health, Novartis, Nu Finish, Office Depot, Olay, Old Spice, Opel, Oracle, P&G, Panasonic, Penguin Random House, Pentland Group,PepsiCo, Pernod Ricard, Peroni, Pfizer, PGA Tour, Pond's, Porsche, Qudrah National Holding, Quicken Loans, Popular Science, Pringles, Prudential, RBS, Red Bull, Reebok, Renault, Reverie, Revlon, Rite Aid, Roche Pharmaceuticals, Rockwell Automation, Rolls-Royce, Royal Exchange Theatre, Russian Standard Vodka, Safeway, Samsung, SAP, Saxo Bank, Scania, Schick, Schwan's, ScoreSense, Sears, Seattle Seahawks, Siemens, Shell, Silk (beverages), Smucker's, Snapfish, Soreen, Southern Comfort, Snip-Snap, Sony, South African Airways, Speedo, Sprite, Standard Bank, Standard Life, Staples, Starbucks, Stoli Vodka, Stouffer's, Subway, Sunbites, Super 8 Motels, Swisscom, Symantec, Tang, Target, Taste Inc., Tesco, The North Face, The Partners (media), The Times, Tidal (music streaming), Time, T-Mobile, Toyota, Travelocity, Travelodge, Travel Republic, UBS, Unilever, United Bankers' Bank, Universal, USA Today, U.S. Bank, Valspar, Vans, Vaseline, Verizon, Viacom, Vimeo, Visa, Vitaminwater, Volkswagen, Volvo, Wall Street Journal, Warner Brothers, Washington Post, Weight Watchers, Wells Fargo, Western Digital, Wrigley, Wyeth, Xactly Corporation, Xaxis, Xbox, Xfinity, Xoom, Yahoo, YOU Technology, Zurich Insurance Group

## Interpublic Group of Companies

Interpublic Group of Companies (IPG) is based in New York, and had $7.6 billion in revenue for 2015, with 49,700 employees working in eighty-eight agencies worldwide. IPG is owned by major investment firms including The Bank of New York Mellon Corporation, Vanguard Group, and Lord Abbett & Co. IPG is represented at the Business Roundtable in the US.

## Interpublic Group of Companies Clients

GOVERNMENTS AND GOVERNMENT-FUNDED ORGANIZATIONS

Boston 2024 Partnership (Olympics bid), California Lottery, Copenhagen Airport, Covered California, El Ministerio de Comercio Exterior y Turismo (Peru), Port of Corpus Christi, UNICEF, US Army

NGOS, NONPROFITS, AND UNIVERSITIES

Ad Council, Bayer HealthCare, BJC HealthCare, Fuels America, National Cancer Institute, National Trauma Institute, NCAA Football, Open Space Institute, Peruvian Cancer Foundation, The Pew Charitable Trust, Singapore Red Cross, Society of Actuaries, St. John Ambulance, Tata Consultancy Services, University of Alabama, University of Pittsburgh Medical Center, University of Southern Mississippi, University of Technology and Engineering (Peru)

MAJOR CORPORATIONS AND BRANDS

4C (media marketing), ABC, Acava Limited, Adelphic, ADmantX, Airbus Group, Amazon, American Standard, America Superconductor, AOL, Applebee's, Atlas Solutions, Bang & Olufsen, BBC America, Bertolucci (watches), Betty Crocker, Bisquick, BJ's Restaurant, BJC HealthCare, BMW, Boehringer Ingelheim, Brand Networks (social advertising), British Airways, Cadbury, Carrera y Carrera, Carrick Brain Centers, Chevrolet, Cisco, Clorox, Coca-Cola, Coffee-mate, Columbia Records, Comfort Inn, comScore, Cross Pixel Media, Crunch Fitness, Daiichi Sankyo, Datonics, Denny's, Depomed, Dr. Phil, Dynamic Glass, eBay, Electronic Arts, Eli Lilly and Company, Entertainment Tonight, Equus (golf), ESPN (Latin America), Expedia,

Experian, ExxonMobil, Eyeota, Facebook, Factual (data management), General Motors, General Mills, Genentech, Gilead Sciences, Glaxo-SmithKline, GOJO Industries, Hamburger Helper, Hot Pockets, Hyundai, IAG Cargo, iHeartRadio, IMS Health, Intel, Inside Edition, Janssen Pharmaceutica, Johnson & Johnson, Juicy Juice, Kaiser Permanente, Kaspersky Lab, Kia, Kohl's, Kwekkeboom, Lancel, Linde North America, LG Electronics, LinkedIn, Machinima, Marriott, MasterCard, McDonald's, Mercedes-Benz, Merrimack Pharmaceuticals, Microsoft, The Mirage (hotel and casino), Nature Valley, NBC, NCR Corporation, Nesquik, Nestlé, New York Sports Clubs, Nielsen, Nintendo, Noble Energy, Norse (cybersecurity), Ocean Spray, Oracle BlueKai, Ormat Technologies, Patrón Tequila, Peer39, Pfizer, Pine-Sol, Purina, Roche, Rocket Fuel, Samsung, Sierra Trading Post (online retailer), Simple Mobile, Sony, St. Regis Hotels, Stouffer's, Subaru, Tesco, The Insider, The Trade Desk, Tiffany & Co., Triad Retail Media, TVTY, TubeMogul, Tumi, TurboTax, Twitter, Unilever, US Bank, VisualDNA, William Hill, Yahoo, Zenith, Zippo

A detailed reading of the above clients lists helps one realize how far the influence of just three firms has spread through market capitalism, governments, and corporate media in the world today.

## PRP FIRMS IN SERVICE TO THE TRANSNATIONAL CAPITALIST CLASS

The US/NATO global military empire is the police force for concentrated transnational capitalism. A few hundred individuals control tens of trillions of dollars. The core agenda for the global empire is the protection of capital growth and the elimination of barriers and restrictions to the free movement of capital. Public relations propaganda firms play a vital role in the continuation of the global capitalist empire. Only thirty-four directors control the three mega-PRP firms. (See the Appendix for a listing of these directors and their remarkably similar backgrounds.) These directors are part of the super class within the global .0001 percent—6,000-plus elites who control half the world's wealth. These people interact in many of same transnational organizations, including the WTO, IMF, World Bank, Council on Foreign Relations, World Economic Forum, Business Roundtable, Trilateral Commission, and Bilderberg Group. They share a common bias for private accumulation, and a deep dislike for public democracies interfering with business practices and profits. The entire PRP industry reflects these leaders' orientation.

The PRP industry is highly concentrated and fully global. Its primary goal is the promotion of capital growth through the hegemonic psychological control of human desires, emotions, beliefs, and values. PRP firms do this by manipulating feelings and cognitions of human beings worldwide. With $35 billion in annual revenue, the big three PRP firms are a key component of the transnational capitalist class. Due to both their global corporate media influence and their increasingly embedded role in the production of government propaganda (including, especially, psychological operations in support of a permanent war on terror), PRP firms are capitalism's ideological engine.

Perhaps democracy movements can offer us some hope for the future. Consciousness of the dark side of PRP and its unrestricted power to warp minds is an important first step. Among some recent positive steps taken by activists to limit the power of the PRP firms, Quebec has become one of the first areas to ban commercial advertising to children under the age of 13.[52] For that matter, three generations of people in Cuba have grown up without product advertising in their lives. A group of graduate students from the University of Havana simply laughed when I asked them four years ago if they ever wanted a "Happy Meal." It seemed absurd to them to even consider the idea. We too need to understand the absurdity, and dangers, of the PRP industry, and move to eliminate its influence from our lives, our cultures, and our world.

---

PETER PHILLIPS is a Professor of Sociology at Sonoma State University and President of Media Freedom Foundation/Project Censored.

*Special thanks to Mary Fitzpatrick, Adjunct College Skills Instructor at College of Marin; and Tom Haseloff, a sociology major at University of California, Berkeley, for additional assistance with editing, formatting, and citations.*

# APPENDIX

## PRP Big Three Boards of Directors

OMNICOM GROUP

*Robert Charles Clark* Director, Trustee. BA in Theology from Mary-knoll College, PhD in Philosophy from Columbia University, and Juris Doctor from Harvard University. Boards: Independent Director of NewBridge Bancorp and Newbridge Bank.

*Leonard S. Coleman, Jr.* has held positions as Director, Independent Director, Commissioner, Chairman, Vice President, Member, and President. Undergraduate degree in History from Princeton University, Master's in Public Administration and Education/Social Policy from Harvard University.

*Errol Cook* has held positions as Director, Senior Advisor, Managing Director, Partner, Senior Partner, and Private Investor.

*Bruce Crawford* has held positions as Chief Operating Officer, Secretary, Senior Vice President, Interim Chief Financial Officer, President, Executive Vice President, Vice President, Director, Operations Consultant, Senior Advisor, and Chairman. He studied Finance at San Jose State University.

*Susan S. Denison* Founding Partner, Partner, Managing Director. BA in Psychology from Connecticut College, Master's in Psychology from the University of Rochester, and Master's in Business Administration from Harvard University.

*Michael A. Henning* has held positions as Chief Executive Officer, Managing Partner, Partner, Vice Chairman, Co-Chairman, Deputy Chairman, Independent Director, Director, and Trustee. Bachelor's in Business Administration from St. Francis College, and a certificate from Harvard University in Advanced Management. Co-Chairman of the Foreign Investment Advisory Board of Russia, where he co-chaired a panel of twenty-five Chief Executive Officers from the G7 countries who advised the Russian government in adopting international accounting and tax standards.

*John R. Murphy* has held positions as Chief Financial Officer, Interim Chief Financial Officer, and Chief Executive Officer. BA in Accounting from Pennsylvania State University.

*John R. Purcell* has held positions as Chairman, Chief Executive Officer, President, Executive Vice President, Senior Vice President, and Director. Graduated from University of Virginia School of Law in 1959.

*Linda Johnson Rice* has held positions as Chief Executive Officer, President, Vice President, Chief Operating Officer, and Director. BA in Journalism from University of Southern California, and Master's in Business Administration from Northwestern University. Specializes in publishing. She was named one of Chicago's 100 Most Powerful Women and was voted one of the Top 10 Women in the Media.

*Gary Roubous* has held positions as Chief Executive Officer, Director, and Chariman. Bachelor of Science in Chemical Engineering from University of Colorado. Specializes in manufacturing and financial services.

*John D. Wren* has held positions as Director, Chief Executive Officer, President, Chairman, Vice Chairman, and Trustee. Bachelor's and Master's in Business Administration from Adelphi University. Specializes in interactive and digital marketing services, investing, and accounting.

WPP

*Jacques Aigrain* Non-Executive Director. Partner at Warburg Pincus LLP. He was on the Executive Committee of Swiss Re Group from 2001 to 2009, including CEO from 2006, and prior to that, he spent twenty years with JPMorgan Chase in New York, London, and Paris.

*Charlene Begley* Non-Executive Director. Served as a Senior Vice President of General Electric Company and the Chief Executive Officer and President of GE Home & Business Solutions at General Electric Company.

*Sir John Hood* Director. Formerly Vice-Chancellor of the University of Oxford and the University of Auckland.

*Roberto Quarta* Director, Chairman.

*Daniela Riccardi* Director. A prominent FMCG, retail-and-fashion products executive, and Chief Executive Officer of Baccarat.

*Paul Richardson* Group Finance Director after four years as Director of Treasury.

*Li Ruigang* Director. Founding Chairman of CMC Capital Partners and CMC Holdings, China's platforms for media and entertainment investment and operations.

*Nicole Seligman* Director. Most recently, Ms. Seligman served as President of Sony Entertainment, Inc. and Sony Corporation of America.

*Hugo Shong* Director. Founding General Partner of IDG Capital Partners and President of IDG Asia/China 1993.

*Timothy Shriver* Chairman of Special Olympics. Member of the Council on Foreign Relations.

*Sir Martin Sorrell* Director, Group Chief Executive. Non-Executive Director of Formula One and Alcoa Inc., and a member of the Trilateral Commission.

*Sally Susman* Director. Currently Executive Vice President of Corporate Affairs for Pfizer.

*Sol Trujillo* Director. Three decades of experience as CEO of high-cap global companies in the US, Europe, the Middle East, Africa, and the Asia-Pacific.

## INTERPUBLIC GROUP OF COMPANIES (IPG)

*Jocelyn E. Carter-Miller* President of TechEd Ventures, a firm that develops and manages charter schools.

*Deborah G. Ellinger* Former Chief Executive Officer of the *Princeton Review*. Previously served as President of Restoration Hardware, and Chief Executive Officer of Wellness Pet Food.

*H. John Greeniaus* President of G-Force, LLC, an investment company. Served as President, Chairman, and Chief Executive Officer of Nabisco, Inc. Began his career with Procter & Gamble in Canada.

*Mary J. Steele Guilfoile* Chairman of MG Advisors, Inc., a privately-owned financial services merger and acquisition advisory and consulting services firm. Worked for twenty years on Wall Street, at times with JPMorgan Chase.

*Dawn E. Hudson* Chief Marketing Officer of the National Football League. Previously CEO of PepsiCo.

*William T. Kerr* Former President and Chief Executive Officer of Arbitron Inc., and Chairman of the Board of Directors of Meredith Corporation, a diversified media company.

*Henry S. Miller* Chairman of Marblegate Asset Management. Previously Cofounder, Chairman, and a Managing Director of Miller Buckfire & Co., an investment bank.

*Jonathan F. Miller* Previously Chairman and Chief Executive of News Corporation's digital media group.

*Michael I. Roth* Chairman and CEO. Previously Chairman and CEO of The MONY Group Inc. Currently a member of the Board of Directors for Pitney Bowes Inc., and the Ad Council.

*David M. Thomas* Former Chairman and CEO of IMS Health, which provides information and consulting for the pharmaceutical and healthcare industries.

# Notes

1   Howard Zinn, *Declaration of Independence: Cross-Examining America* (New York: Harper Collins, 1990), 2.

2   Edward L. Bernays, *Public Relations* (Norman, OK: University of Oklahoma Press, 1952), 1. In earlier days, Bernays, the nephew of Sigmund Freud, cut his teeth in PR as part of the Committee on Public Information, or Creel Committee, on the run up to WWI, where he was instrumental in helping President Woodrow Wilson sway public opinion to support America's entrance into the European war. Afterwards, in 1928, Bernays wrote his classic work *Propaganda*, which boasted of the tactics used to control the public mind. These were later used by many nations and corporations to achieve their varied policy objectives and maintain the appearance of democratic self-governance. For more details about Bernays and public relations, see Stuart Ewen, *PR!: A Social History of Spin* (New York: Basic Books, 1996); and the documentary film *Century of the Self*, directed by Adam Curtis (London: BBC Two, 2002).

3   Fraser P. Seitel, *The Practice of Public Relations*, 8th ed. (Upper Saddle River, NJ: Prentice Hall, 2001), 9.

4   Ibid., 160.

5   Bernays wasn't beyond helping corporations illicitly attain power and profits. He helped the United Fruit Company engineer the overthrow of the Guatemalan government in 1954 and aided the American Tobacco Company in marketing smoking to women (touting cigarettes as great for weight loss and self liberation). See Larry Tye, *The Father of Spin: Edward L. Bernays and the Birth of Public Relations* (Danvers, MA: Crown Publishers, 1998).

6   *World Book Encyclopedia*, s.v. "Propaganda," (Chicago, IL: World Book, Inc., 2015).

7   For an early history of state propaganda, see Jacquie L'Etang, "State Propaganda and Bureaucratic Intelligence: The Creation of Public Relations in 20th Century Britain," *Public Relations Review* 24, no. 4 (1998), 413–41, doi: 10.1016/S0363-8111(99)80109-X.

8   David, L. Robb, *Operation Hollywood: How the Pentagon Shapes and Censors the Movies* (New York: Prometheus Books, 2004).

9   Nima Shirazi, "Revisiting 'Argo,' Hollywood's CIA-Supported Propaganda Fable," AlterNet, April 12, 2016, http://www.alternet.org/grayzone-project/revisiting-argo-hollywoods-cia-supported-propaganda-fable; Rob Williams, "Screening the Homeland: How Hollywood Fantasy Mediates State Fascism in the US of Empire," in *Censored 2014: Fearless Speech in Fateful Times*, eds. Mickey Huff, Andy Lee Roth, and Project Censored (New York: Seven Stories Press, 2013), 297–310; Robin Andersen, "Sony, The Interview and Hollywood Illusions of Creative Expression," *Vision Machine*, December 26, 2014, http://thevisionmachine.com/2014/12/sony-the-interview-and-hollywood-illusions-of-creative-expression/.

10  Douglas Kellner, "Media Propaganda and Spectacle in the War on Iraq: A Critique of U.S. Broadcasting Networks," *Cultural Studies<=>Critical Methodologies* 4, no. 3 (August 2004), 329–38, doi: 10.1177/1532708603262723.

11  James Bamford, "The Man Who Sold the War," *Rolling Stone*, November 2005, republished and available via Common Dreams, November 18, 2005, http://www.rollingstone.com/music/pictures/rolling-stones-biggest-scoops-exposes-and-controversies-2-aa-624/the-man-who-sold-the-war-by-james-bamford-3323040, read the text here http://commondreams.org/headlines05/1118-10.htm.

12  David L. Altheide and Jennifer N. Grimes, "War Programming: The Propaganda Project and the Iraq War," *Sociological Quarterly* 46, no. 4 (2005), 617–43, doi: 10.1111/j.1533-8525.2005.00029.x.

13  David W. Guth, "Black, White, and Shades of Gray: The Sixty-Year Debate Over Propaganda versus Public Diplomacy," *Journal of Promotion Management* 14, no. 3-4 (December 2008), 309–25, doi: 10.1080/10496490802624083. For more accounts of the numerous false statements and propaganda peddled by the Bush administration prior to the invasion of Iraq in 2003, see Charles Lewis, *935 Lies: The Future of Truth and the Decline of America's Moral Integrity* (New York: PublicAffairs, 2014), and Sheldon Rampton and John Stauber, *Weapons of Mass Deception: The Uses of Propaganda in Bush's War on Iraq* (New York: TarcherPerigee, 2003).

14 Dave Gelders, "Government Communication about Potential Policies: Public Relations, Propaganda or Both?" *Public Relations Review* 36, no. 1 (February 2010): 59–62.

15 "Media and PR," Corporate Watch, no date, https://corporatewatch.org/categories/media-pr.

16 Ryszard Lawniczak, "Public Relations Role in a Global Competition 'to Sell' Alternative Political and Socio-economic Models of Market Ecomony," *Public Relations Review* 33, no. 4 (October 2007), 377–86.

17 Edward S. Herman and Noam Chomsky, *Manufacturing Consent: The Political Economy of the Mass Media* (New York: Pantheon Books, 1988).

18 Julia Hobsbawm, "Why Journalism Needs PR," *Guardian*, November 16, 2003, https://www.theguardian.com/media/2003/nov/17/mondaymediasection3.

Ben Bagdikian, author of *The Media Monopoly* and former editor of the *Washington Post*, told this author in late 1999 that he estimated two-thirds of all news stories originated with PR firms.

19 Hill & Knowlton Strategies, "About Us," no date, http://www.hkstrategies.com/about/.

20 Richard Gale and Gary Null, "Monsanto's Sealed Documents Reveal the Truth behind Roundup's Toxicological Dangers," Progressive Radio Network, September 15, 2015, http://prn.fm/monsantos-sealed-documents-reveal-the-truth-behind-roundups-toxicological-dangers-richard-gale-and-gary-null/.

21 Sheldon Rampton and John Stauber, "ConsumerFreedom.org: Tobacco Money Takes on Activist Cash," *PR Watch* 9, no. 1, (2002), 7–8, http://www.prwatch.org/files/pdfs/prwatch/prwv9n1.pdf.

22 Laura Miller, "Global Climate Coalition Melts Down," *PR Watch* (February 27, 2002), http://www.prwatch.org/spin/2002/02/1061/global-climate-coalition-melts-down.

23 "PR Watch Launches the 'Impropaganda Review,'" *PR Watch* 9, no. 1 (2002), 8, http://www.prwatch.org/files/pdfs/prwatch/prwv9n1.pdf.

24 Stephen Adams and Daniel Capparelli, "Knowing When to Quit: Assessing the Nairobi WTO Ministerial," Global Counsel, January 12, 2016, https://www.global-counsel.co.uk/analysis/insight/knowing-when-quit-assessing-nairobi-wto-ministerial.

25 Ray Eldon Hiebert, "Public Relations and Propaganda in Framing the Iraq War: A Preliminary Review," *Public Relations Review* 29, no. 3 (2003), 243–55, http://www.kean.edu/˜jkeil/Welcome_files/PR_Propaganda_Iraq.pdf.

26 Megan R. Wilson, "Feds Shelling Out Billions to Public Relations Firms," Hill, December 8, 2015, http://thehill.com/business-a-lobbying/business-a-lobbying/262387-feds-shelling-out-billions-to-public-relations-firms.

27 Adam Andrzejewski and Tom Coburn, "The Department of Self-Promotion: How Federal Agency PR Spending Advances Their Interests Rather Than the Public Interest, Fiscal Years 2007–2014: Oversight Study," Open the Books, November 2015, http://www.openthebooks.com/openthebooks_oversight_report_-_the_department_of_self-promotion_federal_public_relations/.

28 To give just a single example of these firms' reach, Laughlin, Marinaccio & Owens is a privately-owned PRP company based in Arlington, Virginia, whose clients include the US Department of Homeland Security, Coast Guard Reserve, Army National Guard, Air National Guard, Military Officers Association of America, American Psychological Association, Avis Budget Group, Advantage Rent a Car, Cruise Lines International Association, CRDF Global, U.S. Edelman Financial Services, Evermay Wealth Management, First Virginia Community Bank, George Washington University, Johns Hopkins University, Marriott International, and Associated General Contractors of America.

29 United States House of Representatives, Committee on Government Reform, Minority Staff Special Investigations Division, "Federal Public Relations Spending," January 2005, http://www.savetheinternet.com/sites/default/files/resources/pr_spending_doubles_under_bush.pdf.

30 Johan Carlisle, "Public Relationships: Hill & Knowlton, Robert Gray, and the CIA," *CovertAction Quarterly* 44 (1993), http://whatreallyhappened.com/RANCHO/LIE/HK/HK2.html.

31 Ibid.

32 Ibid.

33 Ibid. For more on the connections between the CIA and corporate media, see Brian Covert's chapter in this volume.

34 Noah Shachtman, "Exclusive: U.S. Spies Buy Stake in Firm That Monitors Blogs, Tweets," *Wired*, October 19, 2009, http://www.wired.com/dangerroom/2009/10/exclusive-us-spies-buy-stake-in-twitter-blog-monitoring-firm/; Noah Shachtman, interview by Amy Goodman and Juan González, "CIA Invests in Software Firm Monitoring Blogs, Twitter," *Democracy Now!*, October 22, 2009, http://www.democracynow.org/2009/10/22/cia_invests_in_software_firm_monitoring.

35 Sarah Lazare, "Meet the Corporate PR Firm Hired to Sell a Muderous Foreign Regime to the American Public," AlterNet, April 15, 2016, http://www.alternet.org/world/meet-corporate-pr-firm-hired-sell-murderous-foreign-regime-american-public.

36 Deirdre Fulton, "UC Davis Spent $175,000 in an Attempt to Scrub This Story from the Internet," CommonDreams, April 24, 2016, http://www.commondreams.org/news/2016/04/14/uc-davis-spent-175000-attempt-scrub-story-internet.

37 See G. William Domhoff, *Who Rules America? The Triumph of the Corporate Rich*, 5th ed. (New York: McGraw Hill, 2006); and Peter Martin Phillips, "A Relative Advantage: Sociology of the San Francisco Bohemian Club," unpublished doctoral dissertation, Sonoma State University, 1994, http://library.sonoma.edu/regional/faculty/phillips/bohemianindex.php.

38 Early studies by Charles Beard, published as *An Economic Interpretation of the Constitution of the United States* (New York: Macmillan, 1913), established that economic elites formulated the US Constitution to serve their own special interests. Henry Klein, in a book entitled *Dynastic America and Those Who Own It* (New York: H.H. Klein, 1921), argued that wealth in America had power never before known in the world and was centered in the top 2 percent of the population, which owned some 60 percent of the country. In 1937, Ferdinand Lundberg published *America's 60 Families* (New York, NY: Vanguard Press, 1937), which documented inter-marrying, self-perpetuating families, for whom wealth was the "indispensable handmaiden of government." In 1945, C. Wright Mills determined that nine out of ten business elites from 1750 to 1879 came from well-to-do families (C. Wright Mills, "The American Business Elite: A Collective Portrait," *Journal of Economic History* 5, no. S1 (December 1945), 20–44.

39 Leslie Sklair, *The Transnational Capitalist Class* (Oxford, UK/Malden, MA: Blackwell, 2001).

40 William I. Robinson, *A Theory of Global Capitalism: Production, Class, and State in a Transnational World* (Baltimore, MD: Johns Hopkins University Press, 2004); William I. Robinson, *Global Capitalism and the Crisis of Humanity* (New York: Cambridge University Press, 2014).

41 William I. Robinson, *A Theory of Global Capitalism*, 155–56.

42 David Rothkopf, *Superclass: The Global Power Elite and the World They Are Making* (New York: Farrar, Straus and Giroux, 2008).

43 William K. Carroll, *The Making of a Transnational Capitalist Class: Corporate Power in the 21st Century* (London/New York: Zed Books, 2010).

44 Peter Phillips and Brady Osborne, "Exposing the Financial Core of the Transnational Corporate Class," *Censored 2014: Fearless Speech in Fateful Times*, eds. Mickey Huff, Andy Lee Roth, and Project Censored (New York: Seven Stories Press, 2013), 313, http://projectcensored.org/financial-core-of-the-transnational-corporate-class/.

45 "America's Navy—The Shield," YouTube video, posted by "America's Navy," December 13, 2014, https://www.youtube.com/watch?v=ThImmlN-I8s.

46 Noam Chomsky, *Media Control: The Spectacular Achievements of Propaganda* (New York: Seven Stories Press, Open Media Book, 2002).

47 TNS, "Political and Social," no date, http://www.tnsglobal.com/what-we-do/political-and-social.

48 GPG, "An Integrated Team, from Idea to Execution," no date, http://gpg.com/services/.

49 Sudler and Hennessey, http://www.sudler.com/.

50 Unless specifically cited, all data about the big three PRP firms was collected from the firms' websites, Bloomberg.com, and http://littlesis.org.

51 Corporate Watch, a UK-based journalism and research group that analyses the impact of corporations and corporate power on the environment, did a profile on one of the company's divi-

sions, Ogilvy & Mather Worldwide, in July 2002. They charged Ogilvy & Mather Worldwide with greenwashing the practices of BP and Ford. See "Ogilvy and Mather Worldwide: Corporate Crimes," Corporate Watch, completed July 2002, posted online June 14, 2005, https://corporatewatch.org/news/2005/jun/13/ogilvy-mather-worldwide-corporate-crimes.

52  Quebec Coalition on Weight-Related Problems, "Quebec Law," http://www.cqpp.qc.ca/en/advertising-to-children/quebec-law.

# CHAPTER 8

# Remote Control
## Electronic Surveillance and the Demise of Human Dignity

Elliot D. Cohen

By surveilling millions of Americans' private electronic communications without warrants, the US government threatens human freedom. Meanwhile, popular government claims—that this colossal spy network preempts terrorism attacks, and poses no significant threat to the civil liberties of the masses—are instances of government propaganda that the corporate media unabashedly propagate. This chapter aims at exploding these well-entrenched government myths, increasing public awareness of important facts about mass, warrantless surveillance not adequately addressed by the corporate media (even in this post-Snowden period), and exposing the dangerous technological trends that drive such surveillance. In this light, it draws some practical conclusions and admonitions regarding this insidious threat to human dignity.

In June 2013, just five days after the *Guardian* broke the story of Edward Snowden's disclosures that the US had been collecting millions of Americans' phone records, a majority of Americans thought that the NSA's phone tracking was an acceptable antiterrorism tactic, according to a Pew Research poll. According to this survey, 56 percent agreed with such a government measure, whereas 41 percent thought that it was unacceptable.[1] In contrast, according to a June 26, 2014, Pew Research survey, these numbers reversed, with 54 percent of Americans disapproving of government collection of telephone and internet data as an antiterrorism tactic and 42 percent approving.[2] It is therefore reasonable to suppose that the American public's perception of government mass surveillance has been, and can be, significantly influenced by what the news media discloses. So, what if the corporate media were to present evidence showing that government collection of millions of Americans' phone records did virtually nothing to stop terrorism plots?

## THE EARLY DAYS OF MASS SPYING

The system of mass, warrantless surveillance did not develop overnight.[3] It is a product of decades of growth dating back to at least the late 1960s, with a system known as Echelon, which captured and filtered signals sent via satellite technologies. Operated jointly by the United States' National Security Agency (NSA) and Great Britain's Government Communications Headquarters (GCHQ), it was officially used for national defense purposes against the Soviet Union during the Cold War. In fact, this early system, like iterations to follow, was also used (and misused) for other purposes, including "eavesdropping on millions of daily communications between ordinary people"[4] as well as "governments, organizations and businesses in virtually every country."[5]

With the advent of fiber-optic cables, satellite technologies were largely replaced, thereby increasing the speed, distance, and amount of data that could be transmitted. By the late 1980s, nations were connected by underwater fiber-optic cables, thus setting the stage for a system of mass surveillance that spanned continents. By the late 1990s, political focus shifted from the Soviet Union (dissolved in 1991) to the Middle East, and, after the attack on the US homeland on September 11, 2001, a new geopolitical basis for the development and deployment of an even more aggressive iteration of the mass surveillance system was born. This time it was "the war on terror"—rather than a "cold war" with the Soviet Union—that became the official rationale for mass, electronic surveillance.

## MASS ELECTRONIC SURVEILLANCE ON STILTS: TOTAL INFORMATION AWARENESS

Unlike conventional wars deserving of the term, this new "war on terror" was to be fought anywhere and everywhere, against an enemy that did not wear a state uniform and could even turn out to be one's neighbor, friend, or peer. The latest iteration of mass surveillance is intended to envelop everyone inside an electronic wall. It brings the "war on terror" into our living rooms and even our bedrooms. Under increasingly pervasive surveillance, everyone is treated as a potential terrorist—guilty until proven innocent. Under the banner of fighting such a ubiquitous "war," within weeks of the 9/11 attacks, the George W. Bush administration established the President's Surveillance Program, also known as the "Total Information Awareness" project. Then, in January 2002, the research and development branch of the Department of Defense, called the Defense Advanced Research Project (DARPA), established an "Information Awareness Office" charged with overseeing the building of this massive surveillance spy network. Its mission was to "imagine, develop, apply, integrate, demonstrate and transition information technologies, components and prototype, closed-loop, information systems that will counter asymmetric threats by achieving *total information awareness.*"[6] That is, its goal was to systematically intercept, store, search, monitor, read, and analyze the electronic communications of 300 million Americans, as well as millions of foreign users passing through switches at telecommunication sites located in the United States.

This system was illegal from its inception, because the 1978 Foreign Intelligence Surveillance Act (FISA), then the law of the land, required court warrants for spying on US persons. Nevertheless, except for a misleading article published by the *New York Times* on December 16, 2005, which reported that the Bush administration only monitored international phone and email messages, such domestic spying operated in secrecy until June 2006, when Mark Klein, an AT&T whistleblower, disclosed AT&T documents proving that the NSA was conducting a far more expansive mass warrantless surveillance program, including the monitoring of *wholly domestic* communications.[7] According to Klein, AT&T's Folsom Street facility in San Francisco, where he worked as chief technician, had a secret "secure room" hidden deep within it, requiring NSA clearance. This room, Klein maintained, contained NSA computing equipment for capturing, storing, and analyzing all incoming data, which was copied and diverted to the room using fiber-optic splitters. "Based on my understanding of the connections and equipment at issue," wrote Klein, "it appears the NSA is capable of conducting what amounts to vacuum-cleaner surveillance of all the data crossing the internet—whether that be peoples' e-mail, web surfing or any other data."[8]

In 2013, classified NSA documents leaked by Edward Snowden confirmed Klein's claims. These documents, including NSA slides, described the latest equipment and provided a clear idea of the substantial technological advances in surveillance capabilities. Whereas Klein disclosed a Narus STA 6400 Semantic Traffic Analyzer, which searched electronic communications based on predefined key terms, the leaked slides also revealed the latest iteration of so-called "deep packet analysis," in particular, a traffic analyzer called Xkeyscore, developed by Science Applications International Corporation (SAIC).[9]

Xkeyscore taps into data flowing upstream, that is, data in transit, before it reaches its destination. Such upstream programs contrast with a collection of programs, code named PRISM, that retrieve data after it has already reached the servers of major Internet companies, including Microsoft, Google, Yahoo, Facebook, Paltalk, YouTube, Skype, AOL, and Apple. Because upstream data is largely unprocessed and encrypted, analysts are instructed to use both upstream and downstream (PRISM) data, which can sometimes circumvent potential challenges such as de-encryption. Analysts for the NSA also have a standard of 51 percent assurance that the targets of PRISM collections are not US persons, which means that there is a 49 percent chance that they are US persons. This probability assessment is also highly subjective.[10] On the other hand, upstream programs, by their nature, tend to indiscriminately capture whatever flows through the fiber-optic cables, which includes both metadata and content of electronic communications of US persons that has been "incidentally" captured.[11] Unfortunately, most media attention has been on PRISM, thus keeping the nature and potential of Xkeyscore relatively hidden from public scrutiny.

In a January 2014 interview with German broadcaster Nord Deutscher Rundfunk, Snowden described Xkeyscore's capabilities:

> You could read anyone's email in the world. Anybody you've got [an] email address for, any website you can watch traffic to

and from it, any computer that an individual sits at you can watch it, any laptop that you're tracking you can follow it as it moves from place to place throughout the world. It's a one stop shop for access to the NSA's information. And what's more you can tag individuals using "XKeyscore." Let's say I saw you once and I thought what you were doing was interesting or you just have access that's interesting to me, let's say you work at a major German corporation and I want access to that network, I can track your username on a website on a form somewhere, I can track your real name, I can track associations with your friends and I can build what's called a fingerprint which is network activity unique to you which means anywhere you go in the world anywhere you try to sort of hide your online presence hide your identity, the NSA can find you and anyone who's allowed to use this or who the NSA shares their software with can do the same thing.[12]

Given Snowden's description, such a system could be quite useful for eavesdropping on the activities of non-terrorists, and this is borne out by the facts. In particular, the NSA, together with its British counterpart, the GCHQ, has spied on senior European Union officials, the former Israeli prime minister and defense minister, the presidents of Brazil and Mexico, the chancellor of Germany, a West African official, United Nations officials, officials at the German Embassy in Rwanda, and a French ambassador, among others. The NSA has also engaged in industrial espionage, including spying on oil giants such as the French company Total, the Brazilian gas and alternative energy company Petrobras, and the French multinational Thales, which builds electrical systems and provides aerospace, space, defense, transportation, and security services.[13]

Clearly, budgeting billions of federal dollars to fund a spy system for these purposes would not pass public muster, so the official purpose of the surveillance programs is to protect the homeland from another attack like 9/11. However, as I will discuss, the NSA's colossal spy network has only very limited uses in conducting terrorist investigations, and these uses do not, by any unbiased assessment, warrant the ever-increasing threat it poses to human freedom and dignity.

## WHAT'S SO PATRIOTIC ABOUT EVISCERATING
## THE FOURTH AMENDMENT?

Indeed, the present state of law makes the protection of these vital human values extremely tenuous. Judicial oversight of NSA data programs largely approximates the Wild West. Although there is a Foreign Intelligence Surveillance Court (FISC) to oversee NSA collection activities and to maintain conformity with FISA "minimization" standards intended to protect US citizens from violations of their Fourth Amendment right to be free from unwarranted searches and seizures, the truth is that enforcement has been inconsistent at best, and entirely absent at worst. For example, in 2011, the FISC concluded that the NSA had been "acquiring annually tens of thousands of wholly domestic communications, and tens of thousands of non-target communications of persons who have little or no relationship to the target but who are protected under the Fourth Amendment."[14] Still, the FISC gave the NSA a pass because the technology being used limited the ability of the NSA to filter out the private communications of US persons. Sadly, the FISC did not even broach the idea of requiring the NSA to find a technological solution to such violations of the Fourth Amendment rights of US persons.

In other cases, there has been no judicial oversight whatsoever. This happens when the NSA collects its data overseas and therefore outside the jurisdiction of the FISC. One particularly egregious instance of this sort involves the program code-named MUSCULAR. Between December 2012 and January 2013, this upstream program collected 181 million records, including email messages and chats.[15] These data streams were collected as they passed between the overseas internal data storage centers of Yahoo and Google. Since overseas routing of data by US companies like Yahoo and Google is primarily motivated by cost-effectiveness and not by the nation from which the data originated, a substantial number of these intercepted communications likely came from US persons. Although this data is collected overseas, it is still routed to Fort Meade, Maryland, for storage, search, and analysis.[16] Thus, through programs like MUSCULAR, the NSA is able to systematically avoid any judicial oversight, summarily violating the Fourth Amendment rights of US persons.

Changes in intelligence law have also made it possible to use the mass, warrantless surveillance network to hunt for more than just terrorists. In particular, the expansive powers of the so-called "Patriot Act," which was hastily enacted following the September 11, 2001, attacks, have broken down the partition between ordinary criminal activities and terrorism by allowing evidence regarding ordinary (non-terrorist) crimes discovered while conducting a terrorist investigation to be admissible for purposes of prosecuting such crimes.[17] So, the illegal-marijuana grower can be prosecuted for her crime if her email about this activity happens to be picked up during a "terrorist investigation." No longer is there a need to show probable cause for investigating such activities, so long as they are discovered in the course of hunting for terrorists. Further, the FISA Amendments Act of 2008, now the law of the land, requires only that "a *significant* purpose of the acquisition is to obtain foreign intelligence information," which opens the door for deploying the system for purposes unrelated to terrorism investigations [emphasis added].[18]

In the face of such a system of mass, warrantless surveillance and the laws under which it presently operates, Fourth Amendment protection against unreasonable search and seizure without probable cause is therefore a relic of times gone by. It was not an accident that the Founding Fathers included such a protection in the US Constitution. The danger of government overreach was seen to be inevitable, over the course of time, without a system of checks and balances to prevent it. Unfortunately, now more than ever before in the history of our nation, unfettered governmental power to inject itself into our private lives threatens citizens' ability "to be secure in their persons, houses, papers, and effects" pursuant to the Fourth Amendment. Like a fire raging out of control, this government power to meddle in our personal affairs is destined to consume human dignity, which entails the ability to live by our own intellectual and moral lights without the encroachment of government. Without a protected sphere of privacy of thought, and feeling, which is none of the government's business, we are not free to be ourselves.

This point has been eloquently stated by John Stuart Mill in his famous treatise *On Liberty*. "It is desirable," wrote Mill, "that, in things which do not primarily concern others, individuality should assert itself. Where, not the person's own character, but the traditions or customs of other people are the rule of conduct, there is wanting one of the principal ingredients of human happiness, and quite the chief ingredient of individual and social progress."[19] Unfortunately, in a culture where government is privy to everything about us—even our more personal and private secrets—the desire to be ourselves is chilled.[20]

## WHAT'S THE PROGNOSIS?

The stakes are simply too high to assume that government will leave us alone. Unconstrained power eventually gets worse, and more abusive, not less. This trajectory ultimately leads to full censorship of anything contrary to the interests of those who wield power. Can a journalist protect his sources when there is no sphere of privacy from government encroachment? How, then, can there be freedom of the press? Can a lawyer protect a client against government encroachment, when, in the process, the client's confidential information is acquired by that very government? How, then, can there be Sixth Amendment rights to trial by jury and the right to counsel? Can a dissenter express antigovernment sentiments when an omnipresent government is bent on suppressing dissent? Can a nonbeliever speak earnestly when a theocratic dictator has her ear to the ground? What about an anti-Muslim demagogue who has branded all Muslims as enemies of the state? Is there freedom of religious worship when mosques are under surveillance? Can we assure that this awesome potential for abuse won't inevitably fall into the hands of a despotic regime that is motivated by hatred, vindictiveness, and paranoia? Predictably, a system of mass, warrantless surveillance will eventually outstrip human dignity, leaving in its tracks an empty shell where creativity, individuality, freedom, vitality, and personal autonomy once lived.

## AND IT'S NOT JUST WHAT YOU SAY!

The history of technology development, especially in the area of brain-computer interfaces, supports the need for constraining this ubiquitous, looming threat to human dignity. On September 17, 2001, just six days after the 9/11 attacks on the US homeland, DARPA issued a memo that stated,

> The brain takes inputs and generates output through the electrical activity of neurons. DARPA is interested in creating new technologies for augmenting human performance through the ability to non-invasively access these codes in the brain in real time and integrate them into peripheral device or system operations.[21]

In practical and blunt terms, this meant that DARPA wanted to be able to remotely control soldiers' minds.

Along these lines, in 2002, DARPA announced that it was "tinkering with a soldier's brain using magnetic resonance" to make severely sleep-deprived soldiers feel rested. According to DARPA, "Eliminating the need for sleep during an operation . . . will create a fundamental change in war fighting and force employment."[22]

Similarly, in 2003, DARPA's brain interface program manager, Alan Rudolph, declared that this program, which investigated the monitoring of brain electrical activity, would focus on

> demonstrations of plasticity from the neural system and from an integrated working device or system that result in real time control under relevant conditions of force perturbation and cluttered sensory environments from which tasks must be performed (e.g., recognizing and picking up a target and manipulating it).[23]

In laymen's terms, the program investigated "reprogramming" soldiers' minds not to experience fear and confusion in extremely threatening environments. This would amount to a kind of short-circuiting of a portion of the brain known as the amygdala, which is hardwired to produce the experience of fear in stressful situations.

In 2014, DARPA awarded contracts to both Massachusetts General Hospital and the University of California, San Francisco, to build electrical brain implants to control human emotions.[24] Although these devices are ostensibly to be tested on mentally ill individuals, DARPA's consistently documented goal in funding this program has been to set the stage for remotely controlling the affect of soldiers on the battlefield. But why stop there when the same devices might be deployed to control the masses?

According to Intel researchers, by 2020 Internet users will have the capability to surf the web using their brain waves.[25] That is, it will be possible to connect human brains to the Internet via brain-computer interfaces, thereby allowing Internet users to upload and download information by their thoughts alone. In fact, it appears that research to develop such a brain-computer interface is now being funded to the tune of $60 million by DARPA.[26] What this portends is the potential for exposing the brains of millions of people to the perils of others bent on acquiring their private information, or manipulating their brains, for self-interested purposes, in ways developed by DARPA. Indeed, cookies clandestinely downloaded on one's computer for nefarious purposes can be problematic; but what if it were a person's brain, not just his or her PC? The technology to turn such disturbing possibilities into actualities is under development, and given the propensity of technology to be marketed when it is available, especially if there are profits to be made, we can reasonably predict that Intel's vision will become reality in the not-so-distant future.

The logical conclusion of a project focused on total information control is to control the source of the information itself, which is the minds of the masses. Information warfare is already a reality. True, as in war in physical space, cyberwars can be fought within the bounds of just war theory (not intentionally targeting noncombatants; not attacking if there are viable alternatives; attacking for purposes of self-defense only, not political gain; and so forth). However, we know from past experience that such principles of just war are not always respected on the battlefield, especially when high-tech solutions to solving conflicts are involved. In actions ranging from the US dropping an atomic bomb on Hiroshima to its use of drone warfare in Afghanistan, the principle of discrimination, calling for the avoidance of "collateral damage," has been overlooked for the sake of expedience.

Here, the analogy with cyberwarfare is not far afield. Instead of wiretaps based on probable cause, we now have mass, warrantless surveillance with little to no judicial oversight. As technologies increasingly develop the potential to access and control the sources of information (including human minds, as the DARPA program intends), we can reasonably expect that the NSA will want to seize control of the minds of those they deem to be potential threats to national security. However, given that we are all now considered guilty until proven innocent, this makes us all potential threats to national security. In fact, few people understand that the technologies of mass surveillance have little capacity to comply with the principle of discrimination as it applies to cyber-investigations. This is because terrorist searches launched with the use of the present system of mass, warrantless surveillance have an incredibly high rate of false positives.

## WHAT ACTIONABLE INTELLIGENCE DOES THIS MULTIBILLION-DOLLAR SPY NETWORK REALLY YIELD?

In January 2014, the New American Foundation, a nonprofit, nonpartisan public policy institute, published a report on the efficacy of the present mass surveillance system, based on its analysis of 225 cases of individuals charged with terrorism after 9/11.[27] The report examined investigations conducted pursuant to Section 702 of the FISA Amendments Act as well as investigations conducted under Section 215 of the US Patriot Act. The former is supposed to target only non-US persons outside of the US, but in fact collects the electronic communications (including the contents of email messages, web searches, chats, Skype exchanges, and phone calls) of millions of Americans; while the latter acquires mass metadata records of telephone use (such as date, time, duration, and number called) of millions of Americans.[28]

According to the New American Foundation's report, the Section 702 program played a role in identifying only 4.8 percent of the 225 documented cases, while the Section 215 program played a role in identifying only 1.8 percent of these cases. The report concluded that bulk surveillance of this sort has made only a "minimal" contribution to identifying terrorist plots before they occur, and that official claims about these programs' role in keeping Americans safe have been "overblown" and "even misleading."[29]

This is not to mention the millions of false positives that were generated in the process of identifying these small numbers of terrorists. In fact, in the case of Section 702 investigations, there appear to have been eleven terrorists out of seventeen that were identified between the years 2009 and 2012. This means that the accuracy rate of the system was 65 percent, which means that the inaccuracy rate (false positives) was 35 percent. Based on FIS Court records, between 2009 and 2012, at least 250 million Internet communications were collected annually pursuant to Section 702. This, in turn, means that, as a modest conjecture, there were *at least* 87.5 million false positives generated to identify eleven terrorists (250 million minus the seventeen true terrorists, multiplied by thirty-five percent).[30]

## WHY SO MANY FALSE POSITIVES?

The obvious question is why the current state of surveillance technology yields such an incredibly high rate of false positives. Why isn't the system more efficient? The answer is that the system uses *pattern matching searches*, which are highly ineffective in catching terrorists.

Pattern matching searches work by developing algorithms for identifying a target group using a set of matching criteria. For example, when an advertiser attempts to market a product to a particular demographic, it collects a data profile about the group in question and targets Internet users who fit this profile. So, suppose it wants to sell Viagra over the Internet. The advertiser would collect information about the most frequent users—in terms of age, sexual behavior, gender, etc. It would then target this group over the Internet by matching the footprint of individual end users with this profile. That is why advertisers install cookies in our computers. With cookies, they can collect information about individuals, and use this data to make inferences about what sort of products would interest them. For example, based on websites visited and web searches, it might infer that a person is a male, 56 years or older, and has sexual interests. If this description matches the profile of individuals most likely to use Viagra, the person would receive a pitch for Viagra from the advertiser.

Even using such a behaviorally oriented approach, the average success rate is only about 6.8 percent.[31] So, if, say, ten million potential Viagra users were targeted, there would be about 9.32 million of these individuals who would not purchase Viagra.

In contrast to targeting potential Viagra users, the use of pattern matching searches to identify prospective terrorists is much more challenging. This is because, unlike in the case of Viagra users, we do not have a clear idea about prospective terrorists' online activities. As a result, algorithms for constructing matching searches for terrorists look for anomalous behavioral patterns on the Internet that do not conform to the web searches of most Internet users. In fact, the NSA has used the profiles of millions of social media users (for example, those who have Facebook accounts) to build such inference engines. However, it is erroneous to conclude that someone is a terrorist simply because he or she does not fit the official profile of an average social media user.[32] As a result of pattern matching searches, the NSA's rate of success in catching terrorists in its electronic net is extremely low, while the rate of false positives is extremely high.

## WHY NOT PUT MORE BOOTS ON THE GROUND?

The success rate in catching terrorist plots pursuant to Section 702 during 2009–12 should have been appreciably less than 65 percent if the NSA relied entirely on pattern matching searches. In fact, however, the NSA did not rely *entirely* on such searches. According to the 2014 New American Foundation Report, 60 percent of the investigations that resulted in thwarting terrorist plots depended on conventional means of evidence gathering, including the use of undercover informants, tips from family members, routine law enforcement, and shared FBI or CIA intelligence.[33] Indeed, as I have discussed elsewhere, leads obtained by conventional "boots on the ground" investigations significantly enhanced the relatively limited success of the Section 702 investigations.[34] More precisely, metadata (so-called "strong selectors") such as names, phone numbers, and email addresses, obtained by conventional means, were used to screen out the millions of false positives from the true terrorists. In the absence of conventionally obtained metadata, the algorithms used by the government to conduct pattern matching searches made only small contributions to their efforts to forestall terrorist plots.

In contrast, a T-shirt vendor stopped the 2010 Times Square car bombing attempt,[35] the passengers and crew of Northwest Airlines Flight 253 stopped the "underwear bomber" on Christmas Day in 2009,[36] and it was passengers on another Northwest flight who thwarted the 2001 "shoe bomber" and tied him to his chair.[37] Such plots as these eluded the multibillion-dollar mass, warrantless, electronic spy system. Yet the United States continues to pour vast amounts of money into it, rather than to invest in antiterrorism programs based on human intelligence, search warrants, and wire taps, all initiated on the basis of probable cause and consistent with US citizens' Fourth Amendment rights. Unless the overreach of the current system of mass, warrantless surveillance is reined in, we are arguably less safe from future terrorist attacks while being remarkably vulnerable to what is worst of all: the undermining of our freedom and dignity as persons.

## SO WHY IS THE CORPORATE MEDIA CENSORING THE STORY?

Clearly, the government wants the American people to believe that the system works well, that it is exclusively aimed at finding and stopping terrorists, and that it poses no significant threat to the civil liberties of non-terrorists. And the corporate media is helping to propagate the myth.

When Edward Snowden leaked government information about the NSA's bulk surveillance program, he was branded a traitor who had betrayed the American people by putting their safety at risk.[38] This was and is the official position taken by the Obama administration (despite the fact that there were no foreign terrorist attacks on the US homeland following the Snowden leaks), and the corporate media helped to propagate this line. It is true that US news media such as the *New York Times* and *Washington Post* covered the story, publishing many of the NSA slides that were leaked. In fact, the *Washington Post* won Pulitzer Prizes for its coverage. Nevertheless, the facts disclosed by Snowden have tended to be buried, and have gotten lost in high-pitched media discussion about whether Snowden was a hero or traitor.[39] Similarly, in 2006, when Mark Klein leaked information about the NSA's massive spy program, corporate media played down the story; today few people have even heard of Mark Klein.[40]

It is important to stress that Snowden did not disclose details about terrorist investigations that were underway, including the names of individuals who were being targeted by the NSA. Clearly, this would have undermined national security. In contrast, information about how the NSA was spying on Americans, without their knowledge or consent, was arguably information to which Americans were entitled. Nevertheless, the media's persistent harping on the question of Snowden's status as a hero or a traitor was a red herring that distracted the public's attention from the more fundamental news story, the government's abuses of power. Isn't the government abusing its power by systematically violating the Fourth Amendment? Shouldn't reporting this abuse of power be the media's central focus?

Here are some disconcerting reasons why the corporate media, and especially network news organizations, failed to do their job. First, the FISA Amendments Act of 2008 requires that electronic communication service providers "immediately provide the Government with all information, facilities, or assistance necessary to accomplish the acquisition in a manner that will protect the secrecy of the acquisition . . ."[41] Network news organizations such as News Corp/Fox News and Comcast/MSNBC are themselves "electronic communication service providers" as this term is defined by the Act.[42] As such, these corporations are complicit with government in spying on millions of Americans—and they are sworn to secrecy about their complicity. As a result, the very media organizations that, pursuant to the First Amendment, are supposed to keep American citizens informed about government abridgments of their rights, at the same time are legally compelled to cooperate with government in violating those same rights. In fact, under the FISA Amendments Act of 2008, such media companies are immune to legal liability for their cooperation with government, and cannot be sued for violating their customers' civil liberties. As a result, the American people are not being told the truth about the system of mass, warrantless surveillance that usurps their constitutional rights.

Another instance of corporate media deception concerns coverage of changes to the telephone metadata collection program, which had been operational since at least 2006. In January 2015, the Obama administration amended the provisions of Section 215 of the Patriot Act by passing the "USA Freedom Act." Corporate media, including the *Washington Post*, claimed that this Act "bans the bulk collection of data of Americans' telephone records and Internet metadata."[43] The USA Freedom Act gave the appearance that the Obama administration was concerned with protecting the privacy of US persons. In fact, the Act did not eliminate bulk collection; rather, it placed some limitations on it by circumscribing the parameters of the selection terms the NSA could use in searching telecommunication company databases. According to the USA Freedom Act, a "'specific selection term' (I) is a term that specifically identifies a person, account, address, or personal device, *or any other specific identifier*; and (II) is used to limit, to the greatest extent *reasonably practicable*, the scope of tangible things sought consistent with the purpose for seeking the tangible things."[emphases added][44] The term also cannot be "a broad geographic region, including the United States, a city, a county, a State, a zip code, or an area code, when not used as part of a specific identifier."[45] But notice the wording I have italicized. The selector does not have to identify a specific person, account, address, or personal device, and the purported purpose of the investigation could dictate what is "reasonably practicable." Thus, for example, it would still be possible to target many Middle Eastern males by searching a series of common Middle Eastern names such as "Muhammad," "Abdul," "Abdullah," "Ahmad," "Ali" . . . Further, the telephone system is now digitized and therefore runs through fiber-optic cables, as do email messages. Because upstream programs intercept electronic communications while they are on route, it is possible to collect the same telephone metadata through a different channel of the mass surveillance system, and specifically one not subject to the legal restrictions of the USA Freedom Act, such as MUSCULAR. In any event, corporate media has succeeded in propagating the myth that the NSA no longer engages in bulk collection of telephone and Internet metadata.

## IF CORPORATE MEDIA IS COMPLICIT, WHAT'S THE SOLUTION?

*Independent* media outlets need to do their best to inform the public about the nature of this system of mass information control and its potential to eviscerate the very values that define humanity: freedom and dignity. Newspapers such as the *New York Times* and *Washington Post* are not as clearly tied to the legal classification of "electronic communication service providers," which may explain why they have done a better job than network news organizations in covering the NSA's mass surveillance program. Unfortunately, these companies are still liable to government "incentives" (tax breaks, FCC media ownership deregulation, government contracts, and other manner of quid pro quo), and, therefore, cannot be counted upon to keep the government honest.

The American public needs to be educated about the dangers and shortcomings of the NSA's bulk electronic surveillance program. Here are just some of the things independent media (and corporate mainstreamers like the *Washington Post* and *New York Times*) need to underscore about the NSA's mass spy network:

1. It is inherently flawed in its capacity to detect and intercept terrorist plots.
2. It produces millions of false positives.
3. Telephone metadata collection is not harmless and can be used to link US citizens' phone numbers to targets of terrorist investigations by a series of "hops," even when these citizens have no real relationships with the targets.[46]
4. By contrast, human intelligence produces the most actionable intelligence.
5. It requires "strong selectors" (particular names, email addresses, telephone numbers, etc.) in order to be useful, but standard wiretaps attained through court warrants can be just as expedient.
6. Presently, upstream programs such as MUSCULAR completely lack judicial oversight.
7. Wholly domestic electronic communications (emails, phone

calls, etc.) have also been illegally collected by the NSA, contrary to current FISA law, and the FISC has given the NSA a free pass to make such illegal collections.

8. NSA analysts have a subjectively applied standard of 51 percent assurance that the targets of PRISM collections are not US persons, which yields a significant probability that many targets are, indeed, US persons. (Theoretically, no more than 49 percent, but, in practice, there are no objective standards to safeguard against highly arbitrary selections).

9. Without judicial oversight, the NSA uses the system for unsanctioned purposes, to eavesdrop on non-terrorists including foreign heads of state, confidential lawyer-client communications, journalists,[47] and industry.

10. The system presently has no privacy safeguards to prevent government overreach.

11. The next generation of surveillance technology presently being developed by DARPA will have the capacity to intercept the target's thoughts themselves, with the potential to change or control those thoughts.

12. Transparency about the above facts is essential if there is to be public pressure leading to constructive change.

Evidence suggests that the American public is prepared to exercise such pressure if told the truth about the dangers, abuses, and inefficacy of the mass, warrantless surveillance network. According to a 2014 Pew Research Poll, 74 percent of Americans deny that they should have to relinquish their privacy and freedom in order to be safe from terrorism, while only 23 percent agree that Americans need to relinquish their privacy and freedom in order to be safe from terrorism. Fifty-four percent of Americans disapprove of the government's collection of telephone and Internet data to thwart terrorist plots, while a substantial minority of 42 percent approve of the program.[48] So, given that 74 percent of Americans do not think they need to give up their freedom and privacy, why is there not a similar overwhelming majority who are against the collection of telephone and Internet data to thwart terrorism plots? The answer appears to be that Americans are not yet adequately informed about the details of the aforementioned modes of collection. But the devil is clearly in the details. When and if public perception is informed by unequivocal evidence about the negative aspects of the surveillance system, as presented here, there will predictably be a change in the tenor of the public outcry. Such transparency will not fall on deaf ears if the media does its job!

## WHAT SORT OF CHANGES ARE NECESSARY?

The absence of privacy safeguards to prevent government overreach is glaring. Inasmuch as the NSA is presently using content filters to sift through an immense amount of private information, most of which has nothing to do with national intelligence, it is curious that the NSA has not installed further filters to avoid collecting private information that is none of its business. For instance, why is the identifying information of US persons not blocked? The potential to add privacy protection was proposed in 2002, by John Poindexter, one of the masterminds of the "Total Information Awareness" project, who suggested that a "privacy appliance" could conceal protected information such as names and addresses, while permitting the acquisition of other information pertinent to terrorist investigations. If the collected information revealed evidence of a possible terrorist plot that warranted access to the concealed information, then the NSA could get a FISA warrant to unblock this information. Unfortunately, research conducted by DARPA at Xerox's Palo Alto Research Center to develop such privacy protection technology was defunded and discontinued in 2003.[49] Sadly, this attests to the low priority the Defense Department has historically placed on protecting the privacy of US persons. Such blatant disregard for building privacy protections into mass surveillance technologies will, predictably, have even bleaker implications for the prospects of preserving human freedom and dignity in the near future.

## REMOTE CONTROL NO LONGER A REMOTE POSSIBILITY

In 2009, researchers at the University of California, Berkeley, funded by DARPA, attached a receiver to a giant flower beetle via six electrodes connected to its optic lobe and flight muscles. Transmitting electrical signals wirelessly by a laptop computer, the researchers were able to control the beetle's flight patterns, including taking off and landing, while interfacing with its natural ability to navigate in flight. The result was a cyborg beetle under direct control of its human operator.[50] The official goal of this research is to eventually develop the technology for search-and-rescue applications as well as surveillance purposes.[51]

Focus on the goal of surveillance. The beetle itself could surely be equipped with a camera to spy on specific targets. But another, more sweeping sense of "surveillance" is also possible. Instead of wirelessly controlling beetles, what if the Pentagon was able to control human beings, remotely, without their informed consent? Of course, this would require sending signals to the brains of human subjects, but remember, as discussed here, DARPA is already working on that component. As Intel predicts, we are on the threshold of being able to receive data downloads from the Internet via brain-computer interfaces. Indeed, there has already been progress in creating removable skullcaps capable of transmitting human brain signals to control flying objects.[52] The next step is to reverse the direction of the signal to remotely control the behavior of human subjects.

This is the next logical step of a government with the insatiable appetite to see and know all. Instead of inferring the actions of targets by acquiring their personal information, why not just cut to the chase and control those actions directly, albeit remotely, surreptitiously, and without the target's informed consent?

So is it really the case that mass, warrantless surveillance ("Total Information Awareness") is in the best interest of our nation, or the world? Only if one believes that placing human freedom and dignity in jeopardy, in the name of preserving these same values, makes sense.

---

ELLIOT D. COHEN is a fellow at the Secular Policy Institute in Washington, D.C., and an ethicist and philosophical consultant. His many published works include four books on media ethics, and two on mass surveillance, including his latest, *Technology of Oppression: Preserving Freedom and Dignity in an Age of Mass, Warrantless Surveillance*. Editor in chief of the *International Journal of Applied Philosophy*, he also writes a popular blog for *Psychology Today* called "What Would Aristotle Do?"

# Notes

1   "Majority Views NSA Phone Tracking as Acceptable Anti-Terror Tactic," Pew Research Center, June 10, 2013, http://www.people-press.org/2013/06/10/majority-views-nsa-phone-tracking-as-acceptable-anti-terror-tactic/.

2   "Views of Privacy, NSA Surveillance," in "Beyond Red vs. Blue: The Political Typology," Pew Research Center, June 26, 2014, http://www.people-press.org/2014/06/26/section-6-foreign-affairs-terrorism-and-privacy/ - views-of-privacy-nsa-surveillance.

3   See, e.g., Trevor Paglen, "Listening to the Moons," in *Astro Noise: A Survival Guide for Living Under Total Surveillance*, ed. Laura Poitras (New Haven and London: Yale University Press, 2016), 104–117.

4   "Spy Network Reading Personal E-mails," *Telegraph*, May 30, 2001, http://www.telegraph.co.uk/news/worldnews/1332199/Spy-network-reading-personal-emails.html.

5   "Echelon: Online Surveillance", WhatReallyHappened.com, no date,   http://whatreallyhappened.com/RANCHO/POLITICS/ECHELON/echelon.html. This WhatReallyHappened webpage includes a reprint of the *Telegraph's* December 16, 1997, "Spies Like Us" article.

6   Elliot D. Cohen, *Mass Surveillance and State Control: The Total Information Awareness Project* (London: Palgrave Macmillan, 2011), 20–21.

7   Elliot D. Cohen, *Technology of Oppression: Preserving Freedom and Dignity in an Age of Mass, Warrantless Surveillance* (London: Palgrave Macmillan, 2014), 14–17.

8   Mark Klein, "Wiretap Whistleblower's Account," *Wired*, April 7, 2006, http://www.wired.com/science/discoveries/news/2006/04/70621.

9   Cohen, *Technology of Oppression*, 21, 115.

10   "NSA Slides Explain the PRISM Data-Collection Program," *Washington Post*, June 6, 2013, http://www.washingtonpost.com/wp-srv/special/politics/prism-collection-documents/.

11   Giuseppe Macri, "Federal Court Dismisses ACLU, Wikipedia Case against NSA's 'Upstream' Surveillance," Inside Sources, October 23, 2015, http://www.insidesources.com/federal-court-dismisses-aclu-wikipedia-case-against-nsas-upstream-surveillance/.

12   "Edward Snowden Speaks in Half-Hour Televised Interview," Common Dreams, January 27, 2014, http://www.commondreams.org/news/2014/01/27/edward-snowden-speaks-half-hour-televised-interview.

13   James Glanz and Andrew W. Lehren, "N.S.A. Spied on Allies, Aid Groups and Businesses," *New York Times*, December 20, 2013, http://www.nytimes.com/2013/12/21/world/nsa-dragnet-included-allies-aid-groups-and-business-elite.html?_r=0; see also Anthony Boadle, "U.S. Spied on Presidents of Brazil, Mexico - Report," Reuters, September 2, 2013, http://in.reuters.com/article/2013/09/02/usa-security-brazil-mexico-surveillance-idINDEE98I08U20130902; and Jonathan Watts, "NSA accused of spying on Brazilian oil company Petrobras," *Guardian*, September 9, 2013, https://www.theguardian.com/world/2013/sep/09/nsa-spying-brazil-oil-petrobras.

14   United States Foreign Intelligence Surveillance Court, "Memorandum Opinion," April 22, 2011, http://nsarchive.gwu.edu/NSAEBB/NSAEBB436/docs/EBB-035.pdf, quotation at 41.

15   "One Month, Hundreds of Millions of Records Collected," *Washington Post*, November 4, 2013, http://apps.washingtonpost.com/g/page/world/one-month-hundreds-of-millions-of-records-collected/554/.

16   "How the NSA's MUSCULAR Program Collects Too Much Data from Yahoo and Google," *Washington Post*, October 30, 2013, http://apps.washingtonpost.com/g/page/world/how-the-nsas-muscular-program-collects-too-much-data-from-yahoo-and-google/543/#document/p2/a129323;   see also Dominic Rushe, Spencer Ackerman, and James Ball, "Reports That NSA Taps into Google and Yahoo Data Hubs Infuriates Tech Giants," *Guardian*, October 31, 2013, https://www.theguardian.com/technology/2013/oct/30/google-reports-nsa-secretly-intercepts-data-links.

17   Deborah C. England, "What Is the Patriot Act and How Can It Affect a Criminal Case?" Nolo: Law for All, no date, http://www.nolo.com/legal-encyclopedia/what-the-patriot-act-how-can-affect-criminal-case.html.

18  FISA Amendments Act of 2008, Sec. 702, (g)(2)(A)(v), https://www.gpo.gov/fdsys/pkg/BILLS-110hr6304enr/pdf/BILLS-110hr6304enr.pdf.

19  John Stuart Mill, *On Liberty*, http://www.gutenberg.org/files/34901/34901-h/34901-h.htm, quote at 105.

20  See, for example, "Fear of Government Spying Is 'Chilling' Writers' Freedom of Expression," in *Censored 2016: Media Freedom on the Line*, eds. Mickey Huff and Andy Lee Roth (New York: Seven Stories Press, 2015), 57–8.

21  "DARPA Brain Machine-Interface," no date, http://dart.stanford.edu:8080/sparrow_2.0/pages/teams/DARPABrainMachineInterface.html

22  Amanda Onion, "The No-Doze Soldier: Military Seeking Radical Ways of Stumping Need for Sleep," ABC News, December 18, 2003, as cited at http://www.sleepnet.com/tech7/messages/625.html.

23  Alan Rudolf, "Brain Machine Interfaces," Defense Sciences Office, DARPA website, March 6, 2003, http://web.archive.org/web/20030306155324/http://www.arpa.mil/dso/thrust/biosci/brainmi.htm.

24  Antonio Regalato, "Military Funds Brain-Computer Interfaces to Control Feelings," *MIT Technology Review*, May 29, 2014, https://www.technologyreview.com/s/527561/military-funds-brain-computer-interfaces-to-control-feelings/.

25  Sharon Gaudin, "Intel: Chips in Brains Will Control Computers by 2020," Computer World, November 19, 2009, http://www.computerworld.com/article/2521888/app-development/intel--chips-in-brains-will-control-computers-by-2020.html.

26  Jessica Hall, "DARPA Devotes $60M to Making an Implantable, Wideband Brain-Computer Interface," Extreme Tech, January 27, 2016, http://www.extremetech.com/extreme/221994-darpa-devotes-60m-to-making-an-implantable-wideband-brain-computer-interface.

27  Peter Bergen, David Sterman, Emily Schneider, and Baily Cahall, "Do NSA's Bulk Surveillance Programs Stop Terrorists?" New America Foundation, January 2014, https://static.newamerica.org/attachments/1311-do-nsas-bulk-surveillance-programs-stop-terrorists/IS_NSA_surveillance.pdf.

28  Cohen, *Technology of Oppression*, 17–18, 20–22.

29  Bergen, et al., "Do NSA's Bulk Surveillance Programs Stop Terrorists?," 1.

30  Here I have applied Bayes' Theorem to calculate false positives. See Sam Savage and Howard Wainer, "Until Proven Guilty: False Positives and the War on Terror: Bayesian Analysis," *Chance*, vol. 21 (March 2008), 55–58, http://www-stat.wharton.upenn.edu/~hwainer/Readings/Wainer%20Savage.pdf; see also Cohen, *Technology of Oppression*, 50–51.

31  Network Advertising Initiative, "Study Finds Behaviorally-Targeted Ads More Than Twice as Valuable, Twice as Effective as Non-Targeted Online Ads," Network Advertising, March 24, 2010, https://www.networkadvertising.org/pdfs/NAI_Beales_Release.pdf.

32  Cohen, *Technology of Oppression*, 49.

33  Bergen, et al., "Do NSA's Bulk Surveillance Programs Stop Terrorists?," 2.

34  Cohen, *Technology of Oppression*, 50–53.

35  Al Baker and William K. Rashbaum, "Police Find Car Bomb in Times Square," *New York Times*, May 1, 2010, http://www.nytimes.com/2010/05/02/nyregion/02timessquare.html?pagewanted=all&_r=0.

36  "Flight 253 Hero Recounts Thwarting Christmas Bombing Attempt," CNN, December 30, 2009, http://www.cnn.com/2009/US/12/30/terror.passenger.account/.

37  "Shoe Bomber: Tale of Another Failed Terrorist Attack," CNN, December 25, 2009, http://www.cnn.com/2009/CRIME/12/25/richard.reid.shoe.bomber/.

38  For critical analysis of corporate news media's Snowden coverage, see *Censored 2015: Inspiring We the People*, eds. Andy Lee Roth and Mickey Huff (New York: Seven Stories Press, 2014), 103–111, 148–150.

39  Alexandra Petri, "Traitor or Patriot? What a Silly Question, after 'Inside Snowden'," *Washington Post*, May 29, 2014, https://www.washingtonpost.com/blogs/compost/wp/2014/05/29/traitor-or-patriot-what-a-silly-question-after-inside-snowden/.

40  But see Klein, "Wiretap Whistleblower's Account."

41  FISA Amendments Act of 2008, h(1)(A), https://www.gpo.gov/fdsys/pkg/BILLS-110hr6304enr/pdf/BILLS-110hr6304enr.pdf.

42  Ibid., Sec. 702 (a)4.

43  "USA Freedom Act: What's In, What's Out," *Washington Post*, June 2, 2015, https://www.washingtonpost.com/graphics/politics/usa-freedom-act/.

44  The USA Freedom Act of 2015, (k)(4)(A), https://www.congress.gov/114/bills/hr2048/BILLS-114hr2048enr.pdf.

45  Ibid.

46  Geoffrey R. Stone, "The NSA's Telephone Metadata Program: Part 1," *Huffington Post*, December 24, 2013, http://www.huffingtonpost.com/geoffrey-r-stone/nsa-meta-data_b_4499934.html; see also, "USA Freedom Act: What's In, What's Out."

47  Warren Mass, "Almost Two-thirds of Journalists Think Government Spies on Them," *New American*, February 6, 2015, http://www.thenewamerican.com/usnews/politics/item/20064-almost-two-thirds-of-journalists-think-government-spies-on-them.

48  Pew Research Center, "View of Privacy, NSA Surveillance."

49  Cohen, *Mass Surveillance and State Control*, 186–87.

50  Emily Singer, "The Army's Remote-Controlled Beetle," *MIT Technology Review*, January 29, 2009, https://www.technologyreview.com/s/411814/the-armys-remote-controlled-beetle/.

51  Noah Shachtman, "Pentagon's Cyborg Beetle Spies Take Off," *Wired*, January 28, 2009, http://www.wired.com/2009/01/pentagons-cybor/.

52  David Szondy, "Mind-Controlled Quadcopter Flies Using Imaginary Fists," Gizmag, June 8, 2013, http://www.gizmag.com/university-minnesota-mind-control-uav/27798/.

# CHAPTER 9

# Ike's Dystopian Dream, and How It Came True

Shahid Buttar

This January marked the sixty-fifth anniversary of a speech by the last victorious military commander to occupy the White House, President Dwight D. "Ike" Eisenhower.[1] His visionary warning holds crucial implications for the US today, and has been overlooked in debates across a range of policy areas, from mass surveillance to police accountability.

Ike was elected to the White House after playing a key role in World War II as supreme commander of the Allied forces in Europe. In his farewell address, he warned the American people of a threat that he had helped create. Even before winning office, then-General Eisenhower coordinated a world-historical industrial mobilization that enabled the US to liberate Europe and defend democracy from the global threat of fascism. But as he retired, Ike expressed concerns about its future consequences.

## FORGOTTEN: A PRESIDENT'S PRESCIENT WARNING

In his departing speech to the American people before leaving the White House,[2] Eisenhower described the necessity of creating a defense industry intertwined with secret government agencies, while predicting—in no uncertain terms—that they would together come to present a threat to democracy in America. President Eisenhower said,

> [W]e have been compelled to create a permanent armaments industry of vast proportions. . . .

This conjunction of an immense military establishment and a large arms industry is new in the American experience. The total influence—economic, political, even spiritual—is felt in every city, every State house, every office of the Federal government. . . . Our toil, resources, and livelihood are all involved; so is the very structure of our society.

In the councils of government, we must guard against the acquisition of unwarranted influence, whether sought or unsought, by the military-industrial complex. *The potential for the disastrous rise of misplaced power exists and will persist.*

*We must never let the weight of this combination endanger our liberties or democratic processes. We should take nothing for granted.* Only an alert and knowledgeable citizenry can compel the proper meshing of the huge industrial and military machinery of defense with our peaceful methods and goals, so that security and liberty may prosper together.[3] (emphasis added)

With the benefit of sixty-five years of hindsight, Ike appears more prescient than Nostradamus. The dangers he predicted have unfortunately grown all too visible today, reflected in several controversies—but rarely discussed in the terms he gave us to connect those issues and expose the threat that they, together, present.

## NSA: BIG BROTHER IS (STILL) WATCHING YOU

Ike's warnings proved prescient in several arenas. Few issues better embody the threat to democracy posed by the military-industrial complex than domestic surveillance.

Despite a continuing international outcry prompted by revelations of facts long kept secret from the public, mass NSA surveillance continues around the world and continues to collect the communications of law-abiding Americans.[4]

Members of Congress from across the political spectrum have expressed outrage at the NSA dragnet capturing telephone and Internet communications.[5] Part of their concern stems from their exclusion from the process: mass electronic surveillance programs were created in secret under the George W. Bush administration without a public mandate.[6]

At the same time that Congress was prevented by executive secrecy from doing its job of imposing checks and balances, courts largely refused to examine mass domestic surveillance on its merits, leaving undefended the First and Fourth Amendment interests it offends.[7]

US history is replete with examples of government agencies and investigators misusing their powers to undermine the right to peacefully promote political perspectives.[8] The advancing technology available to investigators has enabled an aspiration towards state omniscience, which in the wrong hands could threaten values as fundamental as freedom of thought.

Despite these concerns, and continuing controversies in all three branches of the federal government, the NSA's mass surveillance dragnet continues to operate, largely unfettered, in secret.

Advocates continue to challenge unconstitutional domestic spying in the courts.[9] Even over a decade since organizations such as the Electronic Frontier Foundation and the American Civil Liberties Union filed their first challenges, courts have yet to rule on the merits of their concerns.[10]

On the one hand, several court decisions have vindicated widespread concerns about the emergence of "almost Orwellian" systems of domestic spying.[11] Other rulings, however, like the Supreme Court's decision in *Clapper vs. Amnesty International USA* in 2013, have unfortunately allowed those programs to continue.[12]

*Clapper* essentially required plaintiffs to provide evidence of government activity that only government agencies could have, allowing judges to bury their heads in the sand rather than examine allegations that may be difficult to prove. Rulings with similar effects have cited the absurd state secrets privilege, holding that, despite a long history of prolific military and executive lies to evade accountability for everything from mass murders to illegitimate and unprovoked wars (including the very same case establishing the doctrine), US national security requires judges to ignore some topics that are openly discussed in the international press.[13]

The Court thus invites agencies to evade judicial review by maintaining secrets, while also undermining judicial independence by forcing judges to accept official secrecy. From this perspective, *Clapper* undermines the role of the courts envisioned by the founders of our republic in the Federalist Papers No. 78.[14]

Mass surveillance has also forced attention from the executive branch. President Obama promised surveillance reform when running for the White House, writing a campaign pledge to support "any steps needed to preserve civil liberties and to prevent executive branch abuse in the future."[15] He commissioned a review group to issue recommendations, but the administration ultimately declined to adopt most of them, falling short of the president's 2008 campaign pledge.

Meanwhile, Congress last year imposed the first restrictions in two generations on US intelligence agencies, before hastily adopting new surveillance measures at the end of 2015.[16] Even more bizarrely, it enacted both sets of laws before ever conducting an independent investigation to uncover facts as obviously relevant as, for instance, how many Americans have been monitored by the NSA, or how many times the system has been abused by people using the government's powerful tools for their disturbing personal purposes.[17]

## A PATTERN AND PRACTICE: ABUSING CONSTITUTIONAL RIGHTS IN SECRET

On the few occasions that it has examined the intelligence agencies, Congress has discovered recurring violations of constitutional rights, as well as limits on the agencies' powers. Historically, the most significant investigations were in the 1970s, when ad hoc committees convened in the Senate under Senator Frank Church (D-Idaho) and in the House under Representative Otis Pike (D-New York) revealed what the US Senate in 1976 described as "a sophisticated vigilante operation aimed squarely at preventing the exercise of First Amendment rights of speech and association. . . ."[18]

The most prolific target of unconstitutional surveillance during this era was a figure whose memory we now celebrate with a national holiday, the Rev. Dr. Martin Luther King, Jr. His example, involving not only surveillance, but also a character assassination campaign and a coordinated attempt to drive him to suicide, should serve as a stark reminder to anyone today who thinks that because they have nothing to hide, they have nothing to fear.[19]

Indeed, those who have had the most to fear from our government in the past are today celebrated as some of our greatest heroes. Since Dr. King's era, other examples abound of peaceful activists being targeted by intelligence agencies to suppress their voices.[20]

When vulnerable community members are intimidated into silence by the knowledge that their voices and concerns will be publicized or retained, it is not merely they who suffer.[21] The theory of democracy animating the First Amendment presupposes the importance and primacy of public debate, not only as an exercise of a speaker's rights but also to satisfy the rights of listeners to hear from all voices, grow informed by their perspectives, and make better reasoned judgments as participants in the political process.[22]

In 2002 a federal judge ordered the FBI to pay a $4 million judgment to an environmental activist in the Bay Area, Judy Bari, who was severely injured in 1990 by a car bomb that the Bureau (according to the court) falsely accused her of planting before arresting her.[23]

Would US energy policy be any different today had the FBI not criminalized the radical environmental community in the 1990s, driving the supposed "eco-terrorists" of the Earth Liberation Front and Animal Liberation Front into international exile and federal prisons, rather than congressional hearings and political campaigns?[24]

Judy Bari's case, the FBI's plot to suppress the Occupy movement twenty years later, and the Edward Snowden revelations two years after that should each—independently, let alone all together—have sparked the same outrage which, after Watergate, drove the Church and Pike Committees to investigate and reveal the FBI's Counterintelligence Program (COINTELPRO).[25] They still could, if Congress finally does its job and investigates the issues that Snowden and other whistleblowers have raised.[26]

A pattern visible across these historical instances involves what University of Chicago law professor Geoffrey Stone describes as "a national perception of peril and a concerted campaign by government to promote a sense of national hysteria by exaggeration, manipulation, and distortion."[27] While executive secrecy enables violations of powers and rights, in the past we have been fortunate to witness congressional and judicial oversight correct prior abuses.[28] In 2016, a decade and a half since the beginning of the contemporary mass surveillance regime, that accounting still has yet to happen.

While federal agencies like the NSA, CIA, and FBI may be the most prolific bodies monitoring Americans, thousands of local and state law enforcement agencies around the country also practice unconstitutional surveillance of law-abiding residents.[29]

## NEW MARKETS FOR WEAPONS:
## MILITARIZING LOCAL POLICE

The emergence of electronic surveillance not only by federal authorities but also by their local counterparts starkly reflects President Eisenhower's warnings. Surveillance programs, equipment, and training for local and state police serve both as a cause and effect of their militarization.

The Pentagon's 1033 program provides surplus military equipment to local police and sheriffs departments, as well as state law enforcement agencies and the public safety departments of schools and universities.[30] Since the 1033 program began in 1990, it has distributed military gear ranging from tactical vehicles like armored personnel carriers to weapons like assault rifles, to over 13,000 agencies across the US. Over $5 billion worth of military equipment has been transferred to police departments since 2000.[31]

In Utah alone, police departments received over 1,200 military-grade rifles over two years, as well as other weapons like grenade launchers and .45-caliber pistols distributed to agencies across the state.[32] Other gear distributed through the 1033 program ranges from blankets and cars to night vision tools, bomb disposal robots, armored vehicles, body armor, machine guns—and surveillance tools.[33]

For example, International Mobile Subscriber Identity (IMSI) catchers—often known by a trade name, Stingray—mimic cell phone towers in order to monitor voice and data traffic over cell phone networks.[34] In the hands of sheriffs departments and local police, the devices have proliferated across the country.[35]

Domestic surveillance by federal agencies tends to take the form of monitoring communications, or using informants to monitor organizations from within, but local police monitoring takes a variety of forms that includes communications surveillance and human intelligence, but—increasingly enabled by technology—also goes well beyond them.

For instance, police use video surveillance of public spaces enabled by closed circuit cameras mounted in fixed locations, or on aerial drones.[36] Proliferating police body cameras, and agreements allowing police to gain access to private video feeds, present other sources of increasingly pervasive video surveillance not by federal agencies, but by local police.[37]

Beyond allowing authorities to capture video surveillance imagery in public, advanced technology also enables increasingly sophisticated facial recognition, which can automate the process of connecting individuals to specific locations and times.[38]

Real-time and historical location tracking is further enabled by automatic license plate readers (ALPRs), which scan three million records in Los Angeles County alone every week.[39] Corporate ALPR systems have also exposed troves of data to foreign intelligence agencies, malicious hackers, and others who have taken advantage of often weak security to access video feeds without permission.[40]

ALPR systems are often procured and deployed through offensive agreements. Some arrangements, for instance, enable public agencies access to surveillance equipment for free, in exchange for giving police data to private contractors for their commercial purposes, and adding surcharges on court fees payable to the contractors by individuals identified by police.[41] This process essentially turns police into debt collectors.

Local police also use other forms of advanced surveillance. For instance, the ShotSpotter system aims to detect gunshots within a city with microphones so sensitive they are capable of overhearing conversations. Yet in some tests, as many as 90 percent of the warnings delivered by ShotSpotter devices have proven to be false, suggesting that their utility is limited, whatever their impact on rights and communities.[42]

The Pentagon is not the only source of federal resources fueling local police militarization. Local agencies also gain access to military training and tactics through programs like the Urban Areas Security

Initiative (UASI) administered by the Department of Homeland Security.[43] Coordinated by for-profit contractors, UASI is a cross between a marketplace and a testing site, encouraging police departments to bring the military-industrial complex to a town near you.[44]

UASI grants have helped support the proliferation of Special Weapons and Tactics (SWAT) divisions, which epitomize the militarization of police departments. In addition to employing military tactics, SWAT teams also reflect the tendency towards inexplicable violence and so-called "mission creep,"[45] as explained by law professor Jonathan Turley:

> 80 percent of SWAT raids were to serve a search warrant. That is far different from the original purpose of rescuing hostages and capturing armed escaped felons. . . . Conversely, just 7 percent of SWAT raids were "for hostage, barricade, or active shooter scenarios"—the famed purpose of the SWAT unit.[46]

Despite public controversy, UASI funds have helped police departments buy sophisticated surveillance equipment like Stingrays and later versions of IMSI-catchers.[47] UASI grants have also been used to purchase less lethal munitions such as Tasers, which have been abused by police departments in multiple cities, prompting local rules in some of them to restrain their use and curtail recurring deaths.[48]

Similarly, biometric data collection, retention, and dissemination has grown ubiquitous largely through the coordination of local police under an FBI program called the Next Generation Initiative (NGI).[49] While initially presented to the public as the Secure Communities program, billed as a way to streamline the deportation of undocumented migrants who had previously violated the law, NGI involved a more ambitious agenda from the beginning, entailing the creation of a federal biometric database enabling new forms of monitoring and surveillance.[50]

The connection between police surveillance, on the one hand, and the militarization it enables and advances, on the other, may escape the attention of an observer unaware of Eisenhower's parting address. But it emerges in stark relief when informed by Ike's warning that "in every city . . . the very structure of our society" would be influenced by corporate profit motives fueling military operations essentially seeking new targets to justify themselves.[51]

## TRANSPARENCY: FUNDAMENTAL DEMOCRATIC VALUES AT STAKE

Not only are local police using military-grade surveillance equipment to monitor civilian populations, but local oversight of those tools has been essentially absent. It should come as no surprise that local policing and surveillance have been pervaded by the same accountability problems that have plagued federal programs supposedly justified by "national security" concerns.

In Baltimore, for instance, the use of Stingrays became so routine that police deployed the devices thousands of times before policymakers learned and started investigating.[52] Across the country, the North Dakota State Highway Patrol—a single agency among hundreds that receive military equipment under the 1033 program, and one of dozens that have been suspended from it—somehow lost track of over 150 weapons.[53]

The New York Police Department (NYPD) was caught infiltrating college campuses to monitor constitutionally-protected political and religious beliefs.[54] Targets included even schools far beyond New York that, upon learning what happened under the cover of secrecy, expressed outrage at the NYPD's violations.[55]

Concerns about the secret and unaccountable use of Stingray devices have prompted lawsuits in multiple cities including San Diego, policy changes by the Justice Department requiring federal agents to use Stingrays only after receiving a judicial warrant, and legislation in several states, from California to Virginia, forcing greater transparency into the procurement and deployment of IMSI catchers.[56]

While they have grown increasingly controversial in recent years, Stingrays have been used since at least 2007, long preceding revelations of their use and replacement by even more powerful—and constitutionally problematic—devices nearly a decade later.[57] In some communities, that controversy has in turn prompted pointed policy debates, pitting residents and community advocates against police departments and police unions.[58]

Efforts at the state and local level to require greater transparency into the use of surveillance equipment by local and state law enforcement authorities represent some of the most encouraging signs in the movement to reclaim constitutional rights. For instance, the state of California adopted two laws in 2015 that require at least minimal transparency governing two particular kinds of surveillance equipment, while jurisdictions within the state are grappling with proposed measures that would require greater transparency not only for specific surveillance systems, but also any technology method used to monitor residents without their consent.[59]

Distributing military equipment, tactics, and training to domestic local law enforcement officers in itself represents the fulfillment of Eisenhower's vision of a military-industrial complex threatening democratic processes and constitutional rights. The metastasis of domestic surveillance appears even more problematic when considered in historical context.

## A VICIOUS CYCLE: IMPUNITY FOR RECURRING CIA HUMAN RIGHTS ABUSES

In the US, the militarization of domestic policing began in the 1980s, responding to paramilitary narco-trafficking syndicates killing police officers and Drug Enforcement Administration (DEA) agents in Miami and Los Angeles.[60] Official government sources confirmed—but not until the late 1990s—that the organized crime sector, then importing cocaine into US port cities, was largely armed, trained, and equipped by the CIA.[61]

The history of the CIA and its involvement in running drugs and weapons to fuel the Agency's own rogue foreign policy may seem surprising, but it is well established and thoroughly documented: a CIA inspector general's report in 1998 substantially admitted the findings of renowned journalist Gary Webb, who revealed the agency's role in the crack cocaine epidemic at the cost of his own career, and helped set in motion the revelation of the Reagan administration's illegal Iran-Contra affair.[62] After being let go from the San Jose-based *Mercury*

*News* as a result of his reports, which the paper originally supported, Webb documented the entire story in his 1998 book, *Dark Alliance: The CIA, the Contras, and the Crack Cocaine Explosion.* Despite being vindicated in his reporting, Webb's career as a journalist was never resuscitated. Years later, police reported he died of a suicide, which entailed multiple self-inflicted gunshots to the head (an incident that some parties found mysterious).[63]

Beyond its pervasive secrecy, or its work in escalating violence, the impact of CIA international human rights abuses on destabilizing domestic communities has never been systematically explored.

The mere fact that the CIA pursues its own foreign policy should disturb any policymaker or military leader conscious of Eisenhower's legacy. The Agency's commercial interests enable its budget to stretch well beyond its $15 billion federal budget allocation, but there is little transparency to allow the public oversight or opportunity to influence it.[64]

More recently, the CIA has pioneered a new era of human rights abuses by deploying armed drones to conduct extrajudicial assassinations, even of American citizens never accused of committing violence or subjected to a criminal trial.[65] Efforts by the Obama administration to ground drone strikes in some set of principles ultimately merely exposed how arbitrary the process remains.[66]

As in Vietnam, executive officials presumptively classify dead bodies discovered after strikes as those of insurgents, categorically ignoring civilian deaths while downplaying the incalculable strategic costs of deploying unmanned weapons.[67] And what harm to human life could come from CIA drones falling into the hands of our nation's enemies is anyone's guess.[68]

Some of the CIA's most prolific human rights abuses have come in the context of arbitrary detention, international human rights abuses such as torture, and digital espionage operations targeting Congress in order to hide evidence of the Agency's criminal trail.[69]

## A CONTINUING COVER-UP: CIA AND MILITARY TORTURE MOCKING INTERNATIONAL LAW

Under President George W. Bush's administration, the CIA held detainees in secret sites scattered around the globe, hidden from both

Congress and the governments of the countries in which they were situated.[70] The military also continues to openly hold detainees on a US naval base in Cuba.

Interrogation techniques routinely conducted at those sites—such as waterboarding, sleep deprivation, forced "rehydration" using rectal enemas administered so brutally that observers have described the sessions as "rape," and even involuntary human experimentation—violated well-established international laws.[71]

These are not laws in which the US has been historically disinterested. Indeed, our nation—and particularly President Eisenhower—played a critical role in establishing the international human rights regime, by winning the Second World War at enormous cost and litigating the Nuremberg trials that followed its conclusion.[72]

CIA human rights violations committed through the Agency's detention program, however, were just the beginning.[73] Well before torture became politically controversial, Agency personnel took active efforts to obstruct justice by destroying evidence, including videotapes of interrogations confirming accusations of illegally brutal treatment.[74]

Secrecy continues under the Obama administration to prevent transparency into further evidence. Administration officials sought and received authorization from Congress in 2011 to suppress evidence of torture in US military custody.[75] According to the retired US Army major general who wrote a report on detainee treatment, the body of existing evidence that remains suppressed includes thousands of photos, as well as videos, depicting offenses including "torture, abuse, rape, and every indecency."[76]

Later attempts to suppress evidence of CIA crimes reached new heights. In 2014, after concluding an investigation that spanned several years and compiled thousands of pages of documents, the Senate Select Intelligence Committee wrote a scathing report on CIA torture.[77] Committee chair Dianne Feinstein (D-California) fought for years to make even a portion of the report public, and was ultimately forced to publicly decry on the Senate floor an erosion of the separation of powers rising to the level of what the press described as "a constitutional crisis."[78]

After the Senate Select Intelligence Committee demonstrated its independence, resisting pressure from the Obama administration to suppress the Senate's investigation into CIA torture, CIA personnel hacked into congressional computers to steal vital documents.[79] Agency personnel also spied on and even filed false charges against the committee's investigative staff.[80]

An internal CIA accountability board later excused the CIA hack as a "miscommunication," just a week after the inspector general who revealed the hack—contradicting the CIA director's false claims denying it had happened—declared plans to leave the Agency.[81] Less than two years later, his successors claimed to have "mistakenly" destroyed their office's only copy of the Senate's report.[82]

Even the portion of the Senate report released in 2014 is no longer officially available.[83] It was largely based on an internal CIA document memorializing a review by former CIA Director Leon Panetta that has never been released to the public, which former Sen. Mark Udall (D-Utah) felt compelled to focus on in his final speech on the Senate floor.[84]

## "DEMOCRATIC PROCESSES": MILITARIZATION UNDERMINING DEMOCRACY

The CIA's serial assaults on transparency make a mockery of democratic transparency, public oversight of covert operations, and international human rights principles.[85] They reflect—as clearly as police militarization or the recurrence of torture itself—the prescience of Ike's warnings that secrecy, national defense, and industry would combine to form a noxious mix inimical to democracy.

When an executive intelligence agency conducts offensive data exfiltration missions targeting the US Senate specifically in order to hide evidence of human rights abuses by their own agency, there is a grave problem. Perhaps the only thing more astounding than the CIA's audacity is the failure of the political establishment and mainstream media to recognize it in the terms that Eisenhower gave us sixty-five years ago.

In that context, President Obama's willingness to "look forward, not backward" appears like a stratagem to evade the political inconvenience of his administration's responsibility under international law to "promptly and impartially prosecute senior military and civilian officials responsible for authorizing . . . acts of torture."[86]

Torture under the Bush administration violated international law, as does the Obama administration's failure to pursue accountability.[87] The decision to not criminally prosecute any state officials responsible for torture ultimately represents what I have described elsewhere as "an illegal capitulation to illegitimate political interests carrying profound consequences for human rights and freedom both in the US and around the world."[88]

Through another lens, impunity for CIA and military torture—like the torture itself and the continuing lack of transparency into its scope and resounding effects—reflects the subversion of democratic processes by the military-industrial complex that Eisenhower felt compelled to create and grew to fear.

## "LIBERTIES": MILITARIZATION UNDERMINING WE THE PEOPLE

Looking forward, the military-industrial complex threatens constitutional rights, and the American people, even more directly at the local level. Police militarization that may seem offensive in the abstract appears even more constitutionally subversive when it is observed suppressing dissent.

As illustrated during the uprisings in Ferguson, Missouri, and Baltimore, Maryland, military weapons, training, and surveillance tools in the hands of police have been turned increasingly towards suppressing First Amendment rights guaranteed under the speech, association, assembly, and petition clauses.[89]

When the Occupy movement spread across dozens of US cities in Fall 2011, the FBI coordinated a campaign to violently suppress it.[90] The police departments of dozens of major cities participated, all of which used their intelligence and interagency powers justified on national security grounds to instead suppress constitutionally protected domestic dissent.[91]

Local police suppression of dissent continues unabated. A *Truth and Power* mini-documentary explores the use of IMSI-catchers specifically targeting the Black Lives Matter movement, which was simultaneously targeted by a range of other intelligence methods by multiple agencies.[92]

Militarized policing tactics extend beyond surveillance during periods of civil unrest. For example, the Chicago Police Department was caught housing incommunicado detainees in a domestic "black site," Homan Square, at which thousands were routinely beaten, denied access to counsel, and pressured into signing false confessions.[93]

Chicago police effectively denied the Fifth Amendment right against self-incrimination to residents merely suspected of a crime. In that respect, Homan Square resembles other detention centers run by the CIA, or the lawless and counterproductive US military detention facility at Guantánamo Bay in Cuba.[94]

The abuses at Homan Square reflect the domestic impacts of both police militarization and suppression of dissent. Not only were military and CIA violations replicated at the local level, but Homan Square was ironically used to detain and interrogate protesters taking action to challenge US militarism.[95]

Despite being illegal, torture by local police modeled on military practices is hardly unprecedented. In the very same city, a senior police commander was sentenced to prison for lying about a South Side torture ring that for decades sent innocent African American men to prison by the hundreds using torture techniques that were learned in Vietnam.[96]

When Eisenhower warned the American people of the threat presented by a military-industrial complex, he was not likely thinking that law-abiding Americans would be subjected to torture techniques learned by police officers when deployed to fight wars on foreign shores.

It is one thing to relentlessly abuse vulnerable communities' rights for decades, and even centuries.[97] It is another thing to arm and train local police with military weapons and tactics. To then deploy militarized police to suppress demonstrations by communities that have long been victimized compounds an ugly legacy of violence with continuing violations of constitutional rights guaranteed to all Americans.

The circularity—rogue CIA operations importing drugs and sparking a gang war, domestic police deploying military weapons and tactics in response, low-income communities enduring murders with impunity for decades, activists in those communities mobilizing to seek redress for their grievances, and then police responding to their mobilizations with the armed force originally justified by the crisis sparked by the CIA thirty years earlier—offers yet another disturbing reflection of Ike's warnings.[98]

## WHAT TO EXPECT: THE SCHEDULED EXPIRATION IN 2017 OF FISA, SECTION 702

Congress should not be in the business of approving government programs it does not understand. Yet in the surveillance arena, that has become the institution's habit.[99]

Responding to a perceived national security crisis, the Bush administration in secret created a surveillance apparatus in 2001 that remained secret from the American people for several years. The first revelations of the domestic dragnet in 2005 followed an internal struggle within the Bush administration so severe that it nearly led to a mass resignation of the Justice Department's senior leadership.[100]

Yet, three years later, intimidated by the agencies and fear-mongering, Congress changed the law to let the agencies loose from the statutory limits imposed after the Church and Pike Committee investigations thirty years before.[101]

When Congress amended the Foreign Intelligence Surveillance Act (FISA) in 2008, the public did not know how the NSA would use its new powers.[102] It took five years for a whistleblower to reveal how FISA powers have been contorted to pervasively spy on the Internet, using back door searches to effectively target Americans while remaining hidden from public legislative and judicial oversight.[103]

After Edward Snowden revealed the NSA dragnet in 2013, Congress set preliminary limits on domestic telephone surveillance in the USA Freedom Act, while leaving the Internet unprotected. But the key statute enabling Internet spying—FISA—is set to expire in 2017.[104]

As the statutory basis for the PRISM program and upstream collection, FISA must be the subject of further hearings to explore its full scope and impact on the Internet, the constitutional rights of Americans, and freedom of expression around the world.[105]

At a hearing in Spring 2016 in the Senate Select Judiciary Committee, senators explored some basic questions also posed by members of the House, to which no one has yet given an answer.[106] For instance, how many Americans have been subjected to Internet monitoring through programs authorized under FISA? The first senator to pose this question, Ron Wyden (D-Oregon), did so over three years ago and is still waiting for an accurate response.[107]

At a minimum, Congress should insist upon learning how many Americans have been monitored by the NSA. Government officials have had years to produce an answer to that question. But that's just one among many questions that should be answered before Congress can legitimately extend or reauthorize the expiring FISA provisions.

How many times—and in which particular cases—has NSA data been used to circumvent the evidentiary rules of the criminal justice system?[108] How many times has the FBI used NSA databases to find records about US persons?[109] How many times has the Internet dragnet enabled surveillance of peaceful groups and individuals pursuing constitutionally protected political goals, or the former lovers of NSA personnel or government contractors?[110]

We know that Internet spying has already imposed chilling effects on Americans.[111] How many have silenced themselves, and what harm has our democracy suffered as a result?

Congress should also insist on releasing all legal opinions and executive legal analyses about the Section 702 programs, as well as declassifying all relevant documents sent to Congress when FISA was passed and reauthorized in 2008 and 2012.[112]

If the capacity to generate answers does not currently exist, members of Congress should defend their own prerogatives—if not the rights of their constituents and Internet users around the world—by insisting on substantial reform enabling constitutional limits and meaningful congressional and judicial oversight of any programs used to monitor Internet use, traffic, communication, or data.

With the absence of such reform, the law should be allowed to expire as scheduled. Its expiration should force an end to numerous domestic surveillance activities, including PRISM and the upstream collection process.

It would be a mistake to think the process complete once congressional authorization has been allowed to expire. Given longstanding secret interpretations of the USA PATRIOT Act's authorities, or the secret creation of the mass surveillance program in the first instance, or the widespread violations that Congress discovered the last time it actively investigated domestic intelligence efforts, oversight committees should confirm that mass surveillance programs end after the expiration of their legal basis.[113]

We have a great deal to learn from President Eisenhower. Ike told us to "take nothing for granted," while warning the people of the United States not to let our guardians turn their sights on us.

We would do well to remember Ike's words, particularly as policymakers consider whether to reauthorize programs that realize his fears. Connecting seemingly disconnected surveillance and policing issues can help policymakers–from the local level to their counterparts in Congress–better see their decisions through the eyes of the former president and war hero who helped create the military-industrial complex and feared that it would come to threaten our Constitution and democracy in America.

---

SHAHID BUTTAR is a constitutional lawyer focused on the intersection of community organizing and policy reform as a lever to shift legal norms. He led the Bill of Rights Defense Committee from 2009 to 2015 and crafted the organization's platform for advancing transpartisan resistance to domestic surveillance and executive secrecy. Since graduating from Stanford Law School in 2003, he has worked on issues ranging from campaign finance reform and marriage equality for same-sex couples to foreign policy and police accountability. Shahid contributed to this book in his personal capacity. The opinions expressed in this article are his own and do not necessarily reflect the views of his employer, the Electronic Frontier Foundation.

*Special thanks to Brandy Miceli, Project Censored intern and a senior in Print and Online Journalism at San Francisco State University. Miceli is the managing editor for the Xpress Magazine, a student-run publication at the university, and president of the Project Censored chapter at SFSU. For this chapter, Miceli provided additional editing, citation assistance, and formatting.*

## Notes

1    Shahid Buttar, "Ike Had a Dream, and It Unfortunately Came True," Electronic Frontier Foundation, January 17, 2016, https://www.eff.org/deeplinks/2016/01/ike-had-dream-and-it-unfortunately-came-true.

2    Dwight D. Eisenhower, "Farewell Radio and Television Address to the American People," speech, Washington, DC, January 17, 1961, transcript, "Military-Industrial Complex Speech,"

*Public Papers of the Presidents of the United States, Dwight D. Eisenhower, 1960–1961* (Washington, DC: Government Printing Office, 1999), 1035–40, http://www.presidency.ucsb.edu/ws/index.php?pid=12086&st=&st1=.

3　"Eisenhower Warns Us of the Military Industrial Complex," YouTube video, posted by "The 9/11 Truth Movement," filmed January 17, 1961, posted August 4, 2006, https://www.youtube.com/watch?v=8yo6NSBBRtY.

4　The Snowden Files, *Guardian*, no date, http://www.theguardian.com/world/series/the-snowden-files; Shahid Buttar, "Dragnet NSA Spying Survives: 2015 in Review," Electronic Frontier Foundation, December 25, 2015, https://www.eff.org/deeplinks/2015/12/dragnet-nsa-spying-survives-2015-review.

5　Tim Cushing, "Rep. Rush Holt Bill to Repeal PATRIOT and FISA Amendments Acts Now Live, Ambitious," *Techdirt* blog, July 26, 2013, https://www.techdirt.com/articles/20130725/17500723952/rep-rush-holt-bill-to-repeal-patriot-fisa-amendments-acts-now-live-ambitious.shtml; Jessica Schulberg, "Rand Paul Ends Daylong NSA 'Filibuster,'" *Huffington Post*, May 20, 2015, http://www.huffingtonpost.com/2015/05/20/rand-paul-nsa-filibuster_n_7347722.html.

6　Dan Eggen and Paul Kane, "Gonzales Hospital Episode Detailed," *Washington Post*, May 16, 2007, http://www.washingtonpost.com/wp-dyn/content/article/2007/05/15/AR2007051500864.html.

7　Shahid Buttar, "Dragnet NSA Spying Survives: 2015 in Review," Electronic Frontier Foundation, December 25, 2015, https://www.eff.org/deeplinks/2015/12/dragnet-nsa-spying-survives-2015-review; "NSA Spying on Americans," Electronic Frontier Foundation, no date, https://www.eff.org/nsa-spying; Mike Masnick, "How Defenders of NSA Dragnet Surveillance are Stretching a 1979 Ruling to Pretend It's Constitutional," *Techdirt*, July 12, 2013, https://www.techdirt.com/articles/20130625/10084623612/how-defenders-nsa-dragnet-surveillance-are-stretching-1979-ruling-to-pretend-its-constitutional.shtml.

8　"COINTELPRO," Wikipedia, last modified May 28, 2016, https://en.wikipedia.org/wiki/COINTELPRO; Chip Berlet, "The Hunt for Red Menace: How Government Intelligence Agencies & Private Right-Wing Groups Target Dissidents & Leftists as Subversive Terrorists & Outlaws," *Political Research Associates*, 1994, http://www.politicalresearch.org/wp-content/uploads/downloads/2013/02/huntred-1994.pdf; Karen Eng, "Green is the New Red: Will Potter on the Problem of Treating Environmentalists Like Terrorists," *TED Blog*, January 31, 2014, http://blog.ted.com/will-potter-on-of-treating-environmentalists-like-terrorists/.

9　"NSA Spying on Americans."

10　Mark Rumold, "Wikimedia v. NSA: Another Court Blinds Itself to Mass NSA Surveillance," Electronic Frontier Foundation, October 29, 2015, https://www.eff.org/deeplinks/2015/10/wikimedia-v-nsa-another-court-blinds-itself-mass-nsa-surveillance.

11　Dan Eggen and Dafna Linzer, "Judge Rules Against Wiretaps," *Washington Post*, August 18, 2006, http://www.washingtonpost.com/wp-dyn/content/article/2006/08/17/AR2006081700650.html; Andrew P. Napolitano, "'Almost Orwellian'—Why Judge Leon is Right about Massive NSA Spying Program," *Fox News*, December 19, 2013, http://www.foxnews.com/opinion/2013/12/19/almost-orwellian-why-judge-leon-is-right-about-massive-nsa-spying-program.html.

12　Cindy Cohn and Trevor Timm, "Supreme Court Dismisses Challenge to FISA Amendments Act; EFF's Lawsuit over NSA Warrantless Wiretapping Remains," Electronic Frontier Foundation, February 27, 2013, https://www.eff.org/deeplinks/2013/02/supreme-court-dismisses-challenge-fisa-warrantless-wiretapping-law-effs-lawsuit; "Ruling Shields Surveillance Program from Judicial Review," American Civil Liberties Union press release, February 26, 2013, https://www.aclu.org/news/supreme-court-dismisses-aclus-challenge-nsa-warrantless-wiretapping-law.

13　Shahid Buttar, "Clapper v Amnesty: Courts and Congress v Our Constitution," *Before It's News*, March 7, 2013, http://beforeitsnews.com/libertarian/2013/03/clapper-v-amnesty-courts-and-congress-v-our-constitution-2490804.html; Nick Turse, "Was My Lai Just One of Many Massacres in Vietnam War?" *BBC News*, August 28, 2013, http://www.bbc.com/news/world-asia-23427726; Pat Paterson, "The Truth about Tonkin," *Naval History Magazine* 22, no. 1

(February 2008), http://www.usni.org/magazines/navalhistory/2008-02/truth-about-tonkin; Ira Glass, "383: Origin Story, Act Two, The Secret Life of Secrets," *This American Life*, audio podcast, June 19, 2009, http://www.thisamericanlife.org/radio-archives/episode/383/origin-story?act=2; Mike Masnick, "Court Tells US Gov't That 'State Secrets' Isn't a Magic Wand They Can Wave to Make Embarrassing Cases Go Away," *Techdirt*, November 3, 2014, https://www.techdirt.com/articles/20141031/15383329006/court-tells-us-govt-that-state-secrets-isnt-magic-wand-they-can-wave-to-make-embarrassing-cases-go-away.shtml.

14   Alexander Hamilton, "The Federalist Papers, No. 78: The Judiciary Department," *Independent Journal*, June 14, 1788, available via Constitution Society, last updated June 2, 2016, http://www.constitution.org/fed/federa78.htm.

15   Shahid Buttar, "The State of the Union, Ignoring the Elephant in the Room," Electronic Frontier Foundation, January 13, 2016, https://www.eff.org/deeplinks/2016/01/state-union-ignoring-elephant-room.

16   Rainey Reitman, "The New USA Freedom Act: A Step in the Right Direction, but More Must be Done," Electronic Frontier Foundation, April 30, 2015, https://www.eff.org/deeplinks/2015/04/new-usa-freedom-act-step-right-direction-more-must-be-done; Mark Jaycox, "EFF Disappointed as CISA Passes Senate," Electronic Frontier Foundation, October 27, 2015, https://www.eff.org/deeplinks/2015/10/eff-disappointed-cisa-passes-senate.

17   Mark Jaycox, "Note to Congress: The NSA Seizes More Than Just Your Conversations with Israeli Leaders," Electronic Frontier Foundation, January 7, 2016, https://www.eff.org/deeplinks/2016/01/note-congress-nsa-seizes-more-just-your-conversations-israeli-leaders; Andrea Peterson, "LOVEINT: When NSA Officers Use Their Spying Power on Love Interests," *Washington Post*, August 24, 2013, https://www.washingtonpost.com/blogs/the-switch/wp/2013/08/24/loveint-when-nsa-officers-use-their-spying-power-on-love-interests.

18   United States Senate, Select Committee to Study Governmental Operations with Respect to Intelligence Activities, *Supplementary Detailed Staff Reports on Intelligence Activities and the Rights of Americans, Book III, Final Report of the Select Committee to Study Governmental Operations with Respect to Intelligence Activities, United States Senate*, Report No. 94-755, 94th Congress, 2nd session, April 23, 1976 (Washington, DC: Government Printing Office, 1976), http://www.intelligence.senate.gov/sites/default/files/94755_III.pdf.

19   Dia Kayyali, "FBI's 'Suicide Letter' to Dr. Martin Luther King, Jr., and the Dangers of Unchecked Surveillance," Electronic Frontier Foundation, November 12, 2014, https://www.eff.org/deeplinks/2014/11/fbis-suicide-letter-dr-martin-luther-king-jr-and-dangers-unchecked-surveillance.

20   Darryl Cherney, interview by Amy Goodman, "Judi Bari Revisited: New Film Exposes FBI Coverup of 1990 Car Bombing of California Environmentalist," *Democracy Now!*, March 27, 2012, transcript, http://www.democracynow.org/2012/3/27/judi_bari_revisited_new_film_exposes; Ed Pilkington, "Animal Rights 'Terrorists'? Legality of Industry-Friendly Law to be Challenged," *Guardian*, February 19, 2015, http://www.theguardian.com/us-news/2015/feb/19/animal-rights-activists-challenge-federal-terrorism-charges; Kris Hermes, "The NATO 5: Manufactured Crimes Used to Paint Political Dissidents as Terrorists," *Huffington Post*, January 25, 2013, http://www.huffingtonpost.com/kris-hermes/the-nato-5-terrorism-charges_b_2552554.html.

21   Leonard Levitt, "A Black Eye for Democracy," *NYPD Confidential*, March 11, 2013, http://nypdconfidential.com/columns/2013/130311.html#top.

22   Lamont v. Postmaster General, No. 491, United States Supreme Court, 381 U.S. 301, May 24, 1965, http://caselaw.findlaw.com/us-supreme-court/381/301.html.

23   "Judge Enters Partial Verdict in Earth First! Lawsuit Victory," Judi Bari Website, August 26, 2002, http://www.judibari.org/partialverdict.html.

24   "History of the Food Not Bombs Movement," Long Island Food Not Bombs, no date, http://www.lifnb.com/about/history_of_the_food_not_bombs_movement; Keith McHenry, "History of FBI Infiltrating Food Not Bombs to Entrap Volunteers as 'Terrorists,'" *Food Not Bombs* blog, May 21, 2012, http://blog.foodnotbombs.net/history-of-fbi-infiltrating-food-not-bombs-to-entrap-volunteers-as-terrorists/; Andrew Stepanian, Paul Hetznecker, and Will Potter, inter-

view by Amy Goodman, "EXCLUSIVE: Animal Rights Activist Jailed at Secretive Prison Gives First Account of Life Inside a 'CMU,'" *Democracy Now!*, June 25, 2009, transcript, http://www. democracynow.org/2009/6/25/exclusive_animal_rights_activist_jailed_at.

25  "COINTELPRO," FBI Records: The Vault, https://vault.fbi.gov/cointel-pro.

26  David Kravets, "NSA Leak Vindicates AT&T Whistleblower," *Wired*, June 27, 2013, https:// www.wired.com/2013/06/nsa-whistleblower-klein/; Jane Mayer, "The Secret Sharer," *New Yorker*, May 23, 2011, http://www.newyorker.com/magazine/2011/05/23/the-secret-sharer.

27  "Civil Liberties in Wartime," *ShareAmerica*, April 6, 2015, https://share.america.gov/civil-liberties-wartime/.

28  Robert Barnes, "Secrecy of Surveillance Programs Blunt Challenges About Legality," *Washington Post*, June 7, 2013, https://www.washingtonpost.com/politics/secrecy-of-surveillance-programs-blunt-challenges-about-legality/2013/06/07/81da327a-cf9d-11e2-8f6b-67f40e176f03_story. html?tid=a_inl.

29  Jack Gillum and Eileen Sullivan, "US Pushing Local Cops to Stay Mum on Surveillance," Associated Press, June 12, 2014, http://finance.yahoo.com/news/us-pushing-local-cops-stay-174613067.html.

30  Paulina Firozi, "Police Forces Pick Up Surplus Military Supplies," *USA Today*, June 17, 2014, http://www.usatoday.com/story/news/nation/2014/06/15/local-law-enforcement-agencies-surplus-military-equipment/10286485/.

31  "The Texas 1033 Military Surplus Property Program," Texas Department of Public Safety, http://www.txdps.state.tx.us/LawEnforcementSupport/texas1033.htm.

32  Nate Carlisle, "Graphic: Military Weapons Sent to Utah Police," *Salt Lake Tribune*, January 19, 2014, http://www.sltrib.com/news/1542078-155/county-sheriff-param-utah-value-com; Nate Carlisle, "Blankets to Armored Vehicles: Military Gives It, Utah Police Take It," *Salt Lake Tribune*, January 19, 2014, http://archive.sltrib.com/story.php?ref=/sltrib/news/57358599-78/ police-program-utah-1033.html.csp.

33  Dan Gettinger, "How American Police Receive Robots from the U.S. Military," Center for the Study of the Drone at Bard College, August 25, 2014, http://dronecenter.bard.edu/how-american-police-receive-robots-from-the-u-s-military/; Nate Carlisle, "Blankets to Armored Vehicles"; Rhonda Cook, "Military Equipment Flowing to Local Law Enforcement Raises Questions," *Atlanta Journal-Constitution*, January 27, 2013, http://www.ajc.com/news/news/ military-equipment-flowing-to-local-law-enforcemen/nT7ZK/; Hanqing Chen, "The Best Reporting on Federal Push to Militarize Local Police," ProPublica, August 19, 2014, https:// www.propublica.org/article/the-best-reporting-on-the-federal-push-to-militarize-local-police.

34  "Street Level Surveillance," Electronic Frontier Foundation, https://www.eff.org/sls/tech/cell-site-simulators.

35  "Stingray Tracking Devices: Who's Got Them?" American Civil Liberties Union, https://www. aclu.org/map/stingray-tracking-devices-whos-got-them.

36  Fran Spielman, "Alderman Proposes $200 Security Camera Rebate for Homeowners," *Chicago Sun-Times*, May 19, 2016, http://chicago.suntimes.com/news/alderman-proposes-200-security-camera-rebate-for-homeowners/; Peter Aldhous and Charles Seife, "Spies in the Skies," *BuzzFeed*, April 6, 2016, https://www.buzzfeed.com/peteraldhous/spies-in-the-skies.

37  Shahid Buttar, "Police Violence? Body Cams are No Solution," *Truthout*, January 6, 2015, http://www.truth-out.org/opinion/item/28357-police-violence-body-cams-are-no-solution; Hilton Collins, "Video Camera Networks Link Real-Time Partners in Crime-Solving," *Government Technology*, February 1, 2012, http://www.govtech.com/public-safety/Video-Camera-Networks-Link-Real-Time-Partners-in-Crime-Solving.html.

38  Jennifer Lynch, "Written Testimony of Jennifer Lynch, Staff Attorney with the Electronic Frontier Foundation (EFF), Senate Committee on the Judiciary, Subcommittee on Privacy, Technology, and the Law: What Facial Recognition Technology Means for Privacy and Civil Liberties," Electronic Frontier Foundation, July 18, 2012, https://www.eff.org/document/ testimony-jennifer-lynch-senate-committee-judiciary-subcommittee-privacy-technology-and-law.

39    American Civil Liberties Union Foundation of Southern California, Electronic Frontier Foundation v. County of Los Angeles, Los Angeles Sheriff's Department, City of Los Angeles, Los Angeles Police Department, No. S227106, Supreme Court the State of California, County of Los Angeles, June 16, 2016, https://www.eff.org/document/eff-and-aclu-repsonse-amicus-brief-league-california-cities-and-california-state.

40    Dave Maass and Cooper Quintin, "License Plate Readers Exposed! How Public Safety Agencies Responded to Major Vulnerabilities in Vehicle Surveillance Tech," Electronic Frontier Foundation, October 28, 2015, https://www.eff.org/deeplinks/2015/10/license-plate-readers-exposed-how-public-safety-agencies-responded-massive.

41    Dave Maass, "'No Cost' License Plate Readers are Turning Texas Police into Mobile Debt Collectors and Data Miners," Electronic Frontier Foundation, January 26, 2016, https://www.eff.org/deeplinks/2016/01/no-cost-license-plate-readers-are-turning-texas-police-mobile-debt-collectors-and.

42    Wticrblair and Beau Berman, "FOX CT Investigation: Is Costly Gunshot Detection System Worth the Cost?" Fox 61, June 11, 2013, http://fox61.com/2013/05/22/fox-ct-investigation-is-costly-gun-shot-detection-system-worth-the-cost/.

43    Dia Kayyali, "Militarization, Surveillance, and Profit: How Grassroots Groups are Fighting Urban Shield," Electronic Frontier Foundation, September 3, 2014, https://www.eff.org/deeplinks/2014/09/militarization-surveillance-and-profit-how-grassroots-groups-are-fighting-urban.

44    Craig Dziedzic, "Bay Area UASI: Yellow Command 2016, Sustaining Regional Catastrophic Pans [sic] and Enhancing Situations Awareness," Urban Shield, http://urbanshield.org/index.php/about/bay-area-uasi.

45    Radley Balko, "Detroit Girl, 7, Killed in SWAT Raid," Hit and Run blog, May 17, 2010, http://reason.com/blog/2010/05/17/detroit-girl-7-killed-in-swat.

46    Jonathan Turley, "ACLU: 62 Percent of SWAT Team Raids were Searches for Drugs," Jonathan Turley blog, June 26, 2014, https://jonathanturley.org/2014/06/26/aclu-62-percent-of-swat-team-raids-were-searches-for-drugs/.

47    "The Secret Surveillance Catalogue," Intercept, https://theintercept.com/surveillance-catalogue/.

48    Charles Rabin, "Taser Death in Miami Beach Leads to New Policy and Stun Guns," Miami Herald, September 24, 2015, http://www.miamiherald.com/news/local/crime/article36462477.html; Mark Puente and Doug Donovan, "Baltimore Police Use of Tasers in Poor, Black Neighborhoods Questioned," Baltimore Sun, April 9, 2016, http://www.baltimoresun.com/news/maryland/investigations/bs-md-taser-project-baltimore-20160409-story.html; Michael E. Miller, "Miami Cops Misuse Tasers, with Deadly Results," Miami New Times, December 30, 2014, http://www.miaminewtimes.com/news/miami-cops-misuse-tasers-with-deadly-results-6522644.

49    "Transparency Project: FBI's Next Generation Identification Biometrics Database," Electronic Frontier Foundation, https://www.eff.org/foia/fbis-next-generation-identification-biometrics-database.

50    "Secure Communities ('S-COMM')," American Civil Liberties Union, https://www.aclu.org/secure-communities-s-comm; Jennifer Lynch, "FBI Plans to Have 52 Million Photos in Its NGI Face Recognition Database by Next Year," Electronic Frontier Foundation, April 14, 2014, https://www.eff.org/deeplinks/2014/04/fbi-plans-have-52-million-photos-its-ngi-face-recognition-database-next-year; "Next Generation Identification (NGI) Documents," Uncover the Truth, July 6, 2011, http://uncoverthetruth.org/foia-documents/ngi-documents/.

51    Mike Masnick, "NSA, GCHQ Admit That the Public is the Enemy," Techdirt, September 6, 2013, https://www.techdirt.com/articles/20130905/15531224420/nsa-gchq-admit-that-enemy-is-public.shtml.

52    Adam Bates, "Baltimore Police Admit Thousands of Stingray Uses," Cato Institute, April 9, 2015, http://www.cato.org/blog/baltimore-police-admit-thousands-stingray-uses.

53    See the results of Shawn Musgrave's FOIA request for a listing of states and law enforcement agencies that have been temporarily suspended from the 1033 program during FY 2004 – FY 2014, "Redacted Responsive Suspension List," Muckrock, November 13, 2015, https://muckrock.s3.amazonaws.com/foia_files/2015/11/13/Redacted_Responsive_Suspension_list.pdf; Tim Cushing, "Documents Show

1033 Program Still Resulting in Lots of Lost Weapons and Other Abuse," *Techdirt*, November 24, 2015, https://www.techdirt.com/articles/20151117/16050132844/documents-show-1033-program-still-resulting-lots-lost-weapons-other-abuse.shtml.

54 Chris Hawley, "NYPD Monitored Muslim Students All over Northeast," Associated Press, February 18, 2012, http://www.ap.org/Content/AP-In-The-News/2012/NYPD-monitored-Muslim-students-all-over-Northeast.

55 Andrew Theen, "Yale Expresses Outrage at NYPD Monitoring of Muslim Students," *Bloomberg*, February 21, 2012, http://www.bloomberg.com/news/articles/2012-02-21/yale-expresses-outrage-at-nypd-monitoring-of-muslim-students.

56 Kristan T. Harris, "Lawsuit Filed against San Diego Police Department over 'Stingray' Records," *Rundown Live*, December 18, 2014, http://therundownlive.com/lawsuit-filed-san-diego-police-department-stingray-records/; Ellen Nakashima, "Justice Department: Agencies Need Warrants to Use Cellphone Trackers," *Washington Post*, September 3, 2015, https://www.washingtonpost.com/world/national-security/justice-department-agencies-will-have-to-obtain-warrant-before-using-cellphone-surveillance-technology/2015/09/03/08e44b70-5255-11e5-933e-7d06c647a395_story.html; Shahid Buttar, "Victories in California and Virginia alongside a Setback in Florida: 2015 in Review," Electronic Frontier Foundation, December 31, 2015, https://www.eff.org/deeplinks/2015/12/victories-california-and-virginia-alongside-setback-florida-2015-review.

57 Justin Fenton, "Baltimore Police Used Secret Technology to Track Cellphones in Thousands of Cases," *Baltimore Sun*, April 9, 2015, http://www.baltimoresun.com/news/maryland/baltimore-city/bs-md-ci-stingray-case-20150408-story.html; "The Secret Surveillance Catalogue.," *Intercept*, https://theintercept.com/surveillance-catalogue/.

58 Shahid Buttar, "Santa Clara County Weighs Surveillance Reforms to Enhance Transparency and Oversight," Electronic Frontier Foundation, February 18, 2016, https://www.eff.org/deeplinks/2016/02/santa-clara-county-considers-local-reforms-increase-transparency-and-oversight.

59 Buttar, "Victories in California"; Buttar, "Santa Clara County Weighs Surveillance Reforms."

60 "Miami Drug Wars," *Flashback Miami*, http://flashbackmiami.com/2014/09/10/miami-drug-wars/.

61 Ryan Grim, Matt Sledge, and Matt Ferner, "Key Figures in CIA-Crack Cocaine Scandal Begin to Come Forward," *Huffington Post*, October 10, 2014, http://www.huffingtonpost.com/2014/10/10/gary-webb-dark-alliance_n_5961748.html.

62 Central Intelligence Agency, Office of Inspector General, Investigations Staff, "Overview: Report of Investigation Concerning Allegations of Connections between CIA and The Contras in Cocaine Trafficking to the United States (96-0143-IG)," Central Intelligence Agency Library, January 29, 1998, https://www.cia.gov/library/reports/general-reports-1/cocaine/overview-of-report-of-investigation-2.html; Ryan Grim et. al., "Key Figures in CIA-Crack Cocaine Scandal"; Alexander Cockburn, "Alexander Cockburn on the Death of Gary Webb, 'A Very Fine Journalist Who Deserved Better Than He Got,'" *Nation*, October 14, 2014, http://www.thenation.com/article/alexander-cockburn-death-gary-webb-very-fine-journalist-who-deserved-better-he-got/.

63 Larry J. Sabato, "The Iran-Contra Affair—1986–1987," *Washington Post*, 1998, http://www.washingtonpost.com/wp-srv/politics/special/clinton/frenzy/iran.htm; Amy Nicholson, "The Tragedy of Gary Webb Stings Even When *Kill the Messenger* Flags," *Dallas Observer*, October 9, 2014, http://www.dallasobserver.com/film/the-tragedy-of-gary-webb-stings-even-when-kill-the-messenger-flags-6433810.

64 "IQT Mission," In-Q-Tel, https://www.iqt.org/; Wilson Andrews and Todd Lindeman, "The Black Budget," *Washington Post*, August 29, 2013, http://www.washingtonpost.com/wp-srv/special/national/black-budget/.

65 Michael Isikoff, "American Drone Deaths Highlight Controversy," *NBC News*, February 5, 2013, http://usnews.nbcnews.com/_news/2013/02/05/16856963-american-drone-deaths-highlight-controversy.

66 Matt Sledge, "Drone Memo Justifying Anwar al-Awlaki's Killing Released," *Huffington Post*, June 23, 2014, http://www.huffingtonpost.com/2014/06/23/anwar-al-awlaki-drone-

memo_n_5522067.html; Shahid Buttar, "Constitutional Catastrophe: The National Defense Authorization Act vs. the Bill of Rights," *Public Interest Law Reporter* 17, no. 3 (2012), 242–62, http://lawecommons.luc.edu/pilr/vol17/iss3/7/.

67    Mark Benjamin, "Return of the Body Counts," *Salon*, June 11, 2005, https://www.salon.com/2005/06/11/body_counts/; Ned Resnikoff, "Collateral Damage: Brennan's Claims about Civilian Casualties," *MSNBC*, February 8, 2013, http://www.msnbc.com/the-ed-show/collateral-damage-brennans-claims-about-civ; Hassan Abbas, "How Drones Create More Terrorists," *Atlantic*, August 23, 2013, http://www.theatlantic.com/international/archive/2013/08/how-drones-create-more-terrorists/278743/.

68    Lee Ferran, "Iran Claims Video Shows Reverse-Engineered US Drone Can Fly," *ABC News*, November 12, 2014, http://abcnews.go.com/International/iran-claims-video-shows-reverse-engineered-us-drone/story?id=26858830.

69    Dustin Volz, "CIA Admits to Hacking Senate Computers," *National Journal*, July 31, 2014, https://www.nationaljournal.com/s/72881/cia-admits-hacking-senate-computers.

70    Ryan Tate, "Off the Grid," *Intercept*, December 9, 2014, https://theintercept.com/2014/12/09/map-of-cia-black-sites/.

71    Oliver Laughland, "How the CIA Tortured Its Detainees," *Guardian*, May 20, 2015, http://www.theguardian.com/us-news/2014/dec/09/cia-torture-methods-waterboarding-sleep-deprivation; Sharif Mowlabocus, "Rectal Feeding is Rape—But Don't Expect the CIA to Admit It," *Conversation*, December 12, 2014, https://theconversation.com/rectal-feeding-is-rape-but-dont-expect-the-cia-to-admit-it-35437; Jonathan S. Landay, "Did CIA Torture Violate Nuremberg Ban on Human Experimentation?" *McClatchy DC*, December 16, 2014, http://www.mcclatchydc.com/news/nation-world/national/national-security/article24777526.html.

72    Shahid Buttar, "Torturing the Rule of Law," *Augusta Free Press*, June 27, 2009, http://augustafreepress.com/shahid-buttar-torturing-the-rule-of-law/.

73    Erin Dooley, "CIA Torture Report: The Most Stunning Findings," *ABC News*, December 9, 2014, http://abcnews.go.com/Politics/cia-torture-report-stunning-findings/story?id=27473273.

74    Stephen Collinson and Evan Perez, "Senate Report: CIA Misled Public on Torture," CNN, December 9, 2014, http://www.cnn.com/2014/12/09/politics/cia-torture-report/index.html; Cal Colgan, "Justice Dept. Says CIA Destroyed 92 Torture Tapes," *Public Record*, March 2, 2009, http://pubrecord.org/torture/230/justice-dept-says-cia-destroyed-92-torture-tapes/.

75    Daniel Tencer, "Obama Signs Law Blocking Release of Torture Photos," *Raw Story*, October 29, 2009, http://www.rawstory.com/2009/10/obama-law-torture-photos/; Shahid Buttar, "The Failure of the Federalist, No. 10," *Huffington Post*, May 25, 2011, http://www.huffingtonpost.com/shahid-buttar/the-failure-of-the-federa_b_375269.html.

76    "Antonio Taguba," Wikipedia, last modified February 28, 2016, https://en.wikipedia.org/wiki/Antonio_Taguba; Laura Sullivan and David Greene, "Fil-Am General Praised for Report," *Baltimore Sun*, May 8, 2004, available via the Wayback Machine, https://web.archive.org/web/20041124041741/http://www.abs-cbnnews.com/NewsStory.aspx?section=NATIONAL&oid=50564; Zachary Roth, "Taguba: Torture Photos Show Rape," *Talking Points Memo*, May 28, 2009, http://talkingpointsmemo.com/muckraker/taguba-torture-photos-show-rape.

77    Jason Leopold, "DOJ: Feinstein's Committee Controls Torture Report; Has Final Say over Public Release," Freedom of the Press Foundation, January 25, 2014, https://freedom.press/blog/2016/04/doj-feinstein%E2%80%99s-committee-controls-torture-report-has-final-say-over-public-release.

78    "Dianne Feinstein and Her Decision to Release the Torture Report," *CBS News*, December 10, 2014, http://www.cbsnews.com/news/dianne-feinstein-and-her-decision-to-release-the-torture-report/; Dan Roberts and Spencer Ackerman, "Feinstein Accuses CIA of 'Intimidating' Senate Staff over Torture Report," *Guardian*, March 11, 2014, http://www.theguardian.com/world/2014/mar/11/feinstein-accuses-cia-intimidation-torture-report; Dan Froomkin, "CIA Search of Congressional Computer Sparks Constitutional Crisis," *Intercept*, March 11, 2014, https://theintercept.com/2014/03/11/cia-search-congressional-computer-sparks-constitutional-crisis/.

79    Josh Rogin, "Kerry Puts Brakes on CIA Torture Report," *Bloomberg*, December 5, 2014, http://www.bloomberg.com/view/articles/2014-12-05/kerry-puts-brakes-on-cia-torture-report; Pema

Levy, "CIA Hacked Senate Computers," *Newsweek*, July 31, 2014, http://www.newsweek.com/cia-hacked-senate-computers-262387; Jason Leopold, "Government Opposes Preservation Order in FOIA Lawsuit for CIA's 'Panetta Review,'" Freedom of the Press Foundation, March 18, 2014, https://freedom.press/blog/2016/04/government-opposes-preservation-order-foia-lawsuit-cia%E2%80%99s-%E2%80%9Cpanetta-review%E2%80%9D.

80  Mark Rumold, "CIA Spies on Senate Staffers: A Troubling Pattern is Reinforced," Electronic Frontier Foundation, March 14, 2014, https://www.eff.org/deeplinks/2014/03/cia-spies-senate-staffers-troubling-pattern-reinforced; David Lightman and Anita Kumar, "CIA, Senate Democrats Feud over Torture Report for a Second Day," *McClatchy DC*, December 10, 2014, http://www.mcclatchydc.com/news/politics-government/congress/article24777328.html.

81  Dustin Volz and Lauren Fox, "CIA Review Clears Its Spies of Wrongdoing in Senate Hack," *Defense One*, January 15, 2015, http://www.defenseone.com/threats/2015/01/cia-review-clears-its-spies-wrongdoing-senate-hack/102993/; Dustin Volz, "CIA Watchdog Who Revealed Senate Hack is Resigning," *Nextgov*, January 5, 2015, http://www.nextgov.com/defense/2015/01/cia-watchdog-who-revealed-senate-hack-resigning/102201/; John O. Brennan, interview by Andrea Mitchell, "CIA Director Brennan Denies Hacking Allegations," Council on Foreign Relations, March 11, 2014, transcript, http://www.cfr.org/intelligence/cia-director-brennan-denies-hacking-allegations/p32563; Mark Hosenball, "Exclusive: CIA Says Its Inspector General is Resigning at End of Month," Reuters, January 5, 2015, http://www.reuters.com/article/us-usa-cia-inspector-exclusive-idUSKBN0KE1BO20150105.

82  Michael Isikoff, "Senate Report on CIA Torture is One Step Closer to Disappearing," *Yahoo News*, May 16, 2016, https://www.yahoo.com/news/senate-report-on-cia-torture-142963611302303O.html.

83  Link no longer available (furthering Buttar's statement); previously available at http://www.intelligence.senate.gov/study2014/sscistudy1.pdf.

84  Ali Watkins, "The Other Torture Report: The Secret CIA Document That Could Unravel the Case for Torture," *Huffington Post*, December 22, 2014, http://www.huffingtonpost.com/2014/12/22/panetta-review-cia_n_6334728.html; Mike Masnick, "Mark Udall Wants to Release CIA Internal Review of Torture Program," *Techdirt*, December 11, 2014, https://www.techdirt.com/articles/20141210/14511929385/mark-udall-wants-cia-internal-review-torture-program-released.shtml.

85  Charles P. Pierce, "The CIA Wants to Play American Citizens for Fools. Again." *Esquire*, May 16, 2016, http://www.esquire.com/news-politics/politics/news/a44920/cia-destroy-torture-report/.

86  David Cole, "Obama's Torture Problem," *New York Review of Books*, November 18, 2010, http://www.nybooks.com/daily/2010/11/18/obamas-torture-problem/; Murtaza Hussain, "Report to U.N. Calls Bullshit on Obama's 'Look Forward, Not Backwards' Approach to Torture," *Intercept*, October 30, 2014, https://theintercept.com/2014/10/30/un-report-slams-obama-protecting-u-s-officials-torture-charges/.

87  Shahid Buttar, "Unhappy Anniversary: Eight Years of Continuing Lawlessness," *Huffington Post*, August 9, 2010, http://www.huffingtonpost.com/shahid-buttar/unhappy-anniversary-eight_b_673739.html.

88  Shahid Buttar, "Losing Wars We Already Won (Part I): Torture vs. WWII," *Huffington Post*, September 26, 2009, http://www.huffingtonpost.com/shahid-buttar/losing-wars-we-already-wo_b_269189.html.

89  Paul D. Shinkman, "Ferguson and the Militarization of Police," *US News & World Report*, August 14, 2014, http://www.usnews.com/news/articles/2014/08/14/ferguson-and-the-shocking-nature-of-us-police-militarization; Shahid Buttar, "Don't Call It a Curfew: Martial Law in the United States," *Truthout*, May 5, 2015, http://www.truth-out.org/opinion/item/30602-don-t-call-it-a-curfew-martial-law-in-the-united-states; Fruzsina Eördögh, "Evidence of 'Stingray' Phone Surveillance by Police Mounts in Chicago," *Christian Science Monitor*, December 22, 2014, http://www.csmonitor.com/World/Passcode/2014/1222/Evidence-of-stingray-phone-surveillance-by-police-mounts-in-Chicago; Josh Levs, "Ferguson Violence: Critics Rip Police Tactics, Use of

Military Equipment," CNN, August 15, 2014, http://www.cnn.com/2014/08/14/us/missouri-ferguson-police-tactics/index.html.

90 Naomi Wolf, "Revealed: How the FBI Coordinated the Crackdown on Occupy," *Guardian*, December 29, 2012, http://www.theguardian.com/commentisfree/2012/dec/29/fbi-coordinated-crackdown-occupy.

91 Jason Cherkis and Zach Carter, "FBI Surveillance of Occupy Wall Street Detailed," *Huffington Post*, January 5, 2013, http://www.huffingtonpost.com/2013/01/05/fbi-occupy-wall-street_n_2410783.html.

92 Xeni Jardin, "Truth and Power: New TV Series on Ordinary People Exposing Corruption from Brian Knappenberger ('Internet's Own Boy')," *Boing Boing*, January 21, 2016, https://boingboing.net/2016/01/21/truth-and-power-new-tv-series.html; Mike Krauser, "Activists Say Chicago Police Used 'Stingray' Eavesdropping Technology During Protests," *CBS Chicago*, December 6, 2014, http://chicago.cbslocal.com/2014/12/06/activists-say-chicago-police-used-stingray-eavesdropping-technology-during-protests/; George Joseph, "Exclusive: Feds Regularly Monitored Black Lives Matter Since Ferguson," *Intercept*, July 24, 2015, https://theintercept.com/2015/07/24/documents-show-department-homeland-security-monitoring-black-lives-matter-since-ferguson/.

93 "Homan Square," *Guardian*, no date, http://www.theguardian.com/us-news/homan-square; Spencer Ackerman, "The Hidden: How Chicago Police Kept Thousands Isolated at Homan Square," *Guardian*, April 13, 2016, http://www.theguardian.com/us-news/2016/apr/13/homan-square-chicago-police-records-secret-interrogation-facility-new-documents-lawsuit; Spencer Ackerman, "'I was Struck with Multiple Blows': Inside the Secret Violence of Homan Square," *Guardian*, April 11, 2016, http://www.theguardian.com/us-news/2016/apr/11/homan-square-chicago-police-internal-documents-physical-force-prisoner-abuse.

94 John Cook, "At the CIA, Accidentally Kidnapping and Torturing an Innocent Guy Earns You a Promotion," *Gawker*, February 9, 2011, http://gawker.com/5755942/at-the-cia-accidentally-kidnapping-and-torturing-an-innocent-guy-earns-you-a-promotion; Associated Press, "Removal of Judge, Prosecutors Sought in Guantanamo 9/11 Case," Associated Press, May 11, 2016, https://www.yahoo.com/news/removal-judge-prosecutors-sought-guantanamo-9-11-case-185938929.html; Morris Davis, interview by Hala Gorani, "Former Prosecutor: 'No Good Reason for Guantanamo,'" CNN, video, January 21, 2015, http://www.cnn.com/videos/world/2015/01/21/wrn-guantanamo-bay-prosecutor-morris-davis-intv.cnn.

95 Cory Doctorow, "First-hand Reports of Torture from Homan Square, Chicago PD's 'Black Site,'" *Boing Boing*, February 28, 2015, https://boingboing.net/2015/02/28/first-hand-reports-of-torture.html.

96 "Jon Burge Appeal Denied: Court Upholds Perjury Conviction in Ex-Police Commander's Torture Case," *Huffington Post*, April 1, 2013, http://www.huffingtonpost.com/2013/04/01/jon-burge-perjury-convict_n_2994844.html; Hal Dardick and John Byrne, "Mayor: 'Sorry' for Burge Torture Era," *Chicago Tribune*, September 11, 2013, http://www.chicagotribune.com/news/chi-city-council-settles-burge-torture-cases-for-123-million-20130911-story.html.

97 "The Counted: People Killed by Police in the US," *Guardian*, http://www.theguardian.com/us-news/ng-interactive/2015/jun/01/the-counted-police-killings-us-database; E.M. Beck and Stewart E. Tolnay, "Lynching," *New Georgia Encyclopedia*, January 26, 2007, last edited June 27, 2016, http://www.georgiaencyclopedia.org/articles/history-archaeology/lynching.

98 Shahid Buttar, "December Week of Action Challenges CIA and NSA Crimes," *Popular Resistance*, December 4, 2014, https://www.popularresistance.org/54256/.

99 Pete Kasperowicz, "Obama Signs Patriot Act Extension into Law," Hill, February 25, 2011, http://thehill.com/blogs/floor-action/house/146173-obama-signs-patriot-act-extension-into-law.

100 James Risen and Eric Lichtblau, "Bush Lets U.S. Spy on Callers without Courts," *New York Times*, December 16, 2015, http://www.nytimes.com/2005/12/16/politics/bush-lets-us-spy-on-callers-without-courts.html?_r=2; Michael Scherer, "The Ashcroft-Gonzales Hospital Room Showdown," *Salon*, May 15, 2007, https://www.salon.com/2007/05/15/comey_testifies/.

101 Bill Moyers, "The Church Committee and FISA," *Bill Moyers Journal*, October 26, 2007, http://www.pbs.org/moyers/journal/10262007/profile2.html.

102 "FISA Amendments Act of 2008," SourceWatch, last modified March 13, 2010, http://www.sourcewatch.org/index.php?title=FISA_Amendments_Act_of_2008.

103 "NSA Slides Explain the PRISM Data-Collection Program," *Washington Post*, June 6, 2010, http://www.washingtonpost.com/wp-srv/special/politics/prism-collection-documents/; Mike Masnick, "Expanding Unconstitutional Backdoor Searches of Surveillance Data is Easy: Just Change What Words Mean," *Techdirt*, April 22, 2016, https://www.techdirt.com/articles/20160422/07350334243/expanding-unconstitutional-backdoor-searches-surveillance-data-is-easy-just-change-what-words-mean.shtml.

104 Cindy Cohn and Rainey Reitman, "USA Freedom Act Passes: What We Celebrate, What We Mourn, and Where We Go from Here," Electronic Frontier Foundation, June 2, 2015, https://www.eff.org/deeplinks/2015/05/usa-freedom-act-passes-what-we-celebrate-what-we-mourn-and-where-we-go-here; "Domestic Internet Backbone Surveillance," Electronic Frontier Foundation, https://www.eff.org/files/2014/07/24/backbone-3c-color.jpg.

105 Dan Auerbach, Peter Eckersley, and Jonathan Mayer, "What We Need to Know about PRISM," Electronic Frontier Foundation, June 12, 2013, https://www.eff.org/deeplinks/2013/06/what-we-need-to-know-about-prism; Cindy Cohn and Andrew Crocker, "Deeper Dive into EFF's Motion on Backbone Surveillance," Electronic Frontier Foundation, July 26, 2014, https://www.eff.org/deeplinks/2014/07/deeper-dive-effs-backbone-motion.

106 Rainey Reitman, "In Hearing on Internet Surveillance, Nobody Knows How Many Americans Impacted in Data Collection," Electronic Frontier Foundation, May 10, 2016, https://www.eff.org/deeplinks/2016/05/hearing-internet-surveillance-nobody-knows-how-many-americans-impacted-data; "Letter to Director Clapper," Letter from the members of the United States House Committee on the Judiciary to James R. Clapper (Director of National Intelligence), April 22, 2016, Brennan Center, https://www.brennancenter.org/sites/default/files/legal-work/Letter_to_Director_Clapper_4_22.pdf.

107 "Discussion between US Senator Ron Wyden and Director of National Intelligence James Clapper," Wikipedia, video, December 21, 2013, https://en.wikipedia.org/wiki/File:Ron_Wyden_and_James_Clapper_-_12_March_2013.webm.

108 Hanni Fakhoury, "DEA and NSA Team Up to Share Intelligence, Leading to Secret Use of Surveillance in Ordinary Investigations," Electronic Frontier Foundation, August 6, 2013, https://www.eff.org/deeplinks/2013/08/dea-and-nsa-team-intelligence-laundering.

109 Letter from Advocacy for Principled Action in Government, et al. to James R. Clapper (Director of National Intelligence) requesting information on how Section 702 of FISA affects Americans and other US residents, October 29, 2015, Brennan Center, https://www.brennancenter.org/sites/default/files/analysis/Coalition_Letter_DNI_Clapper_102915.pdf.

110 Siobhan Gorman, "NSA Officers Spy on Love Interests," *Wall Street Journal*, August 23, 2013, http://blogs.wsj.com/washwire/2013/08/23/nsa-officers-sometimes-spy-on-love-interests/.

111 Andrea Peterson, "Why a Staggering Number of Americans Have Stopped Using the Internet the Way They Used To," *Washington Post*, May 13, 2016, https://www.washingtonpost.com/news/the-switch/wp/2016/05/13/new-government-data-shows-a-staggering-number-of-americans-have-stopped-basic-online-activities/.

112 David Forscey, "Congress Should Declassify the Legislative Negotiations over the FISA Amendments Act," *Lawfare*, October 14, 2015, https://www.lawfareblog.com/congress-should-declassify-legislative-negotiations-over-fisa-amendments-act.

113 Mike Masnick, "Court Reveals 'Secret Interpretation' of the Patriot Act, Allowing NSA to Collect All Phone Call Data," *Techdirt*, September 17, 2013, https://www.techdirt.com/articles/20130917/13395324556/court-reveals-secret-interpretation-patriot-act-allowing-nsa-to-collect-all-phone-call-data.shtml.

# CHAPTER 10

# Who's Afraid of Critical Media Literacy?

Bill Yousman

> "When I began my schooling in the all-black, segregated schools of Kentucky in the fifties I was lucky to be taught by African American teachers who were genuinely concerned that I, along with all their other pupils, acquired a 'good education.' To those teachers, a 'good education' was not just one that would give us knowledge and prepare us for a vocation, it was also an education that would encourage an ongoing commitment to social justice, particularly to the struggle for racial equality."
>
> —bell hooks[1]

At the 2015 Media Education Summit in Boston, a participant in a roundtable discussion questioned the use of the term "critical media literacy." She challenged the panelists, saying that the term "critical" means many different things to many people: we may know what we think "critical" means, but others may not be interpreting the language the same way we are.

This critique hints at the instability not only of one particular word, but of language itself. Not just the term "critical," but every word in every language is open to multiple and idiosyncratic interpretations. It was the so-called first postmodern president, Bill Clinton, who reminded us of this when he asked us to consider what the definition of the word "is" is.

This essay is an attempt to clarify how we might think about the term "critical media literacy": what it means, how it differs from other forms of media literacy, and what the pedagogical and political implications might be of embracing critical media literacy.

At the same Boston conference, there were two other moments that suggested the title of this essay. During the discussion noted above, another participant voiced her opposition to a critical approach because, she said, she didn't believe that educators should "tell students what they should think." On the following day, a presenter began his talk by noting his personal reluctance about using the term "critical," before delivering a fairly lengthy presentation that seemed, at least to me, to be located firmly in a critical framework.

All of these moments are reflective of a profound reticence, if not outright fear, of the term "critical," even by those who are committed to media literacy education. I see parallels here to other taboo terms like "socialism" or "feminism." The term "socialism" seems to engender dread, especially for those who can't fully define the term or list any of its principles. And while most of my students claim to embrace gender equality, they simultaneously reject identifying themselves as "feminists" or even the notion that they might actually be in agreement with some feminist ideas.

The fear of a critical approach to media education often presents itself as a reasonable response to those who want to indoctrinate young people into their own radical political beliefs; thus, "we shouldn't be telling students what to think." David Buckingham has accused advocates of critical approaches of arrogance, paternalism, and self-aggrandizement, while casting them as mere relics of a bygone era.[2] In a 2003 anthology of essays about new visions of media literacy, Chris Worsnop argued that media education should not be primarily focused on "[h]ealth concerns . . . social concerns . . . moral concerns . . . ideological concerns . . . [or] political concerns . . ."[3] (Without being too flippant, aside from aesthetics and technical skills, I'm not sure what's left after we remove all of the above from any sort of educational project.)

Worsnop also warns educators against "media bashing," a term I have heard several times at media literacy conferences and even from colleagues in academic departments.

So, let's establish from the start what critical media literacy is *not*, so that we can begin to explore what critical media literacy can be.

First, and most simply, critical media literacy is not an empty signifier devoid of any meaning. While it is indeed a phrase that can be interpreted in many different ways, that is true for any abstract terminology. Would it be possible to get a diverse group of people to achieve consensus about what "art" means? Or "beauty"? Or "patriotism"? Or "democracy"? All language is unstable and open to multiple decoding options, yet we still rely on words to propel discourse and create meaning.

Second, despite the fears of some educators, the use of the term "critical" does not imply that we are telling students what they must think. As communication professor Rashmi Luthra says, "The idea is not to have students mimic my analysis and conclusions but to start them on a quest for solutions to pressing problems of global inequities and the interlocking oppressions of race, class, gender, nation, ability, and heterosexuality that result from these inequities."[4] Of course framing inequity as a problem is itself an ideological position. But all cultural and educational practices are ideological. A willingness to directly confront the ideologies in media is one of the distinguishing marks of a critical approach to media education. Rather than political indoctrination, this is actually aimed at encouraging more independent thinking, as Steven Funk, Douglas Kellner, and Jeff Share point out:

> By examining their ideological assumptions, students can learn to question what they consider "normal" or "common sense." "Common sense" is only so because ideas and texts have been produced and disseminated through a dominant frame of thought expressed in powerful master-narratives, often conveyed through media, schools, government, religion, and families.[5]

Encouraging students to deconstruct homophobic imagery in popular culture, for example, by examining the institutional factors behind the production of those images and the influence they might have over viewers, cannot be equated with telling students exactly what they should think about the images themselves or even about the struggle for LGBTQ+ rights. Similarly, a student who has learned that only a small number of profit-driven corporations with close ties to elite interests control most of the commercial news outlets in the US is free to keep relying on those outlets for information, but at least they will do so with more context and from a more informed position about the institutions they rely on.

Providing just this sort of context is key to critical media analysis. Justin Lewis and Sut Jhally offer an example of a contextual, critical approach to, in this case, car commercials:

> When automobile ads invariably show cars driving along empty roads, often across pristine landscapes with cloudless skies, we might ask students not only what is being left out of these images (traffic, pollution, smog), but why? In whose interest is it to see the automobile as a symbol of freedom, exploring rather than despoiling the US landscape? What role do these interests have in media production? What are the consequences of seeing the automobile in only these terms?[6]

This asking of critical questions cannot be equated with simply telling students what to think about those commercials. Instead it is encouraging them to view media in a more informed way and consider alternative ways of thinking about the media they use. And, it should be noted, this critical thinking is exactly the opposite of what is encouraged by the advertising industries themselves, who would much prefer that critical questions not be asked about the stories and images they employ. As Lewis and Jhally point out, "It is important to note that we are not advocating propagandizing in schools for a particular political perspective. We are advocating a view that recognizes that the world is always made by someone, and a decision to tolerate the status quo is as political as a more overtly radical act."[7]

Finally, while I believe that the commercial media industries that dominate our lives certainly do need to be called out for their frequently misogynistic, homophobic, racist, imperialistic, and hyperviolent images and stories, to characterize a critical approach to media education as simply "media bashing" is an oversimplification and distortion of both the methods and goals of critical media literacy. In much the same way that the term "political correctness" is hauled out to distract, deflect, and delegitimize marginalized groups' demands for respect and dignity, "bashing the media" distracts, deflects, and delegitimizes the mission of holding media industries accountable for their propaganda, lies, stereotypes, distortions, omissions, and myriad other ethical breaches.

A crucial figure in the development of critical pedagogy, Paulo Freire, offers an eloquent example of just the sort of critical media literacy exercise that I have in mind:

> For example, as men [sic] through discussion, begin to per-ceive the deceit in a cigarette advertisement featuring a beautiful, smiling woman in a bikini (i.e., the fact that she, her smile, her beauty, and her bikini have nothing at all to do with the cigarette), they begin to discover the difference between education and propaganda. At the same time, they are preparing themselves to discuss and perceive the same deceit in ideological or political propaganda; they are arming themselves to "disassociate ideas." In fact, this has always seemed to me to be the way to defend democracy, not a way to subvert it.[8]

So, to summarize: "Critical media literacy" is not a term that is useless because it can be interpreted in many different ways. Critical media literacy is not political indoctrination of vulnerable young minds. And critical media literacy is not simply "media bashing."

So what is it then?

## WHAT IS THIS "CRITICAL" IN "CRITICAL MEDIA LITERACY"?

One of the most frequently heard phrases in this field of inquiry—and I've even said this myself at times—is that critical media literacy deals with issues of power. But what does that mean? Funk, Kellner, and Share offer a little more specificity: "CML [critical media literacy] calls for examining the hierarchical power relations that are embedded in all communication and that ultimately benefit dominant social groups at the expense of subordinate ones."[9] To hone in on what is pertinent and distinctive about the term "critical," we should start by examining the roots of critical media literacy in critical theories of society, communication, and culture.

Perhaps the best place to start is with a quote from Karl Marx and Friedrich Engels's *The German Ideology* that is frequently referenced in cultural studies scholarship:

> The ideas of the ruling class are in every epoch the ruling ideas, i.e. the class which is the ruling *material* force of society, is at the same time its ruling *intellectual* force. The class which has the means of material production at its disposal, has control at the same time over the means of mental production, so that thereby, generally speaking, the ideas of those who lack the means of mental production are subject to it.[10]

This Marxist conception of ideology is at the heart of what has been called an alternative paradigm of media theory, based in a European tradition of cultural criticism most often identified with the Frankfurt School of the early twentieth century.[11] Rather than looking for the "effects" of media on individual psychology and behavior, as in mainstream social scientific media research, the so-called alternative paradigm concerned itself with power inequities and the role of media in the domination and subordination of particular social groups.

Distancing themselves from approaches to media research sponsored by media industries, writers from the alternative paradigm self-identified as critical theorists because of their acknowledged goal of critiquing powerful institutions like the media rather than unreflectively adopting the agendas and values of these institutions. This distinguishes the critical approach from the more dominant "administrative" approach to media theory and research. Administrative communication research involves projects funded by corporations and governments that examine how media can be used to advance the goals of those sponsoring organizations.[12] We might also think of the administrative paradigm as encompassing any research or theory that either consciously or unconsciously adopts the assumptions, values, and standards of the established and dominant institutions in a given social context.

Todd Gitlin argues that both a cozy relationship with the media industries and a narrow definition of media influence—as simply short-term, behavioral, and individual—prevents scholars in the administrative tradition from even beginning to ask the most fundamental and crucial questions about the role of media in social formations.[13] These unasked questions concern the economic and political structure of media institutions, the material and ideological impact of these structures, and who benefits from the existing patterns of media control. As critical scholar Theodor Adorno wrote about his attempts to work with media researcher Paul Lazarsfeld, "it was . . . implied that the system itself, its cultural and sociological consequences and its social and economic presuppositions were not to be analyzed."[14]

Intellectuals associated with the Frankfurt School of Applied Social Research brought the alternative approach to analyzing and critiquing media and culture to the United States in the 1930s as they fled the Third Reich. The Frankfurt School included Adorno and Max Horkheimer, as well as Leo Löwenthal, Herbert Marcuse, and Walter Benjamin, among others. Rather than an industry-friendly administrative approach, these theorists employed Marxist concepts to focus on questions of power and ideology in the study of the institutions and products of mass communication, or what they called "the culture industries."[15]

Frankfurt School scholars believed that popular forms of entertainment like film, radio, paperback novels, and magazines were nothing more than mass-produced, standardized commodities. As Horkheimer and Adorno wrote, "Culture now impresses the same stamp on everything. Films, radio and magazines make up a system which is uniform as a whole and in every part."[16]

The central concerns of the early critical theorists that are most relevant to critical media literacy can be summed up with two key propositions. First, mass culture promotes conformity and adherence to fashion trends while undermining authentic individuality and intellectual thought. Second, and most importantly, there are specific ideological purposes behind the machinations of the culture industries—legitimizing capitalism, placating workers, distracting the masses from the harsh realities of their existence, and binding them to the prevailing social order:

By subordinating in the same way and to the same end all areas of intellectual creation, by occupying men's senses from the time they leave the factory in the evening to the time they clock in again the next morning with matter that bears the impress of the labor process they themselves have to sustain throughout the day, this subsumption mockingly satisfies the concept of a unified culture . . .[7]

Frankfurt School scholars thus broke with the behaviorist and administrative mass communication researchers of the early twentieth century primarily through their Marxist inquiry into the relationships between culture and power. As Kellner notes, "the critical focus on media culture from the perspectives of commodification, reification, ideology, and domination provides a framework useful as a corrective to more populist and uncritical approaches to media culture which tend to surrender critical standpoints."[18]

Inspired by Marxism and the Frankfurt School's critical paradigm, but interested in problematizing the notion of media audiences as unthinking drones of the culture industries, a critical cultural studies approach to media and power emerged in the 1960s at the Centre for Contemporary Cultural Studies at the University of Birmingham. Here such scholars as Richard Hoggart, Raymond Williams, Stuart Hall, Paul Willis, Angela McRobbie, Paul Gilroy, and many others offered highly influential analyses of the important role that popular culture plays in the daily lives of the public. British Cultural Studies drew inspiration from Louis Althusser's important writing about media as one of several powerful ideological apparatuses that shape our relationship to everyday life,[19] but also from the work of Antonio Gramsci and his notion of an eternal struggle between hegemonic and counterhegemonic forces.[20] Thus, without shying away from sharp ideological critiques of media, cultural studies added "a more sophisticated understanding of the audience as active constructors of reality, not simply mirrors of an external reality."[21] The insights of the cultural studies approach are at the heart of several of the core ideas commonly accepted as key media literacy concepts, including the principle that media are ideological constructions that play a role in constructing our notions of reality, but also, importantly, that this does not amount to absolute ideological control because audiences do have the capacity to negotiate meaning in the media they use.[22]

Influenced by Marxism, the Frankfurt School, and British Cultural Studies, critical media literacy goes beyond more conservative approaches to media education by starting with the recognition that media perform not just as information and entertainment but even more crucially as the voice of the powerful in society. Critical media literacy also adopts the position that this voice can and should be challenged by alternative voices. Advocating for justice and social transformation is thus central to a critical media literacy approach. As Funk, Kellner, and Share summarize, "CML provides a framework that encourages people to read information critically in multiple formats, to create alternative representations that question hierarchies of power, social norms and injustices, and to become agents of change."[23]

The background explored in this section, however, leaves two questions unanswered: First, why do critical media scholars, educators, artists, and activists believe we need alternative systems of representation; and second, why do we think the world itself needs to change? Answering these questions requires us to leave the surface appearance of media messages behind for a bit while we look at why those messages are there and who is actually creating them.

## "YOU CAN'T HANDLE THE TRUTH": COMING TO GRIPS WITH THE "C" WORD

One essential way that critical media education differs from other forms of media literacy is in its willingness to go behind the messages and shine a light on the powerful institutions that control the media environment, as well as their practices of employing engaging visual imagery and storytelling to advance their own economic and ideological agendas. As Shirley Steinberg and Joe Kincheloe put it, "To sustain their privilege, dominant groups must control representation, they must encode the world in forms that support their own power . . . [But] language systems are always multi-accentual, which means that lodged within dominant cultural codes are the preconditions for oppositional interpretations."[24] Opposition, however, can only emerge in conditions of enhanced knowledge that allow us to interrogate the methods and motivations of the powerful. Thus, Julie Frechette, Nolan Higdon, and Rob Williams argue that the goal of critical media literacy is "to analyze how media industries reproduce sociocultural structures of power by determining who gets to tell the stories of a society, what points of view and organizational interests will shape the constructions of these stories, and who the desired target audience is."[25]

Unlike more conservative approaches to media literacy education, the critical approach entails a willingness to take on what media scholar Robert McChesney has called the "elephant in the room." This giant lumbering beast that is too large to ignore, but can't be avoided by any honest investigation of the power of media, is the beast we are often hesitant to name: capitalism. Writing specifically about changes in media since the widespread dissemination of digital technologies, McChesney argues that both those who are suspicious of the Internet and those who embrace it "have a single, deep, and often fatal flaw that severely compromises the value of their work. That flaw, simply put, is ignorance about really existing capitalism and an underappreciation of how capitalism dominates social life. Celebrants and skeptics lack a political economic context. The work tends to take capitalism for granted as part of the background scenery . . ."[26]

McChesney's critique of Internet pundits can easily be applied to conservative media literacy scholars and educators as well. Not just the Internet but the entire commercial media environment is dominated by just a small handful of multinational corporations whose explicit goal is to make as large a profit as possible. This is as true of so-called "new" media as it is of "old" media, as true for Facebook as it is for NBC. In fact, under the US legal system, publicly held corporations are mandated to do everything they can to increase profits in order to benefit their shareholders. Thus, in 1981, Michael Eisner, then CEO of Disney, a company that makes products aimed primarily at children and young people, reported to his investors, "We have no obligation to make art. We have no obligation to make a statement. To make money is our only objective."[27] And in 2003, the founder of the US's largest radio chain, Clear Channel Communications, told *Fortune* magazine, "We're not in the business of providing news and information. We're not in the business of providing well-researched music. We're simply in the business of selling our customers products."[28] And, upon acquiring YouTube in 2008, Google chief executive Eric Schmidt in an interview on CNBC said, "I don't think we've quite figured out the perfect solution of how to make money, and we're working on that. That's our highest priority this year."[29] Most recently, in 2016, the head of CBS, Les Moonves, speaking about the high ratings and the vast amounts of political advertising provoked by the Donald Trump presidential run, admitted, "It may not be good for America, but it's damn good for CBS."[30]

These perspectives from the very top of the corporate media hierarchy provide us with crucial insights about whose interests are really served by capitalist media industries, yet these are truths that many media literacy practitioners are unwilling to acknowledge. While it is true that offering a full-blown critique of capitalism might be an unwise move for public school teachers, the roots of this aversion often seem to grow from ideological dispositions rather than pragmatic career preservation strategies. Several years ago I attended a regional media literacy conference at the University of Connecticut. During a closing plenary session an audience member raised questions about media literacy organizations accepting corporate funding. In defending this practice, one of the world's leading media literacy educators, a college professor protected by tenure, responded, "Hey, I'm a capitalist and I'm not ashamed of that."

Moreover, the dominant media literacy organizations in the US have been partnering with media corporations like Nickelodeon, Time Warner, and Channel One for many years now. Lori Bindig and James Castonguay argue that among many debates about media education, "the issue of whether or not to accept funding from corporate interests is among the most contentious."[31] But, as Sut Jhally and Jeremy Earp point out, "The most influential and pervasive media education initiatives in the country now fit well enough within the demands and logic of the commercial media industry to win its approval and funding."[32]

In contrast to this, alternative groups like the Action Coalition for Media Education (ACME) and the Global Critical Media Literacy Project (GCMLP) refuse to accept corporate funding because they believe it is impossible to honestly and fully critique those who are paying one's bills. In addition to advocating for critical thinking about media images and messages like the more conservative media literacy organizations, ACME and GCMLP go beyond this in their mission statements, advocating for institutional analysis, alternative media production, media reform, and media activism, four aspects of critical media literacy that corporate-funded approaches are unlikely to embrace.[33]

An unwillingness to critique capitalism also disenables the dominant paradigm in media literacy from fully addressing the inequality that capitalist media systems play a role in creating, naturalizing, reinforcing, and justifying. Even an apologist for capitalism, the economist Ha-Joon Chang, is forced to acknowledge many of the problems caused by the innate tendencies of capitalist systems. While he writes, "I still believe that capitalism is the best economic system that humanity has invented,"[34] he then goes on to deconstruct many of the myths about capitalism that corporate media promulgate, including the wrongheaded notions that globalization aids poorer nations, policies that are good for business are also good for the public, and that the stronghold of capitalism, the US, has the highest living standard on the planet.

An unwillingness to confront capitalism means many related "isms," such as militarism, imperialism, nationalism, racism, sexism, classism, heterosexism, ableism, ageism, neoliberalism, hyperconsumerism, antienvironmentalism, and more, may also be considered "too political," and ensures that the crucial role that capitalist media play in advancing these ideologies and practices remains outside the boundaries of acceptable discourse.

bell hooks is one of many critical scholars and educators to point out the mutually reinforcing, intertwined nature of capitalism and other structures of dominance and subordination. She writes, "I often use the phrase 'imperialist white supremacist capitalist patriarchy' to describe the interlocking political systems that are the foundation of our nation's politics."[35] We can be sure that this language would be considered too inflammatory by those who advocate for a type of media education that strives to remain apolitical and neutral. Reflecting on his own experiences working with teachers, Peter McLaren notes, "When I suggest that teaching should be about transforming the injustices of the social order rather than adapting students to that order, many of them feel absolutely threatened. Teachers frequently feel that my position is a 'biased' one and that teachers have an obligation to be neutral and objective . . ."[36]

However, to call on historian Howard Zinn, "You can't be neutral on a moving train." In the documentary film named after this famous quote, Zinn says,

> I don't believe it's possible to be neutral. The world is already moving in certain directions. And to be neutral, to be passive in a situation like that is to collaborate with whatever is going on. And I, as a teacher, do not want to be a collaborator with whatever is happening in the world. I want myself, as a teacher, and I want you as students, to intercede with whatever is happening in the world.[37]

Even if they don't identify as Marxist, many critical media educators believe that when they are silent about the inequality, subordination, violence, and oppression brought on by capitalism they remain complicit with the status quo and they have already chosen a side without acknowledging that the choice has been made. Critical media literacy thus focuses not just on what is visible in media but, crucially, what is invisible. Len Masterman writes about this as media education that emphasizes ideology and the politics of representation and "challenge[s] the media's common-sensed representations by asking whose interests they served, how they were constructed, and what alternative representations were repressed."[38] Critical literacy educator Vivian Vasquez writes about teaching even very young students how to interrogate stories by asking, "Whose voice is heard? Who is silenced? Whose reality is presented? Whose reality is ignored? Who is advantaged? Who is disadvantaged?"[39] Masterman further notes,

> Since the mystification of media's images was tied up with their "naturalization," their "evaporation" of politics and history, the task of the teacher was precisely to provide some sense of the wider political and historical contexts within which these images were produced and could be understood.[40]

Peter McLaren offers a concrete example: Discussing the US government's overthrow of democratically elected leaders around the globe, our adoption of continual "low intensity warfare" as an unstated foundation of our foreign policy, and our employment of chemical weapons—all matters that the corporate media choose to ignore—McLaren asks, "Should such questions form our ongoing debates in our classrooms? Or do we continue to claim that classrooms must be 'neutral' spaces devoid of political debates and discussions and leave such questions to the 'experts' (likely certified by the Pentagon)?"[41]

Asking the difficult questions and encouraging self-reflection and critical dialogue are central tenets of critical pedagogy, an approach to education that has much in common with critical media literacy. In fact, critical media literacy should be understood as grounded not just in the critical theory, cultural studies, and political economic frameworks we have been exploring, but in principles of democratic education and transformative critical pedagogy as well.

## "THE POINT IS TO CHANGE IT": TRANSFORMATIVE PEDAGOGY AND CRITICAL MEDIA LITERACY

Drawing inspiration from Paulo Freire, communication professors Deanna Fassett and John Warren frame critical pedagogy as "[e]fforts to reflect and act upon the world in order to transform it, to make it a more just place for more people, to respond to our own collective pains and needs and desires."[42] Similarly, McLaren notes, "Our interpretation of the world is inseparable from our transformation of the world—both are linked socially and ethically."[43]

The key here is the notion of ethical transformation. Marx noted, "Philosophers have hitherto only interpreted the world in various ways; the point is to change it."[44] This is a crucial difference between conservative educational practices and critical pedagogy. Just as critical media literacy embraces alternative media production and media activism in addition to critical thinking about media messages, critical pedagogy argues that the goal of truly democratic education is not the mere cataloging and memorization of a series of facts (mathematical equations, historical dates and names, conjugation of verbs, etc.). As

Freire argues, "Acquiring literacy does not involve memorizing sentences, words, or syllables—lifeless objects unconnected to an existential universe—but rather an attitude of creation and re-creation, a self-transformation producing a stance of intervention in one's own context."[45] The aim is to allow students the space to explore the actual worlds they inhabit in order to critically reflect on their life conditions and ultimately work for positive change. The idea of transformation, however, is frightening to those who are heavily invested in the status quo—and thus they insist that truly transformative education is not objective, too political, too close to "telling students what to think."

And yet, far from telling students what to think, critical pedagogy is devoted to engaging *with* students in the *process* of thinking. An anecdote from the critical educator bell hooks illustrates this point well:

> Recently, I gave a lecture wherein a young white female student boldly stated during open discussion: "I am one of those evil capitalists you critique and I do not want to be changed by participation in your classroom or by reading your books." After I called attention to the fact that the word "evil" was not used during my lecture or in any work I referred to, I was able to share that in all the classes I teach I make it clear from the start that my intent is not to create clones of myself. Boldly, I affirmed: "My primary intent as a teacher is to create an open learning community where students are able to learn how to be critical thinkers able to understand and respond to the material we are studying together." I added that it has been my experience that as students become critical thinkers they often of their own free will change perspectives; only they know whether that is for the better.[46]

Critical pedagogy is thus *more* open to students arriving at their own conclusions than more teacher-centered approaches. Freire distinguishes between two educational paradigms: The banking model of education assumes that educators are the source of all wealth and that students are empty safe deposit boxes, waiting to be filled up with the riches provided to them by their expert instructors. In contrast to this, the problem-posing model encourages students to struggle with real issues they face in their own lives and engage in constructive dialogue in order to work for change.[47] The problem-posing approach is thus based in Freire's notion of liberatory praxis: "the action and reflection of men and women upon their world in order to transform it."[48] This unavoidably entails dealing with the political: hunger, inequality, violence, disenfranchisement, domination and subordination, etc. Writing specifically about Brazil during the 1960s, Freire's stance is just as relevant to current global realities:

> The education our situation demanded would enable men [*sic*] to discuss courageously the problems of their context— and to intervene in that context; it would warn men of the dangers of the time and offer them the confidence and the strength to confront those dangers instead of surrendering their sense of self through submission to the decisions of others . . . that education could help men to assume an increasingly critical attitude toward the world and so to transform it.[49]

Education is always a political act, as Ira Shor notes: "Not encouraging students to question knowledge, society, and experience tacitly endorses and supports the status quo."[50] The banking model of education encourages passive thinking on the part of students who, no matter the avowed subject, are being taught the meta-lessons of obedience, compliance, and the acceptance of established structures of power. Critical pedagogy is also political, but it acknowledges its politics. Whereas the politics of banking education are the unspoken politics of passivity and conformity, the politics of critical pedagogy are the politics of freedom, liberation, and transgression of rigid boundaries.

This willingness to teach in a way that confronts systems of power is not without risk. Neil Postman and Charles Weingartner point out that those at the top of the social hierarchy "would much prefer that the schools do little or nothing to encourage youth to question, doubt, or challenge any part of the society in which they live . . ."[51] As noted above, even colleagues and other educators may accuse us of politically indoctrinating students (although isn't this exactly what the business schools do?), and there are institutional challenges as well. hooks writes eloquently about the backlash that politically engaged educators face:

> My commitment to engaged pedagogy is an expression of political activism. Given that our educational institutions are so deeply invested in a banking system, teachers are more rewarded when we do not teach against the grain. The choice to work against the grain, to challenge the status quo, often has negative consequences. And that is part of what makes that choice one that is not politically neutral.[52]

The insights of critical pedagogy make it plain that the idea of neutral education is a myth. We can teach with the grain or against the grain, as hooks notes, but either choice is a political choice. Critical pedagogy doesn't entail telling students what political party to vote for or which ballot initiative they should support. Instead it involves engaging students in a process of critical questioning of received wisdom. The process of questioning, researching, introspection, and dialogue is the point, rather than a predetermined outcome that all students are expected to embrace.

When it comes to questions of media, this means encouraging critical thinking not just about media texts, but about the contexts in which media are produced and the ways those media influence their audiences. I've proposed elsewhere that this may be thought of as an integrative holistic approach to media literacy:

> A holistic approach to media literacy, one that encompasses both textual and contextual concerns within a critical framework, argues that to be a citizen rather than a passive consumer in media-saturated societies, one must develop an understanding of the commercial structure of the media industries and the political and ideological implications of this structure. From this perspective, in addition to being able to skillfully deconstruct media texts, the person who is truly media literate is also knowledgeable of the political

economy of the media, the consequences of media consumption, and the activist and alternative media movements that seek to challenge mainstream media norms and create a more democratic system.[53]

By way of example, consider two classroom exercises about fast food advertising: A textual approach might ask students to examine images from a number of different print advertisements and television commercials and discuss the persuasive techniques employed. Teachers might even encourage students to compare the images of food in the ads to what the burgers and tacos actually look like when they are unwrapped. This would allow for critical thinking about the constructed nature of media images. A contextual approach might actually start with this exercise, but then it would go further by asking critical questions about the global reach of the fast food industry, the effectiveness of their advertising in changing people's diets, their labor and environmental practices, their impact on world health and the treatment of farm animals, etc.[54]

In both cases students would be asked to voice their own opinions and insights and use their own research and life experiences to reflect on the questions posed by the teacher. But in the latter case students would be asked to dig a bit deeper and consider not just the words and images in the ads themselves but the context these ads appear in. This does not mean hammering students into submission with the "right" conclusions. After exploring the industrial practices and global impact of the fast food industries, some students might choose to continue patronizing fast food establishments, some might opt for healthier eating choices, and some might actually choose to get involved in activist campaigns to expose the truth about their products and policies, fight for better pay for fast food workers, or exert pressure for more responsible environmental policies, better treatment of animals, regulations on fast food advertising to children, etc. As an exercise in critical pedagogy as well as critical media literacy, all along the way the project would proceed not through forcing students to memorize others' conclusions but by engaging them in dialogue, encouraging them to express their ideas and to do their own research and investigations.

We might contrast this holistic, dialogic approach to the banking approach to education as described by Postman and Weingartner:

> Now, what is it that students *do* in the classroom? Well, mostly, they sit and listen to the teacher. Mostly, they are required to believe in authorities, or at least pretend to such belief when they take tests. Mostly, they are required to remember. They are almost never required to make observations, formulate definitions, or perform any intellectual operations that go beyond repeating what someone else says is true.[55]

Critical media literacy based in a philosophy of critical pedagogy seeks to challenge these patterns while encouraging critical awareness, critical investigation, and critical action around issues of media, culture, and power. Is that a political act? You bet it is. And survival under the present conditions of neoliberal capitalism necessitates just this sort of politically engaged pedagogy.

## WHAT'S AT STAKE: NEOLIBERALISM AND CRITICAL MEDIA LITERACY

"Survival" is admittedly a strong word with powerful implications. In this section I will clarify why I believe this is indeed a matter of survival. To fully understand what is at stake when we are discussing critical pedagogy and critical media literacy, we have to first recognize that we are living in the age of an enormously destructive ideology of global neoliberalism. Secondly, we must appreciate the role that media play in reinforcing neoliberal ideologies and how critical media literacy can serve as a response.

Neoliberalism involves both ideologies and economic and political policies that establish the free market, hyperindividualism, and unfettered global capitalism as the supreme forces in all endeavors related to human life. In an essay published shortly after his death in 2014, Stuart Hall and his coauthors noted,

> For three decades, the neoliberal system has been generating vast profits for multi-nationals, investment institutions

and venture capitalists, and huge accumulations of wealth for the new global super-rich, while grossly increasing the gap between rich and poor and deepening inequalities of income, health and life chances within and between countries, on a scale not seen since before the second world war.[56]

Wendy Brown explains that neoliberalism must be understood as much more than just a capitalist economic policy, but rather as a "normative order of reason" that "transmogrifies every human domain and endeavor, along with humans themselves, according to a specific image of the economic."[57] Thomas Frank points to the emergence of neoliberalism in the US not in right-wing ideology but in the rise to power of Democratic technocrats in the 1980s. This represented a turning away from the traditional constituencies of the Democratic Party as the self-proclaimed neoliberals "blamed unions for the country's industrial problems, mourned all the waste involved in the Social Security program, and called for a war on public school teachers . . . whenever Democrats lost an election it was because their leaders were too weak on crime, too soft on communism, and too sympathetic to minorities . . . it was a bluntly pro-business force—friendly with lobbyists and funded by corporate backers . . ."[58]

Aided and abetted by a media system that embraced the dream of a technologically enhanced free market utopia, neoliberalism became the dominant force in the US and Europe at the end of the Cold War. Today it reigns supreme. In a 2015 interview, media studies and critical pedagogy scholar Henry Giroux explained what neoliberalism does to the public interest:

We're talking about an ideology marked by the selling off of public goods to private interests; the attack on social provisions; the rise of the corporate state organized around privatization, free trade, and deregulation; the celebration of self-interests over social needs; the claim that government is the problem if it gets in the way of profits for the megacorporations and financial services; the investing in prisons rather than schools; the modeling of education after the culture of business; the insistence that exchange values are the only values worthy of consideration; the celebration of profit-making as the essence of democracy coupled with the utterly reductionist notion that consumption is the only applicable form of citizenship. But even more than that, neoliberal ideology upholds the notion that the market serves as a model for structuring all social relations: not just the economy, but the governing of all social life.[59]

From the perspectives of democratic education and critical pedagogy, the purpose of education is to empower students to be thinking citizens, capable of embracing more than just market values. John Dewey's classic call for educational practices that prepare students to be actively engaged members of their communities should thus be a touchstone for critical media literacy.[60] As Masterman argues, "the expression of democratic interests is dependent upon the existence of an educated and informed public."[61] Contrary to this, however, as bell hooks points out, "the interests of big business and corporate capitalism encourage students to see education solely as a means to achieve material success."[62]

Tragically, in the era of imperial neoliberalism the success of the few is being paid for by the misery of the many. As a global society we are facing enormous challenges that have been wrought by decades of capitalism run wild. Dwindling natural resources, ethnic hatred and religious fundamentalism, and abuses by powerful despots (usually supported by the US) are resulting in devastating eruptions of violence around the world. While the wealthiest individuals on the planet continue to accumulate more and more treasure, the gap between the rich and the poor widens and the living conditions for the most desperate become increasingly cruel. The widespread dissemination of guns and violence domestically in the United States mirrors the proliferation of weaponry and state-sponsored terrorism by the American government abroad. Women are subjected to discrimination, misogyny, and sexual violence, while the mass incarceration and slaying of people of color by those who are sworn to "serve and protect" continues despite rising voices of outrage and protest. Governmental and corporate surveillance has become an accepted way of life for many who are placated by smartphones and social media feeds.

Meanwhile, the entire planet is facing the existential crisis of climate change, created by the very same capitalist forces that persist in denying the evidence that can no longer be denied by rational people. Importantly, the same corporate media institutions that provide us with pleasurable distractions play a key role in creating, reinforcing, justifying, and/or hiding most of these trends.

Countering these trends, critical pedagogy and critical media literacy should be understood as the natural enemies of neoliberalism. Critical pedagogy encourages independent thinking and action. Neoliberalism encourages conformity and passivity in the face of authority. Critical pedagogy advocates for fully participatory democracy. Neoliberalism hides behind a façade of democracy while promulgating totalitarian tendencies. Critical pedagogy is about building community and nurturing communal values. Neoliberalism celebrates hyperindividualism and glorifies self-interest. Critical pedagogy is based in an ethical commitment to justice for all. Neoliberalism is devoted to greed and rapacious accumulation whatever the cost.

Approaches to media literacy in the twenty-first century that are unwilling to challenge the neoliberal order are thus destined to be incomplete projects, because it is neoliberalism that is the driving force behind the corporations that dominate the media environment and the stories and imagery those corporations sell to global audiences.

Those stories are extremely influential because media culture performs as a form of public pedagogy that teaches us lessons about power, relationships, ethics, and values. As Carlos Cortés notes, "The mass media teach whether or not media makers intend to or realize it. And users learn from the media whether or not they try or are even aware of it . . . media serve as informal yet omnipresent nonschool textbooks."[63]

It is neoliberal values that are currently being taught across a range of media, from corporate cable news channels and websites; to "reality" television programs that celebrate the police while vilifying communities of color; to the glorification of war, greed, and materialism in Hollywood films; to the spectacles of violent misogyny and hypermasculinity in the best-selling video games; to the hyperindividualistic and consumerist messages that saturate advertising and the content that surrounds it; to the online pornography that teaches dangerous and degrading lessons about gender and sexuality; to the constant allure and intrusive surveillance of social media. Donald Macedo argues, "Because the media represent a mechanism for ideological control, educators need to understand that the popular press and mass media educate more people about issues related to our society and the world than all other sources of education."[64] Thomas Frank offers a mind-boggling example of the corporate media's embrace of neoliberal values and policies:

> The *New York Times* columnist Thomas Friedman has gone so far as to claim that free trade treaties are so good that supporting them doesn't require knowledge of their actual content. "I wrote a column supporting the CAFTA, the Caribbean [*sic*] Free Trade Initiative," he told Tim Russert in 2006. "I didn't even know what was in it. I just knew two words: free trade."[65]

The hyperindividualistic ideological values behind neoliberalism are also nakedly displayed in a recent commercial for a financial services company that features a well-known psychology professor (an expert in "happiness") encouraging us to get involved in a cause: "Today people are coming out to the nation's capitol to support an important cause that could change the way you live for years to come." What is that cause? Fighting climate change? Seeking social justice for people of color? Protesting corporate abuses of power? What can we do, Professor Gilbert?

The ad quickly answers those questions for us: "How can you help? By giving a little more . . . to yourself." We pause. Sorry, what was that? What cause are we talking about? Professor Gilbert answers, "The cause is retirement and today thousands of people came to the race for retirement and pledged to save an additional 1 percent of their income. If we all do that, we can all win."[66]

This, the ad tells us, is what is behind all of our problems: we don't give enough . . . to ourselves. We don't need beneficent government policies or assistance to ensure our safety and security in old age. If we would all just reach into our deep reserves of disposable income, "we can all win." Never mind that most of us owe much more than we have in assets or savings; that increasing numbers of even middle-class Americans are finding it impossible to fund their children's college education; that poverty, homelessness, and hunger are epidemic in the richest nation on the planet. A 2016 survey revealed that only 37 percent of Americans could rely on their savings to pay for an unexpected bill of $500–$1,000. At least 15 percent of Americans live in poverty, and that figure is based on the ridiculously stringent federal poverty standards, which state that in 2016 a family of four that earns $24,300 a year is not impoverished.[67] But in a seamless integration of education and media, a professor on my screen is telling me we can all win if we just practice fiscal restraint and sacrifice a bit in order to be secure in our old age. Wendy Brown identifies the notion of individual sacrifice to the larger economic order as a central aspect of life under neoliberalism: "Human capital for itself bears the responsibility of enhancing and securing its future; it is expected to self-invest wisely and is condemned for dependency."[68]

While this is a particularly blatant example, the ideology behind neoliberalism pervades the entire commercial media system, even down to the time-consuming video game apps on our mobile devices that seduce us into spending hour after hour crushing virtual candy or using exploding birds to kill those elusive pigs, instead of working on community projects, volunteering for schools or nonprofit organizations, getting involved in political campaigns or initiatives, or simply spending time connecting to our neighbors or reading and discussing literature or history, science, current affairs, etc. Giroux argues,

> This retreat into private silos has resulted in the inability of individuals to connect their personal suffering with larger public issues. Thus detached from any concept of the common good or viable vestige of the public realm, they are left to face alone a world of increasing precarity and uncertainty in which it becomes difficult to imagine anything other than how to survive. Under such circumstances, there is little room for thinking critically and acting collectively in ways that are imaginative and courageous.[69]

Faced with the anxiety that Giroux highlights, but bereft of a media system that encourages critical analysis or alternatives to the institutions and forces that have led us to the brink of public collapse, we are overcome by apprehension and fear and tempted to turn to authoritarian solutions that provide an unexamined sort of comfort.

## DECONSTRUCTING FEAR AND LOATHING IN THE CORPORATE MEDIA: CONCRETE EXAMPLES

As the work of the late media scholar George Gerbner demonstrated, for decades the promotion of fear by the media industries has been both a savvy marketing strategy and one of the most profound ways that news and popular culture have made an impact on society. Writing about how to understand the impact of mediated violence, Gerbner explained in his research findings that those who watch the most television

> develop a greater sense of apprehension, mistrust, and alienation, what we call the "mean world syndrome." Insecure, angry people may be prone to violence but are even more likely to be dependent on authority and susceptible to deceptively simple, strong hard-line postures. They may accept and even welcome repressive measures such as more jails, capital punishment, harsher sentences—measures that have never reduced crime but never fail to get votes—if that promises to relieve their anxieties.[70]

During the 2016 US presidential campaign, Donald Trump defied expectations and rose to the top of the Republican slate of candidates by relying on a rhetoric of fear, ethnocentrism, violence, and misogyny. While many corporate media commentators found Trump's appeal baffling, they also tracked his every word and public appearance with avid, if not rabid, enthusiasm as he quickly became the most covered political candidate, the one granted the most airtime, the one discussed the most on social media, and, as noted above, the one guaranteed to raise the ratings for televised debates and political talk shows. A critical media literacy approach is necessary to developing an understanding of the Trump candidacy as a media spectacle.

Drawing on the work of Guy Debord, Douglas Kellner describes media spectacles as

> [t]hose phenomena of media culture that embody contemporary society's basic values, serve to initiate individuals into its way of life, and dramatize its controversies and struggles, as well as its modes of conflict resolution. They include media extravaganzas, sporting events, political happenings, and those attention-grabbing occurrences that we call news—a phenomenon that itself has been subjected to the logic of spectacle and tabloidization in the era of media sensationalism, political scandal and contestation, seemingly unending cultural war, and the new phenomenon of Terror War.[71]

Kellner points out that the US presidency itself has become a media spectacle, and just as Hollywood movies can either triumph and fail, so too can presidencies and political campaigns. While Trump's presentation of himself as the great white savior, coming to "Make America Great Again," enthralled many angry Republican voters, at times his persona faltered with the wider public because of the naked rage that it seemed carefully designed to exploit. The most successful neoliberal projects are generally those that can masquerade as benign: the Obama/Clinton softness that disguises the hardcore corporate imperialism behind the curtain. While Trump blustered like a WWE cartoon, the face of neoliberalism in media culture is often more Tom Hanks than Clint Eastwood. And, indeed, a rich example of a Hollywood-produced neoliberal spectacle designed to turn Western global fears into profit is Hanks's 2013 film *Captain Phillips*.

Ostensibly a true story of the hijacking of an American cargo ship by Somali pirates, *Captain Phillips* depicts a world where good-hearted American businessmen find themselves at the mercy of dark-skinned marauders. Depicted as a loving family man, concerned about his children's future, Captain Phillips is just trying to earn a living when pirates take over his ship and hold him hostage. Physically inferior to the athletic, violent invaders, Phillips must summon all his courage and superior wits to protect his crew and cargo, and, metaphorically, save American white masculinity from the dark forces that threaten its global hegemony. Though constantly met by violence, Hanks portrays Phillips as a kind man, willing to provide medical assistance even to those who threaten and abuse him. Right up until the final moments of the film, he displays compassion and empathy as he tries to reason with the hijackers in order to save their lives. When he believes he might die, he touchingly proclaims his love for his wife. When the US Navy arrives in all its technological glory, with giant ships and helicopters, the audience is reassured. The cavalry is here. All will be set right in the world.

Despite a few throwaway lines about the desperation of life in Somalia, the film mostly ignores the forces of imperialism and global exploitation that brought the real Captain Phillips into contact with Africa. A quintessential neoliberal text, distributed globally by huge media conglomerates Disney, Sony, and Columbia and Universal Pictures working in collaboration with each other, *Captain Phillips* cost $55 million to make and has grossed over $200 million since its 2013 release. By comparison, the United Nations in 2012 estimated Somalia's per capita GDP to be $284. More than 40 percent of the nation's population lives on less than one US dollar per day. Tom Hanks was reportedly paid $15 million to play Captain Phillips. For many who saw the film in the US and Europe, this Hollywood tale of American good threatened by African evil is one of their few referents for any information about Somalia, a nation that is largely ignored by the corporate news media.

Writing about racial ideologies in media and popular culture, Stuart Hall noted that in contrast to the early days of film, racism is now much more likely to be inferential than overt. He describes inferential racism as "apparently naturalized representations of events and situations relating to race, whether 'factual' or 'fictional,' which have racist premises and propositions inscribed in them as a set of *unquestioned assumptions.*"[72] Hall's analysis of how contemporary media contain the traces of past moments of overt racism could not be a more apt description of the binary conflict of *Captain Phillips*:

Popular culture is still full today of countless savage and restless "natives," . . . They are likely to appear at any moment out of the darkness to . . . eat the innocent explorer or colonial administrator . . . against them is always counterposed the isolated white figure, alone "out there," confronting his Destiny and shouldering his Burden in the "heart of darkness," displaying coolness under fire and an unshakeable authority . . .[73]

And while this example is powerful, it is not just fictionalized tales of the US encountering Africa that commercial media use to represent the stark contrast between black and white.

Let's consider media coverage of the Black Lives Matter movement that first emerged after the slaying of Trayvon Martin and the subsequent acquittal of his murderer, George Zimmerman, in 2012. The Black Lives Matter movement embodies the spirit of critical media literacy in its attention to both communication and social justice:

When we say Black Lives Matter, we are broadening the conversation around state violence to include all of the ways in which Black people are intentionally left powerless at the hands of the state. We are talking about the ways in which Black lives are deprived of our basic human rights and dignity . . . #BlackLivesMatter is working for a world where Black lives are no longer systematically and intentionally targeted for demise. We affirm our contributions to this society, our humanity, and our resilience in the face of deadly oppression. We have put our sweat equity and love for Black people into creating a political project—taking the hashtag off of social media and into the streets.[74]

While #BlackLivesMatter is a peaceful protest movement, many voices on the political right and in the corporate media have framed it as a violent, even terrorist, organization. A critical media literacy lens can provide a useful corrective to the mediated discourse surrounding this movement, while placing it in a historical context related to previous social movements that have also been misrepresented, ridiculed, and demeaned by commercial media institutions.

In a new preface to a reissue of his classic study of media coverage of the Vietnam-era protests that he had taken part in, Todd Gitlin noted,

> I wrote *The Whole World is Watching* [1980] out of a wrenching sense of discrepancy—a shock of misrecognition. It was the shock you feel when you discover that what others think they know about you is not what you know, or think you know, about yourself—indeed that what others presume to know is the opposite of what you know. For people in the public eye, this feeling of misrecognition has become one of the common experiences of a media-saturated age.[75]

Activists in the Black Lives Matter movement might also feel this "shock of misrecognition" when they see themselves dissected and distorted by largely white commentators on white-owned, white-run, white-funded cable news outlets. Commercial news media in 2015 blamed the Black Lives Matter movement for encouraging violence against the police, claiming that attacks on police were increasing when in fact they have been decreasing for decades.[76] Some featured commentators have labeled the movement a hate group and a terrorist organization, compared them to the Ku Klux Klan and Nazis, and used the terms "garbage" and "sub-human creeps" when referring to activists.[77]

Gitlin's original study revealed how the commercial news media had framed war protestors in the 1960s as a threat to national security and an affront to patriotic Americans. In the reissue of his book, he notes that news media still seek out isolated moments of violence during otherwise peaceful protests. This violent frame is coupled with what Gitlin calls news "blackouts and deprecations of dissent"[78] to first ignore, then ridicule, and finally demonize protest movements like those that shook Ferguson, Missouri, and other communities around the US as the Black Lives Matter message began to spread throughout the nation.

The public relies on media to provide them with information about issues and events they don't experience directly. However, Frechette, Higdon, and Williams report the results of multiple surveys providing evidence that the corporate media system has led to a public that is largely uninformed or misinformed about key public affairs issues.[79] Miller points out that corporate media have largely abandoned investigative journalism, international coverage, and serious public affairs programming in favor of crime, celebrity, and consumer "news."[80] Even more than this lack of information, commercial media institutions also promote disinformation campaigns such as the one being waged against the Black Lives Matter movement.

"Disinformation is a form of propaganda disseminated by world leaders and media outlets, with an aim to plant false ideas in the public discourse to fulfill an ulterior motive."[81] Critical media literacy is required to combat disinformation, and the Black Lives Matter movement exemplifies this approach through not only deconstructing the distorted messaging of the corporate media, but also by utilizing digital and social media to create their own alternatives to the stories told by the commercial press, while simultaneously working to confront and transform oppressive institutions. Along the way, the Black Lives Matter movement demonstrates the necessary connections between media education and social justice.

## CRITICAL MEDIA LITERACY, TRANSFORMATIVE EDUCATION, AND SOCIAL JUSTICE

A key distinguishing mark of the critical media literacy paradigm is a concern for social justice that inspires and underscores the work of critical media educators, scholars, artists, and activists. Lawrence Frey et al. understand social justice work as being devoted to "the engagement with and advocacy for those in our society who are economically, socially, politically, and/or culturally underresourced."[82] Resistance to the current economic, social, political, and cultural conditions that severely privilege small numbers of the fortunate few while relegating others to lives of diminished resources and possibilities is a necessary component of a critical approach that rejects idealistic notions of pluralistic opportunity and mythic notions of hyperindividualism that portray every human as equally free to prosper and thrive in a libertarian dreamscape of absolute agency and free will. In contrast to these fictions pulled from the twisted mind of Ayn Rand, real human beings inhabit political environments dominated by wealth and corporate power, where those on the outside find their interests and concerns ignored, ridiculed, and/or disparaged by the commercial media system and establishment politics. Frey et al. also argue for more than just critical analysis of injustice, stating that a "social justice sensibility entails a moral imperative to act as effectively as we can to do something about structurally sustained inequalities."[83] A social justice approach thus challenges race, class, and gender inequities while working to transform conditions that marginalize, oppress, and attack people of color, women, sexual minorities, the elderly and/or disabled, and the poor and working classes.

Critical media literacy draws inspiration from feminism, critical race theory, and Marxism, among other radical frameworks, and it applies the lessons of activists, educators, artists, and scholars in those traditions to the analysis of media and popular culture texts and institutions that justify, legitimize, and reinforce cultural, social, political, and economic inequalities. More than just analysis, however, all of these perspectives emphasize the need for action as well as interpretation. For example, writing about feminist media studies, Liesbet van Zoonen notes,

> It is the reciprocal relation between theory, politics and activism, the commitment of feminist academics to have their work contribute to a larger feminist goal (however defined), the blurred line between the feminist as academic and the feminist as activist, that distinguishes feminist perspectives on the media from other possible perspectives.[84]

Inspired by the insights of feminism, critical media literacy practitioners thus challenge media institutions, images, and narratives and the part they play in promoting patriarchal social norms and misogyny. From deconstructing images of homogenized beauty in advertising, to blogging about issues of gender identity and social media, to questioning the equation of violence and masculinity in video games, to organizing protests about discriminatory hiring and compensation practices in the news and entertainment industries, to creating alternative media that treat LGBTQ individuals and communities with dignity and respect, to fighting against porn culture, feminist approaches to critical media literacy shine a spotlight on myriad issues of gender and sexuality in media and popular culture, in order to advance more equitable gender relations.

More broadly, a feminist approach to media education highlights how some voices are dominant in media while others are marginalized or excluded, and that what is considered neutral cultural knowledge is in fact wrapped up in issues of power. Thus, feminist standpoint theory shows that those who live in conditions of oppression are more likely to critically understand unjust hierarchal structures but are less likely to have their insights acknowledged and respected by the dominant forces in society.[85]

By way of example, feminist critical media literacy addresses the relationship between hegemonic masculinity and militarism, and offers a critical analysis of the many ways that media and popular culture equate masculinity with domination, domination with violence, and violence with heroism. Thus, Hollywood films are more likely to celebrate than critique warfare,[86] and candidates for the most powerful political office in the world perform masculinity by suggesting that terrorists should be shot with bullets dipped in the blood of pigs (Donald Trump),[87] or threaten to "carpet-bomb them into oblivion" until Middle Eastern sands "glow in the dark" (Ted Cruz). [88] During the 2015–16 primary season, political rhetoric descended to new lows of hypermasculine posturing, with one candidate egging on an audience member who shouted out that his opponent was a "pussy" (Donald Trump),[89] another making a thinly veiled reference to his rival's small penis (Marco Rubio),[90] and a third bragging (lying?) about spending his teenage years throwing rocks and bricks at people and claiming that he once stabbed someone with a knife (Ben Carson).[91;92] While violent episodes targeting primarily women and people of color were erupting at Trump rallies, the commercial media at first treated this all as a sideshow, a fun-filled entertainment spectacle. This tabloid coverage persisted until elite groups began to fret and their concerns eventually resulted in too-little, too-late "soul searching" by the same corporate media that continued to offer nonstop coverage of Trump, even while lamenting nonstop coverage of Trump.

In addition to highlighting the valorization of patriarchy and violence in media culture, because feminism emphasizes an ethics of care that stresses compassion, connection, community, and our responsibilities to others,[93] bringing a feminist sensibility to media education may also aid in what Antonio López has called the necessary "greening of media education," by heightening our awareness of the relationship between the commercial media system that promotes consumerism and disposability and the environmental destruction humans are wreaking on the planet. López notes: "Ultimately the goal of ecomedia literacy is to encourage mindfulness for how everyday media practice impacts our ability to live sustainably within earth's ecological parameters for the present and future."[94]

Adding another dimension to the social justice emphasis of critical media literacy, critical race theory encourages educators to confront the many ways that media reinforce ethnocentrism, white privilege, and white supremacy. Emerging in the 1970s in the work of legal scholars like Derrick Bell,

> The critical race theory (CRT) movement is a collection of activists and scholars interested in studying and transforming the relationship among race, racism, and power. The movement considers many of the same issues that conventional civil rights and ethnic studies discourses take up, but places them in a broader perspective that includes economics, history, context, group- and self-interest, and even feelings and the unconscious . . . Unlike some academic disciplines, critical race theory contains an activist dimension. It not only tries to understand our social situation, but to change it . . .[95]

Thus, a dialogue with students in a critical media literacy class might ask them to undertake a comparative analysis of media coverage of the 2016 attacks in Brussels and Lahore. Both seem to have been carried out by extremist fundamentalists, both resulted in multiple deaths and misery, but one occurred in Europe and the other in Asia. Why did the attack in Belgium, which resulted in the death of thirty-five people, warrant days of nonstop coverage and mournful special reports while the attack in Pakistan just days later, where over twice as many people were killed, was just another news item reported by US media in March? As media critics have pointed out, this discrepancy was not a one-off occurrence but a pattern in Western media.[96]

Critical race scholars have argued that ethnocentrism, stereotyping, racism, and white privilege are endemic in the US and Europe and must be recognized as normal and indeed functional for those groups that benefit from white supremacy.[97] Funk, Kellner, and Share note: "Discrimination against people of color in the US is also accompanied by underrepresentation and misrepresentations of them in media. While the statistics of incarceration and school suspension among Blacks could be used to highlight the shameful state of race relations in America today, they are instead often exploited by media to attract audiences and increase profit."[98]

Applying critical race theory to media provides a useful way of addressing, and seeking to transform, the ways corporate media promote white supremacy while simultaneously trying to convince the public that it no longer exists. The two examples offered earlier in this chapter, *Captain Phillips* and news coverage of the Black Lives Matter movement, both demonstrate how seeing media through the lens of critical race theory can help illuminate the oft-overlooked white supremacist tendencies in corporate media.

Critical race theory can also play an important role in analysis of the digital technologies that are providing both corporations and governments new and unparalleled avenues for surveillance and domination. People of color have long been aware that they are more closely watched by the police and other representatives of what Althusser called the "Repressive State Apparatus," and that this surveillance has been used to attack and reign in dissenters.[99] Throughout the latter half of the twentieth century, the FBI's COINTELPRO infiltrated the civil rights and peace movements, waged a smear campaign against Martin Luther King Jr., attempted to destroy the Nation of Islam and the Black Panther Party from within, and spied on and ultimately bombed the Philadelphia-based black liberation group, MOVE. A technologically enhanced surveillance campaign is now being used against the Black Lives Matter movement.[100] These examples illustrate the panoptic conditions citizens of supposedly free societies live in, and this has never been more the case than in the era of social media, mobile technologies, and the "always connected" online life-style.

Finally, drawing on the Marxist tradition I described earlier in this chapter allows critical media literacy scholars, educators, activists, and artists to further engage with issues of poverty, economic inequality, disempowerment, and class as they play out in the media environment. Scholars have pointed out, for example, how US television has consistently framed the working class as idiotic, lazy, tasteless, and violent for decades,[101] even as the television industry itself has experienced both economic and technological changes on a grand scale: "On the whole, dominant media such as film and television often celebrate the rich and powerful while presenting negative representations of poor and working people. Traditionally, US television focused on middle and upper class families, and professionals like doctors, lawyers, or corporate executives, while tending to ignore working class life and poor people."[102]

These omissions and distortions offer the viewing public an implicit rationale for why inequality will always persist, why social programs meant to combat poverty are doomed to failure, and why those on the lower end of the economic spectrum are responsible for their own misery. A critical media literacy lens informed by Marxist insights into the machinations of modern-day capitalism thus advances the understanding that amusing forms of popular culture like television comedies, dramas, and "reality" programs are in fact much more than "just entertainment," but actually function as popular pedagogy that instructs us about our proper places in the social hierarchy.

Moreover, as Marxist media scholars like Dallas Smythe and Sut Jhally have argued, while we are consuming media we are actually working for the entertainment industries.[103] The time we spend watching television, for example, is that industry's primary source of profit, as our attention is sold to advertisers and converted into revenue for the corporations that own the television networks. In the era of digital media, as the critical social media scholar Christian Fuchs has pointed out, the same economic strategy is employed even more intensely by companies like Facebook, who rely on users to not only consume the advertising that accompanies the content but to actually create the content itself when they post status updates, comments, photos, and videos.[104] What really counts is the private data we share and the time we spend interacting with targeted commercial messaging, which is increasingly integrated throughout the entire corporate media environment.

A side benefit for corporate interests is that the glorification of consumerism and material wealth on display not just in the advertising but in the content that surrounds, and is increasingly thoroughly integrated with, all the ads, provides an implicit promotion of capitalism while situating the interests of the wealthy as primary and framing the concerns of the less fortunate, including the poor, the elderly, and the disabled, as irrelevant, if not invisible. A form of critical media literacy informed by socialist and feminist principles of sharing, communalism, and equity thus offers insights into why, for example, the *New York Times* has a "Wealth" section but not a "Poverty" section or even a "Labor" section.

Despite these bleak realities, a critical approach to media, education, and social justice can find a sense of purpose in Antonio Gramsci's call for "pessimism of the intellect, optimism of the will."[105] Sut Jhally explains this as a dialectic approach to critical work:

> "Pessimism of the intellect" means recognizing the reality of our present circumstances, analyzing the vast forces arrayed against us, but insisting on the possibilities and the moral desirability of social change that is "the optimism of the will," believing in human values that will be the inspiration for us to struggle for our survival.[106]

When we utilize all of the critical frameworks discussed above and incorporate an intersectionalist approach into critical media literacy education by engaging simultaneously with issues of gender, race, class, sexuality, nationality, age, ability, and more, we position media literacy as not just another subject to be taught in schools but as a social movement, one that is aimed at empowering socially aware and engaged communities, not just better consumers. The goal is, admittedly, big. Truly critical media literacy aims not just to analyze media content but to transform media . . . and the world.

# THE CITIZEN/CONSUMER QUESTION: HOLISTIC, CONTEXTUAL, AND TRANSFORMATIVE MEDIA EDUCATION

> *"A democratic civilization will save itself only if it makes the language of the image into a stimulus for critical reflection— not an invitation for hypnosis."*
>
> —Umberto Eco[107]

According to the Yale Program on Climate Change Communication, while 97 percent of the published research on climate change supports the conclusion that the planet is warming due to human activities, in 2015 only 52 percent of registered voters believe that climate change is caused primarily by humans, and one in three don't believe that it is happening at all.[108] A recent documentary film, *Merchants of Doubt*, based on a book by the same name, presents evidence that this gap between scientific understanding and public opinion is mostly due to a carefully engineered and well-funded communications strategy, sponsored by conservative think tanks and the fossil fuel industries, to plant disinformation in the media and thus seed doubt in the public mind.[109] The commercial news media have largely capitulated to this systematic distortion of the truth by presenting "both sides of the story" in the name of objective reporting.

One version of media literacy might approach this issue by focusing on media content through an examination of the words and images that are used in news reports, advertising and public relations materials, and both documentary and dramatic films that deal with climate change and its consequences. This would, in fact, be a useful place to start. Contrary to what bastardized versions of Marshall McLuhan's theories about media technology would suggest—yes, the medium is the message, but the message is also the message. In other words, while the medium of delivery (television or social media, print or film, etc.) is important, the content of media does indeed matter. Words matter, images matter, stories matter.

The approach critical media literacy scholars and educators advocate for does not preclude textual analysis of media content and the deconstruction of messaging as part of a larger critical process of media education. Paying careful attention to media stories and images is not the problem. The problem is that too much of what is called "media literacy" stops at that point. Lewis and Jhally believe that this is a relatively straightforward issue:

> The argument we wish to make is, in essence, a simple one: Media literacy should be about helping people to become sophisticated citizens rather than sophisticated consumers. The mass media, in other words, should be understood as more than a collection of texts to be deconstructed and analyzed so that we can distinguish or choose among them. They should be analyzed as sets of institutions with particular social and economic structures that are neither inevitable nor irreversible. Media education should certainly teach students to engage media texts, but it should also, in our view, teach them to engage and challenge media institutions.[110]

To return to the example above, a critical media literacy approach to the discrepancy between what climate scientists and the general public know about climate change might start with an analysis of the public relations messages of the fossil fuel industries and their political allies, but it would also move beyond this to a political economic analysis of the institutions behind this messaging, and a cultural analysis of the impact that decades of disinformation have had on public opinion and public policy. An assignment might focus on the creation of alternative media that allows students to present their own take on the relationship between media and climate change. Some students might create culture-jamming projects that expose the deceitfulness of the fossil fuel industries and their strategic communication campaigns. Others might choose to get involved in green activism or local environmental organizations. The introduction of these last few elements is where many in the field of media literacy bail out.

As we near two decades since the publication of the piece Lewis and Jhally called "The Struggle for Media Literacy," it appears that the argument is not as simple as they had hoped. What they proposed at the end of the twentieth century is still derided by many, even those involved in national media literacy organizations, as "too political . . . not the job of teachers . . . bashing the media." Some have even argued that media literacy should not be focused on media at all because it should really only be about the technical skills of literacy more broadly imagined: learning to read an advertisement to see what techniques are used to construct it, just as one would learn to dissect the rhythms and symbolism of a poem in a traditional classroom exercise.[111]

There is nothing wrong with a textual approach to media literacy in and of itself. Arriving at a sophisticated understanding of media texts is a crucial part of critical media literacy. But to go further we also have to understand the context of media messages. Just as Freire and Macedo refer to literacy as both "reading the word and the world,"[112] Lewis and Jhally insist that

> [m]edia literacy, in short, is about more than the analysis of messages, it is about an awareness of why those messages are there. It is not enough to know that they are produced— or even how, in a technical sense, they are produced. To appreciate the significance of contemporary media, we need to know why they are produced, under what constraints and conditions they are produced, and by whom they are produced.[113]

If media educators stop at the level of the text, they may successfully encourage students to become better consumers of media, but critical media literacy is about more than consumption. Some versions of media literacy treat media education as a type of "media appreciation" curriculum, where students are taught to get more out of their media use and to learn how to amplify the pleasures that media produce. While pleasure is indeed important—in fact it is the key to why popular culture is so compelling and is such a powerful force in our lives—pleasurable sensations are not the only thing that media produce. As Postman pointed out, entertainment in the media age has subsumed all other possible ways of relating to the social worlds we inhabit.[114]

Drawing on Teresa Ebert and Mas'ud Zavarzadeh's work, McLaren distinguishes between a pedagogy of desire and a pedagogy of critique, noting, "The pedagogy of desire is about the thrill of corporeal pleasure; it mirrors the conditions of alienated capitalism, because, in reality, the pedagogy of desire is about teaching adjustment to existing social relations . . . not about a commitment to build a more just society."[115] While critical media educators should acknowledge the pleasures that media can provide, if we fall into the seductive trap of a celebratory relationship to the products of the commercial media industries, we run the risk of abandoning the critical edge that makes media education important in the first place. We should consciously ask ourselves: Why do we engage in media literacy education and projects at all? What is the point? Who and what is media literacy for?

Writing specifically about Europe at the end of the twentieth century, Masterman's powerful warning and challenge is applicable globally, and perhaps even more relevant in the age of digital media than it was when he first penned these words:

> One of the greatest areas of inequality across Europe lies in the gap which exists between those who have access to the media and those who do not, between those who have the power to define and those who are always defined, between those who are allowed to speak about the world as they know and understand it and those whose experiences are inevitably framed for them by others. The development of a widespread critical consciousness in relation to media issues must, we believe, be one of the starting points for challenging these inequalities and raising questions about the democratic structures and responsibilities of broadcasting, and questions of human rights in relation to communication issues.[116]

A critical approach to media education is thus focused on equality, democracy, community, and citizenship rather than material accumulation, hyperindividualism, and consumerism. Fully engaged citizens have an interest in the world that extends beyond the marketplace and into the commons that we all must inhabit. Citizens know that being an active member of a functioning society means more than just showing up to vote every few years. Citizens recognize that we are all interconnected and that the communities we live in will only be as democratic, healthy, and just as we make them. Sophisticated media consumers might do a better job of seeing through the deceptions of advertising and making better choices as individuals, but engaged citizens will work to improve the environmental and social conditions that affect us all.[117] Furthermore, Peter McLaren and Rhonda Hammer insist that we must "understand the dangers in considering literacy to be a private or individual competency . . . rather than a complex circulation of economic, political, and ideological practices that inform daily life; that invite or solicit students to acquiesce in their social and gendered positions within a highly stratified society . . ."[118]

The work of media and pedagogy scholar Henry Giroux exemplifies what it means to recognize the connections between citizenship and literacy, pedagogy and media, and social justice and true democracy, and why transformative education is a necessity in the age of neoliberalism. Seeing education as a form of activism, Giroux recognizes both the enormity of the struggles and the limitations on what can be accomplished, as well as the hope and possibilities for achieving real change. He writes,

> While it is true that critical thinking will not in and of itself change the nature of existing society, engaging in an intellectual struggle with the death-driven rationality that now fuels neoliberal capitalism will set the foundation for producing generations of young people who might launch a larger social movement. Such a movement will enable new forms of struggle and, it can be hoped, a new future in which questions of justice, dignity, equality, and compassion matter.[119]

Contrary to being political indoctrination, the approach I have argued for in this chapter should be recognized as unavoidable for any who advocate for forms of literacy that enable free thinking even when we are confronted by tidal waves of governmental and corporate propaganda. Macedo explicitly challenges "educators who falsely believe that education is neutral and is limited to the confines of the classroom."[120] He distinguishes critical education from faux notions of literacy when he writes that "[e]ducators need to courageously reject forms of literacy based on a web of lies . . . Educators need to forcefully expose forms of literacy designed to infuse people with permanent fear under the cover of security . . . Educators not only need to understand the government-media-education nexus in the 'manufacture of consent,' but they must also create pedagogical structures that produce individuals with conviction, ethical posture, courage to speak to power, and willingness to change . . ."[121]

The world of media is not the same as it was when the public had to rely on the daily newspaper, a couple of magazines, the local movie theater, a little bit of radio, and the three major television networks for the majority of their news and entertainment, and the only way to talk back to media was to write a letter to an editor or television producer who would probably never read it. Although really not long ago, this world now seems like the distant past, and it is never coming back. Funk, Kellner, and Share note that "[t]echnology's exponential growth, as well as the convergence of media corporations and new media platforms, are changing society and students to be more mediated and networked than ever."[122]

Young people today grow up in a digital media environment that allows for more choices and more participation, but youth are also more targeted by media, and they still can only participate within the constraints of what the government and the big media and technology giants will ultimately allow. As Kellner and Share point out, "The new technologies of communication are powerful tools that can liberate or dominate, manipulate or enlighten, and it is imperative that educators teach their students how to critically analyze and use these media."[123]

Contrary to Margaret Thatcher's insistence that "there is no alternative" to the capitalist world order, critical media literacy insists on exploring a wide range of alternatives: alternative readings of media content, alternative relationships to corporate media industries, the creation and distribution of alternative media, alternative understandings of the cultural, economic, political, and social conditions we live in, alternative ways of relating to one another as full human beings worthy of dignity and equitable treatment. If we look closely we can find an undercurrent of alternative thought and practices running through the digital and social media that consumes young people's lives in the twenty-first century. Kellner and Share correctly suggest that latter day techno-capitalism has inadvertently placed the digital tools that may be used to challenge its deepest ideologies in the hands of youth around the globe.[124]

But tools can only do so much. More than just tools, a truly democratic society that is committed to social justice needs a critical understanding of both the pitfalls and potential of the new media environment. Wendy Brown contends that "puncturing common neoliberal sense and . . . developing a viable and compelling alternative to capitalist globalization . . . bears no immediate reward, and carries no guarantee of success. Yet, what, apart from this work, could afford the slightest hope for a just, sustainable, and habitable future?"[125]

In the current media-saturated era of neoliberalism and hyper-consumerism; ravaging inequality; capitalism run amok; devastating religious-, ethnic-, and gender-based violence; and an ecological environment on the verge of collapse, rather than being afraid of truly critical media literacy, we should embrace it as truly necessary . . . now more than ever.

---

BILL YOUSMAN, PHD, earned his doctorate in Communication and Media Studies from the University of Massachusetts, Amherst. He is the former managing director of the Media Education Foundation and the current director of the graduate program in Media Literacy and Digital Culture at Sacred Heart University. His first book, *Prime Time Prisons on U.S. TV: Representation of Incarceration*, was published in 2008. His most recent book is *The Spike Lee Enigma: Challenge and Incorporation in Media Culture*.

*Special thanks to Project Censored intern Brandy Miceli for additional editing and citations.*

## Notes

1   bell hooks, *Teaching Critical Thinking: Practical Wisdom* (New York: Routledge, 2010), 1.

2   David Buckingham, *Media Education: Literacy, Learning and Contemporary Culture* (Cambridge, UK/Malden, MA: Polity, 2003).

3   Chris M. Worsnop, "The Future of Media Education," *Visions/Revisions: Moving Forward with Media Education*, eds. Barry Duncan and Kathleen Tyner (Madison, WI: National Telemedia Council, 2003), 180.

4   Rashmi Luthra, "Media Education Toward a More Equitable World," *Rethinking Media Education: Critical Pedagogy and Identity Politics*, eds. Anita Nowak, Sue Abel, and Karen Ross (Creskill, NJ: Hampton Press, 2007), 204.

5 Steven Funk, Douglas Kellner, and Jeff Share, "Critical Media Literacy as Transformative Pedagogy," *Handbook of Research on Media Literacy in the Digital Age*, eds. Melda N. Yildiz and Jared Keengwe (Hershey, PA: Information Science Reference, 2016), 4.

6 Justin Lewis and Sut Jhally, "The Struggle for Media Literacy," *The Spectacle of Accumulation: Essays in Culture, Media, and Politics*, Sut Jhally (New York: Peter Lang, 2006), 229.

7 Ibid., 236.

8 Paulo Freire, *Education for Critical Consciousness* (London: Continuum, 2008), 49.

9 Steven Funk, Douglas Kellner, and Jeff Share, "Critical Media Literacy as Transformative Pedagogy," 23.

10 Karl Marx and Friedrich Engels, *The German Ideology*, ed. C. J. Arthur (New York: International Publishers, 1981 [1846]), 64.

11 Hanno Hardt, *Critical Communication Studies: Communication, History and Theory in America* (London: Routledge, 1992).

12 Todd Gitlin, "Media Sociology: The Dominant Paradigm," *Theory and Society* 6, no. 2 (1978), 205–53.

13 Ibid.

14 Theodor W. Adorno, "Scientific Experiences of a European Scholar in America," *The Intellectual Migration: Europe and America, 1930–1960*, eds. Donald Fleming and Bernard Bailyn (Cambridge, MA: Harvard University Press, 1969), 343.

15 Max Horkheimer and Theodor W. Adorno, *Dialectic of Enlightenment*, tr. John Cumming (New York: Continuum, 1972).

16 Ibid., 120.

17 Ibid., 131.

18 Douglas Kellner, *Media Culture: Cultural Studies, Identity and Politics between the Modern and the Postmodern* (Abingdon, UK/New York: Routledge, 1995), 30.

19 Louis Althusser, *Lenin and Philosophy and Other Essays* (New York: Monthly Review Press, 1971).

20 Antonio Gramsci, *Selections from the Prison Notebooks*, eds. and trs. Quintin Hoare and Geoffrey Nowell Smith (New York: International Publishers, 1971).

21 Douglas Kellner and Jeff Share, "Critical Media Literacy, Democracy, and the Reconstruction of Education," *Media Literacy: A Reader*, eds. Donald Macedo and Shirley R. Steinberg (New York: Peter Lang, 2007), 11.

22 Patricia Aufderheide, *The Daily Planet: A Critic on the Capitalist Culture Beat* (Minneapolis, MN: University of Minnesota Press, 2000).

23 Steven Funk, Douglas Kellner, and Jeff Share, "Critical Media Literacy as Transformative Pedagogy," 2.

24 Shirley R. Steinberg and Joe L. Kincheloe, introduction to *Rethinking Media Literacy: A Critical Pedagogy of Representation*, eds. Peter McLaren, Rhonda Hammer, David Sholle, and Susan Reilly (New York: Peter Lang, 1995), 5.

25 Julie Frechette, Nolan Higdon, and Rob Williams, "A Vision for Transformative Civic Engagement: The Global Critical Media Literacy Project," *Censored 2016: Media Freedom on the Line*, eds. Mickey Huff, Andy Lee Roth, and Project Censored (New York: Seven Stories Press, 2015), 205.

26 Robert W. McChesney, *Digital Disconnect: How Capitalism is Turning the Internet Against Democracy* (New York: The New Press, 2013), 13.

27 Kim Masters, *Keys to the Kingdom: The Rise of Michael Eisner and the Fall of Everybody Else* (New York: William Morrow, 2003).

28 Christine Y. Chen, "The Bad Boys of Radio Lowry Mays and Sons Made Enemies Building Clear Channel into an Empire. Now they want to tell the world they're not . . . ," *Fortune*, March 3, 2003, http://archive.fortune.com/magazines/fortune/fortune_archive/2003/03/03/338343/index.htm.

29 Maria Bartiromo, "Exclusive Interview with Google's Eric Schmidt," CNBC, April 30, 2008, http://www.cnbc.com/id/24387350.

30  Nick Visser, "CBS Chief Les Moonves Says Trump's 'Damn Good' For Business," *Huffington Post*, March 1, 2016, http://www.huffingtonpost.com/entry/les-moonves-donald-trump_us_56d52ce8e4b03260bf780275.

31  Lori Bindig and James Castonguay, "Should I Really Kill My Television? Negotiating Common Ground Among Media Literacy Scholars, Educators, and Activists," *Media Literacy Education in Action: Theoretical and Pedagogical Perspectives*, eds. Belinha S. De Abreu and Paul Mihailidis (Abingdon, UK/New York: Routledge, 2014), 142.

32  Sut Jhally and Jeremy Earp, "Empowering Literacy: Media Education as a Democratic Impera- tive," *The Spectacle of Accumulation: Essays in Culture, Media, and Politics*, ed. Sut Jhally (New York: Peter Lang, 2006), 252.

33  See "Mission," Action Coalition for Media Education (ACME), no date, https://acmesmart- mediaeducation.net/our-mission/; and "About the GCMLP," Global Critical Media Literacy Project (GCMLP), no date, http://gcml.org/about-the-gcmlp/. Full disclosure: I serve on the Boards of both ACME and GCMLP. GCMLP is a partnership of Project Censored, ACME, and the Media Literacy and Digital Culture (MLDC) graduate program that I direct at Sacred Heart University.

34  Ha-Joon Chang, *23 Things They Don't Tell You About Capitalism* (New York: Bloomsbury Press, 2010), xv.

35  bell hooks, *The Will to Change: Men, Masculinity, and Love* (New York: Atria, 2004), 17.

36  Shirley R. Steinberg and Peter McLaren, "Shirley Steinberg Interviews Peter McLaren," *Rethinking Media Literacy: A Critical Pedagogy of Representation*, eds. Peter McLaren, Rhonda Hammer, David Sholle, and Susan Reilly (New York: Peter Lang, 1995), 255.

37  Howard Zinn, *Howard Zinn: You Can't Be Neutral on a Moving Train*, DVD. Directed by Deb Ellis and Denis Mueller (New York: First Run Features, 2004).

38  Len Masterman, "A Rationale for Media Education," *Media Literacy in the Information Age: Cur- rent Perspectives, Information and Behavior, Volume 6*, ed. Robert Kubey (New Brunswick, NJ: Transaction Publishers, 2001), 31.

39  Vivian Vasquez, *Getting Beyond "I Like the Book": Creating Space for Critical Literacy in K–6 Classrooms* (Newark, NJ: International Reading Association, 2003), 15.

40  Len Masterman, "A Rationale for Media Education," 32.

41  Peter McLaren, *Pedagogy of Insurrection: From Resurrection to Revolution* (New York: Peter Lang, 2015), 24.

42  Deanna L. Fassett and John T. Warren, *Critical Communication Pedagogy* (Thousand Oaks, CA: Sage, 2007), 26.

43  Peter McLaren, *Pedagogy of Insurrection: From Resurrection to Revolution*, 11.

44  Karl Marx and Friedrich Engels, *The German Ideology*, 64.

45  Paulo Freire, *Education for Critical Consciousness*, 43.

46  bell hooks, *Teaching Critical Thinking: Practical Wisdom*, 27.

47  Paulo Freire, *Pedagogy of the Oppressed* (New York: Continuum, 2005).

48  Ibid., 79.

49  Paolo Freire, *Education for Critical Consciousness*, 30.

50  Ira Shor, *Empowering Education: Critical Teaching for Social Change* (Chicago/London: The Uni- versity of Chicago Press, 1992), 12.

51  Neil Postman and Charles Weingartner, *Teaching as a Subversive Activity* (New York: Delta Pub- lishing, 1969), 2.

52  bell hooks, *Teaching to Transgress: Education as the Practice of Freedom* (New York/London: Rout- ledge, 1994), 203.

53  Robert L. Duran, Bill Yousman, Kaitlin M. Walsh, and Melanie A. Longshore, "Holistic Media Education: An Assessment of the Effectiveness of a College Course in Media Literacy," *Com- munication Quarterly* 56, no. 1 (2008), 49–68, 51, doi: 10.1080/01463370701839198.

54  Bill Yousman, "Media Literacy: Creating Better Citizens or Better Consumers?" *Battleground: The Media*, eds. Robin Andersen and Jonathan Gray (Westport, CT: Greenwood Publishing, 2008), 238–47.

55  Neil Postman and Charles Weingartner, *Teaching as a Subversive Activity*, 19.

56  Stuart Hall, Doreen Massey, and Michael Rustin, "After Neoliberalism: Analysing the Present," *After Neoliberalism? The Kilburn Manifesto*, eds. Stuart Hall, Doreen Massey, and Michael Rustin (London: Lawrence and Wishart, 2015), 9–10.

57  Wendy Brown, *Undoing the Demos: Neoliberalism's Stealth Revolution* (Brooklyn, NY: Zone Books, 2015), 9–10.

58  Thomas Frank, *Listen, Liberal: Or, What Ever Happened to the Party of the People?* (New York: Metropolitan Books, 2016), 56–57.

59  Henry A. Giroux, *Dangerous Thinking in the Age of the New Authoritarianism* (New York: Paradigm Publishers, 2015), 46.

60  John Dewey, *Democracy and Education* (New York: MacMillan, 1916).

61  Len Masterman, "A Rationale for Media Education," 62.

62  bell hooks, *Teaching Critical Thinking: Practical Wisdom*, 16.

63  Carlos E. Cortés, "How the Media Teach," *Media Literacy: Transforming Curriculum and Teaching*, eds. Gretchen Schwarz and Pamela U. Brown (Malden, MA: Wiley-Blackwell, 2005), 55.

64  Donald Macedo, "Deconstructing the Corporate Media/Government Nexus," *Media Literacy: A Reader*, eds. Donald Macedo and Shirley R. Steinberg (New York: Peter Lang. 2007), xix.

65  Thomas Frank, *Listen, Liberal: Or, What Ever Happened to the Party of the People?*, 88.

66  *The Race for Retirement*, Prudential advertisement, aired April 26, 2016, https://www.ispot.tv/ad/AIHe/prudential-the-race-for-retirement.

67  Sheyna Steiner, "Survey: How Americans Contend with Unexpected Expenses," Bankrate, January 6, 2016, http://www.bankrate.com/finance/consumer-index/money-pulse-1215.aspx; Carmen DeNavas-Walt and Bernadette D. Proctor, "Income and Poverty in the United States: 2014," US Census Bureau, September 2015, https://www.census.gov/content/dam/Census/library/publications/2015/demo/p60-252.pdf; "Poverty Guidelines," US Department of Health and Human Services, Office of the Assistant Secretary for Planning and Evaluation, January 25, 2016, https://aspe.hhs.gov/poverty-guidelines.

68  Wendy Brown, *Undoing the Demos: Neoliberalism's Stealth Revolution*, 211.

69  Henry A. Giroux, *Dangerous Thinking in the Age of the New Authoritarianism*, 36.

70  George Gerbner, "Television Violence: At a Time of Turmoil and Terror," *Against the Mainstream: The Selected Works of George Gerbner*, ed. Michael Morgan (New York: Peter Lang, 2002), 297.

71  Douglas Kellner, *Media Spectacle* (London/New York: Routledge, 2003), 2.

72  Stuart Hall, "The Whites of Their Eyes: Racist Ideologies and the Media," *Gender, Race and Class in Media: A Critical Reader*, eds. Gail Dines and Jean M. Humez (Thousand Oaks, CA: Sage, 2015), 106.

73  Ibid., 107.

74  "About the Black Lives Matter Network," Black Lives Matter, http://blacklivesmatter.com/about/.

75  Todd Gitlin, *The Whole World is Watching: Mass Media in the Making and Unmaking of the New Left* (Berkeley, CA: University of California Press, 2003), xiii.

76  Martin Kaste, "Is There a 'War on Police'? The Statistics Say No," NPR, September 17, 2015, http://www.npr.org/2015/09/17/441196546/is-there-a-war-on-police-the-statistics-say-no.

77  Brennan Suen, "From 'Hate Group' To 'Nazis': Fox News Ramps Up Their War on Black Lives Matter," Media Matters for America, October 26, 2015, http://mediamatters.org/research/2015/10/26/from-hate-group-to-nazis-fox-news-ramps-up-thei/206424.

78  Todd Gitlin, *The Whole World is Watching: Mass Media in the Making and the Unmaking of the New Left*, xviii.

79  Julie Frechette, Nolan Higdon, and Rob Williams, "A Vision for Transformative Civic Engagement: The Global Critical Media Literacy Project."

80  Toby Miller, *Cultural Citizenship: Cosmopolitanism, Consumerism, and Television in a Neoliberal Age* (Philadelphia: Temple University Press, 2007).

81  Julie Frechette, Nolan Higdon, and Rob Williams, "A Vision for Transformative Civic Engagement," 201.

82  Lawrence R. Frey, W. Barnett Pearce, Mark A. Pollock, Lee Artz, and Bren A.O. Murphy, "Looking for Justice in All the Wrong Places: On a Communication Approach to Social Justice," *Communication Studies* 47, no. 1–2 (1996), 110–27, 110, doi: 10.1080/10510979609368467.

83  Ibid., 111.

84  Liesbet van Zoonen, "Feminist Perspectives on the Media," *Mass Media and Society*, eds. James Curran and Michael Gurevitch (London: Edward Arnold, 1991), 34.

85  Sandra Harding, ed., *Feminist Standpoint Theory Reader: Intellectual and Political Controversies* (New York: Routledge, 2004).

86  Carl Boggs and Tom Pollard, *The Hollywood War Machine: U.S. Militarism and Popular Culture* (New York: Routledge, 2015).

87  Tim Murphy, "Donald Trump Trots Out Tale of Muslims, Pig Blood, and Bullets," *Mother Jones*, February 19, 2016, http://www.motherjones.com/mojo/2016/02/donald-trump-john-pershing-pig-blood

88  Philip Rucker, "Ted Cruz Vows to 'Utterly Destroy Isis' and 'Carpet Bomb' terrorists," *Washington Post*, December 5, 2015, https://www.washingtonpost.com/news/post-politics/wp/2015/12/05/ted-cruz-vows-to-utterly-destroy-isis-and-carpet-bomb-terrorists/.

89  Ben Jacobs, "Trump Repeats Crowd Member's 'Pussy' Insult as New Hampshire Votes," *Guardian*, February 9, 2016, https://www.theguardian.com/us-news/2016/feb/08/trump-repeats-insult-from-crowd-member-calling-cruz-a-pussy.

90  Kristinn Taylor, "Rubio Makes Small Penis Joke About Trump," *Gateway Pundit*, February 28, 2016, http://www.thegatewaypundit.com/2016/02/rubio-makes-small-penis-joke-about-trump/.

91  Marina Fang, "Ben Carson Clarifies That He Tried to Stab 'A Close Relative,'" *Huffington Post*, November 5, 2015, http://www.huffingtonpost.com/entry/ben-carson-stabbing_us_563c1115e4b0b24aee49cb2f.

92  On presidential politics and hypermasculinity, see Jackson Katz, *Leading Men: Presidential Campaigns and the Politics of Manhood* (Northampton, MA: Interlink Books, 2013).

93  Carol Gilligan, *In a Different Voice: Psychological Theory and Women's Development* (Cambridge, MA: Harvard University Press, 1982).

94  Antonio López, *Greening Media Education: Bridging Media Literacy with Green Cultural Citizenship* (New York: Peter Lang, 2014), 30.

95  Richard Delgado and Jean Stefancic, *Critical Race Theory: An Introduction* (New York: NYU Press, 2001), 2–3.

96  Neil deMause, "Brussels Bombings Destroy Fiction That All Terrorism Deaths Count as Equal," Fairness and Accuracy In Reporting, March 23, 2016, http://fair.org/home/brussels-bombings-destroy-fiction-that-all-terrorism-deaths-count-as-equal/.

97  Richard Delgado and Jean Stefancic, *Critical Race Theory: An Introduction*.

98  Steven Funk, Douglas Kellner, and Jeff Share, "Critical Media Literacy as Transformative Pedagogy," 10.

99  Louis Althusser, *Lenin and Philosophy and Other Essays*.

100 Julia Craven, "Surveillance of Black Lives Matter Movement Recalls COINTELPRO," *Huffington Post*, August 19, 2015, http://www.huffingtonpost.com/entry/surveillance-black-lives-matter-cointelpro_us_55d49dc6e4b055a6dab24008.

101 Richard Butsch, "Six Decades of Social Class in American Television Sitcoms," *Gender, Race, and Class in Media: A Critical Reader*, eds. Gail Dines and Jean M. Humez (Los Angeles: Sage, 2015), 507–16.

102 Steven Funk, Douglas Kellner, and Jeff Share, "Critical Media Literacy as Transformative Pedagogy," 14.

103 Dallas Smythe, "Communications: Blindspot of Western Marxism," *Canadian Journal of Political and Social Theory* 1, no. 3 (1977), 1–27; Sut Jhally, *The Codes of Advertising: Fetishism and the Political Economy of Meaning in the Consumer Society* (New York: Routledge, 1990).

104 Christian Fuchs, "The Political Economy of Privacy on Facebook," *Television & New Media* 13, no. 2 (March 2012), 139–59, doi: 10.1177/1527476411415699.

105 Antonio Gramsci, *Selections from the Prison Notebooks*. Gramsci attributed this phrase to the French author Romain Rolland.

106 Sut Jhally, "Advertising at the Edge of the Apocalypse," *The Spectacle of Accumulation: Essays in Culture, Media, and Politics*, ed. Sut Jhally (New York: Peter Lang, 2006), 11.

107 Umberto Eco, "Can Television Teach?" *Screen Education Reader* 31 (1979), 15, doi: 10.1007/978-1-349-22426-5_7.

108 Anthony Leiserowitz, Edward Maibach, Connie Roser-Renouf, Geoff Feinberg, and Seth Rosenthal, "Politics and Global Warming, Fall 2015," *Yale Program on Climate Change Communication*, December 14, 2015, http://climatecommunication.yale.edu/publications/voters-prefer-candidates-who-support-climate-friendly-policies/2/.

109 Naomi Oreskes and Erik M. Conway, *Merchants of Doubt: How a Handful of Scientists Obscured the Truth on Issues from Tobacco Smoke to Global Warming* (New York: Bloomsbury, 2010).

110 Justin Lewis and Sut Jhally, "The Struggle for Media Literacy," 225.

111 Faith Rogow, "Shifting from Media to Literacy: One Opinion on the Challenges of Media Literacy Education," *American Behavioral Scientist* 48, no. 1 (2004), 30–34, doi: 10.1177/0002764204267248.

112 Paulo Freire and Donald Macedo, *Literacy: Reading the Word and the World* (Westport, CT: Bergin and Garvey, 1987).

113 Justin Lewis and Sut Jhally, "The Struggle for Media Literacy," 227–28.

114 Neil Postman, *Amusing Ourselves to Death: Public Discourse in the Age of Show Business* (New York: Penguin, 1985).

115 Peter McLaren, *Pedagogy of Insurrection: From Resurrection to Revolution*, 39; Teresa L. Ebert and Mas'ud Zavarzadeh, *Class in Culture* (Boulder, CO: Paradigm Press, 2008).

116 Len Masterman, "A Rationale for Media Education," 61.

117 When using the terms "citizens" and "citizenship" throughout this chapter, I am not referring to the legal status of those living in a particular nation. Wendy Brown notes, "Citizenship in its thinnest mode is mere membership" (Brown, *Undoing the Demos*, 218). Instead, I am referring to a "thick" notion of citizenship that is based in people's active engagement and participation in the civic and cultural life of their communities. In this conceptualization I draw on Toby Miller's articulation of three overlapping zones of citizenship rights: "The political (the right to reside and vote), the economic (the right to work and prosper), the cultural (the right to know and speak)" (Miller, *Cultural Citizenship: Cosmopolitanism, Consumerism, and Television in a Neoliberal Age*, 35). But I would add the notion of obligations to the language of rights to highlight what citizens must do in addition to what they are owed, and to encompass the political obligation to be involved in both electoral and non-electoral action and participation, the economic obligation to work for equitable distribution of resources and material goods, and the cultural obligation to be an informed and articulate voice for democracy, justice, and social progress.

118 Peter McLaren and Rhonda Hammer, "Media Knowledges, Warrior Citzenry, and Postmodern Literacies," *Rethinking Media Literacy: A Critical Pedagogy of Representation*, eds. Peter McLaren, Rhonda Hammer, David Sholle, and Susan Reilly (New York: Peter Lang, 1995), 201.

119 Henry A. Giroux, *Dangerous Thinking in the Age of the New Authoritarianism*, 46.

120 Donald Macedo, "Deconstructing the Corporate Media/Government Nexus," xix.

121 Ibid., xxx.

122 Steven Funk, Douglas Kellner, and Jeff Share, "Critical Media Literacy as Transformative Pedagogy," 2.

123 Douglas Kellner and Jeff Share, "Critical Media Literacy, Democracy, and the Reconstruction of Education," 9.

124 Ibid.

125 Wendy Brown, *Undoing the Demos*, 222.

# ACKNOWLEDGMENTS

Mickey Huff and Andy Lee Roth

Many remarkable people contributed, directly or indirectly, to make *Censored 2017* possible. We are grateful to all involved.

To the courageous independent journalists and vital independent news organizations: without your reporting, Project Censored would be pointless. Faculty evaluators and student researchers at the Project's college and university affiliate campuses make it possible for us to cover the increasingly extensive, dynamic networked fourth estate. The authors who contributed to chapters and sections of *Censored 2017* inspire us with challenging questions and new perspectives. The members of our international panel of judges once again assure that our Top 25 list includes only the best, most significant independent news stories.

As we celebrate the fortieth anniversary of Project Censored, we are mindful to recognize our late founder, Carl Jensen (1929–2015). We honor him for his vision, unwavering support of a free press, and commitment to critical media literacy education.

At Seven Stories Press, our extraordinary publishers in New York, Dan Simon, Veronica Liu, Jon Gilbert, Stewart Cauley, Ruth Weiner, Rachel Nam, Lauren Hooker, Silvia Stramenga, Noah Kumin, Yves Gaston, with interns Azzuré Alexander, Will Bellamy, Allison Paller, and Libby Torres, have our deepest respect and gratitude for their steadfast commitment to publish the Project's research. Thank you also to copyeditor Michael Tencer.

We are pleased to have an ongoing relationship with the very talented and witty Khalil Bendib, whose cartoons have long accentuated our annual book.

To Peter Phillips, whose wisdom, passion, and unrelenting support of the Project and its ideals make him a major force for social justice and equality in the world. Peter is an inspiration to all of us.

The members of the Media Freedom Foundation's board of directors (listed below) continue to provide organizational structure and invaluable counsel. You keep us on course in pursuing Project Censored's mission.

Adam Armstrong is our man behind the digital curtain on the World Wide Web. As our long-time webmaster, he works tirelessly to maintain and expand our online presence at projectcensored.org, as well as our sister sites, including gcml.org and proyectocensurado. org. We could not reach our increasingly global Internet audience without his great skills and dedication to our shared cause.

We thank Christopher Oscar and Doug Hecker of Hole in the Media Productions for their vision and support as filmmakers and allies. Their award-winning documentary, *Project Censored: The Movie—Ending the Reign of Junk Food News*, brings Project Censored's message to new audiences and is now easier than ever to view online in many popular platforms (see the last page of this volume for details). We continue working with them, encouraging student and classroom production of video shorts on Project Censored news stories and analysis.

We are grateful to our friends and supporters at Pacifica Radio, especially KPFA in Berkeley, California. *The Project Censored Show*, coming up on its sixth year on air, continues to broadcast live every Friday owing to the skills and dedication of our amazing producer Anthony Fest and engineers Erica Bridgeman and Pedro Reyes. We also wish to thank all the volunteers there who support the overlapping missions of Project Censored and Pacifica; Bob Baldock for his work on events; and all of the thirty-five stations from Maui to New York that carry our weekly public affairs program across the US.

We are grateful to the people who have hosted Project Censored events or helped to spread the word about the Project's mission over the past year, including Jacob Van Vleet and everyone at Moe's Books in Berkeley; Raymond Lawrason and all at Copperfield's Books in Petaluma; John Bertucci of Petaluma Community Access Television, along with videographers Mark Jaramillo, Michael Martin, and Will Tillman; Sam Freed and Kyle Williams for videography; John Crowley, Diane Gentile, Paul Coffman, and everyone at Aqus Café in Petaluma; Larry Figueroa and the crew at Lagunitas Brewing Company; Kerry McCracken and Farm Fresh Clothing for our wonderful Project Censored T-shirts; Michael Nagler, Stephanie Van Hook, and the Metta Center for Nonviolence; Margli Auclair, Sergio Lub, and everyone at the Mount Diablo Peace and Justice Center; the Peace and Justice Center of Sonoma County; Joan Berezin at Berkeley City College; at Sonoma State University, the Dean of the School of Social Sciences, John Wingard, and School Administrative Manager, Karen Leitsch; all at the Progressive Radio Network and No Lies Radio; Marc Pilisuk; Steven Jay; Chris McManus; Paul Rea; Larry Shoup; David Talbot; Medea Benjamin; Davey D; Sharyl Attkisson; Mark Bebawi; Jim Allgren; Louie b. Free; Ken Walden of What the World Could Be; Mnar Muhawesh and the team at MintPress News; Heather Schreck and everyone at Free Speech TV; Maggie Jacoby and everyone who works on Banned Books Week, including those at the National Coalition Against Censorship and the American Library Association Office of Intellectual Freedom; Bruce Robinson at KRCB Radio; Peter B. Collins; Ralph Nader, the Center for the Study of Responsive Law, and the organizers of "Breaking through Power" in Washington, DC; Abby Martin of the *Empire Files* and Media Roots—each of whom help the Project to reach a broader audience.

We are excited about our partnership with the Action Coalition for Media Education (ACME) and the graduate program in Media Literacy and Digital Culture at Sacred Heart University (SHU). We have collaboratively launched the Global Critical Media Literacy Project (www.gcml.org). Nolan Higdon, who serves on the board of Project Censored, has done tremendous work as the first-year coordinator of the GCMLP helping to get this collaborative effort off the ground. We are grateful to work with Rob Williams and Julie Frechette of ACME and Bill Yousman and Lori Bindig Yousman of SHU as we hope to multiply our efforts promoting critical media literacy education.

We thank Michael McCray, Marcel Reid, Arlene Engelhardt, Mary Glenney, Andrew Krieg, and all those involved with the national Whistleblower Summit held in Washington, DC. Project Censored is honored to be a cohost and supporter of this important annual event. We are also proud members of the National Coalition Against Censorship and a cosponsor of Banned Books Week. We are inspired by our allies who stand against censorship in its many guises.

Colleagues and staff at Diablo Valley College provide Mickey with tremendous support and informed dialogue. Thanks to Hedy Wong and Lisa Martin, history department cochairs Matthew Powell and Melissa Jacobson, Greg Tilles, Manual Gonzales, Katie Graham, John

Corbally, Marcelle Levine, Adam Bessie, David Vela, Lyn Krause, Steve Johnson, Jeremy Cloward, Amer Araim, Mark Akiyama, Bruce Lerro, Bill Oye, English and Social Sciences Dean Obed Vazquez, and Vice President of Student Services Newin Orante, along with current and former teaching and research assistants and Project interns Ellie Kim, Sierra Shidner, Darian Edelman, Crystal Bedford, Lisa Davis, Miya McHugh, Caitlin McCoy, Bri Silva, Brady Osborne, Shelby Wade, Lauren Freeman, Tereese Abuhamdeh, Brandy Miceli, Tom Haseloff, Austin Heidt, Kylene Biaggi, Kamila Janik, and Jason Bud. We thank Mary Fitzpatrick, adjunct college skills instructor at College of Marin, for her editorial assistance. Mickey would also like to thank all of his students for the inspiration they provide, as they are a constant reminder of the possibilities of the future and how privileged we are as educators to have such an amazing role in contributing to the public sphere.

Andy thanks the students in his spring 2016 Introduction to Sociology course at Citrus College for their intellectual curiosity and abiding enthusiasm. At Citrus College, Dana Hester, Lanette Granger, Brian Waddington, and Alicia Longyear each provide steadfast support and encouragement.

The generous financial support of donors and subscribers, too numerous to mention here, literally sustain the Project. This year, we are especially thankful to Julie Andrzejewski, Marcia Annenberg, John Boyer, John Connolly, Dwain Deets, Martha Fleischman, Robert Fojt, Neil Joseph, Peter Kogen, Sergio and Gaye Lub, Sharon Lux, Robert Manning, Sandra Maurer, John Morgan, David Nelson, Leonard and Lynn Riepenhoff, Jeffery Rosenberg, John and Lyn Roth, Basja Samuelson, Marc Sapir, David Schultz, T. M. Scruggs, Bill Simon, Mark and Debra Swedlund, Vince Taylor, Jonathan Ullman, Janice and Tom Vargo, Elaine Wellin, and Derrick West.

On a personal note, we are indebted to and thankful for the love and support of our families and close friends, as they oft make sacrifices behind the scenes so we can continue to do the work we do. Mickey especially thanks his wife, Meg, as he could not do all that he does without her amazing work, counsel, and patience. Andy would like to thank Larry Gassan, Nick Wolfinger, and Liz Boyd for encouragement, inspiration, and loyalty.

CENSORED 2017

Finally, we are grateful to you, our readers, who cherish and demand a truly free press. Together, we make a difference.

## MEDIA FREEDOM FOUNDATION/PROJECT CENSORED BOARD OF DIRECTORS

Peter Phillips (president), Mickey Huff, Andy Lee Roth, Bill Simon, Derrick West, Susan Rahman, Elaine Wellin, Kenn Burrows, Abby Martin, T. M. Scruggs, Nolan Higdon, Arlene Engelhardt, with student representatives Caitlyn McCoy and Brandy Miceli; and bookkeeper Michael Smith.

## PROJECT CENSORED 2015–16 NATIONAL AND INTERNATIONAL JUDGES

ROBIN ANDERSEN. Professor of Communication and Media Studies, Fordham University. She has written dozens of scholarly articles and is author and coauthor of four books, including *A Century of Media, A Century of War* (2006), winner of the Alpha Sigma Nu Book Award. Writes media criticism and commentary for the media watch group Fairness and Accuracy In Reporting (FAIR), the Vision Machine, and *Antenna* blog.

JULIE ANDRZEJEWSKI. Professor Emeritus of Human Relations and cofounder of the Social Responsibility Program, St. Cloud State University. Publications include *Social Justice, Peace, and Environmental Education* (2009).

OLIVER BOYD-BARRETT. Professor Emeritus of Media and Communications, Bowling Green State University, Ohio and California State Polytechnic University, Pomona. Publications include *The International News Agencies* (1980), *Contra-flow in Global News: International and Regional News Exchange Mechanisms* (1992), *The Globalization of News* (1998), *Media in Global Context* (2009), *News Agencies in the Turbulent Era of the Internet* (2010), *Hollywood and the CIA: Cinema, Defense and Subversion* (2011), and *Media Imperialism* (2015).

KENN BURROWS. Faculty member at the Institute for Holistic

Health Studies, Department of Health Education, San Francisco State University. Director of the Holistic Health Learning Center and producer of the biennial conference Future of Health Care.

ERNESTO CARMONA. Journalist and writer. Chief correspondent, teleSUR Chile. Director, Santiago Circle of Journalists. President of the Investigation Commission on Attacks Against Journalists, Latin American Federation of Journalists (CIAP-FELAP).

ELLIOT D. COHEN. Professor of Philosophy and chair of the Humanities Department, Indian River State College. Editor and founder, *International Journal of Applied Philosophy*. Recent books include *Technology of Oppression: Preserving Freedom and Dignity in an Age of Mass, Warrantless Surveillance* (2014), *Theory and Practice of Logic-Based Therapy: Integrating Critical Thinking and Philosophy into Psychotherapy* (2013), and *Philosophy, Counseling, and Psychotherapy* (2013).

GEOFF DAVIDIAN. Investigative reporter and editor, the *Putnam Pit* (Cookeville, TN) and MilwaukeePress.net. Publications included in the *Milwaukee Journal Sentinel, Houston Chronicle, Arizona Republic,* Reuters, *Chicago Sun-Times, New York Daily News, Albuquerque Journal, Seattle Post-Intelligencer,* and the *Vancouver Sun.*

JOSÉ MANUEL DE PABLOS COELLO. Professor of Journalism, Universidad de La Laguna (Tenerife, Canary Islands, Spain). Founder of *Revista Latina de Comunicación Social* (RLCS), a scientific journal based out of the Laboratory of Information Technologies and New Analysis of Communication at Universidad de La Laguna.

LENORE FOERSTEL. Women for Mutual Security, facilitator of the Progressive International Media Exchange (PRIME).

ROBERT HACKETT. Professor of Communication, Simon Fraser University (Vancouver). Codirector of NewsWatch Canada since 1993. Cofounder of Media Democracy Days (2001) and OpenMedia.ca (2007). Publications include *Remaking Media: The Struggle to Democratize Public Communication* (with W. K. Carroll, 2006) and *Expanding Peace Journalism: Comparative and Critical Approaches* (coedited with I. S. Shaw and J. Lynch, 2011).

KEVIN HOWLEY. Professor of Media Studies, DePauw University. Author of *Community Media: People, Places, and Communication Technologies* (2005), and editor of *Understanding Community Media* (2010) and *Media Interventions* (2013).

NICHOLAS JOHNSON.* Author, *How to Talk Back to Your Television Set* (1970). Commissioner, Federal Communications Commission (1966–73). Former media and cyber law professor, University of Iowa College of Law. More online at nicholasjohnson.org.

CHARLES L. KLOTZER. Founder, editor, and publisher emeritus of *St. Louis Journalism Review* and *FOCUS/Midwest*. The *St. Louis Journalism Review* has been transferred to Southern Illinois University, Carbondale, and is now the *Gateway Journalism Review*. Klotzer remains active at the *Review*.

NANCY KRANICH. Lecturer, School of Communication and Information, and Special Projects Librarian, Rutgers University. Past president of the American Library Association (ALA), convener of the ALA Center for Civic Life. Author of *Libraries and Democracy: The Cornerstones of Liberty* (2001) and *Libraries and Civic Engagement* (2012).

DEEPA KUMAR. Professor of Journalism and Media Studies, Rutgers University. Author of *Outside the Box: Corporate Media, Globalization, and the UPS Strike* (2007) and *Islamophobia and the Politics of Empire* (2012). Currently working on a book on the cultural politics of the war on terror.

MARTIN LEE. Investigative journalist and author. Cofounder of Fairness and Accuracy In Reporting, and former editor of FAIR's magazine, *Extra!* Director of Project CBD, a medical science information nonprofit. Author of *Smoke Signals: A Social History of Marijuana—Medical, Recreational, Scientific* (2012), *The Beast Reawakens: Fascism's Resurgence from Hitler's Spymasters to Today's Neo-Nazi Groups and Right-Wing Extremists* (2000), and *Acid Dreams: The Complete Social History of LSD: The CIA, the Sixties, and Beyond* (with B. Shalen, 1985).

DENNIS LOO. Professor of Sociology, California State Polytechnic University, Pomona. Coeditor (with Peter Phillips) of *Impeach the President: The Case Against Bush and Cheney* (2006).

PETER LUDES. Professor of Mass Communication, Jacobs University Bremen. Founder of the German Initiative on News Enlightenment (1997), publishing the most neglected German news (Project Censored, Germany); and editor, *Algorithms of Power: Key Invisibles* (2011).

WILLIAM LUTZ. Professor Emeritus of English, Rutgers University. Former editor of the *Quarterly Review of Doublespeak*. Author of *Doublespeak: From Revenue Enhancement to Terminal Living: How Government, Business, Advertisers, and Others Use Language to Deceive You* (1989), *The Cambridge Thesaurus of American English* (1994), *The New Doublespeak: Why No One Knows What Anyone's Saying Anymore* (1996), and *Doublespeak Defined* (1999).

SILVIA LAGO MARTÍNEZ. Professor of Social Research Methodology and codirector, Research Program on Information Society at the Gino Germani Research Institute, Faculty of Social Sciences, Universidad de Buenos Aires.

CONCHA MATEOS. Professor of Journalism, Department of Communication Sciences, Universidad Rey Juan Carlos (Spain). Journalist for radio, television, and political organizations in Spain and Latin America. Coordinator for Project Censored research in Europe and Latin America.

MARK CRISPIN MILLER. Professor of Media, Culture, and Communication, Steinhardt School of Culture, Education, and Human Development, New York University. Author, editor, activist.

JACK L. NELSON.* Distinguished Professor Emeritus, Graduate School of Education, Rutgers University. Former member, Committee on Academic Freedom and Tenure, American Association of University Professors. Author of seventeen books, including *Critical Issues in Education: Dialogues and Dialectics, 8th ed.* (with S. Palonsky and M. R. McCarthy, 2013) and about two hundred articles.

PETER PHILLIPS. Professor of Sociology, Sonoma State University. Director, Project Censored, 1996–2009. President, Media Freedom Foundation. Editor or coeditor of fourteen editions of *Censored*. Coeditor (with Dennis Loo) of *Impeach the President: The Case Against Bush and Cheney* (2006).

T. M. SCRUGGS. Professor Emeritus (and token ethnomusicologist), University of Iowa. Executive producer, the Real News Network.

NANCY SNOW. Professor Emeritus of Communications, California State University, Fullerton. Part-time resident of Tokyo, Japan. Public Affairs and Media Relations Advisor to Langley Esquire, a leading public affairs firm. Author or editor of ten books, including *Information War: American Propaganda, Free Speech, and Opinion Control Since 9/11* (2003) and the *Routledge Handbook of Critical Public Relations* (with J. L'Etang, D. McKie, and J. Xifra, 2016).

SHEILA RABB WEIDENFELD.* President of DC Productions Ltd. Emmy Award–winning television producer. Former press secretary to Betty Ford.

ROB WILLIAMS. Copresident (with Julie Frechette) of the Action Coalition for Media Education (ACME). Teaches media, communications, global studies, and journalism at the University of Vermont, Champlain College, and Saint Michael's College. Author of numerous articles on media and media literacy education. Coedited *Media Education for a Digital Nation* (with J. Frechette, 2016) and *Most Likely to Secede* (with R. Miller, 2013) about the Vermont independence movement.

*Indicates having been a Project Censored judge since our founding in 1976.*

# ANNUAL REPORT FROM THE MEDIA FREEDOM FOUNDATION PRESIDENT

## Project Censored—Forty Years Of American News Censorship And Propaganda Exposed

Dr. Carl Jensen founded Project Censored in 1976. A former public relations-advertising executive, Carl Jensen earned a PhD in sociology midlife and was hired to teach at Sonoma State University in 1973. Jensen taught classes in media and journalism. In one of these, his students asked him, "How did Richard Nixon get re-elected in 1972, given public knowledge about Watergate?" Jensen went back and checked the "mainstream" media and found that it paid little attention to Watergate before the election. So he began to wonder what else the popular press was not covering. This led to the idea of researching an annual list of the most important news stories not covered in what passed as US mainstream media, and drawing greater public attention to those underreported stories. The first censored news press release was in 1976. Alternative media throughout the US, especially newsweeklies like the *San Francisco Bay Guardian,* published the annual censored news lists. Today, all forty years of Project Censored's annual lists of underreported news stories are archived on the Project Censored website at www.projectcensored.org. Project Censored defines *censorship* as "anything that interferes with the free flow of information in a society that purports to have a free press."

In 1993 Carl Jensen released his first annual yearbook, titled *Censored: The News That Didn't Make the News.* Jensen wrote and edited four *Censored* yearbooks up to 1996, his twentieth anniversary with the Project. Continuing the tradition, in 1997 the Project's new director, Dr. Peter Phillips, completed the annual release of the censored list and the yearbook, and continued to edit both for the next fourteen years, through 2011. Dr. Andy Roth coedited the 2008 and 2009 yearbooks, and Mickey Huff coedited the 2010 and 2011 yearbooks. The 2017 yearbook marks Project Censored director Mickey Huff and associate director Andy Lee Roth's sixth time coordinating the *Censored* yearbook since taking on leadership roles in Project Censored in 2010.

Early in the Project's history, some news reporters, editors, and executives lampooned Jensen for claiming that they "censored" news stories. They argued that the stories were not censored, but that, due to time and space constraints, they could not report every potentially newsworthy story. Responding to these claims, starting in 1984, Jensen began to track the annual range of trivial and non-newsworthy items the press covered, dubbing these reports "junk food news." "Junk Food News" became a regular feature in the annual *Censored* books. Each year's Junk Food News study was added to the annual edition of *Censored*.

The forty-year history of Project Censored closely parallels the consolidation of media ownership in the US. In 1983 Ben H. Bagdikian, former editor of the *Washington Post*, and dean of the Graduate School of Journalism at the University of California, Berkeley, published his first book, *The Media Monopoly*, documenting how fewer than fifty major media companies dominated the media in the US. In five subsequent editions, up through 2004, Bagdikian showed how increasing media consolidation, combined with deregulation, left just six corporations in control of over 90 percent of US media content. The resulting corporate media failed to cover their own consolidation as a consequential news story. Project Censored featured Bagdikian's work as its #1 *Censored* story in 1987, and returned to his theme of media monopoly in several variations over the next thirty years. (See chapter 2 in this volume for an update on our #1 story from 1987, "The Information Monopoly.")

The top-down corporate nature of media led Edward S. Herman and Noam Chomsky to write their 1988 book *Manufacturing Consent: The Political Economy of the Mass Media*, in which they developed a "propaganda model" of corporate media. Herman and Chomsky's propaganda model specified the social, political, and economic forces that led the corporations trusted with informing Americans about news and public affairs to be more concerned with maximizing revenues and avoiding flak than with informing the public.

In line with Bagdikian's and Herman and Chomsky's critical insights, since 2000 Project Censored has used the term "corporate media"—instead of the more familiar name, "mainstream media"—to emphasize consolidated corporate ownership and its impacts on news content.

Project Censored organized the Alternative News Media Expo and Press Freedom Conference at San Francisco State University in April 2001. Over two thousand people attended, networking around information booths from nearly one hundred independent, grassroots media outlets, and attending two days of panels and speeches, which featured Amy Goodman, John Stauber, Laura Flanders, and many more.

The ongoing Iraq War and legacy of 9/11 inspired Project Censored to help organize a Truth Emergency Summit in Santa Cruz, California, in January 2008. Organizers gathered key media constituencies to devise coherent decentralized models for distribution of suppressed news, synergistic truth telling, and collaborative strategies to disclose, legitimize, and popularize deeper historical narratives on power and inequality in the US. In *Censored 2009*, Peter Phillips and Mickey Huff wrote, "In the United States today, the rift between reality and reporting has reached its end. There is no longer a mere credibility gap, but rather a literal Truth Emergency. Americans cannot access the truth about the issues that most impact their lives by relying on the mainstream corporate media."

In 2000, Project Censored came under the oversight of the nonprofit Media Freedom Foundation, Inc., founded by Peter Phillips to ensure the Project's independence and to promote the involvement of students and faculty members from college and university campuses beyond Sonoma State University. Faculty at several universities began incorporating Project Censored research into their courses as early as 2003.

Professor Mickey Huff of Diablo Valley College became director of Project Censored in 2010. Working with associate director Dr. Andy Lee Roth, he has helped to extend the Project's educational reach well beyond Sonoma State University. The campus affiliates program now connects hundreds of faculty and students at colleges and universities across the US and around the world in a collective, networked effort to identify and research each year's top *Censored* news stories, Junk Food News, and News Abuse. Campuses now affiliated with Project Censored include Burlington College, California State University–East Bay, California State University–Maritime Academy, Citrus College, College of Marin, Diablo Valley College, Fordham University, Frostburg State University, Indian River State College, Ohlone College, Purdue University, Sacred Heart University, San Francisco State University, SUNY–Buffalo State, Syracuse University, University of Regina, University of San Francisco, University of Vermont, and more.

In addition to its campus affiliates, Project Censored continues to foster relations with numerous independent media groups and free speech organizations. Since 2010, Project Censored's weekly radio show originating at KPFA in Berkeley has been broadcast on thirty-five Pacifica Network stations across the US from Maui to New York.

Corporate media today are highly concentrated and fully global. Their primary goal is the promotion of product sales and political propaganda through psychological control of human desires, emotions, beliefs, fears, and values. Corporate media do this by manipulating human thought and emotion on a global scale, and by promoting entertainment as a diversion from global inequality and organized efforts to counter it.

To challenge corporate media hegemony, Project Censored is expanding critical media literacy training to thousands of students. Our new Global Critical Media Literacy Project (GCMLP) is scheduled to launch in October 2016. The GCMLP is a social justice education project cosponsored by Project Censored, Action Coalition for Media Education (ACME), and Sacred Heart University's graduate program in Media Literacy and Digital Culture. The GCMLP is the first of its kind to use a service-learning-based media literacy education model to teach digital media literacy and critical thinking skills, as well as to raise awareness about corporate and state-engineered news media censorship around the world.

We could not have persisted in our mission for forty years without your abiding support. With your continued backing, we look forward to sustaining the Project's mission to promote media freedom in service to a more just, equitable, and peaceful world.

Sincerely,

Peter Phillips, PhD
President, Media Freedom Foundation/Project Censored
PO Box 750940
Petaluma, CA 94975
(707) 874-2695
peter@projectcensored.org

# HOW TO SUPPORT PROJECT CENSORED

## NOMINATE A STORY

To nominate a *Censored* story, send us a copy of the article and include the name of the source publication, the date that the article appeared, and the page number. For news stories published on the Internet, forward the URL to mickey@ projectcensored.org, andy@projectcensored.org, and/or peter@projectcen sored.org. The deadline for nominating *Censored* stories is March 15 of each year.

### Criteria for Project Censored news story nominations:

A censored news story reports information that the public has a right and a need to know, but to which the public has had limited access.

The news story is recent, having been first reported no later than one year ago. For *Censored 2017* the Top 25 list includes stories reported between April 2015 and March 2016. Thus, stories submitted for *Censored 2018* should be no older than April 2016.

The story has clearly defined concepts and solid, verifiable documentation. The story's claims should be supported by evidence—the more controversial the claims, the stronger the evidence necessary.

The news story has been published, either electronically or in print, in a publicly circulated newspaper, journal, magazine, newsletter, or similar publi cation from either a domestic or foreign source.

## MAKE A TAX–DEDUCTIBLE DONATION

Project Censored is supported by the Media Freedom Foundation, a 501(c)(3) nonprofit organization. We depend on tax-deductible donations to continue our work. To support our efforts on behalf of independent journalism and freedom of information, send checks to the address below or call (707) 874-2695.

Donations can also be made online at www.projectcensored.org.

Your generous donations help us to oppose news censorship and promote media literacy.

Media Freedom Foundation
PO Box 750940
Petaluma, CA 94975
mickey@projectcensored.org;                          andy@projectcensored.org;
peter@projectcensored.org
Phone: (707) 874-2695

# ABOUT THE EDITORS

MICKEY HUFF is director of Project Censored and serves on the board of the Media Freedom Foundation. To date, he has edited or coedited eight volumes of *Censored* and contributed numerous chapters to these works dating back to 2008. Additionally, he has coauthored several chapters on media and propaganda for other scholarly publications. He is currently professor of social science and history at Diablo Valley College in the San Francisco Bay Area, where he is cochair of the history department. Huff is cohost with former Project Censored director Peter Phillips of *The Project Censored Show*, the weekly syndicated public affairs program that originates from KPFA Pacifica Radio in Berkeley, California. Along with his Project Censored colleagues Peter Phillips and Andy Lee Roth, he is a general editor of the forthcoming *Sage Handbook of Censorship* (2018). He sits on the advisory board for the Media Literacy and Digital Culture graduate program at Sacred Heart University, and serves on the editorial board for the journal *Secrecy and Society*. For the past several years, Huff has worked with the national outreach committee of Banned Books Week, working with the American Library Association and the National Coalition Against Censorship, of which Project Censored is a member. He also represents Project Censored as one of the cosponsoring organizations for the national Whistleblowers Summit held annually in Washington, DC. He is a longtime musician and composer and lives with his family in Northern California.

ANDY LEE ROTH is the associate director of Project Censored. He coordinates the Project's Validated Independent News program. He has coedited six previous editions of Project Censored's yearbook, in addition to contributing chapters on news photographs depicting the human cost of war (*Censored 2008*), the Military Commissions Act (*Censored 2009*), and Iceland and the commons (*Censored 2014*). His research on topics ranging from ritual to broadcast news interviews and communities organizing for parklands has also appeared in journals, including the *International Journal of Press/Politics*; *Social Studies of Science*; *Media, Culture & Society*; *City & Community*; and *Sociological Theory*. He reviews books for *YES! Magazine*. He earned a PhD in sociology at the University of California, Los Angeles, and a BA in sociology and anthropology at Haverford College. He has taught courses in sociology at UCLA, Bard College, Sonoma State University, College of Marin, Pomona College, and, most recently, Citrus College. He serves on the boards of the Claremont Wildlands Conservancy and the Media Freedom Foundation.

For more information about the editors, to invite them to speak at your school or in your community, or to conduct interviews, please visit projectcensored.org.

# Index

Dervin, Brenda, 235–36
desire, pedagogy of, 408
Deutch, John, 276
development, 88
DFAC. *See* Department of Family and Children Services
DHS. *See* Department of Homeland Security
Digital Accountability and Transparency Act (DATA), 48
digital media environment, youth, 410–11
digital technology, 20–21
Dilanian, Ken, 251
Dimopoulos, Eliana, 217
diphtheria-tetanus-pertussis (DTP) vaccine, 77
direct action, 42
Dirty Wars, 205
discrimination
    by law enforcement, 116–18
    racial, 116–19, 402
    in war on drugs, 117–18
disinformation, 398
Disney, 378
Djibouti, 42–43
DNC. *See* Democratic National Committee
DoD. *See* Department of Defense
Dodd-Frank Wall Street Reform and Consumer Protection Act (Dodd-Frank Act), 171–72
DoE. *See* Department of Education
*Domestic Extremism Lexicon*, 229
DPT. *See* diphtheria-tetanus-pertussis vaccine
Draitser, Eric
    on alternative media, 198–202
    on CounterPunch Radio, 202
    on Occupy Movement, 198–200
    on StopImperialism.org, 200–202
drones, 351
Drug Enforcement Administration (DEA), 350
drugs, export of banned, 121
drugs, war on. *See also* narco-trafficking, CIA and
    discriminatory enforcement of, 117–18
    racism in, 112
due process, 114
Dulles, Allen
    on brain warfare, 258
    CIA, Kern and, 254
    CIA, press and, 261–62, 266–68
    *New York Times* connection with, 259–60
    *Reporter* proofs checked by, 260
dumping, international, 121–22
Echelon, 318
Eco, Umberto, 405
ecomedia literacy, 401
eco-terrorists, 345
Edin, Kathryn J., 56–59
education. *See also* charter schools; high schools; transformative education
    as activism, 409
    "A Nation at Risk: The Imperative for Educational Reform" on, 91
    banking model of, 383–85, 387

higher, 119
    neutrality in, 380–81, 385, 409–10
    as political act, 382–87
    problem-posing model of, 384
Ehrlichman, John, 112
Eisenhower, Dwight D., 31–32, 358
    Dulles CIA appointment by, 259
    on human rights, 352
    on military-industrial complex, 341–42
elections. *See* primary, Democratic presidential (2015-2016); voting machines, electronic
    computerized form of, 19
    contributions to, 65–68
    US presidential, 49–52, 264
electronic communication service providers, 331, 333
electronic surveillance, 318–19
electronic waste. *See* e-waste, global epidemic of
Empire, US, 204–5
*The Empire Files*, 204–5
Engel, Friedrich
    *The German Ideology* by, 374
    media theory results of, 374–77
"The Engineering of Consent" (Bernays), 285–86
Environmental Protection Agency (EPA)
    on drinking water contaminated by fracking, 207–8
    on e-waste, 89
EPA. *See* Environmental Protection Agency
Epstein, Robert, 50–52
Eskow, Richard, 132
European Union (EU), 55
"Even It Up: Time to End Extreme Inequality" (Oxfam), 130
e-waste, global epidemic of
    BAN on, 89–90
    EPA on, 89
    GPS tracking of, 88–89
    in Hong Kong, 90
    worker health risks of, 90
extinction, 145–46
extremism
    DHS classification of, 229
    in FBI high school guidelines, 80–81
ExxonMobil, 125
Facebook, 153
facial recognition, 347
fact checking, 20–21
faculty evaluators, 37–38
Fairness and Accuracy in Reporting (FAIR), 167
FBI (Federal Bureau of Investigation)
    eco-terrorists and, 345
    high school spying by, 79–81
    JFK assassination investigation by, 235
    non-terrorists targeted by, 197–98
    sex buyer sentencing by, 98
FCC. *See* Federal Communications Commission
FDA. *See* Food and Drug administration
fear promotion
    in *Captain Phillips*, 394–96
    critical media literacy on, 393–98

in Black Lives Matter movement, 396–97
during Democratic primary, 175–76
"Preventing Violent Extremism in Schools"
on, 80–81
Virginia State Senate, 153
Visible Technology, 292–93
Vladimir Putin, 13–15
Votel, Joseph, 41
voting machines, electronic, 52–53. *See also* elections, computerized
Wall Street, 171–72
*Wall Street Journal*, 56
Walmart, 91. *See also* Walton Family Foundation
Walton, Sam, 91, 93
Walton Family Foundation (WFF), charter school investments by, 91, 93
war, for transnational capitalist class, 294–96
Ware, Leslie, 121–22
Warren, Elizabeth, 173–74
Warren Report, 18
*Washington Post*
censorship, national security and, 277
CIA, Amazon and, 157, 172
CIA and, 267
Sanders negative articles by, 157, 172
Wasserman, Harvey, 52–53
waste, electronic. *See* e-waste, global epidemic of
water, contamination of drinking, 206–9
water, private companies, 210–12
waterboarding, 230
Watergate
news coverage of, 149–50
system correction after, 197
wealth inequality
after 2015, 131–34
corporate news media on, 127–34
from 1970s through 2005, 127–29
of 1 percent in 2015, 129–31
tax shelters and, 129
2003 results of, 129
"Wealth Inequality in 21st Century Threatens Economy and Democracy," 113
Webb, Gary
CIA drug trafficking exposed by, 350–51
on nervous editors, 226
Weill, Kelly, 101–3
Weingartner, Charles, on banking education model, 384–85, 387
Welch, Craig, on ocean acidification, 143–44
welfare reform initiative (1996), job market and, 57–58
Wessler, Seth Freed, on medical neglect in immigrant prisons, 85–86
Western Hemisphere Institute for Security Cooperation, 205
WFF. *See* Walton Family Foundation
Whipple, Chris, 71–72
whistleblowers

Collins on, 192, 195–96
system correction and, 196
white supremacy, 402
Whitney, John Hay, 264
*The Whole World is Watching (Gitlin)*, 397
WikiLeaks, 64, 153
*Wikipedia*, 101–3
Williams, Brian, 153
Williams, Rob, 378, 397–98
wind power, 74–75
Wire & Plastic Products PLC. *See* WPP
wiretaps, 197–98
Wisner, Frank
ACJ and, 253
in Office of Policy Coordination, 257
women, 82–83
women's movements, for social justice
in ArcelorMittal resistance, 88
NDWA in Ferguson, Missouri, 87
in Nepal after earthquake, 88
Woods Hole Oceanographic Institute, 61
working conditions. *See* job market and working conditions
World Bank, 54–55
World Trade Organization (WTO)
corporate news media coverage of, 101
Global Counsel on, 290
on Jawaharlal Nehru National Solar Mission, 99–101
on Ontario Green Energy Act, 101
WPP (Wire & Plastic Products PLC), 288, 293
Burson-Marsteller of, 290, 291
Global Counsel of, 290
Glover Park Group of, 297–98
Hill & Knowlton of, 289–92
history of, 301–2
TNS Company of, 297
WPP, clients of
governments and government funded organizations, 302
major corporations and brands associated with, 303–4
NGOs, nonprofits, and universities, 302–3
WTO. *See* World Trade Organization
Xkeyscore, 320–21
Yale Program on Climate Change Communication, 405
Yanukovych, Viktor, 14
Yousman, Bill, 411
youth, digital media environment for, 410–11
youth vote, presidential primary
Clinton, Bill, on, 164
Maine superdelegates abolishment and, 164
Zinn, Howard, 285, 381
Zodiac Killer, 161–62
Zoonen, Liesbet van, 399
Zubaydah, Abu, 142–43
Zucman, Gabriel, 133

# PROJECT CENSORED THE MOVIE
## ENDING THE REIGN OF JUNK FOOD NEWS

AVAILABLE AT VIMEO, ITUNES, GOOGLE PLAY, AND
AMAZON PRIME VIDEO, STREAMING OR DOWNLOAD.
ALSO AVAILABLE FOR PURCHASE IN DVD FORMAT!
SEE PROJECTCENSOREDTHEMOVIE.COM FOR DETAILS.

Determined to break the grip of Junk Food News on the American public, two California fathers uncover the true agenda of the corporate media while they investigate the importance of a free and independent press.

This award-winning documentary, six years in the making, takes an in-depth look at what is wrong with the news media in the US and what we can do about it. The film highlights the work of forty-year veteran media democracy organization Project Censored and their commitment to providing solutions through media literacy and critical thinking education while celebrating the best in underreported, independent journalism.

*Project Censored: The Movie*, made by former PC Sonoma State University student Doug Hecker and longtime Project supporter Christopher Oscar, features original interviews and montages (edited by Mike Fischer) about the Project and media censorship with Noam Chomsky, Howard Zinn, Daniel Ellsberg, Michael Parenti, Oliver Stone, Cynthia McKinney, Nora Barrows-Friedman, Peter Kuznick, Khalil Bendib, Abby Martin, Project-affiliated faculty and students, as well as Project founder Carl Jensen, former director and president of the Media Freedom Foundation Peter Phillips, current director Mickey Huff, and associate director Andy Lee Roth. Plus much, much more!